IDEOLOGY IN
THE MIDDLE AGES

CARMEN MONOGRAPHS AND STUDIES

This series seeks to explore the movements of people, ideas, religions, and objects in the medieval period. It welcomes publications that deal with the migration of people and artefacts in the Middle Ages, the adoption of Christianity in northern, Baltic, and east-central Europe, and early Islam and its expansion through the Umayyad caliphate. CMS also encourages work that engages with the histories of the Global South and interdisciplinary approaches that explicitly incorporate material culture. The series is a venue for established scholars as well as early career researchers from partners and countries within the CARMEN Medieval Network outside Western Europe and North America. For this reason, the editorial board comprises a new generation of scholars from institutions connected to the CARMEN network, particularly those outside Europe.

Series Editors

IDEOLOGY IN THE MIDDLE AGES

APPROACHES FROM SOUTHWESTERN EUROPE

Edited by
FLOCEL SABATÉ

British Library Cataloguing in Publication Data

A catalogue record for this book is available from the British Library.

© 2019, Arc Humanities Press, Leeds

ISBN (print): 9781641892605
e-ISBN (PDF): 9781641892612

www.arc-humanities.org

Printed and bound by CPI Group (UK) Ltd, Croydon, CR0 4YY

CONTENTS

PART TWO:
IDEOLOGY — THE MANAGEMENT OF POWER

LIST OF ILLUSTRATIONS

FOREWORD

FLOCEL SABATÉ

LET ME BEGIN by using this foreword to explain briefly the aims and ideas that fed into the present book, both through a substantial introduction analysing what we understand by ideology in the Middle Ages, and through specific studies that deepen our knowledge of relevant aspects of the same subject.[1]

This book sets out from a definition of ideology as a set of beliefs or principles, especially one on which a political system is based, in line with common understandings of the word.[2] We seek to interrogate the underlying values that inform the interpretative framework through which we might better understand men and women of the Middle Ages, whether this be their perceptions of the natural surroundings, their spiritual lives or the interaction between the individual and society, and how the latter is organized. In medieval Europe the Christian Church was essential to the ideological framework, and Christian doctrine's adaptability to different social and economic stimuli allowed it to maintain this role for long periods. In Late Antiquity, this flexibility enabled Christian philosophical thought to supersede classical thought to a large extent, earning the Church political and social status. In the Early Middle Ages, the Church cemented its doctrinal and institutional prominence in society, strengthening its relationship to the monarchies of Germanic origin. By the High Middle Ages, the Church had identified feudal order as the model desired by God. And by the Late Middle Ages, Church doctrine informed ideas concerned with the common good, popular power, and "representativity" (the conditions of a representation, from the French word *représentativité*) while supporting (and on occasions challenging) the new market economies in towns and cities, and their ruling elites. Christian discourse provided a coherent vision linking the physical and metaphysical, social order and political power, the collective act and individual responsibility before God. The ideological referent was adaptable to each social group within the tripartite system of orders, because the explanation was always organic, with rights and obligations adapted to each group.

Christianity remained an enduring structural influence (global, permanent, and holistic) throughout the Middle Ages, adapting itself to philosophical, legal, and theological change. The Stoicism of primitive Christianity gave way to the neo-Platonism of late medieval spirituality. The social and economic changes of the Late Middle Ages were accompanied by new perspectives informed by Aristotelian realism. In fact, the renewal of thought in the Late Middle Ages supported a participative and representative social model. Roman law came to be used to sustain both the groups holding power and the

---

1 The reader can find the required secondary referencing for concepts on which I touch in this foreword in subsequent chapters.

2 "[A] set of beliefs or principles, especially one on which a political system, party, or organization is based" from *Cambridge Dictionary*, s.v. "Ideology," accessed November 12, 2016, https://dictionary.cambridge.org/dictionary/english/ideology.

legal framework in order to exercise power based on the alliance of elite groups and the sovereign, and the balance of power between these existing forces.

A particular ideology can contribute to uniting a society by underwriting a controlling and rationalizing narrative of identity. It can be deployed in conjunction with narratives of shared memory to reinforce a shared identity. This volume's two companion volumes deal with the allied concepts of memory and identity as part of a larger project that has sought to map and interrogate the significance of all three allied concepts in the Middle Ages in the West. The fruits of our combined research are here used to demonstrate the ways in which these three concepts provide valuable tools for the researcher of past societies. We think that this is the path for approaching an understanding of the values and interpretative axes that informed the thinking of women and men in Middle Ages. This holistic vision requires interdisciplinary approaches, as opposed to the academic compartmentalization of history, art history, and the study of languages and literatures.

With this in mind, we present a work structured in a particular way, beginning with a long introductory chapter (Sabaté) on the Christian Church in the West as a framing ideology of the Middle Ages, analysing Christianity as a coherent narrative providing people with security through its integrated explanation of physical surroundings, social order, and spiritual hope. The study continues by analysing how this prominent position was maintained thanks to the integration of a multitude of social and economic stimuli; philosophical, theological, and legal reformation; and adaptation to each social group.

This is followed by twenty focused chapters by leading researchers which delve deeper into specific fields. Brought together through the common concern of illuminating medieval thought, these studies focus on concrete cases, giving preference to exemplars from southern Europe, a region with a large amount of documentation but which to date has occupied a relatively minor position in the overall diffusion of research effort into the Middle Ages. It is this emphasis that is acknowledged in the title of this book, *Ideology in the Middle Ages: Approaches from Southwestern Europe*, which is offered as a means of enriching and complicating study of the Middle Ages.

The resulting chapters have been organized according to four fields which equate to the four parts in the book, providing, in our opinion, useful ways of expressing the workings of ideology: ideology as a means of defining power; ideology as a way of managing power; ideology in the mind as an influence on daily living and how we understand societies, and finally, the ways in which ideology associated with the Middle Ages has exerted influence centuries later, conditioning understandings of past and present. We have tried to delve deeper into each of these perspectives through our specialized research endeavours.

Let me summarize the papers in this volume and indicate how, to my mind, they develop an overall picture of the topic at hand. We begin with five studies concerned with ideology as a definition of power. The first chapter explores the relation between ideology and social order, and how the maintenance and perpetuation of the latter justified the existence of the former (Freedman). Chapter two clarifies the meaning of the terms *auctoritas* and *potestas* in Iberian documentary evidence with a view to enhancing our understanding of the legal and political framework (Rucquoi). Ideological discourse and political power in the Middle Ages were usually concerned with sovereignty, its justification, and how this intersects with the social reality. This leads us forward to investigate the evolution of the discourse that combines political power and ideology, firstly to seek to appreciate how, under the Germanic kingdoms in the Early Middle Ages, authors like Isidore of Seville in Visigothic Hispania endorsed sovereign power and justified it using Christianity whilst borrowing arguments from classical thought (Sacchi). Then, the invocation of religion and the contribution of the Church are positioned as the basis of the argument on which the ideology that articulated Carolingian power was built (Hernández). Christian ideology took root in the Middle Ages through the conviction that God had plans for civil society, and that these must be implemented. This is what thirteenth-century jurists and thinkers like the Majorcan Ramon Llull reasoned under the stimuli provided by the late medieval world (Melatini).

The seven chapters that comprise the third section of the book encompass broader interpretations of the workings of ideology in the Middle Ages in its multifarious adaptations to the management of power. Ideology was used to articulate specific propaganda linking political arguments to specific expressions of political memory (Pérez Mariñas). One can distinguish similar effects in the particular invocation of specific objects, such as relics, which could be adapted to the objectives of whoever controlled them (Alonso). The meaning attached to the figures of a particular chronology was adaptable, as can be seen with regard, for instance, to the political use of powerful images of the Magi (Craciun). The links between law and religion can be used to supply the endorsement of an expression of power, even in such extreme cases as duels (Rojas Donat). We can also distinguish clear adaptations of Christianity to the ideological function required to unify society, as it evolved. One can highlight, for instance, the way chivalric ideology was used to unify feudal society during the central centuries of the Middle Ages (Barthélemy). Similarly, the renovation of law from the twelfth century facilitated a legal and political response to the social and economic stimuli of the time, especially from the thirteenth century onwards, to which new impetuses in philosophic and theological thought also contributed. Within this framework, the spread throughout Europe of such political ideas as the ideal of the common good supposedly guaranteed greater participative power and the invocation of representative functions performed by the ruling groups. Urban society accepted and adapted this conceptual vision and generated a veritable civic ideal (Naegle). It was precisely this urban world, with its economic dynamism and religious revision, that blended and led to the ideological renewal required by a society dominated by urban elites, and which gave rise to the Christian market economy (Todeschini).

The success of these expressions of ideology can be traced not only in the way they managed to guide society and mould its political discourse but also, in the ways it can be understood to have become interiorized by the men and women of these times, who accepted it as a natural part of everyday life through their behaviour. It is in this way that we can talk about an ideology in the mind. Accordingly, one can talk about the acculturation of the population during the Early and High Middle Ages (Coira). Similarly, in the Late Middle Ages, with the backdrop of an economy of investment and the new prominence of the market, sovereigns held sway in this booming bourgeois society through an ideology of religious expressiveness focusing on new ideas of poverty (Mancinelli).

Populations interiorized ideological discourse focused on a communal sense of identity and, as a corollary, otherness. This sometimes came close, however, to being a mirror that reflected society's shortcomings and hopes through imaginary characters (Fonseca Antunes). Significantly, the very social and economic dynamism of late medieval society produced further impetus for expansion, which both required ideological justification, by proclaiming the duty to disseminate Christianity, and achieved physical contact with otherness. This can be seen in the Portuguese chronicles documenting early Portuguese expansion in Africa (Bertoli). Moreover, the contrast with other political, social, and ideological realities can contribute to a shaking up of the shortcomings and weaknesses of society, as experienced to some degree by the Florence of Lorenzo de' Medici by coming into contact with the Turks (Salviati). In a final article in this section we are reminded that the ideological framework worked across the whole of society, as evidenced by the penetration of justice's effects among the broader public (Charageat).

Acceptance of ideology at both popular as well as elite levels allows the Middle Ages to be understood as subject to an all-encompassing umbrella-like ideology, despite internal contradictions and although it progressively adapted to different stimuli. This can lead to equating the Middle Ages with a particular ideology. This is of course a simplified and idealized image: medieval society was undoubtedly complex and diverse, although it is sometimes presented as a homogeneous ideological unit. The book ends with two articles that discuss aspects of how ideology associated with the Middle Ages has been perceived in later periods. We are shown how conservative ideologies deployed the medieval model in a search for rationalizing arguments during both the nineteenth and twentieth centuries (Amalvi). The final article focuses specifically on Spain, and the way in which the invoking of an imaginary Middle Ages became a vital part of intellectual life in the first half of the twentieth century (De Murcia).

This perspective enables the use made of the Middle Ages in later centuries also to be defined through an ideological prism. It is evident that ideology acted on concepts of identity while underwriting shared memory and ideas of continuity. Study of this group of ideas was taken up by the Consolidated Medieval Studies Research Group "Space, Power, and Culture," based at the University of Lleida, especially through the research project *Identity, Memory, and Ideology in the Middle Ages* (HAR–2009–08598/HIST) financed by the Spanish government, to concatenate the study of identity, memory, and ideology in the Middle Ages. The works carried out within this framework have enjoyed the backing of three other complementary projects also financed by the Spanish government, centred on the analysis of medieval ideology. These are *Constructing Imagined Identities: Medieval Literature and Ideology* (FFI2011–15215–E), *The Birth of Medieval Linguistic Conscientiousness* (FFI2011–15918–E) and *Ideology and Society in the Middle Ages* (HAR2011–15529–E). Moreover, the momentum generated, even after the objectives of the research had been achieved, led to a continuation of the initiatives through a follow-on research project: *"Auctoritas": Church, Culture and Power (1100–1500)* (HAR2012–31484).

Our research framework favoured intensive interdisciplinary work that integrated the contributions of historians, art historians, and philologists from different geographical backgrounds, and diverse traditions and schools. Central to the varied shared initiatives was a series of scientific meetings held at the University of Lleida. This volume (and its two companion volumes) is the latest in a rich seam of publications that we believe will be the seed for promoting ongoing research.[3] In an effort to make the work in these volumes accessible to as broad an academic audience as possible, all original source texts have been translated into English, with the source quoted in the footnotes. Unless otherwise indicated, the translations have been provided by contributors and editor of this volume.

In producing, selecting, revising, and bringing to fruition the final texts in this volume, the research project *Feelings, Emotion, and Expressivity* (financed by the Spanish government as project HAR–2016–75028–P), the ICREA–Academia award to Flocel Sabaté (2016–2020) and Arc Humanities Press's peer review and pre-press processes have all been instrumental, for which we are sincerely grateful. We hope that this volume, together with *Identity in the Middle Ages: Approaches from Southwestern Europe* and *Memory in the Middle Ages: Approaches from Southwestern Europe* will illuminate in new depth the links between identity, ideology, and memory in the Middle Ages and open new pathways to how we interrogate and understand the Middle Ages.[4]

---

3 Julian Acebrón, Isabel Grifoll, Flocel Sabaté, eds., *La construcció d'identitats imaginades. Literatura medieval i ideologia* (Lleida, 2015); Flocel Sabaté, ed., *Life and Religion in the Middle Ages* (Newcastle, 2015); Javier Terrado, Flocel Sabaté, eds., *El naixement de la consciència lingüística a l'edat mitjana* (Lleida, 2016).

4 Translations into English are generally provided as close to the original text as possible, and the original text and edited source is provided in the notes. We follow the press's practice as a global publisher in retaining native forms as far as possible. Abbreviations to sources from the Monumenta Germaniae Historica (hereafter MGH) follow the guidelines to the *Deutsche Archiv* journal: www.mgh.de/fileadmin/Downloads/pdf/DA-Siglenverzeichnis.pdf.

Introduction

IDEOLOGY IN THE MIDDLE AGES

FLOCEL SABATÉ

The Cardinal responded: Our mother Church tells you expressly: "Beware! don't feel afraid. Only she has the power to dispense good, to defend her sons, to pardon the faults. Serve her humbly and you shall be rewarded."[1]

EUROPE IS A combination of many and diverse cultures. However, in the Middle Ages the powerful reach of the Christian religion imposed an ideology which united European society under a common and coherent understanding of its physical surroundings, social order, and the power of the rulers. Flourishing other cultures, such as those of the Jews and Muslims in southern Europe, were given a secondary place under the growing articulation of society under predominantly Christian rulers.[2] The scope of our task is to analyse why and how Christianity attained this leading position in the Middle Ages and, in this sense, became an ideology: a set of beliefs or principles organizing the whole of a society. Focusing especially on southern Europe, we wish to analyse the ways Christian ideology adapted to the evolution of social and economic circumstances during the

---

[1] "Coms," ditz lo Cardenals, "santa Gleiza'us somon / Que non aiatz temensa ni mala sospeison, / Qu'ela a poder que·us tola e ha poder que·us don / e poder que·us defenda e poder que·us perdon; / e si bé la sirvetz auretz ne gazerdon." Cited from Chanson de la croisade albigeoise (Paris, 1989), 458.

[2] This unequal relation has been the object of important studies. Among many others: David Nirenberg, *Communities of Violence: Persecution of Minorities in the Middle Ages* (Princeton, 1996); Ana Echevarría, *The Fortress of Faith: The Attitude towards Muslims in Fifteenth Century Spain* (Leiden, 1999); Anna Sapir Abulafia, ed., *Religious Violence between Christians and Jews: Medieval Roots, Modern Perspectives* (New York, 2002); John V. Tolan, *Saracens: Islam in the Medieval European Imagination* (New York, 2002); Flocel Sabaté, Claude Denjean, eds., *Chrétiens et juifs au Moyen Âge: sources pour la recherche d'une relation permanente* (Lleida, 2006); Maria Filomena Lopes de Barros, José Hinojosa Montalvo, eds., *Minorías étnico-religiosas na Península Ibérica* (Lisboa, 2008); Flocel Sabaté, Claude Denjean, eds., *Cristianos y judíos en contacto en la edad media: polémica, conversión, dinero y convivencia* (Lleida, 2009); Klaus Herbers, Nikolas Jaspert, eds., *Integration—Segregation—Vertreibung. Religiöse Minderheiten und Randsgruppen auf der Iberischen Halbinsel (7.–17. Jahrhundert)* (Berlin, 2011); José Martínez Gázquez, John Victor Tolan, *Ritus infidelium. Miradas interconfesionales religiosas en la Edad Media* (Madrid, 2013); Sarah Rees Jones, Sethina Watson, eds., *Christians and Jews in Angevin England: The York Massacre of 1190. Narratives and Contexts* (York, 2013); Elisheva Baumgarten, Judah D. Galinsky, *Jews and Christians in Thirteenth-century France* (New York, 2015); Ephraim Shoham-Steiner, ed., *Intricate Interfaith Networks in the Middle Ages: Quotidian Jewish-Christian Contacts* (Turnhout, 2016); Nora Berend, Youna Hameau-Masset, Capucine Nemo-Pekelman, John Tolan, eds., *Religious Minorities in Christian, Jewish and Muslim Law (5th–15th Centuries)* (Turnhout, 2017).

Flocel Sabaté (flocel@historia.udl.cat) is Professor of Medieval History at the University of Lleida, Spain.

medieval millennium, combining with diverse bases of thought and adapting these to relevant social groups. Christian ideology underwrote collective understandings of society's memory and orientated the narratives of identity expressed by otherwise disparate medieval communities. Using case studies grounded in perspectives from southern Europe, and thus focusing our work on Western (Roman) Christendom as opposed to the Eastern (Orthodox) Church, this volume interrogates the workings of ideology in the medieval world, with a view to complicating and enriching scholarly understanding of its diverse and sophisticated effects.

Drivers of Christian Ideology

In 1974, Gonzalo Puente Ojea published the work *Ideología e historia: La formación del Cristianismo como fenómeno ideológico*, stating that he began from the "conviction that without an 'ideological reading' it is impossible to reveal the 'sense of history'."[3] For the historian, ideology should not be a tool but rather a perspective that informs the subject of study. In other words, in conducting analysis of the reasons for the behaviour of the men and women who preceded us, the focus of the study must be placed on the ideology that dictated what was accepted as normal and correct in the society in question. As the legal historian Jesús Lalinde put it, ideology is the narrative that connects the ideal with reality.[4] Our interpretation of a historical reality is thus more comprehensive if we can grasp the governing ideological factors that drove those in authority at various levels.

In this sense, Charles Davis warned that, "Medieval Christianity was the first attempt, an imperfect Christian order," based on a "cultural faith" (*fe cultural*) which meant, depending on each social context, that "the Christian tradition, understood superficially, was accepted simply as part of the culture in which one lived, maintained in deference to the social context."[5] This pre-eminence was justified by divine favour, as Bossuet proclaimed in the seventeenth century.[6] However, in the eighteenth century, Gibbon demanded that it should be interrogated using scientific approaches: "our curi-

---

3 *Convencimiento de que sin una "lectura ideológica" no es posible desvelar el "sentido de la historia."* Cited from Gonzalo Puente Ojea, *Ideología e historia. La formación del Cristianismo como fenómeno ideológico* (Madrid, 1984), 7.

4 Jesús Lalinde, "Notas sobre el papel de las fuerzas políticas y sociales en el desarrollo de los sitemas iushistóricos españoles," *Anuario de Historia del Derecho Español* 46 (1978): 252–53.

5 *El Cristianismo medieval fue el primer intento, imperfecto de un orden cristiano; la tradición cristiana, entendida superficialmente, era acceptada simplemente como parte de la cultura en la que uno vivía, mantenida por deferencia con el contexto social.* Cited from Charles Davis, *La gracia de Dios en la historia* (Bilbao, 1970), 69.

6 Then everything would be the responsibility and will of "God, who gives all his advice to the preservation of his Holy Church and who, rich in means, guides all things towards his hidden ends" (*Dieu, qui rapporte tous ses conseils à la conservation de sa sainte Église, et qui, fécond en moyens, emploie toutes choses à ses fins cachées*). Cited from Jacques-Bénigne Bossuet, *Oraison funèbres* (Paris, 1929), 81.

osity is naturally prompted to inquire by what means the Christian faith obtained so remarkable a victory over the established religions of the earth."[7]

This requires historians to provide a clear articulation of the Christian Church as an institution of power and to analyse it.[8] In this sense, from around the year 150 CE/AD (hereafter we have preferred "CE" for this dating convention), the Church took advantage of political attitudes that facilitated an ideological cohesion with which to overcome internal disparity and impose opposition to the "other."[9] At the same time, a clear hierarchization of the Church was being adopted.[10] This approach enabled the Church to assume greater control over its exclusive claim on "the truth."[11] From the third century, a potentially undermining link between Judaism and Christianity was overcome by the Church's appropriation of biblical discourse. As Raúl González Salinero states, "Christians began the process of Christianizing history to the detriment of the Jewish people, who, by disassociating themselves from the Roman tradition, no longer found a place in the history of salvation."[12] Thus, the history of salvation, the history of Christianity, and the history of humanity became merged together into a coherent whole. In this way, the imposition of Christianity as an official religion across the Empire in 380 as a result of Theodosius's famous edict of Thessalonica enabled other beliefs in the Empire to be countered and annihilated.[13] Beyond the social repercussions of the political decision, an intense conceptual transition took place, sanctioning "the substantial construction of the world by the will of the God," in the expression of Luigi Leoncini Bartoli.[14] Furthermore, from the 370s, this ideological strengthening coincided with the entry of greater numbers of the rich into the Church. This benefited the Church economically, to the detriment of the state;[15] it also reframed history through a Christianized understanding of humanity as one engaged on a path to salvation, and helped to justify the existing social order.[16] The edict of 380 reaffirmed this tendency across the different provinces of

---

7 Edward Gibbon, *The Christians and the Fall of Rome* (London, 2004), 2.

8 Gonzalo Puente Ojea, *El Evangelio de Marcos. Del Cristo de la fe al Jesús de la historia* (Madrid, 1992), 54–127.

9 Elaine Pagels, *Los evangelios gnósticos* (Barcelona, 1982), 170–205.

10 Fe Bajo Álvarez, "Orígens i desenvolupament del cristianisme," *L'Avenç* 54 (1982): 47.

11 Michael Arnheim, *¿Es verdadero el Cristianismo?* (Barcelona, 1985), 119–227.

12 *Los cristianos comenzaron el proceso de cristianización de la historia en detrimento del pueblo judío que, al disociarse de la tradición romana, no encontraba ya lugar en la historia de la salvación.* Cited from Raúl González Salinero, "La idea de 'Romanitas en el pensamiento histórico-político de Prudencio," in *Toga y daga. Teoría de la praxis de la política en Roma*, ed. Gonzalo Bravo, Raúl González (Madrid, 2010), 350.

13 Philip Ellaby Cleator, *Los lenguajes perdidos* (Barcelona, 1963): 44–45.

14 *La costruzione sostanziale del mondo come voluta da Dio.* Cited from Luigi Leoncini Bartoli, *Tempo e potere* (Perugia, 2001), 19.

15 Georges Depeyrot, *Crisis e inflación entre la antigüedad y la edad media* (Barcelona, 1996), 98.

16 Peter Brown, *Through the Eye of a Needle: Wealth, the Fall of Rome, and the Making of Christianity in the West, 350–550 AD*, (Princeton, 2012), 31–90.

the Empire, where Christianization took root among the ruling classes.[17] In this context, between the fourth and fifth centuries "Christianity played a very major role in social change," in the words of Averil Cameron, who draws attention to its visual expression in the form of new temples occupying the public arena, along with the profiling of different models of religious life, the increasingly prominent role exerted by the bishops, and the growth of a mix of private and public religious observance.[18]

Beyond this identification between Empire and Christianity, the conversions of the kings of the Franks in 498 and of the Visigoths in 589, promoted by the respective regional bishops, helped the great popes of the fifth and sixth centuries (Leo I, Gelasius I, and Gregory I) promote catholic universality into these kingdoms. Their position was based on the Roman *ius gentium* and which recognized each king as *rex gentis* and through him the respective dynasty and its rights over the respective *natio*.[19] Christianity and royal power were intertwined everywhere: sovereigns imposed Christian belief, in all its facets, violently if necessary.[20] From the seventh century onwards, both domestic policy and the extension of frontiers, as we see with the Franks, entailed imposing Christian faith in its spiritual component which, at the same time, served as a means of justifying and uniting society.[21]

Christianity started to give sense to all aspects of medieval society. It worked to adapt behaviours, fears, and beliefs and drew directly from popular or traditional beliefs,[22] especially regarding the interpretation of nature, the environment, and interaction with the afterlife.[23] Sovereigns and lords not only enjoyed power through divine will but also became responsible for supervising the religious obligations of the people and the behaviour of the clergy, as Carolingian theocracy and its *pax Christiana* expressed to the full.[24] Extending one's territorial domains was to extend Christendom: war-mongering and evangelization went hand in hand on all the frontiers of the tenth and eleventh centuries, whether those established by the Vikings in Normandy[25] or in the Iberian

---

17 Luis A. García Moreno, "España y el Imperio en época teodosiana. A la espera del bárbaro," in *I Concilio Caesaraugustano. MDC aniversario*, ed. Guillermo Fatás (Zaragoza, 1981), 29–30.

18 Averil Cameron, *The Mediterranean World in Late Antiquity AD 395–600* (London, 1993), 57–80.

19 Émilienne Demougeot, *L'Empire Romain et les Barbares d'Occident (IVe–VIIe siècles)* (Paris, 1988), 327–35.

20 Noël-Yves Tonnerre, *Être chrétien en France au Moyen Âge* (Paris, 1996), 11–25.

21 Bruno Dumézil, *Les racines chrétiennes de l'Europe. Conversion et liberté dans les royaumes barbares Ve–VIIIe siècle* (Paris, 2005), 359–466.

22 Michel Rouche, "Alta Edad Media Occidental," in *Historia de la vida privada*, ed. Philippe Ariès, Georges Duby (Madrid, 1992), 94–137.

23 Flocel Sabaté, *Vivir y sentir en la Edad Media* (Madrid, 2011), 47–50.

24 Eugen Ewig, "La época de Carlomagno (768–814)," in *Manual de Historia de la Iglesia*, ed. Hubert Jedin, 10 vols. (Barcelona, 1970), 3:184–94.

25 Samantha Kahn Herrick, "Heirs to the Apostles: Saintly Power and Ducal Authority in Hagiography of Early Normandy," in *The Experience of Power and Medieval Europe, 950–1350*, ed. Robert F. Berkhofer III, Alan Cooper, Adam J. Kosto (Aldershot, 2005), 11–24.

Peninsula.[26] In short, the strengthening of society, the expansion of Europe, and Christianization became synonyms.[27] This melding of Christian and political power meant a society of private churches and monasteries with an aristocracy whose lineages fed the ruling caste and the senior clerical ranks, and thus led to constant interweaving of the political and religious spheres.

In Walter Ullmann's apt expression, progressive consolidation of the papacy was based on generating a specific ideological memory of the invocation of papal continuity and the memory of the strength of some papal figures.[28] This was combined with an increasing centralization of the Church's structures, and increased conviction concerning its intervention over Christendom, and its power of coercion.[29] While invoking a *restauratio* or *renovatio*,[30] the policies of the Church from the mid-eleventh century did not relate so much to reform of a deformed model, as traditional historiography has reiterated,[31] as to a change of model. If Christianity is understood as having taken control of society in the sixth century, from the eleventh century we might say that the Roman Church then took control of Christendom.[32] From here on, local autonomy disappeared and there would be no churches or monasteries outwith the central authority of the Church.[33] Increased political influence at regional and local levels, the incorporation of Christian doctrine within different aspects of moral philosophy and everyday life, the intensification of the spread of parishes, the growth of a celibate clergy in charge of the ecclesiastical heritage, enhanced access to individual conscience, and increased control over normative models of social behaviour, led to far greater ecclesiastical influence not only over rulers but also, very directly, over the population.[34]

26 Flocel Sabaté, "Occuper la frontier du nord-est péninsulaire (Xe-XIIe siècles)," in *Entre Islam et Chrétienté. La territorialisation des frontières, XIe–XVIe siècle*, ed. Stéphane Boisellier, Isabel Cristina Ferrreira Fernandes (Rennes, 2015), 84–105.

27 Robert Bartlett, *La formación de Europa. Conquista, colonización y cambio cultural, 950–1350* (València, 2003), 323–37.

28 Walter Ullmann, *The Growth of Papal Government in the Middle Ages. A Study in the Ideological Relation of Clerical to Lay Power* (Ann Arbor, 1962), 262.

29 Herbert Edward John Cowdrey, *Pope Gregory VII, 1073–1085* (Oxford, 1998), 584–607.

30 Javier Faci, "Reforma gregoriana, reforma eclesiástica," in *Espacios de poder y formas sociales de la Edad Media. Estudios dedicados a Ángel Barrios*, ed. Gregorio del Ser Quijano, Iñaki Martín Viso (Salamanca, 2007), 78–80.

31 Augustin Fliche, *La Réforme grégorienne et la Reconquête chrétienne (1057–1123)* (Paris, 1950), 12–478.

32 At the end of the process "the Papacy rose institutionally over Christendom" (*o Papado ascendeu institucionalmente sobre a Cristiandade*), as Rust concluded: Leandro Duarte Rust, *Colunas e São Pedro. A política papal na Idade Média Central* (São Paulo, 2011), 513.

33 José Manuel Nieto, *El Pontificado Medieval* (Madrid, 1996), 21.

34 This is clearly perceived when analysing society in different areas. In the case of Catalonia, the Church "embraced Gregorian reform as a means of strengthening the Church's power; it bolstered its physical presence with a wave of newly created parishes; and it provided the discourses on social and political legitimacy and from this stance accentuated its influence over the population, conditioning its consciences, modulating its world view and imposing a model of family based on

In large parts of Europe, with a new feudal setting becoming consolidated in the eleventh century,[35] the Church imposed a model of the family that was based on monogamous, indissoluble, and exogamic marriage[36] and moreover, it took charge of its application, with the corresponding rites of passage. Varied but vital ceremonies of the social structure such as the knighting ceremony (*adoubement*) and marriage, had been essentially secular ceremonies till 1100,[37] apart from in exceptional cases where clergymen played a minor role or offered some basic liturgical rituals for marriage. A century later, in contrast, the Church played a central role, with a well-structured ceremony, especially for weddings.[38]

In reality, the Church was taking over intermediation with the divinity, and this turned the clergy into the middlemen required by each individual in order to obtain the sought-after divine favour. This not only gave new impetus to the numerous religious communities where clergy constantly prayed for the souls of their donors, it became a matter regulating personal conscience from the twelfth century. As a result of the Fourth Lateran Council of 1215 all Christians were obliged to make annual confession. Jean Delumeau emphasizes the importance of this ruling:

> The formalization of this pressure already in force in some dioceses, transformed the religious and psychological life of men and women in the West and weighed enormously on mentalities until the Reformation in the Protestant countries, and until the twentieth century in those that remained Catholic.[39]

Throughout the Late Middle Ages, the Christian message spread by the preachers, especially the mendicants in urban areas,[40] would gradually focus on civic and personal demands. This provoked distress because any deviation from the divine will was said to provoke "the wrath of God,"[41] and lead to a corresponding punishment, frequently

---

monogamous, indissoluble and exogamous marriage." From Flocel Sabaté, "The Catalonia of the 10th to 12th centuries and the historiographic definition of feudalism," *Catalan Historical Review* 3 (2010): 44.

35 Flocel Sabaté, *La feudalización de la sociedad catalana* (Granada, 2007), 190–91.

36 Flocel Sabaté, "La sexualitat a l'època medieval," in *Sexualitat, història i antropologia*, ed. Xavier Roigé (Lleida, 1996), 39.

37 Dominique Barthélemy, "Note sur l'adoubement dans la France des XIe et XIIe siècles," in *Les ages de la vie au Moyen Âge* (Paris, 1992), 113.

38 Dominique Barthélemy, "Parentesco," in *Historia de la vida privada*, ed. Phlippe Ariès, Georges Duby, 10 vols. (Madrid, 1992), 3:125–59.

39 *La generalización de este apremio, ya en vigor antes en varias diócesis, modificó la vida religiosa y psicológica de los hombres y mujeres de Occidente y pesó de forma enorme sobre las mentalidades hasta la Reforma en los países protestantes y hasta el siglo XX en los que permanecieron católicos.* Cited from Jean Delumeau, *La confesión y el perdón* (Madrid, 1992), 15.

40 Jean Longère, "La prédication d'après les status synodaux du Midi au XIIIe siècle," in *La prédication en Pays d'Oc (XIIe–début XVe siècle)* (Toulouse, 1997), 251–74 and Jean-Arnault Dérens, "La prédication et la ville: pratiques de la parole et 'religion civique' à Montpellier aux XIVe et XVe siècles," in *La prédication en Pays d'Oc (XIIe–début XVe siècle)* (Toulouse, 1997), 335–62.

41 *La hira de Déu*. From Carme Olivera, Antoni Riera, Jeròme Lambert, Enric Banda, Pierre Alexandre, *Els terratrèmols de l'any 1373 al Pirineu: efectes a Espanya i França* (Barcelona, 1994), 64.

manifested in bad harvests and other natural calamities. This is what the municipal government of the Valencian town of Elche confirmed in 1379: "For consenting to these sins, pestilences came to our town and our lord God deprived [us] of rain and good weather."[42] Aristotelian realism that came to dominate late medieval theology contributed to increasing popular fears associated with the religious experience. People feared eternal condemnation if death came while they were with sin, or without access to the sacraments as a result of being excommunicated or interdicted. This was frequently the case because the Church used these spiritual arms against individuals or groups in any kind of conflict, including economic demands or jurisdictional disputes.[43] Religion became a guarantee that, in exchange for certain behaviour, one was awarded passage to eternal life. By the end of the Middle Ages, religion had become mainly a system of atonement managed by the Church through its clergy, which is why there was so much focus on confession, indulgences, and purgatory.[44]

This consolidated the powerful influence of the Christian Church on popular behaviour and confirmed the Church as mediator, through the clergy, in all important affairs in the everyday human life. There is no better example than the preoccupation with death.[45] Only one good way of dying was accepted, one described by the Castilian chronicler Diego de Valera when he criticized the carelessness of King Enrique IV of Castile because "no mention was made of confessing nor receiving the Catholic sacraments, nor of making a will or codicil, that is general custom of all men to do in these times."[46] This was normalized behaviour that, at the end of the fourteenth century, the Viscount of Perellós summarized as, "everything those men do who through illness or other dangers await death."[47]

Directive behaviour from the Church affected all aspects of life. Significantly, attempts to remove education from ecclesiastical control generated strong tensions,[48] especially in the thirteenth and fourteenth centuries, when municipal governments

---

42 *Per tals pecats a consentir vinguin pestelençies en la vila e nostre senyor Déu priva pluja e bon temps.* Cited from Pedro Ibarra, "Elig. Noticia de algunes instituciones y costumbres de la Edad Media," in *III Congreso de Historia de la Corona de Aragón (Julio de 1923)*, 2 vols. (València, 2004), 2:39.

43 Flocel Sabaté, "L'Església secular catalana al segle XIV: la conflictiva relació social," *Anuario de Estudios Medievales* 28 (1998): 776–77.

44 Claude Carozzi, *Visiones apocalípticas en la Edad Media. El fin del mundo y la salvación del alma* (Zaragoza, 2000), 175.

45 Johan Huizinga, *El otoño de la Edad Media* (Madrid, 1988), 194.

46 *Ninguna mención hizo de confesar ni rescibir los cathólicos sacramentos, ni tampoco hacer testamento o codicilio, que es general costumbre de todos los hombres de tal tiempo hacer.* Cited from Diego Valera, "Memorial de diversas hazañas," chap. 100 in *Crónicas de los Reyes de Castilla*, ed. Cayetano Rosell, 3 vols. (Madrid, 1953), 3:94.

47 *Tot ço que fan aquests hòmens que per malaltia o per altres perills esperen la mort.* Cited from Ramon de Perellós, "Viatge del vescomte Ramon de Perellós i de Roda fet al Purgatori nomenat de Sant Patrici," in *Novel·les amoroses i morals*, ed. Arsenio Pacheco and August Bover (Barcelona, 1982), 33.

48 Flocel Sabaté, "La formació de la personalitat a l'edat mitjana," in *La formació de la personalitat a l'edat mitjana*, ed. Flocel Sabaté (Lleida, 2016), 14.

worked to gain control of grammar schools[49] and the control of university study was disputed at various levels across much of Europe.[50] Similarly, the consolidation of group identities, either municipal or those relating to trades, offered opportunities for charitable actions as an alternative to ecclesiastical control of charity in the Late Middle Ages;[51] this led to municipal control of hospitals and charitable bodies.[52] Disputes could even extend to concerns with the control of time, and its potential secularization. In València in 1378 the bishop obtained the king's support to prevent the municipal government from having "a bell for the clock that was in the council chamber," because the clock had to be built in the cathedral, so making it an ecclesiastical and not a civil competence.[53]

All this confirms that Christianity acted as a driving doctrine of the Middle Ages and also that the social model envisaged by the Church can be defined as "assisted society," because men and women of the period, under this model, constantly required the help of the clergy and ecclesiastical institutions.[54] Indeed, they could do nothing important without the assistance of the Church via its clergy, from each step in one's life—birth, marriage, and death—to control over knowledge and relief provided by charity.

This domain of the Church not only involved people's livelihoods but also extended to all the lands and countries of the world, since all was created by God. The pope, as representative of Christ on earth, could not only sanction the dethroning of the Merovingians and anoint the new Pippinid monarch in the mid-eighth century,[55] but could also determine to whom territories should belong. In reality, the fate of territories—and, its corollary, the subservience of their rulers to the papacy—were continuously impacted by the will of the Church from the eleventh century until the end of Middle Ages through three arguments: the false donation of the Western Roman Empire to the Roman Church by Emperor Constantine,[56] the assumption by the papacy of feudal domains[57] and the duty to expand Christianity.[58] We can cite here the demand

---

49 Lluís Cifuentes, Gemma Escribà, "El monopoli de la paraula: cura d'ànimes, educació i fe pública a la parròquia de Santa Maria de Piera durant la baixa edat mitjana," *Anuario de Estudios Medievales* 28 (1998): 811–19.

50 Alexander Murray, *Reason and Society in the Middle Ages* (Oxford, 1978), 283–87.

51 Suzanne F. Roberts, "Les consulats de Rouergue et l'assistance urbaine au XIIIe et au début du XIVe siècles," in *Assistance et charité* (Toulouse, 1978), 131–35.

52 Flocel Sabaté, "Assistència a l'edat mitjana," in *Assistència a l'edat mitjana*, ed. Flocel Sabaté (Lleida, 2017), 32–34.

53 *Una campana per alarotge que estigués en la Sala del consell.* Cited from Agustín Rubio Vela, *Epistolari de la València medieval* (València, 1985), 76–77.

54 Sabaté, "Assistència," 40–43.

55 Thomas F. X. Noble, *The Republic of St. Peter. The birth of the Papal state, 680–825* (Philadelphia, 1991), 67–71.

56 Johannes Fried, *Donation of Constantine and Constitutum Constantini. The Misinterpretation of a Fiction and its Original Meaning* (Berlin, 2007), 7–114.

57 Augustin Fliche, *La Réforme grégorienne et la Reconquête chrétienne*, 111–18.

58 Flocel Sabaté, *Fin del mundo y Nuevo mundo. El encaje ideológico entre la Europa medieval y la*

for the vassalage of the Hispanic kingdoms,[59] the enfeoffment of Aragon,[60] involvement in Sardinia,[61] incentives for conquests in the Holy Land[62] and the Iberian Peninsula,[63] guarantee of the domains conquered by the king of Portugal,[64] support for the English conquest of Ireland,[65] the assumption of England and Ireland as enfeoffments,[66] disposition of the domains and jurisdictions of the lords who had collaborated with the Cathars in Occitania,[67] successive enfeoffments of Sicily,[68] the creation of the *Regnum Sardiniae et Corsicae*,[69] donations and arbitrages in the Atlantic expansions of Castile and Portugal[70] and, finally, the 1493 papal concession, in the name of "vicar of Jesus Christ performed on the world," of the new lands beyond the Atlantic to the kingdoms of Castile and Leon, given that their sovereigns had shown such zeal in expelling the "tyranny of the Saracens" from the Iberian Peninsula through the conquest of Granada.[71]

This ongoing catalogue of deeds demonstrates the pre-eminent position for the Church, concordant with the power of the clergy within society. It makes it imperative to analyse now the interpretative capacity and far-reaching effects of Christian ideology in the European Middle Ages.

América moderna en Nueva España (siglo XVI) (Ciudad de México, 2011), 17–22.

59 Demetrio Mansilla, *La documentación pontificia hasta Inocencio III (956–1216)* (Roma, 1955), 42.

60 Paul Kehr, "¿Cómo y cuándo se hizo Aragón feudatario de la Santa Sede. Estudio diplomático?," *Estudios de Edad Media de la Corona de Aragón* 1 (1945): 285–326.

61 Luciano Gallinari, "Les judicats sardes: Un modèle de souveraineté medieval?" (PhD diss., École des Hautes Etudes en Sciences Sociales, Paris, 2009), 117–36.

62 Nikolas Jaspert, *Die Kreuzzüge* (Darmstadt, 2003), 33–34.

63 Flocel Sabaté, "Frontera peninsular e identidad (siglos IX–XII)," in *Las Cinco villas aragonesas en la Europa de los siglos XII y XIII. De la frontera natural a las fronteras políticas y socioeconómicas (foralidad y municipalidad)*, ed. Esteban Sarasa (Zaragoza, 2007), 80–82.

64 Maria Alegria F. Marques, "A bula 'Manifestis probatum'. Ecos, textos e contextos," in *Poder espiritual / Poder temporal. As relações Igreja – Estado no tempo da monarquia (1179–1909) Actas do Colóquio*, eds. Manuela Mendonça, Maria de Fatima Reis (Lisboa, 2009), 114–15.

65 Giraldus Cambrensis, "De rebus a se gestis," in *Giraldo Cambrensis opera*, Rerum Britannicarum Medii Aevi Scriptores (Rolls Series), ed. J. S. Brewer, James F. Dimock, Georges F. Warner, 8 vols. (London, 1861), 1:62.

66 Martin Aurell, *L'Empire des Plantagenêt 1154–1224* (Paris, 2003), 144.

67 Jean-Louis Biget, "La dépossession des seigneurs méridionaux. Modalités, limites, portées," in *La Croisade Albigeoise*, ed. Michel Roquebert (Carcassone, 2004), 263–64.

68 Francesco Giunta, *La Sicília catalana* (Barcelona, 1988), 5–9.

69 Francesco Cesare Casula, *La Sardenya catalano-aragonesa. Perfil històric* (Barcelona, 1985), 13–16.

70 Julieta Araújo Esteves, "Portugal e Castela: o início da disputa pelo Atlântico. Contributo para um estudo," in *Raízes medievais do Brasil moderno*, ed. Margarida Garcez, José Varandas (Lisboa, 2008), 246; Eduardo Aznar, *Evangelización y organización eclesiástica em Canarias (siglos XIV–XVI)* (Santa Cruz de Tenerife, 2007), 12–14.

71 *Vicariatus Ihesu Christi qua fungimur in terris [...] tyrannide sarracenorum*. Cited from Pedro Fernández del Pulgar, *Tropheos gloriosos de los reyes catholicos de España*, 2 vols. (Madrid, 1951), 2:20.

Holistic Christian Ideology

We can define Medieval Christian ideology as holistic because it provided the basis and justification of everything that affected humans in their understanding of their surroundings: world view, social order, belief systems, cultural expressions, and identity. This homogeneity brought social cohesion and facilitated strong individual and collective security. However, the flip side of this was intolerance towards those minorities that were not assimilable to the dominant discourse.

During the Early Middle Ages, religious centres took increasing control of structures of knowledge and thought,[72] while the clergy were the channel for intermediation with the afterlife,[73] bringing systems of knowledge, culture, and religion closer together. The Church thus became the fundamental source of ideas explaining the natural world, the social order, and common-sense beliefs involved in everyday life. From the second half of the eleventh century and into the twelfth, the Gregorian Reform's consolidation of the involvement of the Church in dictating social behaviour and imparting a holistic worldview that incorporated the family and all elements of society, marked a step-change. The clericalization of society and the widespread acceptance of the Church in all domains was remarkable. Conversely, the harshness of the response to religious expressions outwith the Church increased, including those whose thoughts identified them as heretics, non-Christian minorities like the Jews, and enemies of the faith like the Muslims.[74] This change of attitude was particularly marked on the southern frontiers of Europe,[75] and became more pronounced in popular experience of Christianity and attitudes to non-Christian societies abroad in the twelfth century.[76]

The Church did not hesitate to declare a crusade against the (Cathar) heretics in Occitania in 1208,[77] nor to map out a framework for Christian life in 1215, at the Fourth Lateran Council, which included discriminatory measures against the non-assimilable Jews. It was a set of perspectives that gradually became more ingrained in society over the course of the thirteenth and fourteenth centuries through ecclesiastical *pressure*.[78] This change included the growing role of preachers in disseminating to the population a new holistic Christian framework for living, which marked a further consolidation of Christian ideology's influence on society.

Christianity was, of course, based on a book of wisdom. Given that the Holy Scriptures did not supply a code of behaviour, but rather, forced one to deduce this from various narratives framed as history, the basis for interpreting religion lay in applying the hermeneutic with which to convert biblical and evangelical narratives into norms of

---

72 Jacques Paul, *La Iglesia y la cultura en Occidente (siglos IX i XII)*, 2 vols. (Barcelona, 1988) 1:63–89.

73 Oronzo Giordano, *Religiosidad popular en la alta edad media* (Madrid, 1983), 36–38.

74 Dominique Iogna-Prat, *Ordonner et exclure. Cluny et la société chrétienne face à l'hérésie, au judaïsme et à l'Islam (1000–1150)* (Paris, 2000), 103–359.

75 Sabaté "Frontera península," 80–81.

76 André Vauchez, *La espiritualidad del Occidente medieval* (Madrid, 1985), 89–120.

77 Martín Alvira Cabrer, *12 de Septiembre de 1213. El Jueves de Muret* (Barcelona, 2002), 102–6.

78 Solomon Grayzel, *The Church and the Jews in the XIIth Century*, 2 vols. (New York, 1989).

behaviour. Consequently, the philosophical basis of thought conditioned interpretation and oriented religious messages in one or another sense. This is why it was significant that the main line of Christianity from the thirteenth-century scholastics was developed on the basis of Aristotelian realism.[79] From this point on, the focus shifted from duality between the spiritual and the worldly, to teleology, in other words, the explanation of phenomena of the world in terms of the purposes they served according to the will with which God created the world. According to this school of thought, at the moment of creation, absolutely everything was instilled with the divine will's purpose, and thus, everything in the world was implicitly good, it simply had to be adapted to its corresponding purpose. Thus, for instance, sexuality need no longer be distrusted as the fleshly part of human nature that needed to be side-lined in favour of the spiritual. Sexuality could now be appreciated as a creation of God that simply needed to adapt to the purpose for which it was created, that being none other than procreation to guarantee human survival.[80] Conversely, if knowing the divine will enabled a better appreciation of God's purpose, it also meant greater confidence in rejecting what went against God's wishes, such as male homosexuality. Thus, male homosexuality was not only punished with severe late medieval punishments[81] but also with capital punishment in the form reserved for the most serious offences, namely death at the stake.[82]

An important sector of thirteenth-century Christian scholarly thought rejected this dependence on the thoughts of pagan figures like Aristotle, as the Franciscan theologian Peter John Olivi (ca. 1248–1298) explicitly indicated.[83] This school of thought was the root for a separate spiritualist movement, one particularly attentive to divine signals expressed through dreams, revelations, or mystical experience.[84] Although apparently contradictory, both paths—realism and spiritualism—came together in experiencing, in different ways, a proximity to divine thinking that became a fear of provoking God's wrath by opposing his will.[85] Popular behaviour and the actions of leaders, not least municipal authorities, worked to incorporate the Christian dictates in law in response to fear of eternal condemnation or divine punishment.[86] This led to the marginaliza-

---

79 Étienne Gilson, *La filosofía en la Edad Media. Desde los orígenes patrísticos hasta el fin del siglo XIV* (Madrid, 1989), 538–47 and Gilles Perceville, "Entre lógica y mística. La teología universitaria," in *Historia de la teología*, ed. Jean-Yves Lacoste (Buenos Aires, 2011), 210–14.

80 Flocel Sabaté, "Evolució i expressió de la sexualitat medieval," *Anuario de Estudios Medievales* 23 (1993): 169–70.

81 Mark D. Laertes, *La invención de la sodomía en la teología cristiana* (Barcelona, 2001), 51–72.

82 Flocel Sabaté, "La pena de muerte en la Cataluña bajomedieval," *Clio & Historia* 4 (2007): 197–98.

83 François-Xavier Putallaz, *Insolente liberté. Controverses et condamnations au XIIIe siècle* (Fribourg, 1995) 143.

84 José Maria Pou, *Visionarios, beguinos y fraticelos catalanes (siglos XIII–XV)* (Madrid, 1991), 9–33 and Elémire Zolla, *I mistici dell'Occidente* (Milano, 1977).

85 André Vauchez, *Saints, prophètes et visionnaires. Le pouvoir surnaturel au Moyen Age* (Paris, 1999), 95–219 and Flocel Sabaté, "L'Església secular catalana al segle XIV. La conflictiva relació social," *Anuario de Estudios Medievales* 28 (1998): 785–87.

86 Flocel Sabaté, "L'ordenament municipal de la relació amb els jueus a la Catalunya baixmedieval,"

tion, and legal condemnation, of any expression of a relation with the divinity besides through channels established by the Church. In the fourteenth and fifteenth centuries this resulted in accusations of sorcery and witchcraft, while incriminations for heresy were trivialized.[87]

From the thirteenth century on, Thomist thought (based on the works of Thomas Aquinas) enabled faith and reason to be clearly separated. Faith and reason were not in contradiction because each complemented the other due to the shared basis in Aristotelian realism.[88] Even the most specific precepts of faith were explicable by reason: for instance, five rational arguments proved the existence of God.[89] The central tenet of the Catholic Church, the real presence of God within the Eucharist, was reached by the simple application of a law of physics in line with the Aristotelian scheme,[90] transubstantiation was nothing other than the maintenance of form while material composition underwent change.[91]

The supernatural regimes of Heaven and Hell also operated in accordance with physics, as part of a complex universe consisting of seven heavens and three other zones—the circle of the fixed stars, an area of water, and the last, without bodies but responsible for rotations—which opened the way to the Heaven of the blessed, where the souls of the saints lived.[92] Hell was situated inside the Earth in accordance with a belief[93] in the progressive increase in temperature as one penetrated more deeply towards the fiery bowels of the planet. Aquinas did not hesitate to affirm that the passages in the Scriptures referring to suffering physical punishment in Hell, including torment by fire, were

in *Cristianos y judíos en contacto en la Edad Media: polémica, conversión, dinero y convivencia*, ed. Flocel Sabaté, Claude Denjean (Lleida, 2009), 758–75.

87 Sabaté, "La pena de muerte en la Cataluña bajomedieval," 184–85.

88 Maurice de Wulf deduced this: "No one has emphasized the distinction between reason and faith to a greater extent than Thomas [...]. The one is not the other. But reason leads to faith, philosophy to theology": Maurice de Wulf, *The System of Thomas Aquinas* (New York, 1959), 150.

89 Étienne Gilson, *El Tomismo. Introducción a la filosofía de Santo Tomás de Aquino* (Pamplona, 2002), 71–102. See English version: Étienne Gilson, *Thomism. The Philosophy of Thomas Aquinas* (Toronto, 2002).

90 Rafael Gómez Pérez, *Introducción a la metafísica. Aristóteles y Santo Tomás de Aquino* (Madrid, 1991), 90–100.

91 Marilyn McCord Adams, *Some Later Medieval Theories of the Eucharist. Thomas Aquinas, Giles of Rome, Duns Scotus, and William Ockham* (Oxford, 2012), 85–176.

92 Giordano Berti, *Les mondes de l'au-delà* (Paris, 2000), 36–49.

93 "The conception of Hell was related to that of the Last Judgment, that is to say, to places where man necessarily arrived after his earthly death. This conception is universal and present in almost all the world religions. This world of below is a place without life, a place of shadows and confusing disorder." (*La conception de l'Enfer était rattachée à celle du Jugement dernier, c'est-à-dire à des parages ou l'homme arrivait nécessairement après sa mort terrestre. Cette conception est universelle et presente dans presque toutes les religions mondiales. Ce monde d'en-bas est un lieu sans vie, lieu des ombres et du flou informel*). Cited from Martin Zlatoblávek, "Les éléments iconographiques du jugement dernier," in *Le Jugement dernier*, ed. Martin Zlatohlávek, Christian Rätsch, Claudia Müller-Ebeling (Lucerne, 2001), 220.

to be understood literally.[94] To appreciate these torments more fully, Hell was often interpreted as being divided into seven halls, coinciding with the seven deadly sins (lust, gluttony, greed, sloth, wrath, envy, and pride), so that each of the condemned could receive an eternal torture in line with the sin of which he or she was most culpable, as depicted in great detail, for example, in the fresco of the Last Judgment in the cathedral of Albi, dating from around the turn of the fifteenth to sixteenth centuries.[95] Hell was a place conceived as full of activity,[96] in contrast to the passivity associated with purgatory.[97]

Nor did anybody doubt the physical aspect of the other spiritual places, beginning with purgatory, well defined at the start of the Late Middle Ages as a place where minor sinners were temporarily punished, with one entrance on the Irish Station Island on Lough Derg and another on the volcano Etna.[98] The same applied to the other intermediate places, the limbos, defined since the thirteenth century as two rooms, one occupied by the souls of children who died before being baptized and the other, the room of Abraham, for those who lived honestly but before the coming of Christ could redeem them.[99]

In 1396, Juan (John) I of Aragon died suddenly, potentially leading to his eternal damnation through not having been able to prepare for a good death. This was the excuse that the enemies of his circle of councillors had been waiting for to accuse them of negligence with the worst consequences: the king could be in Hell.[100] One of the accused, Viscount de Perellós, travelled to Lough Derg and entered purgatory, only returning after having interviewed the dead king, who assuaged his fears of possible eternal misery: "I talked a lot with the king, my lord, who, by God's grace, was on the way to salvation."[101] It is a very similar story to the journeys of the Cistercian monk Henry of Saltrey, which had been repeated since the twelfth century,[102] which arose from the need to influence the pro-

---

94 "Texts that announce corporal punishment, such as those that predict that the condemned will be tormented by fire in Hell, must be understood literally" (*Quare animabus damnatorum praenuntiant poenas corporeas, utpote quod ad igne inferni cruciabuntur, sunt secundum litteram intelligenda*). Cited from Thomas Aquinas, *Compendium Theologiae*. chap. 179, ed. F. J. H. Ruland (Paderborn, 1863), 152.

95 Jean-Louis Biget, *La cathédrale Sainte-Cécile* (Graulhet, 1998), 9–31.

96 Danièle Alexandre-Bidon, *La mort au Moyen Âge, XIIIᵉ-XVIᵉ siècle* (Paris, 1998), 276–89.

97 Anca Bratu, "L'ici-bas et l'au-delà en image: formes de représentation de l'espace et du temps," *Médiévales. Lange, textes, histoire* 20 (1991): 88–90.

98 Jacques Le Goff, *El nacimiento del Purgatorio* (Madrid, 1985), 205–39.

99 Jerôme Baschet, *Le sein du père. Abraham et la paternité dans l'Occident médiéval* (Paris, 2000), 229–349.

100 Flocel Sabaté, "El poder soberano en la Cataluña bajomedieval: definición y ruptura," in *Coups d'État à la fin du Moyen Âge? Aux fondements du pouvoir politique en Europe occidentale*, ed. François Foronda, Jean-Philippe Genet, José Manuel Nieto Soria (Madrid, 2005), 509–15.

101 *Parlí molt ab lo rei, mon senyor, lo qual, per la gràcia de Deu, era en via de salvació*. From Perellós, "Viatge del vescomte Ramon de Perellós," 41.

102 Maria Teresa Ferrer, "Activitats polítiques i militars de Ramon de Perellós (autor del 'Viatge al Purgatori de Sant Patrici' durant el regnat de Joan I)," in *Medioevo Hispano. Estudios in memoriam del Prof. Derek W. Lomax* (Madrid, 1995), 159–60.

cess against the members of the deceased king's royal council.[103] Indeed, another of the accused, the writer Bernat Metge, also interviewed the deceased (although in this case in dreams),[104] who exonerated him from any responsibility by stating that "the cause of my death [...] was that the deadline stated by Our Lord God arrived at that moment."[105]

The intersections between these spaces was the reason behind the prayers and donations offered by the living to shorten the time spent by their relatives in these intermediate places:[106] "Confronted with this unavoidability of 'post mortem' punishment, and burdened by sin, human beings clearly needed assistance in this world as much as the next."[107] Given the Church's status as intermediary, this need justified both the function of the clergy and the piety of the faithful. The role of relics and the cult of the saints[108] wove an intimate relation between people's everyday problems and these intercessors, rendering them an elemental constituent of medieval belief.[109] Similarly, angels and demons intervened in interrelations between the tangible physical world and spiritual matters, in accordance with Gregory the Great's explanation at the end of the sixth century that God created spirits without flesh, spirits with flesh, and flesh without spirit, in other words, angels, persons, and animals.[110] These intermediate beings inhabited complex societies which were not that different from human society: the angels occupied a strict hierarchy,[111] and a similar arrangement was in place in the regime of the devil.[112]

The coherence between the physical and the spiritual, between scientific explanation and religious discourse, extended to all of creation. The Earth was at the centre of the Universe, in accordance with the special status with which God had endowed man. The sphere with its Outer Ocean held three continents, consistent with the post-Flood biblical narrative: the world repopulated by the human race, with each of Noah's three

---

103 Marina Mitjà, "Procés contra els consellers, domèstics i curials de Joan I, entre ells Bernat Metge," *Boletín de la Real Academia de Buenas Letras de Barcelona* 27 (1957–1958): 375–417.

104 Joan Mahiques, "'Lo somni' de Bernat Metge i els tractats d'apareguts," *Llengua & Literatura* 16 (2005): 7–28.

105 *La causa de la mia mort—dix ell—és estada per tal com lo terme mi constituït per Nostre Senyor Déu a viure, finí aquella hora.* From Bernat Metge, *Lo somni* (Barcelona, 1980), 61.

106 Jean-Loup Lemaitre, "La commémoration des défunts à Saint-Pons de Thomières"; Daniel Picard, "Les suffrages prescrits pour ls défunts par les chapitres provinciaux des dominicains du Midi," in *La mort et l'au-delà en France méridionale XIIᵉ-XVᵉ siècle* (Toulouse, 1989), 77–102; 103–120.

107 Robert N. Swanson, *Religion and Devotion in Europe, c. 1215 – c. 1515* (Cambridge, 1994), 35.

108 Patrick J. Geary, *Furta sacra. Thefts of Relics in the Central Middle Ages* (Princeton, 1990), 3–43 and Pierre Jounel, *Le culte des saints dans les basíliques du Latran et du Vatican au douzième siècle* (Roma, 1977), 97–185; Éric Palazzo, *Liturgie et societé au Moyen Âge* (Paris, 2000), 177–93.

109 José Antonio. González Alcantud, "Seres intermedios: decadència y retroceso en la modernidad," in *Seres intermedios. Ángeles, Demonios y Genios en el Mundo Mediterráneo*, ed. Aurelio Pérez Jiménez, Gonzalo Cruz Andreotti (Málaga, 2001), 11–14.

110 Gregorius I, *Moralia*, chap. 16, 20 (cited from the online Patrologia Latina Database)

111 Claude Carozzi, "Hiérarchie angélique et tripartition fonctionelle chez Grégoire le Grand," in *Hiérarchies et services au Moyen Âge*, ed. Claude Carozzi, Huguette Taviani-Carozzi (Aix-en-Provence, 2001), 31–51.

112 Alfonso M. di Nola, *Historia del Diablo* (Madrid, 1992), 269–71.

sons presiding over a continent: Japheth in Europe, Shem in Asia, and Ham in Africa.[113] This world's centre was Jerusalem and the Mediterranean, while, certain islands, deserts, and mountains, often at the margins or furthest reaches of the world, hosted a wide variety of curious beings: plants (like the mandrake with anthropomorphic roots), animals (basilisks, and manticores, and so on),[114] and mythical humans (pigmies, giants, amazons, cynocephaly, blemmyes, sciapods, and so forth).[115] These lands—such as the Fortunate Islands or the places encountered by St. Brendan in the West,[116] or the land of ferocious and even anthropophagic biblical characters of Gog and Magog, concordant with the prophecies of Ezekiel in the Old Testament, in the East—[117] were believed to exist by virtue of tales, but proved difficult to place. These places were thus relegated to the extremities of the earth by travellers in the thirteenth century, but not denied entirely by them; quite the contrary, their narrations often elaborated with detailed descriptions of sightings of fantastic animals, strange and pagan peoples, and even demons.[118] Such images were edifying to Christians[119] because they reminded them of the evangelizing work that remained to be done given the evidence that there were still "huge regions that were entirely foreign to Christianity."[120]

Moreover, it was believed to be possible to find the place where God had located the earthly Paradise. Belief in the story of Genesis as historical fact left no room for doubt that Paradise inhabited a specific physical and earthly reality.[121] Thus, during the Middle Ages, diverse hypotheses for defining the precise location of Paradise were pursued,[122] whether in an island setting or land-locked, in the Far East, India, Mesopotamia, or

---

113 Pascal Arnaud, "'Plurima orbis imago'. Lectures conventionnelles des cartes au Moyen Age," *Médiévales* 18 (1990): 33–51.

114 Claude Kappler, *Monstruos, demonios y maravillas a fines de la edad media* (Madrid, 1986), 36–41.

115 Juan Casas, "Razas humanas portentosas en las partidas remotas del mundo (de Benjamín de Tudela a Cristóbal Colón)," in *Maravillas, peregrinaciones y utopías: Literatura de viajes en el mundo románico*, ed. Rafael Beltrán (València, 2002), 253–90.

116 Kevin R. Wittmann, *Las islas del fin del mundo. Representación de las Afortunadas en los mapas del Occidente medieval* (Lleida, 2016), 23–111 and Benedeit, *El viaje de San Brandán* (Madrid, 1983), 1–60.

117 Miguel Ángel Ladero Quesada, *Espacios del hombre medieval* (Madrid, 2002), 32–33.

118 Felicitas Schmieder, "Travelling in the 'Orbis Christianus' and beyond (Thirteenth–Fifteenth Century): What makes the difference?," in *Identities on the Move*, ed. Flocel Sabaté (Bern, 2014), 41–42.

119 Chantal Connochie-Bourgne, "L'exemple des peuples d'ailleurs," in *En quête d'Utopies*, ed. Claude Thomasset, Danièle James-Raoul (Paris, 2005), 183–94; Chantal Connochie-Bourgne, "Ailleurs, d'autres vies exemplaires (dans quelques encyclopédies et récits de voyage)," in *Utopies i alternatives de vida a l'edat mitjana*, ed. Flocel Sabaté, (Lleida, 2009), 111–25.

120 Schmieder, "Travelling," 43–51.

121 Jean Delumeau, *Une histoire du paradis. Le jardin des délices* (Paris, 1992), 11–35.

122 Felicitas Schmieder, "Paradise Islands in East and West. Tradition and Meaning in some Cartographical Places on the Medieval Rim of the World," in *Isolated Island in Medieval Mind, Culture and Nature*, ed. Gerhard Jaritz, Torstein Jørgensen (Budapest, 2011), 3–22.

Armenia, though it was suspected by some that it may not have survived the Flood. The search for the lost kingdom of the legendary Christian patriarch Prester John, which was first imagined in Asia and finally agreed to be traceable to Ethiopia, was often linked to a belief that it was located next to Paradise.[123] In any case, it was logical, according to the medieval world-view, to include in depictions of the Earth a place that corresponded to Paradise, although it might be imagined to be somewhere so well protected that super-human resources were necessary to visit it.[124] Late medieval literature contributes vari-ous stories of visits to Paradise depicted in matter-of-fact fashion and including detailed visions of the Tree of Good and Evil mentioned in Genesis, or the Tree of Salvation, whose wood was used to make the cross of Jesus Christ, as well as the source of the four great rivers of the world.[125]

Given the assumption that the Earth was a sphere, the possible existence of human habitation at the antipodes, on the lower part of the globe, had to be entertained. The main problem was that any humans on the other side of the world had to be connected monogenetically to Adam in order to benefit from God's work and Christian redemp-tion. On the basis of the fact that the Holy Scriptures could not lie, Augustine of Hippo proposed the following:

> For Scripture, which proves the truth of its historical statements through the accomplish-ment of its prophecies, gives no false information; and it is too absurd to suggest that some men might have taken ship and traversed the whole wide ocean, crossing from this side of the world to the other, and that thus even the inhabitants of that distant region are descended from that one first man.[126]

The Aristotelian explanation of magnetic attraction, accepted by Thomas Aquinas's mentor, Albert the Great (ca. 1200–1280), dissipated doubts about the physical sustain-ability of humankind on the opposite side of the world, while increased sea travel led people to reason that these human beings would not be so isolated as at first believed, and thus it was likely that they too were descendants of Adam, and worthy of Christ's

---

123 John Roland Seymour Phillips, *The Medieval Expansion of Europe* (Oxford, 1998), 144–45.

124 "The maps of the Middle Ages offer us some of the same materials: paradise is situated to the east, surrounded by a wall or mountains, and sometimes separated by an ocean. Although the barriers hindered access, this region was a place that in reality was located somewhere on the globe, and was thus, somewhere that could be visited, although one had to resort to supernatural means." (En los mapas de la Edad Media nos ofrece algo de los mismos materiales: el paraíso se sitúa al oriente, rodeado por una muralla o montañas, y a veces separado por un océano. Aunque las barreras le hicieran difícil el acceso, esta región era un lugar que en realidad se localizaba en alguna parte del globo, y por tanto, era un lugar que podía visitarse, aunque se tuviera que recurrir a medios sobrenaturales.) Cited from Howard R. Patch, *El otro mundo en la literatura medieval* (Ciudad de México,1983), 161.

125 Patch, *El otro mundo*, 173–75.

126 *Quoniam nullo modo Scriptura ista mentitur, quae narratis praeteritis facit fidem, eo quod eius praedicta complentur: nimisque absurdum est, ut dicatur aliquos homines ex hac in illam partem, Oceani immensitate traiecta, navigare ac pervenire potuisse, ut etiam illic ex uno illo primo homino genus institueretur humanum.* Cited from Augustine of Hippo, *De civitate Dei*, bk. 16, chap. 9, in various online locations (e.g., accessed April 22, 2019 at https://la.wikisource.org/wiki/De_civitate_Dei/Liber_XVI) and with various English translations online.

redemption. Nevertheless, in the fifteenth century, Alonso Fernández de Madrigal (ca. 1400–1455), Castilian bishop and writer, continued to doubt the existence of the antipodes stating that if they did exist, they would have received the attention of the apostles, who travelled all over the world to spread the Gospel, and that there was no evidence that any of them went to the antipodes.[127] At the same time, however, Prince Henrique de Portugal (1394–1460), commonly known as Henry the Navigator, invoked scientific curiosity and the duty to evangelize to justify the Portuguese campaigns of expansion:

> Being convinced through philosophy and cosmography that there were lands below the line of the equinox, and other peoples hidden from us, determined the principle of curiosity and zeal to increase the faith of Jesus Christ in discovering lands.[128]

In the sixteenth century, at the Spanish conquest of America, Francisco López de Gómara remarked that the capacity of the Spanish vessels meant the prior supposition that the antipodes were unreachable could be overcome, confirming that they were also human beings destined to receive the Christian message: "I well believe that they never knew the way from them, as they, the Indians, who we call antipodes, did not have enough ships for such a long and hard sail as the Spanish do in the Ocean."[129]

The coherence between spiritual and physical spaces allowed for a level of permeability, which was the reason why it was easy to believe that God used nature, and especially the celestial spaces, to send messages. The heavenly bodies not only influenced the tides and the growth of plants, but also, according to interpretations of a blend of astronomy and astrology, determined the *fastus* and *nefastus* days.[130] The Holy Scriptures demonstrate how God revealed the relation between the terrestrial and celestial spaces in dreams: Genesis explains the dream in which God showed Jacob the ladder to heaven, which became a symbol of the path to progressive perfection and a route for the blessed according to it featuring regularly in iconography.[131] God also used stars to send specific messages: the Gospel according to St. Matthew describes the "wise men" (Magi) reaching Jesus guided by a star, as repeatedly recounted in the Middle Ages (and beyond).[132] It is no surprise that all unexpected events in the sky and nature were inter-

---

127 Nelson Papavero, Jorge Llorente-Bousquets, David Espinosa, *Historia de la biología comparada desde el Génesis hasta el siglo de las Luces*, 8 vols. (Ciudad de México, 1995), 3:54.

128 *Avendo entendido por la philosophia y cosmographia que avía otras tierras de baxo de la línia equenocial y otras gentes ascondidas a nosotros detreminó al principio por curiosidad y después por selo de aumento de la fee de Jesú Christo descubrir tierras.* Cited from Jerónimo Román, *História das Ínclitas Cavalarias do Cristo, Santiago e Avis* (Porto, 2008), 120.

129 *Bien creo que nunca jamás se supiera el camino por ellos, pues no tenían los indios, a quien llamamos antípodas, navíos bastantes para tan larga y recia navegación como hacen españoles por el mar Océano.* Cited from Francisco López de Gómara, "Hispania victrix. Primera y segunda parte de la Historia General de las Indias," in *Historiadores Primitivos de Indias,* ed. Enrique de Vedia, 3 vols. (Madrid, 1852), 1:160.

130 Flocel Sabaté, "The King's Power and Astrology in the Crown of Aragon," forthcoming.

131 Gérard de Champeaux, Sébastien Sterckx, *Introducción a los símbolos* (Madrid, 1984), 198 and Matilde Battistini, *Simboli e Allegorie* (Milano, 2003), 238–40.

132 Franco Cardini, *Los Reyes Magos. Historia y leyenda* (Barcelona, 2001), 57–163.

preted as direct warnings about great events. What was required was to know how to interpret these signs appropriately, although, in some cases immediate events provided a meaning: a whale stranded at the mouth of the Llobregat in Barcelona in June 1458, brought an omen that was explained a few weeks later when news arrived from Naples concerning the death of King Alfonso the Magnanimous.[133] Messages from the other side harnessed the fascination of medieval men and women for the marvellous, as is the case of comets,[134] where information could either be interpreted as negative, or as something positive, as the announcement of the Magi in the Gospel. The famous Bayeux Tapestry related the crowning of King Harold on January 6, 1066 and the passing of Halley's comet across the English sky on April 24.[135] Rather than bringing bad news for King Harold, the *stella* could be seen as announcing the good news of the coming invasion by William the Conquer. This is the reason why the comet was incorporated in the tapestry that was created, probably at Bayeux itself, as promotion—indeed propaganda—for the new Norman ruler.[136]

The concordance between the physical world and explanations derived from the Holy Scriptures could be extended to all creation, because nature had arisen from the divine design. In line with Aristotelian reasoning, the qualities of each natural element could be learned and, from this, the corresponding interpretation deduced. Lapidaries, herbaries, and bestiaries warned about the properties inherent in each thing.[137] For example, wearing an emerald neutralized poison ingested, or from the bite of an animal, but care had be taken because this protection was destroyed if a maiden lost her virginity while she was wearing the gem.[138] In fact, care was needed to avoid the erroneous use of many products: an inadequate ingestion of plants before sexual relations could mean spawning malformations or dwarfism, for instance.[139] At the same time, all living things carried a specific meaning, which conferred symbolic efficacy on them, as is especially clear with regard to the animal kingdom: the elephant, the beaver, and the unicorn, for example, symbolized chastity.[140] Not only did they represent archetypes, but their qualities as beings created by God, each with its respective characteristics, referred to values interpreted as those of Christian society.[141]

---

133 Flocel Sabaté, *Lo senyor rei és mort!* (Lleida, 1994), 21–22 and *Dietaris de la Generalitat de Catalunya*, ed. Josep Maria Sans, 10 vols. (Barcelona, 1994–2007), 1:142.

134 Jacques Le Goff, *Lo maravilloso y lo cotidiano en el Occidente medieval* (Barcelona, 1985), 9–17.

135 Montserrat Pagès, *El tapís de Bayeux, eina política? Anàlisi de les imatges i nova interpretació* (Barcelona, 2015), 51–52.

136 Xavier Barral i Altet, *En souvenir du roi Guillaume. La broderie de Bayeaux* (Paris, 2016), 91–97.

137 Lluís Cifuentes, *La ciència en català a l'edat mitjana i el Renaixement* (Barcelona, 2001), 274–88.

138 Joan Gili, *Lapidari. Tractat de pedres precioses* (Oxford, 1977), 1–30.

139 J. Ramón Gómez, *Las plantas en la brujería medieval (propiedades y creencias)* (Madrid, 1998), 79–108.

140 Robert Delort, *Les animaux ont une histoire* (Paris, 1990), 76–84.

141 Gerhard Jaritz, "Oxen and Hogs, Monkeys and Parrots: Using 'Familiar' and 'Unfamiliar' Fauna in Late Medieval Visual Representation," in *Animal Diversities,* ed. Gerhard Jaritz, Alice Choyke (Krems, 2005), 107–22.

It was believed that in creating each of these living things, God used different combinations of the four elements: earth, water, fire, and air, corresponding to the four qualities of material: cold, humid, dry, or hot.[142] Knowing the combination of each thing enabled its qualities to be revealed, this being the task of physics, although at the time this was based on observation, as Robert Grosseteste and Roger Bacon stressed in the fourteenth century.[143] Abiogenesis, or spontaneous generation, which was thought to enable worms to be born from earth, flies from rotting meat, and eels from the earth, was an extreme example of the combining of elements. The ability to correctly interpret dreams or diagnose digestive issues provided access to each person's predominant combination. Everything was explained through the same framework of reasoning: sexual attraction was the combination of the woman's cold womb and the man's hot sperm;[144] and the differences between Spaniards and French, as Munzer would state in the sixteenth century, were related to the hotter and drier temperament of the former compared to the cold, humid one of the latter.[145] Everything thus depended on the right balance, as for medicine, which combined four humours concordant with the elements: black bile, blood, bile, and phlegm.[146] Illnesses were imbalances and bleeding had to be applied, but also purgatives, and in other cases, aids to sweating and sneezing in order to restore balance.[147] Imbalance could also occur in nature as a result of human activity, and thus polluting the water or the air through craft activities was seen as a serious issue, especially when, from the thirteenth century on, increases in production led to dumping waste including lime, oil, or the by-products of tanneries, in the elements.[148]

Imbalances in nature were thought to lead to droughts, excessive rains, or even earthquakes, all very significant for a society highly dependent upon nature. Given the link made between natural and spiritual environments, these imbalances were interpreted as punishment for the behaviour of humans and, thus, expressions of anger on the part of an anthropomorphized God annoyed because his dictates were not being followed or due to excessive complicity with his enemies, including the non-assimilable religious minorities. As Joëlle Ducos stated, "meteorology is therefore the sign of the power of

---

142 Edward Grant, *La ciencia física en la edad media* (Ciudad de México, 2016), 145–54.

143 Manuel Sanromà, "El camino hasta el Big Bang," in *La cosmología hasta el siglo XXI: entre la física y la filosofía*, eds. Juan Arana et al. (Tarragona, 2011), 20.

144 Danielle Jacquart, Claude Thomasset, *Sexualidad y saber médico en la edad media* (Barcelona, 1989), 45–82.

145 Alexandra Testino-Zafiropoulos, "Representaciones imaginarias de España en Francia en el siglo XVII. Del saber enciclopédico a los relatos de viaje," in *L'imaginaire du territoire en Espagne et au Portugal (XVIe–XVIIe siècles)*, ed. François Delpech (Madrid, 2008), 25.

146 Luis García Ballester, *La búsqueda de la salud. Sanadores y enfermos en la España medieval* (Barcelona, 2001), 129–76.

147 Antoni Cardoner, *Història de la medicina a la Corona d'Aragó (1162–1479)* (Barcelona, 1973), 128–52.

148 Jean-Pierre Leguay, *La pollution au Moyen Âge dans le royaume de France et dans les grands fiefs* (Paris, 1999), 6–62.

God, a sign sometimes terrible as the flood or, conversely, as beneficent as manna."[149] So, municipal authorities tended to respond to each natural misfortune by calling for divine mercy through the usual devotional practices, beginning with processions and continuing by attempting to correct the customs, while conceding "that God in his mercy wants to bring us this bad weather."[150] It was especially important to find out what had been done wrong and correct it. Faced with the above-mentioned climatic problems suffered in Elche in 1371 and in 1379, the town council discerned that the divine punishment was due to the high number of adulterous women and clergymen who had sexual relations in the town.[151] Late medieval preachers, who travelled around the towns and cities whose people lived in fear of such natural phenomena, helped to root out the causes of divine wrath, often blaming excesses of blasphemy, gambling, or prostitution. The welfare of society depended on not provoking divine wrath. As the famous Dominican Vicent Ferrer stated, the aim was for human behaviour to evoke the opposite response in God: "Our Lord God will say: I like this, I am happy."[152] Given the consequences, the rulers had to take great care, as Ferrer continued, "because some have to account for themselves and others, because they are councillors from villages."[153] The councillors were therefore expected to legislate, for example, to avoid coexistence with God's enemies. Consequently, fears grew about tolerating male homosexuals or coexisting with Jews, and this led to rising levels of tension towards these groups, who found themselves accused of provoking divine wrath.[154]

These fears increased towards the end of the Middle Ages, since millenarian fears[155] were fuelling concerns about the world reaching the end of time without God's people having achieved the evangelical mandate enabling them to be united in obedience to the Church of Christ: "there will be one flock and one shepherd."[156] This led to reflec-

---

149 *La météorologie est donc bien le signe de la puissance de Dieu, signe parfois redoutable comme le déluge ou au contraire bienfaisant comme la manne.* Cited from Joelle Ducos, "Le temps qu'il fait. Signe de Dieu ou de mal. La métereologia du Bourgeois de Paris," in *Le mal et le diable. Leurs figures à la fin du Moyen Âge*, ed. Nathalie Nabert (Paris, 1996), 96.

150 *Que Déus per la sua mercè nos vuylle aquesta mal temps levar.* Cited from Olivera, Riera, Lambert, Banda, Alexandre, *Els terratrèmols*, 64.

151 Ibarra, "Elig," 2:37–9.

152 *Dirà nostra senyor Déus: 'Plau-me, jo só content.* Cited from Vicent Ferrer, *Sermons*, ed. Gret Schib, 6 vols. (Barcelona, 1971–1988), 3:11.

153 *Per què són alguns que han a retre compte de si matex e de altres, axí com regidors de viles.* Cited from Ferrer, *Sermons*, 3:13.

154 Flocel Sabaté, "Les juifs au moyen-âge. Les sources catalanes concernant l'ordre et le désordre," in *Chrétiens et juifs au Moyen Âge: sources pour la recherche d'une relation permanente*, ed. Flocel Sabaté, Claude Denjean (Lleida, 2006), 124–36.

155 Marjorie Reeves, "Pauta y propósito en la historia: los periodos de la baja Edad Media y el Renacimento," in *La teoría del apocalipsis y los fines del mundo*, ed. Malcolm Bull (Ciudad de México, 1998), 109–32.

156 Γενήσεται μία ποίμνη, είζ ποιμήν (*fiet unum ovile et unus pastor*). From the Gospel of John 10:16.

tions about how to achieve the necessary unity.[157] Roger Bacon (ca. 1220–ca. 1292), the English scholastic philosopher and Franciscan friar, anticipated the return of the Greeks (the Eastern Church) and the conversion of the Tartars, but saw no other solution for the recalcitrant Muslims than their destruction.[158] Thus, fear became embedded in a medieval society as an adjunct of its absolute coherence. This fear contributed to intolerance towards that which was not assimilable.

This attitude to otherness was part of the same sense of security that articulated medieval society around its beliefs. We might assert that the strength of the medieval world was not in its physical power or the status of its rulers but in its intellectual mind: people felt sure they were part of a single coherent entity: environment, social order, power, and the concordance between spiritual and physical spheres. All was integrated.

Thus, we can interpret the end of the Middle Ages as the progressive demolition of a well-structured edifice. This can be perceived as part of a long path from the fifteenth to the twentieth century through a sequence of new thoughts symbolized by Copernicus, Luther, Kant, Darwin, and Freud. Certainly, Copernicus's displacement of the Earth from the central position it was previously assumed to inhabit in the universe, meant an end to understanding the universe as an expression of the circular movement of the celestial bodies. Disavowing, with Luther, the central tenets of expiatory religion (confession, indulgences, and purgatory), the physical reality of Paradise and Hell, and the presence of God in the Eucharist, destroyed the central knot of belief that justified the position, power, and behaviour of the Church. Later, following Kant, interpreting the world from the perspective of the subject, Aristotelian realism was displaced as the basis for religion and the interpretation of the world; explaining all living beings, including humanity, through an evolutionary framework, as Darwin did, displaced the central role of creation; and finally, Freud's influential discourse on conscious and unconscious levels of the human mind destabilized our view of human autonomy. At this point, the whole edifice of medieval certainties had collapsed.

With the disavowal of central axes, a variety of truths were destabilized. Thus, in the seventeenth century, Kepler broke with the celestial symbolism based on circular orbits, undisputed synonym of perfection in the medieval sky, and presented the heavenly bodies following elliptical orbits; Reti questioned spontaneous generation; Harvey reconfigured the workings of the body through the circulation of blood; and Boyle questioned a nature explained by the combination of the four elements, which was to be finally displaced by Cavendish and Lavoisier in the eighteenth century. Also in that century, Cuvier would question the Flood and Linnaeus advanced towards a taxonomic classification of animals. Condorcet broke with the identification between universal history and the history of Christian salvation and introduced a new teleology into history, based on the concept of progress. In the nineteenth century, Pasteur discarded spontaneous generation entirely and moved forward with microbial explanations. And in the

---

157 Marjorie Reeves, *The Influence of Prophecy in the Later Middle Ages. A Study in Joachimism* (Oxford, 1969), 399.

158 Aleksey Klemeshov, "The Conversion and Destruction of the infidels in the Works of Roger Bacon," in *Religions and Power in Europe*, ed. Joaquim Carvalho (Pisa, 2007), 23.

twentieth century, Bultmann could imagine God without breaking the cosmic weave to intervene in human affairs.[159]

Even geography has changed: the island of St. Brendan ceased to be depicted on maps from the seventeenth century onwards, in 1790 the entrance to purgatory in Lough Derg was destroyed, and in 2007, Pope Benedict XVI recognized that limbo did not exist. The earth no longer had unknown extremes or wondrous islands. It was well charted by the twentieth century, enabling Paul Valéry to proclaim:

> The era of vacant land, free territories, places that are nobody's, and thus, the era of free expansion, is closed. No more rocks without a flag or blank places on the map [...]. The time of the completed world begins.[160]

Adaptable Christian Ideology

The establishment of Christianity as the official religion of the Roman Empire from 380 sanctioned the use of religious ideology to justify political ends. From then on, as Averil Cameron explains, "emperors undoubtedly involved themselves in religious matters for reason of state."[161] The intertwining of affairs of Church and State involved the acceptance of Christian dictate by the sovereign and legitimized Christianity as the ideology on which the exercise of power was founded and from which the maintenance of social order was derived.

In symbolic terms, the acceptance of Christianity by the Germanic kingdoms converted religion into the backbone of political management and social behaviour: "the State religion in the barbarian kingdoms represented the fundamental pact between the people and the divine."[162] The exercise of power through the Church in the Early Middle Ages can thus be defined as "the formation of the political-religious ideologies of the West."[163] The Carolingian culmination not only brought political power and religious discourse into close conjunction but also charged the clergy with elucidating ideology, as Georges Duby observes: "in the Carolingian tradition, the episcopate is the natural producer of ideology."[164]

Evolution towards a feudal society arose from specific social, economic and, political developments.[165] However, this tended to solidify in a social model clearly defined

---

159 Sabaté, *Vivir y sentir*, 98–99.

160 *L'ère des terrains vagues, des territoires libres, des lieux qui ne sont à personne, donc l'ère de libre expansion est close. Plus de roc qui ne porte un drapeau; plus de vides sur la carte [...]. Le temps du monde fini commence.* Cited from Paul Valéry, *Regards sur le monde actual*, 2 vols. (Paris, 1962), 2:923.

161 Cameron, *The Mediterranean*, 69.

162 *La religion d'État dans les royaumes barbares représente le pacte fondamental qui unit le peuple au divin.* Cited from Dumézil, *Les racines chrétiennes*, 181.

163 *La formación de las ideologías politicoreligiosas de Occidente.* Cited from Paul, *La Iglesia*, 7.

164 *En la tradición carolingia, el episcopado es el productor natural de ideología.* Cited from Georges Duby, *Los tres órdenes o lo imaginario del feudalismo* (Barcelona, 1983), 37.

165 Georges Duby, *Guerreros y campesinos. Desarrollo inicial de la economía europea (500–1200)*

through the ideological contribution of the Church. The arguments flowed from the ecclesiastic environment, continuing the earlier tradition. This made sense because, as Miguel Ángel Ladero has highlighted, "at that time the clergy were the only group with the intellectual capacity to interpret society according to an ideological framework."[166] It was ecclesiastical authors, beginning with Adalberon of Laon and Gerard of Florennes, who first established the idea of society as articulated in three groups, arguing that this tripartite order was God's natural order.[167] The first group ruled and fought, the second prayed, and the third group worked the land. This distilled society to three essential functions (*pugnare, orare, agricolari–laborare*) which, as Georges Duby remarked, was a specific view of society "in the service of an ideology."[168]

The traditional definitions of feudalism from the nineteenth century[169] and those related to the so-called feudal revolution elaborated in the second half of the twentieth[170] presented the medieval Church as an antidote to the excesses of barons or a victim of the process of change. However, analysis of documentary evidence concerned with specific territories, such as Catalonia, shows that the Church played a central role in the adoption of new legal and formal frameworks with which to adapt to new circumstances.[171] Thus the Church was able to intervene decisively in new social and political structures thanks to the so-called Gregorian reform. This can be seen as "a turning point in the long and painful process of adapting pontifical power to the socio-political reality that engulfed the Church in the middle of the eleventh century,"[172] but especially as an adaptation by the Church which enabled it to maintain ideological power over society.

Implementation of the reform of the Church spread throughout the twelfth century, coinciding with the diffusion of Roman law around Europe,[173] which structured the new

---

(Madrid, 1985), 7–197; Jean-Pierre Poly and Éric Bournazel, *El cambio feudal (siglos X al XII)* (Barcelona, 1983), 3–237.

166 *El clero era entonces el único grupo con capacidad de definición ideológica y a través de su mirada intelectual se contemplaba al resto de la sociedad.* Cited from Miguel Ángel Ladero, *Católica y latina. La cristiandad occidental entre los siglos IV y XVII* (Madrid, 2000), 20.

167 Marc Bloch, *La société féodale* (Paris, 1994), 395–493.

168 *Está al servicio de una ideología.* Cited from Duby, *Los tres órdenes*, 26, 33.

169 Flocel Sabaté, "Une histoire médiévale pour l'identité catalane," in *Intégration et disintégration en Europe central et orientale*, ed. Sergiu Miscoiu, Nicolae Päun (Paris, 2016), 47–48.

170 Pierre Bonnassie, *La Catalogne du milieu du Xe à la fin du XIe siècle*, 2 vols. (Toulouse, 1976), 2:550–52.

171 "The Church played a crucial role here: having clearly benefitted from the previous process of encastellation and seigneuralization, it became a pioneer in using the formulations of feudal links and relationships; its rights and revenues benefitted from a veritable clericalization of justice; it protected itself using mechanisms like sanctuary and peace and truce of God, which simultaneously enhanced its social clout." Sabaté, "The Catalonia of the 10th to 12th centuries," 44.

172 *Um ponto de inflexâo do longo e penoso processo de adaptaçâo do poder pontifício à realidade sócio-política que envolveu a Igreja em meados do século XI.* Cited from Rust, *Colunas de Sâo Pedro*, 513.

173 André Gouron, "Un assaut en deux vagues: la diffusion du droit romain dans l'Europe du XXe siècle," in *El dret comú i Catalunya. Actes del Ier Simposi internacional (Barcelona, 25–26 de maig de*

realities and facilitated new social and political frameworks.[174] The Church participated fully in this dynamic, consolidating canon law and articulating a comprehensive legal presence that invigorated the everyday expression of power. The intermixing of law and theology was far-reaching in its effects, as Paolo Grossi argues: "the canonists were able to achieve the result that those who deployed civil law could not because they had an extra arrow in their quiver: the familiarity with explicitly theological reasoning."[175] Certainly, the incorporation in law of concepts borrowed from theology, such as the *corpus mysticum*, strengthened the conceptual toolkit, and was soon accepted by all those involved in the political game.[176]

The legal framework adopted by the Church, the *Codex Iuris Canonici*, included most of the decrees passed by the Fourth Lateran Council IV held in 1215, which ensured the durability of its influence.[177] In fact, the Council was intended to show the power and influence of the papacy over all Christendom,[178] and adapt religion to its contemporary challenges. Certainly, Church and Christianity continued to be authoritative thanks to an extensive set of measures: assuring the full rights of ecclesiastical courts in their sphere; reinforcing episcopal powers; controlling the clergy; using excommunication as a threat in conflicts against civil authorities; stressing the model of the family by imposing exogamic, public, and Christian marriage; permeating the conscience of the faithful through annual confession and Easter communion; articulating a practice of social assistance including the spiritual treatment of the sick by medics; and regulating relations with non-assimilable minorities, like the Jews, who would henceforth be compelled to wear badges on their clothing.

The progressive implementation of these demands, accepted by rulers and disseminated among the population by preachers, was a reflection of the influence of the Church over the people. At the same time, it also showed the Church's enduring capacity for adaptation, both regarding its discourse of self-justification and the model of religion it spread among the populace. We see this in the example of how attitudes towards the wealthy evolved, affecting attitudes to merchant. At the start of the thirteenth century, the devil was described as entering the city of Lleida disguised as a merchant: "he was a devil, who resembling a merchant, entered the city and procured here everything he could."[179]

1990), ed. Aquilino Iglesia (Barcelona, 1991), 47–63.

174 Paul Freedman, "Catalan Lawyers and the Origins of Serfdom," *Mediaeval Studies* 48 (1986): 283–314 and Dieter Mertens, *Il pensiero politicomedievale* (Bologna, 1999), 85–93.

175 *Los canonistas alcanzan el resultado al que no llegaron los civilistas porque tienen una flecha de más en su arco: la familiaridad con razones exquisitamente teológicas.* Cited from Paolo Grossi, *El orden jurídico medieval* (Madrid, 1996), 218.

176 Ernst Kantorowicz, *The King's Two Bodies. A Study in Medieval Political Theology* (Princeton, 1957), 195–270.

177 Hans Wolter, "El Pontificado en la cúspide de su poder (1198–1216)," in *Manual de Historia de la Iglesia*, ed. Hubert Jedin, 10 vols. (Barcelona, 1966–1987), 4:290–91.

178 José Orlandis, *El pontificado romano en la historia* (Madrid, 1996), 141.

179 *Ere un diable, lo qual en semblanza de mercader se n·entrà en una ciutat e procurava aquí tot al que podia.* Cited from *Miracles de la Verge Maria*, ed. Antoni Maria Parramon (Lleida, 1976), 42.

The activity of the merchant was viewed with distrust, and on nearing death some merchants were thus moved to compensate in their wills for the *lucrum* they had earned in life.[180] As a response to this, by the end of that century a model of behaviour was dictated by Ramon Llull who explained that after his son's education was completed, the burgher Evast, who, through inheritance from his father, was "very wealthy in material riches," donated his assets to the poor and dissolved his marriage, for he moved into a monastery and his wife into a nunnery.[181] However, around this same time in Paris, *Le dit des marchéans* not only praised the merchants but also gave them precedence: the "Holy Church was first established by Merchants."[182] This conceptual path culminated in the fourteenth century with views such as those of the Catalan moralist Francesc Eiximenis, who stated that, after the clergy, the most esteemed by God were the merchants, because they were the basis of the wealth necessary for society and the public sphere to exist:

> The moralist Philogolus explained that the merchant must be stressed among the different jobs that put the *res publica* on a good level, because the land where trade runs profusely is always full, fertile and in a good state. Accordingly the same author stated that merchants should be favoured over any other people in the secular world, because, he said, the merchants are the life of the land on which they reside; treasure of the *res publica*; the food of the poor people; and the arm of any good business and fulfilment of all affairs. Without merchants, the communities fall, princes become tyrants, the young are losers, and the poor cry. This situation is reached because neither knights nor citizens living off the rent give large alms; only merchants are generous in giving alms and they become great parents and brothers of the *res publica*, especially when they are good men and have a good conscience.[183]

So much so that the same writer concluded that "all the *res publica* should pray at all times, especially for the merchants."[184] In fact, it was then widely understood that it was good that the bourgeoisie were rich. In 1376, the members of the municipal government of Balaguer expressed this as a matter of fact to their lord, the count of Urgell: "The *res publica* has a strong interest in its citizens, from which it is supported, maintained and

---

180 Lleida, Arxiu Capitular de Lleida, calaix 20, num. 4685.

181 *Molt abundós de les temporals riquees.* Cited from Ramon Llull, *Llibre d'Evast e Blanquerna* (Barcelona, 1987), 31.

182 *Sainte Yglise premierement fu par Marchéanz establie.* Cited from Anatole de Montaiglon, Gaston Raynaud, *Recueil Général et compet des fabliaux des XIIIᵉ et XIVᵉ siècles* (Paris, 1877), 44.

183 *Posa ací Filògolus, moralista, que entre los altres oficis que posen la cosa pública en bon estament són los mercaders, car terra on mercaderia corre e abunda, tostemps és plena, e fèrtil e en bon estament. Per tal, los mercaders diu que deuen ésser favorits sobre tota gent seglar del món, car diu que los mercaders són vida de la terra on són, e són tresor de la cosa pública, e són menjar dels pobres, e són braç de tot bon negoci, de tots afers compliment. Sens mercaders les comunitats caen, los prínceps tornen tirans, los jóvens se perden, los pobres se'n ploren. Car cavallers ne ciutadans que viuen de rendes no curen de gran almoines; solament mercaders són grans almoiners e grans pares e frares de la cosa pública, majorment quan són bons homens e ab bona consciència.* Cited from Francesc Eiximenis, "Dotzè del Crestià," chap. 399; Francesc Eiximenis, *Lo Crestià (selecció)*, ed. Albert Hauf (Barcelona, 1983), 223–24.

184 *Tota la cosa pública deuria fer oració tostemps especial per los mercaders.* Cited from Eiximenis, "Dotzè del Crestià," chap. 399; Eiximenis, *Lo Crestià (selecció)*, 224.

raised, being rich and prominent in temporal wealth, because otherwise, if they are poor, the *res publica* decays and dies."[185]

The public sphere and all the levels of government benefited if its subjects were rich, as the representatives of all the estates in Catalonia—nobles and barons, churchmen, and the men of cities and towns—stated in the court held in Monzón in 1362, concerning negotiations regarding the financial backing demanded by the sovereign: "it is good, for the princes and for the *res publica* that the inhabitants and others who dwell within their kingdoms, principalities, and lands are abundant in wealth and in large quantities of coins."[186]

The wandering friars, in particular the Franciscans, came up with a new definition and specific language adequate for encompassing a public urban space embodying Christian doctrine, a collective expression of identity and the new economic reality.[187] Thus "the conscious effort made by the Friars Minor to annex, re-think, codify, and institutionalize, in both positive and negative terms, both political and economic behaviour, which, up to that point had been on the margins of Christian discourse," can be appreciated.[188] In this way, the Christian ideal became mixed with the public body, a political concept increasingly identified with the municipal.[189] This was justified by the *utilitas rei publicae*, which included, in the words of Thomas Aquinas, the *commune bonum mercatorum*.[190] All components of the equation participated in the ideal of the *bonum commune*,[191] which came to be understood as being as "synonymous with the Christian town as 'Corpus Christi'."[192] In this context, each human being was valued as an indi-

---

185 *Sie gran interès de la cosa pública que·ls singulars per sufragi e ajuda dels quals és sostinguda, mantinguda e exalçada sien richs e abmidats en béns temporals, car per lo contrari, com són empobrits, la cosa pública pereix e decau.* Cited from Dolors Domingo, *Pergamins de Privilegis de la ciutat de Balaguer* (Lleida, 1997), 138.

186 *Als príceps e a la cosa pública sia profitós que·lls habitants et domiciliats dins los regnes e terres e principats d'aquells sien habundants en riqueses e en grans quantitats de monedes.* Cited from Josep Maria Pons Guri, *Actas de las Cortes Generales de la Corona de Aragón de 1362–63* (Madrid, 1982), 72.

187 The people of that time perceived this; for instance, since 1261 St. Francis of Assisi had become patron and protector of the merchants of Pisa. Lester K. Little, *Pobreza voluntaria y economía de beneficio en la Europa medieval* (Madrid, 1983), 267.

188 *Lo sforzo fortemente consapevole compiuto dai Minori di annettere, risemantizzare e, per questa via, codificare ed istituzionazzare in positivo, o in negativo, comportamenti politici, ed economici, sino a quel momento ai margini della dicibilità cristiana.* Cited from Paolo Evangelisti, "I 'pauperes Christi' e i lingiaggi dominative. I franciscani come protagonisti della costruzione della testualità politica e dell'organizzazione del consenso nel bassomedievo. Gilbert de Tournai, Paolino da Venezia, Francesc Eiximenis," in *La propaganda politica nel Basso Medievo. Atti del XXXVIII Convegno storico internazinale, Todi, 14–17 ottobre 2001* (Spoleto, 2002), 392.

189 Pierre Michaud-Quantin, *Universitas. Expressions du movement communautaire dans le Moyen-Âge latin* (Paris, 1970), 271–84.

190 Giacomo Todeschini, "'Ecclesia' e mercato nei linguaggi dottrinali di Tommaso d'Aquino," *Quaderni storici* 35, no. 105 (2000): 614–16.

191 Matthew S. Kempshall, *The Common Good in Late Medieval Political Thought* (Oxford, 1999).

192 *Synonyme de la ville chrétienne en tant que 'Corpus Christi'.* From Giacomo Todeschini, "Participer au Bien Commun: la notion franciscaine d'appartenance à la 'civitas'," in *De Bono Com-*

vidual, although personal identity was understood as inextricably part of the identity of the community to which they belonged.[193] So, the proper development of professional responsibilities benefited both the soul of the individual and that of society because "a good reputation based on daily professional virtue" became "a reason for success and at the same time, salvation for lay people."[194]

The economic activities of those lay people who dominated urban life, guided by the economic norms established by Christian ethics (sound currency, fair prices, credit, and the circulation of capital),[195] produced the profit that benefited the political *caritas* and, at the same time, the *res publica*, which is the object of the redemptive mercy of Christ.[196] In this context, among their Christian duties good rulers included concern for the economic benefits of their subjects, as acknowledged by such authors as Gilles of Rome (ca. 1243–1316), bishop of Bourges and writer on philosophy and theology, who insisted that "the Prince, given his eminence, should run and control the activity in his territory."[197] The ideal of personal poverty and concern for the common good were linked to Christian social care, but "the ideology of poverty" became subsumed within a "reorganization of the public order," which was able to incorporate the new social and economic stimuli.[198] This, then, was the Christian market economy, in the excellent definition by Giacomo Todeschini.[199]

This was the model of society defined by the challenges of the thirteenth and fourteenth centuries by mendicant theologians and accepted by the Church, with the purpose of maintaining, duly adapted, the fit between socio-economic reality and Christian ideological authority. A model of Christian society focused on the traits of the towns and

---

muni. The Discourse and Practice of the Common Good in the European City (13th–16th c.) ed. Elodie Lecuppre-Desjardin, Anne-Laure Van Bruaene (Turnhout, 2010), 231.

193 Flocel Sabaté, "Identities on the move," in *Identities on the Move*, ed. Flocel Sabaté (Bern, 2014), 14–22.

194 *Buona reputazione fondata sulla quotidiana virtù professionale; una ragione del successo e al tempo stesso della Salvezza per i laici.* From Giacomo Todeschini, "Guardiani della soglia. I Fratri Minori come garanti del perimetro sociale (XIII secolo)," *Reti medievali. Rivista* 8 (2007): 15.

195 Flocel Sabaté, "El temps de Francesc Eiximenis. Les estructures econòmiques, socials i polítiques de la Corona d'Aragó a la segona meitat del segle XIV," in *Francesc Eiximenis (c. 1330–1409): el context i l'obra d'un gran pensador català medieval*, ed. Antoni Riera (Barcelona, 2015), 119–31.

196 Paolo Evangelisti, "Per un'etica degli scambi economici. La funzione civile del mercato in Eiximenis e nella pedagogia politica francescana (1273–1493)," *Caplletra* 48 (2010): 211–36.

197 *Le Prince, du fait de son éminence, doit dirigir et gouverner l'activité de son territoire.* Cited from Alain Bourreau, *La religion de l'état. La construction de la République étatique dans le discours théologique de l'Occident medieval (1250–1350)* (Paris, 2006), 269.

198 *La ideologia della povertà [...] riorganizzazione dell'ordine pubblico.* Cited from Giacomo Todeschini, "Povertà, mancanza, assenza come criteri di legittimazione del potere alla fine del Medioevo," in *La légitimité implicite: actes des conférences organisées à Rome en 2010 et en 2011 par SAS en collaboration avec l'École française de Rome*, ed. Jean-Philippe Genet, 2 vols. (Paris, 2015), 1:207–8.

199 Giacomo Todeschini, *Richesse franciscaine. De la pauvreté volontaire à la société de marché* (Lagrasse, 2008).

cities that dominated economy and society coalesced. It was the ideological adaptation of Christianity to the society of the Late Middle Ages that lasted until the Reformation and the Council of Trent, the latter attempting to reach a renewed Christian paradigm adequate for new challenges.[200]

In summary, Christian ideology sustained medieval civilization in the West from the fourth-century Edict of Thessalonica to the Council of Trent in the sixteenth century precisely because, as a framework maintaining a body of norms, it was sufficiently flexible to adapt to contemporary social and economic change.

Christian Ideology for Each Social and Political Group

A narrative reiterated at the end of the Middle Ages stated that a peasant married a woman of a higher social status, who cooked him the meals she knew but that caused him painful indigestion. Her mother made her see that those recipes were too refined and delicate for him, and he had to be fed with food typical of people of lower status, like beans, peas, and bread soaked in milk. When she cooked these things, all the problems ended, because the trouble was that the farmer had tried to elevate himself to a higher plane than his true status.[201]

The Christian model encompassed all society but precisely described behaviour appropriate for each social group, in a fixed and unyielding way, with little permeability. All behaviour, including personal attitudes, eating habits, and dress codes was adapted to fit the corresponding group, and was seen as an expression of a society based on three estates: society operates harmoniously when each person acts according to the order to which he or she is attached.[202] Thus, there was a model of behaviour for each social group affecting all areas of activity and expression.

The social structure accorded with the order desired by God, and each group had its own specific traits in accordance with religious dictates. The clergy spread this ideology, duly adapted to each social group. Thus, for example, under feudalism, Bernard of Clairvaux (1090–1153) could trust that the Christian doctrine would lead the *malitia* (bad qualities) of the knights to be tamed to make a *militia Christi*, thus improving the condition of men at arms and leading to the "incompatibility of malicious warriors with knighthood."[203]

As authors like Linda Paterson and Mary Hackett have warned, care must be taken not to project behaviour onto the past that was not noted by contemporaries.[204] In the

---

200 Odd Langholm, "Economic Ethics of the Mendicant Orders: a Paradigm and a Legacy," in *Etica e Politica: le teorie dei Frati Mendicanti nel Due e Trecento. Atti del XXVI Convegno internazionale (Assisi, 15–17 ottobre 1998)* (Spoleto, 1999), 156–57.

201 Paul Freedman, "Els pagesos medievals. Imatge d'ells mateixos en relació amb el règim senyorial," in *L'Edat Mitjana. Món real i espai imaginari*, ed. Flocel Sabaté (Catarroja, 2012), 95–96.

202 Duby, *Los tres órdenes*, 113–18.

203 Areyh Grabois, "Militia and Malitia: The Bernardine Vision of Chivalry," in *The Second Crusade and the Cistercians*, ed. Michael Gervers (New York, 1992), 55.

204 Linda Paterson, "Knights and the concept of knighthood in the twelfth-century Occitan epic," *Forum for Modern Language Studies* 17, no. 2 (1981): 115–30.

end, during the central Middle Ages, "the man is judged not according to some knightly code, but by whether he is, according to his station, a good vassal or a good lord."[205] However, it is clear that the development of the idea of particular virtues inherent to the respective status of particular groups generated and consolidated specific codes appropriate to each group. As Richard Kaeuper explains, with regard to "knightly ideology," a religious underpinning was precisely what supplied the necessary moderation: good vengeance is valorized, but the knight had to balance this with "an economy of mercy, imitating their Ultimate Lord in their earthly combats."[206] Of course, there were duties, accepted as Christian, that marked out the behaviour of the knights, beginning with maintaining justice, protecting the weak, and upholding the law.[207] Thus knights developed specific forms and cultural values, as Thomas Bisson shows through discussion of twelfth-century Catalan barons and nobles, for whom he notes that customary solidarities and moralities included faith, honour, and shame.[208] This instilled in them virtuous traits: "Knights must have four principal virtues; the good customs those men possess are called virtues and among these, four take precedence: wisdom, fortitude, temperance, and justice."[209]

Linda Paterson stressed the influence of town and bourgeois wealth over knighthood in the southern model of feudalism of twelfth-century Occitania, showing some "types of urban knights."[210] Nevertheless, and especially in northern France between the twelfth century and thirteenth century, those poets who praised the actions of knights, were, at the same time, harshly critical of the bourgeoisie.[211] For instance, the famous Knight of the Lion had to free three hundred maidens imprisoned in a castle in the service of a duke who had been subjected to carrying out tasks with urban links: submitted to a regime of poverty, they had to weave and embroider luxury cloth with gold or

---

205 W. Mary Hackett, "Knights and knighthood in Girart de Roussillon," in *The Ideals and Practice of Medieval Knighthood, II Papers from the Third Strawberry Hill Conference, 1986*, ed. Christopher Harper-Bill and Ruth Harvey (Woodbridge, 1988), 41.

206 Richard Kaeuper, "Vengeance and Mercy in Chivalric 'Mentalité'," in *Peace and Protection in the Middle Ages*, ed. Tom B. Lambert, David Rollason (Durham, 2009), 174, 179.

207 Elspeth Kennedy, "The Quest for identity and the Importance of Lineage in Thirteenth-Century French Prose Romance," in *The Ideals and Practice of Medieval Knighthood, II Papers from the Third Strawberry Hill Conference, 1986*, ed. Christopher Harper-Bill and Ruth Harvey (Woodbridge, 1988), 81.

208 Thomas N. Bisson, *Tormented Voices. Power, Crisis, and Humanity in Rural Catalonia 1140–1200* (Cambridge, MA, 1998), 116–38.

209 *Com los cavallers deuen haver en si IIII virtuts principals; les bones costumes quels homes han en si són appellades virtuts e entre totes son IIII les majors axí com són saviesa, fortalesa, temprança i justícia.* Cited from Próspero de Bofarull, *Procesos de las antiguas Cortes y parlamentos de Cataluña, Aragón y Valencia custodiados en el Archivo General de la Corona de Aragón*, 8 vols. (Barcelona, 1850), 4:36.

210 Paterson, "Knights and the concept of knighthood," 126.

211 Peter S. Noble, "Knights and Burgesses in the Feudal Epic," in *The Ideals and Practice of Medieval Knighthood. Papers from the First and Second Strawberry Hill Conferences, 1986*, ed. Christopher Harper-Bill and Ruth Harvey (Woodbridge, 1986), 104–10.

silk threads.[212] The opposition between the values of the knights and those of the urban populace were highlighted when, in the mid-fourteenth century the former advised King Peter the Ceremonious that the privileges given to the latter led to the worst situations in the world, thinking, especially, of the urban militia who use arms that were traditionally a preserve of the barons.[213]

In any case the Church favoured the notion of authority. Consequently, it backed the position of the lords, while making clear that God had appointed lords to maintain order and justice.[214] It was a rather generalized perspective. In the Catalan town of Valls, in 1357, it was explained as natural that taxes were paid to the lords in exchange for their services of protection and justice: "this is the reason why lords are put in cities, towns, and neighbourhoods and the revenues are given to them, to defend their subjects and do justice against malefactors."[215] These recognitions of corresponding jurisdictional authority were in harmony with the development of municipal power. Concordant with favourable legal, philosophical, and theological guarantees that promoted municipal groups in the Late Middle Ages,[216] the Church, thanks especially to the role of the mendicant orders, was fully involved in urban society, to the point that Comblin estimates that "never did the Church identify itself so deeply with a social regime."[217] Late-medieval urban life, with all its inter-meshings, generated a full civic code,[218] a veritable model of behaviour that embraced all aspects of the connection between the individual and society through specific virtues associated with good citizens and, by extension, with good men.[219] This is coherent with a fully developed medieval European ideal of *civilitas*,[220] shared by

---

212 Chrétien de Troyes, *El caballero del león* (Madrid, 1986), 90–94.

213 "Those who make evil must be punished by the king or his officials, and not by farmers nor a riot of people without any right. It is due to similar determinations and affronts that all the communes that exist have come into the world" (*Aquells qui mal faran, degen esser punits per lo dit Senyor Rey e per sos oficials e no per avalot de pageses ne per gens ses tota raó; per semblants empreniments e ontes sien vengudes totes les comunes que vuy són en lo món*). Cited from *Cortes de los antiguos reinos de Aragón y de Valencia y Principado de Cataluña*, 26 vols. (Madrid, 1896), 1:444.

214 Tàrrega, Arxiu Comarcal d'Urgell, pergamins, Caixa 5, 1345.

215 *Per ço són possats los senyors per les ciutats, per les viles e per los calls e·ls són dades les rendes, per tal que deffenen los lurs sotmesos e façen justícia als mal faytors*. From Valls, Arxiu Comarcal de l'Alt Camp, pergamins, num. 84.

216 Flocel Sabaté, "Municipio y monarquía en la Cataluña bajomedieval," *Anales de la Universidad de Alicante* 13 (2000–2002): 276–79.

217 *Nunca la Iglesia se identificó tan profundamente con un régimen social*. Cited from José Comblin, Francisco Javier Calvo, *Teología de la ciudad* (Estella, 1972), 287.

218 Daniela Romagnoli, "La courtoisie dans la ville: un modèle complexe," in *La ville et la cour. Des bonnes et des mauvaises manières*, ed. Daniela Romagnoli (Paris, 2005), 25–87.

219 Xavier Renedo, "Francesc de Vinatea, el ciutadà ieal segons el Dotzè del Crestià de Francesc Eiximenis," in *Utopies i alternatives de vida a l'edat mitjana*, ed. Flocel Sabaté (Lleida, 2009), 215–52.

220 Paolo Evangelisti, "Construir una identidad: Francesc Eiximenis y una idea europea de 'civilitas'," in *La construcción d'identitats imaginades. Literatura medieval i ideologia*, ed. Julián Acebrón, Isabel Grifoll, Flocel Sabaté (Lleida, 2015), 125–65.

dispersed and diverse experiences of bourgeois governments.[221]

Thus, given the plurality of power-holders, each well justified by a particular discourse, late medieval political practice forced the respective holders to come together, as reflected in the expression "mixed constitution"[222] or *souveraineté partagée*,[223] to define medieval power as an imposed consensus. The government had to continually renew and adapt the ongoing pact between different groups with access to power, configuring the political community to allow for them all.[224] The parliament based on estates of the realm is the best example of this kind of participative government.[225] In parliament, perhaps rather than detailed negotiation between the estates, the most important factor was the justificatory arguments and discourses for creating and holding a notion of "representativity" (or representativeness). This became the key concept around which political community was organized and the name under which it could speak.[226]

The vision of power vested in different holders allowed a general acceptance of different forms of government, either jurisdictional lordships or autonomous urban governments, in each case under the corresponding legal, philosophical, and theological guarantees. The Christian framework and the Romanist legal base were the foundations of specific discourses for each group, justifying a supposed mission and claims for political capacities and aspirations: the sovereign strove to strengthen his position;[227] the nobles reinforced their jurisdictional dominions,[228] the municipalities developed wide autonomy and even full capacities to rule as a political community.[229] Between the thir-

221 John Watts, "The Commons in Medieval England," in *La légitimité implicite: actes des conférences organisées à Rome en 2010 et en 2011 par SAS en collaboration avec l'École française de Rome*, ed. Jean-Philippe Genet, 2 vols. (Paris, 2015), 2:211–22.

222 James M. Blythe, *Ideal Government and the Mixed Constitution in the Middle Ages* (Princeton, 1992).

223 Diego Quaglioni, "La souveraineté partagée au Moyen Âge," in *Le Gouvernement mixte. De l'idéal politique au monstre constitutionnel en Europe (XIIIᵉ-XVIIᵉ siècle)*, ed. Marie Gaille-Nikodimov (Saint-Étienne, 2005), 15–24.

224 Antony Black, *Political Thought in Europe, 1250–1450* (Cambridge, 1992), trans. as *El pensamiento político en Europa, 1250–1450* (Cambridge, 1992), 20–62.

225 Bertie Wilkinson, *The Creation of Medieval Parliaments* (New York, 1972), 55–83.

226 Michel Hébert, *Parlementer. Assemblées representatives et échange politique en Europe occidentale à la fin du Moyen Âge* (Paris, 2014), 81–274.

227 Jacques Krynen, "Droit romain et état monarchique. À propos du cas français," in *Représentation, pouvoir et royauté à la fin du Moyen Âge*, ed. Joël Blanchard (Paris, 1995), 13–24.

228 José Ángel Sesma, "La nobleza bajomedieval y la formación del estado moderno en la Corona de Aragón," in *La nobleza peninsular en la Edad Media. VI Congreso de Estudios Medievales* (Ávila, 1999), 372–7.

229 Georges Jehel, Philippe Racinet, *La ville médiévale. De l'Occidenet chrétien à l'Orient musulman Vᵉ-XVᵉ siècle* (Paris, 1996), 285–300; Ricardo Furini, "Politique et représentation dans le théâtre citadin. L'essor de Florence comme pouvoir souverain au début du XVᵉ siècle," in *Représentation, pouvoir et royauté à la fin du Moyen Âge*, ed. Joël Blanchard (Paris, 1995), 109–18; and Ennio Igor Mineo, "Cose in commune e bene commune. L'ideologia della comunità in Italia nel tardo medioevo," in *Languages of Political Society. Western Europe, 14th–17th Centuries*, ed. Andrea Gamberini, Jean-Philipe Genet, Andrea Zorzi (Roma, 2011), 39–67.

teenth and fourteenth centuries, the respective institutions used these discourses to stabilize their bases, and a framework for action and political management was generated.[230] In each case, a political language was consolidated, which, as Jan Dumolyn commented, reflected and blended elements of a specific political ideology.[231]

These approaches obliged the exercise of a policy that included deals and concord among the holders of power, sometimes emblematically between the sovereign, nobles, and municipalities.[232] In particular, it obliged each holder of power to seek a connection with the corresponding population. It was not only that the *populus* had to be taken into account explicitly, as stated prior to the end of the twelfth century by authors such as Peter the Chanter, Stephen Langton, or Radulphus Niger.[233] The same expression, from the thirteenth century, had also became an agent of political action, one that could be mobilized, agitated, or even for uprising, as shown by a growing number of episodes, especially in urban scenarios.[234] This meant discourse needed to be addressed to the population, to convince them, as the king in Catalonia did in the second half of the fourteenth century, attempting to persuade the people that royal jurisdiction was a "sweet lordship" in contrast to rule by the nobles, which would be arbitrary: the nobles would offer "many oppressions, humiliations, and abuses," according to the king.[235]

In this same late medieval context appeals were made to emotions, and fear and terror were invoked,[236] expressions that were managed through visualization to help ensure their political efficacy.[237] This was consonant with late medieval society's understanding that sentiments and sensations should not be hidden, but rather shown and displayed.[238] So, for instance, on the death of the sovereign, it was expected that even the animals should neigh and howl in pain, like the rest of the population. If the peo-

---

230 John Watts, *The Makings of Polities. Europe, 1300–1500* (Cambridge, 2009), 263–425.

231 "I shall equate the notion of 'ideology', which I personally prefer, with the one of 'political language'." Cited from Jan Dumolyn, "Urban Ideologies in Later Medieval Flanders. Towards an Analytical Framework," in *Languages of Political Society. Western Europe, 14th – 17th Centuries*, ed. Andrea Gamberini, Jean-Philipe Genet, Andrea Zorzi (Roma, 2011), 71.

232 Flocel Sabaté, "Estamentos, soberanía y modelo político en la Cataluña bajomedieval," *Aragón en la Edad Media* 21 (2009): 245–78.

233 Philippe Buc, "'Principes gentium dominantur eorum': Princely Power Between Legitimacy and Illegitimacy in Twelfth-Century Exegesis," in *Cultures of Power. Lordship, Status, and Process in Twelfth-Century Europe*, ed. Thomas N. Bisson (Philadelphia, 1995), 325.

234 Vincent Challet, "Une stratégie de la peur? Complots et menaces populaires en Languedoc à la fin du Moyen Âge," in *Por política, terror social*, ed. Flocel Sabaté (Lleida, 2013), 153–71.

235 *Dolça senyoria [...] moltes opressions, vecsacions e mals tractaments*. Cited from Flocel Sabaté, "Discurs i estrategies del poder reial a Catalunya al segle XIV," *Anuario de Estudios Medievales* 25, no. 2 (1995): 642–43.

236 Flocel Sabaté, "L'abus de pouvoir dans la couronne d'Aragon (XIIIe-XIVe siècles): pathologie, corruption, stratégie ou modèle?," in *La pathologie du pouvoir: vices, crimes et délits des gouvernants. Antiquité, Moyen Âge, époque modern*, ed. Patrick Gilli (Leiden, 2016), 304–20.

237 François Foronda, *El espanto y el miedo. Golpismo, emociones políticas y constitucionalismo en la Edad Media* (Madrid, 2013), 75–200.

238 Sabaté, *Vivir y sentir*, 75–80

ple did not behave in this way, the authorities demanded or concealed it, according to whichever was more useful to the political image.[239] Each of those involved in these late medieval power games used festivals, rituals and symbols as ways of expressing, visualizing, and disseminating power but also unifying identity and consolidating the inherent ideological content of the message.[240] It was a veritable theatricalization of power, as a means of representing a specific political estate, a prevailing code of values and a decisive ideology of power.

The different social and political groups were not internally homogeneous; they were divided into different kinds of subsections. We see this expressed in the efforts of the barons to have their own say in the Catalan court, separate from the nobles in the fourteenth century, reflecting not only differences but also tensions resulting from the intended rise of some and the corresponding efforts of those at higher levels to limit them.[241] Much stronger, clearer, and more widespread were tensions in urban contexts, where socially emerging groups everywhere demanded participation in the political body, generating strong social tensions,[242] augmenting the marked fragmentation within bands,[243] and very often combining with the claims of the political space itself against the corresponding holder of the suzerainty.[244]The corresponding rationalizing discourse in all cases came loaded with formal and legal arguments to be used against opponents.

The marked urban segmentation offers examples of progressive adaptation to the reality of power at each level. Urban social and economic evolution facilitated distinct social and political frameworks and groupings that were rigorously policed and maintained. In the Crown of Aragon, for instance, this took the form of division into three groups, called "upper hand," "middle hand," and "lower hand" (*mà major, mà mitjana, mà menor*) formally these divisions were seen as distinguishing different trades but really this involved different levels of economic capacity, each having different degrees of access to municipal administration.[245] The marked stratification meant a clear and ostentatious separation, defining specific categories, activities, and codes of behaviour for each group, visible in all activities and even in physical appearance.[246]

---

239 Flocel Sabaté, *Cerimònies fúnebres i poder municipal a la Catalunya baixmedieval* (Barcelona, 2003), 15–76.

240 Paola Ventrone, "La construzione dell'identità cittadina in Italia tra XIII e XV secolo: feste, rituali, simboli," in *Identitats*, ed. Flocel Sabaté (Lleida, 2012), 225–54.

241 Francisco Luis Pacheco, "'No y ha bras, no y ha bras, que bones sentencies ni ha'. Las Cortes Catalanas y el problema del cuarto brazo," *Initium* 7 (2002): 99–138.

242 Rodney Hilton, *Les ciutats medievals* (Barcelona, 1989), 43–61.

243 Marco Gentile, *Fazioni al governo. Politica e società a Parma nel Quattrocento* (Roma, 2009), 269–87.

244 Jan Dumolyn, "Privileges and novelties: the political discourse of the Flemish cities and rural districts in their negotiations with the dukes of Burgundy (1384–1506)," *Urban History* 35, no. 1 (2008): 5–23.

245 Flocel Sabaté, "Oligarchies and social fractures in the cities of Late Medieval Catalonia," in *Oligarchy and Patronage in Late Medieval Spanish Urban Society*, ed. María Asenjo-González (Turnhout, 2009), 9–19.

246 Flocel Sabaté, "Ejes vertebradores de la oligarquía urbana en Cataluña," *Revista d'Història*

In another example, in 1447, the municipal government of Barcelona wrote to the council and bishop of Lleida, as being the bodies responsible for the *Studium generale* in Lleida, because in that university tensions had arisen because the upper-level burghers could not sit with the lower-level of the nobility, although they were considered of equivalent social categories:

> They had understood that the students who were sons of knights had their own bench and did not want to sit with the sons of citizens and men of honour of the cities and towns, despite the fact that citizens and men of honour of cities and towns by constitution are of the same degree with knights, in war and in all acts of chivalry.[247]

So, in the Middle Ages, far beyond simple division into estates, people lived in marked stratospheres that affected all aspects of everyday behaviour, where claims for recognition were acknowledged, but not claims for change. It was a sequence of circles that required precise articulation and imposed precise behaviour which was impossible to avoid, as Paolo Grossi stated:

> The protagonist is order, a force from which nothing escapes, the supreme organization of the whole society dominated by a profound diffidence for every individuality and oppressed by a tension to incorporate each individuality into a relational network, that is a communitarian network, to neutralize the subversive charge that the individuality is carrying.[248]

One can nevertheless talk of an organic society, because social behaviour adapted to bodies that fitted together and organized themselves, under the benchmark of the estates, thanks to them sharing the same ideological framework, which did not dilute the existing segmentations, but rather quite the contrary, justified and reinforced these. In that process, the Church supplied the ideological backbone and also the semantics of the discourse, in line with the assessment of Dominique Iogna-Prat: "in a heteronomous world where the social has long been entangled with the ecclesial, any organization or regulation of society (state and city) necessarily evolves in the semantic field of the religious."[249]

---

medieval 9 (1998): 133–40.

247 *Havien entès que los estudiants fills de cavallers feyen banch de per sí y que no volian seure ab fills de Ciutadans y de homens de honor de Ciutats y Viles, majorment que Ciutadans y homes de honor de Ciutats y Viles, per constitucions són de un mateix grau ab Cavallers, axí en guerra com en tots actes de Cavalleria.* Cited from Rúbriques de Bruniquer, *Ceremonial dels Magnífichs Consellers y Regiment de la Ciutat de Barcelona,* ed. Francesc Carreras Candi, Bartolomeu Gunyalons, 9 vols. (Barcelona, 1916), 5:153–54.

248 *Protagonista è l'ordo', una forza a cui nulla sfugge, organizzazione suprema della intiera società dominata da una profonda diffedenza per ogni individualità e sorreta da una tensione a inglobare ogni individualità in tessuti relazionali, cioè communitarii, valevoli a neutralizzare la carica eversiva di cui l'individualità è portatrice.* Cited from Paolo Grossi, "Il sistema giuridico medievale e la civiltà comunale," in *La civiltà comunale italiana nella storiografia internazionale,* ed. Andrea Zorzi (Firenze, 2008), 8–9.

249 *Dans un monde hétéronome où le social se confond longtemps avec l'ecclésial, toute instance d'organisation ou de régulation de la société (l'Etat et la cité) évolue nécessairement dans le champ sémantique du religieux.* Cited from Dominique Iogna-Prat, *Cité de Dieu, cite des homes. L'Église et l'architecture de la société* (Paris, 2016), 137.

The adaptability of these governing ideas, given changing economic and social stimuli, picked out a singular path through the Middle Ages and prefigured a heritage that would continue to influence, and in part condition, later centuries, including the weight exerted by the Church.[250] The most emblematic expressions in immediately subsequent centuries, beginning from what historiography knows as the modern State, were only able to flourish in response to different kinds of evolution, development and contrast from the medieval ideological legacy.[251]

Conclusions

Christianity can be defined as the ideology that brought much of medieval society together, forming its identity, and supplying parts of a common memory. Medieval society, at least in the areas that are the subject of this book, in south-west Europe, might be termed an "assisted society" because all important activities and action, whether individual or collective, needed the intermediation of the Church, which could only be provided by the clergy. Society gained a certain coherence because the whole physical environment (the universe, the Earth and its elements, the human body, and so on) was explained in a way that conformed with the spiritual components of the Christian religion. Ways of thinking and the social order could be manipulated and justified as the Church and its ideology proved capable of adapting to different social and economic stimuli across the medieval millennium. This ideology also offered a specific orientation for each social group at different times. Its historical legacy has been a deep influence on political forms in modern society but, especially, over the European mind and thought. This is the reason why the end of the Middle Ages proved itself far from the conclusion of this medieval ideological coherence.

---

250 Jean-Philippe Genet, "Le problème du pouvoir dans le Moyen Âge latin," in *El poder a l'edat mitjana*, ed. Flocel Sabaté (Lleida, 2004), 42.

251 Marie Gaille-Nikodimov, ed., *Le Gouvernement mixte. De l'idéal politique au monstre constitutionnel en Europe (XIIIᵉ-XVIIᵉ siècle)* (Saint-Étienne, 2005).

Part One

IDEOLOGY — A DEFINITION OF POWER

Chapter 1

IDEOLOGY AND SOCIAL ORDER

PAUL FREEDMAN

SCHOLARS, ESPECIALLY HISTORIANS of other eras, tend to consider the Middle Ages as a period whose outlook was intellectually focused on order and hierarchy. This pertains not only to a political ideology of society being arranged into stable orders and estates, but to a theory of cosmological articulation in which everything has a place in a great chain of being that incorporates all species from earthworms to angels. Within each element of that chain there are further hierarchies, such as within the clerical order or within a university or guild. The very angels themselves are arrayed in a ladder of status according to the model of celestial hierarchies established by Pseudo-Dionysius—nine angelic orders ascending from ordinary angels to seraphim. The circles of Dante's hell, purgatory, and paradise also follow spiritual hierarchical arrangements.

The third chapter of Johan Huizinga's influential *The Waning of the Middle Ages* is entitled "The Hierarchic Conception of Society" and it shows the extension of an ideology of levels of virtue and power into social conceptions of chivalry.[1] Hierarchical ordering is the basis for several famous medievalist enterprises—the "political theology" of Ernst Kantorowicz that joins political theory to religious ideology, or Erwin Panofsky's linking of scholasticism and the Gothic architectural aesthetic.[2] Huizinga himself emphasizes that the medieval conception of society was "static, not dynamic" and that hierarchy was legitimated by cosmic models rendering, in theory, resistance to change. If everything in God's creation is ordered according to ladders or chains of virtue, then disruption of that order is unthinkable, or at least bad. This transitory earth, subject to decay, is faced with disorder, but social change is unnatural, regarded in the traditional view as defiance of God and the order He has established.

The church was the main source of an ideology of order and the grand political theories of social cohesion in the Middle Ages were produced by clerics, from the liturgists of sacred investitures to the advisors of Charlemagne; from the canonists of the collections of decretals and the *Decretum* to the scholastic philosophers. Quarrels between church and state revolved around what Gerd Tellenbach referred to as the "right order in the world"—that is, whether the church as the supreme spiritual power could legitimately be ruled by the empire or a monarchy who were powers of inferior standing according

---

1 Johan Huizinga, *The Waning of the Middle Ages: A Study of the Forms of Life, Thought and Art in France and the Netherlands in the 14th and 15th Centuries* (New York, 1954), 56–57.

2 Ernst Kantorowicz, *The King's Two Bodies: A Study in Medieval Political Theology* (Princeton, 1957); Ernst Kantorowicz, *Laudes Regiae: A Study in Liturgical Acclamation and Mediaeval Rulership* (Los Angeles, 1946); Erwin Panofsky, *Gothic Architecture and Scholasticism* (Latrobe, 1951).

Paul Freedman (paul.freedman@yale.edu) is Professor of Medieval History at Yale University.

to the divine ordering of creation. Subsequent controversies revolved around the assertion of the superiority of the ecclesiastical spiritual power over the material power of secular rulers.[3] To claim this superiority was not so radical, but to argue further that the spiritual should therefore "rule" the material was at the heart of the papal conflict with the Hohenstaufen rulers and the conflict between Pope Boniface VIII and Philippe IV of France. Right order in the world, according to the supporters of the church, was for the spiritual power to rule, a notion expressed in political metaphors like the two swords, or the distinction between *auctoritas* and *potestas*, or Hugh of St. Victor's statement that the spiritual power institutes the material. To reverse this in favour of a secular power that could rule over the church was "monstrous," "unnatural," and so quintessentially disorderly. Those who opposed ecclesiastical claims, such as Marsilius of Padua, denied that the church had an institutional ability to use its spiritual authority in political action; that religious adherence did not confer on the clergy the exercise of practical power in the secular world; so that the papal pretence to do so was in itself monstrous, disorderly, and an inversion of the appropriate role of the spiritual.

All of these arguments, whether about church and state or about the stability of the social hierarchy, assume that the goal of medieval political thought was to exalt and protect unchanging order established once and for all by divine will. Historians no longer tend to believe that the medieval era was uniquely hierarchical in its mind-set, so that these rather theoretical inquiries into political ideology have given way to concern with the more practical and specific performance of rulership. Yet the hierarchical picture is still assumed among historians of modernity who look at the Middle Ages as a kind of beginning point of stasis against which later progressive and interesting movements react. Machiavelli, for example, is often regarded as the first political realist, who dispensed with the idealizing, static conceptions of medieval political theory in favour of a more flexible set of rules based on contingency and human initiative rather than on authoritative (divine or secular) patterns. Equally, medieval art and science are supposedly based on tradition (ancient authorities like Aristotle, or standards set by craft guilds), whereas the Renaissance creates the individual artist or the innovative scientist who is not bound by the imputed superiority of the past or the stability of art and knowledge.

Such assumptions about our period drive medievalists crazy. Over many years a lot of energy has been devoted to refuting these facile ideas, showing that the supposed accomplishments of the early modern centuries took place centuries earlier: that Frederick II was as much a political realist as Machiavelli's Cesare Borgia; that Nicholas of Oresme anticipated the physics of the scientific revolution; that the twelfth century (not the fifteenth) discovered the individual. More recently, rather than the hopeless fight against the Renaissance, attention has turned to the dynamism of the Middle Ages, its richly subversive and creative ideas.

But it is not as if the older view of a hierarchical Middle Ages failed to allow for disorder. It tended to set real disorder in everyday life alongside theoretical stasis. Here again Huizinga is, as it were, iconic. The first chapter of *The Waning of the Middle Ages*

---

3 Gerd Tellenbach, *Libertas: Kirche und Weltordnung im Zeitalter des Investiturstreits* (Stuttgart, 1936).

is entitled "The Violent Tenor of Life" and the entire book is built around contrasts between dreams of chivalry, love, beauty, or social harmony, and the realities of war, pestilence, treachery, and everyday violence.[4] The turbulent does not contradict the orderly as much as it arises out of challenges to order. Honour and its magnified importance provoke constant occasions to fight over insults or precedence. Here too, our colleagues in other fields have built imposing theoretical and historical edifices on the notion of fundamental medieval "disorder." This affects much of the literature of the growth of the state as guarantor of social peace (though here again, medieval historians have tried to argue that the modern state was born long before the end of the Middle Ages). But even more appealing across disciplines are theories of historical development by which anger was subdued in favour of social compromise, notably in the amazingly durable and influential notions of Norbert Elias, whose *Civilizing Process* of 1939 starts with the Middle Ages as violently uncultivated while everything that follows constitutes the taming of those violent instincts.[5] There is also a recent book that has achieved great vogue in the United States, Steven Pinker's *The Better Angels of Our Nature*, which argues that despite the minor altercations of the twentieth century (such as the world wars, genocides, and state-sponsored famines), a much greater percentage of humanity has lived in peace and order in the contemporary era than at any time in the past.[6] That past is seen as incredibly violent, not only in its wars but in quotidian predation, the impossibility of assuring protection from casual murder and robbery. Although the object of Pinker's inquiry is more the violence of very early human history, the Middle Ages is annexed to it.

Let us leave modernity out of the picture for the time being and try to see the Middle Ages in its own right. That is what most medievalists want, after all. We tend to be commendably cautious about our own assumptions or at attempts to link medieval to contemporary concerns. Without completely embracing the lurid colouring of Huizinga, we can acknowledge that the medieval period did produce elaborate theories of order and suffered at the same time considerable and diverse forms of social disorder. There is nothing unique about this—all societies have ideologies of peace that are not fulfilled in reality. What is particular to the Middle Ages is the strength, durability, and complex articulation of its concepts of order. As I have said, and as we all know, medieval political order was not the subject of mere secular social science but the manifestation of a universal harmony so that physics, medicine, metaphysics, politics—indeed all of the Aristotelian disciplines—were linked by the same rules and by a Christianized neo-Platonist theory of hierarchical orders. This was not so much a static view, to use the term that Huizinga and others apply, as one of equilibrium. Joel Kaye has shown how ideas about balance among forces affected thought about the laws of physics, economics, and political ideologies.[7] Equilibrium is also a key to medieval theories of health, in particular of humoral balance.

---

4 Huizinga, *The Waning of the Middle Ages*, 9–31.

5 Norbert Elias, *Über den Prozess der Zivilisation: soziogenetische und psychogenetische Untersuchungen* (Basel, 1939).

6 Steven Pinker, *The Better Angels of Our Nature: Why Violence Has Declined* (New York, 2011).

7 Joel Kaye, "The (Re)balance of Nature, 1250–1350," in *Engaging with Nature; Essays on the*

A second special aspect of medieval ideas of order and disorder, and the one I want to focus on, is that they amount to something more than the drag of social reality on mental constructs. For the medieval period there is a way in which order and disorder are joined and form a unity or paradoxical equilibrium. Order either succeeds disorder or they are mutually reinforcing, or even merely aspects of the same form of oppression. The historiography of the past hundred years reflects these alternative views of social cohesion and exploitation and I wish to offer a four-fold division of the relation between social turmoil and social peace that shows how the inter-dependence of order and disorder can be viewed.

Emergent Order and the Tools of Disorder

In the first instance the forces of order use the tools of disorder. A stable medieval society emerges out of the turbulent militarization brought about by the rise of the *milites* and the decline of central government. Rather than regarding the monarch and state institutions as completely antithetical to private warfare and feudal relations of loyalty, Marc Bloch posited two feudal ages, one built on the institutions established by the other.[8] The first was chaotic and destroyed the structures of royal government in favour of the arrogation by private men of military power of what had previously been aspects of public authority: warfare, judgment, and taxation. Reconstruction of central authority beginning in the twelfth century made use of feudal institutions such as vassalage, castle building, and the assemblage of lands and rights. Eventually the state became distinguished from this background of private exercise of power, but on the basis of coopting its methods rather than in defiance of them.

The relation between feudalism and the emergence of the monarchical state was argued specifically by Charles Petit-Dutaillis in 1933 for the feudal monarchy as developed in France and England.[9] The kings in each nation had powers that were built on different circumstances and institutional bases, but they both profited from the feudal ties that had held society together and were able to manipulate these forms of private loyalty rather than having to destroy them. What turned feudal violence into the rebuilding of state institutions was, according to Jean-Francois Lemarignier, hierarchy— the feudal practice of homage and fidelity turned towards land was arranged in levels with the king eventually able to profit from his position at the top of the feudal chain or pyramid.[10]

Natural World in Medieval and Early modern Europe, ed. Barbara Hanawalt (Notre Dame, 2008), 85–114.

8 Marc Bloch, *La société féodale*, 2 vols. (Paris, 1939–1940).

9 Charles Petit-Dutaillis, *La monarchie féodale en France et en Angleterre, Xe–XIIIe siècle* (Paris, 1933).

10 Jean-François Lemarignier, "La dislocation du 'pagus' et le problème des 'consuetudines' (Xe–XIe siècle)," in *Mélanges d'histoire du Moyen Âge dédiés à la mémoire de Louis Halphen* (Paris, 1951), 401–10; Jean François Lemarignier, *Le gouvernement royale aux premiers temps capétiens, 987–1108* (Paris, 1965).

In the Anglo-American tradition Joseph Strayer described what he called "the medieval origins of the modern state" in a work with that title in which he celebrated the ability of kings to create this aspect of modernity centuries before the Italian Renaissance.[11] Rulers and their advisors moulded state authority out of the materials at their disposal, not from an ideal of order derived from political philosophy. Their ideological and practical implements were those of feudal warfare, loyalty, family alliances, and law.

A variation of order chronologically succeeding disorder is to see greater continuity between the state and the military elite who first formed feudal society. Here the state might impose order, but not in accord with the conventional understanding of public interest. In recent years historians have become disenchanted with the modern state as effective guarantor of peace, so that formerly dominant, progressive teachings that the state emerged out of feudal institutions have been modified or abandoned. Perhaps the medieval state was *not* a civilizing force above the fray, and for that matter neither is the modern one. Elite predation, private interest, the pursuit of war, and fiscal rapacity characterized a society in which the state succeeded not so much in opposition to the aristocracy as in its own interests, even if the make-up of the aristocracy was fluid. Thomas Bisson's intriguing *The Crisis of the Twelfth Century* maintains the traditional picture of administrative kingship and its growth, but points to the perpetuation of social oppression and the efflorescence of harsh conceptions of lordship accompanying this shift so that while government was built on feudal foundations, it did little to temper upper-class extortion, or simply substituted its own system of taxation.[12]

Holding Societies Together

Other views of order and disorder are less chronologically organized as chaos followed by constructive forms of feudal bonds. The anthropological school of medieval historians has studied the rules of the game behind what seem to be constant incidents of violent confrontation. Referred to in France as l'*École américaine*, in fact much of the impetus has come from Germany, including application of the term *Spielregeln* ("Rules of the Game") from the work of Gerd Althoff.[13] The anthropological school sees a complex and durable set of regulations where others see only random warfare. Violence is not anarchic, nor does internal conflict necessarily undermine society. The weakness or absence of state authority is here not a consequence of violence from nobles; rather violence is among the adaptations made to a society without a state, something that Patrick Geary in the title of an article in *Annales* referred to as *vivre en conflit dans une France sans état*.[14] Anthropology supplies models for how societies live in conflict—how they supply forms of order in the absence of what modern observers identify as a state.

---

11 Joseph Strayer, *On the Medieval Origins of the Modern State* (Princeton, 1970).

12 Thomas N. Bisson, *The Crisis of the Twelfth Century: Power, Lordship, and the Origins of European Government* (Princeton, 2009).

13 Gerd Althoff, *Spielregeln der Politik im Mittelalter: Kommunikation in Frieden und Fehde* (Darmstadt, 1997).

14 Patrick Geary, "Vivre en conflit dans une France sans état: Typologie des mécanismes de

Understanding order not in terms of official political institutions but as unwritten social agreements makes it possible to see the feud, skirmishes, gestures of defiance, or ecclesiastical penalties as forms of negotiation, not as evidence of uncontrollable disorder. "Peace within the feud" is a formulation by the anthropologist Max Gluckman of what seems to be a paradox—that kinship feuds, quintessential examples of social chaos and the breakdown of the rule of law, are actually methods of checking greater violence that would result from the lack of private response to provocation.[15] This theory has a certain resonance in the United States where feuds are associated with the Appalachian Mountains, a landscape of imagined lawlessness, or with drug wars in Mexico, or among what was once described as the urban underclass.

The emphasis thus turns to dispute resolution and other means of holding a society together in the absence of official state institutions such as royal courts. The work of Stephen White on legal practices or Barbara Rosenwein on spiritual penalties are examples of this approach for which order is present within what earlier historians regarded as aimless disorder.[16]

Complementary to the effectiveness of informal dispute resolution is what Daniel Smail has found in looking at law courts in a less institutional and more sociological fashion. In late medieval Marseille, according to Smail's evidence, litigation offered opportunities for verbal violence, opinionated and scabrous testimony concerning the character of opponents that would otherwise be punishable as libellous.[17] It was permissible to accuse one's neighbours of heinous crimes and loutish behaviour as long as it was in a court setting, so that far from presiding over a sober adjudication of evidence based on rationality, courts could be manipulated into a means of expanding a feud and destroying the reputation of one's enemies.

Economic Progress

Another way to see disorder as constructive is in terms of productivity and economic progress. The French school identified with Georges Duby and Pierre Bonnassie saw the eruption of aristocratic violence around the year 1000 as marking an abrupt shift from the ancient to the medieval economy; from a mode of production based on large estates, slavery, and centralized power to a feudal model in which the aristocracy directed peasant effort by coercion into something that produced a surplus and a dynamic economy.[18]

---

règlement des conflits (1050–1200)," *Annales. Économies, Sociétés, Civilisations* 41, no. 5 (1986): 1107–33.

15 Max Gluckman, "The Peace in the Feud," *Past and Present* 8 (1955): 1–14.

16 Stephen D. White, *Feuding and Peace-Making in Eleventh-Century France* (London, 2005); Barbara Rosenwein, *To Be the Neighbor to Saint Peter: The Social Meaning of Cluny's Property, 909–1049* (Ithaca, 1989).

17 Daniel Lord Smail, *The Consumption of Justice: Emotions, Publicity and Legal Culture in Marseille, 1214–1423* (Ithaca, 2003).

18 Georges Duby, *L'économie rurale et la vie des campagnes dans l'occident médiéval*, 2 vols. (Paris, 1962); Georges Duby, *Guerriers et paysans: Essai sur la première croissance économique de l'Europe* (Paris, 1973); Pierre Bonnassie, *Société de l'an mil: Un monde entre deux âges* (Bruxelles, 2001).

Subsequent centuries of fortification, trade, urbanization, luxuries, and culture were built on the mobilization of peasant labour by the upper classes, although with scant benefit for the peasants themselves. The concentration of agricultural populations into fortified settlements (*incastellamento*) in many Mediterranean lands and the imposition of seigneurial exploitation ended peasant autonomy and forced the subordinated majority to produce more efficiently and according to the needs of their masters and the larger economy.

This interpretation of events does not deny that coercion and violence accompanied the transition from ancient to feudal systems, but sees disorder as creating wealth rather than destroying it. As with the anthropological school, disorder is actually a kind of order, except that here it is not a negotiated form of peace but an efficient method of coercion.

Radical Responses

Finally, we can identify a tendency to reverse the roles of who foments disorder and who brings about order, or at least a radical re-interpretation of the role of intellectuals and the state. In his influential *The Formation of a Persecuting Society*, Robert I. Moore identifies the church and the architects of royal authority as the instigators of conflict, not the petty knights of the feudal age.[19] There is a *grande mutation* in the eleventh century all right, but this "first European revolution," as Moore later calls it, is the assertion of centralized regional/national/spiritual power in both the papal-dominated church and the European monarchies.[20] While establishing their sway and justifying their role ideologically, administrative bureaucracies identified and, when necessary, sought out enemies against whom tremendous levels of state and ecclesiastical violence were brought to bear. Heretics, foreign powers, and domestic minorities could all be targets of repression and the effect was to increase the power of the people and institutions organizing campaigns against real, exaggerated, or imagined threats. It is not the masses who are the source of social upheaval, nor the barons, but the judges, administrators, and courts. An example of how this plays out is Mark Pegg's approach to the Albigensian Crusade, which he sees as directed against a non-existent heresy, one fabricated by clerical leaders out of a few scraps of irrelevant dissent to serve as an artificial threat whose suppression aided the assertion of both church and state.[21]

This interpretation of medieval order and disorder posits an ideology of order that foments actual disorder or a type of upheaval that actually benefits groups that ideologically purport to stand for order. Such an outlook makes it possible to see a paradoxical element in many medieval movements whose ideological presentation masks other agendas. The Peace of God Movement used to be presented as a form of church

---

19 Robert I. Moore, *The Formation of a Persecuting Society: Power and Deviance in Western Europe, 950–1250* (Oxford, 1987).

20 Robert I. Moore, *The First European Revolution, c. 970–1215* (Oxford, 2000).

21 Mark Gregory Pegg, *A Most Holy War: The Albigensian Crusade and the Battle for Christendom* (New York, 2008).

intervention to restrain violence by nobles and indeed there seems to be a connection between the Peace of God and the later Peace of the Prince or Commune so that the church-enforced peace of the late tenth and early eleventh century anticipates or provides the impetus for the royal or urban peace of the twelfth and thirteenth centuries.[22] But in recent historiography the Peace of God seems not to oppose the interests of the knights but to define their rights to licit private warfare. The limits are established for the church, a set of rules of the game again, but not with the aim of abolishing the game.[23]

Or consider how elaborately the language of peace in the Middle Ages is developed in time of war. The rhetorically extended and complex rituals of peace negotiations could express ways to end wars and also justify their continuation.[24] Hardly unique to the Middle Ages is the notion that the ruler's duty is to defend peace, and this means a willingness to undertake wars made necessary by the intransigence of his enemies.

Some of these recent approaches towards order and disorder in the Middle Ages may go too far in normalizing violence or minimizing the consequences of social turbulence. For example, even if there were rules for the prosecution of feuds in Italian cities, the violence really did adversely affect public order and political stability. Gregory Roberts, a student at Yale, has studied the police powers of the *podestà* especially in Bologna and Perugia.[25] The concern with repressing disorder and maintaining peace was sufficient to warrant elaborate and costly attempts to regulate the carrying of weapons, to punish curfew infractions, and to guarantee public order not so much against criminals as against otherwise respectable or at least economically respectable neighbours. Private violence was in fact seen as a threat to communal order.

Similarly, Thomas Bisson's book about peasant *querimoniae* in twelfth-century Catalonia, *Tormented Voices*, is a re-assertion of the suffering of people who might be seen by the anthropological school as merely the pawns in a rule-bound aristocratic game.[26] One person's negotiating strategy might involve a less fortunate person's death or mutilation.

These are reminders that sometimes disorder really is a bad thing. The actual source of disorder, as we have seen, is not completely agreed upon by medieval historians now. Is it the aristocracy, the *milites*, the state, or the intellectuals? Observers might in certain circumstances emphasize the anarchy of the military elite as the denunciations by monks around the year 1000 show, but for contemporary observers during the central

---

22 Herbert Edward John Cowdrey, "The Peace and Truce of God in the Eleventh Century," *Past and Present* 46 (1970): 42–67.

23 Thomas Head, Richard Landes, eds., *Essays on the Peace of God: Social Violence and Religious Response in France Around the Year 1000* (Ithaca, 1992); Dominique Barthélemy, *L'an mil et la paix de Dieu: La France chrétienne et féodale, 980–1060)* (Paris, 1999).

24 Gisela Naegle, ed., *Frieden schaffen und sich verteidigen im Spätmittelalter / Faire la paix et se défendre à la fin du Moyen Âge* (München, 2012); Sylvie Caucanas, Rémy Cazals, Nicolas Offenstadt, eds., *Paroles de paix en temps de guerre* (Toulouse, 2006); Nicholas Offenstadt, *Faire la paix au Moyen Âge: Discours et gestes de paix pendant la Guerre de Cent Ans* (Paris, 2007).

25 Gregory Roberts, "Policing and Public Power in the Italian Communes" (PhD diss., Yale University, 2013).

26 Thomas N. Bisson, *Tormented Voices: Power, Crisis and Humanity in Rural Catalonia, 1140–1200* (Cambridge, MA, 1998).

and late Middle Ages the source of danger to the stability of society came from the lower classes. This might not be expressed with as much complexity or the citation of biblical or classical precedents as in the higher realms of political theory. But what might be considered a "vernacular theory of order," however, depicted the peasantry and the urban poor as potential as well as actual sources of social chaos.

Peasant Violence

I would now like to discuss particularly the political ideological context and implications of peasant violence in the minds of the articulate clerical and courtly classes. The basic social outlook was, of course, that the peasants were helpless and unarmed in the face of the military elite. Carolingian political theory defined the peasantry as the *inerme vulgus* ("unarmed masses") and as successive centuries came to identify nobility with warfare, this definition of the rustic as incapable of making war became established. In chivalric literature peasants are hapless victims of predation by knights, no more capable of resistance to plunder and despoliation than were their livestock. Bertran de Born famously rhapsodizes about the arrival of spring, the season of campaigning, when rustics and their animals flee in terror before the onslaught of their military exploiters.[27]

But peasants did sometimes form military units and sometimes even proved quite capable in opposing knights. The militias of the Peace of God movement included armed peasant contingents which scandalized clerical conservatives such as Andrew of Fleury, who criticized the inappropriate armed peasant and clerical forces that attempted to enforce the Limoges Peace of 1031. Indeed, as Georges Duby demonstrated in his *Three Orders*, the inventors of the three-part schema of mutuality were responding to the distortion of the function of military action that the Peace Movement represented. In the eyes of Adalberon of Laon and Gerard of Cambrai, it was for the knights to fight, not the other orders, whatever the provocation.[28]

It was also possible for upper-class observers to see peasant armed resistance as logical, even just, a warning to the knights to stay within the terms of the mutuality they so often ignored. Bartholomaeus Anglicus, writing in 1240, admired Frisian peasants who formed free communities and were willing to risk their lives in battle in order to defend themselves from servitude. The thirteenth-century German poet known as "Der Stricker" observed that the peasants are sufficiently competent militarily to dismantle castles and other fortifications erected to coerce and exploit them. In a symbolic animal poem *Beispiel von den Gäuhühnern*, Der Stricker advises respect for peasant anger (*zorn*), depicting this as a reasonable yet formidable response to provocation, not as rebellious disorder. Knights are supposed to defend the other members of society and if they do not, even if they are not guilty of robbery or other forms of violence, they deserve to lose their status, or even their lives. An anonymous German poem of the fifteenth century warns that the nobility neglects its duty to defend the poor. God will not

---

27 Bertran de Born, "Be.m plai lo gais temps de pascor," *The Poems of the Troubadour Bertran de Born*, ed. William Paden, Jr., Tilde Sankovitch, Patricia H. Stäblein (Berkeley, 1986), 339 (poem no. 30).

28 Georges Duby, *Les trois ordres ou l'imaginaire du féodalisme* (Paris, 1978), 35–76.

allow this to continue and some day the common peasants will rise up and slay their masters.[29]

After 1300 concern over the mutuality of the three orders gives way to alarm over the threat of peasant and general lower-class subversion. The idea that peasant rebellions might be justified never disappears, and indeed it has a tremendous resurgence in connection with the Protestant Reformation in Germany, at least until the actual Peasants' Revolt of 1525 which frightened even the reformers, including Martin Luther, who notoriously recommended killing the revolting peasants like wild animals. The image of the peasant as bestial, uncontrollable, and intent on destroying society and civilization becomes a dominant discourse as insurrections became more common and widespread in the fourteenth and fifteenth centuries. It is no longer the knights who provoke social disorder, according to the majority of late medieval writers about society, but the peasants whose proclivities are now not towards passivity but tumult, whose nature is essentially evil and explosive.

It is not just that the peasants are the source of upheaval but that they are by nature violent and destructive. The French *Jacquerie* of 1358 gave rise to stories of peasant atrocities that would be recycled in later histories of peasant rebellions. Once they have power, the peasants are depicted as murderous, sexually depraved, and grotesquely cruel. According to Jean le Bel, for example, a group of French peasants captured a knight whom they murdered and then they forced his wife and children to watch while he was roasted. They raped the wife, forced her to eat the cooked flesh, and then killed her as well. This atrocious story was picked up by the better-known chronicler Froissart who added some embellishments, such as that the knight was roasted on a spit.[30] In the Tuchin revolt of 1384 in Artois and Picardy, the peasants supposedly killed an unfortunate noble Scottish traveller by crowning him with a red-hot iron tripod.[31]

The Hungarian peasant revolt of 1514 offers similar examples of peasant atrocities, with the more oriental addition of impaling (borrowed from stories about the Turks) as a particularly prolonged and hideous form of execution. Historians of this insurrection repeatedly describe peasant rage and furore not being created by the uprising but rather natural forces that have now "boiled over" with the removal of the restraints normally imposed by social coercion. Rape and torture are emblematic peasant atrocities, so that nobles are impaled before the eyes of their families, or the women are raped while the husbands or fathers are forced to watch.[32] Giovanni Vitale, an Italian observer of the Hungarian uprising, describes these horrific incidents, excoriating the peasants as "impudent cattle" who now have an opportunity to fulfil their desire for rape, mur-

---

29 For Bartholomeus Anglicus, Der Stricker and the popular fifteenth-century poems, see Paul Freedman, *Images of the Medieval Peasant* (Stanford, 1999), 182–85.

30 Marie-Thèrese de Medeiros, *Jacques et chroniqueurs: Une étude comparée de récits contemporains relatant la Jacquerie de 1358* (Paris, 1979), 186–89.

31 M. Louis-François Bellagnet, ed. *Chronique du religieux de Saint-Denys*, 6 vols. (Paris, 1839), 2:308–10.

32 Paul Freedman, "Atrocities and the Executions of Peasant Rebel Leaders in Late Medieval and Early Modern Europe," *Medievalia et humanistica* 31 (2005): 101–13.

der, pillage, and the destruction of their betters.[33] Peasants are savages or essentially animals that can be tamed, but which retain the potential for aimless destruction. John Gower, writing about the English Rising of 1381, likens the peasant rebels to domestic animals (asses, swine, oxen, dogs) that have escaped the control of their masters. Once the revolt is suppressed, according to Gower, the peasants revert to their previous status of obedient, productive draught animals.[34]

Such opinions were deeply ingrained and did not require a peasants' revolt to be expressed. The Catalan moralist Francesc Eiximenis said that peasants were naturally inclined to evil and that they must, like cruel or savage beasts, be beaten and starved into submission.[35] Eiximenis notwithstanding, the Catalan peasant war of 1462–1486 is notable for not producing very much in the way of atrocity stories or the kind of apocalyptic tone on the part of the historians or opponents. No examples of human roasting or cannibalism were reported.

Elsewhere what is odd about the atrocities is that some of them were reproduced by the authorities against the peasant leaders as part of the dramatized repression of the revolt. Jacques Calle, one of the leaders of the 1358 *Jacquerie*, was captured by the king of Navarre and executed by being placed naked on a piece of hot iron while he was crowned with a burning iron circlet. The leader of the Hungarian revolt, György Dózsa, was executed by the voivod of Transylvania in a manner similar to the execution of Jacques Calle with the additional detail that once he had been roasted on an iron throne, his followers were forced to eat his flesh.[36] This was not a spontaneous act of revenge but occurred in a public setting ten days after Dózsa's arrest, accompanied by a *Te Deum* and a band of pipes and trumpets.

The borrowing back and forth between peasant and official atrocities shows that there was a vocabulary of cruelty and mockery to be meted out to enemies. We call them atrocities and the Hungarian incident became subsequently sufficiently notorious to be taken up by Montaigne as an example of the violence of the powerful, but initially the details of Dózsa's execution were reported by the perpetrators to the king of Hungary in a casual, even light-hearted fashion, a tone repeated by Vladislav II in a letter to the pope.[37]

Order and disorder are here again complementary or connected in several places rather than being stable, easily identified and always opposed. We are dealing not with high political theory, to be sure, but with everyday expressions of a certain kind of ideology and symbolic political presentation concerning the nature of order. Social cohesion moves from an image of mutuality to a barely-maintained control of the productive but

---

33 Antal Fekete Nagy, ed., *Monumenta rusticorum in Hungaria rebellium anno MDXIV* (Budapest, 1979), 244 (document 200).

34 John Gower, "Vox clamantis," in *The Complete Works of John Gower: The Latin Works*, ed. George C. Macaulay (Oxford, 1902), 79 (book 1, vv. 2093–2096).

35 Jill Webster, ed., *Francesc Eiximenis. La societat catalana al segle XIV* (Barcelona, 1967), 59.

36 Freedman, "Atrocities and the Execution," 102 and 104–5.

37 Lászlo Báti, "Montaignes Aufzeichnung über György Dózsas Tod," *Aus der Geschichte der ostmitteleuropäische Bauernbewegungen im XVI–XVII Jahrhundert*, ed. Gusztáv Heckenast (Budapest, 1977), 457–60; Antal Fekete Nagy, ed., *Monumenta rusticorum*, 175–76 (n. 142).

potentially rebellious lower class. Disorder becomes a peasant characteristic whereas before it was the *milites* who provoked social chaos. But probably such a chronological movement from the first centuries after 1000 to the period after the Black Death is too simplified. There was always fluidity about the sources of political order and disorder, a tendency to slide over from one fear to another. This is not so surprising in view of the confused historiography I mentioned at the outset, or even the contemporary world where it is not always easy to identify the forces of destruction versus the forces of social stability.

Chapter 2

AUCTORITAS, POTESTAS:
CONCEPTS OF POWER IN MEDIEVAL SPAIN

ADELINE RUCQUOI

MEDIEVALISTS WHO TAKE an interest in the history of power tend to come across the words *potestas* or *auctoritas* in historical documents, more rarely the term *imperium*; they are generally translated by "power," "authority," or "empire." The first two are used as synonyms when defining "dominion, empire, faculty, and jurisdiction that one has to command or execute something",[1] in other words the capacity of a king to govern a country, while the latter term refers to a power with universal tendencies. However, the fact that in Spain, some kings of Leon and then Castile bore the title of *imperator* has generated various theories, in many cases controversial, over the last century, and even the idea that the appropriation of such a title responded to the needs of a weak monarchy, with little "power," that required and thus obtained an "increase in legitimacy."[2]

The vast majority of medievalists who have dealt with this problem did so comparing the Hispanic case with contemporary cases or ones not very distant in time. Whoever says "empire" then evokes either the Carolingian empire of the ninth century or the Holy Roman Empire of the eleventh to thirteenth centuries. The comparisons are always established within the traditional "medieval" framework—the years 500 to 1500—, "horizontally" and not "vertically" over time. The division between Antiquity, Middle Ages, and Modern Times often plays the role of an insurmountable frontier: as if each of these epochs invented everything without inheriting anything from the previous age or transmitting anything to the subsequent period. In 1977, Régine Pernoud published a short book with a provocative title: *Pour en finir avec le Moyen Âge*, a work that she began by recalling a question she had been asked: "Could you tell me the exact date of the treaty that officially ended the Middle Ages?"[3] The sentence brought a smile to the

---

1 "Poder : dominio, imperio, facultad y jurisdicción que uno tiene para mandar o ejecutar una cosa," *Diccionario de la Real Academia Española*, accessed November 1, 2016, http://dle.rae.es/?id=TU1KCfY|TU2nLT0.

2 From Ramón Menéndez Pidal, *El imperio hispánico y los cinco reinos. Dos épocas en la estructura política de España* (Madrid, 1950), and Alfonso García-Gallo, "El imperio medieval español," in *Historia de España. Estudios publicados en la revista Arbor* (Madrid, 1953), 108–43, to Thomas Deswarte, *De la destruction à la restauration. L'idéologie du royaume d'Oviedo-León (VIIIᵉ-XIᵉ siècles)* (Turnhout, 2003), and Hélène Sirantoine, *Imperator Hispaniae. Les idéologies impériales dans le royaume de León (IXᵉ-XIIᵉ siècles)* (Madrid, 2012).

3 *Pourriez-vous me dire la date exacte du traité qui mit officiellement fin au Moyen Âge?* Cited from Régine Pernoud, *Pour en finir avec le Moyen Âge* (Paris, 1977), 1.

Adeline Rucquoi (rucquoi@free.fr) is Directeur de recherche at the Centre National de la Recherche Scientifique in Paris.

face of more than a few medievalists who read it from the heights of their discipline and their wisdom. They should not have smiled, because most works dedicated to the Middle Ages display the firm conviction that, one fine day, Antiquity ended and disappeared, remaining as a distant memory, and that the Middle Ages began then, sufficient unto itself; in the same way, the Modern Age will not have any point in common with the centuries that preceded it. Within this perspective, medievalists cannot, and should not, seek origins, causes, and models in Antiquity for the events, concepts, and institutions found in the historical documents. They may look for these in other places, but always within the chronological framework of the "Middle Ages." Between this and Antiquity, there is no continuity.

Potestas, auctoritas, imperium

Potestas and *auctoritas*, together with *imperium*, belong to the terminology of the power of Roma. They may be translated as "faculty to act," "authority," and "power," but the current meaning of these words is far from that which they had under the pen of the Roman jurists. Those who used them in the Middle Ages had found and read them in texts by Cicero, Julius Caesar, Livy, Tertullian, or Lactantius when not in multiple legal texts. They did not invent them, and even less so as Roma had not disappeared for them, continuity persisted. One cannot therefore address the problem of power without first resorting to the meaning of those terms in the sources known in the Middle Ages.

Potestas, auctoritas, imperium: three terms that refer to the exercise of power and that, for more than one and a half centuries, legal historians and social historians have attempted to define as precisely as possible without always managing to do so. At the end of the nineteenth century, in his study about the magistrates in Roma, Theodor Mommsen proposed some elements to distinguish *potestas* from *imperium*, and reached the conclusion that the word *potestas* designated power in its broadest and most general sense, reserving the use of *imperium* for high offices and leaving the lower ones a simple *potestas sine imperio*.[4] In 1925, Richard Heinze took an interest in the concept of *auctoritas*, whose various meanings he inventoried along with their evolution.[5] Several years later, while Álvaro d'Ors was attracted by the "binomial" *auctoritas–potestas*, André Magdelain dedicated numerous works to *auctoritas* and to *imperium*, later combined in a single volume.[6]

Potestas, auctoritas, imperium: the three words refer to power and imply an unequal relationship, of subordination. The concept of *auctoritas*, which in Roma belongs to both private and public law, implies an unequal relationship but without domination or coercion. The *auctor* confirms or completes the act of who is under his authority, ratifies and guarantees it, like, in private law, the tutor validates what his pupil does. Etymologically, it comes from *augere*, which in particular means "increase," "support," "give fulness to

---

4 Theodor Mommsen, *Le droit public romain, 1. La magistrature* (Paris, 1892).

5 Richard Heinze, *"Auctoritas," Hermès* 60 (1925): 348–66.

6 Álvaro d'Ors, *Escritos varios sobre el derecho en crisis* (Madrid, 1973). André Magdelain, *Jus imperium auctoritas. Études de droit romain* (Roma, 1990).

something."[7] In the field of public law and during the Roman Republic, the authority of the *patres* conferred legitimacy on popular decisions, gave full validity to the laws voted by a people who did not have *potestas*. The *auctoritas patrum* was at that time exercised by patrician families who occupied seats in the Senate through having had an ancestor who was a consul and had received the *auspicia maxima*. Until the laws of 339 BC, the Senate offered its *consilium* before the vote and conferred its *auctoritas* on the result obtained. This role evolved over time. In André Magdelain's words:

> It is the intervention of an *auctor* and perfects the operation that another person does not have the ability to perform alone. This relationship is the same between the *patres auctores* and the *populus*. Following later development, it is transformed into a moral power to which it becomes difficult or impossible not to yield.[8]

The *auctoritas patrum* was progressively instrumentalized by the Senate, until it was merged with the *auctoritas senatus*.

For its part, *potestas* in Roma is the generic term that designates the power given by the law to individuals or groups. It applies to both the relationship between a father and his son or family—the *patria potestas*—and to the links between a master and his slave, the tutor and his pupil, the magistrate and the people: Isidore of Seville wrote "just as a slave is in the power of his master, so a child is in the power of his father" (*sicut servus in potestate est domini, sic filius in potestate est patris*) (Etim., 9, v, 17). It is a relation of subordination, of domination, in which he who exercises *potestas* can take decisions, give orders, and demand obedience, with coercion if needed. It is the power that the consuls in Roma wield, only exceeded by that of the censors or, as the case may be, that of the dictator. *Potestas*, Isidore writes in his *Etymologiae*, "is valid wherever it wants and nobody can interfere or oppose it," relating the word with *patens* and the concept of extension.[9]

However, *potestas* in itself is not absolute. To be absolute, *imperium* is required. Characteristic of supreme *potestas*, *imperium* gives its holder power over life and death, and thus, in the Republic, this could only be exercised by the consuls who left the *Urbs* to go to war, preceded by the *lictores* carrying the fasces. The origin of this *imperium* dated back to "immemorial times," did not come from the law, from a vote or a senate consultation, and was transmitted from consul to consul from a first, and indefinite, cession. Obtaining the *imperium* or not depended on the birds. It required that the auspices were favourable to the new consuls who went to "find them" after their election. At the end of the fourth century, in his *De verborum significatione*, Pompeius Festus explained

---

7 Isidoro de Sevilla, *Etimologías* 2.2, ed. José Oroz Reta, (Madrid, 1982): *Auctor ab augendo dictus (Auctor ab agendo).*

8 *Elle est l'intervention d'un* auctor *et parfait l'opération qu'une autre personne n'a pas la capacité d'accomplir seule. Cette relation est la même entre les* patres auctores *et le* populus. *Selon un développement plus récent, elle est un pouvoir moral devant lequel il devient vite difficile ou impossible de ne pas s'incliner.* Cited from André Magdelain, "De l'*auctoritas patrum* à l'*auctoritas senatus*," in *Jus imperium auctoritas. Études de droit romain*, special issue, *Publications de l'École Française de Rome* 133 (1990): 385–403, accessed April 22, 2013, https://www.persee.fr/doc/efr_0000-0000_1990_ant_133_1_3966.

9 Isidoro de Sevilla, *Etimologías* 10.208, ed. Oroz: *Potens, rebus late patens, unde et potestas quod pateat illi qua velit, et nemo intercludat, nullus obsistere valeat.*

that, the year a general was sent to head the army, he went up the Capitol at dawn for the birds to give him their omen, and when he came down he was greeted as the one who had been so designated. The taking of the auspices, essential to being invested with the *imperium*, thus added a celestial—magical—dimension to the function of the one who henceforth exercised this power.[10]

Initiated by Julius Caesar, the accumulation and concentration of powers in the hands of a single person culminated with Octavius around 27 BC. Although he adopted the simple name of prince (*princeps*), which seemed to make him a simple *primus inter pares*, Octavius monopolized the great magistratures being *augustus*—that is, *auctor*—, *pontifex maximus*, *caesar*, and *imperator*, invested with the *imperium consulare et proconsulare*. These prerogatives were granted to him or recognized one after the other by the Senate. The successors of Octavius Augustus were theoretically elected by the Senate but very often by the legions, the Senate restricting itself to giving them a formal investiture, as a concession to the ancient *auctoritas patrum*, immediately followed by a law—*lex imperii*—"voted" by popular acclaim, as concession to the old *iussus plebis*.[11] At the end of the first century, the *lex regia de imperio* evokes the cession—*translatio*—of "*omne suum imperium*" by the "*populus senatusque romanus*" to Octavius forever, thus suppressing the role of the auspices that had set the independence of power from the political body.

The Middle Ages thus inherited from Roman Antiquity the concept according to which, in law, Roma was constituted by two elements: a political body—*populus*, *civitas*, *res publica*—and the group of those who exercised a power with *imperium*, which was transmitted from one magistrate to the next, and whose origin was not in that political body. So *imperium* therefore did not belong to the world of law, but depended on the reading of the divine presages—the auspices.

Christianity attributed to God the various definitions of power drawn up by Roma since the time of the Republic. In the first century, St. Paul claimed that all power came from God—*Omnis potestas a Deo* (Romans 13:1–7)—, and Tertullian, two centuries later, quoting Isaiah 9:5—"For a child is born to us, a son is given to us; upon his shoulder dominion rests"[12]—pointed out that God was the "supernatural" origin of the *imperium*, a divine origin later adopted by the Christian emperors. God thus became the *auctor* of the world, the supreme legislator, and the wielder of the supreme *potestas*. Tertullian (d. ca. 220) evokes this in his *Adversus Hermogenem*: "He says in reply that, even though this is the prerogative of matter, both the authority and the substance of God must remain intact, by virtue of which He is regarded as the sole and prime author, as well as the Lord of all things."[13]

---

10 Festus 276L. Michel Humm, "The curiate law and the religious nature of the power of Roman magistrates," in *Law and Religion in the Roman Republic*, ed. Olga Tellegen-Couperus (Leiden, 2012), 57–84.

11 "*Auctoritas*," in *Dictionnaire des antiquités grecques et romaines*, ed. Charles Daremberg (Paris, 1877–1919).

12 *Filius natus est nobis, cujus imperium factum est super humerum ipsius*. Cited from Tertullianus, "Adversus Judaeos," in *Patrologiae cursus completus*, ed. Jacques-Paul Migne, 221 vols. (Paris, 1844), 2: col. 628.

13 *Vel qua, inquit, et sic habente materia, salva sit Deo et auctoritas et substantia, qua solus et*

For his part, in the sixth book of his *Divinas institutiones*, Lactantius (d. ca. 325) states that "and there will be one common master, and ruler of all, God, the inventor, examiner, and proposer of his law."[14]

Power, as *auctoritas*, *potestas*, and *imperium*, is God's and comes from God. Under divine authority, from the fourth century, the Christian emperor will rule over the people as God's "lieutenant" ("holding the place of"), as his "vicar." To govern adequately, the emperor will have to surround himself with civil administrators—the *comites* and judges—and religious advisers—the patriarchs and bishops—, since, in the end, God will hold his vicar accountable, and only him. Imperial "authority" comes to him by divine delegation.

However, at the end of the fifth century, Pope Gelasius I, in a letter sent to Emperor Anastasius, specifically claimed the *auctoritas* as the power proper to Peter's successor, and coined the phrase "sacred authority of the popes and royal power" (*auctoritas sacrata pontificum et regalis potestas*),[15] a formula that Pope Innocent III took up again at the beginning of the thirteenth century when he talked about "papal authority and royal power" (*pontificalis auctoritas et regalis potestas*). The differentiation between *potestas* and *auctoritas* confers a higher role to the latter, of authorization or ratification of the *potestas*, and will allow the division of power between "spiritual" and "temporal": vicar of God on earth, the pope therefore claimed the divine *auctoritas*, which "authorizes" the powers exercised by the emperor and kings.

Here it is necessary to go forward some centuries, until the middle of the eighth. It is then when in Roma the false "Donation of Constantine" or *Constitutum Constantini* was elaborated, a supposed codicil to the emperor's will that made the bishop of Roma, patriarch of the Occident, the heir to the Western Empire;[16] the pope thus succeeded Emperor Constantine as God's vicar in the western part of the Roman empire, as the only person authorized (by God) to rule, with the help of kings and bishops. As such, Pope Leo III crowned Charlemagne emperor, delegating to him part of the power he had from God, supreme *auctor*. This was recalled by the *rota*, the circular slab of porphyry in the pavement of St. Peter's in Roma, on which occurred part of the coronation ceremony of the emperors by the popes in the eleventh and twelfth centuries: "God ineffable author of the world [...]."[17]

---

primus auctor est, et Dominus omnium censeatur. Cited from Tertullianus, "Adversus Hermogenem," in *Patrologiae cursus completus*, ed. Jacques-Paul Migne, 221 vols. (Paris, 1844), 2: col. 201.

14 *Unusque erit communis quasi magister, et imperator omnium Deus, ille legis hujus inventor, disceptator, lator*. Cited from Lactantius, "Divinarum institutionum. Liber VI," in *Patrologiae cursus completus*, ed. Jacques-Paul Migne, 221 vols. (Paris, 1844), 6: col. 661.

15 *Auctoritas sacrata pontificum et regalis potestas*. Cited from Gelasius I, "Epistolae et Decreta," in *Patrologiae cursus completus*, ed. Jacques-Paul Migne, 221 vols. (Paris, 1862), 59: col. 42.

16 *Das Constitutum Contantini*, ed. Horst Fuhrmann, MGH Fontes iuris 10 (1968). Nicolas Huyghebaert, "Une légende de fondation: le *Constitutum Constantini*," *Le Moyen Âge* 85 (1979): 177–209.

17 *Deus inenarrabilis auctor mundi [...]*. Cited from Michel Andrieu, "La rota porphyretica de la basilique vaticane," *Mélanges d'archéologie et d'histoire* 66 (1954): 189–218.

But what happened in the Hispania dominated by the Visigoths from the end of the sixth century? Are the concepts elaborated in the Carolingian empire or the concepts that arose in the kingdoms of France or England valid? How did the various facets of power evolve in the Peninsula? Did the peninsular kings wield a mere *potestas* under the pontifical *auctoritas*?

Regalis auctoritas

First, let us look at the concept of *auctoritas*. *Auctoritas* has various senses. In everyday life, it was that of the tutor over a legally incapable pupil, or that of the husband over the assets of his wife. However, as it evolved at the end of the Roman Republic, "authority" becomes the power to authenticate records and diplomas, giving them a legal validity, or any act carried out by one who does not have full capacity. Texts and thinkers became "authorities" that empowered those who invoked them to express ideas and develop arguments. The statement by Bernard of Chartres: "We are like dwarves sitting on the shoulders of giants" (*nos esse quasi nanos gigantium humeris insidentes*) can be understood as an expression of modesty, of recognition of the work of his predecessors, but also indicates moral subordination to the *auctores*, those whose works "authorize" the thoughts and writings of those who refer to them. The "author" is not the one who writes, but rather the one who is quoted. The real author of a work is not as important as his sources or as who inspired it, as can be observed in the works placed under the name of the master Gerard of Cremona in Toledo in the twelfth century, or those that appear as "by Alfonso X the Wise." Authorship is always that of the writer or the work that serve as a source. At the end of the fifteenth century, Alfonso of Toledo will complete his *Invencionario* citing all the "authorities" he had used in his work.[18]

The "intellectuals" of the Central Middle Ages therefore raised the problem of "*accessus ad auctores*," of how to cite the "authorities."[19] Adelard of Bath, for example, explained that one had to travel in search of these sources "because what the Gallic schools do not know, is revealed by the transalpines, and what is not learned from the Latins, the fertile Greece will teach it," and added the Arabs among the *auctores* of his own work.[20] Around the same years, 1130–1140, in Barcelona, Plato Tiburtinus sent Johannes Hispalensis his translation of the *Utilitates astrolabii* by Abulcasim (Abu-l Qasim Maslama Ibn al-Saffar); in the prologue, he explains that he had resorted to the Arabs because, after long observations, he had not found in the Latin or Greek authors the astrolabe invented by Ptolemy, but only in Abulcasim, an expert in geometry and astronomy.[21]

---

18 Philip O. Gericke, *Invencionario* (Madison, 1992).

19 Edwin A. Quain, "The Medieval *Accessus ad Auctores*," *Traditio* 3 (1945): 215–64.

20 *Quod enim Gallica studia nesciunt, transalpina reserabunt: quod apud Latinos non addisces, Graecia facunda docebit.* Cited from Charles Burnett, ed., *Adelard of Bath: An English Scientist and Arabist of the Early Twelfth-Century* (London, 1987). Charles Burnett, "Adelard of Bath and the Arabs," in *Rencontres de cultures dans la philosophie médiévale*, ed. Jacqueline Hamesse, Marta Fattori (Louvain-la-Neuve, 1990), 89–107.

21 Città del Vaticano, Biblioteca Apostolica Vaticana, MS Ottob. lat. 309, fols. 136r–143r: *Cum inter universa doctorum instrumenta, post longam et assiduam observationem, nec apud Graecos nec apud Arabes nec etiam apud Latinos, tam subtile tam artificiosum tamque perutile, licet mechanicum,*

However, undoubtedly the person in that time who best defined the "*accessus ad auctores*" and the differences between the Latins and Arabs is Herman of Carinthia, in the prologue to his translation of the *Maius introductorium* by Abu Ma'ashar (Albumasar), which he dedicated to Robert of Ketton in 1140. In his long disquisition about the theme, he specifies that, among the Arabs, seven elements have to appear at the beginning of a work: the author's intention, the utility of the work, the author's name, the name of the book, its place within the field of the discipline, its genre between theory and practice, and finally, the divisions or chapters of the book.[22] In contrast, among Latin writers, there are only five: the title of the work, the intention of the author, the purpose, the way in which it is treated, and its order, that is, the table of contents or chapters.[23] Herman was willing to simplify the *accessus* of the text he was translating, but his friend Robert advised him not to do so because it could be interpreted later as the result of ignorance or laziness. Herman accepted his friend's arguments and took up the seven points of Abu Ma'ashar, attempting to combine them with the Latin tradition. Regarding the "author," he specifies that "the name of the author is necessary for two reasons, on the one hand to return to the authentic work, on the other hand to prevent an unjust glory from falling on someone who does not deserve it."[24]

The problem of the "authority" of the works was thus resolved in five or seven points, and returned to the first "compositor" the authorship of the work. From that time onwards, the *auctor* is both the "inventor" of the work and the person who "authorizes" those who quote him in their own works.[25] In the *General Estoria*, there are

---

invenissem instrumentum, ut est astrolapsus a Ptolomeo subtiliter inventus, et ab eodem artificiose compositus, nec usquam inter Latinos plenariam doctrinam ad ipsius omnes utilitates evidentissimas, cunctisque valde necessarias ostendendas, reperissem, multis atque diversis Arabum voluminibus revolutis, in nullo unquam ita perfectum, ita venustum itaque celeberrimum tractatum, ad eius astronomicas et geometricas diversas utilitates explanandas, et plene elucidandas invenire potui, ut in hoc studiosissimi Abualcasin filii Asafar, tam in geometria quam in astronomia valde peritissimi.

22 *VII., inquit, sunt omnis tractatus inicia: auctoris intentio, operis utilitas, nomen auctoris, nomen libri, locus in ordine discipline, species inter theoricam et practicam, partitiones libri.* From Oxford, Corpus Christi College, MS 95, fol. 60r; Napoli, Biblioteca Nazionale, MS C. 8. 50, fol. 1r.

23 *Quod apud nos quinquipertito sufficeret, operis videlicet titulo, auctoris intencione, finali causa, modo tractandi et ordine.* From Oxford, Corpus Christi College, MS 95, fol. 60r; Napoli, Biblioteca Nazionale, MS C. 8. 50, fol. 1r.

24 *Auctoris nomen duabus de causis necessarium est, tum ut opus autenticum reddat tum ne alii dum vagum et incerti sit nominis immerito ascriptum iniustam parat gloriam.* From Oxford, Corpus Christi College, MS 95, fol. 60r; Napoli, Biblioteca Nazionale, MS C. 8. 50, fol. 1r. Richard Lemay, "De la scolastique à l'histoire par le truchement de la philologie: l'itinéraire d'un médiéviste entre Europe et Islam," in *La diffusione delle scienze islamiche nel Medio Evo europeo* (Roma, 1987), 428–84, esp. 478.

25 In the prologue of his *Sefer ha-Mešalim*, written in the early thirteenth century, the Toledan Jacob ben Eleazar stated: "Following the customs of the Ismaelites of changing the names in the stories I have not kept my name, but have changed it for that of Lemuel ben Itiel, but you should know that I am Jacob ben Eleazar [...], and that whoever steals something of this from me, shall be expelled and annihilated" (*Siguiendo las costumbres de los ismaelitas de cambiarse los nombres en los relatos no he mantenido mi nombre, sino que lo he cambiado por el de Lemuel ben Itiel, pero has de saber que yo soy Jacob ben Eleazar [...], y que el que me robe algo de esto, sea expulsado y aniquilado*).

almost three hundred occurrences of author (*auctor* or *autor*) and authors (*auctores* or *autores*), and four of authority (*autoridad*) or authorities (*autoridades*). Almost all are related to classical or patristic sources that "authorize" the narrative. Thus, Alfonso X of Castile mentions, for example:

> That, in order to prove the Incarnation of our Lord Jesus Christ, they invoke in the lessons of the night of Christmas their proofs from Authorities, as well those from the Gentiles taken from the Arabian, and also from the Jews as well as those of the Christians wherever they found them,

and among the said "authorities" he then refers to the name of "Abul Ubeyt abd Allah, son of Abd Albaziz Albacri, in Chapter 21 of his book about Abraham's birth" or, regarding Ovid, that "he was very wise and fulfilled poet among the authors."[26] "Authority," says the *Tesoro de la lengua castellana o española* by Sebastián de Covarrubias in 1611, is:

> the written reason that we allege to ground some purpose, and the most firm is that which is brought from Holy Scripture, from the Councils, from the traditions of the holy doctors, and in proportion to the others who have written and write.[27]

This is why, in the second half of the eleventh century, the count of Barcelona, Ramon Berenguer I, explains that he completes and amends the "Gothic" laws thanks to the *potestatis regie discrecione* conferred to him by the *Liber Iudicum*—"*libri Iudicum auctoritate*."[28]

However, let us return to *auctoritas* as power. In 916, King Ordoño II glorified God as "king of kings, prince of princes and lord of lords, author of all, shining redeemer of the universes."[29] Shortly after, in 964, the Glossary of San Millán de la Cogolla defined "*auctoritas*" as "dignity of the spirit by which a person is confirmed."[30] When Alfonso X begins the book of the *Siete Partidas*, although he does not use the word, he acknowledges it as well:

Amparo Alba Cecilia, "El *Debate del cálamo y la espada*, de Jacob ben Eleazar de Toledo," *Sefarad* 68, no. 2 (2008): 291–314.

26 *Que pora prouar la Jncarnation de nuestro sennor ihesu xristo. aduzen en las lecciones de la noche de Nauidat. sus prueuas de Auctoridades. tan bien de Gentiles tomadas del arauigo & otrossi de Judios. como delos xristianos donde quier quelas pudieron auer [...] Abul Ubeyt abd Allah fijo de abd Albaziz Albacri en el .xxj. capitulo de su libro sobrel nascimiento de Abraham* [Ovid] *fue muy sabio & muy cumplido. Poeta entre los auctores.* Cited from Alfonso X el Sabio, *General Estoria*, 1.

27 *Autoridad es la razón escrita que alegamos para fundar algún propósito, y la firmísima es la que se trae de la Sagrada Escritura, de los Concilios, de las traditions de los sanctos doctores, y en su proporción de los demas que han escrito y escriven.* Cited from Sebastian de Covarrubias, *Tesoro de la lengua castellana o española* (Madrid, 1611), 105v.

28 *Cortes de los antiguos reinos de Aragón y de Valencia y Principado de Cataluña. Cortes de Cataluña* (Madrid, 1896), 10–11, 1.1.

29 *Rex regum, princeps principum et dominus dominantium, auctor cunctorum, redemtor universorum rutilans.* Cited from Emilio Saez et al., eds., *Colección documental del archivo de la catedral de León*, 18 vols. (León, 1987–), 1:56–58.

30 *Dignitas mentis a quibus confirmata persona.* Cited from Claudio García Turza, Javier García Turza, eds., *El códice emilianense 46 de la Real Academia de la Historia, primer diccionario enciclopédico de la Península ibérica* (Logroño, 1997), 252.

> God is the beginning and end and final of everything, and without him nothing could be; because from his knowledge the things are done, and from his power they are kept, and from his goodness they are maintained.[31]

Within the philosophic concepts that circulated in Spain from the eleventh century, and later in the rest of Europe, God is the primary cause (*causa primaria*), that which has no cause but is universal cause.[32]

Although God is the *auctor* of the world, its creator, from the twelfth century onwards the word has an essentially moral meaning and tends to be limited to the "authorities" under whose shade one writes and produces a work. The *auctoritas sapientialis*, which comes from knowledge, is thus replaced by a more political form of authority. In the *auctoritas–potestas* binomial pair, established by Álvaro d'Ors, the first is "socially recognized knowledge," as opposed to the second, characterized as "socially recognized power"; within this binomial pair, the main purpose of the *auctoritas*—following the classical Roman model—is to limit the *potestas* by virtue of moral precepts.[33] The divine *auctoritas* would be the limit placed on the human *potestas*.

Within this semantic evolution, the vindication of Wisdom by the Hispanic kings from the end of the twelfth century, a vindication that likens them to Solomon, the paradigmatic monarch,[34] implies the vindication of the authority that it confers. Thanks to his wisdom, which comes from God, the king can be the *auctor* of the laws and the supreme sentences, of the writing of history, or of the edification of "temples," be they churches or palaces.[35] Then, although the word is not mentioned, perhaps to reserve it for the moral and literary field, we must see in the constant affirmations that the kings are "God's vicars" in their kingdoms and that "they do not recognise any higher" a vindication of *auctoritas*. In the article "What is the king?" (*¿Qué cosa es el rey?*), the jurists of Alfonso X the Wise respond in the *II Partida*:

> Vicars of God are the kings each in his own realm, placed above the peoples to maintain them in justice and in truth in the temporal, as well as the emperor in his empire. This is proved by two ways. The first of them is spiritual, according to what the prophets and saints demonstrated, to whom Our Lord gave the grace to know things indeed and to

---

31 *Dios es comienzo et fin et acabamiento de todas las cosas, et sin él cosa alguna non puede ser; ca por el su saber son fechas, et por el su poder guardadas, et por la su bondat mantenidas.* Cited from Alfonso X el Sabio, "Prólogo," *Las Siete Partidas* (Salamanca, 1555), 1.

32 Pierre Magnard, Olivier Boulnois, Bruno Pinchard, Jean-Luc Solère, *La Demeure de l'être. Autour d'un anonyme. Étude et traduction du "Liber de Causis"* (Paris, 1990).

33 Álvaro d'Ors, *Escritos varios sobre el derecho en crisis* (Madrid, 1973), 93–108. María Alejandra Vanney, "Libertad, responsabilidad y sentido común en el pensamiento de Álvaro D'Ors," *Thémata. Revista de Filosofía* 41 (2009): 425–40.

34 Adeline Rucquoi, "El Rey Sabio: cultura y poder en la monarquía castellana medieval," in *Repoblación y reconquista. Actas del III Curso de Cultura Medieval*, ed. José Luis Hernando Garrido, (Aguilar de Campoo, 1993), 77–87.

35 Rafael Domingo Oslé, "El binomio auctoritas–potestas en el Derecho romano y moderno," *Persona y Derecho: Revista de fundamentación de las Instituciones jurídicas y de Derechos humanos* 37 (1997): 183–96.

make them understood. The other one is according to nature, as was proved by the wise men who known the things by nature.[36]

King and emperor are equated here, and only differ in their titles. The power they exercise in their kingdom or empire is the supreme power, "authorized" by the Creator. Alfonso X restates this in the *Espéculo*, when he writes that, "thanks to the will of God, we have no one over us in temporal things," and continues explaining that this is:

> by right, since we can prove it by the Roman laws and by the right of the holy Church and by the laws of Spain made by the Goths, in that it says in each of these that emperors and kings have power to make laws and to add to them and to decrease in them and to change everything that needs to be. Therefore, for all these reasons we have the full power to make laws.[37]

The expression "we have no one over us in temporal things" (*non avemos mayor sobre nos en el temporal*) does not mean a concession to the Roman theories related to the *pontificalis auctoritas*, because, by "temporal," Alfonso X understands both the elaboration and promulgation of laws that "belong to the belief in our Lord Jesus Christ" and those that "belong to the government of the peoples."[38]

Due to the Gregorian reform in which the pope vindicated the *pontificalis auctoritas*, the kings in the Peninsula maintained a long quarrel with the bishop of Roma over his *auctoritas* within their respective kingdoms. The independence of the Toledan Church in Visigothic times, obvious in the *Apologeticum* by Julian of Toledo,[39] did not imply a negation of the Roman supremacy in questions of dogma, but a rejection of the control the popes wanted to exert over the kings of Hispania. In the eighth century, after the Muslim invasion, Adrian I's intentions to re-establish the Christian faith in Spain, impose the canonical date for celebrating Easter, excommunicate those who ate meat that had

---

36 *Vicarios de Dios son los reyes cada uno de su reyno, puestos sobre las gentes para mantenerlas en justicia e en verdad quanto en lo tenporal bien assi como el emperador en su imperio. Esto se muestra complidamente en dos maneras. La primera dellas es spiritual, segund lo mostraron los profetas e los santos a quien dio Nuestro Señor gracia de saber las cosas ciertamente e de fazerlas entender. La otra es segund natura, assi como mostraron los omes sabios que fueron conoscedores de las cosas naturalmente.* Cited from Alfonso X el Sabio, *Las Siete Partidas*, Partida 2, Title 1, Law 5.

37 *Que por la merced de Dios non avemos mayor sobre nos en el temporal; por derecho, ca lo podemos probar por las leyes romanas e por el derecho de santa eglesia e por las leys despaña que fezieron los godos en que dize en cada una destas que los emperadores e los reyes an poder de fazer leyes e de anader en ellas e de minguar en ellas e de camiar cada que mester sea. Onde por todas estas razones avemos poder conplidamiente de facer leyes.* Cited from Alfonso X el Sabio, "Espéculo," in *Los Códigos españoles concordados e anotados* (Madrid, 1849), tome 6, book 1, law 13, 7–208.

38 Alfonso X el Sabio, *Las Siete Partidas*, Partida 1, Title 1: "Therefore, we want to make them understand in order to get out of this doubt. What laws are these [...]. Which of these belong to the belief in our Lord Jesus Christ. And which belong to the governance of the people" (*Por ende nos por sacar los desta dubda, queremos les fazer entender. Que leyes son estas [...] E quales dellas pertenescen a la creencia de nuestro señor Iesu Christo. E quales pertenescen al governamiento de las gente [...]*).

39 Santiago Fernández Ardanaz, "El pensamiento religioso en la época hispanorromana," in *Historia de la teología española*, ed. Melquíades Andrés, 2 vols. (Madrid, 1983), 1:285–92. Roger J. H. Collins, "Julian of Toledo and the Education of Kings in Late Seventh-Century Spain," in *Law, Culture and Regionalism in Early Medieval Spain*, ed. Roger J. H. Collins (Aldershot, 1992), 1–22.

not previously been bled, prohibit coexistence with Jews and pagans, and eradicate all the heresies "of the dogma of Priscillian," were seen as an attempt to limit the freedom of the Hispanic Church.[40] The pope commissioned his will to Egila, who was a Frank, which added to the papal attempt Frankish ambitions on the south of the Pyrenees.[41]

Neither the Roman Church nor the emperor created by the same church in the year 800 managed to impose themselves in the Peninsula during the Early Middle Ages. A careful reading of the texts shows, for example, that Alfonso II's embassies to Charlemagne were not a "submission," but rather the notification of the victories obtained by the former.[42] The study of the concession of the pallium to the bishops by the popes highlights the independence of the Hispanic prelates,[43] in kingdoms whose monarchs created the bishoprics and appointed their holders. After addressing Christ as the "light author of the light" (*lux auctor luminis*) and as the "king of kings ruling the heavens as well as the earth" (*rex regum regens celestia simulque terrestria*), the diploma of King Alfonso II from 812 recalled that he, "[his] servant, no, rather [his] slave" (*vernulus famulus immo servus tuus*), founded the church of Oviedo in His honour and endowed it.[44] In the prologue of the diploma, the king evoked the presence of the Goths in Spain as God's will, the loss of the *regnum* because of the presumption of King Rodrigo, and the role of Pelagius who was "exalted to the power of prince" (*in principis sublimatus potentia*) to give the victory to the Christians and to the Asturs. The legitimacy and, therefore, authority of King Alfonso comes to him from God through the *patres* who are the kings of the Visigoths, and allows him to found bishoprics in his kingdom.

In 1073, the rise of Hildebrand of Sovana to the throne of Peter under the name of Gregory VII meant a series of changes in the West. The rupture with the patriarch of Byzantium, the only patriarch left in the East, had occurred almost twenty years earlier. From then on, the pope had full freedom to organize his patriarchy, and he did so taking the false Donation of Constantine as a reference. Without proclaiming himself emperor, he vindicated the imperial powers in the West, powers that the late-Roman tradition attributed to the *pontifex maximus*, God's deputy on earth. The consequences of such claims are well known in relation to the Germanic Empire and the kingdoms that then formed—France, England, Sicily.[45] Regarding the Peninsula, on April 30, 1073, less than

---

40 Beato de Liébana, *Obras completas y complementarias, 2. Documentos de su entorno histórico y literario*, ed. Joaquín González Echegaray, Alberto del Campo, Leslie G. Freeman, José Luis Casado Soto (Madrid, 2004), 382–95.

41 Adeline Rucquoi, "Élipand et l'adoptianisme. Quelques hypothèses," *Bulletin de la Société nationale des antiquaires de France* (2008 [2015]): 292–309.

42 In contrast to the abusive interpretation of Eginhard's text, which we still read in Philippe Senac, *Les Carolingiens et al-Andalus (VIIIᵉ-IXᵉ siècles)* (Paris, 2002), 61.

43 José Martí Bonet, *Roma y las Iglesias particulares en la concesión del palio a los obispos y arzobispos de Occidente* (Madrid, 1976), revd. and updated as José Martí Bonet, *El palio. Insignia pastoral de los papas y arzobispos* (Madrid, 2008).

44 Santos A. García Larragueta, ed., *Colección de documentos de la catedral de Oviedo* (Oviedo, 1962), documents 2, 4–9.

45 Marcel Pacaut, *La théocratie, l'Église et le pouvoir au Moyen Âge* (Paris, 1957). Jean-Marie Mayeur, Charles Pietri, Luce Pietri, André Vauchez, Marc Venard, eds., *Histoire du christianisme*, 14 vols. (Paris, 1991–2001).

a week after his election, Gregory VII reminded the nobles who wished to go to Spain that "from ancient times the kingdom of Spain had belonged to St. Peter" and that, there-fore, any land conquered belonged to him, and he appointed legates in Spain: Cardinal Hugo Cándido, the bishop of Ostia Giraldo, and the subdeacon Raimbaldo.[46] A year later, on March 19, 1074, the pope addressed the kings of Castile and Pamplona stressing the principle of the necessary union of all the faithful under the sole authority of the Church of Roma, and urged them to adopt the Roman rite, warning them that those opposed to the Mother Church were schismatics, infidels, and heretics. In this same letter, Gregory stated that the evangelization of Spain had been done from Roma, by seven bishops sent by the apostles Peter and Paul, thus denying the tradition of an evangelization of the Peninsula by the apostle James, directly from Jerusalem without going through Roma.[47] In 1078, Cardinal Richard, abbot of Saint Victor in Marseille, was appointed papal leg-ate in Spain charged with the task of implanting the Gregorian reform in the Peninsula, which was done two years later in the Council of Burgos, although resistance continued for over two decades.[48]

With the implantation of the Roman rite and, shortly after, the substitution of the Visigothic minuscule by the Carolingian, the bishop of Roma had apparently imposed his *auctoritas* over the *potestas* of King Alfonso VI. This appears not to have been the opinion inside Spain. In the twelfth century, an anonymous *scriptor* copied a chronicle written a century earlier, probably in Sevilla in the Christian media, in which it is suc-cessively explained that no metropolitan should prevail over the bishops of another metropolitan, that the pope, "who is the head of the whole world" had jurisdiction over "Italy, Campania, Capua, Lotharingia, Germany, Teutonia, Avaria, and Bavaria," and that the metropolitan of Hispalis has it "over all Spain and its six metropolis" these being Narbonne, Braga, Tarragona, Toledo, Mérida, and Hispalis itself (Sevilla).[49] The pseudo-Isidorian Chronicle thus acknowledges to the Pope an honorary title, that of *capud totius mundi*, but its jurisdiction in this world does not surpass the borders of Italy and Ger-many, and its power is not exercised in the domain of other metropolitans—"no metro-

---

46 *Desde tiempos remotos el reino de España habia pertenecido a San Pedro.* Demetrio Mansilla, *La documentación pontificia hasta Inocencio III (965–1216)* (Roma, 1955), 12–13, document 6: "[…]We believe that you are not unaware that the Kingdom of Spain has belonged since ancient times to the law of St. Peter and, although it has long been occupied by the Pagans, since the law and justice have not disappeared, it belongs not to any mortal but only to the apostolic see" (*Non latere vos credimus regnum Hyspanie ab antiquo proprii iuris s. Petri fuisse, et adhuc licet diu a paganis sit occupatum, lege tamen iustitie non evacuata, nulli mortalium sed soli apostolice sedi ex equo pertinere*)," and 10–12, document 5.

47 José María Soto Rábanos, "Introducción del rito romano en los reinos de España. Argumentos del papa Gregorio VII," in *Studi Gregoriani, XIV (La riforma gregoriana e l'Europa)* (Roma, 1992), 161–74. Mansilla, *La documentación pontificia*, 15–16, document 8.

48 Adeline Rucquoi, "Cluny, el camino francés y la reforma gregoriana," *Medievalismo* 20 (2010): 97–122.

49 *Que es la cabeza del mundo entero; Italia, Campania, Capua, Lotaringia, Alemania, Teutonia, Avaria y Baviera.* Cited from Fernando González Muñoz, *La chronica gothorum pseudo-isidoriana (MS Paris, Bibliothèque Nationale 6113)* (A Coruña, 2000), 152–55 and 138–41.

politan shall prevail over the bishops of another, nor bind or loose, or exercise any right whatsoever, but by order of the aforesaid metropolitan" (*nullus metropolitanus presumere debet super alterius episcopos vel ligare vel solvere vel aliquid ius habere, nisi iussu vel precatu metropolitani*). The legal vocabulary used here—*ius, iussu, causidicat*—is no coincidence, but instead reveals the desire by the author of the text and the copyist to affirm the independence of the Hispanic Church from Roma.

The independence of the Hispanic Church and the predominant role of the king are clearly manifest in the account of the change of rite, as brought about by Rodrigo Jiménez de Rada's *De rebus Hispaniae liber*, faithfully followed by Alfonso X's *Estoria de España*. In this account, the people, meaning Spain, are adamantly opposed to the introduction of a foreign rite, here called the *officium gallicanum*, introduced by the papal legate. The king orders two ordeals, a fight between two knights, each defending one of the rites, and a bonfire in which the books containing the offices are placed. In both cases, the Toledan *officium* win. The king then intervenes to impose the Roman rite throughout his realm, hence the proverb that states in both the Latin and Spanish texts: "The laws go where kings want."[50] The king imposes the "French" rite, as it is called in the *Estoria de España*, in virtue of his *auctoritas*, even against the will of the people and without any reference to the pope.

The fact is that during the twelfth century the conflict over the collation of benefits, that is, the investiture of the bishops, between the king and the pontiff was settled. In August 1142, Alfonso VII of Castile restored the bishopric of Coria, awarded it to the bishop *novus ordinatus* Navarrón, and endowed its seat; the bull of confirmation was only granted in August 1168.[51] The case of Osma is even more revealing about the strife in Castile between the king and the pope over investitures. A protégé of King Alfonso VII, Bishop Juan II (1148–1173) obtained numerous churches and towns for its see, and in 1152 founded a college of Augustinian canons in Soria.[52] He had inherited a long law-suit with the bishopric of Sigüenza, whose origin dated back to the decision in 1137 by Pope Innocent II to grant the archpriesthoods of Ayllón, Caracena, and Berlanga to Sigüenza.[53] Taking advantage of the disturbances that characterized the death of Sancho II and the minority of Alfonso VIII, the bishop invaded the three archpriesthoods *manu militari*. Immediately excommunicated by Pope Alexander III, in January 1163, the bishop of Osma disregarded the sentences of excommunication and interdict and incited his clergy to do the same. The king of Leon, Fernando II, supported him and wrote to the King of

---

50 *O quieren reys, alla van leys*. See Roderici Ximenii de Rada, *Historia de rebus Hispanie sive Historia gothica*, ed. Juan Fernández Valverde, Corpus Christianorum continuatio medievalis 72 (Turnhout, 1987) 6, 25: "Quo volunt reges vadunt leges." Ramón Menéndez Pidal, Diego Catalán, eds., *Primera Crónica General de España* (Madrid, 1977), 543 (chap. 872).

51 José Luis Martín Martín, *Documentación medieval de la iglesia catedral de Coria* (Salamanca, 1989), 25–28, documents 1 and 2.

52 Juan Loperráez Corvalán, *Descripción histórica del obispado de Osma*, 3 vols. (Madrid, 1978), 3:27–29, document 22.

53 José Manuel Garrido Garrido, *Documentación de la catedral de Burgos (804–1183)* (Burgos, 1983), 205–6, document 117.

France, Louis VII, in that sense. On March 13, 1164, the pope deposed the bishop and ordered the chapter to elect another prelate. The chapter, then, made the pope see that, in Spain, royal assent was required to elect a bishop, and in his response, *Quia requisistis* *[...]*, the pope recognized that an episcopal election in Castile required the king's consent, admitting therefore that the right of investiture in the kingdom did not belong to him.[54]

Although he was the first, the king of Castile was not the only one in the Peninsula who saw his *auctoritas* recognized. In 1205, Pedro II of Aragon (Pere I of Barcelona) punished the canons of Elna for electing a bishop without his authorization; two years later, he renounced "the bad custom" according to which an episcopal election could not be held "without our counsel and agreement" (*sine nostro consilio et assensu*), but specified that royal consent was still necessary and that the newly elected had to present himself before the king "as a sign of royal fidelity" (*in signum regiae fidelitatis*).[55] Innocent III, who in February 1211 had accused King Sancho I of Portugal of having meddled in the collation of ecclesiastic benefits, of having sent the clerics of his kingdom to civil judges or to the army, and of having forbidden them to enter or leave the kingdom, recognized a year later for his successor Alfonso II the right of patronage over the churches of his realm.[56] After the capture of Córdoba in 1236 and in gratitude, Pope Gregory IX expressly authorized King Fernando III of Castile to dispose of the bishoprics as he wished.[57] In 1260, in a donation to the Church of Zaragoza, Pope Alexander IV recalled the concession made to Pedro I of Aragon, for him and his successors, "that they could confer, on any ecclesiastical person they wished, the churches that they might remove from the power of the Saracens."[58] In the conflict for the control of the collation of benefits and, therefore, the appointment of the bishops, the popes lost the battle in the Peninsula, and had to restrict themselves to giving the pallium to the candidates who had obtained the previous consent of the kings. Clement IV (1265–1268) surrendered to the royal supremacy codified in the *Partidas*.[59]

Alfonso X's jurists explained in the first *Partida* that the bishops are to be elected by the cathedral chapter and that:

> [An] old custom was of Spain, and lasted all life, and lasts currently, that when the bishop of a place dies, that the Dean and the Canons inform the King through their messengers

---

54 Peter Linehan, "Royal influence and papal authority in the Diocese of Osma: A note on *Quia requisistis* (JL 13728)," *Bulletin of Medieval Canon Law* 20 (1990): 31–41.

55 Mansilla, *La documentación pontificia*, n. 311, 342–344. *Patrologiae cursus completus*, ed. Jacques-Paul Migne, 221 vols. (Paris, 1855), 215: cols. 568–569, 1243.

56 Avelino Jesus Da Costa, Maria Alegria F. Marques, *Bulário Português. Inocêncio III (1198–1216)* (Coimbra, 1989), n. 154, 295–97 and n. 175, 324. Maria Teresa Nobre Veloso, *D. Afonso II. Relações de Portugal com a Santa Sé durante o seu reinado* (Coimbra , 2000), 125–28.

57 Peter Linehan, *La Iglesia española y el Papado en el siglo XIII* (Salamanca, 1975), 100.

58 *que pudiesen conferir a cualquier persona eclesiástica que quisiesen las iglesias que pudiesen arrancar del poder de los sarracenos*. Cited from Ildefonso Rodríguez de Lama, *La documentación pontificia de Alejandro IV* (Roma, 1976), 450–51, document 481. The grant to Pedro I of Aragon dates from April 16, 1095. See Antonio Durán Gudiol, *Colección diplomática de la catedral de Huesca*, 1 (Zaragoza, 1965), 87–89, document 63.

59 Linehan, *La Iglesia española*, 284.

of the Church, with a letter from the Dean and the chapter of how their prelate has died and request him in his mercy that he allows that they can make their election without pression, and they commend to him the goods of the Church. And the king must accept and send someone to take care of the goods, and when the election is over they must present the elected and the king must give to him what he has received. The kings of Spain have this preeminence and honour for three reasons. The first, because they won the lands from the Moors and made the mosques into churches, and threw out the name of Mohammed, and placed there the name of our Lord Jesus Christ. The second, because they founded them anew, in places where before there had never been any. The third, because they endowed them, and they make well to them, and this is the reason why the kings have the right to ask the canonries about the elections, and they have the right to abide by his request.⁶⁰

In the following section of the first *Partida*, the jurists added that the bishops and other prelates "who had land from the king or any other property" had to participate in the royal military campaigns, and that the clergy had the obligation to participate in the defence of "the castles and the walls."⁶¹

The text of the first *Partida* retakes exactly the arguments brandished at the beginning of the thirteenth century by one of the greatest canonists of the epoch of Innocent III, Vincentius Hispanus. Colleague and rival of another of the great canonists, Johannes Teutonicus, Vincentius never missed an opportunity to affirm Spain's difference in legal matters and even its supremacy over Germany. He writes that, "By virtue alone, the Spaniards won the *imperium* and elected their bishops [...] ¿Have they not exercised their power over the holy lady Spain, power which they themselves created—*dominium pariunt*—and enlarge it by their power, by their virtues of valor and honor?" He also states that "noble Spain is superior to the other provinces" because it was ruled by its own laws—while the Roman-Germanic Empire was ruled by a foreign law, that of the Roman Empire—and rejected and defeated Charlemagne.⁶² In response to the *auctoritas*

---

60 *Antigua costumbre fue de España, e duro toda via, e dura oy dia, que quando fina el obispo de algun lugar, que lo fazen saber el Dean e los Canonigos al Rey por sus mensageros de la Eglesia, con carta del Dean e del cabildo como es finado su perlado e que le piden por merced que le plega que ellos puedan fazer su elecion desembargadamente, e que le encomiendan los bienes de la Eglesia, e el Rey deve gelo otorgar e embiar los recabdar; e despues que la elecion ovieren fecho, presenten le el elegido, e el mande le entregar aquello que rescibio. E esta mayoria e honrra han los reyes de España por tres razones. La primera, por que ganaron las tierras de los Moros e fizieron las mezquitas eglesias, e echaron de y el nome de Mahoma, e metieron y el nome de nuestro señor IESV Christo. La segunda, porque las fundaron de nuevo, en logares donde nunca las ovo. La tercera, por que las dotaron, e de mas les fizieron mucho bien, e por esso han derecho los Reyes de les rogar los cabildos en fecho de las eleciones, e ellos de caber su ruego.* Cited from Alfonso X el Sabio, *Las Siete Partidas*, Partida 1, Title 5, Law 18: "What right the kings of Spain had over the election of the prelates and for which reasons" (*Que derecho ovieron los reyes de España en fecho de las eleciones de los perlados e por que razones*).

61 *Que tovieren tierra del rey o heredamiento alguno; los castillos e los muros.* Cited from Alfonso X el Sabio, *Las Siete Partidas*, Partida 1, Title 6, Law 52: "When the clergy have to guard the walls of the towns or the castles where they live and when not" (*Quando son los clerigos tenudos de guardar los muros de las villas o de los castillos do moran, e quando no*).

62 Gaines Post, *Studies in Medieval Legal Thought. Public Law and the State, 1100–1322* (Princeton, 1964), 482–93: *Sed soli Yspani virtute sua obtinuerunt imperium, et episcopos elegerunt. Nonne [...] Yspani dominantur beate domine Yspane, que dominium pariunt, et dominantes audacie et probitatis*

imperialis that placed the emperor above the kings, Vicentius Hispanus vindicated the independence of his homeland, which, by its own *auctoritas*, exercised supreme power and elected its bishops.

Alfonso X's legal work naturally elicited contrary reactions from the nobility and the clergy, and the end of his reign was not propitious for putting the political theory expressed in the *Partidas* into practice, however traditional it might be in Spain. During the first half of the fourteenth century, other voices made themselves heard defending the primacy of the pope, from whom all the emperors and kings derived their power. The theory of the two swords that granted the pope spiritual supremacy over the temporal powers, was particularly championed by Bishop Egas of Viseu in Portugal,[63] and by Álvaro Pelayo and Juan García de Castrogeriz in Castile.[64] In contrast, others adhered to the idea of the independence of the kings, like the bishop of Burgos Gonzalo de Hinojosa who, in his *Cronice ab origine mundi*, chose the reigns as a measure of time, and not the pontificates or emperors.[65]

In the mid-fourteenth century, the kings reasserted that they were God's vicars in their kingdoms, which implies that they were not subject to the *auctoritas* of the pope or of the emperor.[66] In fact, Pope Urban V confirmed the provision of the bishoprics for

---

virtutibus expandunt? From Paris, Bibliothèque nationale de France, MS lat. 3967, fol. 21 c. 2; "That is why it is assumed that Spain is superior to the other provinces. Indeed, when Charles wanted to enter Spain with all the Franks, the Spaniards opposed their entry into Spain and defeated them in combat and killed the twelve peers (*[…] Immo per hoc colligitur quod Hispania est maior aliis provinciis. Cum enim Carolus vellet cum omnibus Francigenis intrare Hispaniam, Ispani ingressu Ispanie obviaverunt eis, et superaverunt eos in bello et occiderunt xii. paria*)" (Bamberg MS Can. 20 (P.ii.7), fol. 127 c.1, ad v.).

63 Antonio García y García, *Estudios sobre la canonística portuguesa medieval* (Madrid, 1976), 219–81.

64 Álvaro Pais, *Estado e pranto da Igreja (Status et planctus Ecclesiae)*, vol. 7, ed. Miguel Pinto de Meneses (Lisboa, 1988–1997), 1, 56M, [2:518]: "Fifth, it must be considered that the Supreme Pontiff, not only of divine right, but also human, has temporal power (*Quinto considerandum est quod summus pontifex non solum iure divino, sed etiam iure humano, habet potestatem temporalem*) […]." Juan Beneyto Pérez, *Glosa castellana al "Regimiento de Príncipes" de Egidio Romano* (Madrid, 1947), 3, 2, 4, 112: "It is certain that Jesus Christ empowered his vicar with the authority and power over everything spiritual, which is more than the temporal, just as the soul is more than the body; and giving him authority over the judgments of souls, it follows that he should give authority and power over temporal things" (*E cierto es que Jesucristo acomendó a su vicario autoridad e poderío sobre todo lo espiritual, que es más que lo temporal, así como el alma es más que el cuerpo; e dándole autoridad sobre los jucios de las almas, bien se sigue que le devía dar autoridad e poderío sobre las cosas temporales*).

65 Stéphanie Aubert, "Les *Cronice ab origine mundi* de Gonzalo de Hinojosa, de la cathédrale de Burgos à la cour de France (XIVe siècle): biographie et édition d'une chronique universelle" (PhD diss., Université Lumière Lyon 2, 2012).

66 Adeline Rucquoi, "Réflexions sur le droit et la justice en Castille entre 1250 et 1350," in *Droit et justice: le pouvoir dans l'Europe médiévale*, ed. Nilda Guglielmi, Adeline Rucquoi (Buenos Aires, 2008), 135–164. Eduardo d'Oliveira França, *O poder real em Portugal e as origens do absolutismo* (São Paulo, 1946), 103–13.

Pedro I of Castile,[67] and in 1361, the King of Portugal, Pedro I, with the promulgation of the Royal Consent (*Beneplácito regio*) in the Cortes of Elvas, prohibited the publication of papal bulls in his kingdom that had not previously received his approval.[68] The peninsular bishops were therefore loyal servants of the monarchs and of the *beata domina Yspania* before being servants of the popes.

Potestas cum imperio

In May 589, King Recaredo (hereafter Reccared) convoked a council in Toledo. He explained to the sixty-eight prelates present that he had decided to re-establish the ecclesiastical discipline after eradicating the heresy that impeded the holding of councils in the Catholic Church. On May 8, the king opened the session reminding them of his condition as a mortal, "though God Almighty, for the sake of the peoples, has assigned to us the burden of supreme power" (*Quamvis Deus omnipotens pro utilitatibus populorum regni nos culmen subire tribuerit*), and also that:

> The more elevated we are through the royal glory over the subjects, the more we must take care of those things which belong to the Lord, and increase our hope, and look out for the people whom the Lord has entrusted to us.[69]

Therefore, the king, then, and only the king was responsible for the *res divinae*, that is, the faith and orthodoxy of the people. So, the *tomus regius* granted to the bishops "from all Spain and of Gaul" in May 589 defined the faith which must henceforth be that of the Spaniards, that is, the faith proclaimed in Nicaea (325), Constantinople (381), Ephesus I (431), and Chalcedon (451) against all heretics. Proclaimed "true catholic, true orthodox, true lover of God, who truly deserves apostolic merit," the king imposed on all the faithful of the churches of his kingdoms the recitation of the Creed before communion according to the Oriental custom (*iuxta orientalium partium morem*) and demanded that all the constitutions of all councils and synodal letters of the Roman pontiffs be observed. The bishops signed all the canons of the Council, which the king finally sanctioned (*sancimus*), thus giving it force of law.[70] In the letter he later sent to Pope Gregory I to announce the conversion of the kingdom, Reccared recalled that he governed his peoples "after God"—"both to us and to our people who, after God, we rule over."[71]

---

67 Teófilo Ayuso, "El privilegio de los Reyes de España en la presentación de obispos," *Razón y Fe* 9 (1904): 459–73.

68 Fortunato de Almeida, *História das Instituições em Portugal* (Porto, 1903), 50.

69 *Pro qua re quanto subditorum gloria regali extollimur, tanto providi esse debimus in his quae ad Deum sunt vel nostram spem augere vel gentibus a Deo nobis creditis consulere.* Cited from Juan Tejada y Ramiro, *Colección de cánones de la Iglesia española*, 4 vols. (Madrid, 1849–1853), 2:213–60.

70 *Vero catholico, vero orthodoxo, vero amatori Dei, novarum plebium in ecclesia catholica conquisitor, qui apostolicum implevit officium.* Cited from Tejada, *Colección de cánones*, 2:213–60.

71 *Nos gentesque nostras quae nostro post Deum regimine moderantur.* Cited from Tejada, *Colección de cánones*, 2:217. Adeline Rucquoi, "*Cuius rex, eius religio*: Ley y religión en la España medieval," in *Las representaciones del poder en las sociedades hispánicas*, ed. Óscar Mazín (Ciudad de México, 2012), 133–74.

In May 589, in Toledo, Reccared faithfully observed the Roman tradition of Byzantium, in which the emperor convened the councils and then, advised by the prelates, gave legal value to the decisions taken, as stated in book 16 of the Theodosian Code and in the first book of Justinian's Code. Forty years later, King Sisenando convoked the Fourth Council of Toledo. The proceedings of this Council title him indifferently *rex* and *princeps*, and it was specified that the convocation had been done *eius imperiis atque iussis*, terms that have an undoubted juridical connotation.[72]

The royal diplomas, or those signed by the kings during the following centuries, continued to give them indifferently the titles of *rex* or *princeps*. In 917, for example, Ordoño II was titled *rex*, and the year after, he appeared as *princeps*.[73] This last title is that of the emperor and refers to a power *cum imperio*. In fact, in 952, the sentence of a lawsuit that had been initiated in San Feliz de Turió "under the reign of the prince our lord Ordoño, son of the emperor our lord Ramiro," was promulgated "according to what the law commanded and the truth had for sure."[74] The concept of *imperium* was associated with both the power of the king, his *potestas* as *princeps*, and with the law. The *potestas* is evidently that of God, as Bermudo II recalls in July 991 when glorifying the Creator in the prologue of a donation: "To Him therefore praise, honour, virtue, and power (*potestas*) for ever and ever, Amen"; but power was not conceived without the *imperium*, and a document from the previous year was dated *Inperantem Garsea Gomize in Legione*, while, in November 991, the king granted Bishop Sabarigo of León some towns with the jurisdiction over their inhabitants, urging them to abide by what was *iniunctum vel imperatum* by the prelate.[75] One could multiply the examples showing that the *imperium* in Spain, far from wanting to be linked to the Carolingian empire, has its roots in the Roman heritage that, while it was short-lived to the north of the Pyrenees, remained alive on the Peninsula through both law and vocabulary.

Omnis potestas a Deo

The Roman *plenitudo potestatis* required a divine sign, a kind of celestial investiture, the *imperium*, which could only be obtained by taking the auspices. In its origins therefore, power does not come from men but from the gods. If "all power comes from God," in the

---

72 *Fuero Juzgo en latín y castellano* (Madrid, 1815), prologue: "With the care of the love of Christ and with the zeal of the very religious king of Spain and of Gaul Sisnando, we priests have gathered in the city of Toledo in the name of the Lord so that together, by his commands—*imperiis*—and orders, we may make a treatise on the disciplines of the Church" (*Cum studio amoris Christi ac diligentia religiosissimi Sisenandi regis Hispaniae atque Galliae sacerdotes apud Toletanam urbam in nomine Domini in unum convenissemus ut ejus imperiis atque jussis communis a nobis agiteretur de quibusdan ecclesiae disciplinis tractatus* [...]).

73 Saez, ed., *Colección documental del archivo de la catedral de León*, 1:64–68, document 41 [enero, 8, 917]: "*Ego Hordonius rex*," and 1:75–77, document 45 [enero, 8, 918]: "*Ego Hordonius princeps* [...]."

74 Saez, ed., *Colección documental del archivo de la catedral de León*, 1:353–56, document 256: *regnante principe nostro domno Hordonio, prolis domni Ranimiri imperatoris* and *sicut lex imperabat et veritas agnoscebat*.

75 José Manuel Ruiz Asensio, ed., *Colección documental del archivo de la catedral de León*, 3:51–53, document 548: *Ipsi namque laus, honor, virtus et potestas per cuncta secula, amen*; 3:32–33, document 534, and 3:53–55, document 549.

words of St. Paul, the one exercised by the *principes* was obligatorily invested with the *imperium*. The authors of the Glossary of San Millán de la Cogolla, copied in 964, confirm this. They define the word *imperium* as *regale potestate vel iussione*, give "*dominavit*" as a synonym of "*imperavit*" and explain *imperat* by *iudicat*; perhaps more important is their definition of "*imperator*" as "*induperator vel summus sacerdos*" that recalls the definition given by Isidore of Seville of the *rex et sacerdos* in the Fourth Council of Toledo.[76] According to these definitions, to which should be added that of *potestas* as *ditio*, the *imperium* is the royal power, the one that allows him to dominate and judge, which has a sacerdotal nature, and, as such power is that of "saying" the law, that of the *iurisdictio*.

The first task of the one who exercises power is to promulgate the law, "to say it" so that justice exists, hence the authors of the Glossary in the tenth century equate to rule (*imperar*) and to judge (*juzgar*). Therefore, the legal texts, from the *Liber Iudicum* to the Castilian *Partidas* or the Aragonese *Vidal Mayor*, define the law and the legislator:

> Just as the crown on the head of Aaron and the brightness in the middle of the firmament, illuminating all the firmament of the world, so the Law shines in the royal majesty, in which it is established in such a way that, just as from the fountain to the rivers, it is convenient that from him the law comes down and the use of the law to all the others. He who does not receive from him the jurisdiction, like the river, suppressing the feeding in the source, dries by force, thus remains the man separated from the jurisdiction, that is to say from the power of law, and from the use of the law.[77]

"These laws are establishments so that men may know how to live well and in an orderly manner, according to the pleasure of God," writes Alfonso X the Wise in his *Partidas*, and adds: "And also according to the good life of this world, and to keep the faith of our Lord Jesus Christ faithfully, just as it is. Also that men may live with one another in law and in justice."[78] The law—*ius*—, and particularly that of men in general—*ius gentium*—, he adds, "was found by reason, and also by force, because men could not well live among themselves in harmony and peace if all did not use it," because thanks to it,

> each one knows his own separately. And the fields and the lands of the towns are divided. And men are also bound to praise God, and obey their fathers and their mothers, and their land which they say in Latin *patria* [homeland]. Also this law allows each one to protect himself against those who want to dishonor him or force him.[79]

---

76 *El códice emilianense 46*, 377 and 468.

77 *Assi como la corona en la cabeça de Aarón et la resplandor en meyos del firmament, alumpnando todo el firmament del mundo, assi resplandece el dreito en la real magestat, en la quoal es establescida en tal guisa que, assi como de la fuent en los ríos, conviene deill que descienda el dreito et el uso del dreito en todos los otros. Et qui non recibe deill jurisdicción, assi como el río, toilliendo nodricimiento a la fuente, ensequa por fuerça, assi finqua el omne extraniado de la jurisdicción, ço es poderío de dreito, et del uso del dreito.* Cited from María de los Desamparados Cabanes Pecour, Asunción Blasco Martínez, Pilar Pueyo Colomina, eds., *Vidal Mayor. Edición, introducción y notas al manuscrito* (Zaragoza, 1996), 1, 69, 80.

78 *Estas leyes son establecimientos por que los omes sepan bivir bien e ordenadamente, segun el plazer de Dios; e otrosi segund conviene a la buena vida deste mundo, e a guardar la fe de nuestro señor Iesu Christo cunplidamente, assi como ella es. Otrosi como bivan los omes unos con otros en derecho e en justicia.* Cited from Alfonso X el Sabio, *Las Siete Partidas*, Partida 1, Tít. 1, ley 1.

79 *Fue hallado con razon, e otrosi por fuerça, porque los omes non podrian bien bivir entre si en concordia e en paz si todos non usassen del; cada un ome conosce lo suyo apartadamente. E son*

Intimately associated with law, justice rewards those who do good and forces the bad to do good. It is "like something in which all rights are enclosed, of whatever nature they may be"; its commandments are three: to live honestly, not to harm another, to have their rights recognized.[80]

The royal power is thus in the first place that of promulgating laws to maintain justice, and the peninsular monarchs were great legislators, although it is true that only the kings of Castile and Portugal managed to be recognized as the source of law in their respective kingdoms.[81] This power comes directly from God who, as *auctor*, has given them the *imperium*. In the thirteenth century, to explain this relation between God and his vicar, a direct relation in which the latter obtains his *potestas cum imperio* directly from the Creator, Alfonso X resorted to natural law, as it had been elaborated by jurists in the previous century. Through his work, and that of the Spaniards in the following centuries, it is clear that the power of the king is exercised, not over a kingdom but over "the land"—*la tierra*. Those who dwell in that "land" are not the "subjects" of the king, as in France, or his vassals. They are "naturals of the land" - *naturales de la tierra* - that is to say that their primordial bond is with their place of origin; in fact, when they are exiled from it, they are "denaturalized." "We are asked by our naturals," wrote King Jaime (Jaume) I of Aragon in his *Llibre del Feyts* and later specified that the Master of the Temple "was a native (*natural*) of Osona."[82] The obedience and loyalty of the people to the sovereign are due to the fact that he is the "natural lord" of that land.[83]

A philosophical concept inherited from the insight of twelfth-century thinkers, "Nature" (*Natura*) is a polysemic concept which first defines Creation, the world created and ordained by God. Various twelfth-century authors equated Creation with the Creator, God. "Nature, that is, God (*Natura, id est Deus*), write among others the specialists in natural law, for whom natural law is the divine law, which God gave to his

---

departidos los campos e los terminos de las villas. E otrosi son tenudos los omes de loar a Dios, e obedescer a sus padres e a sus madres, e a su tierra que dizen en latin patria. Otrosi consiente este derecho que cada uno se pueda amparar contra aquellos que deshonrra o fuerça le quisieren fazer. Cited from Alfonso X el Sabio, *Las Siete Partidas*, Partida 1, Tít. 1, ley 2.

80 *Como cosa en que se encierran todos los derechos, de qual natura quier que sean.* Cited from Alfonso X el Sabio, *Las Siete Partidas*, Partida 3, Tít. 1, ley 2 and 3.

81 Rucquoi, "Réflexions sur le droit," 135–64. The constitution *Si imperialis maiestas* of Justinian (C. 1, 14, 12), reinforced by the constitution *Leges sacratissimae* (C. 1, 14, 9), attributed the interpretation of the laws, in other words the law, to the emperor and to him alone.

82 *Demanaren-nos nostres naturales; qui era natural d'Osona.* Cited from Jaume I, *Llibre del Feyts* § 10: "and after this, they demand to us our natural people and fought against the French and against this land they had" (*E puys, passat açò, demanaren-nos nostres naturales, e guerrejaren ab franceses e ab aquela terra que ells tenien*).

83 Alfonso X el Sabio, *Espéculo*, 1.1.6, *Los Códigos Españoles concordados y anotados*, 12 vols. (Madrid, 1849), 4:8–9: "Very great and marvellous is the profit that laws give to men because they show them how to know God and, knowing Him, they will know how to love and fear Him. And they also show them how to know their natural lord, and how to be obedient and loyal to him" (*Muy grande es a maravilla el pro que aduzen las leyes a los omes ca ellas les amuestran conoscer Dios e conosciendol sabran en que manera le deven amar e temer. Otrosi les muestran conoscer su señor natural en que guisa le deven seer obedientes e leales*).

creation."[84] In the tripartite rights elaborated by the jurists at the end of the twelfth century, natural law is superior to the law of peoples (*ius gentium*) common to all humanity, and to the civil law (*ius civilis*) specific to each kingdom. It is the order given by God to the Creation, which therefore escapes any human intervention. "Because the wills and understandings of men are divided into many ways, therefore it is only natural that their acts and deeds do not match," states Alfonso X in the prologue of the *Espéculo* before explaining that the king must, therefore, make laws to keep the people "in peace and justice."[85] Therefore, the power wielded by the king, as natural lord, over the natives (*naturales*) of the land belongs to the divine order, to the field of natural law, which is God's law.[86]

So the king, "natural lord" (*señor natural*), exercises his power over "the naturals" (*los naturales*) of a land, Spain, which was blessed by God with all the qualities, according to the *laudes Hispaniae*. Placing the relations between the king, the Spaniards, and the territory in the field of divine and not civil law shows that this relationship is established within the order of the Creation. The *potestas* exercised by the king was conferred on him with the *imperium* by God, the primary cause, the unique *auctor*, and this "concession" or "investiture" allows him to act as a legislator, to create the law, and thus to legitimate. It was not necessary for the kings of the Peninsula to resort to processes of "sacralization" or "legitimation," characteristic of other contemporary monarchs and abusively transferred to the Hispanic sovereigns, since, provided with the *imperium* within the divine order, the natural law, they were at the same time sacred, legitimate, and legitimators.

The concept of power and its practice in the medieval Iberian Peninsula cannot be understood without its origins. The terms used, whether *auctoritas*, *potestas,* or *imperium*, had been defined and employed for centuries in Roma by various authors, first pagan then Christian, who constituted the cultural background that fed the medieval jurists, philosophers, theologians, poets, and moralists. They had no need to seek models or sources of inspiration in other contemporary kingdoms. Their long conflict with the bishop of Roma demonstrates precisely the autonomy of Hispanic thought in this field, their desire to remain faithful to their own tradition.

---

84 *Digesto* 1.1.1. § 3. "Natural law is what nature teaches all animals: in fact this right is not proper to mankind, but is common to all animals, born on land or in the sea, and also to birds. Hence the conjunction of male and female that we call marriage, hence the procreation of children, hence education; in fact we also see various animals, although wild animals, considered as experts in this right." (*Ius naturale est quod natura omnia animalia docuit: nam ius istud non humani generis proprium, sed omnium animalium, quae in terra, quae in mari nascuntur, avium quoque commune est. hinc descendit maris atque feminae coniunctio, quam nos matrimonium appellamus, hinc liberorum procreatio, hinc educatio: videmus etenim cetera quoque animalia, feras etiam istius iuris perita censeri*). Cited from Brian Tierney, "*Natura, id est Deus:* A Case of Juristic Pantheism?," *Journal of the History of Ideas* 24, no. 3 (1963): 307–22.

85 *Porque las voluntades e los entendimientos de los omes son departidos en muchas guisas, por ende natural cosa es que los fechos e las obras dellos non acuerden en uno; en paz e en justicia.* Cited from Alfonso X el Sabio, *Espéculo*, Prologue, 4, 7.

86 Adeline Rucquoi, "Tierra y gobierno en la Península ibérica medieval," in *Las Indias occidentales, procesos de incorporación territorial a las Monarquías ibéricas*, ed. Óscar Mazín, José Javier Ruiz Ibáñez (Ciudad de México, 2012), 43–67. Adeline Rucquoi, "Rei i regne. Conceptes polítics en el segle XIII," in *Jaume I i el seu temps. 800 anys després*, ed. Rafael Narbona Vizcaíno (València, 2012), 407–24.

Assured of being emperors in their kingdom since the Visigothic era,[87] meaning simultaneously defenders of the faith and governors of the people, the kings in the Peninsula rejected the Roman pretensions of *pontificalis auctoritas*. Relying as much on theology—God as *auctor*—as on philosophy—God as primary cause—and on law—God as the origin of the *imperium*—they maintained in their respective kingdoms the concept of absolute power—*auctoritas* and *potestas cum imperio*—inherited from Roma. They claimed it against the imperial and papal jurists in the thirteenth century and the ambassadors of the various nations gathered in Basel in 1434, when the bishop of Burgos, Alfonso de Cartagena, used this argument among others to vindicate the pre-eminence of Castile over England.[88] The candidacies to the imperial crown of Alfonso X the Wise in 1258, as well as that of Carlos I of Spain in 1517, were not candidatures of kings, but rather of monarchs who already wielded "imperial" power in their kingdoms. Not as the result of an "attribution" or a "designation," which would mean that they did not have the right to use the title of emperor,[89] but rather because their power was the same as that of the emperor of Byzantium, the pope, or the Holy Roman emperor.

To seek in the Roman past the origin of the concepts of "empire," "power," and "authority" that defined and characterized the dominion exercised by the kings of the Peninsula during the Middle Ages does not mean, obviously, a stagnation. The "empire" is not the same, nor is it exercised in the same way, in the tenth, twelfth, or sixteenth centuries; however, at any time, it has the Roman legal definitions as a reference and means a supreme power, with the right to life and death, and is protected by a supernatural investiture. The concept of "authority" also underwent an evolution until characterizing the work of creation or writing within the field of knowledge; nevertheless, the idea continued to be expressed through periphrasis or by resorting to philosophy, and the struggle waged by the peninsular kings to be "wise" and not recognise the *pontificalis auctoritas* shows that they were aware of the importance of this form of power. They exercised, therefore, in God's name a unique and indivisible power which was at the same time *auctoritas* and *potestas cum imperio*.

---

87 Céline Martin, *La géographie du pouvoir dans l'Espagne wisigothique* (Lille, 2003).

88 Mª. Victoria Echeverría Gaztelumendi, *Edición crítica del discurso de Alfonso de Cartagena Propositio super altercatione praeminentia sedium inter oratores regum Castellae et Angliae in Concilio Basiliense: versiones en latín y castellano* (Madrid, 1992).

89 Hélène Sirantoine illustrates this in the preface of her book: "The sources [...] testify the attribution of the title of imperator to a certain number of sovereigns of the Asturian–Leonese and then Castilian–Leonese dynasties [...] This was first under a vague use between the ninth century and the first half of the eleventh century, then frequent until the middle of the twelfth century; seventeen of these sovereigns have seen their royal authority dressed in an imperial hue" (*Les sources [...] témoignent de l'attribution du titre d'imperator à un certain nombre de souverains des dynasties asturo-léonaises puis castellano-leónaises [...] D'une manière d'abord diffuse entre le IXe siècle et la première moitié du XIe siècle, puis fréquente jusqu'au milieu du XIIe siècle, dix-sept de ces souverains ont vu habiller leur autorité royale d'une teinte impériale*). Cited from Sirantoine, *Imperator Hispaniae*, 1. The reader is thus warned from the beginning that the title of "emperor" is an "attribution," destined to "disguise"—*habiller*—their power, without foundation or legitimacy. An in-depth study of the terms employed would have helped the author to better analyse the subject.

Chapter 3

KINGSHIP IN ISIDORE OF SEVILLE'S HISTORICAL WORK: A POLITICAL INTERPRETATION OF THE TWO VERSIONS

SAMUELE SACCHI

IN THE WAKE of several recent philological contributions,[1] this paper proposes a reading of Isidore of Seville's historical works (the *Chronica* and *Historia Gothorum Wandalorum et Sueborum*) designed to illustrate the issue of the two versions from a political point of view. I aim to throw light on the cultural hinterland of certain famous legal solutions adopted at the Fourth Council of Toledo in 633.

A reading of this sort can potentially go beyond the tendency to attempt to retrace the characteristics of Isidore's political thought to the analogies between the theory of power illustrated by the third book of his *Sententiae*[2] and the 75th canon of the Fourth Council of Toledo[3] which has been taken to the extent of arguing that the radical change which took place in Isidore's thinking on the "Suintila abdication" (concerning the Visigothic king of Hispania, Septimania and Galicia from 621 to 631) between the *Historia* and the 75th canon represents a change in the Bishop of Sevilla's thought and approach, an inconsistency resulting from the political weakness of an Isidore obliged to go along with those who had removed Suintila.[4]

Before going into the merits of the two versions of Isidore's histories it is worth pausing a moment to consider the contents of the Fourth Council of Toledo's 75th canon.

---

1 Isabel Velázquez Soriano, "La doble redacción de la *Historia Gothorum* de Isidoro de Sevilla," in *L'édition critique des oeuvres d'Isidore de Séville. Les recensions multiples. Actes du colloque organisé à la Casa de Velázquez et à l'Université rey Juan Carlos de Madrid (14–15 janvier 2002)*, ed. María Adelaida Andrés Sanz, Jacques Elfassi, José Carlos Martín (Paris, 2008), 91–126; and in the same collection: José Carlos Martín, "Le problème des recensions multiples dans la *Chronique* d'Isidore de Séville," 127–51.

2 Isidorus Hispalensis, *Sententiae*, ed. Pierre Cazier, Corpus Christianorum Series Latina 111 (Turnhout, 1998).

3 José S. Vives, ed., *Concilios visigóticos e hispano-romanos*, (Barcelona, 1963), 218–21; José Orlandis, Domingo Ramos Lissón, *Historia de los concilios de la España romana y visigoda* (Pamplona, 1986), 261–98.

4 Marc Reydellet, *La Royauté dans la littérature latine de Sidoine Apollinaire à Isidore de Séville* (Roma, 1981), 524; Isabel Velázquez Soriano, "Pro patriae gentisque Gothorum statu (4th Council of Toledo, Canon 75, A:633)," in *Regna and Gentes. The Relationship between Late Antique and Early Medieval Peoples and Kingdoms (The Transformation of the Roman World 13)*, ed. Hans Werner Goetz, Jörg Jarnut, Walter Pohl, Sören Kaschke (Leiden, 2003), 186–217; Peter Heather, *The Goths* (Oxford, 1996), 283–98.

Samuele Sacchi (asmodai@teletu.it) is Researcher at the Università degli Studi di Bologna, Italy.

Drawn up in the context of Suintila's forced abdication for the purposes of legitimizing the succession of usurper Sisenand, the canon preaches a succession of moral warnings designed to define what it meant to be a good prince and politically sanctifies election as the sole valid criterion in legitimate succession, a theme whose flipside involved criticisms of Suintila and the whole of his family, perhaps in a tacit condemnation of the dynastic solution.

Sanctioning elective kingship meant ensuring open political competition to the advantage of the aristocratic factions that periodically fought for the throne against the dynastic solution which Suintila had just attempted (in passing his throne to his son Ricimer).[5] This accords special meaning to the fact that, in the context of the 75th canon, the political subject juxtaposed to kingship (in the election framework applicable to the condemnation of Suintila and his brother Geila) is an ill-defined *gens* who it would perhaps not be stretching a point to identify precisely with that aristocracy whose ambitions were safeguarded by the Council.

Accepting the idea that the writer, or at least he who inspired these norms, was Isidore and in an attempt to get to the roots of a political notion designed to favour aristocratic demands over dynastic considerations, the first passages worth taking a look at here are the canons which the Fourth Council dedicated to the conduct of the good bishop (the 19th and 22nd canons in particular),[6] and the distinctly close relationship which existed between these and Isidore's *Sententiae*[7] (a link which enabled Pierre Cazier to postdate the *Sententiae* themselves to the third decade of the seventh century[8]). In brief, what interests us here is the evolution of a principle, clearly expressed in both the *Sententiae* and the canons, according to which the indispensable characteristics required of potential bishops are morally impeccable conduct and consequently a good reputation. However minimal, the crucial difference in the formulation of this same principle in the *Sententiae* and the canons is that whilst the former emphasizes reputation in the sense of bishops acting as a good example to the faithful, the latter did so in order to conserve the legitimacy of the government.[9]

---

5 Edward A. Thompson, *Los Godos en España* (Madrid, 1971), 193–207; María Isabel Loring, Dionisio Pérez, Pablo Fuentes, *La Hispania tardoromana y visigoda. Siglos V–VIII* (Madrid, 2007), 177–80; Pablo de la Cruz Díaz Martínez, "La Hispania visigoda," in *Hispania tardoantigua y visigoda*. ed. Pablo de la Cruz Díaz Martínez, Celia Martínez Maza, Francisco Javier Sanz Huerma, Historia de España 5 (Madrid, 2007), 402–8; Rosa Sanz Serrano, *Historias de los Godos. Una epopeya histórica de Escandinavia a Toledo* (Madrid, 2009), 296–310; Luis A. García Moreno, "Romanismo y germanismo. El despertar de los pueblos hispánicos (siglos IV–X)," in *Historia de España*, ed. Manuel Tuñón de Lara (Barcelona, 1987), 342–47; José Orlandis, *Historia de España. España Visigótica* (Madrid, 1977), 142–55; Pierre Cazier, *Isidore de Séville et la naissance de l'Espagne catholique* (Paris, 1994), 59–64.

6 Vives, *Concilios visigóticos*, 198–201.

7 Isidorus Hispalensis, *Sententiae*, 275–84.

8 Pierre Cazier, "Les 'Sentences' d'Isidore de Séville et le IVème Concile de Tolède," *Antigüedad y Cristianismo* 3 (1986): 373–86; José A. de Aldama, "Indicaciones sobre la cronología de las obras de s. Isidoro," in *Miscellanea Isidoriana* (Roma, 1936), 57–89.

9 Samuele Sacchi, "La regalità visigotica tra VI e VII secolo," *I Quaderni del M.Ae.S.*, 14 (2011): 63–86.

In other words, the focus shifted from apostolic to political and, from here, it is but a very short step to election as the ideal criterion for the choice of a *rector*. If we accept the idea that Isidore was following the Gregorian lesson of a morality shared by all *rectores*, be they princes or clerics, then it is by no means stretching the point to extend the ideas governing the choice of a good bishop to the king and thus explain the decision to impose election as a criterion for the choice of a monarch. We would thus have a good initial idea of the cultural baggage Isidore was resorting to in the face of the Fourth Council's political imperatives.

If the meaning of the 75th canon truly is pro-aristocracy and anti-dynastic and if it is not simply a case of political opportunism in a writer facing circumstances beyond his control but rather political thought as complex as it is self-aware, then perhaps we can trace the roots of this thought to Isidore's historical work, a work which, significantly, the Bishop of Sevilla revised in the immediate aftermath of Suintila's greatest victory, the reunification of the peninsula at Byzantine expense (in 625), conferring great, but potentially destabilizing, glory on the king.

The *Chronica*

The most recent philological studies have clarified that Isidore wrote two different versions of his *Chronica*, the first dating from the reign of Sisebut and datable to 615 and 616, the second and significantly extended edition dating from Suintila's reign and dated 626.[10]

In this work, Isidore returns to the historical genre of the universal chronicle but compared to the epigones and following Eusebius's and Jerome's examples (composing annual accounts limited to local facts very close at hand, the last of these being the African Victor of Tunnuna and the man who continued his accounts, Giovanni Biclarense), the Bishop of Sevilla composed this work from the starting point of the creation of the world, a full-blown claim to originality in this genre.[11] Such a broad chronological framework offers up a wealth of historical vignettes and anecdotes and, I believe, in the midst of this, a number of political assessments. On the subject of the two versions, Jacques Fontaine has argued that "the comparison between the two versions shows that the longer is no more than a prolongation of the brief version."[12] For my part I would like to

---

10 Isidori Hispalensis, *Chronica*, ed. José Carlos Martín, Corpus Christianorum Series Latina 112 (Turnhout, 2003), 14–15; Martín, "Le problème des recensions, 127–28; Jacques Fontaine, *Isidoro de Sevilla. Génesis y originalidad de la cultura hispánica en tiempos de los visigodos* (Madrid, 2002), 162–78.

11 Isidorus Hispalensis, *Chronica*, 20–25; Pedro Juan Galán Sánchez, *El género historiográfico de la "Chronica." Las crónicas hispanas de época visigoda* (Cáceres, 1994), 175–208; Luis Vázquez de Parga, "Notas sobre la obra histórica de San Isidoro," in *Isidoriana*, ed. Manuel C. Díaz y Díaz (León, 1961), 99–106; Marc Reydellet, "Les intentions idéologiques et politiques dans la *Chronique* d'Isidore de Séville," *Mélanges d'archéologie et d'histoire de l'École française de Rome* 87 (1970): 363–400; José Miguel Alonso-Núñez, "Aspectos del pensamiento historiográfico de San Isidoro de Sevilla," in *Aevum inter utrumque. Mélanges offerts à F. Sanders*, ed. Marc van Uytfanghe, Roland Demeulenaere (Steenbrugge, 1991).

12 *La comparación entre ambas versiones muestra que la larga no es más que una prolongación de la versión breve.* Cited from Fontaine, *Isidoro de Sevilla*, 169.

try to interpret certain excerpts from the second version paying special attention to the most significant difference between this and the first version, namely its gallery of brief moral portraits accompanying the actions of the Roman emperors.

The suspicion that Isidore's intentions went beyond mere historical comprehensiveness derives from the fact that when he returned to his work ten years after the first version, he used the same sources which he had at his disposal in 615/616.[13] The principal source of Isidore's *Chronicle* is Eusebius–Jerome's *Chronicle*[14] and it covers chapters 34 to 351 out of a total of four hundred and seventeen.[15] In the 615/616 version, Isidore makes use of Eusebius–Jerome's *Chronicle* no more than four times, using Eutropius's *Breviarium ab urbe condita*.[16] In the 626 version, the references from the *Breviarium* have multiplied to twenty-nine (twenty-six entirely new ones and three partial chapters) almost all of which are anecdotes on the character, actions, and crimes of the Roman emperors and very evidently no longer simply chronological entries.

This is the most important practical change from one version to the other. It is systematic and might be described as monographic additions to its contents. In addition to Eutropius's work, Isidore also made use of Rufus Festus's *Breviarium rerum gestarum populi romani* from which he took eleven new chapters for a total of forty additions, all devoted to good or bad conduct by emperors and their relative military successes and failures. The relevant chapters from Eutropius are the following: 235 (Octavian), 238 (Tiberius), 241 (Caligula), 243 (Claudius), 246 (Nero), 250 (Vespasian), 253–254 (Titus), 257 (Domitian), 262 (Nerva), 264–265 (Trajan), 268 (Hadrian), 273 (Antoninus Pius), 276 (Antoninus the Younger), 278 (Commodus), 283 (Severus), 288 (Caracalla), 290 (Macrinus), 291 (Aurelius), 294 (Alexander), 300 (Gordian), 305 (Decius), 307 (Volusianus), 316 (Aurelian), 320 (Probus), 326 (Diocletian), 335 (Constans), 347 (Jovian); from Rufus Festus: 233 (Caesar), 265 (Trajan), 268 (Hadrian), 273 (Antoninus Pius), 276 (Antoninus the Younger), 283 (Severus), 300 (Gordian), 326 (Diocletian), 329 (Constantine).

After correcting chapter 347 dedicated to Jovian, the text continues without significant alterations from the first to the second versions for forty chapters to 386 when a new sequence of substantial modifications starts again. These too are dedicated to the emperors and are all drawn from a single source, Victor of Tunnuna, who was available to Isidore already in 615/616 (he was the main source for chapters 380 to 400). The relevant chapters are as follows: 386 (Zeno), 389 (Anastasius), 394 (Justin), 397–399 (Justinian), and 401 (Justin the Younger, drawn from Biclarense).

---

13 Isidorus Hispalensis, *Chronica*, 28.

14 St. Jérôme, *Chronique, continuation de la Chronique d'Eusèbe, années 326–378*, ed. Rudolf Helm, Benoît Jeanjean, Bertrand Lançon (Rennes, 2004).

15 Isidorus Hispalensis, *Chronica*, 25–35. For chapters 1–33 the author refers to Genesis, the *City of God*, and the *Chronicle* of Prosper Aquitanus; for chapters 352–79 he uses Prosper Aquitanus again, sourced from the *Ecclesiastical History* by Cassiodorus; for chapters 380–417 Isidorus refers to the *Chronicle* by Vittorio di Tutunna and Giovanni Biclarense.

16 *Eutropii Breviarium ab urbe condita*, ed. Carlo Santini, Nino Scivoletto (Leipzig, 1979); Eutropius, *Breviarium ab urbe condita*, ed. Franz Ruehl (Leipzig, 1887–1919).

As mentioned above, José Carlos Martín, the editor of the *Chronicle*, has argued that Isidore already had access to Eutropius in 615/16 and it is certain that he used Victor of Tunnuna in his first version of the work. I believe that this may mean that Isidore decided to use these sources much more extensively for reasons which go well beyond considerations of completeness. If he had wanted to make his work more thoroughgoing using Eutropius, Rufus Festus, and Victor he could have done so in the first version. Why wait a decade to do so?

Summarizing, then, there are no significant changes from one version to the next except in two groups of chapters (232–347 and 386–401) which, as we have seen, were systematically corrected almost chapter by chapter, transforming chronological data on the emperors into vignettes of good and bad kingship.

Given the considerably precise, specifically identified, and monographic nature of the information which Isidore seeks out in the works of Eutropius and Victor, I believe that we can hazard a hypothesis that the writer's intention in adjusting the work was not simply historiographical.

Whatever the imperial portraits themselves, in an almost entirely regular sequence of good and bad sovereigns, there are a number of constants which, I would argue, show the outlines of coherent political thought which was increasingly clear. If we take a look, for example, at chapters 150, 172, 281, 282, and 298, it is clear that, included in the context of the extreme synthesis required by the chronicle genre, Isidore looked to the Senate (the aristocratic institution *par excellence*) as a legitimate political entity worthy of the greatest respect, a point of view which is reinforced from the first to the second version if we take a look at details such as the use of the epithet "father of the nation"[17] for senators alone and its non-application to Antoninus Pius,[18] who effectively lost this title in the newer version of the work. The same type of rethinking is at work when Isidore amends the Senate's stance in its attitude to Aelius, *supplicant* in the first version, *poscente* in the second. Parallel with this perspective on the Senate is Isidore's admiring attention to the consuls (208, 210, 216, 221, 227), a cycle which concludes emblematically with the effectively ambivalent Caesar story (232, 233, 234) that juxtaposes Caesar's military glory during his mandate as consul, while the onset of his rule is linked to civil war.[19]

Now it is a question of allusions, clearly, but allusions which are meaningful when taken together. If we observe the alternation of good and bad emperors from Octavian onwards, we can see that it is their attitude to the senatorial class that marks out the good emperors and harassment and persecution of the aristocracy by the bad ones. (On the subject of Isidore's stance on the matter and what most interested him, Domitian is perhaps most exemplary in chapters 257–260: in correcting his explanation from the first to the second versions Isidore focuses on the persecution of the aristocracy, relegating the persecution of the Christians to second place, a choice which recurs elsewhere.) This constant seems to come to fruition when Isidore assesses the reign of Vespasian

---

17 Isidorus Hispalensis, *Chronica*, 74–75.

18 Isidorus Hispalensis, *Chronica*, 132–33.

19 Isidorus Hispalensis, *Chronica*, 110–13.

(250) and Titus (252–255), textbook cases for sovereigns, the former of "forgiveness of offence" and the latter of indulgence to plotters. Note that Domitian, the oppressor of senators, follows on from Titus, who is his mirror image. Next come Antoninus (272–273) whose second version, as we have seen, no longer calls him "father of the nation," Aelius (281–282) who debated with the Senate to great advantage (as we will see), Macrinus and his son (290), victims of a plot, Aurelius Antoninus, victim of a plot, Alexander, on the other hand, once again much loved by the *cives* and Maximinus (298), favoured by the Senate. Isidore is especially interested in the theme of plots. The evil and inept emperors stand out and Isidore expresses no disapproval of them whatsoever, a perspective that complements his praise of Vespasian and Titus's indulgence.

Summarizing, this implicit respect for the Senate is underlined and completed in the story of the consular victories (to which we could add the triumphs of the "patrician" Belisarius and Narses, ideally juxtaposed with the heretical decadence of the Justinian dynasty in the period 394–401), of an aristocracy that is a victim of evil emperors, regicide as an implicitly legitimate reaction (a theme which we find reiterated in *Historia*), and good princes forgiving plotters and adversaries.

Thus, if the intent is illustrative, the positive model indicated by Isidore could be the senatorial–consular model, namely an aristocratic regime and elective rulers. It would thus come as no surprise if the negative model were diametrically the opposite. In the long catalogue of negative examples brought together by the *Chronicle*, a certain tendency by the writer to associate inept rule with dynastic succession and the related occasional divisions of power can be observed. Almost all the dynasties and those that the narrative associates with them coincide with decadent and unsuccessful rules: Cleopatra and Ptolemy (232), Domitian, Titus's son (257–266), Antoninus Pius and Antoninus the Younger (272–273), Caracalla, son of Severus (288), Macrinus and his son (290), Gallus and Volusian (307), Valerian and Gallienus (309–311), Carus, Carinus, and Numerian (322, 323), Diocletian and Maximilan (324–326), Constantius and Constans (335), Valentinian and Valens with Fridigern and Alaric (348, 349), Arcadius and Honorius (365–373), Justin I, Justinian, and Justin II (394–401), and Liuvigild and Hermenegild (405).

In accordance with the *Chronicle*'s essential style, Isidore lets the facts, or rather the anecdotes, talk without ever openly theorizing or espousing political principles. When he does decide to do so, rather than contravene the requirements of the genre, he lets his characters speak for him.

In chapters 262 and 265, first Nerva and then Trajan state that they were not at all different from other men, emphasizing the fact that good rulers are in no way superior to their subjects and thus not distinct from them. In chapter 282, Pertinax responds to senators demanding that he associate his family (wife and son) with the crown, that is, form a royal family, saying that anyone taking on the responsibilities of power must deserve the invitation to rule: he expresses his denial of the division of power, of contemporary dynastic policy and argues by contrast for election and consent based on merit (the idea of the invitation to rule leaves no room for doubt). Lastly, in the dialogue between the *princeps* and the army in chapter 347, Isidore expresses the bonds of reciprocity which link kingliness, consent, and Christianity (in what seems to be a correction of the Reccared model at the Third Council of Toledo in 589).[20] In each of these four passages, Isidore reports the words of an emperor and, on each occasion, he expresses and exemplifies one of the key elements in the model of kingliness which he is perhaps seeking and illustrating over the course of his work: a modest ruler is in no way superior to his subjects; opposition to the dynastic solution; election; and consent.

Of the four chapters we have looked at, the only additions from the first to the second versions are those in which Nerva and Trajan express their ordinariness (262 and 265) while 282, with its denial of dynasty, and 347, on Jovian's election, are present in both versions. This is the basis for two further considerations. Firstly, the fact that certain key parenetic considerations are present right from the first version of the work and so it would appear that Isidore set to work on these for the purposes of highlighting and underlining them with new examples. Secondly, we can see that the additions for Trajan and Nerva are mirror images of the condemnation of imitations of divinity which we find in the chapters on Caligula and Domitian, criticism of whom appears only in the second version. Perhaps this is the new element which Isidore introduces from one version to the next (developing models which were potentially already there): both an awareness of their humanity and imitation of the divine as the distinction between good and bad kings.

Isidore's kings are more favourably presented the more moderate and modest they are (Nerva excels in considering himself a common man, a perfect contrast with "execrable" Domitian who dared to define himself a god) and this brings us to two further subjects which seem to emerge from a reading of the *Chronicle*: disapproval of ostentatious power, its formalization in investitures, and royal dress and, complementary to this, scorn for the imitation of the divine in an explicit condemnation of Domitian and Caligula.

The analogy between these two ways of exalting kingliness comes across: both Domitian and Caligula, and also Diocletian, raise kingliness to an evident and accentuated state of holiness which separates it definitively and irredeemably from the community of subjects. Domitian and Caligula do this by asserting and exhibiting divinity, Diocletian takes the luminous splendour of his vestments to its apex. There is nothing accidental about the fact that it is their persecutions which Isidore recalls of Domitian and Diocletian and the cruelty and luxury of Caligula. To complete these thoroughly negative examples, Domitian is presented as being as brutal with the senators as with the Christians and this is underlined by contrasting Domitian with Nerva, who saw himself as a common man and Trajan, who stated that a good prince should consider himself

---

20 Vives, *Concilios visigóticos*, 107–45; Orlandis, *Historia de los concilios*, 197–226; Santiago Castellano, *Los Godos y la Cruz, Reccared y la unidad de España* (Madrid, 2007), 212–35; Cristina Godoy, Josep Villela, "De la Fides Gothica a la Ortodoxia nicena: inicio de la teología política visigoda," *Antigüedad y Cristianismo* 3 (1986): 117–45; Sanz, *Historias de los Godos*, 289–296; Díaz, "La Hispania visigoda," 378–89, esp. 383–89; Loring, *La Hispania tardoromana*, 166–71; Luis A. García Moreno, *Historia de España Visigoda* (Madrid, 1989), 131–43; Thompson, *Los Godos en España*, 113–21; José Orlandis, "Baddo, gloriosa regina," in *Des Tertullien aux mozarabes. Mélange offerts à Jacques Fontaine*, ed. Louis Holtz, Jean Claude Fredouille, Jacques Fontaine, Marie-Hélène Jullien, 2 vols. (Paris, 1992), 1:84–91.

a citizen like any other. It is worth underlining the adherence of these contents to the power theory Isidore sets out in the third book of his *Sententiae*, where his condemnation of the *lumina lapillorum* is explicit[21] and illuminating: an illustration in which Caligula, Domitian and, in particular, Diocletian are depicted in the *Chronicle* as extremely apt examples.

I would argue that Isidore's implicit advocacy of the aristocratic historical subjects which we come across in the *Chronicle* is strictly correlated to the ambiguous use he makes of the word *gens* and the fact that it is not synonymous with the term *populus* to be found in the *Etymologiae*,[22] an issue which Velázquez Soriano has also highlighted.[23] This comes out most clearly in the 7th canon of the Fourth Council in the rhetorical reflection of the struggle for power between the aristocratic managerial class and a royalty which, from time to time, attempts to consolidate its power in hereditary ways. I believe that in outlining his political model in the *Chronicle*, Isidore's intention is to draw precisely on this contrast.

What emerges from the examples selected by Isidore as a whole is the model of a respectful sovereign with a sense of responsibility towards his subjects and the aristocracy in particular, a sovereign who resists the temptation to add a formal, dynastic aspect to his rule, presumably because a dynasty destabilizes in a detrimental way the relationship between forces internal to the ruling elite. Many of the crucial issues in the 75th canon are recognizable from this.

If a strong link between the contents of the *Sententiae* and the canons of the Fourth Council does exist, if it is Isidore's personality and thought which underlies crucial canons like the 75th, then perhaps it is not stretching a point to trace this process backwards in the Bishop of Sevilla's work and consequently link legal solutions such as the electoral requirement (and the political weight guaranteed to the *gens*) to the examples which Isidore underlines in the *Chronicle*.

As we have seen, the addition of these brief vignettes and moral judgments on the emperors are the most significant change from the first to the second versions of the *Chronicle*. I believe that the numerous, however brief, references to the dominant features of each emperor's reign represent a certain change in the orientation of the work itself or, at the very least, an extension of the author's interests and intentions; for, in the first version he limited himself to constructing a chronological time-frame for a series of crucial events in Christian history, using the reigns as little more than chronological reference points.

The new approach does not take the form of precise and explicit assertions by the writer (which would not be consistent to the chronicle genre). I believe, however, that a credible proof of the presence of a political model and Isidore's intention to make it explicit and promote it lies in the fact that it is the model itself that constitutes the difference between the two versions. Consider again the year 626, when he decided to take

---

21 Isidorus Hispalensis, *Sententiae*, 297.

22 Isidorus Hispalensis, *Etimologie o Origini*, ed. Angelo Valastro Canale (Turin, 2004), 9, 2.1, 1, 706; 9, 4.5, 1, 752

23 Velázquez, "*Pro patriae gentisque*," 186–217.

up his work once again, the first year of rediscovered territorial unity, the apex for a king whose victory perhaps prepared the way for centralization and a future dynastic direction, there would be nothing surprising about Isidore renewing, on one hand, his own historiography to celebrate the victorious king (making him quite literally go down in history) and, on the other, to warn him against making negative use of his victory. In my view this was why the *Chronicle* was revised, as too the *Historia*.

The *Historia*[24]

In the case of the *Historia*, the best-known changes are in the chapters dedicated precisely to Suintila in the *Laus Hispanie* and the *Recapitulatio*, on which a great deal has been written. Here I would like to shift the focus onto a whole series of minor modifications.

There is no space here to go into greater textual detail on the many passages worthy of note and I will thus concentrate on listing the most emblematic personalities and group them on the basis of their relevance in an attempt to bring out a certain parenetic exercise of power archetypes both positive and negative. Of the sixty-five chapters of *Historia Gothorum*, it is the first fifty that I will consider here (the last fifteen relate to Isidore's own contemporary world, the kingdom he lived in, the king he himself met, and thus, I believe, should be discussed separately). Twenty-two kings are described in chapters one to fifty of the second version (the only version with numbered chapters) and nineteen of these deal with nineteen appalling instances of leadership: Athanaric (6), Fridigern (7), Radagaisus and Alaric (13), Ataulf (19), Teodoret (23), Turismond (30), Euric (34), Alaric (36), Gisaleric (37–38), Odoacer and Onoulphus (39), Amalaric (40), Theudis (41), Theudigisel (44), Agila (45), Athanagild (46–47), Liuva and Liuvigild (48–49). I have included Odoacer and Onoulphus because I believe that Isidore's intention in judging his characters and making examples of them in no way revolves around ethnic identity. For this reason we can also add to the list of bad kings those in the *Historia Vandalorum* and the *Historia Sueborum*: Gunderic (73), Genseric (74–77), Huneric (78–79), and Gelimer (83–84), Retiarius (88), Maldra, Franta, Reccimondus, and Frumar (88–90).

On the basis of this catalogue of around thirty vignettes, we can perhaps summarize the qualities of a bad king: violent tendencies; war for the purpose of sacking and military defeat as its consequence; immorality; luxury; weak will; cowardice; treason: avidity. These are the faults which return again and again and which the *Historia*'s bad kings and the *Chronicle*'s bad *principes* share. (What marks them out is perhaps Isidore's insistence on underlining the brutal and predatory nature of their invasions and the criminal illegitimacy of those involved in them.) In addition to these archetypes of moral and behavioural defects, there are at least two concrete political themes which Isidore seems to be focusing on: on one hand, oppression of the aristocracy by their kings, placing the aristocracy in the narrative role of victim; on the other hand, the division of power, dynastic or otherwise, that is fatally destined to encourage civil war or, at any

---

24 Cristóbal Rodríguez Alonso, ed., *Las historias de los godos, vándalos y suevos de Isidoro de Sevilla. Estudio, edición critica y traducción* (León, 1975); for the chapters mentioned in this work, see the Latin text edition by Cristóbal Rodríguez Alonso.

rate, leads to a degeneration in moral and political leadership. In the course of these opening fifty chapters (three-quarters of the part of the work devoted to the Visigoths), Isidore never misses a chance to underline cases of civil war or to associate dynastic succession with execrable men and failed reigns, a narrative feature we find throughout the *Chronicle* and, in brief, a catalogue of associations and dynasties to be condemned and destined to ill fortune: Fridigern and Athanaric, Alaric and Radagaisus, Ataulf and Galla Placidia, Teodoret and Turismond, Euric, Alaric, Gisaleric, Odoacer and Onulphus, Liuva and Liuvigild, Liuvigild and Hermenegild, all the Vandal kings with a clash between the defeated dynasty of Hilderic and the new dynasty of Gelimer and the pair of Suebian kings of whom we will speak below.

Telling of the joint reign of Liuva and Liuvigild (49), as if to wrap up and sum up the theory of examples he has put together, Isidore allows himself an explicit and personal judgment written in the first person arguing that "two cannot occupy the space of one."[25] The specific example is found in chapters 88, 89, and 90 and these passages recount the division of power between two subsequent pairs of kings: Franta and Maldra and then Reccimondus and Frumar. In both chapters 88 and 89, Isidore chooses to put to one side the military events from the first to the second version insisting on the dysfunctional nature of power sharing. This is also the theme of the amendments made to chapter 90 which specifies the law on the strength of which Frumar finally brings all the Suebians together under his rule, that is *regali iure*, and creating an explanatory contrast with the two previous chapters. The effect of this change is that the group of chapters from 88 to 90 illustrates good and bad ways of managing leadership, contrasting the violent anarchy of power division with the legitimacy of a power centred on *regali iure*, examples which accord fully with the personal views Isidore expressed in chapter 48.

Let us now look at a few examples of the other principle which, reading between the lines, Isidore would appear to be expounding and to do so, we need to delve into the subject of potentially positive examples of leadership. We have seen that in narrative terms, the aristocracy (whether Roman or Goth) is subject to royal bullying. The feral nature of the invasions concerned gives the writer the opportunity to contrast the virtues of an aristocracy, victim of the vices of a frequently degenerate royalty, and make them exemplary, and presenting the emperors specifically within the category of incompetent rulers (Valens, Constantius, Valentinian, Theodosius, Majorian). This further strengthens the impression that for Isidore the clash was not so much between two civilizations or ethnic groups, i.e., following the dynamic of the invasion, but rather he cuts across these and explores two political models. Athanaric, Alaric, and Radagaisus are Roman oppressors and the idea that Roman-ness was generally noble (or rather *ultra noble*) is clear to us from the raids by Thedoret, Euric, the Vandals, and Suebians in general and Gelimer in particular. On his part Theudigisel dishonoured his aristocrats, Amalaric was assassinated by his soldiers, and lastly Theudis how had killed one king fell victim to regicide himself and died commanding that his assassin remain unpunished as he had deserved his end (which the *Chronicle* reminds us is a homage to indulgent *principes*). The point I am making is the considerably coherent political opinion which would seem to underlie

---

25 Rodríguez, *Las historias de los godos*, 250–52.

this series of anecdotes. This is reinforced by the positive portrayal of the only two kings Isidore presents positively across twenty-two of his first fifty chapters: Valia (21) and Thedoric (39).

Valia was elected, "inspired by divine providence" to enter a *foedus* with the Romans and place his arms at the service of the *respublica*. It is of note that it is Ataulf who precedes Valia in the account, the man who married Galla Placidia with the explicit objective of founding a dynasty, a childless marriage according to Daniel's prophecy. Valia is followed by Theodoret, a marauder who broke his *foedus* and sacked "the most noble" of Roman cities, implying that *chiaroscuro* worked both ways.

Theodoric, on the other hand, was "consul" before he was king and came to Italy, triumphing over his brothers Odoacer and Onulf and devoting himself to restoring Roma to greatness with the consent and the applause of the Senate.

Thus, the only kings who Isidore judges favourably in these fifty chapters are a confederate (and elected) and a consul.

Let us see who else is undeniably cast in a positive light: we have "consul" Pompey (3), Caesar's adversary against the backdrop of the civil wars and the man the Goths bravely sided with; we have *dux* Stilicho (14) who triumphed over bloody Radagasius; we have "virtuous" *dux* Aetius (23) who "punished" warmonger Theodoret and then triumphed at the Battle of the Catalaunian Fields (it is worth noting that in narrative terms Theodoret could just as well have been the heroic victor over Attila instead of a Roman *dux*); we have two anonymous "patricians" (62) who only Suintila succeeded in defeating, the high water mark of his military valour; we have Didimeus and Veridian (71) "the most noble and powerful Roman brothers" who defended Hispania against the Vandals and fell blameless victims to Constantius; lastly we have *magister militum* Belisarius (83–84) who, as the *Chronicle* highlights, in triumphing over Gelimer and his brothers, brought down the tyrannical and heretical reign of the Vandals (while noting in an aside that Belisarius's mission came to Justinian when Bishop martyr Lieto appeared to him).

These are, in brief, the positive examples in the *Historia*: a gallery of Roman aristocrats, patricians, and *duces* all exclusively victorious both militarily and morally over an equal number of degenerate royals. It is a gallery to which only two *reges* are clearly to be added, one confederate and the other, and not accidentally, a consul. The theory behind this historiographical juxtaposition can be found by consulting the *Etymologiae* in which consuls are contrasted with kings as the elective post *par excellence*, preferable to kings precisely because of the consensus required (in the form of the Senate), the service they embody, and the consultation which is their role's semantic root (in this sense it is precisely Theodoric of the *Historia* who seems to reflect the consuls of the *Etymologiae*). *Dux* in turn in the *Etymologiae* appears a few sentences after the passages devoted to comparing *rex* and *consul*,[26] fitting into the list of the definitions of those holding and managing power. *Dux* is paralleled as much with *rex* as with *princeps* but no degeneration is inferred and it has positive associations thanks to a quotation from Sallust who says that soldiers ardently desire to show their courage before generals.[27]

---

26 Isidorus Hispalensis, *Etimologie o Origini*, 9, 3.4–7, 1, 736–8.

27 Isidorus Hispalensis, *Etimologie o Origini*, 9, 3.21–22, 1, 742.

In the last analysis, it strongly appears that Isidore is promoting a positive image of these late Roman military and political men which tends implicitly to show them as positive models, always juxtaposed as a counter-balance to cases of kingly degeneration. *Duces* and, above all, *consules*, embody a series of political themes relating to the exercise of power which Isidore seems to identify and promote overall in his work: service, consent, consultation, and election as a guarantee of consent. It is clear that the *Historia*'s negative figures betray these principles while the positive ones hold offices which represent them and it is equally clear that this perspective coincides with the theories expressed by enlightened emperors in the *Chronicle* (Nerva, Trajan, Aelius) and represents an institutional model which is diametrically opposed to the dynastic one.

Now that we have collected and more or less summarized all these royal and other vignettes in the *Historia*, I would like to highlight the differences in the two versions and analyse the way in which this difference enables us to refine (in the same way as occurs with the *Chronicle*'s two texts) the writer's thought and intentions in reworking his own text.

Let us group the corrections together according to a thematic criterion: it is only the second version that contains an account of Pompey, Stilicho, Didimeus, and Veridian in addition to the extremely noble and anonymous patricians overcome by Suintila. All these figures are absent from the first version.

Equally, only the second version insists explicitly on Aetius's worth, crediting him with victory over the Huns (at the expense of Theodoret and Turismond). Only the second version places so much attention on Belisarius's North-African exploits. Lastly, only the second version tells of the "providential" merits of "confederate" Valia and Theodoric's triumphant consul. It looks very like a coherent model underlying conscious narrative and rhetorical choices. In a precise counterpoint to the appearance and promotion of these "Romanly correct" figures, the 626 version tends to introduce negative portraits (where it is necessary to worsen those already existing) of the main players. This is the fate of Radagasius, Ataulf (Galla Placida's husband—the whole detailed juxtaposition between this sterile dynastic marriage and the "providential" election of Valia is a narrative construct only present in the later version), Theodoret, Turismond, Odoacer, and Onulph, to the still anonymous Vandals who overthrew Didimeus and Veridian and Gelimer. The sensation is that Isidore's intention is to define (and in certain cases construct) mirror image textbook *chiaroscuro* relationships. As a result many kings have undergone artfully deteriorated cameos depicting them as seemingly lifelike examples of bad kingship.

I believe that a comparison between the two versions of the *Historia*, as in the *Chronicle*, provides us with an opportunity to highlight the ideas and perhaps political intentions of Isidore not simply updating but practically revising his history, and that underlying his praise of Suintila's greatness lies a coherent parenetic discourse, an intentional illustration (an intention showed by the need for amendment) of positive and negative models not just of the exercise of power but also in the way it was conferred. These models were refined and honed from one version to the next of the work examined here and perhaps preceded the legal outcomes of the Fourth Council's 75th canon.

We cannot but note the parallels between the *Chronicle*'s positive examples and those of the *Historia*, nor the fact that Nerva, Trajan, and Jovian's words are confirmed by the conduct of kings such as Valia and Theodoric, the fact that approval for the consulate and the patriciate expressed in the *Chronicle* and theorized in the *Etymologiae* is specifically illustrated in the *Historia*'s worthy and victorious *duces*. Equally we cannot fail to note that, as we will see shortly, Isidore's open condemnation of the formal excesses of emperors like Caligula, Domitian, and Diocletian in the *Chronicle* is reflected in the judgment on Luivigild expressed by the *Historia*.

A certain underlying coherence is detectable, an ideal of kingship tending to push sovereigns towards promotion of consensus and election contrasted with repeated condemnation of dynasty and ceremonial aggrandizement of kingship. In this perspective let us now take a look at the example of Luivigild.

Luivigild

Chapter 51 is the only one devoted to Luivigild whose contents Isidore decided to change. He left the chapter on the military campaigns unchanged (49) as well as that of the relationship between this Aryan king and the Catholics (50). The only chapter modified is the one which tells of the relationship between the king and the *gens*, between the king and the aristocracy. This alone tells us a great deal about Isidore's intentions, his desire to give advice to sovereigns, and on which subjects (we have also seen that Domitian and Gelimer were considered evil more for their harassment of the aristocracy than for that of the Christians—the second version focuses on the former rather than the latter). The first version reserves especially harsh criticism for the behaviour of Reccared's father, openly accusing him of having harassed and tormented the aristocracy for greed and personal gain.

In the second version, Luivigild is no longer guilty of envy or particularly of *cupiditas*. As Luivigild is not guilty of *cupiditas* in this later version, the passage describing him expropriating the assets of the aristocracy has also disappeared.

The concept of rapacity is still there but it is now associated with the positive fact of it having filled the state's coffers and the expropriations at the expense of the *cives* are linked to those at the expense of the *hostes* in accordance with a decidedly less serious image of a strong sovereign gradually replacing the concept of the enemy of the people and the aristocracy.

In the first version, the exiles and executions were presented as the result of Liuvigild's *cupiditas*, a means with which to get his hands on the goods of those persecuted and this, in essence, was the king's sin. In the 626 version, there is no relationship between this harassment and Luivigild's rapacity, which Isidore presumably intended to constitute an improvement in the king's reputation and bring him within the sphere of legitimacy.

The themes of property, respect for property by kings, the indispensable distinction between the goods of the state and the crown and those of the individual acting as king were crucial ones in the context of the Toledan conciliar debates in the second half of the seventh century (themes that consciously suggest a concept of kingship, one far from dynastic considerations) and on closer examination, we already find them in embryonic form in the relationship between the two versions of chapter 51—the superior Luivigild does not act for personal gain but to fill the coffers of the state he legitimately rules.

The improved Luivigild does not even dress as a king.

If Isidore is improving his portrait of Luivigild, it is coherent of him to condemn the vanity of those he calls *lumina lapillorum* in the *Sententiae*.

The most highly visible change in the context of chapter 51 relates precisely to Luivigild's adoption of kingly costume and pomp. The disappearance of this passage from the second version accords perfectly with the other changes and contributes to softening Luivigild's attitude to the aristocracy and conferring greater legitimacy on him. This confirms that Isidore considered formal pomp negatively, a highly debatable expectation by kings.

It is also worth noting that it is precisely the passage dealing with the adoption of purple dress which underlines that this was the way Luivigild distinguished himself from the *gens*, making the term *gens* clearly conjure up the sense of "nobility." This alteration gives us an insight into the type of relationship which Isidore saw as desirable between king and *gens*, a relationship which is ultimately sanctioned by the 75th canon.

Velázquez Soriano has underlined that some manuscripts transmitting the 626 version adopted the phrase relating to Liuvigild's kingliness using *populus* instead of *gens*.[28] This is actually the solution adopted by Mommsen's 1894 version[29] while Rodriguez Alonso's more recent version (of 1975, which I have used here) uses *gens*:[30] on this subject Velázquez Soriano advances the hypothesis of an intermediate version in which Isidore had yet to decide to eliminate the passage in question entirely.

The idea of an intermediate version, a first amendment in which Luivigild no longer marked himself out from the *gens* but from the *populus*, would show that Isidore's issue with this passage was precisely the relationship between *rex* and *gens*, that the information to be eliminated was the king's claim to superiority over the *gens* distinguished by royal costume and ceremony.

Velázquez Soriano has hypothesized that in the second version of the *Historia*, Isidore decided to omit the famous passage relating to the plagiarism of the imperial purple for the purposes of freeing Gothic kingliness from the Byzantine model and reclaiming cultural and political autonomy with pride.[31] I personally believe that the problem underlying the omission is not so much a matter of the Roman-Byzantine origin of the kingship model being imitated as much as the political content of the model itself. It is plausible that Isidore decided to eliminate this passage not because it told of

---

28 Velázquez, "La doble redacción de la *Historia Gothorum*," 122.

29 Isidorus Hispalensis, *Historia Gothorum Wandalorum Sueborum*, ed. Theodor Mommsen, MGH Auct. ant. 2 (1894), c. 51.

30 Javier Arce, "*Leovigildus rex* y el ceremonial de la corte visigótica," in *Visigoti e Longobardi. Atti del Seminario (Roma 28–29 aprile 1997)*, ed. Javier Arce, Paolo Delogu (Firenze, 2001), 84–85.

31 Velázquez, "*Pro patriae gentisque*," 186–217; Velázquez, "La doble redacción," 122; Arce, "*Leovigildus rex*," 79–92; Marcelo Vigil, Abilio Barbero, "Sucesión al trono y evolución social en el reino visigodo," *Hispania antiqua* (1974): 379–93.

a somewhat undignified imitation of Byzantine kingship but rather because it told of the advent of kingship *per se* with the hierarchical political definition this brought with it. In the 621 version, Isidore speaks only of "royal costume" not of "imperial" or "Roman purple." In other words he makes no mention whatsoever of the origin of the kingship in question or of the fact that Luivigild imitated the emperors in Constantinople. I believe that the character of the anecdote may be political and social rather than cultural and ethnic.

The issue of Luivigild's regal pose is the very same issue that Isidore brought up and dealt with in the *Chronicle* on the subject of Tullus Hostilius[32] and, in particular, Diocletian. (On this subject he also refers to the much-cited Domitian and Caligula and it is worth noting that his condemnation of these two dates precisely to the year 626 in common with his softer portrayal of Luivigild, further proof of Isidore's coherence in his case studies.) The anecdote, the stereotype Isidore highlights is practically the same in all three cases: that of kings who elevate themselves and mark themselves out formally from their predecessors at the expense of their peers. This tells us much about the attention the writer pays to the issue of kingship as decisive formalization and its disastrous impact on the social and political equilibrium.

The fact that Isidore chooses to eliminate this passage in order to temper his portrait of Luivigild is indicative of his opinion on the subject and clearly anticipates his judgment in the *Sententiae*, the absolute condemnation of the *lumina lapillorum* (a theme that is not coincidentally linked to his repudiation of Christomimesis in the *Etymologiae*).[33]

Wanting to present a parenetic model of kingship to the king, Isidore's intention is perhaps to start right from Luivigild who, on one hand, was Reccared's father and, on the other, the sovereign who set in motion the process of unification brought to fruition by Suintila.

In the shift from the first to the second version, Isidore's portrayal of Luivigild is toned down, his judgment of his behaviour tempered, his energetic centralization brought back within the confines of legitimacy for the purposes of presenting an at least partially positive model. Thus, the Luivigild of 626 is not greedy but fills the coffers of the state and no longer marks himself out from the aristocrats with formal claims. His kingship is more institutional and less personal; he looks after the state's interests rather than his own and, at the same time, keeps a low profile.

His conquests extend the domain of the *gens* and he no longer marks himself out from it. It is a kingship which is no different from that which Isidore exemplified on many occasions in the *Chronicle* in 626, where good emperors reconquered the provinces of the Empire and certainly made no claims to be anything but straightforward men (Nerva and Trajan).

---

32 Isidorus Hispalensis, *Chronica*, 76–77.

33 Isidorus Hispalensis, *Etimologie o Origini*, 7, 2.2–9, 1, 552–54.

Some Conclusions

The reading I have proposed here of certain passages from Isidore's work revolves principally around the theme of kingship in an attempt to go beyond the model drawn up on the basis of the more explicit and famous vignettes left by the Bishop of Sevilla, namely Reccared[34] and Suintila.[35] Examining these in relation to the contents of the *Sententiae* has enabled me to establish an effective *trait d'union* between Isidore's political thought and Gregory the Great's lessons, one which translates into an image of the providential prince, a predestined middleman between God and man, a centre-stage player in a privileged and exclusive dialogue with God. This model marries effectively with the idea of a Toledo kingship strongly influenced by the Byzantine imperial archetype and so, with the institutional and formal outcomes testified to by the acts of the Third Council of Toledo (589) where, with Leander of Seville (Isidore's brother), Reccared presented himself as apostle king and the new Constantine.[36]

The point is that this kingship model does not marry equally well with the legal solutions adopted forty years later by the Fourth Council of Toledo which Isidore himself inspired and in which he played a centre-stage role. It was precisely Reydellet who, while identifying and describing Isidore's dependence on Gregory's lesson, detected this discrepancy and explained it by attributing the 75th Canon to an elderly, unwell Isidore no longer capable of defending his thoughts and victim to pressure from the usurper Sisenand's faction.[37]

On my part, I have attempted to go beyond this position in the belief that the 75th Canon was much more integral to Isidore's work than might appear from a comparison of the two opposing judgments on Suintila and also in the belief that Isidore was capable of revisiting Gregory's lessons and forming his own thought over the decades on the basis of the urgent institutional requirements facing him and on the strength of a powerful and original political personality.

It is plausible that in 626 Isidore perceived the risk of an authoritarian turn by a sovereign whose enormous charisma and power expanded enormously with the reconquest of Byzantine Baetica. Is it not possible that Isidore's intention is (also) to warn Suintila not to fall victim to a series of errors and behaviour that would make an enemy of the ruling class? It is clear that both revised works have had to take the need for flattery into account. I am, however, convinced that Isidore does not miss the chance

---

34 Isidorus Hispalensis, *Chronica*, 262–66.

35 Isidorus Hispalensis, *Chronica*, 278–80.

36 For a comprehensive introduction to the subject of the Visigothic kingship, see María R. Valverde Castro, *Ideología, simbolismo, y ejercicio del poder real en la monarquía visigoda: un proceso de cambio* (Salamanca, 2000); Manuel A. Rodríguez de la Peña, *Los reyes sabios. Cultura y poder en la antigüedad tardía y la alta edad media* (Madrid, 2008), 245–97; José Orlandis, "El rey visigodo católico," in *De la Antigüedad al Medioevo. Siglos IV–VIII* (Madrid, 1993); Claudio Sánchez-Albornoz, "La *ordinatio principis* en la España goda y postvisigoda," in *Viejos y nuevos estudios sobre las instituciones medievales españolas*, Claudio Sánchez-Albornoz (Madrid, 1980); Barbero, "Sucesión al trono."

37 Reydellet, *La Royauté dans la Littérature Latine*, 524.

(between the lines but not excessively so) to communicate to the glorious sovereign his idea of a kingship which is certainly victorious but also modest and responsible to an even greater extent than it is religious. That Isidore's concerns are principally political in nature, linked to an extremely concrete vision of the exercise of power and the power relationships which the latter influences and modifies, is demonstrated by the fact that his argument on kingship touches not so much on the theme of the faith and religiosity of the prince (an obvious superlative and little more) as much as on the issue of the relationship between king, subjects, and *gens*. The theme of consensus reappears frequently. Dynasticization is a problem in this sense as is ceremonial pomp (as well as the imitation of divinity) to the extent to which they create a breach between kings and their subjects with the former being accorded excessive majesty.

Isidore's historiographical work repeatedly conjures up models of the exercise of power relating to Republican Roma and late antiquity, models which in some cases (given the author's choice of vocabulary) contain echoes of consular rule, models which are always cast in a positive light in direct contrast (as militarily and morally victorious) with examples of monarchical degeneration.

The sense that Isidore judges these archetypes positively is confirmed by a reading of the *Etimologiae* in which *senatus*, *consul*, and *dux* represent positive case studies of oligarchical rule juxtaposed with kingship. In particular, the relationship between *consul* and *senatus* (and the simultaneous dualism with *rex*[38]) illustrates a model which exemplifies a whole series of socio-political motives (service, responsibility, consent, and election as guarantees of legitimacy and consent) which Isidore may have been establishing as norms in the canons of Fourth Council.

What has changed in the Bishop of Sevilla's thought from the 620s in which he revised his histories to the 630s when he began work at the Council and on the *Sententiae* is not the content of kingship as such, but more the concrete examples that Isidore moves the figure of the king towards.

If in 626 he looked to the consulate and the patriciate as models of the moderation he had in mind for the king of Toledo, in 633—on the point of legislating on the subject of kingship—he finds that same moderation in the episcopal models on the strength of the example of Gregory the Great (remember the powerful analogies between the *Sententiae* and the canons in the wake of a single moral code for princes and clerics to the extent that all are *rectores*). The substance is the same—legitimacy based on consent, election as a guarantee of legitimacy—but passing from the historiographical literature of the 620s to his legislative work in the 630s, Isidore simply seems to have abandoned the purely literary models of the past in favour of references to contemporary models— active, concrete episcopal ones.

---

38 Isidorus Hispalensis, *Etimologie o Origini*, 9, 3.4–6, 1, 736–78.

Chapter 4

THE QUEST FOR IDEOLOGY IN CAROLINGIAN TIMES: ECCLESIOLOGICAL PATTERNS IN THE LATIN WEST FROM THE EIGHTH TO THE EARLY TENTH CENTURIES

ALFONSO M. HERNÁNDEZ RODRÍGUEZ

BEFORE DISCUSSING IDEOLOGY in the Carolingian period let us make a few basic assertions. First of all, between the eighth and early tenth centuries in the Frankish kingdom, any ideology that could be articulated was built upon Christian tradition, and this was the sole ideological tool capable of unifying the regional elites of the Empire.[1] Accordingly, ideology would be presented in the terms of ecclesiology, as I will soon describe (that is, the theological doctrine of the Christian Church).[2] And the Western Christian tradition drew on two main textual sources: Scripture[3] and patristic

---

1 On the use of the concept of "elite" during the Early Middle Ages, see Steffen Patzold, "Zu den Chancen und Problemen des Elitenbegriffs für eine Typologie frühmittelalterlicher Führungsgruppen," in *Théorie et pratiques des élites au Haut Moyen Âge*, ed. François Bougard, Hans-Werner Goetz, Régine Le Jan (Turnhout, 2011), 127–46.

2 Yves Congar, *L'ecclésiologie du Haut Moyen Age* (Paris, 1968); Jean Chélini, *L'aube du Moyen Âge. Naissance de la chrétienté occidentale. La vie religieuse des laïcs de l'Europe carolingienne (750–900)* (Paris, 1991). Raffaelle Savigni, "La place des laïcs dans l'ecclésiologie carolingienne: normes statutaires et idéal de 'conversion' (à propos de Paulin d'Aquilée, Jonas d'Orléans, Dhuoda et Hincmar de Reims)," in *Guerriers et moines. Conversion et sainteté aristocratique dans l'Occident médiéval (IXe–XIIe)*, ed. Michel Lauwers (Nice, 2002), 41–92; Raffaelle Savigni, "La *communitas christiana* dans l'ecclésiologie carolingienne," in *Hiérarchie et stratification sociale dans l'Occident médiéval (400–1100)*, ed. François Bougard, Dominique Iogna-Prat, Régine Le Jan (Turnhout, 2008), 83–104.

3 The history of the biblical text from Jerome's translation to the Carolingian period is quite a complex one; see Samuel Berger, *Histoire de la Vulgate pendant les premiers siècles du moyen âge* (Paris, 1893); Bonifatius Fischer, "Bibeltext und Bibelreform unter Karl der Grosse," in *Karl der Grosse*, ed. Wolfgang Braunfelds, 4 vols. (Düsseldorf, 1965–67), 2:156–216; Bonifatius Fischer, "Bibelausgaben des frühen Mittelalters," *Settimane* 10 (1963): 519–600; John J. Contreni, "Carolingian Biblical Culture," in *Johannes Scottus Eriugena. The Bible and Hermeneutics. Proceedings of the Ninth International Colloquium of the Society for the promotion of Eriugean Studies*, ed. Gerd Van Riel, Carlos Steel, James McEvoy (Leuven, 1996), 1–23; Bernice M. Kaczynski, "Edition, Translation, and Exegesis: The Carolingians and the Bible," in *The Gentle Voices of Teachers: Aspects of Learning in the Carolingian Age*, ed. Richard E. Sullivan (Columbus, 1995), 171–185; Geoffrey William Hugo Lampe, ed., *The West from the Fathers to the Reformation*, The Cambridge History of the Bible, 2 (New York, 1969); Laura Light, "Versions et révisions du texte biblique," in *Le Moyen*

Alfonso M. Hernández Rodríguez (alfonsohernandez1974@gmail.com) is Investigador adjunto at the Consejo Nacional de Investigaciones Científicas y Técnicas in Argentina, and Professor of Medieval History at the Universidad Pedagógica Nacional, Buenos Aires.

writings, comprising texts written in Latin and Eastern Christian texts translated into Latin.[4]

Secondly, a Carolingian ideology became a necessity for Carolingian rulers after the development of a large Christian state that covered much of Western Europe. For the first time since the dissolution of the Western Roman Empire, almost all Latin Christendom was contained in a single political structure. The Carolingian conquest took place in stages between Charles Martel and Charlemagne, and it ended with the victories of Louis the Pious. By the end of the ninth century, by inheritance or by his own wars of conquest, Charlemagne dominated a vast territory. This is a matter of *Realpolitik*, but once the conquest was over, it was necessary to provide a unifying ideology to all the subjected territory; it was necessary to move on from a kingdom built by conquest to an empire unified, and this was done via Christianity.

For some historians of Late Antiquity, as Robert Markus, the Christianization of Europe was a *fait accompli* by the end of that period.[5] It is true that the European states of the sixth century—the famous Barbarian Kingdoms of traditional historiography— declared themselves Christian, and that Christianity was a varnish that covered these societies. But Christianized Europe, before and after the conversion of the last Arian Visigothic king Reccared in 589, was actually, as Peter Brown pointed out, a sum of micro-Christianities. They were very loosely united by the same Nicene–Constantinopolitan creed, they had distinctive pious, liturgical, and calendrical practices, and in some cases they even included syncretic pagan beliefs. Brown believes that the Carolingian conquest put an end to this Christianity of Late Antiquity and gave birth to something new: medieval Christianity.[6]

Western Christianity is thus, in many ways, an "invention" of the Carolingian period, the product of collaboration between Pippinids, Roma, and the regional aristocracies of the Empire.[7] This Franco-Roman Christianity, with strong influences coming from the former Visigothic Kingdom, Lombard Italy, and the British Isles, presented itself as the only real one. This specific kind of Christianity would be the most powerful cultural innovation bequeathed by the great Carolingian kings and intellectuals to Western Europe, and it was a leading ideological instrument in the construction of medieval Europe.

At the beginning of the ninth century there was a Carolingian social order, which embraced a Christian empire, whose boundaries were the boundaries of the "true"

Age et la Bible, ed. Pierre Riché, Guy Lobrichon (Paris, 1984), 55–94; Laura Light, "La Bible et la vie politique dans le haut Moyen Age," in *Le Moyen Age et la Bible*, ed. Pierre Riché, Guy Lobrichon (Paris, 1984), 385–400; Beryl Smalley, *The Study of the Bible in the Middle Ages* (Oxford, 1952).

4 Willemien Otten, "The Texture of Tradition: The Role of the Church Fathers in Carolingian Theology," in *The Reception of the Church Fathers in the West: From the Carolingians to the Maurists*, ed. Irena Backus (Leiden, 1996), 3–50.

5 Robert Markus, *The End of Ancient Christianity* (Cambridge, 1991).

6 Peter Brown, *The Rise of Western Christendom: Triumph and Diversity, A.D. 200–1000* (Oxford, 2003).

7 This collaboration is quite clear, not only in the political field, but also in religion and culture: Éric Palazzo, "La liturgie carolingienne: vieux débats, nouvelles questions. Publications récentes," in *Le monde carolingien: Bilan, perspectives, champs de recherche*, ed. Wojciech Falkowski, Yves Sassier (Turnhout, 2009), 219–41.

Christianity and the one and only Church.[8] In Carolingian ideologies society, Empire, Christianity, and church identified themselves with each other. Consequently, the models to explain each of these socio-political realities or the programs proposed by Carolingian intellectuals to reform, order, or give shape to them, may be interpreted as ecclesiologies. Ecclesiology seeks to lay down the place of each individual or group of individuals within the Church, according to the divine will. In the period under investigation, "Church" was the main concept capable of including every part of society. Hence ideological, theological, and ecclesiological discourses came to be inseparably linked.

We arrive now at another problem: there was not one single Carolingian ecclesiology but several. The differences between them are due to the social and ecclesiastical place that each of the Carolingian writers of the extant sources occupied in his time. We can nonetheless establish a taxonomy within Carolingian ecclesiologies: an ecclesiology in which the head of the Church is a secular authority; or ecclesiologies with religious leadership.

Ecclesiology with Secular Leadership: Church, Kingdom, and Empire

Before the late eleventh century, that is, before the cultural revolution of the Gregorian reform, according to Florian Mazel's expression,[9] it was natural for Carolingian, and even for Ottonian, kings to consider themselves as head of the Church by divine will, and it was also expected that intellectuals subject to them—mostly ecclesiastics—proposed a social and ecclesiastical order headed by the king or emperor.

It is impossible to do justice to the number of studies devoted to the figure of the Carolingian kings and emperors in this paper. Therefore, this chapter considers two key elements to define a royal or imperial Carolingian ecclesiology: first, comparing Carolingian rulers to the kings from the Old Testament; secondly, the image of the king as builder of the Church in ninth-century royal biographies.

The likening of Carolingian sovereigns to biblical kings was at the core of their primacy in Carolingian society and the Church. In the *Admonitio generalis* Charlemagne is shown to be ruling both the kingdom and the Church as if it were the same task.[10] In this text, he is compared to Josiah, king, priest, and restorer of the Temple;[11] the use of the image of Josiah is important here but it was not very successful in later developments of Carolingian ecclesiology. Instead, other kings like David and Solomon were preferred to him.[12]

---

8 An excellent summary of current studies on Carolingian society can be found in Régine Le Jan, "Histoire carolingienne et sciences sociales: quelques perspectives," in *Le monde carolingien: Bilan, perspectives, champs de recherche*, ed. Wojciech Falkowski, Yves Sassier (Turnhout, 2009), 301–21.

9 Florian Mazel, *Féodalités 888–1180* (Paris, 2010), 235.

10 Yves Sassier, *Royauté et idéologie au Moyen Âge, Bas-Empire, monde franc, France (IVe-XIIe siècle)* (Paris, 2002), 126.

11 *Die Admonitio generalis Karls des Großen*, ed. Hubert Mordek, Klaus Zechiel-Eckes, Michael Glatthaar, MGH Fontes iuris 16 (2013), 54.

12 Isabel Rosé, "Le roi Josias dans l'ecclésiologie politique du haut Moyen Âge," *Mélanges de l'École française de Rome (Moyen Âge)* 115 (2003): 683–709.

The first reference to a relationship between David and a Carolingian king appeared in Pepin the Short's anointing by the Frankish bishops in 751 and by Pope Stephen II in 754. The anointing of a king, as described in the *Clausula de unctione Pippini regis*,[13] had Visigothic precedents, probably known to the Frankish world. There was an important difference in 754: the pope anointed not just Pepin, but also his sons, Charles and Carloman, and he also blessed his wife Bertrada. What was at stake in this act, according to Yves Sassier, was the creation of a royal dynasty whose aim was to prepare the Christian people for the *parousia* or Second Coming of Christ.[14] During the reign of Charlemagne, David was the most exalted example of a ruler, to the point that it became the nickname of the king himself. The king became the anointed of the Lord—like David—and that condition entitled him to rule over his kingdom, as Alcuin said in one of his letters (794–795).[15]

Dominique Iogna-Prat noted the centrality of the figure of the sovereign as builder of the Church in panegyric and biographical texts written before 850: Einhard's *Vita Karoli*, the two lives of Louis the Pious written by Thegan, and the anonymous author called the "Astronomer," and the biographical poem/panegyric of Ermoldus Nigellus. To these texts we may add many other references in other writings of the period.

According to Iogna-Prat, Einhard's, Thegan's, Astronomer's, and Ermoldus's writings have some interesting peculiarities. They were all written between 817 and 840, during the reign of Louis the Pious, a period when the imperial ecclesiological model was at its zenith. Moreover, they appear together in the manuscript tradition.[16] The Carolingian ruler as builder of the Church was the main image of all these biographical texts. As builder, he was also head of the Church, which denotes a Caesaro–Papist—using a traditional but criticized expression—[17] Constantinian ecclesiology: the king built the Church while he built churches. He increased the Church by converting subjected people; he supported and protected it, hence he had the right to rule over it. The texts in fact presented the ruler as builder and sovereign head of the Church.[18] This Carolingian Caesaro–Papism was also visible in the councils of the Church presided over by the rulers, following the example of Constantine at Nicaea.[19] The council of Frankfurt is the most cited example of this attitude.[20] But identification of the emperor and the Church

---

13 "Clausula de unctione Pippini regis," in *Archives de la France sous la direction de Jean Favier. Tome 1. V^e-XIe siècle*, ed. Jean-Pierre Brunterc'h (Paris, 1994), 204–18.

14 Sassier, *Royauté et idéologie*, 122–24.

15 Alcuin of York, *Epistolae*, ed. Ernst Dümmler, MGH Epp. 4 (1895), 84.

16 Rosamond McKitterick, "L'idéologie politique dans l'historiographie carolingienne," in *La royauté et les élites dans l'Europe carolingienne (du début du IXe siècle aux envierons de 920)*, ed. Régine Le Jan (Lille, 1998), 59–70.

17 Gilbert Dagron, *Empereur et prêtre. Étude su le "cesaropapisme" byzantin* (Paris, 1996), 290–322.

18 Dominique Iogna-Prat, *La Maison Dieu. Une histoire monumentale de l'Église au Moyen Âge (v. 800-v.1200)* (Paris, 2006), 119–52.

19 Arnold Angenendt, "Karl der Große als *rex et sacerdos*," in *Das frankfurter Konzil von 794. Kristallizationspunkt karolingischer Kultur*, ed. Rainer Berndt (Mainz, 1997), 255–78.

20 The famous *Libri carolini*, more exactly called *Opus Caroli regis contra synodum*, were written

is also present in the political ideas of thinkers from the ninth century, like Hrabannus Maurus.[21]

The idea underlining this ecclesiology headed by the king was the sacredness of the ruler. He was not just a layman, a simple baptized Christian; he was a sacred person, the Lord's anointed, the successor of David and Constantine. He was closer to Christ than any ecclesiastic. In the eyes of Charlemagne and other pre-Gregorian kings and their intellectuals, this was not simply an ecclesiology with secular leadership because kings and emperors were in fact religious characters (though many ecclesiastics, including popes, would disagree).

Ecclesiologies with Religious Leadership: Bishops, Popes, and Monks

Let us now consider two main ecclesiological patterns led by religious authorities during the Carolingian period in the Frankish kingdoms. The first one had episcopal leadership and the other a kind of monastic leadership. A particular case of episcopal ecclesiology, because of its future developments in western medieval Christianity model of the bishop or pope in Roma.

Clerical-led ecclesiologies—especially the papal one—would eventually overcome the secular ecclesiology, although its triumph would be clearly visible only after the Gregorian Reform.[22] One of the main intellectual tools for the triumph of clerical ecclesiologies was the "hierarchical" concept, taken from Pseudo-Dionysius's neo-Platonic texts translated into Latin by John Scotus Erigena. This allowed clerics—bishops, popes, and abbots—to set up a hierarchy of spiritual degrees and to deny the highest grades of it to secular rulers.[23]

---

by Theodulph in the context of the struggle against adoptionism and Byzantine worship of icons. *Opus Caroli regis contra synodon (Libri Carolini)*, ed. Ann Freeman, MGH Conc. Supplementum 1 (1998). The text asserted Charlemagne's power over church and kingdom, trying to respect papal spiritual primacy, see Thomas F. X. Noble, *Images, Iconoclasm and the Carolingians* (Philadelphia, 2009), 158–206.

21 Geneviève Bührer-Thierry, "Raban Maur et l'episcopat de son temps," in *Raban Maur et son temps*, ed. Philippe Depreux, Stéphane Lebecq, Michel J.-L. Perrin, Olivier Szerwiniack (Turnhout, 2010), 74; Mayke de Jong, "The Empire as *ecclesia*: Hrabannus Maurus and biblical *historia* for rulers," in *The Uses of the Past in the Early Middle Ages*, ed. Ytzhak Hen, Matthew Innes (Cambridge, 2004), 191–226.

22 On the development of the hierarchy inside the order of priests, see Alain Rauwel, "Les hiérarchies internes à l'ordre sacerdotal et la question de la sacramentalité de l'épiscopat dans l'Église romaine de saint Augustin à Pierre Lombard," in *Hiérarchie et stratification sociale dans l'Occident médiéval (400–1100)*, ed. François Bougard, Dominique Iogna-Prat, Régine Le Jan (Turnhout, 2008), 105–15.

23 Sassier, *Royauté et idéologie*, 133–40. The complex implications of the reception of Pseudo-Dionysius's texts in the Latin west were thoroughly studied by Dominique Iogna-Prat, "Penser l'Église, penser la société après le Pseudo-Denys l'Aréopagite," in *Hiérarchie et stratification sociale dans l'Occident médiéval (400–1100)*, ed. François Bougard, Dominique Iogna-Prat, Régine Le Jan (Turnhout, 2008), 55–81.

The Episcopal Model

From Late Antiquity to the Gregorian Reform the government of the Church rested on the bishops. Each of them was the leading independent authority of his Church in his diocese. The religious episcopal authority also involved the exercise of some kind of secular power, which was quite visible in post-imperial Roma.[24] The relationship between Carolingian kings and bishops is complex. For instance, at certain times and places, bishops worked as officers of the government and were thus subjected to the secular authority of the kings but, in others, they had more freedom of action and could even take part in conspiracies against them. Apart from this, the role of bishops during the Carolingian period constitutes a field which requires further research.[25] Episcopal ecclesiology was developing and this was visible in the political practice of bishops during the crisis of the reign of Louis the Pious, showing one of the outstanding characteristics of ideology during the middle of the ninth century: the administering of secular and religious power.[26]

Mirrors of princes and lay people are Carolingian texts that have received much attention in modern historiography. The goal of these texts was to provide Christian moral models for powerful lay persons.[27] Jonas of Orleans, for example, was the author of two of these texts,[28] one dedicated to the sovereign, called *De institutione regia,* and another addressed to the laity in general, *De institutione laicali.*[29] Both texts showed a laity under clerical tutelage and compelled, *inter alia*, to secure the material support of the Church through tithing but, at the same time, they were to provide a moral function for conjugal love within the Church.[30] However, the place of the laity within the Church was secondary and involved clerical monopoly of the sacred,[31] which was one of the objectives of eighth-century missionaries like St. Boniface when fighting against non-

---

24 Thomas X. Noble, *The Republic of St. Peter. The Birth of the Papal State 680–825* (Philadelphia, 1984).

25 Geneviève Bührer-Thierry, "Épiscopat et royauté dans le monde carolingien," in *Le monde carolingien: Bilan, perspectives, champs de recherche*, ed. Wojciech Falkowski, Yves Sassier (Turnhout, 2009), 143–55.

26 Sassier, *Royauté et idéologie*, 133–40; Janet L. Nelson, "National synods, kingship as office, and royal anointing: an early medieval syndrome," in *Politics and Ritual in Early Medieval Europe*, ed. Janet L. Nelson (London, 1986), 239–57.

27 Hans Huber Anton, *Fürstenspiegel und Herrscherethos in der Karolingerzeit* (Bonn, 1968).

28 Jonas of Orleans is, in modern scholarship, one of the most explored authors in the study of Carolingian ideology; see especially Raffaelle Savigni, *Giona di Orléans. Una ecclesiologia carolingia* (Bologna, 1989).

29 Jonas d'Orléans, *Le Métier de Roi (De institutione regia)*, ed. Alain Dubreucq (Paris, 1995); Jonas d'Orléans, "De institutione laicali," in *Patrologiae cursus completus*, ed. Jacques-Paul Migne, 221 vols. (Paris, 1864), 106: col. 121–278.

30 Iogna-Prat, *La Maison Dieu*, 228–36; Pierre Toubert, "La théorie du mariage chez les moralistes carolingiens," *Settimane* 24 (1977): 233–85.

31 A monopoly which will not be achieved during the Carolingian period: Régine Le Jan, "Histoire carolingienne et sciences sociales: quelques perspectives," in *Le monde carolingien: Bilan, perspectives, champs de recherche*, ed. Wojciech Falkowski, Yves Sassier (Turnhout, 2009), 317–19.

Roman ways of Christianity[32] or the reformers of the rural clergy during the eighth and ninth centuries.[33]

Episcopal capitularies written in the years 800–950 were produced to adapt the great royal or imperial capitulary texts to the life of each diocese.[34] Among other things, capitularies defined the place of the clergy within society: clerics were beyond the secular world, or at least away from the secular behaviour which might affect the purity required to perform the eucharistic sacrifice.

Another relevant Carolingian development that affected the relationship between laity and clergy was the assertion of the ecclesiastical building as the privileged sacred place for Christianity.[35] It is no coincidence that in the middle of the ninth century, within the context of the hierarchization of the Church, the first major Western eucharistic controversy took place. The discussion was not only about the actual or symbolic presence of Christ in the eucharistic sacrifice, but also about the status of the place where the sacrifice was accomplished (the church building) and also about the status of the man who controlled that space and carried out the sacrifice (the priest).[36] The other major controversy of the century concerned predestination and also had important ecclesiological overtones, since predestination, especially the double predestination proposed by Gottschalk of Orbais, implicitly put into question the need for a mediating salvific institution like the Church itself.[37]

The canonical collection known as the "False Isidorian Decretals" is an important source for the study of Carolingian episcopal ecclesiology.[38] Written around 846–852

---

32 Jeffrey B. Russell, "Saint Boniface and the Eccentrics," *Church History* 33 (1964): 235–47.

33 Charles Mériaux, "Ordre et hiérarchie au sein du clergé rural pendant le Hau Moyen Âge," in *Hiérarchie et stratification sociale dans l'Occident médiéval (400–1100)*, ed. François Bougard, Dominique Iogna-Prat, Régine Le Jan (Turnhout, 2008), 117–36.

34 *Capitula episcoporum. Die bischöflichen Kapitularien des 9. und 10. Jahrhunderts*, ed. Peter Brommer (Turnhout, 1985).

35 Iogna-Prat, *La Maison Dieu*, 236–49.

36 Gary Macy, "The dogma of transubstantiation in the middle ages," *The Journal of Ecclesiastical History* 45 (1994): 11–31. Celia Chazelle, "Exegesis in the Ninth-Century Eucharistic Controversy," in *The Study of the Bible in the Carolingian Era*, ed. Celia Chazelle, Burton Van Name Edwards (Turnhout, 2003), 167–87; Giulio D'Onofrio, *Storia della teologia nel Medioevo*, 3 vols. (Casale Monferrato, 2003), 2:83–94; Alain Boureau, "Visions of God," in *The Cambridge History of Christianity c. 600-c. 1100*, ed. Thomas F. X. Noble, Julia M. H. Smith (Cambridge, 2008), 503–4; Joseph Goering, "The Invention of Transubstantiation," *Traditio* 46 (1991): 147–70; Ian Christopher Levy, Gary Macy, Kristen Van Ausdall, *A Companion to the Eucharist in the Middle Ages* (Leiden, 2012).

37 Gillian R. Evans, "The grammar of predestination in the ninth century," *Journal of Theological Studies* 33 (1982): 134–45; Peter Von Moos, "Le secret de la prédestination," in *Il Segreto nel Medioevo. Potere, Scienza e Cultura*, ed. Agostino Paravicini Bagliani, Francesco Santi, *Micrologus* 13 (Firenze, 2006), 9–40 (online version accessed April 22, 2019 from *Reti Medievali*, www.rmoa.unina.it/2208/); Klaus Schatz, "Der Beitrag des Johannes Scottus Eriugena zum Prädestinationsstreit," in *Die Iren und Europa in frühen Mittelalten*, ed. Heinz Löwe (Stuttgart, 1982), 819–65; Gangolf Schrimpf, "Die ethischen Implikationen der Auseinandersetzung zwischen Hraban und Gottschalk um die Prädestinationslehre," *Archiv für Geschichte der Philosophie* 68 (1986): 153–73.

38 *Capitularia spuria. Canones ecclesiastici. Bullae pontifium*, ed. Georg Heinrich Pertz, MGH LL 2/2

near Reims, the *Decretals* aimed at strengthening the position of bishops against the pressures from secular authorities, but also from archbishops,[39] appealing to the higher authority of Roma.[40] In the long term they would be important tools for the construction of papal monarchy, especially during the Gregorian Reform.

The division of the Carolingian Empire in 843 did not disturb the basic premises of the government of Church and kingdom: the Carolingian kings in their kingdoms remained as head of their churches. But before the partition of the kingdom, from the reign of Louis the Pious onwards, this situation began to be questioned by an "episcopal party," whose chief representative was Jonas of Orleans. This does not mean that the episcopate was a coherent and homogeneous group looking to impose episcopal rights over lay powers; most of the bishops took sides depending on their interests and those of their kin.[41] Instead, we are here in the presence of the emergence of an independent Episcopal ecclesiology.

The ruler, the *rector ecclesiae*, became *filius ecclesiae*. Although he was still considered a partner in the construction of the Church, it also meant that some bishops considered him no longer the head of the Church.[42] From the years 850–880 a clericalization of the ecclesiological discourse took place, at a time when we see the disappearance of eulogies and biographical texts aimed at exalting the sovereign and the emergence of coronation *ordines*. This shows the transition from a notion of rulership grounded on the sovereign king as lieutenant of Christ to a ritualized kingship under clerical ward[43] with a manifest aim of restraining Christian kingship using elements like law and liturgy—as Janet Nelson showed in several papers—[44] or admonition—as Mayke De Jong indicated.[45] There was also a visible change from synods summoned by kings, during the times of Charlemagne and Louis the Pious, to synods summoned by the king with the collaboration of bishops during Charles the Bald's kingship.[46]

(1837). The most complete work on this subject remains: Horst Fuhrmann, *Einfluß und Verbreitung der pseudoisidorischen Fälschungen. Von ihrem Auftauchen bis in die neuere Zeit*, 3 vols. (Stuttgart, 1972–1974).

39 The settlement of an archbishopric *ordo* seeking to submit the bishops to its authority is one of the outstanding church developments of the Carolingian period; see Steffen Patzold, "Eine Hierarchie im Wandel: die Ausbildung einer Metropolitanordnung im Frankenreich des 8. und 9. Jahrhunderts," in *Hiérarchie et stratification sociale dans l'Occident médiéval (400–1100)*, ed. François Bougard, Dominique Iogna-Prat, Régine Le Jan (Turnhout, 2008), 161–84.

40 Peter R. McKeon, *Hincmar of Laon and Carolingian Politics* (Chicago, 1978).

41 Bührer-Thierry, "Épiscopat et royauté."

42 Iogna-Prat, *La Maison Dieu*, 150–52.

43 Iogna-Prat, *La Maison Dieu*, 147; Geneviève Bührer-Thierry, "L'épiscopat en Francie orientale et occidentale à la fin du IXe siècle: Substitution ou soutien du pouvoir royal?," in *La royauté et les élites dans l'Europe carolingienne (du début du IXe siècle aux envierons de 920)*, ed. Régine Le Jan (Lille, 1998), 347–64.

44 Nelson, "Kingship," 133–171; Nelson, "National synods," 239–57.

45 Mayke de Jong, "Admonitio and criticism of the ruler at the court of Louis the Pious," in *La Culture du Haut Moyen Âge: une question d'élites?*, ed. François Bougard, Régine Le Jan, Rosamond McKitterick (Turnhout, 2009), 315–38.

46 Nelson, "National synods," 254–55; Wilfried Hartmann, "Eliten auf Synoden, besonders in der

In this context Carolingian monarchs were still likened to king David, but from the middle of the ninth century onwards, David became not only the powerful king chosen and anointed by God, but also represents the sinner who murdered Uriah and was rebuked by the prophet Nathan.[47] Louis the Pious suffered the indignity of losing his throne and being compelled to submit to a humiliating penance by a group of bishops. A few years later, the ninth century would witness a steady ecclesiastical pressure on kings looking to recover or emancipate church property in secular possession.[48] This pressure was also apparent in the legal collection of Benedict Levita, a compilation of imperial and royal edicts aimed at counteracting the misuse of ecclesiastical resources.[49]

Papal Ecclesiology

The rise of the Pippinids to power and the conquest of the Empire were contemporary with a special moment for the papacy, unique in Western history. It was the time when the Roman See affirmed itself as a spiritual monarchy. This implies not only the papacy's claim of superiority over other spiritual authorities of the Latin Church (the other bishops and archbishops), but also the construction of a true territorial state in central Italy under papal government: "it is the divine fixed here below as an instance of power."[50]

When Roma was abandoned by the imperial administration, the pope took over the government of the city. This meant that Roman bureaucracy was subsumed under episcopal bureaucracy and, therefore, there was a deep coincidence between sacred and secular administrations. This happened in many western cities, but Roma was a special case.

The prestige that emanated from Roma as former imperial capital and See of Peter did not prevent hostile movements coming from Byzantine and Lombard powers. But during the late seventh and the middle of the eighth centuries, there was a vacuum of power in central Italy filled by the aristocracy of Lazio.[51] This vacuum allowed the pope to gain control over central Italy, since the papacy was the most important institution of the Roman elite. This situation, which in the long term lasted until the mid-nineteenth

---

Karolingerzeit," in *Théorie et pratiques des élites au Haut Moyen Âge*, ed. François Bougard, Hans-Werner Goetz, Régine Le Jan (Turnhout, 2011), 352–54.

47 Lawrence Nees, "Carolingian Art and Politics," in *The Gentle Voices of Teachers: Aspects of Learning in the Carolingian Age*, ed. Richard E. Sullivan (Columbus, 1995), 202–6; Dominique Alibert, "Pécheur, avare et injuste: remarques sur la figure du mauvais roi à l'époque carolingienne," in *Le monde carolingien: Bilan, perspectives, champs de recherche*, ed. Wojciech Falkowski, Yves Sassier (Turnhout, 2009), 121–42.

48 Gaëlle Calvet-Marcadé, "Les clercs carolingiens et la défense des terres d'église (Francie du nord, IXe siècle)" (PhD diss., Université Paris I Panthéon–Sorbonne, 2012).

49 Janet L. Nelson, "Charles the Bald and the church in town and countryside," *Studies in Church History* 16 (1979): 103–18, reprinted in Janet L. Nelson, *Politics and Ritual in Early Medieval Europe* (London, 1986), 75–90.

50 *C'est le divin qu'on essaie de fixer ici-bas comme instance de pouvoir.* Cited from Iogna-Prat, *La Maison Dieu*, 155.

51 Noble, *The Republic of St. Peter*.

century, did not happen in any other place in Europe, at least not over such a long period and in such a prestigious bishopric.[52]

Even at the height of imperial power, Carolingian capability to act in the territories of central Italy was very limited and the papacy, as head of the Roman elite, competed for control of the region against other regional aristocracies, with little intervention from the Franks.[53] The need to defend Roma against the Saracens was another crucial element that contributed to the elaboration of papal ecclesiology. This situation forced John VIII to construct a wall and a fleet, and allowed him to identify the defence of the dependent territories of the Holy See with the *Defensio totius Christianitatis*.[54]

The *Constitutum Constantini*, the infamous "Donation of Constantine," is another example of papal ecclesiology in the Carolingian period.[55] This text aimed to establish the right of the pope to both religious and temporal government over territories vaguely defined, but likely to be those confirmed or assigned by Pepin the Short.[56]

Leo III's coronation of Charlemagne, the architectural ambitions of Pascal I,[57] some epistles of John VIII,[58] and the *Constitutum Constantini* are all expressions of the self-consciousness of the papal monarchy seeking to identify Christianity with the See of Peter and also claiming the right to rule over it.

The Monastic Model

Monasteries were central to early medieval society and to Carolingian rule. Monasteries were religious centres containing holy men, living or dead. They were also cultural and educational foundations and they even had some of the administrative functions that

---

52 An interesting and fairly well-documented case of a bishopric controlling secular and ecclesiastical power over the hinterland of its see with complete sovereignty is that of the bishops of Auxerre, before the conquest of Burgundy by Charles Martel; see Yves Sassier, "Les caroligiens et Auxerre," in *L'École Carolingienne d'Auxerre. De Murethach a Remi. 830–908*, ed. Dominique Iogna-Prat, Colette Jeudy, Guy Lobrichon, (Paris, 1991), 21–36.

53 Costambeys recently studied the case of the elite in the region of Farfa Abbey. He states that Carolingian interventions do not always seek to defend Roman interests, but to keep a balance of power between the Roman elite and the elites of other regions, against papal interests if necessary. He even denies the status of state to the Republic of St. Peter: Marios Costambeys, *Power and Patronage in the Early Medieval Italy: Local Society, Italian Politics, and the Abbey of Farfa, c.700–900* (Cambridge, 2007).

54 Iogna-Prat, *La Maison Dieu*, 199–203.

55 There were always doubts about the Roman origin of the *Constitutum Constantini*. Nevertheless, this chapter follows Furhmann's traditional thesis, since the hypothesis of the Frankish origin of the text, as presented by Johannes Fried, has generated more controversy than certitude. *Constitutum Constantini*, ed. Horst Fuhrmann, MGH Fontes iuri 10 (1968); Johannes Fried, *"Donation of Constantine" and "Constitutum Constantini." The Misinterpretation of a Fiction and Its Original Meaning* (Berlin, 2007).

56 Iogna-Prat, *La Maison Dieu*, 167.

57 Caroline J. Goodson, *The Rome of Pope Paschal I. Papal power, urban renovation, church rebuilding and relic translation, 817–824* (Cambridge, 2010).

58 *Epistolae Karolini aevi (VI). Hincmari archiepiscopi Remensis epistolae*, ed. Ernst Perels, MGH Epp. 8 (1985).

belonged to the city in Antiquity.[59] The ascetic way of Christian life preached by monks had permeated the entire religious life, not only inside the cloister but also beyond their walls,[60] and to some Carolingian authors it represented the ideal church of apostolic times.[61] This situation makes the study of a specific monastic ecclesiology quite difficult, since the whole Christian discourse is tinged with asceticism. Nevertheless, it is still possible to discuss the existence of a specific monastic ecclesiology by using a *corpus* of texts that have been poorly studied so far, the exegetical texts of monastic origin.[62] The existence of this monastic ecclesiology as part of Carolingian ideological discourse is additionally important because one of its by-products was the tri-functional scheme of society.

Contrary to Duby's idea that the appearance of the famous scheme of three orders of society (*oratores*, *bellatores*, *laboratores*) during the eleventh century was a product of the transformations around the year 1000,[63] Dominique Iogna-Prat and Edmond Ortigues have shown that this kind of representation of society already existed in the ninth century in the *Commentary on Saint Paul's Epistle to the Romans* of Haimo, monk and biblical exegete from the monastery of St. Germaine of Auxerre.[64] The three orders model proposed by Haimo seems *a priori* clear but there are some ambiguities. One in particular interests us in this chapter: who are the *oratores*? All the clergy? Just the priests? Or only the bishops? The monks themselves, perhaps? This is not clear in the *Commentary on Romans*. The study of other texts by the same author allows us to suggest that according to him, monks (and in particular those dedicated to biblical exegesis)

59 Madge M. Hildebrandt, *The External School in Carolingian Society* (Leiden, 1992); Matthew Innes, *State and Society in the Early Middle Ages. The Middle Rhine Valley, 400–1000* (Cambridge, 2000); Mayke de Jong, "Carolingian monasticism: the power of prayer," in *The New Cambridge Medieval History, 2, c. 700-c. 900*, ed. Rosamond McKitterick, (Cambridge, 1995), 622–53; Otto Gerhard Oexle, "Mönchtum und Hierarchie im Okzident," in *Hiérarchie et stratification sociale dans l'Occident médiéval (400–1100)*, ed. François Bougard, Dominique Iogna-Prat, Régine Le Jan (Turnhout, 2008), 185–204.

60 Mary Alberi, "'The Better Paths of Wisdom': Alcuin's Monastic 'True Philosophy' and the Wordly Court," *Speculum* 76 (2001): 896–910; Thomas F.X. Noble, "The monastic ideal as a model for empire: the case of Louis the pious," *Revue Bénédictine* 86 (1976): 235–50.

61 Patzold, "Hraban, Gottschalk und der Traktat," 105–18.

62 On the use of biblical exegesis as a source for Carolingian ecclesiology, see Sumi Shimahara, "L'éxégèse biblique et les élites: qui son les recteurs de l'Église à l'époque carolingienne?," in *La Culture du Haut Moyen Âge: une question d'élites?*, ed. François Bougard, Régine Le Jan, Rosamond McKitterick (Turnhout, 2009), 201–15.

63 George Duby, *Les trois ordres ou l'imaginaire du féodalisme* (Paris, 1978).

64 Dominique Iogna-Prat, "Le 'baptême' du schéma des trois ordres fonctionnels: l'apport de l'école d'Auxerre dans la seconde moitié du IXe siècle," *Annales. Économies, Sociétés, Civilisations* 41, no. 1 (1986): 101–26; Edmond Ortigues, "L'Elaboration de la théorie des trois ordres chez Haymon d'Auxerre," *Francia* 14 (1987): 17–43; Edmond Ortigues, "Haymon d'Auxerre, théoricien des trois ordres," in *L'École Carolingienne d'Auxerre. De Murethach a Remi. 830–908*, ed. Dominique Iogna-Prat, Colette Jeudy, Guy Lobrichon (Paris, 1991), pp. 181–227; Goetz offers strong criticism of the three estates scheme as a hierarchical system: Hans-Werner Goetz, "Les ordines dans la théorie médiévale de la société: uns système hiérarchique," in *Hiérarchie et stratification sociale dans l'Occident médiéval (400–1100)*, ed. François Bougard, Dominique Iogna-Prat, Régine Le Jan (Turnhout, 2008), 221–36.

replaced the prophets from the Old Testament (whose position in Israel is as ambiguous as that of the Carolingian monks, since they were simultaneously inside and outside the world, that is, society). They had originally been lay Christians living ordinary lives but became mostly clerics in Carolingian times.[65] But they could consider themselves chosen for salvation because of their penitential condition, making them the true moral guides for Christian people's salvation, above kings, emperors, or bishops.[66]

When Heiric, another monk from St. Germain of Auxerre and Haimo's student, developed the scheme of his master in his account of the miracles of St. Germanus of Auxerre,[67] he stated that monks were the true *oratores*, replacing priests and bishops.[68] Heiric's outlook may be explained by the primarily monastic reception of the writings of Pseudo-Dionysius, fundamental for the construction of the hierarchical world-view. In those texts monks were at the lowest level of the hierarchy, but they embodied the perfect philosopher.[69] The tradition asserting monastic oversight of secular and spiritual power is also present in the texts of Odo of Cluny, whose writings were fundamental to Cluniac spirituality and, by extension, to the latter development of Benedictine monasticism.[70] But we do not have to infer that there was a "natural" rivalry between monks and secular clergy. There were many cases of bishops becoming abbots and vice versa. Monastic and secular clergy were at some levels easily interchangeable.

Conclusions

The Carolingian Empire was born out of military conquest by the Franks under the command of the Pippinid dynasty. Its historical development included the final disappearance of the political and religious order of Late Antiquity and the unification of much of Latin Christendom under a single "state." It also included the spread of Christianity over former pagan territories. Once Frankish rule was established, it was necessary to find a unifying ideology. This ideology was found in Roman Christianity and it was enriched with contributions coming from Gallo-Frankish, Lombard, Visigoth, and Insular Christian traditions. The definition of the one and only kind of Christianity also led to a struggle against regional and syncretic forms of Christianity and to the concentration of

65 Otto Gerhard Oexle, "Mönchtum und Hierarchie im Okzident," in *Hiérarchie et stratification sociale dans l'Occident médiéval (400–1100)*, ed. François Bougard, Dominique Iogna-Prat, Régine Le Jan (Turnhout, 2008), 199–201.

66 On this issue, see my own doctoral research: Alfonso Hernández Rodríguez, "Antropología y eclesiología en la exégesis bíblica carolingia según según *el comentario al profeta Oseas* de Haimón de Auxerre" (PhD diss., Universidad de Buenos Aires, 2009). Available online at http://repositorio. filo.uba.ar/handle/filodigital/1398.

67 Heiric, "Miracula sancti Germani," in *Patrologiae cursus completus*, ed. Jacques-Paul Migne, 221 vols. (Paris, 1879) 124: cols. 1208–1270.

68 Iogna-Prat, *La Maison Dieu*, 227.

69 Iogna-Prat, "Penser l'Église," 72–73.

70 For the reception of the monastic *Auxerroise* ecclesiology in Odo of Cluny see Isabelle Rosé, *Construire une société seigneuriale. Itinéraire et ecclésiologie de l'Abbé Odon de Cluny (fin du IXe–milieu du Xe siècle)* (Turnhout, 2008).

"the sacred," in the words of Peter Brown, in a hierarchical institution: the Church. This also meant leaving the monopoly of religion in the hands of individuals who formed the apex of the pyramid of the Church. But to make this possible it was necessary to clarify this ecclesiastical hierarchy, to establish an upward path from the mundane and secular to the heavenly and spiritual plane. It was a path that could only be traversed through church doors and under the guidance of the clergy. Three things made this development possible: the establishment of the temple as the only possible place of worship; clerical control of that space; and the construction of a spiritual hierarchical scale, using neo-Platonic texts of Pseudo-Dionysius as ideological weapons.

In ecclesiological terms this process involved the final separation of secular power from sacred power. In the long term, under its influence the initial Constantinian ecclesiology became ideologically unfeasible, centred in an ecclesiological model led by a secular ruler, which I prefer to call Caesaro–Davidic instead of Caesaro–Papist. Henceforth, kings and emperors and other powerful laymen would have *de facto* control over the churches in their territories, but they would have lost the ideological battle for the government of the Church. It was also the defeat of secular power to control Christianity as a whole.

Ecclesiological models would ultimately be headed by future religious leaders. In those models, laymen would play a secondary role, based on the support or protection of the Church, whereas the clergy would have the most important task, that of leading the people of God to salvation. This situation left lay secular power at pains to elaborate a secular ideology in a Christian society.

Chapter 5

SPIRITUAL AND TEMPORAL POWER IN RAYMOND LLULL'S *ARBOR SCIENTIAE*

CHIARA MELATINI

RAMON LLULL HAD a complex and multi-faceted thirteenth-century intellectual profile, which gave him an eminent position in the cultural history of the Late Middle Ages, so much so that his scholastic accolade was *Doctor Illuminatus*. He was simultaneously a poet who experienced court life, a man of letters attentive to social issues, a philosopher, and Christian theologian who tried by means of reason to prove the truth of faith, a mystic, a Christ apologist, a scientific writer, and an encyclopaedist who enquired into the laws of creation. Mixing these profiles, he was able to suggest a specific way to understand and promote the Christian ideology adapted to contemporary human society through what he called the "Tree of Science."[1]

The Importance of the *Arbor scientiae* within Llull's Literary Output

The events in Ramon Llull's life are suffused with his strong character, his constant involvement in the frenetic evangelization activity which took him travelling untiringly around the Mediterranean, prompted him to form personal bonds with popes and sovereigns, and generated an extraordinary volume of work (around two hundred and fifty writings are mentioned) in Latin, Catalan, and Arabic. In the face of such a vast volume of work critics generally identify a series of works considered especially representative of the author's thought and focus on them, thus applying a selection process in the light of the fact that it would otherwise be problematical to deal with the full range of ideological and thematic issues appearing in such a rich corpus. This explains why Llull's *Arbor scientiae* has not been accorded the attention paid, for example, to *Libre de contemplació, Libre d'Evast e d'Aloma e de Blanquerna, Doctrina pueril, Libre de les meravelles*, his work promoting the Crusades and, his work on logic, the *Ars magna*. The presence, however, in European libraries of a considerable number of manuscript versions of *Arbor* (in addition to Latin, versions in exist in, sometimes incomplete, Catalan, French, Castilian, and even Hebrew) is indicative of the fact that in the past this work must have reached a wide readership.[2]

---

1 Another work, on the same subject and by the same author, can be seen in: "La teoria politica dell'Arbor Scientiae di Ramon Lull," *Picenum Seraphicum: Rivista di studi storici e francescani*, 30 (2017): 8–46.

2 For a more thorough understanding of the manuscript tradition of the *Arbor scientiae*, see Ramon Llull, *Arbor Scientiae*, ed. Pere Villalba i Varneda, Raimundi Lulli Opera latina / Corpus

---

Chiara Melatini (melatini.chiara@gmail.com) is Researcher at the Università degli Studi di Macerata, Italy.

Written during a stay in Roma in 1295–1296, *Arbor scientiae* was intended as a compendium of the universal science contained in the *Ars magna*, Llull's greatest work. In its constituent sixteen books (or *arbores*) Llull's intention was to enquire into the general principles regulating both earthly and divine worlds which, in accordance with a commonly shared medieval notion, responded to a unitary vision of an ordered cosmos structured according to eternal laws dictated by God.

This present study looks at *Arbor scientiae* on the basis of its being in no way marginal to Llull's more famous work to the extent that I believe it gives us an insight into the writer's stance on a central issue in medieval political thought, namely the relationship between *regnum* and *ecclesia*, in other words between temporal and spiritual power. It is an aspect of Llull's thought which has not yet been studied in sufficient depth despite its interest and multi-faceted character.

A study of the seventh and eighth books of *Arbor scientiae*, namely *Arbor imperialis* and *Arbor apostolicalis*, two brief treatises on the roles and functions of sovereigns and popes respectively, is an opportunity to analyse and study in depth the political themes of *regnum* and *ecclesia* because in them Llull theorizes the ideal form of government of both Empire and Church from the perspective of the implementation of divine plans for a single civil and religious entity.[3]

Papal and Sovereign Power Compared

Arbor scientiae is full of symbolism. The work develops according to its own internal symmetry and thus the order in which the various books are organized takes on a precise meaning which is worthy of analysis for a more holistic vision of the work and its single parts. Pring-Mill has brought to light the logical connections between *Arbor*'s contents and the numerology within it;[4] of its sixteen books,[5] the last two—*Arbor exem-*

Christianorum: Continuatio Mediaevalis 24–26, 3 vols. (Turnhout, 2000), 1:14*–19*; Chiara Melatini, "L'Arbor Scientiae: un'opera 'italiana' di Lullo. La tradizione manoscritta latina," in *Il lullismo in Italia: itinerario storico-critico. Volume miscellaneo in occasione del VII centenario della morte di Raimondo Lullo*, ed. Marta Romano, Francesca Chimento (Palermo, 2015).

3 At the beginning of the *Arbor*, Llull gives the reader a brief description of the various issues addressed in the individual books. He writes about the *Arbor imperialis* and the *Arbor apostolicalis* respectively: Llull, *Arbor Scientiae*, 8–9, lines 111–16. Jürgen Miethke, "Die Arbor imperialis des Ramon Lull," in *Arbor Scientiae, der Baum des Wissens von Ramon Llull: Akten des internationale Kongreßes aus Anlaß des 40-jährigen Jubiläums des Raimundus Lullus, Instituts der Universität Freiburg*, ed. Fernando Dominguez Reboiras, Pere Villalba i Varneda, Peter Walter (Turnhout, 2002), 175–96; Francesco Santi, "*Arbor apostolicalis*: la vita dell'organismo apostolico," in *Arbor Scientiae, der Baum des Wissens von Ramon Llull: Akten des internationale Kongreßes aus Anlaß des 40-jährigen Jubiläums des Raimundus Lullus, Instituts der Universität Freiburg*, ed. Fernando Dominguez Reboiras, Pere Villalba i Varneda, Peter Walter (Turnhout, 2002), 197–205.

4 Robert Pring-Mill, "The role of numbers in the structure of the *Arbor scientiae*," in *Arbor Scientiae, der Baum des Wissens von Ramon Llull: Akten des internationale Kongreßes aus Anlaß des 40-jährigen Jubiläums des Raimundus Lullus, Instituts der Universität Freiburg*, ed. Fernando Dominguez Reboiras, Pere Villalba i Varneda, Peter Walter (Turnhout, 2002), 35–63.

5 In order, the books are: 1. *Arbor elementalis*, 2. *Arbor vegetalis*, 3. *Arbor sensualis*, 4. *Arbor imagi-*

plificalis and *quaestionalis*—play an auxiliary role and do not thus constitute an independent argument, but simply rework the material of the first fourteen books by means of *exempla* and *quaestiones*. Given this, the presence of *Arbor imperialis* at the seventh level and *Arbor apostolicalis* at the eighth level must perform a specific function. The following is a possible classification: the first part of the tree of science (from book 1 to book 7) examines themes related to earthly life, while *Arbor apostolicalis*, on the other hand, marks the passage to higher matters concerning spiritual life and celestial bodies. The last two books, *exemplificalis* and *quaestionalis*, analyse the overall contents of the work in greater depth. Pring-Mill also proposes a further reading: he sees *Arbor moralis* (bk. 6) and the two trees which follow on from it—the subjects of this analysis—as a compact triad deliberately designed by the writer to explore the three levels of man's "government" in this world. It is the task of the moral tree to analyse self-control or rather "self-governance" (using an expression of Pring-Mill's):[6] every individual must conform to the dictates of a solid and upright conscience. Rising a level, *Arbor imperialis* shows the importance of secular government founded on the loyalty and justice of the Christian "emperor or prince" (*imperator sive princeps*) and the rectitude of those working for him to ensure community peace and prosperity. Lastly, spiritual power, presented in *Arbor apostolicalis*, occupies the highest rung of this ladder with the task of governing the Church. In this way ecclesiastical power takes on a pre-eminent role in the structure of the work.

Llull's intention is to construct a sort of brief treatise structured using the symbolism of a tree on the overall duties of prince and pope and thus of the government of the public sphere and the Church, supplying general guidelines which can then be concretely applied to specific cases.

Princes must be the ultimate examples of uprightness and morality and represent the tangible culmination of love for the Creator. If the purpose for which man was created was to love and serve God, anyone not bringing his or her existence in line with the teaching of the Gospels will not be accepted into the Kingdom of Heaven. *Arbor imperialis*, in order to be able to transmit "the knowledge and the way to govern people and the kingdom in peace,"[7] the final objective for which it was conceived, must have deep roots in a solid ethical system[8] on which to base a stable *regimen* working to serve God and the common good. Right from the outset Llull defines a sovereign's functions in this world: *Imperator et princeps est imago Dei in terra*.[9] As archetype of perfection, God is always

---

nalis, 5. *Arbor humanalis*, 6. *Arbor moralis*, 7. *Arbor imperialis*, 8. *Arbor apostolicalis*, 9. *Arbor caelestialis*, 10. *Arbor angelicalis*, 11. *Arbor aeviternalis*, 12. *Arbor maternalis*, 13. *Arbor Iesu Christi*, 14. *Arbor divinalis*, 15. *Arbor exemplificalis*, 16. *Arbor quaestionalis*.

6 Pring-Mill, "The role of numbers," 48.

7 *Cognitio et modus ad regendum in pace populum et regnum.* Cited from Llull, *Arbor Scientiae*, 333, lines 17–18.

8 These are: *bonitates, magnitudines, durationes, potestates, sapientiae, voluntates, virtutes, veritates, delectationes, concordantiae, principia, media, fines, maioritates, aequalitates et minoritates* (Llull, *Arbor Scientiae*, 333–34, lines 1–5).

9 Llull, *Arbor Scientiae*, 334, lines 17–18. The sovereign is re-defined as "*imago Dei*" also in *Arbor*

presented as the ideal model on which both the figure of the king and all manifestations of *potestas regia* must be inspired. Llull's *Libre de les bèsties* also offers a virtually identical explanation of the role of the prince: "that holy man [...] asked the king what king means in this world; and the king said: King is established in this world as a meaning of God."[10]

In both cases, kings reflect divine *podestas* in this world and, as figures at the apex of the social scale, their conduct should also theoretically be as far as possible in line with the virtues of the Creator. In the definition put forward to princes in *Arbor imperialis*, Llull clearly identifies the sphere of influence of princely powers, circumscribed "to govern the moral properties of the material reality of the prince's subjects,"[11] thus avoiding any potential misunderstandings. His concern is to guarantee good government and the utmost morality among subjects. Thus a clear dividing line is drawn right from the start between the roles of emperors and popes: the former is entrusted with good management in the temporal sphere, and the latter with care of souls as specified in *Arbor apostolicalis*: "It is the universal Tree that governs things and the structure of the spiritual sphere."[12] The figure of the *princeps* is in no way diminished, however. It is, in fact, a role corresponding to God's direct desire ("God placed him to govern")[13] and one which contributes fully to the creation of *civitas mundi*.

As a general rule, princes are to take on great responsibility for their peoples: their goodness, greatness, and are to inspire great specific goodness, greatness, and will in their people. Thus, they act "as a shepherd obligated to govern many sheep."[14] In exchange for just administration of the public sphere, the people are to accord kings honour, merit, and respect, but to ensure these kings were never to give into sycophancy leading to pride. Their humility and respect for their public roles are to safeguard them against falling into sin. *Malus princeps* is the worst evil imaginable for the realm and Llull

---

quaestionalis, *Quaestio 96: Quaestio: Princeps, quare plus honorem diligit quam denarios? Solutio: Princeps dixit, quod ipse per honorem magis erat imago Dei quam per denarius* (Llull, *Arbor Scientiae*, 1064).

10 *Aquell sant hom [...] demanà al rei cual cosa significa rei en est món; e el rei dix: Rei és establir en est món a significança de Déu.* Cited from Ramon Llull, *Libre de les bèsties*, Obres essencials (Barcelona, 1957), 1, chap. 40. He also states in *Doctrina Pueril*: "God has a more earthly lord between him and you: and do you know why? Because loving and honouring and fearing your earthly lord, you are loving and honouring God and that you fear his power" (*Deus ha mes senyor terrenal entre sí metex e tu: ¿e sabs per que? Per so que amant e honrant e tement ton senyor terrenal, sies amador e honrador de Deu e que temes son poder*). Cited from Ramon Llull, *Doctrina pueril*, Obres de Ramon Llull, ed. Mateu Obrador i Bennàssar, 5 vols. (Palma, 1986), 1:150. Pedro Ramis i Serra, "Libre de les bèsties: el príncipe y la sociedad," *Studia lulliana* 31 (1991): 149–65; Francesca Chimento, "Il felix e la teoria politica di Raimondo Lullo: spunti di riflessione," in *El pensamiento politico en la Edad Media*, ed. Pedro Roche Arnas (Madrid, 2010), 391–402.

11 *Ad regendum bonitates morales rerum corporalium sui populi.* Cited from Llull, *Arbor Scientiae*, 333, line 18.

12 *Est arbor generalis ad res et ordines spirituales.* Cited from Llull, *Arbor Scientiae*, 375, lines 4–5.

13 *Deus ipsum posuit ad regendum.* Cited from Llull, *Arbor Scientiae*, 334, line 22.

14 *Sicut unus pastor obligatus ad regendum plures oves.* Cited from Llull, *Arbor Scientiae*, lines 25–26.

insisted on highlighting the serious damage which could be incurred by an unworthy sovereign as a veritable cancer within the community blocking its very life blood. Above all, his concerns stemmed from the knowledge that "in the bad prince the purpose and completion of his people get lost."[15]

Good sovereigns, on the other hand, are associated with respect for the wellbeing of the community and all their actions are to be for the public good. The best way to bring this about is through the correct administration of justice by kings with the objective of combating subversion by individuals' private *utilitas*. Justice, the first of the *Arbor*'s branches, is to guarantee peace for the people.[16] It is to be the result of the joint action of the king and other functionaries of the realm and implemented by means of *prudentia, fortitudine et aliis virtutibus.*

Llull argued for a close interrelation between popular morals and exemplary conduct by the *princeps*. A sovereign's *flores* are to be more virtuous than those of any other component of the realm and, on the other hand, *malus princeps* generates *turpes flores* (that is, bad government and unjust laws), corrupting popular morals. For the people to emulate the conduct of their sovereigns, they have to demonstrate their virtue and commitment to governing the public sphere well at all times. It is thus unacceptable, in the eyes of this *Doctor Illuminatus*, that kings should spend their time in laziness or idle pursuits. Kings must not "be negligent, neither sleep a lot, nor hunt, nor be inactive."[17]

The writer underlines the capital importance of a sovereign's virtue: the whole structure of temporal power is built around the absolute moral rectitude of the *princeps* who, as image of God on earth, is to govern his people by means of his virtues. Civil society mirrors royal behaviour and for this reason the greatest attention is to be paid to the choice of ruler. Thus Llull concludes his brief treatise on princes in this way: "there is no other tree that makes such a bad, dangerous, harmful fruit, from which so much evil arises, as that of the tree of the bad prince."[18]

Llull dedicates an equally meticulous analysis to the figure of the pope in *Arbor apostolicalis* in which, to ensure its validity and theological foundations, he brings together

---

15 *In malo principe perditur finis et complementum sui populi.* Cited from Llull, *Arbor Scientiae*, 733. The following are some proverbs drawn from the same section: (5 "Stupidity of a bad prince took and jailed the wisdom of his people" (*Stultitia mali principis cepit et incarceravit sapientiam populi sui*); 8."The mouth of a bad prince has no shame in lying" (*Os mali principis verecundiam mentiendi non habuit*); 9. "Vainglory of a prince breeds work in his kingdom" (*Vana gloria principis laborem in suo regno seminavit*); 10. "The evil prince gives his people a confused conscience" (*Malus princeps confusam conscientiam sui populi facit*); 13. "Once a prince starts doing bad things, his people soon follows" (*Incepit princeps malefacere, cuius populus ipsam sequebatur*)).

16 Llull, *Arbor Scientiae*, 876: ("Peace for the people comes from the king's justice" (*In iustitia regis est pax sui populi*)) and it is repeated on p. 1062: *Iustitia non consentit, quod plus bonum speciale quam bonum publicum diligatur*).

17 *Esse negligens, nec multum dormire, nec venari, nec quiescere.* Cited from Llull, *Arbor Scientiae*, 358, lines 18–19.

18 *Non est alia arbor, quae faciat ita malum fructum, ita periculosum, ita damnosum, nec a qua tantum de malo veniat, sicut de arbore mali principis.* Cited from Llull, *Arbor Scientiae*, 360, lines 52–54.

and reworks the material dealt with previously in *Liber de sancto Spiritu* (1274–1283), *Liber de quattuordecim articulis sacrosantae Romanae Catholicae Fidei* (1283–1285) and the contemporary *Liber de articulis fidei* (part of *Liber de apostrophe* sent to Boniface VIII).[19] The spiritual premises underlying the whole apostolic organism make up the tree's roots, branches, leaves, and flowers. Trunks (popes) require robust roots on which their greatness is based.

Cardinal and theological virtues are the principles on which the Church rests and which guarantee papal solidity and moral rectitude. As for princes, justice is the cardinal virtue guiding the actions of popes and guarantees the Church's peace and internal harmony. Through justice, Peter's successors must avoid the disputes which can arise in the heart of ecclesiastical institutions; they must become guarantors of justice among the faithful. The expression "Papal justice should be the medium between God and his people"[20] fundamentally implies that popes must act as mediators between Heaven and Earth, between God and his people, and that by means of this Christians can be transformed by divine love and teachings. For this reason, virtues in general, and justice in particular, must take root in the soul of the head of the Church; in the absence of this, divine virtues will be unable to filter down to the faithful due to papal vice and sin. As with kings, as ultimate expressions of *persona communis*, popes are obliged by their role to act for the public good because it is for this purpose that they were appointed.[21] In parallel, in the *Arbor imperialis*, the prince also possesses a general power: "Power belongs to the prince because power is an instrument of his office. Power is such a general instrument of the prince, just as the hammer is a general instrument for a blacksmith for making a sword and a nail."[22]

In the text the adjectives *communis* and *generalis* identify figures performing a public role, a function within the governing mechanisms of the realm and the Church, individuals who influence—or rather determine with their ethical behaviour and work— the attitudes of *particolaris* subjects whether *civis* or *fidelis*.

As vicar of St. Peter (*vicarius Petri*),[23] the Pope's duty is to match both Peter's moral greatness and, above all, his profound faith, the virtues for which Christ chose him as his successor.[24] On the faith of the pope depends the faith of the whole community. The

---

19 Llull, *Arbor Scientiae*, 123*–124*.

20 *Iustitia papae debet esse medium inter Deum et suum populum.* Cited from Llull, *Arbor Scientiae*, 376, lines 26–27.

21 See Llull, *Arbor Scientiae*, line 31.

22 *Ad principem pertinet potestas, quia potestas est instrumentum sui officii. Et est potestas ita generale instrumentum principis, sicut martellus qui est instrumentum generale fabro, ut gladium et clavum faciat.* Cited from Llull, *Arbor Scientiae*, 347, lines 84–87.

23 See Antoni Oliver, "El papa 'vicarius Petri' en Ramón Llull: origen, vicisitudes y justificación del título papal," *Estudios lulianos* 3 (1959): 53–58.

24 Llull, *Arbor Scientiae*, 379, lines 47–49, 379 ("It is necessary that the Pope has a huge faith, because St. Peter's faith was big. And it is necessary that the Pope has also a huge faith because the people respond to his faith" (*Et oportet, quod papa habeat magnam fidem, quia fides sancti Petri fuit magna. Et oportet, quod papa ita magnam fidem habeat, quod fidei sui populi respondeat*)).

head of the Church's love for God is made even steadier by the virtue of *fortitudo*. It is precisely this virtue that enables popes—who had received the ancient Roman Empire as a gift—to work to convert non-believers with the support of temporal power. It is the pope's task to defend the Christian faith against the dangers represented by infidels—mainly Muslims and Jews—and against internal divisions within the Church itself. By means of their good example, the faith of the popes is to light the way of the Christian people towards God just as the sun, receiving its light from God, illuminates it to a greater extent than the moon and the lesser stars. This light shows the way by which a holy life of contemplation and penitence is to be achieved.[25] After Peter the Apostle, bishops of Roma were to be the new shepherds of God's flock and their task is to transmit his love and faith to the Christian people in such a way as to enable them to benefit from his greatness. To make this more comprehensible to his readers Llull uses an effective image:

> As the fire that bows to the air, which has not got a great virtue like the fire, so it causes it to ascend to a higher degree, to the extent that it makes him grow in virtue. The sun does the same with the fire, because it causes it to ascend to the extent that it multiplies its heat.[26]

In this initial part of *Arbor apostolicalis*, dedicated to *radices*, the writer goes no further on all seven cardinal and theological virtues, but limits himself to applying the principles first espoused in *Arbor moralis*, solely justice and faith, in accordance with a model which can then be reworked for all other virtues. In this section of *radices* Llull condenses the principal arguments which act as the foundation for the rest of his work right from the outset. In this way, he demonstrates that the pope's task is the greatest in the world as far as the cure of souls and the defence of the Church is concerned, greater in honour than that of sovereigns despite the fact that they are *imago Dei,* as the previous *Arbor* notes. It is important to underline that this is not an attempt by Llull to espouse wholesale the hierocratic thesis previously adopted by other authors, theologians, or popes in support of *plenitudo potestatis*, which was soon to reach its apex during the dispute between Boniface VIII and Philippe IV of France. Llull was moving parallel to this struggle between the exponents of the papal and imperial causes respectively. He limits himself to registering the natural human limits of the holders of these two offices due to their shared inclination to sin and desire for glory; Llull offers a chance for redemption in the form of guidelines to ensure that the *cives–fideles* people live in peace and harmony, bringing divine plans to fruition without one power getting the upper hand over the other.

At the head of each power sphere God had placed two distinct figures and Llull thus devoted a specific treatise to each to take a closer look at their respective duties and spheres of action and define a judicial science to regulate their internal relationships.

---

25 Llull, *Arbor Scientiae*, 380, lines 92–99.

26 *Sicut ignis, qui se inclinat ad aerem, qui non est de ita magna virtute, sicut ipse est, et ipsum ascendere facit supra, in quantum in virtute ipsum maiorificat, et idem facit Sol de igne, quoniam ipsum ascendere facit, in quantum multiplicat calorem ipsius.* Cited from Llull, *Arbor Scientiae*, 380–81, lines 106–10.

Llull recognises this separation of power and clearly sets out distinct spheres of influence: the *princeps* was to rule over temporal things and the pope over spiritual matters.
On this subject we read in *Arbor imperialis*: "For this reason emperor and prince are
God's image on earth to govern the moral aspects of material affairs for their subjects,"[27]
while the pope manages the spiritual sphere.[28] Between care for souls and care of the
body, in accordance with an approach which was universally shared in the Christian
milieu, Llull recognises the primacy of saving souls but the satisfaction of material needs,
he acknowledges, is a precondition for this. Royal or imperial power is born out of God's
will, just like apostolic power, and responds to the civil community's need for wellbeing
and peace. It is, in fact, not solely by means of the contemplative and religious life that
one can love and serve the Lord, but also via everyday life in the towns and cities where
every action must be guided by feelings of mutual charity and in which individual interests must bend to the collective will. Llull reiterates a great many times in *Arbor imperialis* that the duty of a sovereign is to "govern the people and realm in peace"[29] and, as far
as possible (we read in *de fructu*), "also to worship, to understand, and to love, worship,
and serve God."[30] At heart, it is the same objective as that of the Holy Father: "Apostolic
fruit is the salvation of the people, so that God may be worshipped, understood, loved,
worshipped, and served more than any other."[31] The similarity of intention between
the two heads brings with it similarity of action. The tasks of ruling are both guided and
constantly enlightened by divine teachings and marked out by profound moral rectitude
which takes concrete form in a range of contexts.

The faith of the pope must nurture and sustain the faith of the Christian people
and Jesus Christ has made the pope shepherd of all men to show them the truth of the
gospel and to combat lies and errors.[32] Alluding to a passage from the Gospel of John

---

27 *Idcirco imperator et princeps est imago Dei in terra ad regendum bonitates morales rerum
corporalium sui populi.* Cited from Llull, *Arbor Scientiae*, 334, lines 17–18.

28 Llull, *Arbor Scientiae*, 375, lines 4–5.

29 *Regere in pace populum et regnum.* Cited from Llull, *Arbor Scientiae*, 333, line 18.

30 *Deum etiam recolere, intelligere et amare, honorare et servire.* Cited from Llull, *Arbor Scientiae*,
359, lines 3–5.

31 *Fructus apostolicalis est salvatio gentium [...], ut Deus recolatur, intelligatur, et ametur,
honoretur et ei serviatur plus quam alicui alii.* Cited from Llull, *Arbor Scientiae*, 483, lines 10–12.

32 "The faith of the Pope must be sincere, because it must be against falsehood and error. The
Lord Jesus Christ said to St. Peter: 'Peter, if you love me, feed my sheep.' And he told him a threefold
signification, because the sheep are God the Father, God the Son, and God the Holy Spirit, which are
one God, one Christ, who chose one shepherd for his sheep, and give to them the truth of faith to
eat, and with which truth they live. And in the person of St. Peter the sheep are under the care of the
faith of the Pope" (*Item fides papae debet esse vera, ut sit contra falsitatem et errorem. Et ideo dixit
dominus noster Iesu Christus ad Beatum Petrum: 'Petre, si diligis me, pasce oves meas'. Et dixit ei ter
ad significandum, quod oves sunt Dei Patris, et Dei Filii et Dei Spiritus Sancti, qui sunt unus Deus, unus
Christus, qui unum pastorem suis ovibus elegit, ut daret eis veritatem fidei ad comedendum, cum qua
veritate viverent. Et in persona beati Petri sunt oves commissae fidei cuiuslibet papae*). Cited from
Llull, *Arbor Scientiae*, 379, lines 65–72. Sebastián García Palou, "La infalibilidad pontificia en *Arbre
de sciencia* del Beato Ramón Llull," *Revista Española de Teología* 4 (1944): 229–55, esp. 247–49.
To go deeper into the Lullian posture on the question of papal power, see Antoni Oliver, "El poder

(21:15–17) Llull designates the pope as the Church's ultimate shepherd and an example to be followed for the faithful. Popes who do not work to reinforce the faith in the community of *fideles* and expand it amongst those who do not yet know of it are acting contrary to God's will. God's flock must grow and get stronger because "The grace of spiritual life is greater than the corporeal one."[33] Despite this note on the subject of the pre-eminence of the spiritual over the temporal world, Llull equally recognises the sovereign's role as shepherd for the *cives*: "God placed him to govern with his one goodness, many goodnesses, [...] as a shepherd obligated to govern many sheep."[34] Without the guidance of a prince and a blameless council, the kingdom was in disarray "as the sheep who are afflicted by a wolf, when there are no shepherds."[35] He uses a similar expression in *Arbor apostolicalis* where we read: "because God humiliates himself and inclines towards the lesser of his people or towards sheep, in order to protect the sheep from greedy wolves."[36] Note that ultimately, despite repeated affirmations of the superiority of the spiritual over the temporal, Llull treats the heads of both spheres of power in the same way in the majority of instances.

The structure of the pope's tree—in the correspondence between the various parts—echoes that of the sovereign's tree. Thus the roots of both are represented by the virtues set out in the first part of *Arbor moralis*: the two trunks are made up of the apex of the ecclesiastical institution and the head of the civil institution respectively. The main branches host the respective subordinates (on one hand the college of cardinals and the rest of the clergy, on the other all the royal officials). The seven lesser branches of the *Arbor imperialis* (justice, love, fear, wisdom, power, honour, and liberty [*iustitia, amor, timor, sapientia, potestas, honor, et libertas*]) are echoed in the various lesser branches of the papal tree where the ten commandments are added. In the section devoted to the leaves, Llull underlines the fundamental importance of a reorganization of civil law for the management of the public sphere and of ecclesiastical law to regulate relations internal to the Church. The leaves of the *Arbor apostolicalis* also encompass the seven sacraments, the means by which God makes direct contact with his children and the clergy and eradicates sin from the world. The fourteen articles of the Creed, on the other hand, take the place of the apostolic flowers while the *Arbor imperialis* encompasses the multiple concrete forms of royal government and legislation. Lastly the fruit of the two trees—that is, the ultimate purpose of both spheres of power—is, as we have seen, peace in the world, enabling God's people to love and serve the creator.

---

temporal del papa según Ramón Llull y postura de éste relativa a las controversias de su tiempo," *Studia lulliana* 5 (1961): 99–132, esp. 100–12.

33 *Maior est gratia vitae spiritualis quam corporalis.* Cited from Llull, *Arbor Scientiae*, 380, line 75.

34 *Deus ipsum posuit ad regendum cum una sua bonitate plures bonitates, [...] sicut unus pastor obligatus ad regendum plures oves.* Cited from Llull, *Arbor Scientiae*, 334, lines 22–26.

35 *Sicut oves, quae tribulantur per lupos, quando pastores non habent.* Cited from Llull, *Arbor Scientiae*, 341, line 108.

36 *[...] quod Dominus maior se humiliet et inclinet ad minoritates sui populi sive ad oves, ut ipsas custodiat a lupis rapacibus.* Cited from Llull, *Arbor Scientiae*, 376, lines 40–42.

The fruit of the papal tree brings together all the fruit of the previous trees and ensures the concord and serenity required for men to nurture their love for God.[37] The matter of all the other trees is encompassed within this fruit which conjures up the perfection of the creation to the extent that everything converges on the pope, the central node in this universe and the highest general office towards which all specific interests flow. The pope's charge is "dominion over all people",[38] namely over all Christians, rulers included. In guiding the people to the fulfilment of the purpose for which they were created, the pope ensures "ordered ministry" (*ordinatum ministerium*), namely the management of the ecclesiastical institution and "to save people" (*salvatio gentis*).[39]

Sovereigns, like popes, were to ensure peace in this world, but Llull also entrusted to the Church hierarchy a further onerous task: salvation for God's people. While the prince was to take a role in this, too, the writer makes no explicit mention of this in *Arbor imperialis* while he does for the pope. This salvation-related duty was to follow two trajectories: one internal to the Church, involving defending men against damnation for sin, and the other external, involving the dissemination of God's word amongst the infidels. Llull's work focused on the latter task, as his biography and written work make clear. In *Arbor apostolicalis* he states:

> And with his faith, the pope should be against those who are against the faith. Because of this contrariety, he should try to destroy the errors, which are spread among Saracens, Tartars, and Jews, with these errors they are against the Christian faith: he must destroy the divisions that have been sown among Christians or schismatics, diverted from the true Christian faith.[40]

Llull explicitly demonstrates his clear desire to convert infidels to the word of Christ in much of his work and writings and directly invites the pope to get involved in this project: *Epistola ad papam Nicholaum IV* (also known as *Quomodo Terra Sancta recuperari potest*) and the *Tractatus de modo convertendi infideles* (1292), *Petitio Raimundi pro conversione infidelium ad Coelestinum V papam* (1294), *Petitio Raimundi pro conversione infidelium ad Bonifacium VIII papam* (1295), *Liber de fine* (1305), *Liber de acquisitione Terra Sanctae* (1309) and *Petitio Raimundi in Concilio generali ad acquirendam Terram Sanctam* (1311), a work that goes in considerable depth into the theology of Llull's mission, though his belief in the need to convert non-Christian peoples dates to well before this. Already in the first synthetic explanation of this doctrine in *Libre de contemplació*

---

37 *Fructus Arboris apostolicalis est ille, in quo colliguntur omnes fructus aliarum arborum, de quibus dictum est, quoniam omnia, quotquot sunt in hac vita praesenti secundum divinam ordinationem, quam Deus posuit in creaturis istius vitae, in qua sumus, se ita dirigunt ad Arborem apostolicalem et generalem, sicut plures lineae ad unum punctum ex illis constitutum et centrum, in quo sibi invicem obviant, sicut plures partes in suo toto.* Cited from Llull, *Arbor Scientiae*, 482–83, lines 1–9.

38 *Dominium super omnes homines.* Llull, *Arbor Scientiae*, 483, line 15.

39 Llull, *Arbor Scientiae*, line 10, 483.

40 *Et cum sua fide debet papa esse contra illos, qui sunt contra fidem, ratione cuius contratietatis conari debet errores destruere, qui sunt seminati inter Saracenos, Tartaros et inter Judeos cum quibus erroribus sunt contra fidem christianam: debet etiam destruere schismata, quae sunt seminata inter Christianos sive schismaticos derivatos a vera fide christiana.* From Llull, *Arbor Scientiae*, 380, lines 83–88.

(chap. 346), whilst also underlining that the duty to disseminate gospel teachings is the responsibility of the faithful as a whole, Llull makes clear that God has entrusted this high task to the popes to a greater extent than to any other members of the Church because the contributions of the whole Christian community depend on his decisions on the subject. Our *Doctor Illuminatus* plans a structured programme of conversions moving in two directions: on one hand an attempt to show Muslims the errors of their faith via public *disputationes* between wise men and, on the other, where the force of Christ's reason and truth are not sufficient to convince infidels to embrace the Christian religion, armed crusades are espoused. Llull was always an exponent of dialogue between cultures and religions, and the dream of building colleges on the model of the Miramar convent, which he himself founded, to train Christian missionaries in the theology and language needed to take on their adversaries with reasoned argument, never left him. This type of conversion activity, known as a "spiritual crusade" (based on dialectic debate), if not sufficient, could, he argued, be accompanied by a "material crusade," namely armed action aimed in particular at winning back the Holy Land.[41]

In *Arbor*, Llull reserves a quasi-marginal space to the mission theme which is so central to his thought[42] and never achieves that argumentative energy which is to be found, for example, in *Petitio ad Bonifacium*, written in the same period. In the document sent to Boniface, Llull asks the pope to act "to provide that all those who don't know the true worship of God, come to the light of truth",[43] proposing that he set up schools to train

---

41 The theme of the crusade is present in two variants, spiritual and material, in Llullian writing from the beginning, as we read in *Libre de contemplació*: "10. Glorious Lord, [...] I see that many knights go to the Holy Land overseas and attempt to conquer it by force of arms. Where, when the end came, everyone has exhausted their efforts without having reached the objective they aimed for. Where, I believe, Lord, that the Holy Land can only be conquered in the way you and your apostles conquered it, who conquered it with love and with prayers and with the shedding of tears and blood. 11. Given that the Holy Sepulchre, Lord, and the Holy Land overseas seems to be better conquered by preaching than by the force of arms, and that before, Lord, the holy religious knights covered themselves with the sign of the cross, and filling themselves with the grace of the Holy Spirit, and went to preach the truth of your passion to the infidels and shed for your love all the water from their eyes and all the blood from their hearts, like you for love of them" (*10. Gloriós Senyor, [...] molts cavallers veig que van en la sancta terra d'outramar e cuiden aquella conquerre per força d'armes. On, com ve a la fi tots s'hi consumen sens que no vénen a fi de ço que.s cuiden. On, par'me Sènyer, que lo conqueriment d'aquella sancta terra no.s deja conquerir sinó per la manera on la conquesés vós e.ls vostres apòstols, qui la conquerís ab amor e ab oracions e ab escampament de làgremes e de sang. 11. Com lo sant sepulcre, Sènyer, e la sancta terra d'outramar par que.s deja conquerre per predicació mills que per força d'armes, faer'se a avant, Sènyer, los sants cavallers religioses e guarnesquen'se del senyal de la creu, e umplense de la gràcia del sant Espirit, e vagen preïcar veritat de la vostra passió als infeels e escampen per la vostra amor totes les aigües de lurs ulls e tota la sang de lurs cors, així com vós feés per amor d'ells!*). Cited from Ramon Llull, *Libre de contemplació en Déu*, Obres de Ramon Llull, ed. Mateu Obrador i Bennàssar (Palma, 1986), 340, chap. 112, lines 10–11.

42 For details of the vast literature on the theme of mission and crusade in Ramon Llull, see: Jordi Gayà Estelrich, *Raimondo Lullo: una teologia per la missione* (Milano, 2002).

43 *Ad procurandum, quod omnes qui verum Dei cultum ignorant, ad veritatis lumen perveniant.* From Ramon Llull, "Petitio Raymundi pro conversione infidelium ad Bonifacium VIII papam," in

missionaries and organize a crusade to win back Jerusalem. He also suggests, in characteristically practical spirit, that Church tithes could be used to fund this war and gives advice on the importance of well-prepared missionaries to stand up to Saracen learned men. Worried about continued Arab expansion, he offers his own services on an evangelization mission.

In the second part of *De secunda parte foliorum Arboris apostolicalis*, Llull gives indirect indications on the right approach to spiritual crusades. With the objective of re-organizing canon law, he chooses a theme—applicable in all specific cases—that had often been at the centre of the debate between Christian theologians and Muslim learned men: the Holy Trinity. Reading these pages, a hypothetical missionary (or the pope himself) would have been supplied with a well-structured example, reusable on other occasions, of the arguments supporting the Christian position and the potential objections which their Muslim counterparts might raise: with the force of reason even the mysteries of the faith can be demonstrated.

For the Christian religion to be embraced by the infidels and the pope to become a universal lord, the support and action of the temporal powers was needed. On this subject we read: "And the judgment of God was that the dominion of Roma was given to the pope, in order that with the secular arm he would be strong enough to resist the enemies of faith."[44] The crusading motif is interwoven with the equally well-known *Donatio Constantini* theme. It is no simple matter to identify the importance which Llull attributes to the Donation of Constantine, in the first place because his use of it is not systematic or frequent and, in the second place, because his use of and the meaning he attributes to the *Donatio* shifts over time.[45] First and foremost he sees it as an apologetic argument supporting the divinity of the Church and a help given by God to the pope in the debate with the opponents of the Christian faith. It is not a thesis supporting papal hierocracy. Quite the contrary, aware that it is generally emblematic of the Church's claims to temporal power, Llull encompasses it within his missionary theory, asking himself not if and how the *Donatio* legitimizes spiritual power in this temporal "contract," but rather how it can be used for the good of the Christian community in accordance with divine will. Given his proximity to the mendicant orders, moreover, Llull foresees a renewal of the Church according to ideals of moral rectitude and austerity which did not marry well with the image of a clergy preoccupied with material affairs.

In *Libre de demostracions* Llull is clearly alluding to the *Donatio Constantini*, interpreting it as a vehicle offered by God to be used to strengthen the dissemination of the Christian faith with Arab peoples:

> Whereas the Church in the beginning had few people and they were poor so that they did
> not conquer lands by force of arms but rather through preaching and martyrdom they

---

Politics and Culture in Medieval Spain and Italy, ed. Helene Wieruszowski (Roma, 1971), 147–72, esp. 161.

44 *Et ordinatio Dei fuit, quod imperium Romanum datum fuit papae, ut cum brachio saeculari papa foret fortis ad resistendum inimicis fidei.* Cited from Llull, *Arbor Scientiae*, 379, lines 54–56.

45 Oliver explores these aspects in his study: Antoni Oliver, "La *Donatio Constantini* en los escritos y en la mente de Ramón Llull," *Estudios Lulianos* 8 (1964): 155–70.

multiplied the Christian peoples, and as the Empire of Roma, or many other principalities, were given to them, that showed that the belief of the Christians is agreeable to our Lord God; because they were surely in agreement that the miracles and divine work have given the empire to the Roman Church.[46]

The aim of Llull's reading is not to increase the pope's power as compared to the emperor, but ensure that the Church was capable of fulfilling its evangelizing mission, namely to conquer the world with the Christian faith. Thus the question the writer poses in *Arbor quaestionalis*—"Why did the Christian emperor give the empire to the Roman Church?"[47]—receives an answer in the roots of *Arbor apostolicalis*: "in order that with the secular arm he would be strong enough to resist the enemies of faith."[48] Constantine entrusted the Roman Empire to the pope not for him to take precedence over imperial jurisdiction, but because with it the popes would be able to extend Christ's truth to the whole world.

Llull sanctions the use of force to combat the infidel enemy and in this struggle sovereigns were to act in accordance with the orders imparted them by the apostolic see "so that emperor can maintain peace on earth and destroy rebellious infidels by the apostolic orders of St. Peter, in order that the fruit is picked under his management."[49] The management of the crusades is entrusted in *Arbor* entirely to the pope, who was to exert his power also over the person of the prince who must, in turn, act according to the demands and instructions of the head of the Church. Llull's words echo one of the themes characteristic of the struggle between pope and emperor, namely ownership over the "two swords" (*duo gladii*) used generally by the exponents of the papal cause as a biblical sign of his possession of both the powers placed in Peter's hands.[50] Llull must have had in mind St. Bernard's stance in which sovereigns were to use the temporal sword according to the indications of the Church and in its defence:

> Therefore both swords belong to the Church, namely spiritual and material; but one is surely to be used to defend the Church, the other must even be brandished by the Church:

---

46 *On, com la Eglesya en lo comencament fos en poques persones e aquelles fossen pobres e tals que per forsa d'armes non conquistassen terres, ans per precaició e per martire multiplicassen lo poble crestians, e com l'Emperi de Roma, o molts d'altres principats, sia donat a ells, per assò es demostrar que la creensa dels crestians es agradable a nostre Senyor Deus; cor de necessitat se cové que miracles e obra divina ajen donat l'emperi a l'Eglesya romana.* Cited from Ramon Llull, *Libre de demostracions*, Obres de Ramon Llull, ed. Mateu Obrador i Bennàssar (Palma, 1986), 589.

47 *Quare christianus imperator dedit imperium Ecclesiae Romanae?* Cited from Llull, *Arbor Scientiae*, 860.

48 *Ut cum brachio saeculari papa foret fortis ad resistendum inimicis fidei.* Cited from Llull, *Arbor Scientiae*, 379, lines 54–56.

49 *Ut imperator pacem possit tenere in mundo et destruere infideles rebelles mandatis Sanctis Patris apostolicis, ut fructus colligatur sub sua administratione.* From Llull, *Arbor Scientiae*, 484, lines 43–45.

50 The theory of "two swords" originates from a passage in the Gospel of Luke, where, during the Last Supper, Peter turns to Christ with these words: *Domine, ecce gladii duo hic* and Jesus responds: *satis est* (Luke 22:38).

the one is wielded by the priest, the other by the soldier, but, of course, with priest's consent and with emperor's order.[51]

In *Arbor scientiae*, Bernard's expression *ad nutum sacerdotis* has been replaced with *mandatis Sancti Patris*, namely the invitation or instruction given by the spiritual powers to the secular powers to take up the temporal sword by St. Bernard becomes a command by the pope to the emperor in Llull,[52] limited, however, to action in defence of the Church itself. In his *opus*, Llull returns frequently to the image of the two swords and always in connection with the missionary theme.[53] In *Liber de fine* Llull writes:

> and for this reason, why do you sleep and don't you work, since such a great treasure relies on you through the spiritual sword and even through the temporal one? [...] This distinction indicates the spiritual sword, that is truth against falsehood, ignorance, or misunderstanding. Right after it follows the second sword, that is the temporal one. Since human being is made up only by body and soul, two swords are enough.[54]

The Church is presented as bearer of both powers (the spiritual and temporal swords) in the context of the struggle against the infidels, which was to be fought by means of the two treasures given by God to the ecclesiastical institution in order to fulfil the divine plan to constitute a single *Res publica christiana*. Llull had previously illustrated the characteristics of the two treasures given by the Lord to the earthly Church in the dual form of the practical application of Llull's mission theory as described above. With *thesaurus spiritualis*,[55] Llull indicates a training programme for missionaries designed to prepare them for systematic preaching in infidel lands where they were to disseminate God's word and demonstrate the dogmatic error of other religions. The Church's spir-

---

51 *Uterque ergo Ecclesiae et spiritualis scilicet gladius, et materialis; sed is quidem pro Ecclesia, ille vero et ab Ecclesia exserendus: ille sacerdotis, is militis manu, sed sane ad nutum sacerdotis, et jussum imperatoris.* Cited from Bernardus Claraevallensis, "De consideratione," in *Patrologiae cursus completus*, ed. Jacques-Paul Migne, 221 vols. (Paris, 1841), 182: col. 776 (book 4, chap. 3).

52 The Llullian term *mandates* used to define the action command of the pope over the sovereign is closest in meaning to the formula *ad jussum* (translated as "with the order") rather than *ad nutum*. Note, however, that Bernard accompanies the formula *ad jussum* with *imperatoris*, while Llull links the term *mandatis* to *Sancti Patris*.

53 Ricardo da Costa, Tatyana Nunes Lemos, "Com ferro, fogo e argumentação: Cruzada, Conversão e a Teoria dos Dois Gládios na filosofia de Ramon Llull," *Mirabilia: Revista Eletrônica da Antiguidade e Idade Média*, 10 (2010), accessed January 6, 2019, www.revistamirabilia.com/sites/default/files/pdfs/2010_01_12.pdf.

54 *Et ideo, ecclesia, quare dormis, et non laboras, postquam tantus thesaurus est tibi commendatus per spiritualem gladium et etiam per corporalem? Forte non poteris dum voles [...] Et ista distinctio gladium spiritualem significat, videlicet veritatem contra falsitatem, ignorantiam et errorem. Modo sequitur de secundo gladio, videlicet corporali. Et quia homo non est compositus, nisi ex corpore et anima, gladii sufficiunt isti duo.* Cited from Ramon Llull, "Liber de fine," in *Raimundi Lulli Opera Latina*, ed. Alois Madre (Turnhout, 1981), 233–291, esp. 268–69, lines 607–17.

55 *Thesaurus spiritualis potest ipsis infidelibus communicari, hoc modo scilicet, quod in diversis locis ad hoc aptis per terram christianorum ac in quibusdam locis etiam tartarorum fiant studia idiomatum diversorum, in quibus viri sacra scriptura competenter imbuti tam religiosi quam seculares, qui cultum divinum per orbem terrarum desiderant ampliari.* Cited from Llull, "Petitio Raymundi pro conversione," 161.

itual sword consisted precisely in the power to teach, divulge the Gospel truth, and show the way to heavenly salvation within and without the Christian community. *Thesaurus corporalis*,[56] also to be attributed to the pope was, on the other hand, designed to convert the Saracens by freeing the Holy Land from Muslim dominion by means of the help of temporal power, that is, the sovereign. This is how the supremacy of ecclesiastical over secular power was to be read: material arms were to be at the service of spiritual arms, or in other words civil power is subject to spiritual power where the affirmation and defence of the Christian faith is concerned.[57]

In neither *Arbor imperialis* nor *Arbor apostolicalias* does Llull present an explicit and systematic theory of the two powers by means of the *duo gladii*, although this is implied in the papal tree in the expressions: "with the secular arm he would be strong enough to resist the enemies of faith"[58] and "the emperor should destroy rebellious infidels by the orders of the Pope."[59]

---

56 *Thesauro temporali uti poteris, isto modo scilicet, quod similiter uni domino cardinali ordinatio committatur ad procurandum et tractandum passagium pro Terra Sancta laudabiliter acquirenda et acquisita et etiam conservanda).* Cited from Llull, "Petitio Raymundi pro conversione," 161.

57 Da Costa, "Com ferro, fogo e argumentação," 212. It is also interesting to read two passages from the Llullian opus where the author again emphasizes the need for the intervention of the temporal power on the orders of the Church in the fight against the Muslims. He wrote the *Disputatio Petri clerici et Raimundi phantastici* in 1311: "The universal catholic Church has two swords, as is said in the Gospel, that is a corporal sword and a spiritual sword, which means learning and devotion. With these two swords the Church has enough to turn all unbelieving people to the path of truth. Firstly, the pope should send wise and discreet men, prepared to meet their death, to Muslims, Turks, and Tartars, to show unbelievers their errors and open up the truth of the Holy Catholic faith and these unbelievers can return to a bath of rebirth. If they, instead, resist, the pope must call the secular sword against them. It is legal and right to do this, and he who is against this command is culpable, out of reality, and consequently no longer ordained" (*Nam universa catholicorum Ecclesia duos gladios habet, ut in Evangelio dictum est, scilicet gladium corporalem, ensem videlicet, et spiritualem, scilicet scientiam et devotionem. Cum istis autem duobus gladiis sufficeret Ecclesia omnes infideles ad viam reducere veritatis. Primo, si papa sapientes et discretos, mortem sustinere paratos, apud saracenos, turcos et tartaros mitteret, qui infidelibus suos errores ostenderent et sanctae fidei catholicae veritatem aperirent, ut ipsi infideles ad sacrum regenerationis lavacrum venirent; deinde si resisterent, tunc papa contra ipsos procurare deberet gladium saecularem. Licitum et debitum est talem esse ordinationem, et qui in aliquo contra ordinationem est, phantasticus est et culpabilis, atque per consequens inordinatus).* Cited from Ramon Llull, *Disputatio Petri clerici et Raimundi phantastici*, ed. Antoni Oliver, Michel Senellart, Fernando Domínguez, Raimundi Lulli Opera Latina 16 / Corpus christianorum Continuatio mediaevalis 78 (Turnhout, 1988), 1–30, esp. 117; and also in 1314, in the *Liber de civitate mundi* he writes: *De quo damnum est quia imperium est propter hoc ut teneat iustitiam et cum gladio defendat romanam Ecclesiam contra infideles et contra schismaticos, etiam contra iniustos christianos et contra infideles qui possident Terram sanctam. Et quis est qui curet de hoc?* (from Ramon Llull, *Liber de civitate mundi*, Raimundi Lulli Opera Latina, ed. Johannes Stöhr (Palma, 1960), 169–201, esp. 195).

58 *Cum brachio saeculari papa foret fortis ad resistendum inimicis fidei.* Cited from Llull, *Arbor Scientiae*, 379, lines 54–56.

59 *Imperator [...] possit [...] destruere infideles rebelles mandatis Sancti Patris apostolici.* Cited from Llull, *Arbor Scientiae*, 484, lines 43–45.

In both cases, he makes a brief reference to the pope's responsibility to spread the Christian faith among non-believers and the king's duty to support the Church in this task on God's wishes. In *Arbor quaestionalis*, in the part dealing with the imperial tree, mention is made of the king's sword with a focus on the need for a council made up of learned men to ensure that the government of the realm (i.e., the temporal sphere) is good and just.[60] So, with regards to the king, there is no reference to any duty by the king—and thus the temporal power—to take part in the struggle against the infidels. In contrast to his other work, in *Arbor scientiae* Llull does not link the figure of the prince to mission except in an aside in *Arbor apostolicalis* where he goes into greater depth on *sacerdotium*. As Paolo Evangelisti has rightly noted, the issue of the "recovery" (*recuperatio*) of the Holy Land appears not only in Llull's treatises promoting the crusades and addressed to the pope but is also present in work targeting Christian princes or the lay public, which present the Christian king as duty-bound to become directly involved in forced conversion.[61]

The fact that *Arbor scientiae* makes marginal reference to mission and conversion, an issue that is central to the thought of the *Doctor Illuminatus*, is an indication of the work's doctrinal originality within the context of Llull's corpus. This originality consists in its unitary vision of society conceived of as a single organism in which every single component contributes to the good functioning of the whole. Cooperation between spiritual power and the *brachio saeculari* ensures peace in the world, the indispensable precondition for the Christian people's ability to pursue the end for which it was created: loving and serving God. The submission of the temporal powers to the dictates of the Church is limited to crusading and does not apply to the whole temporal sphere. Quite the contrary, Llull makes plain his efforts to show the independence of the imperial office as far as the government of the realm is concerned. The presence of two powers on earth and their respective hierarchies is part of the divine plan. Each has been entrusted with a specific sphere of competence with no interference by one over the other. *Magna concordia* must reign within each power and between the two[62] for "one pope and one sovereign should acquire the whole world."[63] The popes and the kings are absolute lords within the *ecclesia* and *regnum* respectively and both are at the apex of institutions recognized by God and organized according to a hierarchical structure in which rules sanctioned by canon and civil law are abided by. The *bonus princeps* is a model for the *cives* who, inspired by the good example of their rulers, will act virtuously in their daily lives, in their relations with others, in trade, and in respect of the pre-established order. Llull sees the need for moral renewal but never gives way to reformist proposals which might undermine the *status quo*. As the *imago Dei in terris*, sovereigns

---

60 *Quaestio: Ab ense regis quarebatur, quare non erat rectus. Solutio: Dixit ensis, quod ipse obliquus erat quia rex bonum consilium non habuit.* Cited from Llull, *Arbor Scientiae*, 1026.

61 Paolo Evangelisti, *I Francescani e la costruzione di uno stato: linguaggi politici, progetti di governo in area catalano-aragonese* (Padova, 2006), 140–43.

62 *Contrarietas praelati et pricipis est valde mala atque periculosa.* From Llull, *Arbor Scientiae*, 734.

63 *Unus apostolicus et unus imperator totum mundum acquirere possent.* From Llull, *Arbor Scientiae*, 880.

must, by nature of their office, be acknowledged, honoured, and obeyed by the people and, in the event that they do not fulfil their duty, the people must not rebel, as we read also in the chapter *De paciencia et ira*[64] in *Libre de les meravelles*.

Within the framework of the potential *Res publica christiana* imagined by Llull in *Arbor*, the pope's powers are circumscribed to the spiritual sphere and their direct influence is over the clergy and the faithful, not over the civil community in general subject to royal jurisdiction. When the writer states, "The pope has been appointed as universal prelate and general prelate to all the prelates",[65] he would appear to be limiting the Church's sphere of action to the Church itself and those subject to it, a stance which would seem to be confirmed in *Arbor imperialis* in which Llull argues for the need for a single emperor ruling over the various lordships to ensure peace and stability in the kingdom, just as the popes rule over the various prelates: "so, it would be necessary to have just one emperor on earth, over many kings and princes, just as there is only one pope over many prelates."[66]

---

64 "In a city there was a very wise burgher, noble and powerful in riches and in friends. The prince of that city was an evil man and rude. That prince was of such evil customs that he misused and destroyed that city. As the burgher loved the city, and as he was a fair and wise man, there was a great ire at the badness of the prince and the destruction of that city. One day it happened that the prince did a great misdeed against the city, and for that reason the burgher became very angry, and thought about how to move all the people of the city and make them assassinate the prince. The burgher willingly put the plot he had thought up into action, until he remembered justice, loyalty, and charity, and understanding that he should have patience under God's will, who had given them that prince as their natural lord; and regretting his mad idea he had had in wanting to kill his lord. The burgher was surprised that the ire, a deadly sin, he had towards his lord, had been able to affect him, given that he desired the good and useful things for the city; but he understood that the ire he had felt because of the damage to the city was not a vice, but rather had some similarity with the ire he had felt in wanting to kill his lord. That is why he lacked the fortitude to destroy the similarity that one ire had with the other, which could be destroyed with patience" (*En una ciutat havia un burguès molt savi, noble e poderós de riqueses e d'amics. Lo príncep d'aquella ciutat era malvat hom e de mala manera. Aquell príncep era de tan malvades costumes, que aquella ciutat malmetia e destrovia. Car lo burguès amava la ciutat, e car era hom just e savi, havia molt gran ira de la malea del príncep e del destroviment d'aquella ciutat. Un dia s'esdevenc que el príncep hac fet un gran falliment contra la ciutat, e lo burguès ne fo en tan gran ira, que ell cogità com mogués-li tot lo poble de la ciutat e que auciés lo príncep. En volentat fo lo burguès que metés en obra ço que cogitava, tro que remebrà justícia, leialtat, caritat, e entès que ell devia haver paciència sots la volentat de Déu, qui aquell príncep los havia donat per senyor natural; e penedí's de sa folla consideració la qual havia haüda en auciure son senyor. Meravellà's lo burguès com la ira, que és pecat mortal, la qual hac contra son senyor, poc en ell venir, pus que ell desijava lo bé e la utilitat de la ciutat; emperò entès e dix que la ira que havia del mal de la ciutat no era vici, mas que havia alcuna semblança ab la ira que hac en auciure son senyor, per ço com li defallí fortitudo a destrovir la semblança que la una ira havia ab l'altra, la qual poc ésser destrovida ab paciencia*). Cited from Ramon Llull, *Libre de les meravelles*, book 8, chap. 75. Júlia Butiñá, "El *Libre de les bèsties* de Llull y el comportamiento político," in *El pensamiento politico en la Edad Media*, ed. Pedro Roche Arnas (Madrid, 2010), 321–32, esp. 324.

65 *Papa [...] est creatus universalis praelatus et generalis ad omnes praelatos.* From Llull, *Arbor Scientiae*, 376, lines 30–31.

66 *[...] Oporteret, quod esset unus imperator tantummodo in mundo, ita supra multos reges et principes, sicut est unus papa supra multos prelatos.* From Llull, *Arbor Scientiae*, 338, lines 39–41.

A parallel is hereby established between the figure of the *imperator* and that of the pope, the former at the apex of the political pyramid and the latter at the apex of the ecclesiastical pyramid. *Civitas mundi*, where there is no distinction between earthly and celestial cities, where the needs of the soul cohabit with bodily needs, emerges from the joint contribution of popes and sovereigns.

As an intellectual and rational man, Llull is aware of the importance of temporal over spiritual power but, at the same time, as a man of great faith, he cannot avoid recognizing the Church's supremacy over the world. These two stances, however, coexist rather than contradict one another. As I have shown, the very sequence of the various books in the work is meaningful and the fact that *Arbor apostolicalis* follows *imperialis* in the intellect's ascension towards God automatically determines the superiority of the former over the latter. From an eschatological perspective, the salvation of souls is assured by the Church, which looks after the Lord's flock and protects it from the infidel threat. From this point of view popes are authorized to guide temporal action in the struggle against Islam. Beyond being rulers of a realm princes are Christians and as such they are duty-bound to offer their services as *defensor* of the pope, the faith, and the Christian dominions, acting by order of the pope to fulfil divine will. This is how Llull's statements in *Arbor quaestionalis* can be explained: "no man has greater office than a prelate"[67] and "no man is more perfect in honour than a good prelate";[68] the papacy is universally recognized as the world's ultimate office and honour because the pope is actively involved in spreading the word of God by means of the spiritual and moral treasures for the purposes of creating a single great universal Church.

Conclusions

The absence of concrete or direct references to the historic and political vicissitudes of the era in *Arbor scientiae* bears witness to the timeless character of the work. Llull puts forward general principles, almost ideals, on the basis of which the real world should be structured. It is thus not a question of looking to the figure of the *imperator sive princeps* or the pope for a specific image of a sovereign or pope of the era, and even less should we be looking for support for one side or the other. It should not be forgotten that the idea behind *Arbor scientiae* was the writer's desire to rework his *Ars magna* in a more intelligible version for a wider readership.

Llull's great faith, his strong desire to see the Gospel alive in the world, his vision of a unitary society, moved him away from discussing contemporary secular or religious controversies. In the work we have examined Llull never took sides in defence of either the papal or the imperial causes. He sidesteps them, but intentionally. The same arguments used by the exponents of papal supremacy take on an original meaning in *Arbor scientiae* and are interpreted differently—in the context of conversion and mission.

The issues examined by *Arbor imperialis* and *Arbor apostolicalis* do not attempt an in-depth theological analysis of temporal and spiritual power. The writer's intention

---

67 *Nullus homo maius habet officium quam praelatus.* Llull, *Arbor Scientiae*, 734.

68 *Nullus homo bono praelato est honore perfectior.* Llull, *Arbor Scientiae*, Proverbium 15.

is, on the other hand, to bring to light the way in which the two offices—imperial and papal—both desired by God can best bring to fruition the divine plan for Christianity. One is at the apex of the civil institutions and the other of the ecclesiastical hierarchy and cooperation between the two is fundamental.

For man's spiritual and material well-being, God desires two leaders enabling his people to live in peace, a necessary pre-requisite for the affirmation of gospel teachings. Spiritual care has been entrusted to the head of the Church who must watch over his flock (the faithful), a task Christ entrusted to Peter, as a good shepherd. The sovereign's task, on the other hand, is to look after citizens' material needs to enable them to act virtuously and serve God in their daily lives. In Llull's approach to the creation of a single world city, as defined by him in a work written after *Arbor*, *Liber de civitate mundi*, a prince's mission in civil society and a pope's in the Church converge on a single objective: loving and serving God.

This is the basis for the need for Church and Empire, or rather *Christianitas* as a whole, to constitute a common front in the struggle against the infidels. The aim of converting the Islamic and Jewish peoples absorbed all Llull's physical and mental energies and shaped his view of the balance between temporal and spiritual power. The pope has been placed by God at the head of action to disseminate Christ's teachings via preaching and crusades to win back the Holy Land. To this end he can and must demand help from the secular arm in the pursuit of new Christian converts among Muslims and Jews. As Christians and leaders of a Christian realm, princes must take up the sword according to the dictates of the Church and fight to defend it.

However, by its nature temporal power is independent of spiritual power and must work for the *utilitas publica*, the common good of kingdom or city but, from the perspective of the triumph of the Christian model in the world, princes must subordinate their will to that of the head of the Church.

Part Two

IDEOLOGY — THE MANAGEMENT OF POWER

Chapter 6

REGNUM GOTHORUM AND REGNUM HISPANIAE IN MEDIEVAL SPANISH CHRISTIAN CHRONICLES: CONTINUATION, END, OR TRANSLATION IN THEIR ACCOUNTS OF THE ARAB CONQUEST

IVÁN PÉREZ MARINAS

THIS CHAPTER ANALYSES the view that medieval Spanish-Christian historiography provided on the effects caused by the Arab-Berber conquest in the Iberian Peninsula of the *regnum Gothorum* (in terms of its end or its transfer northwards) and the *regnum Hispaniae* (its exclusive continuation in al-Andalus, its partial possession by Christians to be fully recovered later, or its continued existence limited to Christian territory). The two terms are not identical, since in all medieval chronicles consulted the *regnum Gothorum* refers to the rule, government, and the authority of the Visigoths, while the *regnum Hispaniae*, or simply *regnum*, designates the political and public institution established on Spanish territory, that is, the Kingdom of Spain.[1]

I shall examine preserved medieval chronicles dealing with these historiographical issues that were written by Christians in territories of the former Visigothic Kingdom, which also included Septimania in today's southern France. Later sequels (*Chronicle of Sampiro* and *Chronicle of Bishop Pelagius*) and specific narratives of famous kings (*Chronica Adephonsi imperatoris* or the Catalan late-medieval chronicles about the Aragonese kings) are not considered. I also exclude annals, deeds, and chronicles of kingdoms and counties that do not attempt to explain their origins in the uprising against Andalusian rule (*Chronica latina regum Castellae* and *Crónica de los estados peninsulares*) or that look for other ways of legitimization, such as through the Carolingian Empire (*Gesta Comitum Barchinonensium* and the diverse annals and genealogies from the Pyrenean regions). Therefore, the chapter focuses on the following historiographical texts: the *Arab-Byzantine Chronicle of 741*, *Mozarabic Chronicle of 754*, *Chronologia regum Gothorum*, *Chronicon Moissiacense*, *Chronicle of Albelda*, *Chronicle of Alfonso III*, *Annales Portugalenses Veteres*, *Chronicon Compostellanum*, *Chronicon Iriense*, *Historia Legionensis*, *Chronica Naierensis*, *Liber regum*, *Chronicon Mundi*, *De rebus Hispaniae*, *Historia Arabum*, *Estoria de España general*, *Chronicle of San Juan de la Peña*, *Crónica d'Espayña*, *Chronicle*

---

1 This chapter attempts a comprehensive study of the topic. An earlier approach, limited to the chronicles of the eighth and ninth centuries, has been published in Iván Pérez Marinas, "*Regnum Gothorum* y *regnum Hispaniae* en las crónicas hispano-cristianas de los siglos VIII y IX: continuación, fin o traslado en el relato de la conquista árabe," *Estudios Medievales Hispánicos* 2 (2013): 175–200.

Iván Pérez Marinas (ivanperez@bne.es) is Técnico de biblioteca at the Biblioteca Nacional de España in Madrid.

of Garci López de Roncesvalles, Crónica de los reyes de Navarra, and *Anacefaleosis o Genealogía de los reyes de España*. I shall deal with them chronologically.

Andalusian-Christian Chronicles

The earliest surviving evidence on the course of the *regnum Gothorum* and the *regnum Hispaniae* are the *Arab-Byzantine Chronicle of 741* and the *Mozarabic Chronicle of 754*. Both come from al-Andalus, particularly the south-eastern quadrant of the Iberian Peninsula, and were written by Mozarabs a few decades after the Arab conquest. Although their close proximity in time might have permitted oral sources, it seems that the authors, both anonymous, relied on written records.

In addition, despite the chronicles disagreeing on whether the Arab conquest was a positive or negative event, it is noteworthy that they offer a similar historiographical vision, even considering that they must have shared an Arab source. This group of chronicles makes clear that the *regnum Gothorum* was eliminated by the Arabs, specifically by caliph al-Walid through Musa ibn Nusayr, while the *regnum*, that is, the *regnum Hispaniae*, continues as an entity under the control of and taxation by by the new rulers.

Arab-Byzantine Chronicle of 741

Studying each of these literary works separately, the *Arab-Byzantine Chronicle of 741*,[2] whose place of composition was recently placed in the south or east of al-Andalus, is described as a text that tries to link the particular history of Spain to the general history of the Arab Empire as a continuous process to show that the Kingdom of Spain is part of a global future under Arab dominion. For this reason, the chronicler, heavily influenced by Byzantine culture,[3] which is why he is assumed to have been born outside Spain, continues the chronicle of the Spanish-Gothic John of Biclar until the rule of Hisham I and Leo III. The author tries at all times to present a positive image of the Arab Empire, an indifferent vision of the Visigothic Kingdom, and a negative view of the Empire of Constantinople. Considered to be a Christian serving a Muslim official,[4] the author aims to highlight the Mozarabs, who could read Latin, and whose history connects perfectly with the evolution of the political entities incorporated, that is, the Roman Empire and the Visigothic Kingdom, as a globalizing force.

This ideology is clear from the passage that deals with the conquest of the Iberian Peninsula:

> In the western regions the rule of the Goths [*regnum Gothorum*], settled with old solidity in the Spains [*Spanias*], was subdued when an army whose general was called Musa arrived and he subjected the abject kingdom [*regno*] to tribute.[5]

---

2 For the general description of this chronicle I rely on the interpretations presented in José Carlos Martín, "Los *Chronica Byzantia-Arabica*," *e-Spania. Revue interdisciplinaire d'études hispaniques médiévales et modernes* 1 (2006), accessed February 11, 2013, http://e-spania.revues.org/329.

3 He mainly used Greek and Syrian sources to compose this work.

4 In the study by Jose Carlos Martin in *e-Spania* (above) he also offers the possibility that the chronicler was a Muslim because his references to God seem to belong to the Islamic tradition.

5 *In occiduis quoque partibus regnum Gothorum antiqua soliditate firmatum apud Spanias per*

In line with the ideological background of the whole work, this text shows the conclusion of the *regnum Hispaniae* after its take-over by the Arabs and the persistence of the *regnum*, that is, the *regnum Hispaniae*, without any qualifier (e.g., "of Spain") apart from the dismissive adjective (*abiecto*), since the lack of any identifier seeks to place this kingdom as part of a greater political entity. However, the spatial reference to *Spanias* provides some trans-historical element suggesting historical progression without rupture. It is therefore possible to conclude that the *regnum*, belonging to the Goths or pertaining to the Arabs as part of a larger political entity, is still Spain.

Mozarabic Chronicle of 754

Historiographical focus on the *regna* is evident in the *Mozarabic Chronicle of 754*. It shares an Arabic source with the *Arab-Byzantine Chronicle of 741*, resulting in shared ideological attitudes among the two Andalusian-Christian chronicles. According to recent philological opinions,[6] this *Mozarabic Chronicle of 754* comes from the southeast of al-Andalus, specifically the area between Guadix and Murcia, and was written in several phases completed in 742, in 744, in 750, and in 754, with the latter developed by an author different from the rest. Like the previous work, it traces history back to the Visigothic age, since it is a continuation of the *Historia Gothorum* of Isidore of Seville. In addition, it uses the events of the Byzantine Arab empires as milestones, but even so rejects Arab rule, considering it harmful to Spain's earliest history.[7]

The first episode in which the fate of the *regnum Gothorum* and *regnum Hispaniae* caused by the Arab conquest is mentioned is as follows:

> In the western regions the rule of the Goths [*regnum Gothorum*], settled with ancient solidity for almost three hundred and fifty years from the start and beginning in the four hundredth era, spread out peacefully in the Spains [*Spanias*] by Liuvigild for almost one hundred and forty years until the era 750, was subdued when an army whose general was called Musa arrived and he subjected the taken kingdom [*regno*] to tribute.[8]

The textual parallelism with the passage from the *Arab-Byzantine Chronicle of 741* is obvious; both chroniclers have clearly used a common source. Unlike the previous

---

ducem sui exercitus nomine Musae adgressus edomuit et regno abiecto uectigalis fecit. Cited from *Corpus scriptorum Muzarabicorum*, ed. Juan Gil, 2 vols. (Madrid, 1973), 1:13.

6 *Continuatio Isidoriana Hispana. Crónica mozárabe de 754*, ed. José Eduardo López Pereira (León, 2009), 46–61.

7 I would not venture to reject the possibility that the text refers to the *regnum Hispaniae*, but I am inclined to the other option because Spain becomes a character with human attributes (i.e., it has honour or disgrace, and is delectable or miserable), as will be seen below in one of the texts inserted.

8 *In occiduis quoque partibus regnum Gothorum antiqua soliditate pene per trecentos quinquaginta annos, ab era quadringentesima ab exordio et principio sui firmatum, aput Spanias uero a Liuuigildo pene per CXL annos pacifice usque in era DCCL porrectum, per ducem sui exercitus nomine Muze adgressum edomuit et regno ablato uectigale fecit.* Cited from the *Continuatio Isidoriana*, 222 and 224. Note that I have erred on the side of literalness in these translations, retaining some Latin constructions, since many of the words and phrases in one chronicle appear later, and I wish to preserve the original phrasing.

Mozarabic work, the duration of the *regnum Gothorum* is specified,[9] which highlights the fact that it is now considered extinct, and the conquered kingdom is not insulted (*ablato* "taken over", instead of *abiecto*), since the author was a native of Spain and respected his kingdom.[10] However, the similarities to the previous chronicle are more noticeable than the differences and, thus, the *regnum Hispaniae* survives, while the rule of the Goths has been replaced by one of exogenous origin.

The following excerpt of the *Mozarabic Chronicle of 754* illustrates the political situation in the early years of the Andalusian Wilayah:

> At the same time in the era 753, the year of the Empire 9, the year of the Arabs 97, since Abd al-Aziz, who pacified all Spain [*omnem Hispaniam*] in three years under the yoke of the tax census, ardently desired the queen of Spain, to which he had been united in marriage, and to the daughters of the kings and princes, with whom he was emancipated and recklessly abandoned, with riches and honours in Sevilla, promoted a conspiracy of his people, he was killed by Ayyub's advice when he was engaged in prayer and, holding this one Spain a whole month, he was succeeded by Al-Hurr in the Kingdom of Hesperia [*regno Esperie*] by imperial order. He was informed of the death of Abd al-Aziz thus, as if with Queen Egilona's advice, the spouse of King Roderic previously, with whom he had allied, he would have tried to get rid of the Arab yoke from his neck and to hold the invaded Kingdom of Iberia [*regnum Iberie*] for himself.[11]

This fragment shows clearly the conception of the existence of a *regnum Hispaniae* after the Arab conquest. Thus, in addition to referring to Queen Egilona of Spain, presented as the character who gives political continuity between the rule of the Goths and the new Arab government, the Mozarabic chronicler mentions the *regnum Hispaniae* with different poetic epithets from the Greek tradition, perpetuated in the Isidorian renaissance: *regno Esperie* and *regnum Iberie*. Besides, the mention of *omnem Hispaniam* may refer to a political *regnum* but it may refer to a geographical territory. Finally, the chronicle continues with the subsequent Arab *walīs*, with the Mozarabic chronicler indicating that each one reigns in Spain (*regnat in Spania*).[12]

---

9 This custom is seen in chronicles from Christian lands, as discussed in the following presentation of Septimanian chronicles. It is possible that in the middle of the eighth century this type of chronicle with the duration of the *regnum Gothorum* existed, but unfortunately has not survived.

10 Perhaps the difference between *abiecto* and *ablato* in both chronicles is due to an error in the textual transmission, most likely located in the *Arab-Byzantine Chronicle of 741*, the text of which is not well- preserved.

11 *Per idem tempus in era DCCLIII, anno imperii eius VIIII, Arabum LXLVII, Abdellazis omnem Spaniam per annos tres sub censuario iugo pacificans, cum Spalim diuitiis et honorum fascibus cum reginam Spanie in coniugio copulatam uel filias regum hac principium pelicatas et inprudinter distractas extuaret, seditione suorum facta orationi instans ob consilio Aiub occiditur atque eo Spaniam retinente mense impleto Alaor in regno Esperie per principalia iussa succedit. Cui de morte Abdillazis ita edicitur, ut quasi consilio Egilonis regine coniugis quondam Ruderici regis, quam sibi sociauerat, iugum Arabicum a sua ceruice conaret euertere et regnum inuasum Iberie sibimet retemtare.* Cited from the *Continuatio Isidoriana*, 232 and 234.

12 For example: "Anbasa ibn Suhaym held the princedom of enlarged Spain for four years" (*Ambiza semis cum quattuor annos principatum Spanie aucte retemtat*). Cited from the *Continuatio Isidoriana*, 246.

The last extract I wish to show from the *Mozarabic Chronicle of 754* is widely known by scholars today:

> In fact, who would be able to narrate so many dangers? Who would be able to enumerate unbearable misfortunes to such an extent? Since if all the limbs became tongue, it could not absolutely at all say in a human way the catastrophes of Spain [*Spanie ruinas*] or its many great evils. [...] since everyone knows from experience that once Spain was delectable and now it has finished miserable both in honour and in dishonour.[13]

A misunderstanding of this piece became fixed among a section of historians, currently a small minority, but important for the purpose of this investigation. Traditionally, this text has been used as the first evidence for the concept of "the loss of Spain," and is usually linked to the rise of the idea of Reconquista from the need to regain the lost Spain. Without entering the large current historiographical debate about the concept of Reconquista, I want to emphasize that the Mozarab chronicler never describes Spain as "lost" or "disappeared," but complains that Spain, as a historical entity and even as a way of referring to the Spanish population, is suffering a deep crisis unlike the situation in an earlier, idealized time. Thus, according to the chronicler's point of view, Spain has never ceased to exist. Furthermore, as discussed in the previous piece of his work, the anonymous Mozarab explains that *Spania* survives as a kingdom under the rule of Arab leaders and shows no desire to restore the Visigothic order. Finally, analysing the text of the *deploratio Hispaniae*, the origin of its misreading is probably due to the erroneous translation or interpretation of *Spanie ruinas*, since some historians consider that *ruinas* means "destruction," when actually *ruinas*, besides being plural, means "catastrophes" or "misfortunes."

Septimanian Chronicles

Although the Septimanian chronicles are outside the geographical framework of this study, they are included because, as Septimania formed part of the territory of the former Visigothic Kingdom, the chronicles recount both the history of the Gothic kings and of Spain, and also because one of them greatly influenced the *Chronicle of Albelda*, as we will see below.

Both the *Chronologia regum Gothorum* and *Chronicon Moissiacense*[14] not only have in common their Septimanian origin and chronological proximity (797 and 818 respectively), but also and above all they share an expressly stated perception that the *regnum Gothorum* has concluded and that Saracens do not possess the *regnum Hispaniae* com-

---

13 *Quis enim narrare queat tanta pericula? Quis dinumerare tam inportuna naufragia? Nam si omnia menbra uerterentur in linguam, omnino nequaquam Spanie ruinas uel eius toth tantaque mala dicere poterit humana natura. [...] omnia et toth ut Spania condam deliciosa et nunc misera effecta tam in honore quam etiam in dedecore experibit.* Cited from the *Continuatio Isidoriana*, 228 and 230.

14 These chronicles have been studied in Georges Martin, "Un récit (la chute du royaume wisigothique d'Espagne dans l'historiographie chrétienne des VIIIᵉ et IXᵉ siècles)," in *Histoires de l'Espagne médiévale. Historiographie, geste, romancero*, ed. Georges Martin (Paris, 1997), 17–23. This famous French Hispanist investigated the concepts of the *regnum Gothorum* and *regnum Hispaniae* in line with this chapter and arrived at similar conclusions to me.

pletely since part of it is in Christian hands.[15] Thus, these two chronicles show the first appearance of an ideology that will be perpetuated in the historiography of the rest of the Middle Ages and even later, that is, the belief that Christians are the legitimate owners of the *regnum Hispaniae*, that they are a group radically opposed to the Saracens, and that they are predestined by God to recover it.

Chronologia regum Gothorum

This new approach is most evident in the *Chronologia regum Gothorum*, since it is roughly a list of reigns of all the Visigothic kings (from Athanaric to Roderic), supplying the duration of each reign, each king's noteworthy actions, and the emperors who ruled during each reign. Significantly, the chronicle ends with a mention of Charlemagne, then king of the Franks and patrician of Roma, but not yet emperor of the Romans. A passage related to the future of the *regnum Gothorum* and the *regnum Hispaniae* concludes the work:

> Roderic reigned three years. At that time, era 752, the Saracens, attracted by the false promise of the land, occupied the Spains [*Hispanias*] and seized the Kingdom of the Goths [*regnum Gothorum*], which they have forever retained in part until now; and they wage wars against the Christians day and night, and they fight every day, until divine predestination orders that from now on they are to be cruelly expelled. The kings of the Goths ended. They are under one rule for 314 [*sic*] years; from Alaric in era 301 the Goths entered Italy. After the years of this one [Alaric] the Gothic kings entered Gaul. After seven years the Goths migrated to Spain. In the era 835, Charles, King of the Franks and Patrician of Roma, reigned.[16]

Besides establishing the year 714 CE for the Arab conquest, not surprising considering it has linked the time of the Arab incursion and the domination of the north-eastern region of the Visigothic Kingdom, the *Chronologia regum Gothorum* states that the *regnum Hispaniae*, belonging to the Goths, was taken and that their rule has been extinguished, indicating its duration; therefore, the *regnum Hispaniae* remains, though in the hands of the Saracens. However, the chronicler specifies that not all of it belongs to them, implying that a part is under Christian control, a group to which the writer belongs. Thus, this group replaces the Goths in the irreducible fight against the Saracens

---

15 It should be noted that, at this time, the Carolingians were conquering the Spanish areas close to the Pyrenees, that is, the counties of the future Catalonia, the Aragonese lands, and Pamplona. But the *regnum Hispaniae* was considered indivisible, since it was not considered to be a Christian kingdom on one side and a Muslim kingdom on the other. It is also not asserted that Spain must only be held by Christians to be considered as such.

16 *Rudericus regnavit ann. III. Istius tempore era DCCLII, farmalio terrae Saraceni evocati Hispanias occupaverunt, regnumque Gothorum ceperunt; quod adhuc usque ex parte pertinaciter possident; et cum Christianis die noctuque bella ineunt, et quotidie confligunt, dum praedestinatio usque divina dehinc eos expelli crudeliter jubeat. Reges Gothorum defecerunt. Sunt sub uno ann. CCCXIIII; Alarico regnante ab era CCCI, ingressi sunt Gothi in Italiam. Post hujus annos reges Gothi Galliam ingressi sunt. Post septem annos Gothi Hispaniam migraverunt. In era D. IX. LXV. [forte, DCCCXXXV] regnavit Carolus Francorum rex, et patricius Romae.* Cited from Isidorus Hispalensis, "Chronologia regum Gothorum," in *Patrologiae cursus completus*, ed. Jacques-Paul Migne, 221 vols. (Paris, 1850), 83: col. 1118.

and is fated to defeat them because, at some point in the future, it is certain that God will support the Christians.

Therefore, there are no Goths because there are no Gothic kings; this syllogism mirrors the following: there are Christians because there is now a Christian king, who can be none other than Charlemagne. The chronicler clearly shows that the *regnum Christianorum* under the command of Charles the Great is the legitimate successor of the *regnum Gothorum* for the Kingdom of Spain, since he places the reign of this character just following the era of the Goths. So, Charlemagne becomes the champion of the conquest of the *regnum Hispaniae*, which should be in Christian hands, fighting against the Saracens under divine auspices. The chronicler does not write of neo-Gothicism, but of Christian restoration.[17]

---

17 It is possible that at this time there was the same political ideology in the Kingdom of Asturias, also heir of the whole *regnum Hispaniae* because the Asturian rulers identify themselves as Christians, not as Goths. This is plausible according to the information contained in the *Testament of Alfonso II*, a copy made in the tenth or eleventh centuries from a donation diploma written in the year 812 (María Josefa Sanz Fuentes, "Transcripción," in *Testamento de Alfonso II el Casto. Estudio y contexto histórico*, ed. Juan Ignacio Ruiz de la Peña Soler, María Josefa Sanz Fuentes (Granada, 2005), 85): "But because their prepotent vanity offended You, in the 749th era, the glory of the kingdom, together with King Roderic, left. In fact, he suffered the Arab sword deservedly. With your right hand, Christ, You took out from this plague your servant Pelagius, who, risen with the authority of the prince, destroyed the enemies fighting victoriously and, rising victorious, defended the people of the Christians and Asturians" (*Sed quia te offendit eorum prepotens iactantia in era DCC CL VIIII[ª] simul cum rege Roderico regni amisit gloria. Merito etenim arabicum sustinuit gladium. Ex qua peste tua dextera Christe famulum tuum eruisti Pelagium. Qui >in< principis sublimatus potentia, uictorialiter dimicans hostes perculit et christianorum asturumque gentem uictor sublimando defendit*). Cited from María Josefa Sanz Fuentes, "Transcripción," 87–88.

This fragment shows Pelagius as a survivor of the Arab conquest without identifying him as "a Goth" and he is mentioned just after the end of the *regnum Gothorum*, turning him into the historical successor of these due to his new *regnum*, described in the diploma as Christian and simultaneously Asturian. Thus, the rule of the Goths was succeeded and replaced by the rule of the "Christians," a word also in the Septimanian chronicles, along with "Asturians," a term of ethnicity or geography. However, this ideological approach does not fully coincide with the information provided on the possible remains of the hypothetical *Chronicle of Alfonso II* or other historiographical texts of this reign in the *Chronicle of Alfonso III*, whose presence is proposed in Claudio Sánchez-Albornoz, "¿Una crónica asturiana perdida?," *Revista de Filología Hispánica* 7 (1945): 105–46, and in Juan Gil Fernández, "Introducción," *Crónicas asturianas*, ed. Juan Gil Fernández (Oviedo, 1985), 76.

There are hints that the Asturians of Alfonso II did not consider themselves as the depositories of Spain by similar material in the *Chronicle of Albelda* according to Claudio Sánchez-Albornoz, "¿Una crónica asturiana perdida?" It is also my opinion that some fragments of chap. 15 of this chronicle could not have been written in the neo-Gothic and pro-Spanish reign of Alfonso III: there is the consideration that the Asturians are not Spanish because of their qualification of the Andalusian Wilayah and Emirate as *Hispania*. So, they would not be in it, but in Asturias, a different political entity, and would not control a part of this kingdom (see the next note).

For textual examples, see the following: "[Silo] had peace with Spain because of his mother" (*Cum Spania ob causam matris [Silo] pacem habuit*) cited from *Chronicle of Albelda*, 15.6. "And in his time a certain Mahmud who had fled from the Cordovan king from Spain was welcomed with his people in Asturias by this prince" (*Suoque tempore quidam de Spania nomine Mahamut a rege Cordouense fugatus cum suis omnibus Asturias ab hoc principe est susceptus*) from *Chronicle of Albelda*, 15.9. "And he invaded this castle, in which he beheaded the fifty thousand Saracens

Chronicon Moissiacense

Meanwhile, the *Chronicon Moissiacense* addresses these issues in a tangential way, since the purpose of this work is to relate the history of the Frankish kings, and the passages relate to Saracen attacks in Gaul. However, this chronicle agrees with the previous chronicle in its view that the *regnum Gothorum* is finished and that there is a part of Spain that does not belong to the Saracens,[18] as shown in the following passage:

> Then the Saracens enter Spain. The Goths place King Roderic over them. King Roderic goes into battle against the Saracens with a great army of Goths; and in the battle the Goths are defeated by the Saracens, and thus the rule of the Goths [*regnum Gothorum*] in Spain ends, and in less than two years the Saracens subdue almost all of Spain.[19]

In addition, this literary work provides an element that we do not see in the *Chronologia regum Gothorum*:

> After nine years of the Saracens entering Spain, Al-Samh, King of the Saracens, besieged Narbonne and took it by siege, and ordered the men of this city to be executed by the sword; they carried the captive women and children to Spain. [...] After the fifth year, Anbasa, King of the Saracens, invaded the Gauls with a huge army, defeated and took Carcassonne, and without interruption conquered Nîmes peacefully, and sent their hostages to Barcelona. [...] Year 732. Abd al-Rahman, King of Spain, who crossed Pamplona and the Pyrenean Mountains with a large army of Saracens, besieged the city of Bordeaux.[20]

With an approach more centred on the political situation of the Cordovan Wilayah than on his own, the chronicler called the rulers of al-Andalus kings of the Saracens and kings of Spain. This interpretation follows the distinction in the Christian-Andalusian

---

who came to its aid from Spain, and happily the victorious Alfonso returned in peace to Oviedo" (*Ipsutque castrum inuaditur, in quo fere quinquaginta milia Sarracenorum, qui ad auxilium eius ab Spania confluxerunt, detruncatur, atque feliciter Adefonsus uictor reuersus est in pace Oueto*) from the *Chronicle of Alfonso III, Ad Sebastianum*, 22. There are also passages for the subsequent reigns of Alfonso II in which al-Andalus is called *Hispania*, but it is easy to argue that this is due to an imitation of texts created in the reign of the Chaste King.

18 As in this passage the name of the Kingdom of Spain is not specified, it is possible the chronicler was referring to the Iberian Peninsula, since in the following extracts it is mentioned that the walī of Córdoba was the king of Spain. Therefore, the kingdom would have been under Arab rule, but would not cover the entire Peninsula. This concept may also be present in the supposedly lost *Chronicle of Alfonso II* or other texts with an anti-neo-Gothic outlook.

19 *Sarraceni tunc in Spania ingrediuntur. Gothi super se Rudericum regem constituunt. Rudericus rex cum magno exercitu Gothorum Sarracenis obviam et in proelio; sed inito proelio, Gothi debellati sunt a Sarracenis, sicque regnum Gothorum in Spania finitur, et infra duos annos Sarraceni pene totam Spaniam subiciunt*. Cited from *Annales et chronica aevi Carolini*, ed. George Heinrich Pertz, MGH SS 1 (1826), 290.

20 *Soma Rex Sarracenorum, nono anno postquam Spaniam ingressi sunt Narbonam obsidet, obsessamque capit, virosque civitatis illius gladio perimi jussit: mulieres et parvulos captivos in Spaniam ducunt [...]. Ambisa Rex Sarracenorum cum ingenti exercitu post quantum annum Gallias aggreditur, Carcassonam expugnat et capit, et usque Noemauso pace conquisivit, et obsides eorum Barchinona transmisit [...]. Anno DCCCXXII. Abderaman, rex Spaniae, cum exercitu magno Sarracenorum per Pampelonam et montes Pireneos transiens, Burdigalem civitatem obsidet*. Cited from *Annales et chronica*, 290–91.

chronicles: the *regnum Gothorum* was succeeded by the *regnum Sarracenorum* while the *regnum Hispaniae* continues without interruption. Thus, unlike the *Chronologia regum Gothorum*, the part of the Iberian Peninsula not controlled by the Saracens was probably not considered by the Septimanian chronicler as part of the *regnum Hispaniae*. In this way, the reference to the transfer of captives to Spain does not refer to a geographical territory but to the Kingdom of Spain, controlled by the king of the Saracens.

Interestingly, the title *rex Spaniae* used to refer to the walī of Córdoba also appears in Frankish contemporary works, such as Einhard's *Annales*,[21] although here the most common nomenclature is *rex Sarracenorum*.

Asturian Chronicles

Asturian chronicles from the ninth century represent a fundamental change that will mark all subsequent medieval Spanish-Christian historiography. They present a neo-Gothic ideology. According to this, the *regnum Gothorum* had not disappeared, but moved to the Asturias because the new kingdom was controlled by royal Visigothic lineages, either only that of Pelagius or Pelagius's plus those of several aristocrats. This new political ideology, reflected in the chronicles, arises in Asturias in the second half of the ninth century, coinciding with the reign of Alfonso III or perhaps earlier, during the rule of Ordoño I, though no chronicles from then have been preserved. Conversely, we find in these chronicles remnants of their sources written in the reign of Alfonso II containing elements against the neo-Gothic ideal,[22] whilst also asserting that the *regnum Gothorum* is over.

Furthermore, adapting the ideal of the Septimanian chronicles and texts of the reign of Alfonso II,[23] the Kingdom of Asturias is presented as part of the *regnum Hispaniae* and is the rightful owner of all of it by the mere fact that Asturias is governed by Christians, although implicitly this does mean recognizing that the Emirate of Córdoba is also part of the *regnum Hispaniae*. Besides, in the neo-Gothic passages this legitimacy is reinforced with the fact that the *regnum Gothorum* continues uninterrupted in Asturian territory.

Chronicle of Albelda

The *Chronicle of Albelda*,[24] an Asturian compilation of the years 881–883 that was probably made in a religious centre because of its encyclopaedic character, is the result of the recasting of several earlier works, which lends it a contradictory approach to neo-Gothicism and anti-neo-Gothicism. It is composed of Visigothic chronicles and geographies with Mozarabic additions (Isidore of Seville's *Historia Gothorum* and Julian of Toledo's *Historia Wambae*), Christian-Andalusian texts (the basis-work of ar-Razi's *Ajbâr Mulûk al-Andalus*), Septimanian chronicles (*Chronologia regum Gothorum*), Asturian historio-

---

21 *Annales et chronica*, 198.

22 See notes 17 and 18 above.

23 See notes 17 and 18.

24 For the description of this chronicle, I rely on the work of Juan Gil Fernández, "Introducción," 88–104.

graphical works (*Chronicle of Alfonso II*),[25] and also works contemporary to its period of compilation which give it a neo-Gothic nuance. Later, in the tenth and eleventh centuries, it was extended in the Kingdom of Nájera, where the oldest manuscripts were produced: Codex Albeldensis (972–974), MS Emilianensis 39 (end of tenth century) from the Real Academia de la Historia [hereafter RAH], and Codex Rotensis (eleventh century).[26] The first two codices share textual variants from Nájera, with notable differences in Chapters 13 and 14, while the third codex contains a very interesting textual fragment of Chapter 17 that is not contained in the other two codices.

As each chapter of the chronicle offers a different interpretation of the trajectory of the *regnum Gothorum* and *regnum Hispaniae*, an individual analysis is necessary. Chapter 13 of the *Chronicle of Albelda*, entitled "Incipit ordo Romanorum regum," concerns the succession of Roman kings, indicating important events in the history of Christianity and noting the correspondence of their reigns with those of the Gothic kings. Its end is very significant because it is not neo-Gothic, but quite the opposite. Thus, the Codex Albeldensis says: "At last, in the time of Emperor Tiberius, Wittiza was for nine years and Roderic reigned for three years. [In the margin] Then the Saracens possessed Spain and the rule of the Goths [*regnum Gothorum*] in the era 752."[27] And RAH-Emilianensis 39 says: "At last, in the time of Emperor Tiberius, Wittiza reigned for nine years and Roderic reigned for three years. Then the Saracens exterminated the rule of the Goths [*regnum Gothorum*]. It is ended."[28] Both fragments state that the Saracens possess the *regnum Hispaniae*, without indicating that there is some territory dominated by Christians, implying that Asturias was not part of that. In addition, they do not argue that the *regnum Gothorum* continues in Asturias, but even in RAH-Emilianensis 39 it is said to have been destroyed. In a way, it seems that the scribe of the Codex Albeldensis tried to avoid this conclusion, relegating it to the margin of the folio. Luckily, he did not omit it, since the mention of the year 714 makes it possible to locate the origin of the source of this text in the north-eastern part of the Iberian Peninsula or in Septimania: in that year these areas were conquered by the Arabs.

---

25 On the possible existence of this chronicle, mentioned several times in this chapter, I recommend reading the classic study of Claudio Sánchez-Albornoz, "¿Una crónica asturiana perdida?" This great scholar based its existence on the textual similarity between the *Chronicle of Albelda* and the *Chronicle of Alfonso III*, only possible due to dependence on the same source; the change of style in the *Chronicle of Alfonso III* shortly after the account of the reign of Alfonso II; the presence of the history of the Asturian kings until Alfonso II in Ibn al-Atir's *Kamil fi-l-Ta'rij*, caused by the handling of ar-Razi's *Ajbâr Mulûk al-Andalus*, whose writer would in turn use an Asturian text with this information; and a testimony of Ambrosio de Morales, who had in his hands a chronicle that related the history of the Asturian kings from Pelagius to Alfonso II. Juan Gil Fernández, "Introducción," 76, also defended the existence of some *Chronicle of Alfonso II*. However, if this chronicle did not exist, the presence of Asturian texts created in the reign of Alfonso II seems evident (see note 17).

26 All codices with chapters of the *Chronicle of Albelda* are studied in Juan Gil Fernández, "Introducción," 81–8.

27 *Tiberio denique imperante Uittizza peragit an. VIIII et Rudericus rg. an. III. [Ad marginem] Tunc Sarrazeni Spaniam possederunt et regnum Gotorum era DCCLII.* Cited from *Crónicas asturianas*, 166.

28 *Tiberio denique imperante Uittizza peragit an. VIIII et Rudericus rg. an. III. Tunc Sarraceni Spania obtenta regnum Gotorum exterminatur. Finit.* Cited from *Crónicas asturianas*, 166.

Chapter 14, "Item ordo gentis Gotorum," deals with the Visigothic kings explaining the important events of each reign. This is the first part of the chronicle showing the sense that the whole of the *regnum Hispaniae* has not been occupied because one group of Christians resisted the invaders. The Septimanian source of this passage is obvious because the chronicler copies the *Chronologia regum Gothorum* almost verbatim. However, unlike this chronicle, the region free of Muslim rule is not the Pyrenees, but the territory of the Kingdom of Asturias, and the Christians who succeed the Goths are not the Carolingians, but the Asturians. According to the Codex Albeldensis:

> Roderic reigned three years. At that time, era 752, the Saracens, drawn by the troubled land, occupy the Spains [*Spanias*] and seize the Kingdom of the Goths [*regnum Gothorum*], which they have forever retained in part until now. And they wage wars against the Christians day and night and they fight every day, until divine predestination orders from now on that they will be cruelly expelled. Amen.[29]

According to RAH-Emilianensis 39:

> Roderic reigned three years. At that time, era 752, the Saracens, drawn by the troubled land, occupy the Spains [*Spanias*] and seize the Kingdom of the Goths [*regnum Gothorum*], which they have forever retained in part until now. And they wage wars against the Christians day and night and they fight every day, but they are not able to snatch them Spain at all. It is ended.[30]

Both variants are virtually identical except for the ending and, compared with the *Chronologia regum Gothorum*, they share the omission of the part declaring the end of the Gothic kings and linking their history with Charlemagne. The wording of RAH-Emilianensis 39 defends more the idea of division of the *regnum Hispaniae* because, in this text, it emphasizes that the whole of Spain has not been occupied. Moreover, in this version, a few paragraphs earlier on Wittiza, there is a brief comment on the Visigothic ancestry of Pelagius, the first leader of the Asturians; but this is likely not enough to qualify it as neo-Gothic because it continues to base the legitimacy of recovery of the *regnum* on Christianity and not on Gothicism. Furthermore, the fact that the reference to the ancestry of Pelagius is only in that copy may imply that it was added later by a scribe.

Chapter 15, whose title is "Item ordo Gotorum Obetensium regum" in Codex Albeldensis and "Item ordo Gotorum regum" in RAH-Emilianensis 39, deals with the Asturian kings, is totally neo-Gothic and shows the strong influence of the *Chronicle of Alfonso III* in word and in spirit.[31] The beginning of this chapter is essentially the same

---

29 *Rudericus rg. an. III. Istius tempore era DCCLII farmalio terre Sarraceni euocati Spanias occupant regnumque Gotorum capiunt, quem aduc usque ex parte pertinaciter possedunt. Et cum eis Xpiani die noctuque bella iniunt et cotidie confligunt, dum praedestinatio usque divina dehinc eo expelli crudeliter iubeat. Amen.* Cited from *Crónicas asturianas*, 171.

30 *Rudericus rg. an. III. Istius tempore era DCCLII farmalio terre Sarraceni euocati Spanias occupant regnumque Gotorum capiunt, quem aduc usque ex parte pertinaciter possedunt. Et cum eis Xpiani die noctuque bella iniunt et cotidie confligunt, sed eis ex toto Spaniam auferre non possunt. Finit.* Cited from *Crónicas asturianas*, 171.

31 This influence is chronologically possible because the text of the *Chronicle of Alfonso III* was already developed in the reign of Ordoño I, except for the final part about this king, added under the rule of Alfonso III.

in both codices: "First in Asturias Pelagius reigned in Cangas eighteen years. He, [as we said above][32] when expelled from Toledo by King Wittiza, he entered Asturias. And after Spain was occupied by the Saracens, first he rebelled against them in Asturias, when Yusuf was reigning in Córdoba and Munuza administering in Gijón, city of the Saracens, over the Asturians."[33]

The neo-Gothicism is clear both in the title of the chapter and in the fact that Pelagius is linked with Toledo and King Wittiza; therefore, although it is not specified in the text, the chronicler of this chapter considered the *regnum Gothorum* to have moved from Toledo to Asturias by Pelagius. In addition, the rebellion means the emergence of a Christian part of the *regnum Hispaniae* that is fighting against those who hold illegitimate tenure of that *regnum* in Córdoba.

Finally, Chapter 17, which deals with the entrance of the Saracens into Spain and includes a list of the walīs of al-Andalus, reverts to an anti-neo-Gothic tone, showing no information to indicate that the *regnum Hispaniae* still survives in Christian hands. With the obvious influence of Christian-Andalusian sources (e.g., the use of the nomenclature *amir al-muminin* replacing the typical *rex* for the rulers of Damascus), the origin of this chapter seems completely independent from the rest of the *Chronicle of Albelda*. It was likely composed by a Mozarab in al-Andalus, perhaps in the Upper March because of the presence of the traditional date of conquest of this region of the Visigothic Kingdom, although this could be the result of a modification of the Asturian compiler to match the dates of conquest in other chapters. The chronicler may have considered it essential to include this Mozarabic work to present the history of al-Andalus in his global vision of Spanish history. Even so, it is significant that he did not refine the text to introduce neo-Gothic elements or, at least, the idea that the Kingdom of Asturias was the part of Spain fighting against the Saracens. All this can be seen in the following excerpt, virtually identical in both the Codex Albeldensis and RAH-Emilianense 39:

XVII. [In addition,][34] the entrance of the Saracens in Spain is so.

As we already mentioned above, Roderic was ruling the Goths in Spain, through King Wittiza's sons a range of disputes arose among the Goths, since a part of them wished to see [his] rule [*regnum*] overthrown; both by their favour and by deceitfulness, the Saracens entered Spain in the third year of King Roderic, the third day of the Ides of November of the 752nd era, when Amir al-Mu'minin Al-Walid ibn Abd al-Malik was reigning in Africa, in the hundredth year of the Arabs. First Abu Zuhra entered Spain whilst remaining under General Musa in Africa and leaving the homelands of the Moors.

The following year Tariq arrived.

---

32 An addition in RAH, MS Emilianensis 39. It refers to the addition mentioned above about Chapter 14 on the Gothic ancestry of Pelagius.

33 *Primum in Asturias Pelagius rg. in Canicas an. XVIII. Iste [, ut supra diximus,] a Uittizzane rege de Toleto expulsus Asturias ingressus. Et postquam a Sarracenis Spania occupata est, iste primum contra eis sumsit reuellionem in Asturias, regnante Iuzep in Cordoba et in legione cibitate Sarracenorum iussa super Astures procurante Monnuzza.* Cited from *Crónicas asturianas*, 173.

34 Only in the Codex Albeldensis.

In the third year, Tariq already having already fought against Roderic, Musa ibn Nusayr arrived and the rule of the Goths [*regnum Gotorum*] perished and then all the glory of the Gothic people perished through fear or with iron. And nobody knows the cause of King Roderic's death until the present day.[35]

The Codex Rotensis contains, just following this text, a fragment similar to a passage of the *Rotense* version of the *Chronicle of Alfonso III*. Therefore, there are two hypotheses: it could be an addition created from this historiographical work in the eleventh century, at which time the manuscript, which also contains the Alfonsine chronicle although with a significant textual difference,[36] was produced. Alternatively, and more likely, it could be the original text of both the Mozarabic work and the *Chronicle of Albelda*. So, it was eliminated in the common version of the Codex Albeldensis and RAH-Emilianensis 39, remained in the variant of the Codex Rotensis, and coincides with the passage of *Chronicle of Alfonso III*, both using the same Mozarabic source. The version of the beginning of this chapter in the Codex Rotensis is:

XVII. Explanation about the entrance of the Saracens in Spain

While Roderic was ruling the Goths in Spain, the Saracens entered Spain in the third year of King Roderic, the third day of the Ides of November of the 752nd era, when Amir al-Mu'minin Al-Walid ibn Abd al-Malik was reigning in Africa, in the hundredth year of the Arabs. In the era and the year above, first Abu Zuhra entered Spain remaining under General Musa in Africa and leaving the homelands of the Moors.

The following year Tariq arrived.

In the third year, Tariq already having already fought against Roderic, Musa ibn Nusayr arrived and the rule of the Goths [*regnum Gotorum*] perished and then the glory of the Gothic people perished through fear or with iron. And about King Roderic nobody knows the cause of his death until today.

Nevertheless, the Arabs possessed the region along with the kingdom [*regno*]; all the glory of the Gothic people perished through fear or with iron. Since there was no worthy penance in them for their faults and since they abandoned the established precepts of the Lord and the holy canons, the Lord abandoned them so that they do not possess desirable land. And those who, always helped by the right hand of the Lord, overcame the enemy's

---

35 *XVII. [Item] ingressio Sarracenorum in Spania ita est. Sicut iam supra retulimus, Ruderico regnante Gotis in Spania pre filios Uittizani regis oritur Gotis rixarum discesio, ita ut una pars eorum regnum dirutum uidere desiderarent; quorum etiam fabore atque farmalio Sarraceni Spaniam sunt ingressi anno regni Ruderici IIIº, die IIIº Idus Nouembris era DCCLIIª, regnante in Africa Ulith Amir Almauminin filio de Abdelmelic, anno Arabum centesimo. Ingressus est primum Abzuhura in Spania sub Muzza duce in Africa commanente et Maurorum patrias defecante. Alio anno ingressus est Tarik. Tertio anno iam eodem Tarik prelio agente cum Ruderico ingressus est Muzza iben Nuzzeir, et periit regnum Gotorum et tunc omnis decor Gotice gentis pauore uel ferro periit. De rege quoque eodem Ruderico nulli causa interitus eius cognita manet usque in presentem diem.* Cited from *Crónicas asturianas*, 182–83.

36 The difference is that, in the corresponding passage of the *Chronicle of Alfonso III* in the Codex Rotensis (see further below), a date, unique among the extant copies and not present in the passage of the *Chronicle of Albelda* from the same codex, is written at the beginning of the paragraph. This may invalidate this hypothesis because, if this passage was taken from the text of the *Chronicle of Alfonso III* from the copy of the same manuscript, the scribe would not have forgotten to include information as significant as a date.

attacks and prostrated the lands of wars, were reduced almost to nothing, and many of them are discernibly humbled, due to God's judgment. In addition, the city of Toledo, victor of all the peoples, succumbed defeated by the Ismaelite triumphs and submitted to them. And so, due to the bloody sins, Spain fell in the year of the Goths 380.[37]

In line with the rest of Chapter 17 this part, which is only preserved by this codex, indicates that the *regnum Gothorum* has ended and the *regnum Hispaniae* is in Arab hands.

Chronicle of Alfonso III

After the contradictory *Chronicle of Albelda*, the so-called *Chronicle of Alfonso III* is much more consistent in its ideology. Interest in the detail of its contents inspired the drafting of two versions of the same chronicle, with similar approaches but different nuances: the *Rotense* and the *Ad Sebastianum*.[38] This great twofold work was made in the court of Oviedo, though historians differ to its process of composition and date. According to the traditional theory,[39] the *Chronicle of Alfonso III* was written shortly after the year 884 because it does not refer to the *Prophetic Chronicle*, meaning that the date on which Alfonso III was expected to recover all Spain and restore the *regnum Gothorum* would have passed.

However, currently there are two new theories arising when Bonnaz and Gil Fernández noticed that the similarities and differences between the versions follow a common pattern.[40] According to Bonnaz, Alfonso III ordered the original text in the ninth century, then this text was recast with the famous letter to Sebastian during the reign of Garcia I (910–914), and finally a scribe from the reign of Garcia I and one from the time of Ordoño II (914–924) created the archetypes of the two versions.[41] Instead, for Gil Fernández,

---

37 *XVII. Ratio Sarracenorum de sua ingressione in Spania. Ruderico regnante Gotis in Spania, Sarraceni Spaniam sunt ingressi anno regni Ruderici IIIº, die IIIº Idus Nouembris era DCCLIIª, regnante in Africa Ulith Amir Almauminin filio de Abdelmelic, anno Arabum centesimo. Era et anno quo supra, ingressus est primum Abzuhura in Spania sub Muzza duce in Africa commanente et Maurorum patrias defecante. Alio anno ingressus est Tarik.Tertio anno iam eodem Tarik prelio agente cum Ruderico ingressus est Muzza iben Nuzzeir, et periit regnum Gotorum et tunc omnis decor Gotice gentis pauore uel ferro periit. De rege quoque eodem Ruderico nulli causa interitus eius cognita manet usque in odiernum diem. Arabes tamen regionem simul cum regno possessam, omnis decor Gotice gentis pabore uel ferro periit. Quia non fuit in illis pro suis delictis digna penitentia, et quia derelinquerunt precepta Domini et sacrorum canonum instituta, dereliquid illos Dominus ne possiderant desiderauilem terram. Et qui semper dextera Domini adiuti hostiles impetus deuincebant tellasque bellorum prostrabant, iudicio Dei a paucis superati pene ad nicilum sunt redacti, ex quibus multi ucusque dinoscuntur manere humiliati. Urbs quoque Toletana cunctarumque gentium uictrix Ismaeliticis triumfis uicta subcumbuit eisque subiecta deseruit. Sicque peccatis concruentibus Ispania ruit anno Gotorum CCCLXXX.* Cited from *Crónicas asturianas*, 182–83.

38 There are some parallels with Alfonso X's *Estoria de España*, because this chronicle has a "Primitive Version" and a "Critical Version," and the differences are not based on proximity to the original draft but on ideology. On this, I recommend consulting Inés Fernández-Ordóñez, *Las estorias de Alfonso el Sabio* (Madrid, 1992).

39 See Juan Ignacio Ruiz de la Peña, "Estudio preliminar: la Cultura en la Corte Ovetense del siglo IX," in *Crónicas asturianas*, 39.

40 *Chroniques asturiennes (fin IXᵉ siècle)*, ed. Yves Bonnaz (Paris, 1987), 28–29. Juan Gil Fernández, "Introducción," 61–63.

41 *Chroniques asturiennes*, 28–29. If this theory is true, the two versions were made in León

whose proposal seems to me more reasonable, the final part of the work, which includes the end of the reign of Ordoño I and the history of the Banu Qasi, shows that originally the *Chronicle of Alfonso III* ended in the early years of the reign of Ordoño I and, years later, Alfonso III decided to add the reign of his father to honour him, including among other things his great victory over the Banu Qasi. Accordingly, Gil Fernández proposed that the texts of the *Rotense* and *Ad Sebastianum* were originally produced in the reign of Ordoño I and they have an almost identical conclusion added by order of Alfonso III.[42]

With regard to its sources, let me highlight the use of the lost *Chronicle of Alfonso II* or another historiographical work from this reign.[43] This has been demonstrated by the parallels between the *Chronicle of Alfonso III* and the *Chronicle of Albelda* in texts dealing with the first Asturian kings, and by a break in style in the account from the reign of Alfonso II, a section with more clerical inspiration.[44]

In terms of its contents, the *Chronicle of Alfonso III* relates the reigns of Gothic and Asturian kings from the death of Reccared and Wamba's reign until the death of Ordoño I, thus covering 672 to 866. In this way, the main objective was to produce a chronicle which recounted the history of these kings, continuing the tradition of Isidore of Seville's *Historia Gothorum*.[45] It was also intended to dignify the Asturian throne: in the ninth century the Kingdom of Asturias became conscious of its importance, and the Mozarabic immigrants who came north throughout the century projected their past onto Asturian history, giving light to some shadowy events. This brought to Asturias the concepts of neo-Gothicism and the recovery of all Spain.[46]

This neo-Gothicism is more present in the *Chronicle of Alfonso III* than in the *Chronicle of Albelda*, because while the latter only contains a few explicit references, the former retains a Gothic spirit that emerges from the account, such as the mention of the lineages of Pelagius and Alfonso I and the choice of Pelagius as leader.[47] Neo-Gothicism was on the rise during the time in which the *Chronicle of Alfonso III* was written for the following reasons: the arrival of Mozarabs in Asturias in a time when Toledo was linked more to the Arab culture; military expansion south towards the Douro/Duero river, which opened up the possibility of recovering Toledo, considered a Jerusalem for neo-Gothicism; the need for a unifying and stabilizing element against successive political upheavals in the Kingdom of Asturias which had tried to usurp the throne or to split the territory; and the weakness of the Carolingians, who had also declared themselves heirs to the Goths, due to them being Christians and holding Septimania and the Spanish March.[48]

---

because in this time Asturias was ruled by Fruela II.

42 Juan Gil Fernández, "Introducción," 74–75.

43 See notes 17 and 26.

44 *Chroniques asturiennes*, 76–83.

45 *Chroniques asturiennes*, 46.

46 Juan Gil Fernández, "Introducción," 70.

47 *Chroniques asturiennes*, 88–89.

48 *Chroniques asturiennes*, 92–93.

On the differences between the two versions of the *Chronicle of Alfonso III*, the *Rotense* is sometimes more erudite and careful than the *Ad Sebastianum*, with more quotations and more knowledge of books. The *Rotense* has a literary style influenced by homeop-toton, with rhymed prose, while the *Ad Sebastianum* tries to avoid it; so the *Rotense* has a Visigothic style. The *Ad Sebastianum*, instead, has a classical style similar to that used by the Carolingians. From the two accounts of the Battle of Covadonga, it can be demonstrated that the *Rotense* always provides more information about the original text and is closer to it. The greater movement of the *Ad Sebastianum* away from the original text lies in its departure from a more clerical profile in favour of a neo-Gothic political ideal: exalting the Asturian kings as the true and worthy successors of the Visigothic kings.[49]

In my opinion, both texts should be considered as two independent chronicles, the *Rotense Chronicle* and the *Ad Sebastianum Chronicle*, belonging to the cycle of Alfonso III with the *Prophetic Chronicle* and the *Chronicle of Albelda*, because even with their similarities, they differ both in content and in ideological approach. Refining the hypothesis of Gil Fernández, I propose that each version-chronicle was a reworking and reinterpretation of the same lost chronicle of the reign of Ordoño I. Thus, each one would have been made in the last third of the ninth century by a writer or group of writers with a different mindset leading to different ideological approaches.[50]

Having set out the ideology behind the *Chronicle of Alfonso III*, let me include the following passage on the conception of the *regnum Gothorum* and the *regnum Hispaniae* after the Arab conquest in the *Rotense*:

> And in fact, in our rough times, when the city of Viseu and its suburbs were looted [*populata*] by our order, in a certain basilica there a monument was discovered above which an epitaph is inscribed in this way, "Here rests Roderic, the last king of the Goths." But let us go back to the time when the Saracens invaded Spain.

> [On the third day of the Ides of November of the era 752][51] the Arabs killed with the sword many in the region as well as in the oppressed kingdom [*regno*]; they subjugated the rest who agreed acts of peace to subdue them. In addition, the city of Toledo, victor of all the peoples, succumbed defeated by the Ismaelite triumphs and it submitted to them. They placed prefects throughout the provinces of Spain and for many years they made them pay tributes to the Babylonian king <until they elected their king>, and they consolidated a kingdom [*regno*] for themselves in the patrician city of Córdoba. During this hard time in this region of the Asturians the prefect Munuza, a partner of Tariq, was in the city of Gijón. Then, taking a stand, a certain Pelagius, sword-bearer of kings Wittiza and Roderic, oppressed under the dictat of the Ismaelites, entered Asturias with his own sister.[52]

---

49 Juan Gil Fernández, "Introducción," 65–71 and 77–80.

50 On my hypothesis about the creation of the *Chronicle(s) of Alfonso III*, see my article: Iván Pérez Marinas, "Las obras de las crónicas de Alfonso III: *Crónica de Alfonso II sobre el final de los reyes godos, Leyenda de Covadonga, Crónica de Sebastián de Salamanca* y *Crónica de Ordoño I*," *Journal of Medieval Iberian Studies* 7, no. 2 (2015): 249–65.

51 Only in the Codex Rotensis.

52 *Rudis namque nostris temporibus quum ciuitas Uiseo et suburbis eius iussum nostrum esset populatus, in quadam ibi baselica monumentus inuentus est, ubi desuper epitafion huiusmodi est conscriptus: "Hic requiescit Rudericus ultimus rex Gotorum." Sed redeamus ad illum tempus quo Sarrazeni Spaniam sunt adgressi.*

And in the *Ad Sebastianum*:

> And in fact, in our rough times, when the city of Viseu and its suburbs were looted [*populata*] by us, in a certain basilica there a monument was discovered above which a sculpted epitaph says, "Here rests Roderic, the last king of the Goths."

> In the homeland as well as in the oppressed kingdom [*regno*] for many years the Arabs forced tributes through their chiefs to the Babylonian king, until they elected their king, and they consolidated the kingdom [*regno*] for themselves in the patrician city of Córdoba. The Goths died, partly by the sword, partly from hunger. But those of royal lineage who remained, some of them went to France, but most entered the homeland of the Asturians and elected Pelagius, son of a certain Favila, duke of royal lineage, as prince.[53]

Both versions, which are theoretically neo-Gothic, contain the surprising reference to Roderic as the last king of the Goths, so that would suggest that the *regnum Gothorum* was over. It is very difficult to know whether this statement, perpetuated in the Spanish-Christian medieval historiography and only amended by Lucas de Tuy deleting the word *ultimus*, comes from a text from a previous reign before neo-Gothicism came to the fore and this relic explains the reference to Roderic being the last Visigothic king. But since the passage indicates that the discovery of the epitaph was contemporary with its writing, this text is supposed to have been created in the reign of Alfonso III, who also is credited with the conquest of Viseu in the *Chronicle of Albelda*. Even so, I propose the following hypothesis. Just as the *Chronica Naierensis* copied from the *Chronicle of Alfonso III*, this passage, as it stands, including references to the contemporaneity of the discovery and conquest of Viseu, perhaps in the time of Alfonso III or Ordoño I,[54] may have literally copied from a chronicle drawn up in the reign of Alfonso II (maybe the *Chronicle of Alfonso II*). This would explain the expression *nostris temporibus*. Similarly, the action directed against Viseu might not refer to its conquest, but a previous looting,[55]

[III Idus Nouembris era DCCLII] Araues tamen regionem simul et regno opresso plures gladio interfecerunt, relicos uero pacis federe blandiendo siui subiugauerunt. Urbs quoque Toletana, cunctarum gentium uictris, Ismaeliticis triumfis uicta subcubuit et eis subiugata deseruit. Per omnes prouincias Spanie prefectos posuerunt et pluribus annis Bauilonico regi tributa persolberunt <quousque sibi regem elegerunt>, et Cordoba urbem patriciam regnum sibi firmaberunt. Per idem ferre tempus in hac regione Asturiensium prefectus erat in ciuitate Ieione nomine Munnuza conpar Tarec. Ipso quoque prefecturam agente, Pelagius quidam, spatarius Uitizani et Ruderici regum, dicione Ismaelitarum oppressus cum propia sorore Asturias est ingressus. Cited from *Crónicas asturianas*, 122.

53 *Rudis namque nostris temporibus quum Uiseo ciuitas et suburbana eius a nobis populata esset, in quadam ibi baselica monumentum inuentum est, ubi desuper epitaphion sculptum sic dicit: "Hic requiescit Rudericus ultimus rex Gotorum." Arabes tamen patria simul cum regno oppreso pluribus annis per presides Babilonico regi tributa persoluerunt, quousque sibi regem elegerunt et Cordoba urbem patriciam regnum sibi firmauerunt. Goti uero partim gladio, partim fame perierunt. Sed qui ex semine regio remanserunt, quidam ex illis Franciam petierunt, maxima uero pars in patria Asturiensium intrauerunt sibi que Pelagium filium quondam Faffilani ducis ex semine regio principem elegerunt.* Cited from *Crónicas asturianas*, 123.

54 As mentioned above, according to Gil Fernández, this king ordered the creation of the two versions of the *Chronicle of Alfonso III*.

55 The translation of the Latin word *populare* is much discussed, since in classical Latin it means

an unknown event which is not reproduced in the chronicle corresponding to the reign of Alfonso II.[56] This explains the words *iussum nostrum* and *a nobis*.[57]

Certainly, these words about the end of the Gothic kings contrasts with the neo-Gothic ideology contained in the second paragraph of both fragments. According to *Rotense*, the *regnum Gothorum* continues in Asturias because Pelagius was the sword-bearer (*spatarius*) of the two previous Gothic kings, while according to *Ad Sebastianum*, the continuity of the Gothic kings is clear because Pelagius hasd the same royal lineage as the refugees who fled with him in Asturias. It is noteworthy that this version of the chronicle recognizes that France, perhaps specifically Septimania and the Spanish March, was another repository of Gothicism.

Finally, the *Rotense* accepts more than the *Ad Sebastianum* that the Arabs control the *regnum Hispaniae*. As stated above, we can see the similarity between *Rotense* text, and even *Ad Sebastianum* text, with the passage of Chapter 17 of the *Chronicle of Albelda* contained in the Codex Rotensis. They differ in that the text of *Chronicle of Albelda* seems to be more complete and to have an anti-neo-Gothic ideology belonging to the eighth century or the first half of the ninth century.[58]

Galician-Portuguese Chronicles

A significant historiographical gap in the tenth century and the first three quarters of the eleventh century follows, and the next group of chronicle texts represent what I call Galician-Portuguese chronicles. They date to the late eleventh and twelfth centuries. Besides coinciding in their north-western Iberian origin, they share the same historiographical ideology on the two points we have been studying in this chapter. They show no hints of neo-Gothicism, so the Asturian chronicles of the second half of the ninth century clearly did not influence this region (Galicia-Portugal). They maintain the historiographical schemes of the late eighth and early ninth centuries. Therefore, the Galician-Portuguese chronicles consider that the *regnum Gothorum* had been extinguished at the hands of the Saracens, the new holders of the *regnum Hispaniae*, and, although it was not made explicit as it was in the Septimanian chronicles, they do imply the existence of a perpetual struggle between Christians and Muslims for the control of this *regnum* since, after the end of the Goths, the line continues in the kings of Asturias, where they are presented as its legitimate successors.

---

to "plunder or devastate a village," but it seems that this sense does not fit in certain passages of the chronicle and might be replaced by *settle*.

56 The *Chronicle of Alfonso III* also omits a similar event, the sacking of Lisboa, conducted by the same king, Alfonso II, and known thanks to Frankish sources, primarily Einhard's *Annals*: see *Annales et chronica*, 185.

57 If these hypotheses are true, it would be interesting to explore if such status can be observed in the reign of Alfonso II, since it would occur in a time close to the discovery of the tomb of St. James. This would be a clear ideological linkage of the Asturians, or rather the royal Asturian lineage, with the Goths as their legitimate successors, no longer Goths but Asturians and Christians.

58 Previously I have shown that the ideology of this chapter of the *Chronicle of Albelda* is seen in its status as a Mozarabic work in favour of Arab rule.

Annales Portugalenses veteres

Let us consider first the *Annales Portugalenses veteres*, preserved in various Portuguese manuscripts. These were a collection of similar chronicles developed from a common text in the late eleventh century and throughout the twelfth century in the County of Portugal or Porto, though we should not preclude the possibility that these Portuguese annals influenced each other. All the *Annales Portugalenses veteres* begin with the end of the Goths; they continue with a listing of the Asturian kings until the reign of Alfonso II; and then, suddenly, present the main events of the invasion of al-Mansur in Galician lands and of the conquering progression to the south, specifying the king who took over each city. Obviously, the later annals complete the accounts with the events that occurred until the date of its composition.[59]

The beginning text of all versions of the *Annales* is virtually identical. Their chronological order is: the "Long Recension" (1079), preserved in the *Livro da Noa II* and the *Chronica Gothorum*; the "Short Recension" (1111), conserved in the *Homiliarium of 1139* and the *Summa Chronicarum*; and the "Short Recension Continued until 1168" (1168), whose passage about the end of the Goths has survived only in the *Livro da Noa I*. The texts are:

> Era 349 the Goths left their land. Era 366 they entered Spain and reigned there 383 years; they arrived in Spain from their land in seventeen years. In the seven-hundred and forty-ninth era they were expelled from the Kingdom of Spain [*regno Hispaniae*]. Era 749 the Saracens obtained Spain.
>
> Before Lord Pelagius reigned, the Saracens reigned in Spain for five years.[60]
>
> In the 349th era the Goths left their land. 366th era they entered Spain. The people of the Goths dominated Spain 383 years and they arrived in Spain from their land in seventeen years. Era 749 they were expelled from their kingdom [*regno*]. 750th era the Saracens obtain Spain.
>
> Before Lord Pelagius reigned, the Saracens reigned in Spain for five years.[61]
>
> In the 349th era the Goths left their land. 366th era they entered Spain, dominated it 383 years and arrived in Spain from their land in seventeen years.
>
> Before Lord Pelagius reigned, the Saracens reigned in Spain for five years.[62]

---

59 Pierre David, *Études historiques sur la Galice et le Portugal du VIᵉ au XIIᵉ siècle* (Coimbra, 1947), 257–59. For more information about the creation of these historiographical works, see David, *Études historiques sur la Galice*, 261–90.

60 *Era CCC XL IX egressi sunt Gotti de terra sua. Era CCC LX VI ingressi sunt Hispaniam et regnaverunt ibi annis CCC LXXX III; de terra autem sua pervenerunt ad Hispaniam per XVII annos. Era septingentesima quadragesima nona expulsi sunt de regno Hispanie. Era 749 Sarraceni Hispaniam adepti sunt. Antequam Dominus Pelagius regnaret Sarraceni regnaverunt in Hispania annis V.* Cited from David, *Études*, 291–92.

61 *In era CCCᵃ XLᵃ IXᵃ egressi sunt Goti de terra sua. Era CCCᵃ LXᵃ VIᵃ ingressi sunt Ispaniam. Dominati sunt Ispaniam gens Gotorum annis CCC LXXX III et de terra sua pervenerunt in Ispaniam per annos XVII. Era DCC XL VIIII expulsi sunt de regno suo. Era DCCᵃ Lᵃ Sarraceni Ispaniam obtinent. Antequam Domnus Pelagius regnaret Sarraceni regnaverunt in Ispaniam annis Vᵉ.* Cited from David, *Études*, 303.

62 *In era CCCᵃ XLᵃ IXᵃ egressi sunt Goti de terra sua. Era CCCᵃ LXᵃ VIᵃ ingressi in Spaniam et*

In a summarizing fashion the chroniclers merely state the duration of the *regnum Gothorum*, commenting that the Goths were the owners of the *regnum Hispaniae* until it was obtained by the Saracens, who preserved this kingdom under their rule. However, this introduction may be regarded as the leitmotif of all of the annals, as they point out one by one the cities conquered by the Saracens in the western Peninsula. Regardless, the lack of ideological interpretation is significant, both in the fragments studied here and in the rest of the work, because at no point are neo-Gothic principles or the struggle between Christians and Muslims mentioned, but only the conquest undertaken by leaders, either al-Mansur or Pelagius's successors, to whom remarkably neither origin nor leadership of a particular people are assigned.

Chronicon Compostellanum

The *Chronicon Compostellanum* takes the same non-ideological line. However, unlike the previous annals, its chronicler is more interested in the rule of the Asturian-Leonese kings, explaining their actions in more detail from the reign of Fernando I and Sancha I and adding partisan touches to praise Alfonso VI, to criticize Urraca I, and to conclude the story significantly with the enthronement of Alfonso VII in 1126, the year around which this literary work was written. Turning to consider the interpretation of the *Chronicon Compostellanum* on the two historiographical issues analysed here, the chronicle begins with these words:

> In the era 400 the Goths began to reign until the era 747. They obtained Spain for 352 years, four months and five days, until Tariq, overseas general of the Saracens, entered and killed Roderic, the last king of the Goths, on Thursday at noon the era 748, and took almost all of Spain by force. And then the Saracens reigned in Asturias five years.[63]

Like the *Annales Portugalenses veteres* and the Septimanian chronicles, there is interest in the duration of the *regnum Gothorum* because of the authors' belief that it had ended. In this case, it shows clear knowledge of the Asturian chronicles because of the mention of Tariq and the expression *ultimo rege Gotorum* referring to King Roderic, coming from the passage concerning the discovery of his grave. Perhaps due to the influence of Septimanian chronicles or, more likely, the proximity of the Asturian ones, it suggests that the whole *regnum Hispaniae* is in the hands of the Saracens, a view not present in the *Annales Portugalenses veteres*, and this may presume, without saying so explicitly, an ideology of there being a Christian–Saracen struggle for complete domination of this kingdom. In addition, as neo-Gothic elements are not evident, but rather anti-neo-Gothic ones, it is possible that the Asturian chronicles managed by the chronicler were not the

---

dominati sunt eam annis CCC^{tis} LXXX^{a} III^{bus} et de terra sua pervenerunt in Spaniam per annos decem septem. Antequam Domnus Pelagius regnaret Sarraceni regnaverunt in Spaniam annis V^e. Cited from David, *Études*, 306.

63 *In era CCCC ceperunt Goti regnare usque in eram DCCXLVII. Qui per CCC et LII annos et menses quatuor et dies quinque Hispaniam obtinuerunt, donec ingressus fuit transmarinus dux Sarracenorum nomine Taruc, qui, Roderico ultimo rege Gotorum die V feria ora VI era DCCXLVIII interfecto, fere totam Yspaniam armis cepit. Et tunc Sarraceni in Asturiis annos V regnauerunt.* Cited from Emma Falque, "Chronicon Compostellanum," *Habis* 14 (1983): 73–83 at. 77.

ones of Alfonso III's cycle, but the *Chronicle of Alfonso II* or other non-conserved historiographical texts of this time in Oviedo, the content of which would probably be similar to that manifested in the Septimanian chronicles because of their contemporaneity.[64]

Chronicon Iriense

The *Chronicon Iriense* is the last Galician-Portuguese historiographical work that includes a passage about the conquest of Spain by the Arabs. In spite of concluding its story in 984, Isla Frez has dated it, because of the topics discussed in it, as contemporary with the *Historia Compostellana*, completed around 1139 on the death of Bishop Diego Gelmírez of Compostela,[65] though García Álvarez had previously proposed 1080 as its date of composition due to the vocabulary and documentary information.[66] According to the interpretations of Isla Frez,[67] its author, a clergyman of the Church of Santiago de Compostela,[68] seeks primarily to relate the feats of the bishops of Iria and highlight the role of this see in the history of the Asturian-Leonese Kingdom. At the same time, this clergyman wants to alienate this see from the Church of Toledo, indicating that the See of Iria was founded by Suevi kings, in order to emphasize their ecclesiastical autonomy and to defend their native liturgical tradition against the arrival of new trends promoted from Toledo. Finally and above all, the writer wishes to stress the importance of the chapter of canons at Compostela, since they are portrayed as the protagonists of the history, beyond the bishops and even the kings.

Thus, the *Chronicon Iriense* has little interest in political events unless they affect the See of Iria–Compostela. The institution of the monarchy influenced the foundation of the Church around Galicia; the following passage reflects the replacement of the Visigothic monarchy with the Asturian one:

> Then Tariq, king of the Moors, entered Spain in the 747th era and Roderic, the last king of the Goths, was killed [on Thursday] in the 748th era and his body was buried in a church in the city of Viseu, where the epitaph is written: HERE RESTS RODERIC, THE LAST KING OF THE GOTHS. Then Pelagius Favílaz invaded Asturias, at the time of Emila, the tenth Bishop of Iria.[69]

From the textual overlaps we can see that common writings utilized for the preparation of the other Galician-Portuguese chronicles were also used in the *Chronicon Iriense*,

---

64 See note 17.

65 Amancio Isla Frez, *Memoria, culto y monarquía hispánica entre los siglos X y XII* (Jaén, 2006), 214–19.

66 Manuel Rubén García Álvarez, ed., "El Cronicón Iriense," in *Memorial histórico español. Colección de documentos, opúsculos y antigüedades que publica la Real Academia de la Historia* (Madrid, 1963), 80–92.

67 Isla, *Memoria*, 191–214.

68 This authorship is also defended in García, ed., "El Cronicón Iriense," 92–4.

69 *Tunc ingressus est rex maurorum, nomine Tarich, Hyspaniam, in era DCCªXL VIIª, et interfectus est Rudericus, ultimus rex gothorum, [die Vª feria] in era DCCªXL VIIIª, cuius corpus sepultum est in ecclesia in Uisensem ciuitatem, ubi scriptum est epitaphyon: HIC REQUIESCIT RUDERICUS, ULTIMUS REX GOTHORUM. Tunc Pelagius Faphilaz Asturias inuasit, sub quo Emila Hylliensis decimus episcopus fuit.* Cited from García, ed., "El Cronicón Iriense," 109.

so they share the anti-neo-Gothic belief that the *regnum Gothorum* ended. However, *Chronicon Iriense* differs from the other Galician-Portuguese chronicles in that its chronicler is not interested in the course of the *regnum Hispaniae*, perhaps because he identified this kingdom entirely with the domain of the Saracens in the Iberian Peninsula, and because he assumes the parentage of Pelagius that appears in the *Ad Sebastianum* version of the *Chronicle of Alfonso III* and his exogenous origin outside Asturias. At this point, it is interesting that this chronicler gives a military touch to the appearance of Pelagius in this region, because he uses the word *inuasit* ("he invaded") instead of *ingressus est* or *intrauit* ("he entered"), the more neutral descriptions we find elsewhere.

The Leonese *Historia Legionensis*

At the same time that some of the Galician-Portuguese chronicles were being written, in the royal city of León, the cleric Ordoño Sisnández composed the *Historia Legionensis*, which until very recently has tended to be known as the *Historia Silense*.[70] Dated between 1110 and 1125,[71] the main objectives of this unfinished literary work are characterizing the reign of Alfonso VI as an idealized time, presented at the beginning of the history with a strong Leonist ideology, and defending the archetype of *imperium* of this king which was continued with his grandson, Alfonso Raimúndez. The interest in these two characters is inferred from the recurrent parallels that Sisnández made between them and the earlier Asturian-Leonese monarchs, mainly Fernando I, the last king described in the work.[72]

This historiographical ideology is the product of the survival in Leon of the Asturian chronicles created in the second half of the ninth century, unlike what happened in Galicia and Portugal as discussed in the previous section. Because of this, when they write about the Arab conquest, discussed below, there is clear neo-Gothic thought plus a new ideological concept: the Hispanicity of the kingdom. In this way, transforming neo-Gothic ideology, the legitimacy of the rule of the *regnum Hispaniae* by the kings of Leon is based not so much on their being heirs of the *regnum Gothorum* due to their Christian character or their Gothicity, but from their Spanish identity (*Hispani*). Before, the *regnum Hispaniae* was just a political institution, ruled by one or two authorities (Saracen or Christian); now it is also a government, a political regime, and a domain of a people, classified as Hispanic. Therefore, the Leonese chronicler uses a political ideology which considers both *regna*; the *regnum Gothorum* and a new conception of the *regnum*

---

70 The authorship of this chronicle has been ascertained by Georges Martin, who offered a preview of his findings to the attendees of the International Symposium *Convivencia de lenguas y conflictos de poder en la Edad Media Ibérica*, held at the Universidad Autónoma de Madrid on November 3–4, 2011. Besides, in Isla, *Memoria*, 232–39, Amancio Isla had already deduced that the chronicler was a clergyman of the basilica of St. Isidore of León. Moreover, I also took from Martin the new nomenclature of this historiographical work because it better indicates its true origin and its strong "Leonist" ideology.

71 Isla, *Memoria*, 239–41 and 271. This historian reduces the time frame to 1118–1125 as a possible hypothesis.

72 Isla, *Memoria*, 269–73.

Hispaniae, also known as the *regnum Hispanorum* (not "of Spain" but "of the Spanish"). The two senses were inextricably bound together to form the imperialist foundation of Alfonso VI, as well as that of his grandson, Alfonso VII the Emperor.[73] Obviously, the Saracens, by now commonly referred to as Moors (*Mauri*), are excluded from this new conception of *regnum Hispaniae*, but they still rule part of the *regnum Hispaniae* in the traditional view, referring to a political entity.

> But also they [the loyals of Wittiza], who travelled by boat to the province of Tingitania, joined Count Julian, whom King Wittiza had as a close friend among his loyals, and they, who complained there about the affronts received, disposed that the ruin was brought both for them and for the Kingdom of all Spain [*totius Ispanie regno*] by introducing the Moors. [...]

> So, 752nd era,[74] Al-Walid, very mighty King of the Barbarians [Berbers] of all Africa, sent ahead Tariq the Squint-eyed, one of the generals of his army, with 25 thousand infantry warriors to the Spains under the guidance of Count Julian and the sons of Witiza, so that, knowing the fluctuating fidelity of Julian, he would undertake the war against the Spanish king [*Yspano rege*].[75]

The first passage clearly shows how the conception of the *regnum Gothorum* has been diluted into the one of *regnum Hispanorum*, since Ordoño Sisnández explains that the Goths are so much *Hispani* that Roderic is called "Spanish king" (*Yspano rege*), unlike all other chronicles who describe him as *Gothorum rex*. In addition, the chronicler never refers to the *regnum Gothorum* at the time of their conquest because he considered that, in the Kingdom of Spain, there was a rule of Spanish (*regnum Hispanorum*), which is replaced, exclusively at first, by a rule of Moors or Berbers ("Barbarians").

Moreover, it is significant that an adjective (*tota* or "all") is added to *Hispania*, referring to a public political entity, and also the plural *Hispaniae*. This recalls the notion of the two domains of the *regnum Hispaniae*, present in previous chronicles and now preserved as a fixed name for the *regnum*, as in this passage Sisnández is not referring to two rules, formerly called Christian and Saracen and now considered as Spanish and Moorish.[76]

---

73 For the concepts of *imperium* and *Hispania* in the reign of Alfonso VI, see the interesting work of Isla, *Memoria*, 130–84.

74 Justo Pérez de Urbel, editor of this chronicle, has transliterated "DCCXLVII" based on the extant copies. But, in my opinion, the original date should be "DCCᵃLᵃIIᵃ," as it is written in Lucas de Tuy's *Chronicon Mundi*; a medieval scribe confused the abbreviations with letters of the date.

75 *Sed et isti ad Tingitanam prouintiam transfretantes, Iuliani comitti, quem Victica rex in suis fidelibus familiarissimum habuerat, adheserunt, ibique de illatis contumeliis ingemiscentes, Mauros introducendo, et sibi et totius Ispanie regno perditum iri disposuerunt. [...] Igitur, era DCCXLVII, Hulit, fortissimus rex barbarorum totius Africe, ducatu Iuliani comittis filiorumque Victice, Tarich strabonem, vnum ex ducibus exercitus sui, cum XXV milibus pugnatorum peditum ad Ispanias premisit, vt, cognita Iuliani dubia fide, bellum cum Yspano rege inciperet.* Cited from *Historia Silense*, ed. Justo Pérez de Urbel, Atilano González Ruiz-Zorrilla (Madrid, 1959), 127–28.

76 The plural designation of *Hispania* has existed since Antiquity and was taken up by various medieval chronicles, including Christian-Andalusian, Septimanian, and Asturian ones, from the works of Isidore of Seville. These texts recalled the Roman division into Ulterior and Citerior Hispania; but, the *Historia Legionensis* employs the plural term with a new meaning after having forgotten the original, since, for example, applying it to the time of Alfonso VI does not make sense.

In fact, He had withdrawn the hands of the Lord from Spain because of the ingrained evil of the kings, so that He would not protect it at the time of this ruin, and one by one all the soldiers of the Goths, dispersed and fled, were reached almost until the deadly blow of the sword.

After this, as no man was an obstacle, the Moors took possession of all Spain, consumed by iron, fire, and hunger, with their lord. Indeed, what would be opposed to them, to those who completely defeated the whole mob of the Spains in a public battle with triumphant might? Those who surely have made so great slaughters and so great ravages of the Christians with horrifying sword narrate in abundance and over testimony devastated [*depopulate*] provinces, demolished city walls, and destroyed churches, in whose place the name of Muhammad is worshipped.[77]

For this Pelagius, sword-bearer of King Roderic, who wandered through indeterminate places due to the oppression of the Moors until, trusting in the divine oracle, he arrived with some soldiers of the Goths, was confirmed by the Lord to defeat the Barbarians [Berbers], and also all the Asturians, gathered together, conferred Pelagius as their prince.[78]

In the first of these two fragments it is explicitly mentioned that the Kingdom of Spain is left in Moorish hands. The chronicler refers to the Goths, but they do not appear as possessors of a *regnum,* but rather as a social group, a warrior elite. Yet neo-Gothicism is latent, since these Goths are those that provide the continuity of the *regnum Hispaniae,* understood as a political entity, in Asturias because Pelagius was one of them and won his victory against the Berbers thanks to them.

The Castilian *Chronica Naiarensis*

The *Chronica Naiarensis* (ca. 1180) was written possibly by a French Cluniac monk linked to the monastery of Santa María of Nájera.[79] Whether it was a Cluniac or not, the provenance from around Nájera is certain due to both the pro-Castilian positions of the chronicler and the use of chronicles with textual variants preserved in this region.[80] The

---

77 *Receserat enim manus Domini ob inueteratam regum malitiam ab Ispania, ne in tempore huius ruyne eam protegeret, omnesque deinceps Gotorum milites fusi fugatique fere vsque ad iteremptionem gladii peruenere. Post hec Mauri, viribus nullis obstantibus, totam Yspaniam ferro, flama et fame atritam suo domino mancipauerunt. Quid enim illis officeret, qui publico bello omnem Yspaniarum multitudinem triumfali potentia deuicerant? Qui nimirum quantas cedes, quantasue orrifero ense christianorum strages fecerint, depopulate prouintie, subuersa ciuitatum menia, destructe ecclesie, in loco quarum Mahometis nomen collitur, habunde et super testimonium perhibent.* Cited from *Historia Silense*, 129.

78 *Ad quam Pelagius, Roderici regis spatarius, qui oppressione Maurorum incertis locis vagabatur, dum peruenit, fretus diuino oraculo, cum quibusdam Gotorum militibus, ad expugnandos barbaros a Domino corroboratus est, sed et omnes Astures, in vnum colecti, Pelagium super se principem constituunt.* Cited from *Historia Silense*, 131–32.

79 According to *Chronica Naierensis*, ed. Juan Antonio Estévez Sola (Turnhout, 1995), 74–7, this dating is based on the references of the chronicle to Peter Comestor's *Historia Scholastica*, completed in 1173 and quickly influential. Moreover, it's interesting how soon a Castilianist chronicle was written in the region of Nájera after its conquest by Alfonso VIII against the Kingdom of Navarre (1176).

80 *Chronica Naierensis*, 89–93.

author purposefully divides the history into three books, making them correspond to three periods: Antiquity (from the Creation to the end of the Visigothic time), the period of Asturian-Leonese predominance (Pelagius to Bermudo III), and the time of Navarrese-Castilian rise (Sancho III the Great to Alfonso VI). Although compositionally the *Chronica Naiarensis* is a compilation of earlier chronicles, it alters the historiographical model and does not seek to propound a traditional succession of kings, but to provide, especially in the third book, an account of events that affect mainly the Castilian lands.[81]

Because of this historiographical approach, the writer is less interested in the conceptions of *imperium* and *Hispania*, so present in the Leonist, royalist chronicle of Ordoño Sisnández, and adopts the neo-Gothic ideology as he found them in the Asturian chronicles of Alfonso III's cycle. Thus, the chronicler of Nájera takes over the interpretation that the *regnum Gothorum* was moved to Asturias and the *regnum Hispaniae*, understood in its original sense of political entity, was divided into two areas controlled by Christians and Saracens without identifying the first ones as Spanish.

> But also they [the loyals of Wittiza], who travelled by boat to the province of Tingitania, joined Count Julian, whom King Wittiza had as a close friend among his loyals. And they, who complained there about the affronts affronts, disposed that the ruin was brought both for them and for the Kingdom of all Spain [*tocius Yspanie regno*] by introducing the Moors.[82]

This fragment is almost identical to the one written in the *Historia Legionensis*. The chronicler of Nájera copied it and thus took the concept expressed in the phrase "tocius Yspanie regno," for which there are two Spains as parts of a homogeneous whole.

> And in fact, in our rough times, when the city of Viseu and its suburbs were looted [*populata*] by our order, in a certain basilica there a monument was discovered above which an epitaph is inscribed in this way, "Here rests Roderic, the last king of the Goths." But let us go back to the time when the Saracens invaded Spain, the third day of the Ides of November of the 752nd era. The Arabs killed many in the region as well as in the oppressed kingdom [*regno*]; but they subjugated the rest who agreed to peace. In addition, the city of Toledo, victor of all the peoples, succumbed defeated by the Ismaelite triumphs. Here ends the first book.

> The second book begins. With the death of Roderic, King of the Goths, the land was devoid of kings of the Goths four years.

> They placed prefects throughout the provinces of Spain and for many years they made them pay tributes to the Babylonian king until they elected their king, and they consolidated a kingdom [*regno*] for themselves in the patrician city of Cordova.[83]

---

81 *Chronica Naierensis*, 79–86.

82 *Set et isti ad Tingitanam prouintiam transfretantes Iuliani comiti, quem Vitiza rex in suis fidelibus familiarissimum habuerat, adheserunt. Ibique de illatis contumeliis ingemiscentes, Mauros introducendo et sibi et tocius Yspanie regno perditum iri disposuerunt.* Cited from *Chronica Naierensis*, 96.

83 *Rudis namque nostris temporibus, cum ciuitas Viseo et suburbia eius iussu nostro essent populata, in quadam ibi basilica monumentum inuentum est ubi desuper epitaphion huiusmodi est conscriptum: "hic requiescit Rudericus, ultimus rex Gotorum." Set redeamus ad tempus quo Sarraceni Hispaniam sunt adgressi, III <idus> nouembris era DCCLIIª. Arabes tamen regione simul et regno opresso plures*

These two passages, divided by the end of the first book and the beginning of the second, are a replica of the *Rotense* version of the *Chronicle of Alfonso III*. Thus, the chronicler endorses the historiographical tradition by which the Arabs possessed the *regnum Hispaniae* as direct continuation of the Visigothic kings. There is a remarkable contradiction here, already present in the *Chronicle of Alfonso III*, specifying that Roderic is the last king of the Goths and, later, clearly indicating that his death was just a brief interregnum of Gothic kings:

> Disposed this the command to all Asturians, they were together assembled and elected Pelagius as their prince in the 756th era. In fact, the rule of the Goths [*regnum Gotorum*] had been emptied for 4 years, that is, from the 752nd era.[84]

Finally, this text demonstrates the neo-Gothicism of this chronicle in naming Pelagius as successor in the *regnum Gothorum*. In fact, beside the title of Chapter 15 of the *Chronicle of Albelda* ("Item Gotorum Obetensium regum ordo"), the *Chronica Naierensis* expresses this continuity most clearly, without indirect allusions to lineages or Pelagius's links with former Gothic kings.

The Navarrese *Liber regum*

The *Liber regum*, also known as *Libro de las generaciones y linajes de los reyes* (*The Book of the Generations and Lineages of the Kings*), is a historiographical *unicum* because there are no Spanish chronicles that tries to concatenate all the successive generations of history: biblical characters, kings of Jerusalem, kings of Persia, Alexander the Great as King of Greece, Ptolemaic kings of Egypt, emperors of Roma, Gothic kings of Spain, kings of the lineage of Pelagius,[85] judges and counts of Castile, Sancho the Great and his sons, Fernando I and his sons, the Emperor Alfonso VI of Castile,[86] Urraca I and her marriages, and the Emperor Alfonso VII and his sons. Then, this chronicle continues with the kings of Navarre, from Arista up to present time; the ones of Aragon, from Sancho the Great to present time; and the ones of France, from Charlemagne onward.

Dated between 1194 and 1211, that is, during the first years of the reign of Sancho VII,[87] it is evident that the *Liber regum* is a Navarrese work since it appears in a Romance

---

tamen interfecerunt, reliquos uero pacis federe blandiendo sibi pace subiugauerunt. Vrb[i]s quoque Toletana gentium uictrix Ysmaeliticis triumphis ui<c>ta subcubuit. Explicit liber primus.

Incipit liber secundus. Mortuo uero Roderico rege Gotorum uacauit terra regum Gotorum IIII annis. Per omnes prouintias Yspanie prefectos posuerunt et pluribus annis Bauilonico regi tributa persoluerunt, quousque ibi regem elegerunt et Cordobam urbem patriciam regnum sibi firmauerunt. Cited from *Chronica Naierensis*, 96–98.

84 *Quo omnes Astures mandatum dirigente, in unum concilium collecti sunt et sibi Pelagium principem elegerunt era DCCLVIª. Vacuerat enim per IIII annos regnum Gotorum ab era scilicet DCCLIIª.* Cited from *Chronica Naierensis*, 99.

85 The *Liber regum* only deals with the descendants of Pelagius, that is, it ends with Alfonso II, and does not name these kings as Asturian or in any particular way.

86 Significantly, this king is described as Castilian instead of Leonese. This is probably because of the Navarrese origin of the chronicle.

87 Louis Cooper, *El Liber regum. Estudio lingüístico* (Zaragoza, 1960), 7.

language with typical features of Navarrese, contains references to both Navarrese and French kings, and gives an important role to Sancho the Great. Ideologically, this chronicle does not show neo-Gothicism either in the passage below about the conquest of the Iberian Peninsula or in the general account of the chronicle, as it has no particular interest in the Visigothic Kingdom. It presents that period as one of wars among the inhabitants of Spain and avoids mention of Visigothic kings, even some as outstanding as Reccared I, except for the final monarchs (Wamba, Erwig, Wittiza, and Roderic). Even so, I believe that the *Liber regum* traces a historical continuum at the political level from the Gothic kings to the kings of Asturias, probably because, as Christians, they were considered the successors of a new kingdom.[88] As for the conquest of Spain (*Espanna*), the Navarrese chronicler presents it with this text:

> Era 753. At the time when King Roderic reigned in Spain, King Al-Walid and Abu Zuhra came from Africa. And King Amir Al-Muminin[89] was king in Morocco, and then Tariq came to Spain and arrived in Gibraltar. These kings Abu Zuhra, Al-Walid and Amir Al-Muminin, with many other kings and with great forces of Moors came to King Roderic in battle and found him in the field of Sagnera. In the first fight the Moors were damaged, but later they recovered and the Christians were defeated. In that battle King Roderic was lost, and they did not find him either dead or alive; but long after, in Viseu in Portugal, they found a tomb where the letters written above stated that there laid King Roderic, who was lost in battle in the time of the Goths.
>
> When King Roderic was lost, the Moors conquered all the land until Portugal and Galicia, outside the mountains of Asturias. All the people of the land who ran away from the battle sought shelter in those mountains, and elected King Lord Pelagius, who was in a cave in Auseva, as their king. This King Lord Pelagius was a very good and loyal king; and all the Christians who were in the mountains were all taken in by him, and fought the Moors and did many battles and won them.[90]

This text does not talk of a *regnum Gothorum* as such, because the chronicler believes that Roderic's rule was a *regnum Christianorum*. Even so, he argues for a "time of the Goths" (*tiempo de los godos*), which is understood to have already concluded, probably with the

---

88 It should be noted that Andalusian kings do not appear in this chronicle and that Arista, first ruler of the Navarrese, is not mentioned until after the presentation of all the Castilian kings.

89 The chronicler wrongly believed that the title *amir al-muminin* was itself a character.

90 *Era DCLII. A la sazon que regnaua el rei Rodrigo en Espanna, uinieron d'Affrica el rey Aboali & Aboçubra. Et era rei en Marruecos el rei Amiramozmelin, & estonz uino Taric en Espanna & arribo a Gibaltaric. Est rei Aboçubra & Aboali & Amiramozmelin, con otros reies muitos e con grandes poderes de moros uinieron al rei Rodrigo a la batalla e li dioron con el en el campo de Sagnera. En la primera fazienda foron mal treitos los moros; mas pues cobroron e foron rancados los christianos. En aquella batalla fo perdido el rei Rodrigo, e no lo troboron ni muerto ni biuo; mas pues a luengos tiempos, en Uiseu en Portugal, troboron un sepulcre que dizian las letras qui de suso eran escritas que alli iazia el rei Rodrigo, el qui fo perdido en la batalla en el tiempo de los godos. Quando fo perdido el rei Rodrigo, conquerieron moros toda la tierra tro a en Portogal & en Gallicia fueras de las montannas d'Asturias. En aquellas montannas, s'acuellieron todas las hientes de la tierra los qui escaporon de la batalla, e fizieron rei por election al rei don Pelaio, qui estaua en una cueua en Asseua. Est rei don Pelaio fo muit buen rei e leial; e todos los christianos qui eran en las montannas acullieron se todos ad el, e guerreioron a moros e fizieron muitas batallas e uencieron las.* Cited from Louis Cooper, *El Liber regum*, 32.

defeat of King Roderic. The Christian character of the extinct *regnum* link to the new monarchy founded by survivors of the Battle of Sagnera, who were specifically defined as Christians, after the enthronement of Pelagius. Pelagius curiously is not given a clear origin and the text simply mentions his presence in Asturias so he might be identified as either a member of the group of warriors defeated by the Moors or an Asturian native.

Therefore, according to this narrative, the successor of the *regnum Gothorum* wass established in the lands of Asturias, unlike the rest of the Iberian Peninsula, which lay in the hands of the Moors. This worldview can lead to the Septimanian interpretation that the *regnum Hispaniae*, or *Espanna*, has been divided into two domains: Christian and Muslim. However, it is difficult to be sure if the chronicler interpreted these two areas in a political sense, with the consequent continuation of Spain as an entity, or in a merely geographical vision, because lands and regions figure prominently in his writing.

Castilian-Leonese Chronicles

In the thirteenth century, during the reigns of Fernando III and Alfonso X, the historiographical ideology on the progression of the *regnum Gothorum* and the *regnum Hispaniae* had become definitively established and becomes official, since chronicles were commissioned under the direction of Castilian-Leonese monarchs. In this period, new historiographical views were not developed, because the chroniclers of this time just used the same ideas that had endured for posterity. New texts, with new points of view about the Arab conquest of the Iberian Peninsula were not devised until more than a century later.

The three main chronicles of this historiographical set take the approach of universal histories, although they do end up focusing on the Iberian Peninsula. The major vernacular work, the *Estoria de España*, is the fusion of Lucas de Tuy's *Chronicon Mundi* and Rodrigo Jiménez de Rada's *De rebus Hispaniae* with an ideological predilection for the second one where the texts dissent.

Chronicon Mundi

Chronicon Mundi is a Leonist work in the sense that it follows the ideological tradition which favours the Kingdom of Leon as it appeared in the *Historia Legionensis*. Like its predecessor, it was written in the city of León by a clerical member of the community of St. Isidore: Deacon Lucas de León, who, shortly after the conclusion of this work, received the episcopal staff of Tuy in 1239. The chronicle was commissioned by the Queen Mother Berengaria of Castile, to whom it is dedicated by Lucas de Tuy , and was made during the 1230s, and finished around 1238.[91]

This work of universal history is composed in four books. The first and second books are copies, revised with additions, of two historiographical works of Isidore of Seville: the *Chronicle*, concerning the six ages of the world until the rule of Heraclius, and the *Historia Gothorum*, which deals with each of the Germanic peoples that were present in

---

91 Lucas de Tuy, *Chronicon Mundi*, ed. Emma Falque, Corpus Christianorum Continuatio Mediaevalis 74 (Turnhout, 2003), 16–21.

Spain (Vandals, Suevi, and Goths) until the reign of Suintila. The third book completes the history of the Goths until the Arab-Berber conquest using Visigothic chronicles of the second half of the seventh century and the *Chronicle of Alfonso III*. Finally, the fourth book, the largest of all because of the political importance of its contents, tells the history of the kings of Asturias and Leon. It also includes information about the rulers of Castile (judges, counts, independent kings), the most relevant kings of Navarre (Sancho Abarca, Garcia III, Sancho the Great, and Garcia IV) and Ramiro I of Aragon as the founder of this kingdom, and shows a special interest in detailing the reigns of some Leonese kings: Fernando I, Alfonso VI, Alfonso VII, and Fernando III.[92]

Lucas de Tuy's account of the Arab conquest of Spain shows the strong textual influence of two previous chronicles, namely the *Chronicle of Alfonso III*, from Asturias, and the *Historia Legionensis*, from Leon. Their ideological projection into his work is evident: the *Chronicon Mundi* takes a neo-Gothic view, through which the *regnum Gothorum* continues its spread to Asturias by Pelagius, and sees the division of the *regnum Hispaniae* into two opposing domains.

> So, 752nd era, Al-Walid, very mighty King of the Barbarians [Berbers] of all Africa, sent ahead Tariq the Squint-eyed, one of the generals of his army, with twenty-five thousand mighty warriors to Spain under the guidance of Julian and the sons of Witiza, relied on the help since he knew that there were no weapons and horses in Spain and the cities were without walls, so that, knowing the fluctuating fidelity of Julian, he would undertake the war against the King of Spain [*Yspanie rege*].[93]

This excerpt was taken from the *Historia Legionensis* by Lucas de León, but its presentation of Roderic is quite different, since here he is not the Spanish king (*Yspano rege*), but the king of Spain (*Yspanie rege*). So, Lucas de Tuy has not adopted Ordoño Sisnández's theory that there is a *regnum Hispanorum*; he seems to prefer writing only about the *regnum Hispaniae* as a political institution.

> And in fact, after that, in our rough [times], in the city of Viseu a stone grave in whose epitaph was written above, "Here rests Roderic, the King of the Goths," was discovered. He had withdrawn the hands of the Lord from Spain because of the ingrained evil of the kings, so that He would not protect it at the time of this ruin. One by one all the soldiers of the Goths dispersed and fled, died from extermination by the sword and the lack of food. They succumbed not only because of the persecutions of the Barbarians [Berbers], but also because of the weapons of the Franks from the region of the Gauls.
>
> After this, as no Gothic man was an obstacle, the Moors took possession of almost all of Spain, the province of Burgundy [Bordeaux] and Poitiers, consumed by iron, fire and hunger, with their lord.

---

92 This information on the main contents of *Chronicon Mundi* is from Lucas de Tuy, *Chronicon Mundi*, 21–25.

93 *Igitur, era DCCᵃ Lᵃ IIᵃ Hulit fortissimus rex barbarorum, totius Africe ducatu, Iuliani et filiorum Vitice fretus auxilio, ut cognouit quod arma et equi non essent in Yspania et ciuitates essent absque muris, Tharich strabonem, unum ex ducibus exercitus sui, cum uiginti quinque milibus forcium pugnatorum ad Yspaniam premisit, ut cognita Iuliani dubia fide bellum cum Yspanie rege inciperet.* Cited from Lucas de Tuy, *Chronicon Mundi*, 220.

[...] They put prefects throughout the provinces of Spain and for many years they made them pay tributes to the Babylonian sultan, until they elected Luza [Musa?] as their king, and consolidated for them the patrician city of Cordova and the kingdom [*regno*].[94]

These passages show the textual fusion between the *Ad Sebastianum* version of the *Chronicle of Alfonso III* and the *Historia Legionensis*. Thus, Lucas de Tuy supports the idea that only some Goths perished in battle, allowing him to argue that the *regnum Gothorum* continued in Asturias, and he even amends the incongruous reference to Roderic as the last of the Gothic kings, as shown in the neo-Gothic *Chronicle of Alfonso III* and *Chronica Naierensis*. Moreover, these fragments show that the larger part of the *regnum Hispaniae* remains in the hands of the Moors and that the new Saracen domain, the *Sarracenorum regnum*, has developed over it. Finally, Lucas de Tuy makes interesting references to French territories conquered by the Moors, probably mistaking the Bordeaux region for Burgundy due to the similarity of words, and the attack of the Franks against the Visigoths, taking advantage of the Arab-Berber conquest, an event not depicted in any other known chronicle.

> However, the remaining Goths, secluded in the heights of the Pyrenees mountains, Asturias, and Galicia, escaped in whatever manner, the Saracens gained the planes and the better lands with the vengeful sword, and in the churches, in which the name of Christ was praised, they proclaim the profane name of Muhammad in public voice.

> [...] For this Pelagius, sword-bearer of King Roderic, who wandered through indeterminate places due to the oppression of the Moors until, trusting in the divine oracle, he arrived with some soldiers of the Goths, was confirmed by the Lord to defeat the Barbarians [Berbers].

> All the Asturians, gathered together, raised Pelagius as their prince.[95]

These last two excerpts, of which the second is virtually identical to the text found in the *Historia Legionensis*, explain that the surviving Goths were exiled both in Galician-Asturian lands and in Frankish lands, as detailed in the *Ad Sebastianum* version of the

---

94 *Rudis tamen postea in ciuitate Viseo inuenta est lapidea sepultura, in qua epitafium est desuper scriptum, scilicet: "Hic requiescit Rodericus rex Gotorum." Recesserat manus Domini ab Yspania ob inueteratam regum malitiam, ne in tempore huius ruine eam protegeret. Omnes deinceps Gotorum milites fusi fugatique fere usque ad internicionem gladio et inedia perierunt. Non solummodo insecutionibus barbarorum, uerum etiam Francorum armis ex parte Galliarum consumpti sunt.*
    Post hec Mauri, uiribus Goticis non obstantibus, totam Yspaniam fere atque Prouinciam Burgundiam et Pictauiam ferro, flamma, fame atritas suo domino manciparunt. [...] Post hec Sarraceni prefectos per omnes prouincias Yspanie posuerunt et pluribus annis Babilonico soldano persolberunt tributa, quousque sibi regem nomine Luza elegerunt et Cordubam urbem patriciam regnumque sibi firmaberunt. Cited from Lucas de Tuy, *Chronicon Mundi*, 221–22.

95 *Tamen residui Goti in arduis montium Pireneorum, Asturiarum et Gallecie se recludentes, qualitercumque euaserunt, Sarracenis queque plana et meliora gladio uindice obtinentibus, et in ecclesiis, quibus laudabatur nomen Christi, Machometi nomen prophanum uoce publica proclamantes; [...] Ad quam Pelagius, regis Roderici spatarius, qui fugiens oppressionem Maurorum in locis vagabatur incertis, dum peruenit, diuino fretus oraculo cum quibusdam Gotorum militibus ad expugnandos barbaros a Domino corroboratus est. Omnes Astures in unum collecti Pelagium super se principem erexerunt.* Cited from Lucas de Tuy, *Chronicon Mundi*, 222; 224.

Chronicle of Alfonso III. Thus, by this diaspora, the continuity of the *regnum Gothorum* was linked to the Asturian monarchy of Pelagius.

Rodrigo Jiménez de Rada's Chronicles

The Navarrese Rodrigo Jiménez de Rada, Archbishop of Toledo and Primate of the Spains, is the great abridger of the history of Spain, having not only combined Christian and Arab sources, but also created a great historiographical work from a disparate group of chronicles to form a universal history. In the chronicles, in which he treats the conquest of the Iberian Peninsula, both in *De rebus Hispaniae*, from the perspective of the Christian kingdoms in history, and in *Historia Arabum*, with an Andalusian focus, the Toledan Archbishop assumes that the *regnum Gothorum* had succumbed, although he did attribute the several *regna* that were formed in the north as their worthy successors to by the fact that they were Christians like the Goths. Jiménez de Rada also believes that the *regnum Hispaniae* continues, under the rule of the Arabs, and by the grace of God it will be fully recovered by the Christians of the northern mountains, although he does not specify any particular kingdom.

De rebus Hispaniae

Jiménez de Rada composed the *De rebus Hispaniae*, completed in 1243 at the request of King Fernando III,[96] to reconstruct the history of Spain through a remarkable historiographical project of contrasting sources.[97]

De Rada's objective was to reconstruct the entire past of Spain, with Spain as the historical protagonist, without distinguishing domains, peoples, cultures, or religions. In this way, the work set up a Spanish identity, as was happening in France and England at the same time, with the aim that Castile-Spain would be considered one more *natio* in Christendom. Significantly, Jiménez de Rada dismisses neo-Gothicism, though this does not mean that he was anti-Gothic; he presents the extinct *regnum Gothorum* as an example to imitate in his ideal of *regnum Hispaniae*. In relation to the content of the work, in imitation of the Navarrese *Liber regum*, although in this case centred on the Iberian Peninsula, after referring to Japhet, the first European, Jiménez de Rada traces all the peoples of Spain from its earliest inhabitants until his lord, King Fernando III of Castile and Leon, going through the Iberians, Greeks (Hercules), the Romans, the Goths, the Gothic kings, the Asturian-Leonese kings, the Navarrese kings, the Aragonese kings, the Castilian kings, and the Almohads.[98]

---

96 According to Rodrigo Jiménez de Rada, *Historia de los hechos de España*, trans. Juan Fernández Valverde (Madrid, 1989), 49–50, this date appears at the end of the historiographical work, but some of the chronological dates do not fit reality (e.g., the day of week).

97 Unlike Lucas de Tuy, the archbishop of Toledo constructs the text of the whole work by his own hand, that is, he does not reuse the texts of earlier chronicles, and he incorporates Arabic sources from al-Andalus, which explains the dates from the Hijri calendar and of the year of each caliph's reign.

98 All information is based on the opinions and the data presented in Jiménez, *Historia de los hechos*, 42–49.

In the Middle Ages the success of Jiménez de Rada's *De rebus Hispaniae* was so great that, besides being widely copied as shown by the large number of manuscripts, it was translated in the second half of the thirteenth century into the Romance language, with the title of *Estoria de los godos*:[99]

> But advising and helping the senate and the still living Wittiza, began to reign together with Roderic, the last king of the Goths, in the fourth year of Al-Walid, the ninety-first year of the Arabs, era 748, seventh year of Wittiza, and reigned only three years, one by himself, two with Wittiza. [...] But what would happen to his corpse is completely ignored except that in modern times in Viseu, city of Portugal, an inscribed tumulus was discovered: "Here lies Roderic, the last king of the Goths."[100]

I chose this passage because of the way in which Jiménez de Rada defines Roderic as the last king of the Goths, meaning he ignored the omission of "last" from the Viseu epitaph in Lucas de Tuy's account, but he also provides this ending when he presents King Roderic for the first time.

> But with Count Julian and the Goths who were with him facing stern menaces, the lines of the Christian armies, who due to the long peace and abundance were found to be lazy, unprepared and ignorant for battle, broke apart, and turning their backs as barriers on Sunday, fifth day of the month of Shawwal, year 92 of the Arabs, era 752, King Roderic and the Christian army were defeated and they died in useless flight.
>
> And instantly the lines of the Gothic armies fled almost everywhere, King Roderic thought one moment of flight and the other of fighting, but finally, with the battle over, one part of the people of the Goths was killed and the other part was freed with the protection of flight.
>
> Chapter 21 On the destruction of the Goths and the reputation of Spain:
>
> Alas, pain! Here ends the glory of the Gothic greatness in the era 752 and it, which subdued so many kingdoms in many battles, had the flags of its glory hauled down in a single battle.[101]

---

99 The Romance version is edited in Rodrigo Jiménez de Rada, *Estoria de los godos del Arçobispo don Rodrigo* (Vaduz, 1966). There is an interesting commentary on this chronicle in Aengus Ward, "La *Estoria de los godos*: ¿la primera crónica castellana?," *Revista de poética medieval* 8 (2002): 181–98.

100 *Hortante autem et adiuuante senatu et adhuc Witiza uiuente, cepit conregnare Rodericus ultimus rex Gothorum anno Vlit IIIIº, Arabum uero LXXXX primo, era DCCXLVIIII, anno VIIº Witize, et tantum tribus annis regnauit, uno per se, duobus cum Witiza. [...] Quid autem de corpore fuerit factum, penitus ignoratur, nisi quod modernis temporibus apud Viseum ciuitatem Portugalie inscriptus tumulus inuenitur: "Hic iacet Rodericus ultimus rex Gothorum."* Cited from Jiménez de Rada, *Historia de rebus Hispanie*, 99, 104.

101 *Set Iuliano comite et Gothis qui secum aderant dure instantibus, franguntur acies christiane, qui longa pace et habundancia desides, imbelles et ignaui certaminis sunt inuenti, et obicibus terga dantes die Dominica, Vº idus mensis Xauel, anno Arabum LXXXII, era DCCLII, rex Rodericus et christianus exercitus uincitur et fuga inutili perierunt [...] Iam iamque Gothorum aciebus fere undique consternatis, rex Rodericus interdum fuga, interdum occursibus nitebatur, set aliquandiu bello protracto gens Gothorum in parte ceditur, in parte fuge presidio liberatur. [...] Cap. XXI. De destrvctione Gothorvm et conmendatione Hispanie. Pro dolor! Hic finitur gloria Gothice maiestatis era DCCLII, et que pluribus bellis regna plurima incuruauit, uno bello uexilla sue glorie inclinauit.* Cited from Jiménez de Rada, *Historia de rebus Hispanie*, 103–4.

These passages show Roderic's army as Christian, as well as Gothic. This feature of the *regnum Gothorum* would then serve as a link with the new *regna* formed in the Cantabrian Mountains and the Pyrenees. It is also noteworthy that, despite the claim that part of the Gothic people survived, it shows a belief, even including the date (the year 714), that the *regnum Gothorum* ended through destruction by the Arabs, although their defeat in the battle was under Goths led by Count Julian.

> Fourth book. Chapter I. About the rebellion of Pelagius against the Arabs, about his sister and about his kingdom.

> And at the same time that they chopped Spain into so many payments, God Almighty, who did not forget mercy in His wrath, wanted to preserve Pelagius as if he were a small spark in His gaze. This Pelagius, who, as it has been said, fled from the face of Wittiza, who wanted to blind him despite having been his sword-bearer, retired to Cantabria; but hearing that the army of the Christians had succumbed and the Arabs had invaded anything desirable, taken his own sister with him, he gifted himself in Asturias so that at least in the defiles of Asturias some little spark of the name of Christ could be preserved, since the Saracens occupied all of Spain by not resisting anywhere the already consumed force of the Gothic people, except for a few remaining ones that stayed in the mountains of Asturias, Biscay, Álava, Gipuzkoa, Rucconia, and Aragon, whom the Lord saved for this reason, so that the lamp of the saints would not be extinguished in the Spains in the presence of the Lord.[102]

Finally, this fragment shows that the extinct *regnum Gothorum* was replaced by pockets of resistance across the northern Peninsula, from Asturias to Aragon, not because they were Goths or were under the leadership of someone related to an earlier Gothic king, but because they were Christians. In addition, Jiménez de Rada claims that the *regnum Hispaniae* just about survived under the Arabs, although it was in a terrible situation. He also shows the origin of the division of the *regnum* into two domains with Christian members who would act as the seeds of the various kingdoms to carry out the complete recovery of Spain as rightful owners due to their Christian faith.

Historia Arabum

With the writing of *Historia Arabum* around 1245, Rodrigo Jiménez de Rada completed his historiographical output.[103] In this chronicle, he explains the history of the Arabs,

---

102 *Liber Qvartvs. Cap. I. De rebellione Pelagii contra Arabes et de sorore sva et de regno eivs. Et dum tot dispendiis Hispaniam dissecarent, Deus omnipotens in ira sua misericordie non oblitus Pelagium quasi cintillam modicam in suo conspectu uoluit conseruare. Hic Pelagius, ut est dictum, fugiens a facie Witize, qui eum uoluerat, excecare, licet spatarius eius fuisset, apud Cantabriam se recepit, set audiens subcubuisse exercitum christianum et Arabes queque desiderabilia inuasisse, sumpta secum sorore propria Asturiis se donauit, ut saltem in Asturiarum angustiis posset christiani nominis aliquam scintillulam conseruare, Sarraceni enim totam Hispaniam occupauerant gentis Gothice fortitudine iam contrita nec alicubi resistente, exceptis paucis reliquiis que in montanis Asturiarum, Biscagie, Alaue, Guipuscue, Ruchonie et Aragonie remanserunt, quos ideo Dominus reseruauit ne lucerna sanctorum in Hispaniis coram Domino extingueretur.* Cited from Jiménez de Rada, *Historia de rebus Hispanie*, 114.

103 Juan Fernández Valverde, Juan Antonio Estévez Sola, "Introducción," in Rodrigo Jiménez de Rada, *Historiae minores. Dialogus libri vite*, ed. Juan Fernández Valverde, Juan Antonio Estévez Sola, Corpus Christianorum Continuatio Mediaevalis 72C (Turnhout, 1999), 28–33.

beginning with the life of Muhammad and the reigns and conquests of the first caliphs, to soon focus on the events of Spain: as wilayah, emirate, caliphate, its division into taifas, and the arrival of the Almoravids under the leadership of Yusuf. His sources were from al-Andalus, both Latin and Arabic, among which we can see that the Toledan Archbishop used Al-Razi's *Ajbar muluk Al-Andalus*, Ibn Ishaq's *Sira*, Ibn Idari's *al-Bayan al-Mugrib*, and Ibn al-Atir's *Kamil fi-l-Tarij*.[104] Although he worked with these Arabic sources and dated events according to the Hijri calendar, Jiménez de Rada does not hold a neutral stance and is always in favour of the Christians in his interpretations, considering the Arab-Berber conquest a negative event.

Following the ideological line of *De rebus Hispaniae*, now reinforced by the Andalusian sources, the Navarrese chronicler relates the end of the *regnum Gothorum* and its succession by the Arab government in the *regnum Hispaniae*. As he only focuses on the history of al-Andalus, he does not discuss the *regnum*'s division into Christian and Muslim powers; and so, Spain comes under the full control of the *regnum Arabum*:

> In the western regions he gained and overthrew the rule of the Goths [*regnum Gothorum*], settled with ancient solidity, which, in continual peace from the time of Leovigildo for one hundred and forty years, was destroyed. He dominated the Spains by means of General Musa's army, took away the dignity of the kingdom [*regni*] and established tributes. In the fourth year of the imperial rule of Al-Walid, Musa ibn Nusayr, leader of King Al-Walid's army, sent Tariq ibn Zarqa[105] with an army to this side of the sea, and he put Roderic, the last king of the Goths, to flight in a battle and subjugated the Spains.[106]

This fragment has an obvious kinship with the texts from the *Arab-Byzantine Chronicle of 741* and the *Mozarabic Chronicle of 754*, described in the first section of this chapter. Jiménez de Rada mainly follows the latter, perhaps because the text is a derivative of the Arabic source common to both chronicles or a copy of this source. Regarding the contents, Jiménez de Rada considers the duration and end of the *regnum Gothorum*, specifying Roderic as the last king. He also indicates that the kingdom, that is, Spain, was left safely in the hands of Al-Walid.

> And because Ayyub, of whom we have spoken, had some consanguinity with Musa, the *amir al-muminin* removed him from the Kingdom of Spain [*regno Hispanie*] and for the Kingdom of Spain [*regno Hispanie*] he chose Al-Hurr ibn Abd al-Rahman as a replacement, who lasted two years and nine months in the kingdom [*regno*].[107]

---

104 On the Arabic sources, see Juan Fernández Valverde, Juan Antonio Estévez Sola, "Introducción," 26–28.

105 I think Jiménez de Rada refers to Tariq ibn Zayid, but it could also be Abu Zuhra Tarif.

106 *In occiduis partibus regnum Gothorum antiqua soliditate firmatum optinuit et afflixit, quod a tempore Leouegildi per annos CXL pace continua fuit letum. Hic per ducem exercitus sui Muzam Hispanias domuit et regni abstulit dignitatem et constituit uectigales. Anno imperii Vlit IIIIº Muza Abennozayr princeps milicie Vlit regis misit Taric Abenzarcha cum exercitu citra mare, qui et Rodericum ultimum regem Gothorum bello fugauit et Hispanias subiugauit.* Cited from Jiménez de Rada, *Historiae minores*, 100.

107 *Et quia Ayub, de quo diximus, Muze consanguinitate aliqua atinebat, Ammiramomenin fecit eum a regno Hispanie remoueri et Alohor filium Abderramen in regno Hispanie subrogauit, qui duos annos et nouem menses in regno expleuit.* Cited from Jiménez de Rada, *Historiae minores*, 101.

Finally, this text explicitly mentions that the Arabs rule the *regnum Hispaniae*, so Jiménez de Rada takes the Andalusian view that the Spanish political institution survived in the southern Iberian Peninsula without interruption, and it had not partially relocated to lands ruled by Christian leaders or kings.

Estoria de España general

This great historiographical work, the *Estoria de España general* (*General History of Spain*), was personally commissioned by King Alfonso X *"el Sabio"* to a group of expert historians in the court of Toledo in the 1270s. The aim was to make a compendium of the history of Spain, as a historical subject, from the beginning of time until the reign of Alfonso X, although it was never completed. The work underwent an important revision by philologists, called the *Versión crítica* (1282–1284), concerning the chapters on the Asturian, Leonese, and Castilian kings, in the last years of the Wise King when he was in his Sevilla redoubt during the war against his son, Sancho IV. Divided into two volumes, the significant historical event of both books was the Arab conquest of Spain and the rise of Pelagius in Asturias as a bastion of Christendom. The main sources were Jiménez de Rada's *De rebus Hispaniae* and Lucas de Tuy's *Chronicon mundi*, giving preference to the first work where there was a discrepancy in facts, although they also used other chronicles, both in Latin and Arabic, and even *chansons de geste*, whose contents have been preserved thanks to the *Estoria de España*. Thereafter, it was enlarged in the reign of Sancho IV in 1289 in the *Versión o Crónica Amplificada de 1289* and reworked in the reign of Alfonso XI in 1345 in the *Primera Crónica General*. It heavily influenced later chronicles, such as the *Crónica de veinte reyes*, the *Estoria del fecho de los godos*, and the *Crónica de Castilla*.[108]

This group of Alfonsine historians not only favoured Jiménez de Rada's *De rebus Hispaniae* in their selection of sources. They also adopted his ideological approach to the Arab conquest of the Iberian Peninsula, since the historians borrowed the Toledan Archbishop's rejection of neo-Gothicism, which is clear by their downplaying the work of Lucas de Tuy. So, the *Estoria de España* never states that the *regnum Gothorum* (*el poder de los godos* in Romance) continued in Asturias thanks to Pelagius; it follows the idea that the Asturians are the legitimate successors of the Goths through their Christianity (although it avoids explicit reference to the end of the Goths, leaving the event to be inferred). In addition, this chronicle is the first to emphasize the loss and destruction of Spain,[109] but I would suggest that almost all of these references concern human losses among the Spanish people and the destruction of farmland and buildings, mainly

---

108 I gratefully owe my information provided about the *Estoria de España general* to the lessons taught by one of the leading experts on this great chronicle, Prof. Dr. Mariano de la Campa, on the subject "Cronística medieval hispanocristiana" ("Spanish-Christian medieval chronicles"), whose class I attended in the Máster en Estudios Medievales Hispánicos at the Universidad Autónoma de Madrid in 2010–2011. I also highly recommend reading Fernández-Ordóñez, *Las estorias de Alfonso el Sabio*.

109 A study is needed on whether this expression appears in other sources, contemporary or not to the *Estoria de España general*.

churches, since these Alfonsine historians believed that the kingdom, *Espanna*, continued in the south until the duplication of *regna* following the enthronement of Pelagius.

> Tarif[110] and Count Julian arrived in Spain and began to destroy the province of Baetica,
> that is, Guadalquivir, and that of Lucena. When King Roderic knew this, he gathered all
> the Goths that were with him; [...] but Count Julian and the Goths who went with him
> fought so fiercely that they broke the lines of the Christians. [...] And from here on they
> never knew more about what happened, until after a time in the city of Viseu in the land
> of Portugal a stone grave on which was written, "Here lies King Roderic, the last king of
> the Goths," was discovered.

> After King Roderic and the Christians were defeated and killed, the very noble people of
> the Goths, which won many battles and subdued many kingdoms, were then beaten and
> subdued, and their precious flags were brought down.[111]

In these and the following fragments, the textual similarity to Jiménez de Rada's *De rebus
Hispaniae* is evident. Moreover, like Jiménez de Rada, Alfonso X's team of historians suggests that the Goths who were with the king in the fight with Roderic and Julian were
Christians, which allows a link between them and the Christians of the *regnum* inaugurated by Pelagius. In addition, these passages reveal the interpretation, somewhat veiled
and not as explicit as in the works of Jiménez de Rada, that the rule of the Goths is over,
because they indicate that Roderic is the last king of the Goths. Revisiting the account
of the *Chronicle of Alfonso III*, the earliest documented evidence of the event, these passages show that the defeat of the Goths left them in the same state of submission that
they once brought upon other kingdoms.

> 559. About the mourning of the Goths of Spain and about the reason why it was destroyed.
> [...] Miserable Spain! Its death was so afflicted that nobody remained here to lament it;
> [...] Its affliction and its destruction were so disturbing that there is no whirlwind nor
> rain nor sea storm that a man could compare to. What evil or what storm did not Spain
> go through? [...] Who would give me water that washed this moment from my head and
> [who would give] springs that flow tears always to my eyes so that I cry and weep the loss
> and the death of the ones of Spain and the meanness and the terrorization of the Goths?[112]

---

110 Tarif is Abu Zuhra Tarif, not to be confused with Tariq ibn Ziyad.

111 *Tarif et el cuende Julian arribaron en Espanna et començaron de destroyr la prouincia de
Bethica, esta es Guadalquiuir, et la de Luzenna. El rey Rodrigo quando lo sopo, ayunto todos los godos
que con ell eran; [...] mas el cuende Julian et los godos que andauan con el lidiaron tan fieramientre
que crebantaron las azes de los cristianos. [...] E dalli adelante nunqua sopieron mas que se fizo, si
non que despues a tiempo en la cibdad de Viseo en tierra de Portogal fue fallado un luziello en que
seye escripto: "aqui yaze el rey Rodrigo, el postrimero rey de los godos." [...]. Pues que el rey Rodrigo
et los cristianos fueron uençudos et muertos, la muy noble yente de los godos que muchas batallas
crebantara et abaxara muchos regnos fue estonces crebantada et abaxada, et las sus preciadas sennas
abatidas.* Cited from *Primera Crónica General*, 1, 310.

112 *559. Del duello de los godos de Espanna et de la razon porque ella fue destroyda [...] ¡Espanna
mezquina! Tanto fue la su muert coytada que solamientre non finco y ninguno que la llante; [...]
Tan assora fue la su cueta et el su destroymiento que non a toruellinno nin lluuia nin tempestad de
mar a que lo omne pudiesse asmar. ¿Qual mal o qual tempestad non passo Espanna? [...] ¿Quien me
darie agua que toda mi cabeça fuesse ende bannada, e a mios oios fuentes que siempre manassen
llagrimas por que llorase et llanniesse la perdida et la muerte de los de Espanna et la mezquindad et
ell aterramiento de los godos?* Cited from *Primera Crónica General*, 1, 312–13.

This text references the destruction and loss of Spain. It is likely that, as in the *Mozarabic Chronicle of 754*, this *deploratio Hispaniae* is actually a lament of the suffering caused by the Arab conquest in Spain and reflects the misfortunes and deaths of its inhabitants, while it offers a poetic conclusion to the idealized Visigothic Spain. This marks the beginning of a new period, a new Spain, because we must not forget that the protagonist of this *estoria* is none other than Spain. We can assume that the Alfonsine historians here are not referring to the *regnum Hispaniae*, especially if we realize that in the following chapters it is still in existence.

> 560. About how Tarif commanded to devastate land of Spain and about how Córdoba was seized. After the battle was concluded as we told, Prince Lord Pelagius, who was in Cantabria, arrived in Asturias with those Christians that remained, as we will say later in the history. And since no lord remained in the land to protect the Christians except this Lord Pelagius, we bring up for him the account of the years that the land was without lord and they were five [years] until they raised him [to the throne] as king; and when he arrived in Asturias and remained as lord of the Christians it was in the era that we said of seven hundred and fifty two years, when it was the year of the Incarnation in seven hundred and fourteen, that of the imperial rule of Leo in one, that of Pope Gregory in four, that of Al-Walid, King of the Moors, in seven, that of the Arabs in ninety-four, and that of Clovis, King of France, in three.

> [...] And when he heard that the Christians were defeated and all the cavalry was lost, he took the sister that he had, and went with her to Asturias so that at least in the narrowness of the mountains some luminary could be preserved for the Christianity to take shelter, because the Moors had already conquered all the most of Spain, as we said, and broke out the rule of the Goths [*el poder de los godos*] in such a way that nobody was there to defend them, but a few ones that remained and also arrived in Asturias, Biscay, Álava, and Gipuzkoa, because they are very big mountains, and in the Ruccones mountains and Aragon. And God wanted to save them so that the flame of Christianity and His servants would not go out completely in Spain.

> [...] In the book of history that starts with how Moses made the book of Genesis, and also about the generations that came to populate Spain, it is contained how the Goths came to Spain and conquered it and how they had it in their rule until they lost it in the time of King Roderic. And since after that the Moors had Spain five years without any battle, the history will tell the beginning of King Lord Pelagius, who was the first king of Leon.[113]

---

113 *560. De como Tarif enuio destroyr tierra de Espanna et de como fue presa Cordoua. Pues que la batalla fue uençuda assi como dixiemos, ell infante don Pelayo, que era en Cantabria, açosse a las Asturias con aquellos cristianos que fincaran, assi como adelante diremos en la estoria. E por que otro sennor non fincaua en la tierra pora amparamiento de los cristianos si este don Pelayo, traemos por ell el cuento de los annos que la tierra estido sin sennor, et fueron cinco fasta quel alçaron a el por rey; e quando se ell alço a las Asturias et finco por sennor de los cristianos fue en la era que auemos dicha de sietecientos et cinquaenta et dos annos, quando andaua el anno de la Encarnacion en sietecientos et catorze, e el dell imperio de Leo en uno; e del papa Gregorio en quatro, e el de Vlit rey de los moros en siete, e el de los alaruaes en nouaenta et quatro, e el de Glodoueo rey de Francia en tres. [...] E quando oyo que los cristianos eran uençudos et toda la caualleria perduda, tomo una hermana que auie, et fuesse con ella pora las Asturias que siquier entre las estrechuras de las montannas pudiesse guardar alguna lumbrera pora la cristiandad a que se acogiesse, ca los moros auien ya conquerida todo lo mas de Espanna, assi como auemos dicho, e crebantaron el poder de los godos de guisa que non auie y ninguno que se les defendiesse, sinon unos pocos que fincaran et se alçaran otrossi en las Asturias et en Vizcaya et en Alaua et en Guipuzcua por que son mui grandes montannas, et en los*

These excerpts show that the *regnum Gothorum* (*el poder de los godos*) was succeeded by the *regnum Christianorum*, since the Christians, whose first leader is Pelagius, must undertake the task of recovering the *regnum Hispaniae* after its loss by the Goths.[114] In addition, the non-continuity of the Goths is evidenced by the fact that Pelagius is considered a Christian refugee and not as a Goth, although he is briefly linked with Wittiza as his sword-bearer in a text not included here. Moreover, in the first of these fragments, it is written that Spain was without lord until Pelagius was erected as a king, but this must be understood to mean that Spain was without a Christian king, that is, without a legitimate king, since the third fragment discusses the Moors' rule of Spain during the Christian interregnum. These northern Christians from Asturias and other mountainous regions will be the rivals of the Moors for total domination of "Spain," also ruled by Muslims, as we shall see below.

> This year the Arabs killed Abd al-Aziz, the son of Musa who was king of Sevilla, where one day he was making his prayer, because they thought him to be Christian; and this was on advice of Ayyub ibn Habib; and he had been reigning for three years. And because this Ayyub was very wise in the sect of Muhammad, they made him king; and he populated the city of Calatayud,[115] and returned to Córdoba the seat of the kingdom and the court of the Arabs, which was previously in Sevilla. Then Al-Walid sent to Spain one who was called Al-Hurr ibn Abd al-Rahman, and made him king, and ordered him to expel Ayyub, which we said above, from the kingdom because he was a relative of Musa. And he reigned in Spain two years and nine months.[116]

Finally, these two excerpts illustrate the historiographical idea that there is another power controlling the Kingdom of Spain, that of the Arabs, located first in Sevilla and later in Córdoba.

---

montes Rucones et en Aragon. E a estos quiso los Dios guardar por que la lumbre de la cristiandad et de los sus sieruos non se amatasse de tod en Espann. [...] En el libro de la estoria que comiença de como Moysen fizo el libro Genesis, et otrosi de las generaciones que uinieron poblar a Espanna, se contiene de commo los godos uinieron a Espanna et la conquirieron et comm la touieron en su poder fasta que la perdieron en tiempo del rey Rodrigo. Et por que despues desto los moros touieron Espanna çinco annos sin contienda ninguna, la estoria contara el comienço del rey don Pelayo, que fue el primero rey de Leon. Cited from *Primera Crónica General*, 1, 314, 319; 2, 32

114 In this passage, unlike the previous one, the Castilian-Leonese historians use the concept of loss in the meaning of Reconquista. Even so, we must realize that it is a loss of the total control of the Kingdom of Spain by the Christians, and not the disappearance of the kingdom itself, since it remained but under the power of the Arabs.

115 The name of Calatayud literally means "Citadel of Ayyub" (*Qalat Ayyub*).

116 *Esse anno mataron los alaraues a Abdullaziz el fijo de Muça que era rey de Seuilla o estaua vn dia faziendo su oracion, porque tenien que era cristiano; et esto fue con conseio de Ayub Auenhabib; et auie ya tres annos que regnaua. Et por que aqueste Ayub era muy sabio en la secta de Mahomat, alçaron le por rey; et este poblo la cibdat de Calatayub, et torno a Cordoua la siella del regno et la corte de los alaraues, la que ante era en Seuilla. Vlit enuio estonces a Espanna uno que auie nombre Alohor, fijo de Abderrahmen, et fizol rey, et mandol que echasse del regno a Ayub, el que de suso dixiemos, por que era pariente de Muça. Et regno ell en Espanna dos annos et nueue meses.* Cited from *Primera Crónica General*, 2, 322.

The Catalonian-Aragonese *Crónica de San Juan de la Peña*

After establishing the historiographical ideology of the conquest of the Iberian Peninsula and its consequences in the *Estoria de España general*, chronicles in the fourteenth and fifteenth centuries rarely dealt with these topics; they didn't cover the general history of Spain, but specific reigns of the different kingdoms, and new ideological approaches on these events did not develop in the late medieval mindset. It seems that the success of *De rebus Hispaniae*, the Romance translation of this work, and the *Estoria de España* made new pan-Hispanic historiographical creations unnecessary in the western kingdoms of the Iberian peninsula.

However, the *Crónica de San Juan de la Peña*[117] was written between 1369 and 1372 at the initiative of King Pedro IV of Aragon (also known as Count Pere III of Barcelona or Peter the Ceremonious), when he requested codices to the monasteries of San Juan de la Peña and Ripoll. The original version was written in Latin at least partly by this king-count and by several collaborators under his supervision, including Tomàs Canyelles. Soon after its completion, the chronicle was translated almost simultaneously into Aragonese and Catalan with minimal textual variations from the original, with copies sent to the territories of these two languages. The main source is Jiménez de Rada's *De rebus Hispaniae*, whose ideology on the issues discussed here were followed in the Catalonian-Aragonese chronicle. In addition, the Aragonese *Crónica de los estados peninsulares*, the Catalan *Gesta Comitum Barchinonensium*, and the Sicilian *Liber de gestis siculorum sub Friderico rege et suis* developed the chapters on these domains.

In terms of content, although this chronicle is a work concerning Spain's general history, most of it is dedicated to the kings of Navarre and Aragon and the counts of Barcelona. Briefly at the beginning it tells the history of the first peoples of Spain and the Goths. On the Arab conquest, this chronicle says:

> This king was defeated and all Spain was occupied by the Saracens to the place of Arles in Provence. [...] Indeed, after the aforesaid persecution and occupation, the Christians who were able to escape were dispersed fleeing to the hideaways and fortresses of the mountains of Sobrarbe, Ribagorza, Aragon, Berriozar, Artieda, Ordoñana, Biscay, Álava, and Asturias, where they built many castles and many other fortresses where they were able to take refuge and defend themselves from the Saracens. And all those lands remained in the possession of the Christians, so that the Moors did not possess them at any time.[118]

---

117 The information on this chronicle comes from *Crónica de San Juan de la Peña*, ed. Antonio Ubieto Arteta (València, 1961), 9–13; Amadeu-Jesús Soberanas Lleó, "Prefaci," in *Crònica General de Pere III el Cerimoniós, dita comunament Crònica de Sant Joan de la Penya*, ed. Amadeu-Jesús Soberanas Lleó (Barcelona, 1961), 5–16; and Carmen Orcástegui Gros, "Presentación," in *Crónica de San Juan de la Peña (Versión aragonesa). Edición crítica*, ed. Carmen Orcástegui Gros (Zaragoza, 1986), 5.

118 *Idem rex fuit deuictus et tota Ispania occupata per sarracenos usque ad locum de Arleto Prouintie. [...].Facta quidem persecutione siue occupatione predicta, christiani qui euadere potuerunt, dispersi sunt, fugientes uersus latebras seu fortitudines muntanearum Suprarbii, Rippacurtie, Aragonum, de Bierroça, de Artide, Ordonya, de Biscaya, de Alaua et de Asturiis, ubi construxerunt pluria castra et plures alias fortitudines, in quibus se receptare ualerunt et deffendere a sarracenis. Et omnes ille terre remanserunt in posse christianorum, sic quod eas mauri nullo tempore possederunt.* Cited from *Crónica de San Juan de la Peña*, 24–5.

In these passages the ideological influence of Jiménez de Rada is evident. The *Crónica de San Juan de la Peña* assumes that the *regnum Hispaniae* remains under Saracen rule and reinforces its division into two domains, Muslim and Christian, without Gothic connotations. Thus, the continuity comes through the Christian element, emphasizing the Christian presence in the Pyrenean and Cantabrian territories under Navarrese-Aragonese control; these Christian refugees will see the origin of the domains of King Peter the Ceremonious and the legitimacy of the conquests of his predecessors on the throne against Muslim rulers.

It is noteworthy that a textual fragment was added to the Aragonese translation of the *Crónica de San Juan de la Peña*, located before the account of the history of the Goths and their kings: "The Goths threw out those nations from Spain and later they were in it until the treason of Count Lord Julian, almost 400 years, because the last king of the Goths was Lord Roderic."[119] The Aragonese translator establishes the timespan of the *regnum Gothorum*, besides highlighting the last place of King Roderic among the Gothic kings, so he supports the conclusion of the *regnum Gothorum* as post-dating the Arab conquest, an idea inferred from the context in Latin and Catalan versions, but stated explicitly in the Aragonese translation. It is difficult to determine the source of the Aragonese chronicler's statement that the Visigothic kingdom lasted four centuries instead of three: it could be the *Mozarabic Chronicle of 754*, the *Chronologia regum Gothorum*, or another historiographical text of the eighth and ninth centuries no longer in existence.

Navarrese Chronicles

As in the previous Catalonian-Aragonese case, chronicles on the universal history of Spain were written in the Kingdom of Navarre, although the authors' interest was focused on the kings of Navarre and events affecting that kingdom. Despite this, probably because the struggle for the Reconquista was by then so pertinent, the passages relating to the Arab-Berber conquest of the Peninsula follow the ideology made official in the Toledan chronicles of Jiménez de Rada and Alfonso X of Castile. Therefore, with a slight difference in the work of Charles of Viana,[120] the Navarrese chronicles perpetuate the theory that the *regnum Gothorum* ended with King Roderic, starting then a reign of Christians in the northern regions of the *regnum Hispaniae*. This kingdom endured under the new Moorish rule in the south until it was shared by two domains after the previously mentioned Christian uprisings in the north.

---

119 *Las quales naciones los godos echaron de Espannya et después estaron en ella fasta la traición del conde don Yllan, quasi CCCCos annos, porque el çaguer rey de los godos fue don Rodrigo.* Cited from *Crónica de San Juan de la Peña (Versión aragonesa)*, 8.

120 As shall be seen later, it seems that Charles of Viana's *Crónica de los reyes de Navarra* accepts the Gothic continuation in Asturias, probably under the influence of Lucas de Tuy. Even so, the heir of Navarre favors the Christian element in this Asturian continuity; he confines the neo-Gothicism to this region, while he qualifies the Navarrese and Aragonese refugees as Christians exclusively.

Crónica d'Espayña

The *Crónica d'Espayña* was composed shortly after 1387 under the direction of García de Eugui, Bishop of Bayonne and close associate on his diplomatic missions of King Charles II of Navarre, as well as confessor for his successor, Charles III.[121] Structurally, one half of the chronicle is dedicated to ancient history (the six ages, Greek, Carthaginian, and Iberian legendary characters, the history of Carthage, history of Roma, and the history of the Gothic kings) and the other half to the history of the Christian kingdoms (Asturias–Leon–Castile and Navarre[122]). The main sources are the *Estoria de España* and the *Estoria de los godos*, the Romance translation of Jiménez de Rada's *De rebus Hispaniae*,[123] so it is not surprising that the chronicle of García de Eugui is permeated with the ideology transmitted by the Archbishop of Toledo and that of King Alfonso the Wise. In addition, specifically for the chapter of Pelagius, the *Liber regum* is used as a secondary but significant source,[124] and also offers a similar view to that of the two other historiographical works in relation to the account of the Arab conquest.

> R about the King Vaticano or Wittiza, the penultimate king of the Goths. [...] R about the sins that the Goths were destroyed for. [...] R about the evils that Spain suffered [...]. Alas, pain! There was then nobody who lifted a hand to defend Spain, and it remained plain, waste of people. The evils of Hercules, the Greeks, the Alans and the Vandals were renewed, now the Muslim lineage began to rule [*regnar*] in Spain. [...]

> This Lord Pelagius heard about the death of the Christians and the defeat of the Goths, took his sister and fled with her to Asturias. And the Arabs seized all Spain except a few men who remained in the mountains, such as in Biscay, Álava, Gipuzkoa, and Recovia [Rucconia] in Aragon, which God retained so that His name would not be forgotten in Spain, because there was enough great evil in what they had seized.

> In addition, this Lord Pelagius was son of the sister of King Roderic, the old queen [...].

> In addition, this King Lord Pelagius was very good, loyal, and a warrior, and all the Christians who were in the mountains went to him, fought the Moors and made many battles and he won them all and killed many Moors.[125]

---

121 Aengus Ward, "El autor ¿fray García de Eugui?," *Crónica d'Espayña de García de Eugui*, ed. Aengus Ward (Pamplona, 1999), 13–28.

122 The Aragonese kings are not included, except Alfonso I the Battler, in virtue of his being king of Leon and Castile, and the kings of Navarre, who also ruled Aragon (Sancho V and, again, Alfonso I).

123 Aengus Ward, "Fuentes y antecedentes históricos de la *Crónica d'Espayña* de García de Eugui," in *Crónica d'Espayña de García de Eugui*, ed. Ward, 36 and 51–57.

124 Ward, "Fuentes y antecedentes," 66.

125 *R del rey Vaticano o Utiçia, el penultimo rey de los godos. [...]. R delos peccados delos godos por que fueron destruidos. [...]. R delos males que sufrio Espayña.¡Ay dolor! Ya non abia qui alçase la mano a defender Spayna, & finco llana, yerma de gentes. Renobaron se los males de Hercules & de los griegos & delos alanos & delos vandalos, agora començo de regnar en Espayña el linage ageno [...] Este don Pelayo oyo muerte delos xristianos & quebrantamiento delos godos, priso asu hermana & fuyo conella alas Ysturias. & los arabes prisieron toda Espayña sino pocos homes que fincaron enlas montaynas como en Vizcaya et en Alaba et en Ypuzcoa & en Recovia en Aragon que Dios retovo por que su nombre non fuesse olbidado en Espayña, que asaz abia grant mal enlo preso [...]. Jtem este don Pelayo fue fijo dela hermana del rey don Rodrigo la reyna viella, [...]. Jtem est rey don Pelayo fue muy bueno leal & guerrero, & todos los xristianos que eran enlas montaynas acudieron se ael et guerrearon con moros*

The sum of these headings and fragments gathers all the information that emerges in several chapters, some of them containing popular legends, such as the death of Roderic in Viseu, about the *regnum Gothorum* and the *regnum Hispaniae*. These texts explain the end of the dominion of the Goths and their succession, only by the Arabs at first, until in the mountains the Christians forged a new kingdom led by King Pelagius who, despite being recognized as Gothic by García de Eugui, does not make the kingdom founded in Asturias a Gothic one. Moreover, this Navarrese bishop indicates that the rule of the Arabs took over the *regnum Hispaniae* but, as with the *Liber regum*, there is no discussion of the *regnum*'s two domains being in permanent struggle and rivalry, since the reference to Spain in the fourth text above can be understood as both territorial and institutional.

The Chronicle of Garci López de Roncesvalles

Garci López de Roncesvalles, treasurer of the kingdom during the reign of Charles III of Navarre, wrote his chronicle in 1405 as a preface to the book of *Comptos* ("Accounts") of 1404, although he later added an event from 1406.[126] The treasurer's role was to recount briefly the succession of the kings of Navarre, starting with the evangelization of Spain, a topic he addresses in the opening paragraphs, to show the legitimacy of the royal house which had just admitted him as official of the Navarrese Kingdom.[127] His main source is Jiménez de Rada's *De rebus Hispaniae* but, relying on Garci López's summary, he also worked in some chronicles of ecclesiastical history written by Ptolomeus of Fiadonibus, Vincent of Beauvais's *Speculum Historiale*, the *Fuero general de Navarra*, and the *Book of Genealogies*.[128]

Garci López de Roncesvalles did not have a particular ideological interest in the events that occurred during the Arab conquest of the Iberian Peninsula. They did not significantly affect his work, focused as it was on the kings of Navarre. So his words on this topic are limited to the following:

> And they [the Goths] were Christians from the said time of the conversion to the great pain of the destruction and ruin that the overseas Moors made and Count Lord Julian, nephew of King Roderic, brought here because of the betrayal that he made to his nephew by laying with his wife, as it is largely in the histories of Spain and the charter makes mention of it. And this was in the era of Caesar 702 years.

> And thus from the time of the conversion of Pamplona and the Spains to the ruin the Christians lasted 610 years; and the Christians who could be saved were saved in the mountains of Portugal, Galicia, the Asturias, Navarre, Roncal, Jaca, and the mountain chains of Aragon.[129]

& fizieron muchas batallas & ranço las todas & mato muchos moros. Cited from *Crónica d'Espayña*, 280, 286, 287, 291, 293–94.

126 Carmen Orcástegui Gros, "Estudio," in *Crónica de Garci López de Roncesvalles. Estudio y edición crítica*, ed. Carmen Orcástegui Gros (Pamplona, 1977), 15–16.

127 Orcástegui, "Estudio," 31–33.

128 Orcástegui, "Estudio," 35–41.

129 *Et fueron christianos del dicho tiempo de la conversión ata la grant dolor de la destrución et*

Garci López never discusses the Goths because the element of continuity from the period before the conquest to the next one is the presence of Christians. Besides, he does not mention the *regnum Hispaniae* per se, because the references to *las Spannas* have more a geographical than a political significance. Even so, the Navarrese chronicler includes the ideology, then traditional and completely assumed due to its frequent repetition in the chronicles, that the legitimate continuation of the *regnum Hispaniae* survived in the north because the people of this region were Christians.

Crónica de los reyes de Navarra

The *Crónica de los reyes de Navarra* was created under the supervision of the heir to the throne, Charles of Viana, who wanted to have an official history of the Kingdom of Navarre with a Navarrist ideology. To produce a particular history of this kingdom, the prince of Navarre followed the historiographical pattern of Garci López de Roncesvalles' chronicle; the prince copied much of its content verbatim, since the writing of chronicles about kingdoms had been abandoned in Spain in favour of official chronicles about recent reigns.[130] This unfinished work was written between 1453 and 1455, although the preface specifies 1454,[131] by two writers: the first produced a draft with chapters divided into three books; on Charles of Viana's order, the contents were expanded with new information by the second chronicler.[132] As for sources, the main pillar is the *Chronicle of Garci López de Roncesvalles*; below that are the works of Jiménez de Rada and Lucas de Tuy, and in a lesser degree can be seen the influence of the *Estoria de España general* and the Aragonese *Crónica de San Juan de la Peña*.[133]

In terms of structure, the first book ends with the unification of Pamplona and Aragon on the death of Sancho IV in 1076, that is, it contains the origins of the kingdom and the first dynasties; the second book is about the Navarrese-Aragonese dynasty begun by Sancho V and the Navarrese dynasty restored by Garcia V; and the third book begins with the dynasty of Champagne and ends with King Charles II.[134] Although the Prince of Viana's main objective was to tell the history of Navarre, before focusing on it he wanted to link with the general history of Spain in the first five chapters of Book I, among which

---

perdición que fizieron los moros de Ultramar que y fizo venir el conte don Jullián, sobrino del rey don Rodrigo, por la trayción que él fizo a su sobrino de iazer con su mujer, como desto largament iaze en las ystorias de Spanna et eno faze mencion el fuero. Et esto fue era de Cesar VIIc IIo annos.

Et assí del tiempo de la conversión de Pamplona et las Spannas ata la perdición duraron christianos VIc X annos; et los christianos que podieron salvarse, se salvaron en las montañas de Portogal, Galicia, las Asturias, Navarra, Roncal, Iaqua et las sierras de Aragón. Cited from *Crónica de Garci López de Roncesvalles*, 58–59.

130 Carmen Orcástegui Gros, "Estudio," in *La Crónica de los reyes de Navarra*, ed. Carmen Orcástegui Gros (Pamplona, 2002), 17–21.

131 Orcástegui, "Estudio," *La Crónica*, 21–23.

132 Orcástegui, "Estudio," *La Crónica*, 32–33.

133 Orcástegui, "Estudio," *La Crónica*, 43–55.

134 Orcástegui, "Estudio," *La Crónica*, 57–70.

are those containing the passages in this article: the second chapter deals with the Goths and the fifth chapter with the northern haven of the Christians.

> And when the Christians were overrun by the Moors, they had to desert the Spains, which in a few days was conquered by the said Moors, except Galicia, the Asturias, Biscay, Gipuzkoa, Álava, the Cinco Villas, Baztán, La Berrueta, Valdelana, Améscoa, Deierri, Aézcoa, Salazar, Roncal, Ansó, Echo, Jaca and the mountains of Santa Cristina [de Somport], Canfranc, Aísa and Sobrarbe. In whose lands some Christians were preserved, as we will say onward [...].

> Prince Pelagius withdrew to the Holy Cave, which is between the Asturias and Galicia, with some few Gothic faithful that persevered in the faith of Our Lord. [...]

> And up to three hundred Christians took refuge in the land of Aragon with Count Lord Aznar, that is, in a mount called Oroel, near the city of Jaca. And the Naverrese lived in the old Navarre with Count Lord García Jiménez.[135]

Although in the first fragment Charles of Viana considers Christianity to be the element of continuity with the period before the conquest, he probably borrows Lucas de Tuy's neo-Gothic approach, considering that the *regnum Gothorum* was perpetuated in Asturias. However, I find it significant that the heir of Navarre used the term "Christians," without Gothic connotations, for the Aragonese and perhaps also for the Navarrese. Moreover, Charles of Viana shows the idea of a Christian–Muslim division of domains in control of the Spains, although, as in all the Navarrese chronicles relying on the same source, the *Liber regum*, the text does not reveal whether he refers to the land or to the kingdom.

The Castilian *Anacefaleosis o Genealogía de los reyes de España*

The *Anacefaleosis o Genealogía de los reyes de España* of Alfonso de Cartagena, Bishop of Burgos and a prominent Spanish humanist, was completed in 1456 and written in Latin to give the work a universalizing character; the author wanted to show the prominent place occupied by Spain across Christendom. Because of its success, a few years later it was translated into Castilian in two versions, one of which was produced by Juan Rodriguez de Villafuerte before 1463. The other was perhaps written by Fernán Pérez de Guzmán at a date close to the conclusion of the Latin version.[136]

---

135 *Y por cuanto los cristianos fueron rebasados por los moros, tuvieron que desamparar las Españas, las cuales en breves días conquistaron los dichos moros, salvo Galicia, las Asturias, Vizcaya, Guipúzcoa, Álava, las Cinco Villas, Baztán, La Berrueta, Valdelana, Amescua, Deyerri, Aezcoa, Sarasaz, Roncal, Ansó, Echo, Jaca y las montañas de Santa Cristina, Canfranc, Ainsa y Sobrarbe. En cuyas tierras se preservaron algunos cristianos, como adelante diremos.[...] El infante Don Pelayo se retiró a la Cueva Santa, la cual está entre las Asturias y Galicia, con algunos pocos fieles godos, perseverantes en la fe de Nuestro Señor.[...] Y hasta trescientos cristianos se refugiaron en la tierra de Aragón con el conde Don Aznar, a saber en un monte llamado Oroel, cerca de la ciudad de Jaca. Y los navarros habitaban en la antigua Navarra con el conde Don García Ximénez.* Cited from Carmen Orcástegui Gros, ed., *La Crónica de los reyes de Navarra*, 80, 92.

136 Alfonso de Cartagena, *El Libro de la Genealogía de los reyes de España de Alfonso de Cartagena*, ed. Bonifacio Palacios Martín, 2 vols. (València, 1995), 65, 67, 89 (all citations from vol. 2, since vol. 1 is the facsimile).

With a humanist methodological approach, this historian seeks to bring to light historical truth based on objectivity and textual criticism and, for that, he uses a wide range of historiographical sources, among which, for the topics discussed in this chapter, are *De rebus Hispaniae* and *Estoria de España general*. However, this does not stop him including legends, following the general trend of late medieval chronicles.[137]

The aim of Alfonso de Cartagena is to show the legitimacy of the lineage of the kings of Castile with a succession of genealogies of Spanish kings, beginning with the indigenous, Greek, and Roman kingdoms of Antiquity (the First Age), passing through the *regnum Gothorum* (the Second Age), and ending with the feudal kingdoms after the Arab conquest (the Third Age). Thus, the axis of the historical narrative turns on the *regnum Hispaniae*, through which all the kingdoms with their dynasties pass. Obviously, with his ideology the Bishop of Burgos disdains the Arabs as legitimate kings of Spain for their religious impiety, unlike the Goths, who have legitimacy in the *regnum Hispaniae* because they established order and social peace after defeating tyrannical barbarians, and unlike the Asturian-Leonese, whose legitimacy is due to the royal, indeed messianic, choice of Pelagius through divine providence. Significantly, the chronicler does not link the Gothic and Asturian-Leonese kings dynastically, considering that after the victory of the Saracens against the Christian army, the *regnum Gothorum* ended and the Third Age began, an age that was based on the struggle between Christians and Muslims for the restoration of the *regnum Hispaniae*. As an aside, although the historiographical work's title names the kings of Spain and focuses on the Christian reigns, we should note that Alfonso de Cartagena does not consider the kings of the Crown of Aragon, Navarre, and Portugal as legitimate Spanish kings; he places the line of genealogies of Spanish kings exclusively through Asturias, Leon, and Castile.[138]

The fragments in the *Anacefaleosis* relating the course of the *regnum Gothorum* and the *regnum Hispaniae* are the following:

> Roderic, the last king of the Goths, who, with Wittiza living, began to reign together. [...] However, he heard of the ravages of his people and the devastation of the province. King Roderic opposed the arrival of the Arabs with all the gathered Goths and he hurried diligently to meet them. [...] King Roderic and the Christian army were defeated and died in a useless flight. [...] After a long time in Viseu, city of Portugal, an inscribed tumulus was discovered: "HERE LIES RODERIC, THE LAST KING OF THE GOTHS." [...] In fact, he had a great cause to lament when in his time the monarchy of the Spanish Kingdom [*hispani regni*] was humiliated and the name of the Goths completely ceased among the Spanish. In fact, although the kings of Spain descended from that lineage, they nevertheless renounced the Gothic title and were appointed other royal titles.[139]

---

137 *El Libro de la Genealogía*, 92, 112.

138 *El Libro de la Genealogía*, 116–24.

139 *Rodericus, ultimus Rex Gothorum, qui vivente Vetiza conregnare ceperat. [...] Rex autem Rodericus audita strage suorum et provincie vastatione, gothis omnibus congregatis adventui arabum se obiecit et ad occursum eorum strenue properavit. [...] Rex Rodericus et christianus exercitus devincuntur et fuga inutili perierunt. [...] Post multa tempora apud Viseum civitatem Portugali inscriptus tumulus fuit inventus. HIC IACET RODERICUS ULTIMUS REX GOTHORUM. [...] Habuit enim magnam lamentandi causam; cum eius tempore hispani regni Monarchia humiliata est et gothorum nomen apud hispanos prorsus cessavit. Nam licet Hispanie reges a genere illo descenderant, titulum*

In these fragments Alfonso de Cartagena declares the end of the *regnum Gothorum* with emphasis on the last place of King Roderic, presenting the famous passage whose earliest use is attested in the *Chronicle of Alfonso III*. The author also makes clear that, although the Asturian-Leonese kings descend from Goths, they are not Goths, since the new kings are identified with other royal denominations. In addition, he clearly distinguishes the concepts of *regnum Gothorum* and the *regnum Hispaniae,* indicating that the first one ended while the second one continues with the kings of the Third Age. Finally, he introduces the element of continuity with the later kingdom by naming as Christian the army of the Goths.

> After the disaster Pelagius managed to rebel against the Hagarenes and obtain the Princedom of Spain [*principatum Hispanie*] among the Christians. [...] Therefore, counting the periods of his rule it is estimated that he managed to reign in the seven-hundred and twelfth year of the Lord. The three-hundred and twentieth [year] of the Kingdom of Spain [*Regni Hispanie*]. [...] He, descendant from the royal lineage of the Goths, took many cities of the Hagarenes and won many battles against the Hagarenes. But, otherwise, the other kings were not called kings of the Goths but kings of Leon or Asturias.[140]

In these extracts, the chronicler writes that the kingdom or princedom located in Asturias is Spain and is based on Christianity. In addition, the reign of Pelagius is part of the larger structure that is the *regnum Hispaniae*, a transhistorical political entity, because Alfonso de Cartagena placed this reign in the year of the foundation of the *regnum*, in this case 320. Moreover, as in the previous fragments, the historian of Burgos reiterates the blood relationship of the new genealogy of Spanish kings to the extinct Gothic kings, and reminds readers that the new kings are not Goths since they identify themselves as Asturians and Leonese. Finally, unlike previous chronicles, there is no notice that this historiographical work considers the Andalusian as rulers of a part of the *regnum Hispaniae* despite their illegality; therefore, the sole owners of it are the Asturian kings because of being Christians like the previous Gothic kings of Spain.

Conclusions

This chapter has tried to present an overall assessment of the ideological progression of Spanish-Christian historiography throughout the Middle Ages on a theme, the *regnum Gothorum* ("rule of the Goths") and the *regnum Hispaniae* ("kingdom of Spain"), through a specific episode: the Arab-Berber conquest of the Iberian Peninsula. The following is a brief summary of the chronicles, organized by place, time, and ideology.

---

tamen gothicum dimiserunt et aliis regiis titulis sunt insigniti. Cited from *El Libro de la Genealogía*, 250, 251–52.

140 *Pelagius post cladem cepit rebellare agarenis et principatum Hispanie inter christianos obtinere. [...] Sic ergo regni eius tempora computando regnare illum cepisse existimandum est anno Domini septingentesimo duodecimo. Regni Hispanie trecentesimo vicesimo. [...] Hic de regio Gothorum genere descendens, plurimas agarenorum civitates cepit et multa prelia contra agarenos devicit. De cetero autem alii reges nuncupati non fuerunt reges gothorum, sed Reges Legionis, vel Asturiarum.* Cited from *El Libro de la Genealogía*, 253.

The mid-eighth century Christian-Andalusian chronicles are convinced that the *regnum Gothorum* was eliminated by the Arabs, while the *regnum*, that is, the *regnum Hispaniae*, continued as an institution under the control by and the imposition of taxes to its new rulers. Shortly after, in the late eighth and early ninth centuries, the Septimanian chronicles present the end of the *regnum Gothorum* and the fact that Saracens only rule part of the *regnum Hispaniae* because the rest lies in Christian hands. Thus, we see the first instance of an ideology that will appear in the historiography of the rest of the Middle Ages and even later: the belief that the legitimate owners of the *regnum Hispaniae* are the Christians, a group radically opposed to the Saracens, and that they are predestined by God to recover it.

Making its own the ideal of the Septimanian chronicles, in the second half of the ninth century the Asturian chronicle cycle presents the Kingdom of Asturias as part of the *regnum Hispaniae* and the rightful owner of all it by the mere fact that Asturias is governed by Christians. Furthermore, these texts incorporate a neo-Gothic ideology, by which the *regnum Gothorum* is considered not to have disappeared, but it has moved to Asturias because the new kingdom is under a Visigothic royal lineage.

In the eleventh century and the first third of the twelfth century, the Galician-Portuguese chronicles were developed. They maintain an ideology that does not follow the line from the Asturian cycle, but a previous one that has not been preserved. In this way, they confirm the termination of the *regnum Gothorum* with King Roderic, ignoring the notion that the *regnum Hispaniae* subsists in the north as its legitimate repository simply by the fact of it being in Christian hands.

Even so, the historiographical ideology created in the Asturian cycle persisted in Leonese lands, now based on new arguments and the elimination of certain ambiguous passages on neo-Gothicism and the Spanish quality of the northern Christian kingdoms. Its recovery occurred in the first half of the twelfth century in the royal see of Leon, where the chroniclers added the component of "Hispanity," whereby a domain must be considered Spanish for it to be legitimate in governing the *regnum Hispaniae*. This neo-Gothicism, minus the ideology of Hispanity, expanded into the kingdom of Castile-Nájera in the second half of the twelfth century, recorded for posterity thanks to the Leonese Lucas de Tuy slightly later.

However, the dominant historiographical ideology came to give precedence to the Christian aspect and relegated, even ignored, the Gothic component. This ideology accepted the rule of the Goths ending with King Roderic followed by the emergence of a new kingdom in Asturias and, depending on the specific chronicle, various successor kingdoms in other northern mountainous regions. In the pioneering *Liber regum*, this ideological approach became established thanks to the Navarrese Rodrigo Jiménez de Rada and gained official sanction with the *Estoria de España general*, composed by Alfonso X's team of historians in the second half of the thirteenth century.

In the fourteenth and fifteenth centuries, the Romance translations of *De rebus Hispaniae* and the derivatives of the great work of Alfonso the Wise definitively established the notion of the Christian legitimacy of the northern kingdoms standing against the Muslim domains for the government of the *regnum Hispaniae*, which remained in infidel hands after the destruction of the *regnum Gothorum*. This interpretation of history influenced the chroniclers and writers of the Kingdom of Navarre and the Crown of Aragon, albeit without displacing, particularly among Catalan authors, the social and political influence of narratives that linked the original fight against Muslims with the Carolingian past.

Lastly, in the mid-fifteenth century, the historiographical work of Alfonso de Cartagena added a final element destined to influence its contemporaries and pass into modern ages: the idea that the *regnum Hispaniae* only survives in the northern kingdoms because the line of historical progression is determined by the Christian character of the rulers.

Chapter 7

THE DUEL IN MEDIEVAL WESTERN MENTALITY

LUIS ROJAS DONAT

THE TWO-PERSON CONTEST known as the "duel" (*duellum, Zweikampf, duel, pugna*) was customary in England, Italy, Germany, France, and Spain. It was used by the Slavs and the Normans from Sicily and the Crusaders introduced it in Palestine.[1] Like other ordeals, it is definitely not a typical Germanic institution. It is, however, present throughout the history of the West with different nuances and special circumstances that may be evidence, usually camouflaged, of its use up to the early twenty-first century outside the judicial system. Indeed, in medieval and modern literature, there is plenty of evidence for judicial combat.[2]

The duel has occupied a prominent place in historiography. It was considered a practice inherited from the Germanic peoples to regulate their conflicts, affirmed by Paul Fournier and placed in historical context by Jean Gaudemet.[3] It is originally an ordeal, a "primitive and religious trial," according to Jean-Philippe Levy, and it is mainly attributed to people of the feudal era.[4] It is truly the symbol of the accusatory system: it begins with a complaint and the procedure compels the accused to prove his innocence; the two parties become adversaries subjected to the same obligation.

The duel, also called single combat, was a small-scale mirror of collective combat. There have been two types of duels, as Charles de Smedt wrote in 1894: firstly, the conventional public duel involving two heads of state or army chiefs or two champions chosen by agreement; and secondly, the conventional private duel, which takes place

---

1 Charles de Smedt, "Les origines du duel judiciaire," *Études religieuses, philosophiques, historiques et littéraires* 63 (1894): 337–62. Joseph Declareuil, "Les preuves judiciaires dans le droit franc du Vᵉ au VIIᵉ siècle," *Nouvelle revue historique de droit français et étranger* 23 (1899): 320–54. Kurt Georg Cram, *Iudicium Dei: Zum Rechtscharakter des Krieges im deutschen Mittelalter* (Münster, 1955).

2 Marco Cavina, *Il sangue dell'onore. Storia del duello* (Roma, 2005), 8–11. Gerardo Ortalli, "Premessa," *Il duello fra medioevo ed età moderna: prospettive storico-culturali*, ed. U. Israel, G. Ortalli (Roma, 2009), 9–16. Sergio Valzania, "Il giusto duello," in *La civiltà del torneo (ss. XII–XVII). Giostre e tornei tra Medioevo ed Età Moterna*, ed. Maria Vittoria Baruti Ceccopieri (Narni, 1990), 12ff.; Richard Howard Bloch, *Medieval French Literature and Law* (Berkeley, 1977), esp. chap. 1: "Trial by Combat and Capture: Twilight of the Arthurian Gods" and chap. 2: "Warfare in the Feudal Epic Cycle."

3 Paul Fournier, "Quelques observations sur l'histoire des ordalies au Moyen Âge," *Mélanges Gustave Glotz*, 2 vols. (Paris, 1932), 1:368. Jean Gaudemet, "Les ordalies au Moyen Âge, doctrine, législation et pratique canonique," in *La Preuve*, Recueils de la Société Jean Bodin 17, 4 vols. (Bruxelles, 1965), 2:104–5.

4 Jean-Philippe Levy, "L'évolution de la preuve, des origines à nos jours," in *La Preuve*, 2:11.

Luis Rojas Donat (lsrojas.donat@gmail.com) is Professor of Medieval and Modern History at the Universidad del Bío-Bío, Chillán, in Chile.

between two individuals without any intervention by public authority, in which conditions are freely agreed to and outside the law. The reasons leading to either type of duel are clearly different: in the public duel, the victory of a nation or an army is at stake, whereas a private duel may be fought over an insult, an enmity, or even as a demonstration of obvious superiority.[5]

Historiographical Approaches

The *riepto* is closely related to the duel; it is a special procedure that appears in high medieval Spain and is rooted in a previous conflict, that is, the breakdown of peace or truce among members of the nobility. Its origins date back to much earlier times when private revenge dominated. Cases involving serious accusations, such as acting against the king, the homeland, or the Goths,[6] were brought before the royal curia.

The duel cannot be simply perceived as a combat with a victor and a loser. It drew from a profoundly religious mentality because it was not possible to know the right judgment, "good law," in many circumstances, and truth was not clearly discernible. Personal oath and testimony were insufficient and untrustworthy. It was therefore necessary to invoke divine intervention, to invite God to decide. God was somehow required to make a judicial decision, a divine judgment. The moral significance of the duel was thus inscribed, that is, the victor, who was assisted by God, obtained the right itself.

At the end of the nineteenth century, De Smedt demystified judicial combat, arguing that the duel should be understood as a restricted application of the law of private war where the idea of divine judgment was merely accessory:

> I believe that the duel must be put quite in the same line as other judgments of God or ordeals [...] I understand the duel primarily as the restricted application of the law of private war, which the ancient Germans used; the idea of the judgment of God was only included as an accessory, but it constituted the main and fundamental character of the ordeals.[7]

Taking the opposite view, Paul Rousset in the middle of the twentieth century argued that the duel itself could be considered as "divine judgment," that is, an ordeal.[8]

The combat again came under discussion thanks to the contributions of juridical anthropology, especially with regard to its nature and the role it played in the admin-

---

5 Smedt, "Les origines du duel judiciaire," 337–38. Gerardo Ortalli, "Dall'ordalia al duello per punto d'onore," *Il duello fra medioevo ed età moderna: prospettive storico-culturali*, ed. U. Israel, G. Ortalli (Roma, 2009), 17–34.

6 Alfonso Otero Varela, "El riepto en el Derecho castellano-leonés," in *Dos estudios histórico-jurídicos*, ed. Alfonso Otero (Roma, 1955), 9–82.

7 *Je n'admets pas que le duel doive être mis tout à fait sur la même ligne que les autres jugements de Dieu ou ordalies [...] je regarde le duel comme étant principalement une application restreinte du droit de guerre privée dont se prévalaient les anciens Germains; l'idée de jugement de Dieu ne s'y joignit que comme accessoire, tandis que, dans les ordalies proprement dites, elle constituait le caractère principal et fondamental de l'institution.* Cited from Smedt, "Les origines du duel judiciaire," 337n1.

8 Paul Rousset, "La croyance en la justice immanente à l'époque féodal," *Le Moyen Age* 54 (1948): 235.

istration of justice. Examining the French region of Vendôme, Dominique Barthélemy addressed trial by combat (hereafter "the judicial duel") and reintegrated it into global conflict resolution processes, demonstrating the existence of a logic that he called "graduated tension strategy."[9]

The duel was tailor-made for the Middle Ages, in which the survival of the fittest prevailed. It was a frequent recourse both judicially and extrajudicially; both parties having sworn to be in the right, the dispute had to be solved by duel or another ordeal. Under these circumstances, one of the parties must have committed perjury, a problem that was widespread during that era and, undoubtedly, ours.

The duel's main principle is that the parties themselves resolve the conflict, each one convinced that he who feels "strong" in his "good law," that is, innocent of the accusations, will win with the help that God always provides to any honest person. The duel's religious origins connect it to medieval society's value system: God helps the good and punishes the bad. Given that divine intervention has always been difficult to verify, the duel's spectacle demanded the attendance of qualified witnesses, all of whom could confirm that God was with the victor.

For that reason, rather than endorsing the written norm, given that the high medieval legislator prescribed the duel for situations difficult to solve, it must be understood that frequent recourse to the duel reflected its deep roots in popular customs. Socially validated, it was frequently used in court proceedings: it did not show the power of the priest who blessed the instruments and invited God to participate, as in single-person ordeals; rather, it extolled the strength of the free man, likely a knight or an aristocrat, that is, a landowner.

Let us agree that war—or revenge—exists in all human cultures as the final recourse for resolving disputes, whatever the cause. Dominique Barthélemy argues that, between justice and revenge, there seems to be no other recourse, because when justice was done, it reflected "consensual reparation." On the other hand, revenge meant "imposed reparation" which, in certain circumstances, could be legitimate and measured.[10] The duel therefore represented a limited prolongation of war that took place within a limited space, sanctioned both socially and legally, avoiding the widespread damages of unleashed hostilities on a larger scale.

The largely peasant society of the Middle Ages was open to convincing solutions, served by the existing precarious judicial system, and conceived the duel as evidence to be presented before a tribunal. In this sense, combat between two people meant the containment of violence; otherwise, in the absence of judicial authority and to compensate for damage, the solution would be channelled through private war or feuds undertaken by the families of both parties.[11]

---

9 Dominique Barthélemy, *La société dans le comte de Vendôme de l'an mil au XIVe siècle* (Paris, 1993), 653–80.

10 Dominique Barthélemy, *El año mil y la paz de Dios. La Iglesia y la sociedad feudal* (Granada, 2005), 120. Franco Cardini, *Onore* (Bologna, 2016).

11 Xavier Rousseaux, "De la négociation au procès pénal: la gestion de la violence dans la société médiévale et moderne," in *Droit négocié, droit imposé?*, ed. Philippe Gérard, François Ost and Michel

The duel was used to satisfy disputes provoked by many different causes. The law prescribed it for crimes such as robbery and homicide, but it was also considered as evidence in civil cases. If the authorities struggled to channel or contain the confrontation within a judicial framework, there was room for doubt about its legality. This element of doubt is intriguing for the historian because the value system of medieval society is revealed. Doubt could only arise from the most cultured men of the era, the clergymen, who never accepted the duel with goodwill.

Trust in the Justice of God

The internal logic of the duel reveals that contenders were seeking justice by trusting in God to help them win. It is difficult to believe with our modern mentality that one would only rely on God's help to solve the conflict, without recourse to one's own abilities.

This trust in divine help is reflected in the donations that some great monasteries made for God to favour them in war or in a duel; the same behaviour would certainly occur if they were victorious. The documents reporting duels and wars make clear that the victorious party triumphed thanks to God; the winning was a *victoria* and the litigator or successful warrior, *victor*.[12]

In the Early Middle Ages, the initiative for using combat to resolve disputes could arise from either the parties or a judge. Gregory of Tours related in 584 that Childebert II, King of Austrasia, sent a delegation to his uncle Gontran, King of Neustria and Burgundy, to claim some villas that Childebert intended to put under his domain. King Gontran treated the delegates rudely and sharply criticized Bishop Aegidius, who led the group. King Gontran later reproached Gontran Boson for betraying him by favouring the manoeuvres of Gondovald, an adventurer who sought to impersonate the son of Chlothar I. Undisturbed and offended, Gontran Boson said:

> You are the king, and the royal dignity of which you are clothed does not allow me to make a denial. I claim my innocence. If someone of my rank has accused me in secret before you, let him show himself and speak, and I ask you, Oh my pious King, put my cause before the judgment of God, He who will make the truth shine, giving me the victory in single combat in the arena.[13]

The proposed fight did not occur because the interview was interrupted by an exchange of insults by those present.

The same chronicler related that another duel took place under the rule of King Gontran. While hunting in the royal forest of the Vosges in 590, the king found the remains

---

van de Kerchove (Bruxelles, 1996), 273–312.

12 Hélène Couderc-Barraud, "Le duel judiciaire en Gascogne d'après les cartulaires," in *Le règlement des conflits au Moyen Âge. Actes du XXXI Congrès de la Société des Historiens Médiévistes de l'Enseignement Supérieur Public* (Paris, 2001), 97–115, esp. 108.

13 *Tu dominus et rex regali in solio resedis, et nullus tibi ad ea quae loqueris ausus est respondere. Insontem enim me de hac causa profiteor. At si aliquis est similis mihi, qui hoc crimen inpingat (imputat) occulte, veniat nunc palam et loquatur. Tunc, o rex piissime, ponens hoc in Dei iudicium, ut ille discernat, cum nos in unius campi planitiae viderit demicare.* Cited from Grégoire de Tours, *Histoire des Francs*, trans. Henri-Léonard Bordier (Paris, 1859), 7, 14.

of a wild bull. He immediately summoned the forest warden and strongly reproached him for allowing such poaching. The forester accused the king's chamberlain, Chundon, of the offence, who was arrested and sent to Chalon-sur-Saône. The accused denied the charge, so the king demanded that he justify himself by a duel. To avoid combat, the chamberlain presented his nephew as his representative. The duel had just started when the young man speared the forester's foot; he was severely wounded and fell. The young man took a knife from his waist and rushed upon his opponent to cut his throat, but the wounded forester buried his own knife in the young man's belly. Both died on the battlefield. Chundon realized that his champion's death condemned him, so he fled to take refuge in the basilica of St. Marcel. However, the king immediately ordered his arrest; before crossing the threshold of the church, he was tied to a pole and was stoned to death. Later, the king regretted the rash decision he had made during an outburst of anger against a faithful vassal who had committed a minor offence.[14]

The case of Austregisilius, bishop of Bourges, is interesting. He had been close to Gontran, King of Burgundy. While still a member of the court, a king's officer had unrightfully occupied some property belonging to the monarchy and was reprimanded by the king. In response to the monarch's criticism, the officer showed Gontran a document that he claimed he had received from Austregisilius. The king was very irritated because Austregisilius denied the fact and he ordered them to fight in the ring, so that the judgment of God would reveal who was lying. Austregisilius got up very early on the day of the combat and ordered his servants to carry his shield and spear to the place where the combat was to take place in the king's presence. Once there, Austregisilius entered St. Marcel's basilica in Chalon-sur-Saône and prayed. He met someone poor along the way to whom he gave the only coin he carried. After praying, he crossed himself and departed without fear to the site of combat, trusting in the justice of God and the certainty of his innocence. While waiting for his opponent, one of the latter's servants appeared and told the king that his master had died when his usually docile horse had reared; his master fell and the furious animal trampled his body until he was horribly disfigured. The king immediately looked at Austregisilius and said, "The Lord, whom you have invoked for help, has fought for you. Your accuser has died struck by divine vengeance." The pious bishop did not rejoice at the death of his enemy and thanked God for not having blood on his hands.[15]

---

14 Grégoire de Tours, *Histoire des Francs*, trans. Bordier (Paris, 1859), 10, 10.

15 "There was then in the palace of the king a certain wild man called Bethelenus who was endowed with power and excessive pride. He fraudulently governed the affairs of the treasury in a reckless way. When it came to be known by the king that he showed him false authority, the king said, 'Who, has given this order?' He said, 'Austrigisilus the naperer'. Having been sent for and questioned, Austregisilius denied what he had not done. The king was turned into rage and as he was judging them, he ordered that they should fight in the field of combat on account of this matter so that the judgment of the Lord would show who lied. When it was the day instituted for deciding, Austregisilius rose in the morning and directed two of his boys to take a round shield with a javelin into the field where the king was accustomed to watch the fighters. Meanwhile he went to the basilica of the holy Marcellus to offer prayers of thanks according to his custom. He met a certain poor man and he would have given him more but he did not have more than a triens because he

Another testimony is that of Gondeberga, the daughter of King Agilulf of the Lombards and wife of Caroaldus, or Arioald, the second in line of succession to Agilulf; she was wrongly accused of infidelity by her husband and sent to a small village among his domains. Chlothar, King of the Franks, who was kin to Gondeberga, sent a delegation to Arioald to complain about the way the lady was being treated. The King of the Lombards told the emissaries the cause of the queen's misfortune. An emissary named Ansoaldus took the initiative to argue that the accuser had to prove the truth of his claims by the

---

had already given away those which he had possessed to similar causes. Then there came into his mind that prophecy which says, 'Blessed is he who watches over the destitute and the poor. The Lord freed him in the day of evil and will not hand him over to the hand of his enemy'. Having given the man the triens he entered the basilica. Having sent out prayers he defended himself with the sign of the cross, which is the armour of God. Being faithful in his justice and not daunted by the just judgment of the Lord, he went hurrying to the contest. When he stood ready for the coming of the enemy in that place behold a certain man who was a servant of Bethelenus came up panting. He announced to the king with a face full of mourning that the noble Bethelenus was dead. The king began to inquire how his destruction had happened so quickly. The messenger spoke to the king in this way with these words,'When your servant Bethelenus came to the palace yesterday he stayed at Aury. Today when the day dawned he ordered an extremely tame horse to be prepared for him and having mounted it he remained fixed and immovable. When he pierced the horse with his heels it sprang up with great speed and with great zeal. It began to bend his limbs in divers ways and to put its head down with its forelegs and to shake its hind legs in the air. Then at length either because it struck a short tree or by the impetus of a whirlwind it swung and threw the noble Bethelenus onto the ground from on high yet this was not enough. The horse turned on him and bashed his brains with all his feet so that gore thrust forth through his nose and ears so that he gave out his spirit even before he was lifted from the ground. This was done according to what is written: 'You lose, those of you who are called liars' and 'A false witness will not be saved'. Having heard this, the king summoned Austregisilius to him and said to him: 'The Lord has fought for you. You have displayed his help most faithfully. Bethelenus is dead because he was punished by divine power'." (*Erat tunc in palatio Regis quidam potestate praedictus, homo ferus et superbiae nimiae deditus Bethelenus nomine, qui temerario ordine quiddam de fiscalibus rebus fraudulenter occuparet. Unde dum argueretur a Rege, ostendit illi falsam auctoritatem. Quis, inquit, Rex hanc praeceptionem dedit? Dixit: Austregisilus Mapparius. Accersitus Austregisilus, interrogatus, quod non fecerat denegavit. Illos deceptantes Rex in furorem versus iussit eos ex hoc in campo certare, ut quis falleret Domini iudicio monstraretur. Jam advenerat dies institutus certandi. Manes urgens Austregisilus, clypeum cum jaculo per pueros suos direxit in campum, ubi Rex agonistas exspectare solitus erat. Ipse autem cum ad Basilicam S. Marcelli a orandi gratia pergeret, habuit quemdam pauperem obvium, et quid ei amplius largiretur non habebat quam unum trientem. Nam et si fuerant, in simile opus abierant [...] Dato treinte ingreditur Basilicam, praemissa oratione vexillo Crucis se munivit, quod est armature Dei, fidus de sua iusticia et de Domini iusto iudicio imperterritus festinusque ad certamen pergerat. Cum ibidem praestolaretur adversarii adventum, ecce veniens quídam ex ministris Betheleni, anhelabundus et lugubri vultu nuntians Regi mortuum esse Bethelenum. Rex indagare coepit tam celerem ejus interitum, qualiter contigisset. Ille his verbis et eo ordine exponebat Regi. Cum venire Bethelenus servus tuus hesterno ad Placitum, mansit sub Auriaco. Et hodie cum illucesceret dies iussit sibi parari equum mansuetissimum. Quo adsenso, tamquam fixus mansit immobilis. Cujus cum calcaribus latera perforaret, exsiliens summa velocitate, ingenti impetus coepit in diversa flectere membra, caput jungere pedibus, pedes superiores in sublime excutere [...] Hoc audito Rex accersivit ad se Austregisilum et ait ei: Pugnavit pro te Dominus, cujus auxilium fideliter poposcisti. Mortuus est, inquiens, Bethelenus Divina ultione punitus.*) Latin cited from Johannes Mabillon, *Acta Sanctorum Ordinis Sancti Benedicti*, 9 vols. (Paris, 1669), 2:95–96.

judgment of God and fight against Gondeberga's champion in the ring. Arioald accepted the proposal, and the slanderer was killed. The queen's honour and rank were restored. The chronicles of Fredegar and Paul the Deacon record this episode.[16]

---

16 Fredegarius, 51: "Queen Gondeberga, who was very beautiful, pleasant with everyone, merciful, and generous with alms, was much loved for her kindness. A man called Adaluph, who belonged to the Lombard nation, frequently visited the palace to perform his duties before the king; on such an occasion, the queen, who appreciated him just as she did everyone, told him that he was of great stature. Adaluph heard this and spoke to the queen in secret saying, "You have deigned to praise my stature; allow me into your bed. The queen rejected him forcefully and contemptuously, and she spat at him. Seeing that his life was in danger, Adaluph went rapidly to King Arioald to tell him secret news. Granted an audience, he said to the king: 'My lady, Queen Gondeberga, has secretly been with Duke Tasson for three days; she plans to poison you in order to wed Tasson and put him on the throne'. King Arioald believed these lies, exiled the queen to Lumelle, and locked her up in a tower. Chlothar, annoyed with Arioald, sent emissaries to inform him of the reason why he humiliated Queen Gondeberga, akin to the Franks, and had her exiled. Arioald responded that the lies were true. Therefore, a man called Ansoald, of his own initiative, said to Arioald: 'You could resolve this matter without guilt; order the man who has said these things to arm himself and that another man, representing the queen, combat in a duel. By the judgment of God, it can be known if Queen Gondeberga is guilty or innocent of this offence'. The advice pleased King Arioald and all the grandees of the Court, and he ordered Adaluph to arm himself for the combat. Gondeberga's cousin, Pitton, confronted Adaluph. They fought and Adaluph was killed. After three years of exile, Gondeberga was restored to the throne." (*Gundeberga regina cum esset pulchra aspectu, benigna in cunctis, et pietate plenissima, christiana, eleemosynis larga, praecellente bonitate ejus, diligebatur a cunctis. Homo quidam, nomine Adalulfus, ex genere Langobardorum, cum in aula palatii assidue ad obsequium regis conversaretur, quadam vice ad reginam veniens, cum in ejus staret conspectu, Gundeberga regina eum sicut et caeteros diligens, dixit honestae staturae Adalulfum fuisse formatum. Ille haec audiens ad Gundebergam secretius ait, dicens: Formam status mei laudare dignata es, stratui tuo jube me subjungere. Illa fortiter denegans, eumque despiciens in faciem exspuit. Adalulfus cernens se vitae periculum habere, ad Charoaldum regem protinus cucurrit, petens ut secretius quod ad suggerendum habebat, exponeret. Loco accepto, dixit ad regem: Domina mea regina tua Gundeberga apud Tasonem ducem secretius tribus diebus locuta est, ut te veneno interficeret, ipsumque sibi conjugatum sublimaret in regnum. Charoaldus rex his mendaciis auditis credens, Gundebergam in Caumello castro in unam turrem exsilio trudit. Chlotharius legatos dirigens ad Charoaldum regem, inquirens qua de re Gundebergam reginam parentem Francorum humiliasset, ut exsilio retrudisset. Charoaldus his verbis mendacibus quasi veritate subsisterent, respondit. Tunc unus ex legatariis, nomine Ansoaldus, non quasi injunctum habuisset, sed ex se ad Charoaldum dixit: Liberare poteras de blasphemia hanc causam; jube illum hominem qui hujuscemodi verba tibi nuntiavit armari, et procedat alius de parte reginae Gundebergae; quique armatus ad singular certamen, ut judicio Dei, his duobus confligentibus, cognoscatur utrum hujus culpae reputationis Gundeberga sit innoxia, an fortasse culpabilis. Cumque haec Charoaldo regi et omnibus primatibus palatii sui placuissent, jubet Adalulfum armatum conflictum adire certaminis, et de parte Gundebergae procurrentibus consobrinis Gundebergae et Ariberto, homo, nomine Pitto, contra Adalulfum armatus aggreditur. Cumque conflixissent certamine, Adalulfus a Pittone interficitur. Gundeberga statim de exsilio post annos tres regressa sublimatur in regnum*). Latin cited from Fredegarii et al., *Chronica. Vitae sanctorum*, ed. Bruno Krusch, MGH SS rer. Merov. 2 (1878), 146.
     Also Pauli, *Historia Langobardorum*, ed. Georg Waitz, MGH SS rer. Germ. 4 (1878), 47: "Rodoalf then received the kingdom of the Longobards after the death of his father, and united with himself in marriage Gundeberga the daughter of Agilulfus and Theudelinda. This Gundeberga in imitation of her mother, just as the latter had done in Modicia, so the former within the city of Ticinum built a church in honor of St. John the Baptist, which she decorated wonderfully with gold and silver and draperies

In the Early Middle Ages, the initiative to employ combat to solve a dispute could rest with the judge; depending on the region, he had freedom to choose for or against the practice. There was no standard norm in the medieval West; in the south of France, the judge would ask the parties which law they were subject to before opening the case: whether Roman law or Romanized local rights, the Salic law of the Franks, or Gothic law; this explains why the judge's advisors would be divided into *romani*, *salici*, and *gothi*, respectively.[17]

Popular pressure, as always, desired a resounding and severe solution that only the duel could satisfy and influenced the decision of an indecisive and fearful magistrate. The demand for the duel fell on one of the parties, who responded to the claims and oaths of the other. Thus, judges were often required to declare the combat because to oppose it or doubt its effectiveness would have been considered as blasphemy, aberrant behaviour, and contrary to venerable traditions.

An example of traditional practices is shown by the case of the Vandals and Alamanni who were on the verge of war in 400. Both monarchs, according to Gregory of Tours, decided not to sacrifice all their people in a confrontation. Instead, both nations were to be represented by a champion to reveal the victor by the duel. According to the chronicler, the king of the Alamanni addressed his adversary in the following way:

> How long should war have to fall on a people? I ask you to not make suffer the legions of either army, but instead, only two of our men could fight with war gear on the battle field. The victorious party will win the region without fighting.

The representative of the Vandals was defeated, his throat probably slit by his Alaman opponent.[18]

---

and enriched bountifully with particular articles, and in it her body lies buried. And when she had been accused to her husband of the crime of adultery, her own slave, Carellus by name, besought the king that he might fight in single combat for the honor of his mistress, with him who has imputed the crime to the queen. And when he had gone into single combat with that accuser he overcame him in the presence of the whole people. The queen indeed after this was done, returned to her former dignity." (*Rodoald igitur post funus patris Langobardorum regnum suscipiens, Gundipergam Agilulfi et Theudelindae sibi filiam in matrimonium sociavit. Haec Gundiperga Regina ad instar suae genetricis, sicut illa in Modicia, sic et ista intra Ticinensem civitatem basilicam in honerem beati Iohannis baptistae construxit, quam mire ex auro et argento peplisque decoravit rebusque singulis optime ditavit; in qua et [deest] eius corpus tumulatum quiescit. Haec dum de crimine adulterii aput virum accusata fuisset, proprius eius servus Carellus nomine a rege expetiit; ut cum eo qui reginae crimen ingesserat pro castitate suae dominae monomachia dimicaret. Qui dum cum criminatore illo singulare certamen inisset, eum cuncto populo adstante superavit. Regina vero post hoc factum ad dignitatem pristinam rediit.*)

17 Jean Pierre Poly, Eric Bournazel, *El cambio feudal. Siglos X al XII* (Barcelona, 1983), 254.

18 "After this the Vandals left their own country and burst into the Gauls under King Gunderic. And when the Gauls had been thoroughly laid waste they made for the Spains. The Suebi, that is, Alamanni, following them, seized Gallicia. Not long after, a quarrel arose between the two peoples, since they were neighbours. And when they had gone armed to the battle, and already at the point of fighting, the king of the Alamanni said: 'Why are all the people involved in war? Let our people, I pray, not kill one another in battle, but let two of our warriors go to the field in arms and fight with one another. Then he whose champion wins shall hold the region without strife' [...] And in the conflict of the champions the side of the Vandals was overcome" (*Post haec Wandali a loco suo*

It was sometimes impossible for the court to judge between opposing testimonies, which could lead to a dead end. If neither party expressed willingness to use weapons, then the judge imposed a combat with shields and sticks, and he reserved to himself the right to choose the combatants from each competing group. Among the Franks, this was clearly imposed by the Capitulary of Pepin in 816:

> If the witnesses of both parties disagreed, and neither of them wanted to favour the other, two champions had to be chosen from the two groups; these champions would fight with shields and sticks, and one would lie in truth and the other in falsehood.[19]

As for the quality of the combatants, sources reveal that only free men could legally fight. Among the Carolingians, especially in France, such a requirement constituted a categorical assumption. This explains why the duel was exclusively practised by the aristocracy in judicial proceedings as the way best suited to defend their honour sullied by an accusation.

The duel does not appear in the last codes promulgated by the Visigoths, the *Liber iudiciorum* (*Book of Judges*). It is not possible to conclude from this, however, that its introduction in Spain was due to the Franks. Perhaps its absence is due to combat not being part of the scope of the judiciary, but rather an extrajudicial procedural recourse. In addition, we should remember that there was no impediment for certain accusations between members of the nobility, frequently voiced publicly, to be solved through the duel in the absence of evidence. This special procedure was adopted by the nobility to resolve accusations of infidelity to king or kingdom, which had to be revealed before the monarch. Other social classes could also resort to the extrajudicial duel when the conflicting parties committed themselves to accepting the outcome of combat. However, this was always outside the law. It should be pointed out that in Castile, according to Otero Varela, a duel among serfs was characterized as an ordeal; meanwhile, nobles never sought to kill their opponent, but simply wanted to provoke a retraction.[20]

In Visigothic Spain, the duel was not established by law, but if the parties agreed, judges could accept practices not included in Gothic legislation. A failed proposal for a duel occurred in Catalonia in 1019. Hugo, Count of Ampurias, invited Ermesinda, Count-

---

degressi, cum Gunderico rege in Gallias ruunt. Quibus valde devastatis, Spanias adpetunt. Hos secuti Suebi, id est Alamanni, Gallitiam adpraehendunt. Nec multo pos scandalum inter utrumque oritur populum, quoniam propinqui sibi erant. Cumque ad bellum armati procederent ac iamiamque in conflicto parati essent, ait Alamannorum rex: 'Quousque bellum super cunctum populum commovetur? Ne pereant, quaeso, populi utriusque falangae, sed procedant duo de nostris in campum cum armis bellicis, et ipse inter se confligant. Tunc ille, cuius puer vicerit, regione sine certamine obtenebit' [...] Confligentibus vero pueris, pars Wandalorum victa succubuit.) Latin cited from Grégoire de Tours, *Histoire des Francs*, trans. Bordier (Paris, 1859), 2. §2, 44–45. Marguerite Boulet-Sautel, "Aperçu sur le problème des preuves dans la France coutumière," in *La Preuve*, Recueils de la Société Jean Bodin 17, 4 vols. (Bruxelles, 1965), 1:276.

19 [S]i ambae partes testium ita inter se dissenserint, ut nullatenus una pars alteri cedere velit, eligantur duo ex ipsis, id est ex utraque parte unus, qui cum scutis et fustibus in campo decertent, utra pars falsitatem, utra veritatem sequatur. Cited from *Capitularia Regun Francorum*, ed. Alfred Boretius, MGH Capit. 1 (1883), 267–68.

20 Otero, "*El riepto*," 73.

ess of Barcelona, to resolve their differences through combat. The Countess refused the duel because "Gothic law does not command that business be resolved by combat."[21]

There is evidence of two testimonies in which a duel was agreed to beforehand. This was the case of the counts of Barcelona and Urgell in 1064, who agreed by a treaty to resolve their disputes under oath or by a challenge between mounted soldiers of the two counties under the guidance and judgment of four good men, two from each county. The count of Barcelona and viscount of Carcassonne and Coserans did the same in 1080 when they resolved their territorial differences by a combat between two knights using shields and sticks; these representatives were also named and approved by four good men, two from each party.[22]

But there were cases in which, if the parties agreed, judges admitted practices unforeseen in Gothic legislation; a case occurred in 1073 when Abbot Guitart and someone named Bernard resolved a property boundary conflict through ordeal by cold water.[23]

It is known that this type of evidence was clearly accepted in Germanic legislation.[24] Emperor Otto I pointed it out explicitly in the Constitution of 967, adding that if a servant were accused of theft, he cannot defend his innocence by his own testimony, but his lord must do so by taking an oath and paying compensation. On the other hand, a free man could be "justified" by resorting to arms against his accuser.[25]

---

21 *Lex Gothica non jubet ut per pugnam discutiantur negotia.* Cited from Walter Kienast, "La pervivencia del derecho godo en el sur de Francia y Cataluña," *Boletin de la Real Academia de Buenas Letras de Barcelona* 35 (1973–1974): 277–80 (document 35). Eduardo Hinojosa, "La admisión del Derecho romano en Cataluña," in *Obras* (Madrid, 1955), 2, 391. Michel Zimmermann, "L'usage du droit wisigothique en Catalogne du IXe au XIIe siècle: aproches d'une signification culturelle," *Mélanges de la Casa de Velázquez* 9 (1971): 233–81. Javier Alvarado Planas, "El problema de la naturaleza germánica del derecho español altomedieval," in *VII Semana de Estudios Medievales*, ed. José Ignacio de la Iglesia Duarte (Logroño, 1997), 121–48.

22 Juan Francisco de Masdeu y Montoro, *Historia crítica de España, y de la cultura española*, 20 vols. in 10 (Madrid, 1794), 13:92–93. Alvarado, "El problema," 126.

23 "With respect to this conflict, Gislibert judged that the bishop and Bernard had to submit to the law, and the guarantors opined that the dispute had to be directly sanctioned according to the *Book of Judges*. Abbot Guitart and the guarantors agreed that the trial would be directly resolved according to the law of the *Book of Judges*. However, Bernard opposed this solution and said: 'I do not want this to be solved with the law nor that we reach a direct agreement, but that we resolve it by subjecting two of our representatives to the judgment of God Almighty through the ordeal by cold water.'" (*De hoc altercantes atque inter se contendentes iudicavit Gislibertus, suprascriptus episcopus, et donno Bernardus, ut ambobus partibus misissent se sub lege, et dedissent fideiussores ut secundum sanccionem legis Libri Iudicum fecissent sibi inter se directum. Ad quem supradictus abba Guitardus prestus fuit et fideiussores dare et secundum sanccionem legis Libri Iudicum directum facere. Supradictus vero Bernardus noluit se mittere sub iugo supradicte legis, nec ullumque alium directum facere, nisi tantum modo verbis suis afflatus est dicens: Ego nullum alium directum faciam neque recipiam, sed si vultis mittamus singulos puerulos ad iudicium Dei Omnipotentis in aqua frigida, ut inde appareat cuius directum sit.*) Latin cited from *Cartulario de San Cugat del Vallés*, ed. José Rius Serra, 4 vols. (Barcelona, 1946–1950), 2:203–5 (document 545).

24 Javier Alvarado Planas, "Ordalías y derecho en la España visigoda," in *De la Antigüedad al Medievo. Siglos VI-VIII* (Madrid, 1993), 468–79.

25 "If a free man is accused of robbery and has property, he proceeds to justify himself before

A servant named Stabilis, around 970, is mentioned in the chronicle called the *Miracula Sancti Benedicti*. He refused to admit his direct dependency on the abbey of Fleury-sur-Loire. He considered himself to be a free man, having married a noble woman and lived as if he were part of the nobility. The abbot of Fleury claimed otherwise, so Stabilis was forced to prove his claims of freedom by the duel. Considering himself to be a bad warrior, he thought of resolving the problem by refusing the *champion* presented by the monastery because he was unequal to him; he expressed his indignation and refused to be forced to deal with a man who was not a free man like him.[26]

Clerics could also be involved in judicial combats, as expressly foreseen by numerous capitularies of the Carolingians for France; Otto I did this for Germany and Italy with the previously cited Constitution of 967. However, the Church rejected combat as evidence whenever possible. The evolution of medieval Christianity, increasingly Romanized, can probably explain the prevailing reluctance of the Church for the judicial duel. The Church did not create any ritual or liturgical *ordo* for combat, but it did so for the single-person ordeals, such as the ordeal by cold water, hot water, and hot iron, which had many liturgical rituals called *ordines*. The Church accepted them because it considered that personal ordeals could be more easily tolerated within the framework of Christianity by interposing God, Jesus Christ, the Virgin Mary, or the saints as guarantors of the test.[27]

The Site of the Combat

Combat was certainly violent and this primitivism was especially noticeable when the combat was part of a judicial process in which attempts to find a "reasonable" solution by the authorities contrasted with the basic, elementary, or "para-rational" logic of the duel. It was carried out before a secular court, which could be that of a count or a sovereign, or before a judge, who only acted as a qualified minister of faith, confirming the triumph of one of the parties and the defeat of the other.

---

the tribunal in presence of the count. If he has no property, he will find guarantors who justify him, and he will be brought to the assembly. The first time, it is lawful to exonerate himself by an oath according to the law. If two or three accuse him of robbery at another time, it is lawful for him to confront one of them with a shield and stick in the ring." (*Si liber homo de furto accusatus fuerit et res proprias habuerit, in mallo ad praesentiam comitis se adhramiat; et si res non habet, fideiussores donet qui eum adhramire et in placitum adduci faciant. Et liceat ei prima vice per sacramentum se secundum legem idoneare, si potuerit. At si alia vice duo vel tres eum de furto accusaverint, liceat ei contra unum ex his cum scuto et fuste in campo contendere. Quod si servus de furto accusatus fuerit, dominus eius pro eo emendet aut eum sacramento excuset, nisi tale furtum perpetratum habeat propter quod ad supplicium tradi debeat.*) Latin cited from *Capitularia Regum Francorum*, ed. Alfred Boretius, MGH Capit. 1 (1883), 284.

26 Adrevald de Fleury, *Miracula Santi Benedicti*, ed. Eugène de Certain (Paris, 1858), 218–22.

27 Michel Rubellin, "Combattant de Dieu ou combattant du Diable? Le combattant dans les duels judiciaires aux IXe et Xe siècles," in *Le combattant au Moyen Age. Actes du XVIII Congrès de la Société des Historiens Médiévistes de l'Enseignement Supérieur Public* (Paris, 1991), 111–22. Alexander Coulin, *Verfall des offiziellen und Entstehung des privaten Zweikampfes in Frankreich* (Wroclaw, 1909), 30–60. Bernhard Schwenter, "Die Stellung der Kirche zum Zweikampfe bis zu den Dekretalen Gregors IX," *Theologisches Quartalschrift* 3 (1930): 190–234.

The joust was fought on foot and the combatants were armed with primitive weapons that did not cause injuries as serious as those caused by swords or spears. These were shields and sticks, as some Carolingian capitularies indicated: "with shields and sticks fighting in the arena" (*cum scutis et fustibus in campo decertent*). Another capitulary states *exeant in campum cum fustibus*.[28] These weapons may seem unusual for adversaries often belonging to the aristocracy or high secular officials. These weapons prevented bleeding by one or both combatants; divine intervention was therefore more necessary, as pointed out by Pierre Bonnassie.[29]

The combat was usually very violent and therefore brief; in the first blows that were exchanged, he whose bad faith was evident would fall to the ground as a manifestation of the defeat imposed by God and this fall was usually aggravated by serious injuries. This dramatic scene reinforced the popular belief in divine signs. The chronicler Thietmar of Merseburg, in his *Chronicon*, relates the episode in which Liutgard, daughter of Otto I (912–973), was accused of adultery by Conon. Conon was contradicted by Count Burchard, who decided to defend the honour of the princess; Conon persisted in his accusation, but then under oath. The chronicler narrates that Conon was obliged to settle the conflict by a duel, andin the very first blow lost his right hand, the one he had used for lying (*in primo aditu dexteram mendacem perdidit*).[30]

We also find testimonies of very long combats, so long that it was impossible to judge the victor and the vanquished. In those cases, when the confrontation could not reveal the truth, it was necessary to find another resolution for the dispute. Such was the case in Saint-Sernin in Aveyron in 960 when Bernard and Gerbert disputed the rights to the church of Saint-Médard-de-Presque. In the presence of the count of Rouergue the combat began at the second hour and lasted until sunset, producing no results. The count then decided to transfer the goods in dispute to the abbey of Beaulieu, to which this

---

28 *Capitularia Regum Francorum*, ed. Alfred Boretius, MGH Capit. 1 (1883), 268.

29 Pierre Bonnassie, *La Catalogne du milieu du Xe à la fin du XIe siècle* (Toulouse, 1976), 1: 729.

30 "The emperor was gravely offended that a certain Conon was slandering his daughter, who was his wife, with shameful news. Very annoyed and wishing that she be justified, the emperor spoke with her in private to know if she was guilty. She excused herself by the sacraments and put Christ as her witness. All the princes of the kingdom were summoned, and the emperor said that if someone wished to take up arms to defend his daughter, he would forever consider him as a friend. Upon hearing this, Count Burchard stood amid them all and said that Conon was a liar. When the former claimed that it was true, he stayed for a duel. At the first blow, Conon lost his right lying hand and confessed his wickedness." (*Filiam vero suimet, uxorem eius, a quodam Conone, eo quod sibi satisfacere noluisset, late diffamatam et conjugem suam clam fore ab eodem dictam, cesar hoc graviter ferens, sic eam expurgavit. Convocatis omnibus regni suimet principibus, primo secretis allocutionibus eandem, si huius rei culpabilis esset, diligenter inquirit; posteaque cum illam adhibito Christi testimonio et sacramentis se nimis excusare vidisset, presentibus cunctis indixit, si aliquis ex numero sibi familiarium eam armis defendere voluisset, ut se firmum in die hac et in perpetuum acquirere potuisset amicum. Burchardus comes haec audiens, in medium prosiliit, et Cononem per omnia mentitum fore, coram omnibus dixit. Ille autem cum id verum esse sacramentis afirmaret, cum eodem congressus, in primo aditu dexteram mendacem perdidit, et iniusticiam suimet devictus innotuit*). Latin cited from Thietmari Merseburgensis episcopi, *Chronicon*, ed. Robert Holtzman, MGH SS rer. Germ. N. S. 3 (1935), 755–56.

same property had been originally donated.[31] Given the outcome, it is obvious that the combat between the two champions was not the solution.

The internal logic of the judicial duel reveals that God would designate the defeated party as guilty. Together with the obligation to accept the sanction provided for the offence committed, the established penalty must be added because the guilty party, aware of his guilt in his conscience, had not acknowledged it. For this crime Louis the Pious stipulated in 816 that "the combatant who had committed perjury before the combat, cut off their right hand."[32]

Some duels had unexpected outcomes that altered this intrinsic logic and questioned divine intervention in the result. Such a case occurred in Magdeburg in 979 when Count Gerus and someone named Waldo fought a duel. The reasons the count was accused by Waldo before Emperor Otto II are unknown, but the dispute had to be settled by a duel that would take place on an island. Once the battle started, Waldo was severely wounded, but he overcame his critical state and managed to seriously injure his adversary, knocking him to the ground. He asked Gerus if he were able to continue the battle, but Gerus responded that he was not. Then, Waldo jumped into the water and swam back to reach the nearby shore. Extremely exhausted, he was only able to take off his weapons before collapsing dead. Given the unexpected and surprising outcome, Otto II ordered that the victor, Count Gerus, be beheaded. Michel Rubellin has questioned whether it was the right punishment for the guilty party, and that God's sign had appeared in such a strange way.[33] It is possible to think that the emperor wanted to mercilessly intervene in the result of the duel, intending to interpret divine will through a human sign—but in harmony with divine justice—in accordance with traditional respect for the religious nature of the duel. It seemed inconceivable that the victor had died, but the vanquished was alive. Perhaps to justify *a posteriori* the sentence, our chronicler Thietmar of Merseburg adds that on the day of the duel, Liudolf, Abbot of Corvey, had had a vision while celebrating mass; he saw the head of the count on the altar, thus confirming God's intervention.

---

31 Chap. 47: "The two champions fought from the second hour until sunset and neither party was declared victorious. The count and his advisers decided that neither contender, Bernard and Gerbert, had the right to the church in dispute. Therefore, they transferred this property to the Abbey of Beaulieu, which had received it long before that." (*nam secunda dici hora certantibus usque ad solis occasum, neminem quippe cernerent eorum vincere, judicaverunt memorati Regi mundus comes, caeterique ei in circuitu sistentes, cuiquam eorum Bernardi vel Gerberti nihil ad possidendum jure debere habere, in usus usurpare, sed potius Domino omnium creatori et S. Petro Bellilocensi, apostolorum principi, in usibus monachorum inibi desidentium, expendi, cui praedictus Rigaldus, pro remedio animae suae, devoverat offerri.*) Latin cited from *Cartulaire de l'Abbaye de Beaulieu en Limousin*, ed. Maximin Deloche (Paris, 1859), 85–6. François Bougard, "Rationalité et irrationalité des procédures autour de l'an mil: le duel judiciaire en Italie," in *La justice en l'an mil. Actes du colloque de Paris, 12 mai 2000* (Paris, 2003), 93–122.

32 *Camphioni qui convictus fuerit propter periurium quod ante pugnam commisit dextera manus amputetur.* Cited from "Capitularia Regum Francorum," *Capitularia Regum Francorum*, ed. Alfred Boretius, MGH Capit. 1 (1883), 268.

33 Rubellin, "Combattant de Dieu," 116.

This interesting episode is related by Thietmar:

> Waldo accused Count Gerus in front of the emperor [...] Then all the princes of the king-
> dom were summoned and agreed that this trial should be resolved by a combat on an
> island. Waldo, wounded twice in the head, struck a strong blow to his opponent's head
> that made him fall violently onto the ground. Count Gerus was asked by Waldo if he could
> continue fighting, and he declared that he could not. Then, Waldo went into the water
> [...], took off his weapons and fell flat on his back and died. Then, the Emperor issued the
> decree that Gerus be beheaded by an executioner. [...] I would like to state that Liudulf
> [Abbot] of Corvey, by the merits of God, vigils, and fasts, God deigned to reveal [to him].
> The day of the fight, having celebrated the morning mass with humility and fear, as he
> used to, Corvey saw the head of Count Gerus on the altar, and once mass was said, he
> prayed for the deceased. The priests took off their robes in silence and gathered all the
> church members to insistently ask them to say a common prayer for the count. His decap-
> itation would occur during sunset.[34]

Legality of Duels

Two types of case encouraged duels as a judicial solution. Firstly, cases that could be
considered as fundamental: the legislative documents of the Franks—the capitularies—
clearly prescribe duels as permissible evidence in cases of theft, crime, or property disputes. But in view of the testimonies in accounts of the combats, another reason must be
added: adultery, a serious accusation involving honour. The Count of Barcelona, Bernard
of Septimania (826–844), a member of the French court of the Emperor Louis the Pious,
was accused in 831 of having an illicit liaison with the monarch's wife, the Empress
Judith of Bavaria.[35] It is impossible to forget too the case in which Lothar II confronted
his wife Theutberge, whom he accused of adultery.[36] Between 879 and 883, Adele,
Countess of Gatinais, was accused of both adultery and her husband's death.[37] Richardis,
wife of Charles the Fat, the German king, was accused of a relationship with Liutward,

---

34 *Accusatus apud inperatorem Gero comes a Waldone [...] Deindeque convocatis ad Magathaburg
cunctis regni principibus, congressi sunt hii iudicio in insula quadam singulari certamine,
vulneratusque in cervicem bis Waldo, ardencius insequitur hostem, percuciensque ictu valido capud,
prostravit eundem. Interrogatus autem Gero comes ab eodem, si plus potuisset pugnare, coactus est,
quod iam defecisset, profiteri. Waldo tum egressus, aqua refocilatur depositis armis, et post tergum
mortuus cecidit. Tunc Gero iussus est decreto iudicum et voce inperatoris a carnifice quodam decollari
[...] Libet paucis exponere Liudulfi Corbensis meritum patris, cui multum vigiliis ieiuniisque laboranti,
plurima Deus dignatus est revelare. Hic in die prefati certaminis cum diluculo missam humiliter et
timorate, ut semper solebat, celebraret, vidit super altare comitis capud Geronis, finitaque hac aliam
pro defunctis cantavit; exutisque sacerdotalibus vestimentis, cum silentio exivit, congregatisque
fratribus obitum eius indicavit, orationemque pro eo fieri communem suppliciter postulavit.
Decollatio autem eius in ipso solis occasu fiebat.* Latin cited from Thietmari Merseburgensis episcopi,
Chronicon, ed. Robert Holtzmann, MGH SS rer. Germ. N. S. 3 (1935), 761.

35 Astronomus, *Vita Hludowici imperatoris*, ed. Ernst Tremp, MGH SS rer. Germ. 2 (1995), 634. I
continue with Smedt, "Les origines du duel judiciaire," 359.

36 "Letter of Pope Nicholas I to Charles the Bald," in *Patrologiae cursus completus*, ed. Jacques-
Paul Migne, 221 vols. (Paris, 1852), 119: letter 148, 1144.

37 "Gesta consulum Andegavorum," chap. 3 of *Chroniques des comtes d'Anjou et des seigneurs
d'Amboise*, ed. Louis Halphen, René Poupardin (Paris, 1913), 136–37.

Bishop of Vercelli and minister of the monarch.[38] Finally, we have looked at the case of Conon who accused Liutgard, the daughter of Emperor Otto I, of adultery in 755–756.

Secondly, procedural reasons also explain how easily the duel could intervene to resolve conflicts. It was used as an ancillary ordeal to confirm or affirm the "doubts" expressed by one of the two parties or to validate the oaths taken by the other party. It was also used to elucidate the truth when there was a discrepancy among the witnesses.[39]

The judicial duel always had to be carried out before witnesses, who made the final decision binding on both parties. Testimonies confirm that combats always occurred before a secular court, which could be that of a count or a sovereign. Bernard of Septimania defended himself before the court of Louis the Pious. The court of Charles the Bald witnessed the dispute for the innocence of Richardis; likewise, Otto I witnessed the defence of his daughter Liutgard and the dispute between Count Gerus and Waldo.

It seems that the Ostrogoths knew the judicial duel, just as the Burgundians and the Salian Franks (sixth century), and the Ripuarians (seventh century). Given that the duel became popular throughout Italy, legal historians share the opinion that the Lombards introduced it to the peninsula because they continually resorted to the duel to solve disputes. The Normans did the same in southern Italy and in England, where the judicial duel became common for resolving both civil and criminal matters after 1066.

In the medieval West, the duel was preferred to the oath. The judge had no option other than combat to avoid the extraordinary proliferation of perjury. To address the situation of irreconcilable opposition provoked by the diverse testimonies of the witnesses, the parties had to be subjected to the duel to settle disputes, as established by Louis the Pious among the Franks. This solution prevailed for a long time in judicial practice.

But there were always opposing positions regarding the evidentiary value of the duel. While the Church preferred Roman ordeals, the population seemed rooted in the duel's tradition. When Louis the Pious ordered the use of the duel in 816, the real purpose was to restrain perjurers:

> If someone had a conflict with another for any reason, and witnesses against that person were presented, who were suspected of being false, it should be allowed to oppose him with other witnesses, the best ones to be found, so that the testimony of the good witnesses against the perversity of the bad ones can overcome. But if the witnesses of both parties disagreed with each other, and in no way wanted to yield, two individuals were to be chosen, one from each party, to fight with shields and sticks in the arena and obtain the veracity of one party and the falseness of the other. [...] [I]n secular causes, the diversity of the witnesses was proven in the arena.[40]

---

38 "She declared that she had never had a virile bond with any man; to defend the integrity of her virginity she offered that her husband test her by combat or ordeal by fire." (*[A]b omni virili commixtione se immunem esse profitetur, et de virginitatis integritate gloriatur, idque se approbare Dei omnipotentis iudicio, si marito placeret, aut singulari certamine aut ignitorum vomerum examine.*) Latin cited from Reginonis abbatis Prumiensis, *Chronicon ad an. 887*, ed. Friedrich Kurze, MGH SS rer. Germ. 1 (1890), 597. Germana Gandino, *Contemplare l'ordine. Intellettuali e potente dell'alto medioevo* (Napoli, 2004), 73.

39 Capitulare Karoli M., *De latronibus*, ed. Alfred Boretius, MGH Capit. 1 (1883), 180.

40 *Si quis cum altero de qualibet causa contentionem habuerit, et testes contra eum per iudicium producti fuerint, si ille falsos eos esse suspicatur, liceat ei alios testes, quos meliores potuerit, contra*

The duel was unknown in Visigothic law and the only reference mentioned in the first millennium is the duel fought by a Gothic noble, Count Bera, before Louis the Pious in 820. Having taken Barcelona after many efforts and defeats, the Frankish monarch left Count Bera as his royal appointee, who also became the first count of Barcelona. After a nineteen-year government, the Gothic Sanila accused him of planning an attempt at independence together with others, that is, betrayal, forcing him to appear before the king in Aachen for his defence. The count denied all of Sanila's accusations. To ensure his trustworthiness, he appealed to the judgment of God following Visigothic traditions in which the two adversaries had to fight on horseback, rather than the Frankish custom of fighting on foot. Bera was defeated and King Louis commuted his death sentence to banishment in Rouen, where he lived the rest of his life.[41]

However, at the Council of Valence held in 855, the church fathers in southern Gaul strongly condemned the practice of the judicial duel because of the bloodshed and its tendency to inspire a thirst for revenge in society.[42] This measure failed because the duel was so firmly rooted as a judicial resolution in Occitan tradition as well as in the northern regions and in the rest of Europe.

The Church found it difficult to tolerate duels among the laity, something beyond its control and approval, and especially the aristocracy who adhered to this practice for a very long time.[43] According to Paul Rousset, the Church likely contributed to its omnipresence by the widespread belief in God's immanent justice, thus emphasizing divine intervention in decisive moments.[44]

---

eos opponere, ut veratium testimonio falsorum testium perversitas superetur. Quod si ambae partes testium ita inter se dissenserint, ut nullatenus una pars alteri cedere velit, eligantur duo ex ipsis, id est ex utraque parte unus, qui cum scutis et fustibus in campo decertent, utra pars falsitatem, utra veritatem suo testimonio sequatur [...] in seculari quidem causa huiuscemodi testium diversitas campo conprobetur. Latin cited from Hludowici Pii, *Capitula Legi Addita*, ed. Alfred Boretius, MGH Capit. 1 (1883), 268.

41 Ermoldus Nigellus, *In honorem Lodovici. Liber III*, ed. Georg Heinrich Pertz, MGH SS 1 (1826), 549–60. Charles Romey, *Historia de España*, trans. and revd. Antonio Bergnes de las Casas, 4 vols. (Barcelona, 1839–1849), 2:48 (trans. from orig. *Histoire d'Espagne depuis le premiers temps jusqu'à nos jours*). Alvarado, "Ordalías y derecho," 518–28. Aquilino Iglesia, "El proceso del conde Bera y el problema de las ordalías," *Anuario de Historia del Derecho Español* 51 (1981): 1–221.

42 Giovanni Domenico Mansi, *Sacrorum Conciliorum nova et amplissima collectio*, 31 vols. (Venezia, 1759–1778), 15:9. Charles-Joseph Hefele, Henri Leclercq, *Histoire des Conciles*, 11 vols. in 22 (Paris, 1907–1952), 4:197. The metropolitans Rémy of Lyon, Agilmar of Vienne, Rotland of Arles and the bishops of Grenoble, Avignon, Vaison and Valence were present at Valence. Rubellin, "Combattant de Dieu," 117.

43 Jean Marie Carbasse, "Le duel judiciaire dans les coutumes méridionales," *Annales du Midi* 87 (1975): 385. Paul Ourliac, "Les coutumes du sud-ouest de la France (1953)," in *Études d'histoire de droit médiéval*, ed. Paul Orliac (Paris, 1979), 3–15. Paul Ourliac, "Le duel judiciaire dans le Sud-Ouest," in *Mélanges dédiés à la mémoire de Raymond Monier* (Lille, 1958), 345–48.

44 Rousset, "La croyance," 235ff. See: Aron Gurevich, "Représentations et attitudes à l'égard de la propriété pendant le haut Moyen Âge," *Annales. Économies, Sociétés, Civilisations* 27, no. 3 (1972): 523–47.

As can be seen, opinion at the time was both favourable and hostile to the ordeals. A good testimony to this is a curious account by Adrevaldus de Fleury (ca. 814–879) in his chronicle *Miracula Sancti Benedicti*, summarized now. It is about a claim made by the monks of the abbey of Saint-Denis to the abbey of Fleury over ownership of some servants. The allegation was brought before two of the king's envoys, that is, Jonas, Bishop of Orleans and Donatus, Count of Melun, in 834; each party was supported by its own lawyers (*legum magistri*). They had apparently not found a judge in Paris who could apply Roman law, or what they understood Roman law to be at that time. They only found a few judges of the Salic law (*salicae legis judices*), who failed to resolve the return of the servants as prescribed in Roman law; probably because the judges either did not know Roman law or did not know it well. The case was moved to Orleans where a group of legal experts from that city and from the Gatinais met to provide a satisfactory solution, which in the end, was not reached. The idea of using two champions then materialized; these champions would dispute the right of each party, an initiative that was generally approved. It would certainly have been unusual to oppose this traditional solution. However, against all common sense, a jurist from the Gatinais, that Adrevaldus called *Bestiale*, argued that the procedure was not applicable to church affairs which had to be resolved by Roman law instead of by duel. Adrevaldus, who belonged to the abbey of Fleury, disagreed with this resolution, claiming that the judge must have acted venally by receiving payment from the abbey of Saint-Denis (*ex parte S. Dionysii munere advenerat corruptus*). The monks from Fleury were horrified by the decision to divide the servants between both abbeys. Faced with such injustice, according to the chronicler, St. Benedict punished the jurist who had audaciously dismissed the duel by striking him mute. Perhaps Adrevaldus meant to teach a lesson by condemning those who preferred the Roman tradition by pointing out that the supreme *iudicium Dei*, arrogantly rejected by the lawyer, could not be questioned.

The text follows:

Many judges and men of law from both sides got together to discuss for or against each of them. The king's guests, Jonas, Bishop of Orleans and Donatus, Count of Melun were present. The dispute urged a solution to determine if an ecclesiastical matter should be judged by the Salic or Roman law. Unable to resolve the quarrel properly, they decided to move it to Orleans where a group of professors and jurists from that city and the province of Gatinais would try to clarify the dispute. Although the dispute lasted for a long time, neither one nor the other yielded nor wished to withdraw their demand. It was decided to choose representatives from both sides to put an end to the controversy with sticks and shields. It was clear for everyone that it was fair and honest, except Bestiale from Gatinais. He had been bribed by the monks of Saint-Denis. He thought that it was not appropriate that ecclesiastical matters be resolved by a duel because he feared that his combatant would die in battle; it was therefore more convenient to equally divide the servants. Viscount Genesius, accepting this solution, ordered the division and forced the court to go back to its first choice. However, Benedict knew how to punish the wicked judge that, according to the significance of his name, had cleverly and bestially proposed the idea of dividing the servants between the two monasteries. Once the division occurred by the righteous judgment of God, the judge lost his voice, so he could not speak a word. His relatives, who were with him and knew well the cause of his illness, led him to the monastery of the holy confessor. He remained there nearly a month begging the relief of the great patriarch. Finally, when he started to feel better, his health improved. He never said the name of St. Benedict again for the rest of his life.[45]

This famous case contradicts the relatively popular belief among medieval historians that monks preferred ordeals to the judicial duel. The choice of one or the other depended on which was favourable for a desirable outcome. Duels and ordeals were usually avoided whenever the parties could reach an agreement. Bruno Lemesle suggested that, according to the account, the monk named *Bestiale* justified his position according to law because he had in mind the 818–819 capitulary of Louis the Pious, in which judicial duel was excluded when two ecclesiastical parties in conflict did not reach an agreement. In such a situation, they had to bring the case before the count for him to act as mediator, which was precisely what happened in Orleans.[46]

It was a fact that ecclesiastics considered it unfair to settle disputes by duel. However, according to the chronicle of Adrevaldus, the saint contradicted this himself, believing the duel would have revealed the abbey was in the right. The miracle reveals the injustice of *Bestiale*, the injustice of avoiding the ordeal because the monks admitted its validity.

Despite the divided opinions prevalent in the first millennium, the duel and ordeals continued throughout the medieval West. The Council of Lillebonne in 1080 prescribed punishment for the cleric who participated in a judicial duel without the authorization

---

45 *Colliguntur ab utrisque partibus plurimi legum magistri et judices, qui pro partibus decertarent. Praeterea aderant in eodem placito missi a latere regis, Jonas episcopus Aurelianensis, et Donatus comes Milidunensium. Sed cum litem in eo placito finire nequirent, eo quod Salicae legis judices ecclesiasticas res sub Romana constitutas lege decernere perfecte non possent, visum est missis dominicis placitum Aurelianis mutare. Venientes itaque ad condictum locum, magistri et judices, utraque ex parte, acerrime decertabant. Aderant namque legum doctores, tam ex Aurelianensi quam ex Wastinensi provincia. Enim vero, longiuscule litem judicibus protrahentibus, eo quod nec hi cedere illis, nec illi assensum aliis praebere vellent, tandem adjudicatum est, ut ab utraque parte testes exirent, qui, post sacramenti fidem, scutis ac baculis decertantes, finem controversiae imponerent. Sed cum id justum rectumque visum fuisset omnibus, quidam Wastinensis regionis legis doctor, cui, quodam praesagio, bestiale nomen pro humano indictum erat, quique ex parte S. Dionysii, munere corruptus, advenerat, verens ne si duo inter se decertarent, testis eorum reprobus inveniretur, judicium protulit: non esse rectum ut bello propter res ecclesiasticas testes decernerent; immo magis inter se advocati mancipia partirentur. Cujus sententiae Genesius vicecomes favens, rectius dixit esse mancipia dividi quam testes bello decernere, in eamque sententiam concilium omne deflexit. At vero S. Benedictus nequaquam judicis illius ac legislatoris oblitus est, qui primus sententiam dividi mancipia, versute juxta nomen suum ac bestialiter, protulit. Namque continuo, ut eadem in duas divisa sunt partes mancipia, ille justo Dei judicio ita percussus est, ut nullomodo aliquid loqui posset, evacuato totius linguae officio. Cognoscentes autem familiares ejus, qui inibi aderant, veritatem rei gestae, deduxerunt eum ad monasterium S. confessoris Christi quem graviter offenderat; ibique per unum ferme demoratus est mensem, nutibus quibus poterat, auxilium deposcens egregii patris. Denique aliquantulam sanitatem consecutus, ad sua regreditur; nunquam tamen donec advixit, impetrate voluit ut nomen sancti lingua propria exprimeret Benedicti.* Latin cited from *Patrologiae cursus completus*, ed. Jacques-Paul Migne, 221 vols. (Paris, 1879), 124: col. 928–92. Adrevald de Fleury, *Miracula Santi Benedicti* 1, 25. Smedt, "Les origines du duel judiciaire," 361.

46 Bruno Lemesle, "La pratique du duel judiciaire au XIe siècle, à partir de quelques notices de l'abbaye Saint-Aubin d'Angers," in *Le règlement des conflits au Moyen Âge. Actes du XXXI congrès de la Société des historiens médiévistes de l'enseignement supérieur public* (Paris, 2001), 163–64.

of a bishop (*duellum sine licentia episcopi susceperit*, canon 12); in other words, it was not explicitly prohibited.[47] In many parts of France, the duel was the practice traditionally imposed on a servant who claimed his freedom.

Recognizing both the importance of circumventing perjury and the search for resolution, which meant retaining ordeals, Nottarp's diligent research shows that the judicial duel continued to be preferred to the purgatory oath. He shows that the duel became accompanied by a religious ritual: a vigil of the weapons together with the combatant's companions in the church, mass, communion, blessing of the weapons before the duel, presentation of the sword and shield by the priest; everything was carefully regulated as to locations, time, conditions, and weapons (*benedicti oscuti et baculi ad duellum faciendum*).[48]

Representation

The parties were not always able to face the ordeal themselves. In such a case, they could resort to a representative to undertake the duel for them. This option was intended for women, sick people, old people, and also monks, who were forbidden to combat; they all had champions (*campiones*). This obligation usually fell on a servant of the accused or on the witnesses who supported the testimony.

These representatives were required to meet certain conditions to be able to carry out the duel, which converted them into "legitimate men" (*legitimi viri*). They had to be strong and well-built to bear execution of the judgment of God with real chances of success. All these requirements could become a serious obstacle for the party obliged to prove that its claims were just. If on the day of the duel no champion was found that met the requirements, the party had to reject the obligation of being subjected to the ordeal. However, the contest was normally carried out and the judicial duel (variously called *bellum*, *duellum*, or *pugna*) was usually chosen. Each fighter was armed with a stick and a small shield and was publicly introduced in the arena; the combat proceeded until one of the parties was overpowered and fell to the ground.

Thuringian law prescribed this procedural recourse in the case of a woman who was suspected of attacking her husband. It was arranged that she would prove her innocence by allowing a relative to fight in her place (*proximus mulieris campo eam innocentem efficiat*).[49] However, if a woman declined to be represented and preferred to defend herself "like a man," Bavarian law allowed it (*Si [femina] pugnare voluerit per audatiam cordis sui sicut vir*);[50] the bishop of Lausanne and the judicial regulations of Bohemia (*ordo iudicii terrae Boemiae*) had the same provisions.[51] According to an ancient practice, clerics were usually represented by another person. In 775, a conflict between the bishop of

---

47 Domenico, *Sacrorum Conciliorum*, 20, 558.

48 Hermann Nottarp, *Gottesurteilstudien* (München, 1956), 193–203.

49 "Lex Thuringorum," in *Leges Saxonum*, ed. Karl Friedrich von Richthofen, MGH LL 5 (1875), 140.

50 In *Leges Langobardorum*, ed, Friedrich Bluhme, Alfred Boretius, MGH LL 4 (1868), 29.

51 Jean Gaudemet, "Les ordalies," 114.

Paris and the abbot of Saint-Denis was solved by an ordeal in which men from their own lands participated.[52]

The duel was intended to solve diverse disputes, such as an intriguing case that occurred in Castile in 1077. Pope Gregory VII, the successor of Alexander II, initiated a reforming and centralizing policy. Gregory VII longed for liturgical unity in Christianity and wanted the Hispanic rite, that is, the Mozarabic liturgy, to be abolished on the peninsula. Moreover, he wanted the Roman ritual to be imposed just as in the rest of Christianity. The Hispanic episcopate expressed its refusal to such a change, although some bishops, such as Muño of Calahorra and Jimeno of Burgos, approved the initiative. The decision in favour of the pontiff by the King of Leon and Castile, Alfonso VI, incited opposition and people rose up to protest against its imposition. According to the sources, the dispute then, at the request of the knights, had to be settled following the customs in use, with God providing judgment in the course of a duel. The nobles and the people chose a knight named Juan Ruiz from the house of Matanzas (by the Pisuerga River) to defend the Hispanic rite. Meanwhile, the king chose another knight, a native from Toledo, to defend the Roman rite. The jousting took place in Burgos on Palm Sunday, April 9, 1077 and the Mozarabic knight was victorious to the great joy of the people.[53] Another chronicle states that a French knight defended the Roman rite and that he won "through falseness."[54] However, the king resolved to annul the victory, emphasizing the illegality of the duel (*duellum iudicans ius non esse*). The conflict was therefore solved through an ordeal by fire, in which the Roman rite was victorious.

Jurisdictional disputes were frequent in the West; whether between the laity and religious institutions or between religious institutions themselves. The monks would cancel duels within their jurisdiction, as the cartulary of the abbey of Saint-Aubin of Angers describes regarding a land dispute between the abbey and Renaud Giraud. Once they decided to reach an agreement through a duel, the monks arrived at the location chosen for the combat with the relics of a saint. According to the author of the account,

---

52 Jean Gaudemet, "Les ordalies," 118.

53 "That year two knights fought for the Roman and Mozarabic rite on Palm Sunday. One was Castilian and the other Toledan, and the Toledan won." (*[I]n ipso anno pugnaverunt duo milites pro lege Romana et Toletana in die Ramis palmarum, et unus eorum erat Castellanus, et alius Toletanus, et victus est Toletanus a Castellano.*) Cited from "Cronicon Burgense," *España Sagrada*, ed. Enrique Flórez et al., 51 vols. (Madrid, 1747–1879), 23:309.

54 "As related to the cause and dispute that arose from the introduction in Spain of the Roman rite to replace the Mozarabic rite, a duel was fought by two knights and the knight representing the Franks won maliciously." (*Pro qua extitit causa et contentio de lege Romana quam legem Romanam voluit introducere in Hispaniam, et Toletanam mutare, et ideo fuit factum bellum inter duos milites, et falsitate fuit victus miles ex parte Francorum.*) Latin cited from *La chronique de Saint-Maixent (751–1140)*, ed. Jean Verdon (Paris, 1979), 221. Charles-Joseph, *Histoire des Conciles*, 5:285. Colin Morris, "Judicium Dei. The social and political significance on the ordeal in the eleventh century," *Studies in Church History* 12 (1975): 99. Julia Montenegro, "El cambio de rito en los reinos de León y Castilla según las crónicas: la memoria, la distorsión y el olvido," en *La construcción medieval de la memoria regia*, ed. Pascual Martínez Sopena-Ana Rodríguez López (València, 2011), 72 and ff.

the duel was avoided with a peaceful solution,[55] thanks to both the sanctity of the place and the relics of the saint.

The consequence of a duel was not always in accordance with expectations. According to the same cartulary, there was a case in Méron in the second half of the eleventh century in which a monastic writer described how the representative (*vicarius, voyer*) of the viscount of Thouars wanted the monks of the priory to suffer for some terrible practices. A farmer from the abbey had unjustly fought a duel with this representative and, having lost the combat, took advantage of his opponent and demanded a fine. However, the monk, named Fulcrade, who was in charge of managing the properties of the abbey, protested before the court of the viscount and won his case. The document states that the monks had jurisdiction in their domains, except in cases of bloodshed, robbery, abduction of women, and fires. Nonetheless, they could use justice by blood over their own vassals and, more explicitly, the duel.[56]

The following case is interesting because of the details submitted by Paul Marchegay.[57] His account involves a dispute between three abbeys in 1098, that is, the abbey of Marmoutier near Tours, the abbey Sainte-Croix of Talmont, and the abbey of Sainte-Marie of Angles. Marmoutier was associated with the other abbeys in a priory located in Fontaines in Bas-Poitou. This priory had been founded by William II, Prince and Lord of Talmont, in 1050. Among the properties Fontaines received from the prince was the land of Angles. The lord of Talmont had donated the property in full ownership and with no restriction, but he had not listed what it consisted of, as was common among church benefactors. The priory of Fontaines had exploited the land of Angles under the first successors of William II of Talmont. However, William's nephew Pepin II seized the land in

---

55 "When the duel was about to start, the monks arrived at the location with the relics of the saint, and in this way, thank God, amity was reached" (*[J]udicio duellum ceperunt et usque ad reliquias Allethe armati venerunt, ibique, Deo disponente, hoc modo facta est concordia*). Latin cited from *Cartulaire de l'Abbaye Saint-Aubin d'Angers*, ed. Arthur Bertrand de Broussillon, 3 vols. (Paris, 1903), 1:241. Lemesle, "La pratique du duel judiciaire au XIe siècle," in *Le règlement des conflits au Moyen Âge*, 160.

56 "A villein of the monks called Durand Granvelle had a duel in the monastery. Given that he was defeated, and the custom points out that a sum must be paid to the victor, the vicar demanded that the monastery pay [...] The viscount and his council judged that this was unjust because the vicar had no jurisdiction over the properties of the monastery, except in the four cases of bloodshed, robbery, abduction of women, and fires. However, because men from the monastery participated, the vicar never paid for the bloodshed [...] because the duel does not cover any of the four cases." (*Quidam villanus monachorum, nomine Durandus Gravella, in Monasteriolo fecit quoddam bellum injuste, quia cecidit et consuetudinem quam victi emendare solent vicario Mosterioli emendavit... Judicavit itaque vicecomes et curia ejus hoc esse injustum, quia non habent prepositus vel vicarius consuetudinem in terra monachorum nisi pro quattor forsfactis, id est pro sanguine facto, pro furto, pro rapto mulieris, pro incendio. Sanguis autem vicario nunquam emendabitur, si inter homines Sancti Albini factus erit [...] bellum illud non fuit factum pro aliquot quattor forsfactorum.*) Cited from *Cartulaire de l'Abbaye Saint-Aubin*, 270–71. Bruno Lemesle, *La société aristocratique dans le Haut-Maine (XIe-XIIe siècles)* (Rennes, 1999), 190–92.

57 Paul Marchegay, "Duel judiciaire entre des communautés religieuses. 1098," in *Bibliothèque de l'École de Chartres* 1 (1840): 552–64.

1080. To avoid a possible claim by the abbey, he donated a part of the land to the canons of Angles, who were the natural enemies of the priory of Fontaines.

Trying to take advantage of the situation, Pepin greatly improved the land, making it more productive and increasing the value of the property. The monks of Marmoutier reacted, remembered their ancient rights, and unsuccessfully demanded the restitution of the property to the canons of Angles. However, the claim was heard before Pepin, who acknowledged it and compensated the monks with the tithe of the confiscated land. In addition, an official record explicitly forbade that the land be donated to any other abbey. On his deathbed, pressed by the monks of Sainte-Croix for him to give alms to their church and for the salvation of his soul, Pepin donated to them, among other things, the land he had promised to the other abbey. The monks then appealed to William IX, Duke of Aquitaine and Count of Poitou, to resolve the dispute.

The conflict was not presented before an ecclesiastical court probably because of the nature of the conflict, which was the responsibility of the feudal lord. The land of Angles belonged to the county of Poitou, and it was crucial to have the count's consent for the monks of Marmoutier to receive the land from William of Talmont, who had the most knowledge about the dispute. Reluctant to make a decision that compromised his interests with respect to both parties, William entrusted that responsibility to a baron of the region whom the feudal court considered more knowledgeable. Otto de la Roche had to decide whether the land of Angles belonged to the abbey of Marmoutier or the abbey of Sainte-Croix. Like the count, Otto was linked to both parties and was unable to make a decision. Therefore, he decided to subject the parties to the judgment of God, a duel, that is, by the strength and skill of the combatants chosen by the two abbeys; these would fight in the presence of Otto and the lords of the region. The place chosen for the combat was Moutiers-les-Maufaits, a sandy esplanade fenced with palisades, including a platform for the judges.

Shortly before noon, the combatants were introduced; each one was bareheaded, barefoot, with short hair, and wearing a tunic. They attended a religious service with Lord de la Roche. Their weapons and clothing were examined to safeguard against fraud, and they were asked to swear that they had practised neither witchcraft nor other evil spells to ensure victory. They left the church and went to the place designated for the combat. Amidst the crowd, Lord de la Roche ordered the start of the combat. The exchange of blows using sticks was brief and doubts were dispelled when the champion of the usurpers fell with a blow from his adversary. Many religious ceremonies were held by the monks of Tours to thank God for the sign revealed in the duel.

In the absence of other contests, the duel became common practice. Stephen of Tournai, the abbot of Sainte-Geneviève in Paris, was involved in a conflict about the nature of his personal services with some tenants of Rosny-sous-Vincennes in 1179. Stephen put the situation in the hands of the court of King Louis VII. Given that there were no documents to clarify either the tenants' or the abbot's obligations, the king decided to resolve the dispute through a judicial duel according to Frankish custom. When the champions for Rosny-sous-Vincennes left the arena after the combat with the adversary of the Parisian abbey, the king indicated to the vanquished the personal services to which they were obliged. The dispute was attended by a large number of witnesses, including the

Parisian clergy, the abbots of Saint-Germain-des-Prés and Saint-Denis, and the dean and archdeacon of Notre-Dame. The decision was made by Popes Lucius III and Clement III, as written in Stephen's own letters.[58]

Clerics and Jews were obliged to have a representative, usually a relative. Otherwise, it was necessary to choose a mediator who was paid for his services. It was therefore natural for representation to gain ground, especially among the affluent. Many preferred a strong man, known as a champion, to intervene in their favour even if they could have fought personally. Monasteries could also engage a "warrior" (*bellator*) to be their representative or champion in a dispute in which the duel was ruled as evidence. The champions received an *allodium* for life. Many German cities had a paid representative for this purpose.

Hélène Couderc-Barraud has studied cartularies in the region of Gascony in southern France during the eleventh and twelfth centuries to understand details of trial by combat and its role in the concepts of peace and war. A summary of her contributions is worth mentioning in this chapter.[59] If the jurists Paul Ourliac and Jean-Marie Carbasse used traditional documents from southwestern France to present the duel as a common practice between the twelfth and thirteenth centuries,[60] Couderc-Barraud reveals a significantly different evolution by analysing judicial sources from Gascony. The duel started to decline early due to endogenous societal factors, not because of the influence of Roman law. Documents are sparse on the details of the procedure used to settle disputes. The cases of interest were those in which a duel is mentioned and where combat actually took place. Even so, and considering regional differences, the cases of single combat are few.[61]

As elsewhere in the West, law-suits covered territorial extensions, churches, and the rights derived from the control over a certain domain. These controversies involved clergymen and lay people, clergymen among themselves, and duels among lay people, most of whom belonged to the upper strata of society. However, the parties' social backgrounds are not sufficient to explain the preference for the duel; other recourses for resolution of conflict mentioned elsewhere here were actually the most used means of evidence.

Although legal documentation is particularly laconic, all the accounts have one thing in common regarding the duel, that is, the intervention of generally prestigious mediators. Legal proceedings were brought before the court of an important individual, who was

---

58 Étienne de Tournai, *Lettres*, ed. Jules Desilve (Paris, 1893), 421. Joseph Warichez, *Étienne de Tournai et son temps* (Paris, 1936), 53–6. John Baldwin, "The intellectual preparation for the canon of 1215 against ordeal," *Speculum* 36 (1961): 613–36 at 621.

59 Couderc-Barraud, "Le duel judiciaire en Gascogne," 97–115. Hélène Couderc-Barraud, "Justice d'Église et justice laïque: complémentarités et rivalités en Gascogne (milieu XIᵉ–début XIIᵉ siècle)," in *Les justices d'Eglise dans le Midi (XIᵉ-XVᵉ siècle)*, ed. Hélène Couderc-Barraud (Toulouse, 2007), 21–46.

60 Paul Ourliac, *Les pays de Garonne vers l'an mil* (Toulouse, 1993). Carbasse, "Le duel judiciaire dans les coutumes méridionales," 385–403.

61 Couderc-Barraud, "Le duel judiciaire en Gascogne," 99.

surrounded by nobles, ecclesiastics, or witnesses who judged the relevance of the trial by duel. A large and important assembly of "nobles," sometimes called *proceres eiusdem terrae* ("princes of the earth"), "good and honest men," "powerful men," or "wise men," listened to the allegations. The parties could also negotiate settlement of the dispute by a duel. However, this had to be proposed to the assembly for confirmation, although other procedures could also be dictated, such as the oath or evaluation of the testimonies.

The duel was therefore closely related to the act of judging because the mediators would decide on the evidence to settle the dispute, but not on the merits of the matter. This court was crucial at the moment of combat because its members were witnesses and were always in the presence of the highest presiding authority, a count or viscount considered "prince of the whole region" (*tanquam in principe totius terrae*). The expression commonly used in the cartularies is that the duel will be put "in their hands" (*in manu*), that is, under their authority.

Historians wonder why the duel was used rather than other methods. Was it the consequence of a deficient law or lack of judicial authority? The answer must be nuanced; when a party was convinced of having or wanting certain rights and was not able to reasonably prove them, the duel would remedy the lack of evidence. Frequently, when other practices failed, such as the appearance of "conjurators" who supported the demands, the duel could become the last recourse. In such instances, the judges had no other choice but to order the chosen champions to execute the duel to resolve the conflict.

In other cases, the value of the duel compared to other means of evidence is indeed ambiguous. Although the parties could claim ownership with the aid of documents or by presenting witnesses, they might accept the duel. This indicates that the judicial duel still had some supernatural meaning despite its continuing demystification.

According to Stephen White, if a trial was considered less effective and less fair, the decision to promote the duel was not intended to establish or create a right, but rather to find a solution that would be convenient for both parties.[62]

Therefore, it does not seem that the duel owes its existence to the weakness or deficiency of public power. However, its importance should not be exaggerated because litigants and mediators, at least in eleventh-century Gascony as studied by Couderc-Barraud, had a range of recourses available to them, with the duel only one of them.

The Duel and War

The duel and war are so closely linked that it is sometimes difficult for historians to distinguish the difference between them. Medieval terminology does not help to clarify the situation: *duellum* is the most used term, but is followed by *bellum* ("war"), *certamen*, and its derivatives *decertare* ("to combat") and *certatores* ("combatants"), and finally, *bataille*, which is *batalla* or "combat" in Latin. *Pugna* ("struggle"), which jurists eventually used to wisely analyse the duel, is rarely found.

---

62 Stephen White, "Pactum ... legem vincit et amor judicium: The Settlement of Disputes by Compromise in Eleventh-Century Western France," *The American Journal of Legal History* 22 (1978): 281–308.

In eleventh-century documentation, the terms are combined, such as *duellum bellum*, meaning that the duel was war. In the vernacular people said *batalla* ("battle") when referring to the duel (*duellum, que vulgo batala dicitur*), or "make war as a duel" (*facere duelle bellum*).[63] This connection is quite interesting because it clearly indicates a "war of the duel"; the duel is a particular, well-defined, and limited war. It is not a war presented as pure violence or as contrary to the law, but a ritualized war between representatives of the parties (*campiones*) in a closed field before a prince, an element of aristocratic culture in which members of the same family could confront each other.[64]

The judicial duel was a war minus violence and injustice, employed to motivate the parties to avoid a confrontation and find a solution. The goal of the resolution was negotiation and peace, which required the two parties to agree on the terms; negotiations could continue until the start of the battle. When one of the parties was defeated, negotiations must end. However, the mediators, that is, those who supported the adversaries, tried to convince the victor to listen to reason and agree to compromise.[65]

According to Claude Gauvard, war and revenge both incited violence against property and individuals, and they should not be confused. The objective of war was domination outside of one's territory, while revenge was interpersonal and occurred within one's domain. This could also include war as in the case of the feud (*faida*), the existence of which is not confined to the first centuries of the Middle Ages.[66] In Gascony, a few cases of revenge are documented, but violence is extreme, such as decapitation or ripping out the eyes of the enemy.

However frightening these transgressive situations may be, the historian must not see anarchic violence in them. Seen against the backdrop of political structures, these acts obeyed ritualized practices that expressed the power of a group united by solidarity because violence, inherent in the power of the great, was an element of social differentiation. Much ambiguity is found in the documents, in which the evaluation of violence differs according to social class. In other words, the meaning of violence depends on its practitioner; for example, *pignoratio* (seizure) was used if the person was noble and *furtum* (theft) if not.

For such reasons, there is a difference between duel and war. Two "enemies" confront each other in war; it is a term never used in judicial documents to refer to two combatants, indicating the duel is not strictly considered as war. The duel's parameters guided, without social damage, the conflict between friendship and hatred. Furthermore, the ritualization behind trail by combat distinguished it from war. It was held in a closed field before a secular authority and a large assembly in the context of a judi-

---

63 See Frédéric Boutoulle, "Homicides et violences dans les conflits familiaux de la Gascogne occidentale (XIe-XIIe siècle)," in *La Parenté déchirée: les luttes intrafamiliales au Moyen Âge*, ed. Martin Aurell (Turnhout, 2010), 208.

64 Hélène Couderc-Barraud, *La violence, l'ordre et la paix: résoudre les conflits en Gascogne du XIe au début du XIIIe siècle* (Toulouse, 2008), 296.

65 Couderc-Barraud, *La violence, l'ordre et la paix*, 296.

66 Claude Gauvard, "Prefacio," in *La violence, l'ordre et la paix: résoudre les conflits en Gascogne du XIe au début du XIIIe siècle* (Toulouse, 2008), 3.

cial process; only the champions confronted each other, not the litigants, even when the combat became very violent.

The judicial duel is often described as a special combat, a ritualized war that differed from violence and injustice because the duel allowed the parties to impose a solution. There is a particularly interesting case found in the Bigorre cartulary in which lay people confronted each other. In the first conflict, Sanche Garcie was the adversary of his cousin, Arnaud Laudig, because Laudig was a vassal recognised by Centulle II, the count of Bigorre. Sanche Garcie was then involved in a second conflict in which three duels sought a solution. The first duel between the cousins had to be fought under the authority of the count of Comminges. On the day of the duel, Arnaud Laudig refused to fight, while he promised loyalty and released the hostages to the count of Bigorre. The judges from Toulouse decided to impose the duel again, but Arnaud Laudig did not appear on the battlefield and war broke out between the parties. The third duel seems to be different because alliances were restored, leaving the count of Bigorre in conflict with Sanche Garcie. They all appeared before the court of the king of Aragon to declare their demands, and the duel once again arose as a solution. This time, Sanche Garcie refused to fight and, unlike the two previous occasions, he had to yield to the demands of the count of Bigorre and surrender the castle ceded to him by the count years earlier.[67]

In addition, this case reveals a significant weakness. In these law-suits, the opposing parties, the count of Bigorre and Arnaud Laudig, and then Sanche Garcie, benefit from their power relations in the region. The two cousins play with the rivalries and wars that opposed the counts of Bigorre and Comminges, and when Sanche Garcie and his cousin agreed to go against Centulle II, the latter was forced to ask both the count and bishop of Comminges to exert pressure on their former vassal, but to no avail. Finally, the solution appeared in the court of the king of Aragon, who held the highest authority and, considering Sanche Garcie's reluctance to fight in the duel, the litigation concluded with acceptance of the clause stating that his enjoyment of the castle implied possession but not ownership (*château rendable*). However, the situation remained fragile: the count of Bigorre was captured by the count of Comminges a few years later. Seeing the weakness of his lord, Arnaud Laudig refused to restore the castle demanded by the count. He later left the castle. For a duel to achieve its aim, it was necessary for the two adversaries to truly submit to the result. Herein lies the role of the mediators, the persuasion of the religious, or the intervention of an authority who would oblige them.

On the other hand, while the outcome of combat was certainly God's decision, it was sometimes difficult to accept, as written in the same source referring to a law-suit that involved the monastery of Saint-Mont and the son of Centulle V, the count of Bigorre, and the viscount of Bearn. The monastery paid a large sum of money to the count so he could proceed with the duel without difficulty. The document recounts how the friends of the vanquished party, the allies of Centulle V, and himself, pounced on the victorious champion of the monastery and attacked him. He and his friends defeated them again, and this second victory served as a second duel.[68]

67 Couderc-Barraud, "Le duel judiciaire en Gascogne," 113.
68 Couderc-Barraud, "Le duel judiciaire en Gascogne," 114.

It is clear that for the laity the abyss between the judicial duel and war was not insurmountable, as for the clerics. Such cases were not restricted to southwestern France, since Dominique Barthélemy finds evidence of them in the county of Vendôme in the north.[69] However, it is clear that the solution to the conflict was finally achieved. Hélène Couderc-Barraud suggests that the common use of the judicial duel in Gascony is explained as a *mise-en-scène*: "a ritualized war that differs from violence and injustice, is conceived under the gaze of God, and makes the parties emerge from a power struggle to impose a resolution." It is a compromise between the power of the count and secular aristocracy.[70]

Evidence in secular proceedings until the mid-twelfth century shows a preference for taking the purgatory oath and, even more, the judicial duel. This is rarely documented because there are so few conflicts that bear witness to the duel, and even fewer testifying that it indeed took place. Duels were often conducted under the jurisdiction of a prince and before a large audience, as decided by lords who could not themselves resolve the dispute.

The clergy was generally in favour of duels, at least until they were banned in 1215 by the Fourth Lateran Council, although clerics had always been forbidden to directly take part in the confrontation. In fact, they never did, and that is why they turned to representatives when there was no other solution. Clerics were permanently in conflict with the laity and the duel allowed them to enter more effectively into social negotiations, changing the power relations when they were unfavourable. They also attempted to present the duel as a special combat, a ritualized war in which divine will was manifested in the outcome. However, this view was not always accepted by their adversaries, especially when they were aristocrats; war was an important element of aristocratic culture, that is, an appropriate recourse in accordance with their status, as Pierre Bonnassie showed when studying feudal Catalonia.[71]

We must remember that the ultimate goal of the duel as well as the other practices was the triumph of peace over war (*pacem malens quam bellum*), and it was usually achieved through negotiation. In the meantime, the purpose of the judicial duel was to force the parties to find common ground to avoid confrontation. For this reason, there were occasions when an attempt was made to stop the combat. Those attending, the secular, ecclesiastic, noble, and other authorities, played a crucial role in achieving compromise between parties.

There are cases in which a settlement arose from a request set forth by one of the litigants; however, a negotiation could even take place during the execution of the combat when the champions fought violently (*campiones sese ad invicem maxime percuterent*). All these efforts were carried out by mediators who, during a negotiation, had to say when the proposal of one party was acceptable to the adversary or determine whether the conflict should be prevented or stopped. Any initiative had to be approved by the designated mediators.

---

69 Barthélemy, *La société dans le comté de Vendôme*, 680.

70 Couderc-Barraud, *La violence, l'ordre et la paix*, 296.

71 Bonnassie, *La Catalogne du milieu*, 685.

Compensation, usually economic (such as grazing rights), not only inspired the aggrieved parties to rebuild social peace (*ut amore Dei pacis causa pacis*), but also to certify that the resolution was definite and unwavering. These and other initiatives were healthy for a society eager to restore peace because, in trials where the duel actually took place, negotiation ensured that the vanquished litigant did not leave empty-handed.

Conclusion

Mistrust of the duel later became widespread. Although there are many examples in the Middle Ages (and indeed the modern world) indicating the persistence of deeply rooted traditions that are difficult to eradicate, by the late fourteenth century, trial by combat and other ordeals are rarely mentioned in documents. Where the use of these practices lasted over time in judicial settings, such tenacity seems to be explained by the fact that those crimes prosecuted either by ordeals or duels were punishable by the death penalty. However, the bare legal facts underestimate the seriousness of these crimes to medieval society. When the ordeal is used in a trial, it is not just that the fate of the accused is to be judged in this world; his salvation or damnation in the afterworld is also at stake. The strong medieval religious belief system held that when the accused was condemned he went directly to hell. Abundant literature, including hagiography and *exempla*, bear witness to the widespread nature of this belief. As such, the religious character of the death penalty explains how both the single-person ordeal and the two-person ordeal—or duel—had a continuing presence in judicial settings. In public under-standing of the death penalty, the sacred and profane converged, and were manifested in the need to ask God for his decision as judge.

Chapter 8

ROYAL POWER AND THE EPISCOPACY: ELEVENTH- AND TWELFTH-CENTURY RELICS FROM OVIEDO CATHEDRAL

RAQUEL ALONSO ÁLVAREZ

THE PRESTIGE CONFERRED by relics was used in the Middle Ages by both lay and clerical powers. This shared interest is an indication of the importance of religious ideology at this time, given that the same material resources—relics—served to cement the legitimacy, weight, and authority of abbots and bishops as well as kings, emperors, and aristocrats. This chapter analyses a case study involving the relics of the cathedral of Oviedo.[1]

The worship of relics in Oviedo was consolidated between the eleventh and twelfth centuries and played a very important role in both the memorial construction of the see and the organization of its apparatus of propaganda. The process was not homogenous, but rather divided into various phases that responded to different interests.

In the initial phase it was Alfonso VI, King of Leon and Castile who directed the *inventio* of the relics contained in the Holy Ark. Later, Bishop Pelagius of Oviedo promoted a deep transformation that benefited the bishops of the see, who were seen from this moment onwards as directors, controllers, and organizers of the cult of relics. The same religious elements served, therefore, various interests.

Relics and Power

Christianity in Late Antiquity developed an intimate relation between power and relics, the latter used by lay and episcopal élites as an element of prestige and legitimation. Individuals who participated in the finding, transfer, and exhibition of holy remains attributed this to their own *merita*, consequently considering themselves responsible for the protection of the *sacra pignora* exercised over the populations they protected.[2] The association between relics and rulers had already appeared in the *De obitu Theodosi*, by Ambrose of Milan (340–397), which narrated the legendary finding of the True Cross to the initiative of St. Helena and the consequent despatch of the nails from the crown and her horse's stirrup to her son, the Emperor Constantine.[3] The same prelate con-

---

1 This chapter was prepared as part of the Research Project PAPI-17–PPUENT-4 at the Universidad de Oviedo.

2 Peter Brown, *The Cult of the Saints. Its Rise and Function in Latin Christianity* (Chicago, 1981), 95.

3 Chiara Mercuri, *"Stat inter spinas lilium*: le Lys de France et la couronne d'épines," *Le Moyen Age*

Raquel Alonso Álvarez (raquelaa@uniovi.es) is Profesora titular at the Universidad de Oviedo in Spain.

sidered the relics guarantors of the safety of the communities that housed them.[4] This was undoubtedly the reason for the progressive accumulation of the remains of saints in the city of Constantinople, promoted by the emperors starting with Constantius II (317–361), and their use in certain solemn court ceremonies.[5]

From the sixth and seventh centuries, relics were used in the ceremony of the *circuitus murorum*, which consisted of solemn processions around the walls of cities besieged by enemies, with the clear aim of seeking salvation. Processions of this type are documented in Constantinople and Apamea, but also, according to the story by Gregory of Tours, in the city of Zaragoza. There, during the Frankish siege of 541, the shroud of St. Vincent was taken out in procession. At the end of the seventh century, the custom had also been taken up in the Frankish domains, as indicated by the *ostentatio* promoted by Bishop Leodegar in the besieged city of Autun.[6]

In Latin and Greek churches, relics were used, as a result, as instruments for consolidating power and as protection against the enemy. Merovingian monarchs especially favoured those Parisian churches that held remains, trusting in the cloak of St. Martin for protection in battle. Charlemagne inherited and extended the collection, which he gathered in Aachen and used in the necessary legitimation of the new dynasty.[7] According to the eleventh-century Montecassino Chronicle, Duke Arechis II (758–787) deposited a series of relics *ad tutelam et honorem patrie* on the high altar of the church of Santa Sofia in Benevento.[8]

In the Iberian Peninsula, apart from the early Zaragozan *circuitum murorum* mentioned above, the Visigothic monarchs used relics as protection in battle and to promote worship at the tombs of the martyrs. The use of a cross that included a fragment of the *lignum crucis* is known. It was housed in the church of San Pedro y San Pablo in Toledo, and the king raised it when leaving on military campaigns, a ceremony probably of Byzantine origin described in the *Liber ordinum*.[9] The *Historia Wambæ regis* recalls the gift

---

3–4 (2004): 498n2; Chiara Mercuri, *Corona di Cristo, corona di re. La monarchia francese e la corona di spine nel Medioevo* (Roma, 2004), 29–31, esp. 30–31 for the Ambrosian landscape that interests us.

4 Edina Bozóky, *La politique des reliques de Constantin à Saint-Louis* (Paris, 2006), 7.

5 Bozóky, *La politique*, 85–118; Gilbert Dagron, *Emperador y sacerdorte: Estudio sobre el "cesaropapismo" bizantino* (Granada, 2007), 115–16 (orig. ed.: *Empereur et prêtre. Étude sur le "cesaropapisme" byzantin* (Paris, 1996)).

6 Michael McCormick, *Eternal Victory. Triumphal Rulership in Late Antiquity, Byzantium, and the Early Medieval West* (Cambridge, 1986), 343–44.

7 Bozóky, *La politique*, 120–153; Mercuri, *Corona di Cristo*, 57.

8 "In which temple twelve holy bodies of the saint martyr brothers beheaded in diverse place of Apulia were stored in two similar boxes hidden in an altar in order to be brought safely and treated with honour to the homeland" (*In quo videlicet templo, sanctorum martyrum dudodecim fratrum corpora diversis in locis per Apuliam, in quibus et decollati fuerant, quiescentia honorabiliter allata ad tutelam et honorem patrie in singulis capsis pariter sub uno altare recondidit*. Cited from *Chronica monasterii casinensis*, ed. Hartmut Hoffmann, MGH SS 34 (1980), 37–38 (I, 9); Bozóky, *La politique*, 131–32.

9 *Le "Liber ordinum" en usage dans l'église wisigothique et mozarabe d'Espagne du cinquième au*

of a crown by Reccared to the *martyrium* of St. Felix of Girona.[10] A story contained in the *Lives of the Fathers of Mérida* is especially significant: Bishop Mausona refused to give the Arian Leovigild the cloak of St. Eulalia, a possession desired by the king for the prestige it conferred.[11] Wamba, now a Catholic, built some relics into the walls of Toledo, undoubtedly as a means of protection against enemies.[12]

Relics and the Kings of Asturias and Leon

The relation between the Asturian monarchy and relics is more difficult to establish as most of the sources that refer to them are of dubious credibility. Mentions in Asturian chronicles are insignificant, restricted to linking those deposited in the ceremony consecrating the altars of the Oviedo churches and to reproducing those included by Isidore of Seville in the *Chronica maiora*.[13]

Both the remains of St. Eulalia and those of Eulogius and Leocritia, as well as those included in the Holy Ark, do not appear in the documentation linked to the kings of Asturias until the twelfth century, and are dealt with in a later epigraph in this work.

The protective role of the apostle James is better documented from the end of the eighth century.[14] The hymn *O dei uerbum*, dedicated to Mauregatus (783–788), presents the "Son of Thunder" as *patronus* and *tutor* of Hispania, although it does not yet localize his tomb in Compostela.[15] The tradition situates the *inventio* of his sepulchre to

onzième siècle, ed. Marius Férotin (Paris, 1904; repr. Roma, 1996), 109–11; McCormick, *Eternal Victory*, 314.

10 *Sancti Juliani Toletanae sedis episcopi opera. Pars 1*, Corpus Chritianorum Series Latina 115, ed. Jocelyn N. Hillgarth, Wilhelm Levison, Bernhard Bischoff (Turnhout, 1976), 26, 240–241.

11 *Vitas sanctorum patrum emeritensium*, Corpus Christianorum Series Latina 116, ed. Antonio Maya Sánchez (Turnhout, 1992), 5–6, 63–71.

12 According to the *Chronica muzarabica* for 754. *Corpus scriptorum muzarabicorum*, ed. Juan Gil, 2 vols. (Madrid, 1973), 1:26–27.

13 *Crónicas asturianas*, ed. Juan Gil Fernández, trans. José L. Moralejo, study by Juan Ignacio Ruiz de la Peña (Oviedo, 1985), 158–68; *Chronica Albendensia*: "Hallazgo de la cruz por santa Helena," xiii, 43; "Traslado a Constantinopla de las reliquias de Andrés y Lucas," xiii, 44; "Traslado a Constantinopla de la cabeza de Juan Bautista," xiii, 49; "Descubrimiento de los cuerpos de Habacuc y Miqueas," xiii, 51; "Descubrimiento del cuerpo del apóstol Bernabé y del evangelio de Mateo," xiii, 56; "Hallazgo del cuerpo de san Antonio y traslado a la iglesia de San Juan de Alejandría," xiii, 59; "Profanación del sepulcro de san Acisclo de Córdoba por el rey Agila," xiv, 16. For the *Chronica maiora* as the source of these passages: *Chronica minora saec. IV. V. VI. VII*, ed. Theodor Mommsen, MGH Auct. ant. 11 (1894), 2:466, 467, 470, 471, 474 and 476. The episode of Agila and St. Acisclus, by the same author and in the same volume: *Historia gothorum, wandalorum, sueborum*, 285.

14 For this question, Raquel Alonso Àlvarez, "*Tocius Hyspanie presidio et saluti adsistencia*. La protección del reino: de Santiago al Arca Santa de Oviedo," in *Los reyes de Asturias y los orígenes del culto a la tumba del apóstol Santiago*, ed. Francisco Javier Fernández Conde, Raquel Alonso Álvarez (Gijón, 2017), 127–29.

15 Study and edition in Manuel Díaz y Díaz, *Asturias en el siglo VIII. La cultura literaria* (Oviedo, 2001), 83–93.

the epoch of Alfonso II, granting the monarch a leading role in promoting his worship.[16] Although the detailed story of the finding was not known until the end of the eleventh century, in the so-called *Concordia de Antealtares* (1077), the documentation echoes the *martyrium* of James from the ninth century.[17] If, as Henriet believes, the epistle from Alfonso III to the clergy of Tours was authentic, in the monarch's time the apostle's tomb would already have been the subject of a thaumaturgical veneration, equivalent to that of St. Martin of Tours.[18]

Thus, the rise of the worship of the remains of Santiago in Compostela from the ninth century onwards can be accepted, although the late or suspicious nature of the more expressive sources impedes a precise estimation of the role of the kings at the beginning of the process. Perhaps, as Guiance supposes, the veneration was initially an episcopal endeavour, later accepted and promoted by the monarchy.[19]

Sancho I (935–966) inaugurated a policy of accumulating relics in the new royal seat of León by beginning the process of acquiring the body of St. Pelagius, which arrived in the city during the time of his successor, Ramiro III (961–958).[20] With the land threatened by the terrible incursions of Almanzor, the remains of the Córdoban saint were moved to the monastery of San Juan Bautista in Oviedo, then renamed.[21]

Kings Fernando I (ca. 1016–1065) and Sancha (1013–1067) provided new impulse for the policy of collecting and dignifying relics. On one hand, they continued to protect

---

16 For the origins of the worship of the apostle see: Luis Vázquez de Parga, José María Lacarra, Juan Uría Ríu, *Las peregrinaciones a Santiago de Compostela*, 3 vols. (Madrid, 1948; repr. Pamplona, 1993), 1:27–36; Jan van Herwaarden, "The origins of the cult of St. James of Compostella," *Journal of Medieval History* 6, no. 1 (1980): 1–35; Fernando López Alsina, "Cabeza de oro refulgente de España: los orígenes del patrocinio jacobeo sobre el reino astur," in *Las peregrinaciones a Santiago de Compostela y San Salvador de Oviedo en la Edad Media. Actas del Congreso Internacional celebrado del 3 al 7 de diciembre de 1990*, ed. Juan Ignacio Ruiz de la Peña (Oviedo, 1993), 26–36. Thomas Deswarte, *De la destruction à la restauration. L'idéologie du royaume d'Oviedo-Léon (VIIIᵉ–XIᵉ siècles)* (Turnhout, 2003), 97–110; Adeline Rucquoi, "Saint-Jacques de Compostelle: un pèlerinage et ses textes," in *Études sur les Terres saintes et pèlerinages dans les religions monothéistes*, ed. Daniel Tollet (Paris, 2012), 77–92; Adeline Rucquoi, "Los reyes de Asturias y los orígenes del culto a la tumba del apóstol Santiago," in *Los reyes de Asturias*, 17–37.

17 A recent study of the "Concordia de Antealtares" in: José Miguel Andrade Cernadas, "La Concordia de Antealtares en su contexto histórico," in *Los reyes de Asturias*, 109–27. The earliest appearances of the tomb in the documentation in Rucquoi, "Saint-Jacques de Compostelle," 77–78.

18 Patrick Henriet, "La lettre d'Alphonse III, rex Hispaniae, aux chanoines de Saint-Martin de Tours (906)," in *Retour aux sources. Textes, études et documents d'histoire médiévale offerts à Michel Parisse* (Paris, 2004), 155–66.

19 Ariel Guiance, "'Pignora sanctorum'. Reliquias y devoción en Hispania tras la conquista musulmana," in *Christ, Mary and the Saints. Reading Religious Subjects in Medieval and Renaissance Spain*, ed. Lesley K. Twomey (Leiden, 2018). My thanks to the author for allowing me to consult the pre-publication version.

20 *Sampiro, su crónica y la monarquía leonesa en el siglo X*, ed. Justo Pérez de Urbel (Madrid, 1952), 337–40.

21 According to Pelagius of Oviedo. *Crónica del obispo don Pelayo*, ed. Benito Sánchez Alonso (Madrid, 1924), 65–66.

those of St. Pelagius in their home in Oviedo, attending his *elevatio* and the rebuilding of his tomb in 1053.[22] Under their auspices, the *translatio* of the brothers Vicente, Sabina, and Cristeta, took place. They were buried in Ávila and transported to León, Palencia, and Arlanza respectively.[23]

The main *translatio* in their reign was undoubtedly that which brought St. Isidore of Seville to San Juan Bautista in León, in 1063. The oldest reference is found in the *Acta translationis corporis S. Isidori*, from the end of the eleventh century, which served as the basis for the story in the *Historia Silense*.[24] Fernando I would have sent a mission led by the bishops Alvito of León and Ordoño of Astorga to Sevilla, to ask the king for the body of St. Justa, whose exact location was unknown. Alvito pleaded for a revelation, and an ancient bishop appeared to him in a vision. This was St. Isidore telling him where his own tomb was, asking him to have his remains, found incorrupt and fragrant, moved instead of those of St. Justa. The Sevillan monarch finally granted permission and also handed over a rich shroud to wrap the body in. Although Alvito died before finishing the task, the relics reached their destination, where they were solemnly received by Fernando I. The story undoubtedly has some historical basis but is transformed by the stereotypes characteristic of the literature of *inventiones*.[25] After being installed in León, the veneration of Isidore reached an extraordinary brilliance thanks to this promotion by the royal house.[26]

---

22 On November 7, 1053. *Colección diplomática de Fernando I (1037–1065)*, ed. Pilar Blanco Lozano (León, 1987), 136–38 (document 47).

23 The *translationes* are contained in the *Crónica de Pelayo* (Pelagius of Oviedo, *Crónica del obispo don Pelayo*, 74) but are corroborated by the documentation (*Colección diplomática de Fernando I*, 183–84 (document 72) (1065, May 19: Donation by the kings to the Church of Palencia for the exhumation of the martyrs).

24 An analysis of the phases of creation of the history in Patrick Henriet, "Un exemple de religiosité politique: saint Isidore et les rois de León (XIe-XIIIe siècles)," in *Fonctions sociales et politiques du culte des saints dans les societés de rite latin au Moyen Âge et à l'époque moderne: approche comparative*, ed. Marek Derwich, Mikhail Dmitriev (Wroclaw, 1999), 79–80. For the first version, *Sancti Isidori hispalensis episcopi opera omnia*, in *Patrologiae cursus completus*, ed. Jacques-Paul Migne, 221 vols. (Paris, 1850), 81: col. 39–43. See *Historia Silense*, ed. Justo Pérez de Urbel, Atilano González Ruiz-Zorrilla (Madrid, 1959), 198–205.

25 Its echo is similarly found in the documentation of the epoch. (1065, December, 23: Donation to Ordoño of Astorga for his participation in the *translatio*). *Colección diplomática de Fernando I*, n. 72, 183–84. For a general panorama of the common places that appear in the *translationes*, Patrick J. Geary, *Furta sacra. Thefts of Relics in the Central Middle Ages* (Princeton, 1978), esp. 12–13, 61–63, 122. Pierre André Sigal, "Le déroulement des translations de reliques principalement dans les régions entre Loire et Rhin aux XIe et XIIe siècles," in *Les reliques. Objets, cultes, symboles. Actes du colloque international de l'Université du Littoral–Côte d'Opale (Boulogne-sur-Mer). 4–6 septembre 1997*, ed. Edina Bozóky, Anne-Marie Helvétius (Paris, 1999), 213–27.

26 Henriet, "Un exemple de religiosité politique," 78.

Alfonso VI and the Opening of the Holy Ark of Oviedo

Alfonso VI employed the political use of relics with a purpose even more clearly defined than his predecessors. An analysis of the primal *corpus* related to the opening of the Holy Ark in 1075 will help to show this.

The earliest certain references to the worship of relics in Oviedo are from the end of the eleventh century. The mentions in the documentation relating to the church of San Salvador in the ninth and tenth centuries refer to the consecration of the altars.[27] The *Chronicle of Alfonso III*, in its *Ad Sebastianum* version, undoubtedly also refers to these:

> He also built a basilica with admirable work, dedicated to our Lord Jesus also called San Salvador Church. On both sides of the main altar, twelve altars with hidden relics of the Apostles were added.[28]

The formulae used coincide significantly with some passages from the Roman *ordines*, like number 41: "On reaching the altar, a veil spread between the relics and the people, the Bishop, with his own hands, hides them in the hollow in the altar."[29]

Thus, the oldest mentions correspond, as stated above, to the final years of the eleventh century.

The Act of Opening the Holy Ark (1075)

According to the so-called *Acta de apertura del Arca Santa*, on March 13, 1075, during Lent, an assembly in Oviedo Cathedral took place, made up of King Alfonso VI, his sister Urraca, Bishop Arias of Oviedo, and holders of the sees of Palencia, Dumio, and Oca. The document refers to an ark full of relics that had reached Oviedo, having been saved from the Muslim invasion, from Toledo, and that had remained hidden for many years. During the time of Bishop Ponce de Tabérnoles (1025–1035), there was said to have been an unsuccessful attempt to open it that left some of those in attendance blind because of the dazzling light that emanated from the reliquary. What the virtuous prelate failed to obtain was achieved years later by King Alfonso VI, leading to an even more rigorous penitence than usual during Lent, and ordering that prayers be offered to the Lord by both the *tholetanos* priests in Oviedo and the practitioners of the *romanus ritus*. After these propitiatory acts, at nine o'clock in the morning on March 13, after mass, a solemn procession walked to the place of the ark (which is not specified) among chants and incense. Christ revealed the location of the long-hidden treasure to the *fidelissimo principe*. As a consequence of the holiness of the relics found in it, the king granted the church of San Salvador the *mandación* of Langreo the day after the ceremony, which is

---

27 This problem, in detail, in Raquel Alonso Àlvarez, "'Patria uallata asperitate moncium'. Pelayo de Oviedo, el 'archa' de las reliquias y la creación de una topografía regia," *Locus amœmus* 9 (2007–2008): 17–29.

28 *Basilicam quoque in nomine Redemptoris nostri Saluatoris Ihesu Xp̄i miro construxit opere, unde et specialiter ecclesia sancti Saluatoris nuncupatur, adiciens principali altari ex utroque latere bis senum numerum titulorum reconditis reliquiis omnium apostolorum.* Cited from *Crónicas asturianas*, 139.

29 *Venientes ante altare, extenso velo inter eos et populum, recondit ipse pontifex manu sua ipsas reliquias in locum altaris.* . Cited from *Les Ordines Romani du Haut Moyen Age. IV. Les textes (suite)*, ed. Michel Andrieu (Leuven, 1956), 346–47.

Figure 8.1: *Act of Opening the Holy Ark* (1075). Thirteenth-century copy. Oviedo, Archivo de la Catedral, serie B, folder 2, no. 9A. (© Catedral de Oviedo, photo: Lorenzo Arias Páramo).

the date on the document. A long list of laymen and clergy appear as witnesses, among them the king, together with his sisters Urraca and Elvira, the bishops of Palencia, León, Astorga, Oca, Dumio, and Oviedo, various abbots, and a series of aristocrats including Rodrigo Díaz de Vivar, called El Cid. Juan, the king's notary, was in charge of writing and validating the document, indicating on finishing that a copy was placed in the ark before closing it again.

The original version of the diploma has not survived, but two copies dated from the thirteenth century have.[30] The A copy has been used as a basis for most transcriptions and editions, as the B version did not reach Oviedo until 2005, thanks to the generous donation to the cathedral archive by the García-Trelles family. Fernández Conde and

---

30 Oviedo, Archivo de la Catedral, serie B, folder 2, nos. 9A and 9B.

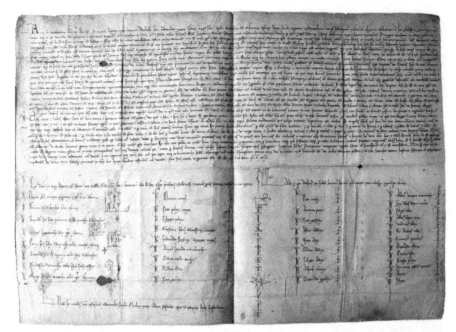

Figure 8.2: *Act of Opening the Holy Ark* (1075). Thirteenth-century copy. Oviedo, Archivo de la Catedral, serie B, folder 2, no. 9B. (© Catedral de Oviedo, photo: Lorenzo Arias Páramo).

Alonso Álvarez have recently carried out a study of the two versions, which is the one used in this work.[31]

Given that the original has not survived, the authenticity of the copies has been questioned on occasion. Without ruling out the possibility that an authentic document served as a basis, Reilly considered the report a falsification resulting from Oviedo's desire to compete with Santiago as a destination for pilgrims. He based this belief on the document's unusual dating according to the year of the Incarnation, and on the use of the formula *rex Legionensis et Gallecie atque Castelle et Asturiarum*, which he claims did not appear until the twelfth century.[32] Gambra considers the piece to be the result of the combination of two independent documents, a set that differed from those used in Alfonso VI's chancellery. As it does not appear in the collection of the *Liber Testamentorum ecclesiae ouetensis,* it should be considered later than the time of Pelagius of Oviedo. Although Gambra believes it possible that the donation of Langreo actually occurred,

---

31 Francisco Javier Fernández Conde, Raquel Alonso Álvarez, "Los catálogos de las reliquias de la catedral de Oviedo," *Territorio, Sociedad y Poder* 12 (2017): 55–81. This article brings together the main earlier editions. Our thanks to the archivist canon of Oviedo Cathedral, Agustín Hevia Ballina, for facilitating the study of the documents.

32 Bernard F. Reilly, "The Chancery of Alfonso VI of León-Castile (1065–1109)," in *Santiago, Saint-Denis, and Saint Peter: The Reception of the Roman Liturgy in León-Castile in 1080*, ed. Bernard F. Reilly (New York, 1985), 7 and 25n40.

the story of the ark's opening could be a creation of the Oviedo *scriptorium*: its style is close to the Pelagian and it draws attention to the monarch's use of the title *imperator*, an anachronism in Gambra's opinion, or the simultaneous appearance of clergy who followed the Hispanic and Roman rites. In contrast with Reilly, he does not consider the use of the term *rex* at that time problematic.[33]

Regarding the structure of the document, made up of an *inventio* followed by the royal privilege, its apparent rarity can be explained by analysing it in a wider context. In the Catalan counties, these combinations in which a donation was preceded by a liturgical, hagiographic, or consecratory text, one a consequence of the other, were habitual.[34] Although more infrequent, the model is not unknown in the Leonese documentation. Fernando I and Sancha, Alfonso VI's parents, participated in the *translatio* by St. Pelagius to his monastery in Oviedo in 1053. The monarchs are also presented here instigating the *elevatio*, which they attended together with magnates, bishops, and relatives: "Finally, we came to this holy place with our bishops and offspring, and all the magnates of our land, and we made a wonderful transfer of the Holy Body."[35]

The act was followed by a royal donation motivated by the saintliness the martyr's remains conferred on the place. It is probable that a document similar to this inspired the writers of the *Act of Opening the Holy Ark*.

Nor does it seem that the use of the term *imperator* as a royal title clashes with the date in the Act. Sirantoine, who has analysed this problem, highlights its use by some Asturian-Leonese kings and in diplomas from Fernando I. She suggests that Alfonso VI may have adopted it in a curia in 1077 as a method of territorial unification.[36] Given that Alfonso's chancellery was already organized in 1073, I see no reason not to accept that, in reality, the earliest appearance of the title was the one in the *Act of Opening the Holy Ark*.

The formal elements, especially those in the B copy, also back this possible fidelity, in general terms, of the thirteenth-century copies to a supposed original from 1075. Large and oblong in shape, roughly the bottom half is covered with subscriptions, accompanied by elaborate monograms, as we find in many originals from between the tenth and twelfth centuries. Thus, the one that contains the donation by Bermudo II to the monastery of San Pelayo, in 996, or the diploma, mentioned above, that describes the *elevatio* of the martyr in the Oviedo nunnery under the auspices of Fernando I and Sancha in 1053.[37]

---

33 Andrés Gambra, *Alfonso VI. Cancillería, Curia e Imperio. II. Colección diplomática* (León, 1998), 61–62.

34 My thanks to doctor Daniel Rico Camps for drawing my attention to this typology of document. There are a good number of examples in Ramon Ordeig i Mata, *Les dotalies de les esglésies de Catalunya (segles IX-XII)* (Vic, 1993), such as 14–16 (document 2) (833, November 17).

35 *Denique uenimus in hunc sanctum locum cum episcopis et proles nostri et omnes magnati terre nostre et fecimus translacionem mirificam ipsius corporis Sancti.* Cited from *Colección diplomática de Fernando I*, 136–38 (document 47).

36 Hélène Sirantoine, *Imperator Hispaniæ. Les idéologies impériales dans le Royaume de León (IXᵉ-XIIᵉ siècle)* (Madrid, 2012), 123, 158 and 205.

37 Reproduced in *San Pelayo. Mil años de Historia* (Oviedo, 1994), 21 and 23.

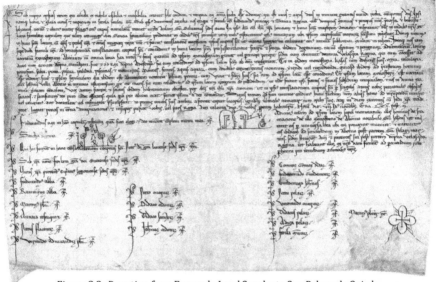

Figure 8.3: *Donation from Fernando I and Sancha to San Pelayo de Oviedo* (1053). Oviedo, Archivo del Monasterio de San Pelayo, Fondo documental de San Pelayo, file A, no. 3. (© Real Monasterio de San Pelayo de Oviedo).

In both cases, as in the B copy of the *Act*, the subscription of the king occupies a central position, the queen being placed one line lower on the left half of the document.

The B copy of the *Act* includes monograms with the subscriptions of Alfonso VI, Infanta Urraca Fernández, and the bishops Pelagius of León and Pedro of Astorga.

The A copy is simpler, smaller, and quadrangular in shape, with only Urraca's monogram appearing on it. The comparison with earlier royal diplomas and those from the end of the eleventh century suggests that, if a prototype were to be imitated, the B copy would be closest to it.

If we compare the monograms in the copies of the *Act* with those corresponding to the same characters in original documents, we have to admit that either the copier had a document from the times of Alfonso VI before him, or a good copy, or he was an excellent forger. Alfonso used a monogram inspired by that of his predecessors of the same name,[38] very similar to the contents in the donation by the king and his sister Urraca in 1071.[39] The later Alfonsos abandoned this style in favour of other solutions: the seventh used a cross and the legend *signum imperatoris* inscribed on a cartouche. From Fernando II on, the kings preferred the wheel inspired in the papal rotas that Diego Gelmírez introduced into the kingdom.[40]

---

38 The confirmatory signs of the Leonese monarchs are contained and classified in Elsa de Luca, "Royal misattribution: monograms in the León antiphoner," *Journal of Medieval Iberian Studies* 9, no. 1 (2017): 25–51 (published November 9, 2015, and accessed December 28, 2017, http://dx.doi.org/10.1080/17546559.2015.1101521). The monograms of Alfonso III, IV, and V in fig. 5a.

39 Madrid, Archivo Histórico Nacional, Clero, folder 959, no. 3.

40 Antonio Sánchez González, "Los "*Privilegios Rodados*" originales del Archivo Ducal de Medinaceli: I. Alfonso VIII de Castilla," *En la España medieval* 35 (2012): 369–72.

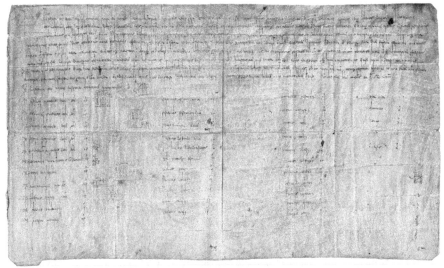

Figure 8.4: *Donation from Alfonso VI to the Infanta Urraca* (1071). Madrid,
Archivo Histórico Nacional, CLERO–SECULAR–REGULAR, folder 959, no. 3.
(© Ministerio de Cultura y Deporte, Gobierno de España, Madrid).

Bishops Pedro of Astorga and Pelagius of León are identified in the *Act* through
monograms comparable to those found in the original from 1071 mentioned above.

The analysis of the monogram of the Infanta that does not appear in any original
document is more complex. Urraca Fernández either did not use it or no diploma that
contains it has survived. However, another Urraca used the monogrammatic sign found
in both copies of the *Act*: the queen, daughter of Alfonso VI (1109–1126), who used it in
an instrument in 1110 and another in 1120.[41]

It is not inconceivable that, as was frequent, ladies of the same name in the royal family used similar monograms. Nevertheless, what is difficult to find is the reason, in the
A copy, the Infanta was the only subscriber to use this element. The problem would be
clarified if an intermediate copy had been made in the queen's time. This would explain
the special relevance given to her aunt in the two copies of the *Act*, as any spectator of
the time would visually identify the monogram with the sign of the queen.

Leaving these questions concerning the documentary *traditio* aside, other aspects of
the document are relevant, some reinforcing its reliability.

In short, I believe that the simplicity of the story of the *translatio* in the *Act* indicates
that this is a pre-Pelagian state of the story of the Holy Ark.[42] While the later versions
included novelesque and fantastic elements, the one presented in the document of 1075

---

41 1110, December 16. AHN, Clero, folder 1591, no. 15; 1120, April 27. AHN, Clero, folder 1591,
no. 17. Edited in *Diplomatario de la reina Urraca de Castilla y León (1109–1126)*, ed. Cristina
Monterde Albiac (Zaragoza, 1996), 46–47 and 226–227 (documents 20 and 144).

42 Alonso Àlvarez, "*Patria uallata asperitate moncium*," 22.

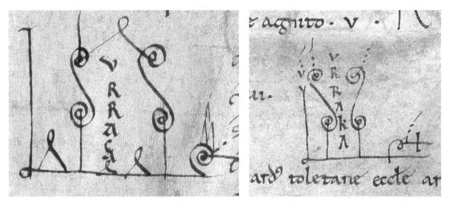

Figure 8.5: (left) Infanta Urraca Fernandez's monogram (*Act of 1075*, copy A) and (right) Queen Urraca's monogram. Madrid, Archivo Histórico Nacional, CLERO–SECULAR–REGULAR, folder 1591, no. 17. (© Ministerio de Cultura y Deporte, Gobierno de España, Madrid).

indicates simply that the holy remains reached safe territory fleeing from Toledo before the Muslim invasion.

More significant is the extraordinary importance given to the king in the development and organization of the ceremony, a characteristic shared in all the *corpus* corresponding to the epoch of Alfonso VI, as shown below.[43] Despite highlighting the qualities of the *magne uirtutis vir Poncius* (Bishop Ponce de Tabérnoles), the attempt to open the ark was not only a failure, but also had dramatic consequences for those attending, some being blinded for life. It would be King Alfonso who was chosen by the divinity to triumph on the mission on which the prelate had failed. If this is surprising in a story originating in a cathedral, it is even more so given the decision by the monarch to lead the Lenten penitence, a prerogative exclusive to bishops at that time.[44]

Gambra also considered the presence of the "clerics of Toledo who lived there [in Oviedo], and the remaining following the Roman Rite" in the *Act* as another indication of forgery.[45] Given that other authors accept the possibility of this coexistence,[46] it seems difficult to take part in this debate. What interests me most in this passage is the territorial segregation of the clergy following the ancient and modern rites. The *tholetanos* would be residents in Oviedo, so it appears that the *reliquos* should be identified with the members of the royal entourage. The appearance among the latter of Pelagius of León, a reformist prelate on the margins of Gregorianism, as Peter Linehan discovered,[47]

---

43 Raquel Alonso Álvarez, "El obispo Arias y la apertura del Arca Santa de Oviedo: la reforma litúrgica antes del Concilio de Burgos (1080)," *Medievalia* 17 (2014): 79–102.

44 Mary C. Mansfield, *The Humiliation of Sinners. Public Penance in Thirteenth Century France* (Ithaca, 1984), 169–88.

45 *Clericos tholetanos illic habitantibus esse precepit et reliquos romanum ritum tenentibus*. From Gambra, *Alfonso VI*, 61–62.

46 Francisco Javier Fernández Conde, *La religiosidad medieval en España. Alta Edad Media (siglos VII-X)* (Gijón, 2008), 368.

47 Peter Linehan, "León, ciudad regia, y sus obispos en los siglos X-XIII," in *El Reino de León en la*

Figure 8.6: Holy Ark, Holy Chamber in the Oviedo Cathedral.
(© Catedral de Oviedo, photo: Lorenzo Arias Páramo).

suggests that the aim of this clear differentiation was not to reflect the true liturgical composition of the Oviedo assembly, but to present the king as the principal backer of the religious renewal confirmed in the Council of Burgos in 1080.[48] As a matter of fact, it comes as no surprise that the person charged with formalizing the *Act* was the notary to the monarch.

The Holy Ark (Prior to 1102)

Alfonso VI not only appears as the organizer of the ceremony of the opening of the Holy Ark, but also as the donor of the splendid silver reliquary that holds it. This is an unusually large prismatic piece (119 × 93 × 73 cm), made up of various sheets of silver covering a wooden box.

The *Maiestas Domini* is depicted on the front between the apostles distributed in levels under arches, two on each side. The scenes on the left correspond to the cycle of Christ's infancy: the Visitation, Annunciation to the Shepherds, Annunciation, Nativity, and Flight to Egypt. The right-hand side is reserved for the Ascension, another series of apostles, and St. Michael spearing the dragon. The back is decorated with a geometric reticulate pattern. The scenes include explanatory Latin *tituli*, while Kufic inscriptions that were recently reviewed, read, and translated by Martínez Núñez border the panels.[49]

Alta Edad Media (León, 1994), 409–57.

48 Alonso Álvarez, "El obispo Arias," 79–102.

49 María Antonia Martínez Núñez, "Inscripciones àrabes en la catedral de Oviedo: El Arca Santa, la Arqueta del obispo Arias y la Arqueta de Santa Eulalia," *Territorio, Sociedad y Poder* 11 (2016): 23–62.

To finish, the table bears a scene of the crucifixion with Christ between the thieves. The edge of the lid has a long Latin inscription, the second documentary evidence corresponding to the epoch of Alfonso VI analysed in this work.[50] It contains an inventory of relics, and mentions the king as the donor of the work and the date, partially missing, of its execution. Reference is made to the assembly constituted for the opening, composed of an unspecified series of clergy and bishops, King Alfonso, and his sister, Urraca. The text ends with the mention of a final group of relics.

The chronology of the Holy Ark has also been a subject of controversy. The date generally accepted was the one reconstructed by Gómez-Moreno in coincidence with the dating of the *Act*: 1075.[51] The suspicions, mentioned above, questioning the validity of the diploma and some other arguments, motivated Harris's chronological revision, who moved the work's creation forward to ca. 1120, under the diocesan administration of Pelagius.[52] Leaving aside questions concerning the authenticity of the *Act* mentioned above, neither the typology nor stylistic characteristics of the piece support this chronological postponement.[53]

The arguments proposed by Moralejo are still valid for this purpose. On one hand, the stylistic parallels that can be adduced for the work correspond to the end of the eleventh century. Moreover, there is a small box in Oviedo Cathedral for the eucharistic reservation commissioned by Bishop Arias as indicated in its inscription. It also contains a Kufic text that allows its execution to be reasonably connected to that of the Holy Ark. The baffling isolation of the great reliquary is probably due to the loss of contemporary works linked to Alfonso VI, especially the *Tabula argentae* in Santiago de Compostela and the antipendium from Sahagún.[54]

Although the part of the inscription that dates the Holy Ark is only partially conserved, the mention of Alfonso VI (d. 1109) as the donor guarantees that it was done prior to his death. To consider it "a commemorative rather than a descriptive notice," composed by Bishop Pelagius,[55] is incongruent in this context. If we were to follow this proposal, it would be difficult to understand the reasons for both the mention of a long

---

50 The most recent edition and transcription corresponds to Daniel Rico Camps, "La inscripción histórica del Arca Santa de Oviedo. Nueva transcripción y edición," *Territorio, Sociedad y Poder* 12 (2017): 37–53.

51 Manuel Gómez-Moreno, "El Arca Santa de Oviedo documentada," *Archivo Español de Arte* 69 (1945): 125–36.

52 Julie A. Harris, "Redating the Arca Santa of Oviedo," *The Art Bulletin* 77, no. 1 (1995): 84–93, esp. 90 for the proposed date. The author presents her interpretation, much more briefly, in "Arca Santa of Oviedo," in *The Art of Medieval Spain A.D. 500–1200* (New York, 1993), 259–260.

53 This problem, in detail, in Alonso Àlvarez, "*Patria uallata asperitate moncium,*" 21–22.

54 Serafín Moralejo, "Les arts somptuaires hispaniques aux environs de 1100," *Les Cahiers de Saint-Michel de Cuxa*, 13 (1982): 285–310 (2nd ed. in *Patrimonio artístico de Galicia y otros estudios. Homenaje al prof. Dr. Serafín Moralejo Álvarez*, ed. Ángela Franco Mata, 3 vols. (Santiago de Compostela, 2004), 1:219–37). Serafín Moralejo, "Ars sacra et sculpture romane monumentale: le trésor et le chantier de Compostelle," *Les Cahiers de Saint-Michel de Cuxa* 11 (1980): 189–238 (2nd ed. in *Patrimonio artístico de Galicia,* 1:161–88).

55 Harris, "Redating the Arca Santa," 91.

dead monarch (and one of his sisters!) and the omission of the bishop who supposedly promoted the work. The most recent revision of the epigraphic text recovers the interpretation by Gómez-Moreno of 1075.[56]

Pelagius himself resolved the question by placing the Holy Ark in its current location in 1102 on the occasion of the *elevatio* of the relics of St. Eulalia of Mérida, to which we shall return below.[57] With some variation, all reviews after 2008[58] accept a date earlier than this for the great Oviedo reliquary.[59]

The Epistle of Bishop Osmundo (Before 1096)

The letter from Bishop Osmundo of Astorga to Ida of Boulogne closes this early *corpus*. The prelate responds to a communication from the countess, which has not survived, in which she requests the sending of some of the hairs of the Virgin conserved in Astorga. According to Osmundo, the relic was taken from Jerusalem to Toledo by Torcuatus and Hesychius, two of the Seven Apostolic Men. The relics deposited in the city were taken northwards, in flight from the Muslims, and the collection was split between Astorga and Oviedo. The bishop finally sent the hair to Bishop Ida, not without previously obtaining authorization from Alfonso VI.[60] Henriet suggests this version of the tradition of the Holy Ark is a variant eliminated later by Pelagius of Oviedo, fearful of possible competition.[61]

The King and the Bishops

Both bishops mentioned in the ancient tradition of the Holy Ark were closely linked to Alfonso VI.

Arias Cromaz (d. ca. 1098) was from the comital family that founded the monastery of Corias, and was its first abbot (1043–1062). Between 1069 and 1072, he occupied the episcopal chair of Oviedo as auxiliary to Froilán, and as the holder from ca. 1075. Around 1093 or 1094, he withdrew to the monastery, where he probably died a few years later.[62]

---

56 Rico Camps, "La inscripción histórica," 37–53.

57 The episode is part of a long interpolation incorporated by the bishop tino the Chronicle of Alfonso III. Jan Prelog, *Die Chronik Alfons' III. Untersuchung und kritische Edition der vier Redaktionen* (Frankfurt-am-Main, 1980), 89–90.

58 Alonso Àlvarez, "*Patria uallata asperitate moncium*," 17–29.

59 Isidro Bango Torviso, "La renovación del tesoro sagrado a partir del concilio de Coyanza y el taller real de orfebrería de León. El Arca Santa de Oviedo (1072)," *Anales de Historia del Arte* 2 (2011): 11–67. Rose Walker, "Becoming Alfonso VI: the king, his sister and the *arca santa* reliquary," *Anales de Historia del Arte* 2 (2011): 391–412. Etelvina Fernández González, "El Arca Santa de Oviedo y sus precedentes. De Alfonso II a Alfonso VI," in *Alfonso VI y su legado*, ed. Carlos Estepa Díez, Etelvina Fernández González, Javier Rivera Blanco (León, 2012), 311–43. César García de Castro Valdés, "Datos y observaciones sobre el Arca Santa de la Cámara Santa de la catedral de Oviedo," *Nailos* 3 (July 2016): 121–63.

60 A recent analysis of the epistle in Patrick Henriet, "La lettre d'Osmundus, évêque d'Astorga, à la comtesse Ide de Boulogne (avant 1096)," *Territorio, Sociedad y Poder* 11 (2016): 63–75.

61 Henriet, "La lettre d'Osmundus," 71.

62 The origins and career of Arias in Alonso Álvarez, "El obispo Arias," 83–91.

According to the *Anales Caurienses*, it was the king who appointed Arias bishop,[63] as was habitual in the Kingdom of Leon. The Leonese monarchs followed the custom of Theodosian origin that called on them to protect the religion, and gave them the right to call councils and appoint bishops.[64] This situation still persisted in the second half of the eleventh century, as we know that the monarch intervened in the appointments of Pedro and Diego in Astorga, Miro in Palencia, Pelagius in León, and Munio in Sasamón, as well as that of Arias.[65] The bishop of Oviedo appears frequently in the royal retinue confirming the donations or privileges granted or subscribed by Alfonso VI.[66] This proximity explains why the prelate was able to summon the distinguished assembly that gathered in Oviedo in 1075.

Osmundo of Astorga is less well known. He was bishop of Astorga between 1082 and 1096, and seems to have been one of the foreign prelates in León around these years. Henriet has highlighted his close relation with Alfonso VI as, before rising to the chair, he resided in the royal household.[67] Although it is not found in any document, it is likely that he obtained the post through the monarch. Thus, both owed their careers to the king, whom they accompanied and served.

Among all the pieces corresponding to the first phase of the creation of the history of the Holy Ark, royal primacy stands out. In the *Act* of 1075, the *inventio* denied to the virtuous Poncio was granted to the prince, who also appears in this puzzling leading of the Lenten penitence.

The epigraph on the reliquary recalls the presence of Urraca and Alfonso in Oviedo and indicates the latter's role as a donor, but omits the name of the clergy present. It does not even specify the identity of the bishop who ruled the see at that time, in contrast with the *Act*, which does refer to Arias, although without presenting him as the opening's promotor.

Lastly, Osmundo requested the king's authorization before despatching the requested hair of the Virgin to the countess. Other cases similarly required the monarch's approval for *translationes*. In 1090, the relics of St. Felices were transferred to

---

63 *Corpus pelagianum* (Corpus Pelagianum). Madrid, Biblioteca Nacional de España, MS 1358, fol. 4v; Manuel Risco, *España sagrada*, vol. 34 (Madrid, 1784), 65.

64 Adeline Rucquoi, "*Cuius rex, eius religio*: Ley y religión en la España medieval," in *Las representaciones del poder en las sociedades hispánicas*, ed. Óscar Mazín (Ciudad de México, 2012), 137–50.

65 Carlos Reglero de la Fuente, "Los obispos y sus sedes en los reinos hispánicos occidentales. Mediados del siglo XI – mediados del siglo XII: tradición visigoda y reforma romana," in *La reforma gregoriana y su proyección en la Cristiandad occidental. Siglos XI-XII* (Pamplona, 2006), 222–27.

66 1073, November 10: Donation to Santa María de León: José Manuel Ruiz Asensio, ed., *Colección documental del archivo de la catedral de León*, 18 vols. (León, 1987–), 4:439–47 (document 1190). 1077, September 3: *Colección documental del archivo de la catedral de León*, 4:474–76 (document 1207). 1080, May 8: Donation to Sahagún: *Colección diplomática del monasterio de Sahagún*, ed. Marta Herrero de la Fuente et al., 7 vols. (León, 1976–), 3:68–70 (document 781). 1080, April 30. Donation to St. Servandus of Toledo: *Colección diplomática del monasterio de Sahagún*, 3:152–53 (document 848). 1093, September 2: Release: *Colección documental del archivo de la catedral de León*, 4:583–84 (document 1277).

67 Henriet, "La lettre d'Osmundus," 66.

the monastery of San Millán de la Cogolla. Abbot Blas requested royal consent to do so. Alfonso himself decided that the remains from Domingo de Silos should be installed in a more appropriate place.[68]

Alfonso VI was undoubtedly aware of the propaganda possibilities and the prestige conferred through control of the relics, and used this in a more conscious and generalized way than his predecessors.

To finish, we can extract another consequence from this first textual group: the unanimity with which it is accepted that royal involvement in the worship of the relics disappears from Oviedo sources in the twelfth century, to be replaced by other strategies. This shared characteristic, closely linking the *Act*, the epigraph, and the epistle to Osmundo, supports a date for it before Alfonso VI's death in 1109.

The Oviedo Relics as an Element of Diocesan Vindication

The central figure here is Pelagius of Oviedo (1089–1153). His life, prior to his episcopal career, is insufficiently known. Fernández Conde suggests he was of Asturian or Leonese origin, highlighting his links to the monastery of Sahagún. The *Liber Testamentorum* includes the genealogies corresponding to the lineage of the founder of Corias and Lapedo, perhaps because of some family connection. On the other hand, the donations of certain Leonese properties to the chapter of Oviedo in 1136 and his excellent topographic knowledge of the city of León might suggest he had close links to that area.[69]

Other authors have attempted to identify him with other people of the same name documented in Oviedo, like the presbyter who *notuit* an act of the monastic sources in San Pelagius in 1097, or the notary who registered various cathedral documents, the earliest in 1096.[70] The sign used by the notary of Pelagius was a cross inside a tetrobule that Sanz Fuentes believes was the nucleus of the well-known sign of the bishop, in which tetrobule is incorporated into an outstretched arm. Fernández Conde warns that the inscribed cross was used systematically by the cathedral notaries, which precludes its ascription to a specific person. So, Sanz Fuentes believes that it would be precisely Pelagius's old profession that would explain the use of this sign.[71] In fact, the sign we are

---

68 Ariel Guiance, "Entre la hagiografía y la historiografía: la *translatio* de san Felices de Bilibio," in *Legendario cristiano. Creencias y espiritualidad en el pensamiento medieval*, ed. Ariel Guiance (Buenos Aires, 2014), 243. My thanks to Dr. Guiance for drawing my attention to these episodes.

69 Francisco Javier Fernández Conde, *El Libro de los Testamentos de la Catedral de Oviedo* (Roma, 1971), 36–37. Emiliano Fernández Vallina, "El obispo Pelayo de Oviedo. Su vida y su obra," in *Liber Testamentorum Ecclesiae Ouetensis* (Barcelona, 1995), 244, judges these pro-Leonese arguments to be inconsistent, as the properties granted to the church were not necessarily from the family assets of Pelagius.

70 The former in Marcos García Martínez, "Regesta de don Pelayo, obispo de Oviedo," *Boletín del Instituto de Estudios Asturianos* 52 (1964): 214. For the latter, María Josefa Sanz Fuentes, "Estudio paleográfico" in *Liber Testamentorum*, 140–41.

71 One can follow the controversy in Fernández Conde, *El Libro de los Testamentos*, 37 (document 9). Sanz Fuentes, "Estudio paleográfico," 140–141. A range of the signs used by Bishop Pelagius in Vicente José González García, "El obispo don Pelayo, clave para el estudio de la Historia de Asturias,"

referring to is far from the exclusive use by notaries. Count Álvaro Rodríguez used it in a donation to Caaveiro.[72] As shown below, a review of the documentation precludes the identification of Pelagius with any presbyter or notary from these years.

Some clues reinforce his Asturian origins. Fernández Conde recalls that the only genealogical relationship in the *Liber Testamentorum* was that of the offspring of Munnio Ruderíquiz and Enderquina, the parents of Esloncia, the founder of Corias, together with her husband, Count Piniolo Xeméniz.[73]

Personally, I believe that an analysis of some of the passages in the *Corpus Pelagianum* reinforce his links to the count.[74] The medieval copies corresponding to the so-called *Compilación B* have been transmitted in the manuscripts 1358 and 2805 in the Biblioteca Nacional de España (hereafter "BNE"), MS 9/5496 from the Real Academia de la Historia (hereafter "RAH") and MS VLO 91 at the University of Leiden (hereafter "Leiden"). On analysing BNE MS 1358, Rodríguez Díaz proposed that this was done in the monastery of Corias, as it includes the *Anales Caurienses*.[75] In fact, the historical connection appears in all the copies in group A mentioned above, although not so extensively. To accept their execution in Corias as a reason for their inclusion, we must accept that BNE 2805, RAH 9/5497 and Leiden VLO 91 are derived from BNE 1358. This line presents a difficult hurdle to surmount: BNE 2805 and RAH 9/5497 are clearly related from an aesthetic point of view. Some iconographic archaisms indicate a common Pelagian model. This characteristic makes it impossible for them to be copies of BNE 1358,[76] suggesting at the same time the inclusion of the *Anales Caurienses* in the original project, we know not whether for reasons of kinship with the prelate or because of the church of San Salvador's interests in the monastery.[77]

The Leonese connection also sends us in that direction. Among the property gifted by Pelagius to the canons of Oviedo in 1136, the first is of particular interest, as the second was not part of his family's assets. This was located in Villademoros, very near

---

El Basilisco 8 (1979): 72–84.

72 This is a donation of suspect authenticity granted in 1117, copied around 1135, and confirmed by the count. The authenticity of the document is irrelevant for this discussion, in which the only interest is in the sign of the count. José Luis López Sangil, "Un nuevo documento de 1117 del monasterio de Caaveiro," *Cátedra. Revista eumesa de estudios* 13 (2006): 165–88, accessed April 12, 2019, www.estudioshistoricos.com/wp-content/uploads/2014/10/jlls_04.pdf. My thanks to Mr. López Sangil for his kind information on this document and the loan of the photograph.

73 Fernández Conde, *El Libro de los Testamentos*, 37 (document 9). "Commes Munnio Ruderiquiz maior et uxor eius comitissa domna Henderquina fuerunt parentes de istas quatuor comitissas: domna Esloncia, uxor comites Piniolo Xemeniz habuit filios." María José Sanz Fuentes, "Transcripción" in *Liber Testamentorum*, 577–78 (document 38).

74 Both the *Liber Testamentorum* and the *Corpus Pelagianum* are analysed in a later chapter in this same work.

75 Elena E. Rodríguez Díaz, "Producción libraria en la Asturias medieval: el ms. 1358 de la Biblioteca Nacional de Madrid," *Boletín del Real Instituto de Estudios Asturianos* 152 (1998): 21–46.

76 More details about these links in Raquel Alonso Àlvarez, "El obispo Pelayo de Oviedo (1101–1153): historiador y promotor de códices iluminados," *Semata* 22 (2010): 334–39.

77 Fernández Conde, *El Libro de los Testamentos*, 235–38, explains what type of interests these were.

the city of León.[78] As was common, the counts owned properties on both sides of the Cantabrian range, but while the Piniolo patrimony appears concentrated in Babia, Esloncia's family had land in León, as shown by the founding of a monastery in the city on the initiative of one of her brothers.[79] Bear in mind that it is precisely this line that is in the genealogical list in the *Liber Testamentorum*.

Lastly, the nature of Pelagius's links with Sahagún are difficult to specify, given that it is absolutely impossible to distinguish the future bishop of Oviedo from among the dozens of characters of the same name cited in the monastery's documentation. It is true that he appears much more frequently there than his predecessors in the chair. As bishop, he is found in Sahagún in 1103, 1104, 1105, 1106, 1110, 1116, 1117, 1118, 1121, and 1127,[80] during the reigns of Alfonso VI and Urraca, although such assiduity is not necessarily due to an education in the abbey of St. Facundus,[81] but rather simply to his closeness to the monarchs.

Pelagius's access to the see of Oviedo is equally confusing. The news of his appointment is contained in a well-known passage from the *Corpus Pelagiatum*:[82] *Pelagius ouetensis ecclesiae episcopus fuit consecratus sub era MCXXXVI, IIII Kalendas Januarii* (December 19, 1098). His predecessor, Martín, still appears as head of the see until his death on March 1, 1101.[83] Risco explains this contradiction by assigning Pelagius the role of auxiliary bishop during these years,[84] a post that, according to Reilly, did not exist in eleventh- and twelfth-century Spain.[85]

In fact, Pelagius is first documented as bishop of Oviedo in an original from 1089,[86] although Arias still headed the see at that time. The same year, the abbot of Corias

---

78 Santos A. García Larragueta, ed., *Colección de documentos de la catedral de Oviedo* (Oviedo, 1962), 384–86 (document 151). This was *Uilla de Mauris*, on the banks of the Torío, a place near *Uilla Episcopo*.

79 María Élida García García, *San Juan Bautista de Corias. Historia de un señorío monástico asturiano (siglos X–XV)* (Oviedo, 1980), 49–57.

80 *Colección diplomática del monasterio de Sahagún*, 3:440–47, 3:449–50, 3:457–59, 3:489–90, 3:499–500, 3:502–3, 3:506–9 (documents 1092, 1093, 1094, 1097, 1103, 1127, 1133, 1135, 1138 and 1139). *Colección diplomática del monasterio de Sahagún*, ed. Marta Herrero de la Fuente et al., 7 vols. (León, 1976–), 4:10–12, 4:16–24, 4:47–49, 4:51–57, 4:64–65, 4:114–15 (documents 1177, 1180, 1195, 1197, 1199, 1200, 1205 and 1233). The 1102 document published by Romualdo Escalona, *Historia del Real Monasterio de Sahagún* (Madrid, 1782), 502 (document 135), is the one in *Colección diplomática del monasterio de Sahagún*, 3:420–21 (document 1081), without Pelagius appearing. This must be an error by Escalona.

81 As supposed by Sanz Fuentes, "Estudio paleográfico," 141, and Fernández Vallina, "El obispo Pelayo," 246–49.

82 Madrid, Biblioteca Nacional de España, MS 1358, fol. 4v; Risco, *España Sagrada*, 38:99.

83 Fernández Conde, *El Libro de los Testamentos*, 37.

84 Risco, *España Sagrada*, 38:99.

85 Bernard F. Reilly, *The Kingdom of León-Castilla under King Alfonso VI, 1065–1109* (Ann Arbor, 1988), 269 (document 37).

86 León, Archivo de la Catedral. 1089, September 30: "Pelagius in sede Ouetensis"; *Colección documental del archivo de la catedral de León*, 4:531–32 (document 1245). My thanks to Dr.

appears confirming a donation by Alfonso VI to San Salvador de Peñafiel, and successively until 1093.[87] Despite Reilly's claim, it was not infrequent to find two bishops simultaneously in the same post. Between 1069 and 1075, Froilán and Arias coincided,[88] confirming the same document on one occasion.[89] We again find Pelagius in 1097, in an instrument of donation to San Salvador, while the see was headed by Bishop Martín, in presence of *domnus Pelagius episcopus et clerici canonici Ouetensi sedis.*[90] A year later, he confirmed some donations by Alfonso VI to the chapter of León.[91] Martín, for his part, continues to appear as bishop of Oviedo until shortly before his death in 1010.[92]

The figure of the auxiliary bishop appears in some passages from Gregory of Tours highlighted by Lynch.[93] One Austrapius was placed in the post to prepare the succession of the holder:

> When King Lothar returned to his kingdom, he showed great favour to the Duke [Austrapius]. During his reign, Austrapius was admitted to the priesthood, in the castle of Selle, located in the Diocese of Poitiers, where he was ordained Bishop to take the place of Bishop Pientus, ruler of the church of Poitiers, when he died.[94]

Gregoria Cavero for supplying me with a photograph of the document. An advance of the analysis of the chronology of Pelagius and the simultaneity of two bishops in the post, in Raquel Alonso Àlvarez "La obra histórica del obispo Pelayo de Oviedo (1089–1153) and his relation with the *Historia legionensis* (llamada *silensis*)," *e-Spania* 14 (December 2012), accessed December 20, 2017, http://e-spania.revues.org/21586.

87 *Colección diplomática del monasterio de Sahagún* 3:152–53 (document 848). *Colección de documentos de la catedral de Oviedo*, 269–74, 280–81, 283–86 (documents 96, 97, 98, 99, 101, 103, and 104). *Colección documental del archivo de la catedral de León*, 4:557–59, 563–65, 569–70, 583–84 (documents 1262, 1265, 1269, and 1277).

88 Froilán: *Colección de documentos de la catedral de Oviedo*, 204–5, 209–13 (documents 67, 70, 71); *Colección diplomática del monasterio de San Vicente de Oviedo*, ed. Pedro Floriano Llorente (Oviedo, 1968), 141–44 (documents 74 and 75). Arias: *Colección de documentos de la catedral de Oviedo*, 202–6, 209–11, 214–25 (documents 66, 68, 70, 72, 73, and 74); *Colección documental del archivo de la catedral de León*, 4:439–47, 450–57 (documents 1190, 1193 and 1195); *Colección diplomática del monasterio de Sahagún*, 3:6–7 (document 730); *Colección diplomática del monasterio de San Vicente de Oviedo*, 141–44 (documents 74 and 75).

89 730; *Colección diplomática del monasterio de San Vicente de Oviedo*, 141–42 (document 74): "Froylani episcopi" and "Ariani Dei gratia episcopus ouetense."

90 Arias: *Colección de documentos de la catedral de Oviedo*, 306–7 (document 114).

91 *Colección documental del archivo de la catedral de León*, 4:612–14 (document 1295).

92 *Colección diplomática del monasterio de Sahagún*, 3:403–4 (document 1060); *Colección documental del archivo de la catedral de León*, 4:626–27 (document 1304).

93 George Edward Lynch, *Coadjutors and Auxiliaries of Bishops. A Historical Synopsis and a Commentary* (Washington, DC, 1947), 7.

94 *Redeunte autem in regnum suum rege Chlotario magnus cum eo est habitus. Tempore vero eius ad clericatum accedens, apud Sellensis castrum, quod in Pectava habitur diocisi episcopus ordenatur; futurum, ut, decedente Pientio antestite, qui tum Pectava regebat ecclesiam, ipse succederet.* Cited from *Gregorii episcopi turonensis historiarum libri X*, ed. Bruno Krusch, MGH SS rer. Merov. 1/1, fasc. 1 (1937), 151 (IV, 18).

The existence of this type of dignity is also confirmed in Visigothic Spain. Isidore of Seville included the *corepiscopus* on the roster in his *De ecclesiasticis officiis* as an assistant to the bishop.[95] In the *Vitas sanctorum patrum emeritensium*, as in Gregory of Tours, the post of auxiliary is preparation for the succession. Thus, Fidel would replace his uncle Paulo through this procedure.[96]

There are many examples of this overlapping in the Kingdom of Leon during the eleventh century. In Astorga, Sampiro and Pedro Gundúlfiz coincided in 1041, and Diego and Ordoño in 1060 and 1061. We find Ordoño in 1066 together with his successor, Pedro Núñez. Gudesteus, and his nephew Cresconius occupied the see of Iria-Compostela in 1068, Cipriano and Alvito that of León between 1047 and 1057, and in Palencia, Bernardo and Miro in 1043 and the subsequent two years.[97]

The figure of the *corepiscopus* would be regulated by the Decretals of Gregory IX (1234) and become reserved for cases of infirmity of the holder.[98] From Boniface VIII (ca. 1235–1303), such appointments were reserved for *causae maiores*, and could only be done by the Holy See. The coadjutors were no longer considered prelates and lost the post on the death of the bishop they assisted.[99] Before these restrictions, the auxiliary helped the holder and, frequently, succeeded him on his death.[100]

Remember that the first appearance of Pelagius as bishop of Oviedo in the documents occurs in a see still occupied by Arias, who was intimately related to the county house that founded Corias. The family had supplied some other bishops to the see: two forebears of Piniolo on his mother's side, Oveco and Bermudo, had also sat on the Asturian cathedral chair.[101] If, as we suppose, Pelagius was also from this aristocratic circle,

---

95 "The chorbishops, that is, the vicars of the bishops, according to what the canons teach, were established after the example of the seventy old men, in the likeness of priests, in order to provide for the poor. These, appointed for the villages and rural areas, run the churches committed to them, and they are allowed to appoint lectors, subdeacons, exorcists, and acolytes, but they must not dare to ordain presbyters or deacons, except with the permission of the bishops of the area. And they are ordained only by the bishops of the nearest town" (*De corepiscopis. Corepiscopi, id est, uicarii episcoporum, iuxta quod canones ipsi testantur, instituti sunt ad exemplum septuaginta seniorum tamquam consacerdotes propter sollicitudinem pauperum. Hii in uicis et uillis constituti gubernant sibi commisas ecclesias, habentes licentiam constituere lectores, subdiaconos, exorcistas. Presbiteros autem aut diaconos ordinare non audent praeter conscientiam episcopi in cuius regione praese noscuntur. Hii autem a solo episcopi ciuitatis cuius adiacent ordinantur*). Cited from Sancti Isidori episcopi hispalensis. *De ecclesiasticis oficiis*, Corpus Christianorum Series Latina 113, ed. Christopher M. Lawson (Turnhout, 1989), 46.

96 *Vitas sanctorum patrum emeritensium*, 25–41 (IV, I–VIII).

97 These are documented by Pablo Dorronzoro Ramírez, *Poder e identidad de los obispos del Reino de León en el siglo XI. Una aproximación biográfica (1037–1080)* (Madrid, 2012), 24, 52–53, 56, 112–19, 192, and 379. The author did not notice the existence of this figure, and attributed the coincidences to errors in dating.

98 "De clerigo aegrotante vel debilitato." *Decretales D. Gregorii papae IX, suæ integritate una cum glossis restitutæ* (Lyon, 1634), III. VI, col. 1026–27.

99 Lynch, *Coadjutors and auxiliaries*, 18, 22–25.

100 Lynch, *Coadjutors and auxiliaries*, 7, 12–25.

101 Alfonso Sánchez Candeira, "El obispado de Oviedo entre 976 y 1035," in *Estudios dedicados*

one can imagine that it was Arias himself who called him to his side. Perhaps he was too young to succeed his mentor after his retirement, being obliged to wait another turn before acceding to the chair. In any case, what interests us especially about these circumstances is that it can be assured that Pelagius was aware, from an early age, of the propaganda operations taking place in Oviedo as a result of an alliance between Alfonso VI and Arias that, some years later, would not be so convenient for the Oviedo bishops.

The early years of his pontificate were marked by his closeness to the kings, first to Alfonso VI and later to his daughter and heiress, Urraca.[102] His relations were less cordial with Alfonso VII, who promoted his deposition in the Council of Carrión (1130), in obscure circumstances and, it seems, instigated by Diego Gelmírez. This decision has been attributed to the prelate's opposition to the consanguineous marriage between the monarch and Queen Berenguela, perhaps as a pretext for the real motive: the support given by Pelagius to the rebel Asturian aristocrats.[103] Reilly blames this on the king's fear of a group of independent bishops difficult to control.[104] Whatever the reason, Pelagius was forced to step down, briefly recovering the post between 1142 and 1143, in unknown circumstances. He died in 1153.[105]

Pelagius of Oviedo created an extensive body of work that has reached us in the *Liber Testamentorum Ecclesiae Ouetensis* and the *Corpus Pelagianum*.

The *Liber Testamentorum* is a spectacular cartulary, catalogued number 1 in the Archive of Oviedo Cathedral. Written in Visigothic calligraphy, by then already archaic, it contains a series of donations and privileges conceded by kings, aristocrats, and popes to the cathedral of Oviedo. As Fernández Conde shows in his detailed study, a good part of them are false or interpolated.[106] To these, a series of historical, legendary, and epigraphic passages is added, among which the reworked history of the arrival of the Holy Ark in Asturias stands out.[107] The date of its writing is disputed. Rodríguez Díaz sup-

---

a Menéndez Pidal, 7 vols. in 8 (Madrid, 1950–1962), 3:609. Francisco Javier Fernández Conde, *La iglesia de Asturias en la Alta Edad Media* (Oviedo, 1972), 57. García García, *San Juan Bautista de Corias*, 37–39.

102 Fernández Conde, *El Libro de los Testamentos*, 45–49; Francisco Javier Fernández Conde, "El obispo don Pelayo. Reorganización eclesiástica y señorial en la diócesis de Oviedo/Uviéu," in *Orígenes: Arte y Cultura en Asturias. Siglos VII-XV* (Barcelona, 1993), 348.

103 Fernández Conde, *El Libro de los Testamentos*, 37; Fernández Conde, "El obispo don Pelayo," 352–53.

104 Bernard F. Reilly, "On getting to be a bishop in León-Castile: the 'emperor' Alfonso VI and the post-Gregorian church," *Studies in Medieval and Renaissance History* 1 (1978): 48–53.

105 Fernández Conde, *El Libro de los Testamentos*, 41–44.

106 Fernández Conde, *El Libro de los Testamentos*. He vigorously defends the authenticity of the Pelagian Fernández Vallina, "El obispo Pelayo," 233–401.

107 Sanz Fuentes, "Transcripción," 456–61 (document 4). For a general analysis of these passages, Alonso Álvarez, "El obispo Pelayo de Oviedo," 331–50; Raquel Alonso Álvarez, "El 'Corpus Pelagianum' y el 'Liber Testamentorum Ecclesiae Ouetensis': las "reliquias del pasado" de la catedral de Oviedo y su uso propagandístico en la obra del obispo Pelayo de Oviedo (1101-1153), in *Texte et contexte. Littérature et historie de l'Europe médiévale*, ed. Marie-Françoise Alamichel, Robert Braid (Paris, 2010), 519–48; Raquel Alonso Álvarez, "El rey Alfonso VI (m. 1109) en la obra del obispo

poses that its initial nucleus was composed ca. 1109, with other booklets being added later.[108] The date most generally accepted covers a range between 1118 and 1130.[109]

The original codices of the *Corpus Pelagianum* have not survived, but there is a set of copies, a good number of which are medieval, arranged and classified by Jerez.[110] Three collections would have been done in the cathedral *scriptorium* of Oviedo commissioned by Bishop Pelagius.

The first, contained in the so-called *Codex uetustissimus ouetensis*, is known through the copy commissioned by Ambrosio de Morales, in BNE 1346.[111] This would be a first compilation, collecting somewhat reworked earlier material.[112]

The historical interests of the *Corpus Pelagianum* appear better defined in the "Compilación A." Its contents have been transmitted through BNE 1358, BNE 2805, RAH 9/5496, and Leiden VLO91.

The most mature stage of the *Corpus Pelagianum*, the "Compilación B," corresponds to the contents of the BNE MS 1513, the well-known Batres Codex.

The chronology of this complex *corpus* is difficult to establish, although it is usually dated around 1132, with Pelagius recently deposed from the Oviedo chair, as Fernández Conde proposes.[113] According to Jerez, the process of compilation would have begun ca. 1120–1130, although the "Compilación B" would not have been done until after the death of its promotor.[114] I believe this to be extremely difficult to prove, especially because it is complicated to explain BNE 1513 without the composition of the *Liber Testamentorum*, with which it is closely connected. The date defended by Fernández Conde seems acceptable.

The numerous versions of the *Corpus Pelagianum* hinder drawing up a complete and coherent list of its contents. For our interests, the historical contents of the A and B compilations are particularly relevant. In BNE 1513, we find the *Liber cronicorum*, a collection of old chronicles interpolated by Pelagius that closes with the prelate's own

Pelayo de Oviedo (m. 1153)," in *Imágenes de poder en la Edad Media. Estudios* in memoriam *del Prof. Dr. Fernando Galván Freile*, ed. Etelvina Fernández González (León, 2011), 2:13–32; Raquel Alonso Álvarez, "Les évêques d'Oviedo (XIᵉ-XIIᵉ siècles) et la réutilization de la tradition dans de nouveaux contextes historiques et liturgiques: textes et objets," *Revue d'Auvergne* 614 (2015): 225–39.

108 Elena E. Rodríguez Díaz, "Estudio codicológico," in *Liber Testamentorum*, 36; Sanz Fuentes, "Estudio paleográfico," 132–43.

109 Fernández Conde, *El Libro de los Testamentos*, 87–88; Francisco Javier Fernández Conde, "229. Libro de los Testamentos," in *Orígenes*, 355; John Williams dates it ca. 1118, "Liber Testamentorum," in *The Art of Medieval Spain*, 295–97.

110 Enrique Jerez, "Arte compilatoria pelagiana. La formación del *Liber cronicorum*," in *Poétique de la chronique. L'écriture des textes historiographiques au Moyen Âge (péninsule Ibérique et France)*, ed. Amaia Arizaleta (Toulouse, 2008), 47–87.

111 For its characteristics, see *Inventario General de manuscritos de la Biblioteca nacional, IV (1101 a 1598)* (Madrid, 1958), 198–205.

112 Diego Catalán, "Desenredando la maraña textual pelagiana (I)," *Revista de Filoloxía Asturiana* 3-4 (2003–2004): 61–87.

113 Francisco Javier Fernández Conde, "230. Corpus pelagianum," in *Orígenes*, 357–58.

114 Jerez, "Arte compilatoria pelagiana," 69–78, 86.

composition, the *Chronicon regum legionensium*. To understand the historical conception of the work, it is necessary to handle both the *Liber Testamentorum* and the *Corpus Pelagianum*, which present a notable coherence and complementarity. The congruence that links the two indicates a unitary and planned conception, one that places in doubt Jerez's chronological proposal for BNE 1513.

Old and New Relics

New versions of the history of the Holy Ark appear in both the *Liber Testamentorum* and the *Corpus Pelagianum*. These coincide along general lines but are complementary in other respects.

The list of relics mentioned by Pelagius repeats those catalogued from approximately the eleventh century.[115] However, some significant novelties appear. Some accounts seek to update earlier remains, but most insist on linking the sacred collection with the Asturian kings. Almost all pursue a re-contextualization that guarantees their validity in subsequent epochs and circumstances. The collections of documents in the cartularies, as in this case, supported and completed with historical texts, frequently played an important role in building the European institutional memory.[116] The Hispanic territory was no exception, as Rucquoi has demonstrated for Santiago and Oviedo.[117] As Fernández Conde has shown, in Oviedo they were put into the service of the independence of the see and the development of worship of the relics.[118]

The old and valuable objects, Geary's "relics of the past,"[119] were used as material proof of these memorial creations, as with the material and texts in the abbey of Saint-Denis brilliantly studied by Theis.[120] These strategies were also widely used in Oviedo, as we shall see below.[121]

Pelagius had the material previously prepared by Arias under the auspices of Alfonso VI; at least, a story of *inventio* which indicates the Toledan origins of the ark and a splendid reliquary. A more complex and novel-like narrative would be composed

---

115 A comparison of the different lists in Fernández Conde, Alonso Álvarez, "Los catálogos de las reliquias."

116 Jean-Phillipe Genet, "Cartulaires, registres et histoire: l'exemple anglais," in *Le métier d'historien au Moyen Âge. Études sur l'historiographie médiévale*, ed. Bernard Guenée (Paris, 1977), 95–129; Patrick Geary, "Entre gestion et gesta," in *Les cartulaires. Actes de la Table ronde organisée par l'École nationale des chartes et le G.D.R. 121 du C.N.R.S. (Paris, 5–7 décembre 1991)*, ed. Olivier Guyotjeannin, Michel Parisse, Laurent Morelle (Paris, 1993), 13–26; Patrick Geary, *Phantoms of Remembrance. Memory and Oblivion in the End of the First Millenium* (Princeton, 1994).

117 Adeline Rucquoi, "La invención de una memoria: los cabildos peninsulares del siglo XII," *Temas Medievales* 2 (1992): 67–80.

118 Fernández Conde, *El Libro de los Testamentos*; Fernández Conde, "El obispo don Pelayo," 347–53.

119 Geary, *Phantoms*, 7–8, 128.

120 Laurent Theis, "Dagobert, Saint-Denis et la royauté française au Moyen Âge," in *Le métier d'historien au Moyen Âge*, 19–30.

121 Alonso Álvarez, "El *Corpus Pelagianum* y el *Liber Testamentorum Ecclesiae Ouetensis*," 519–48.

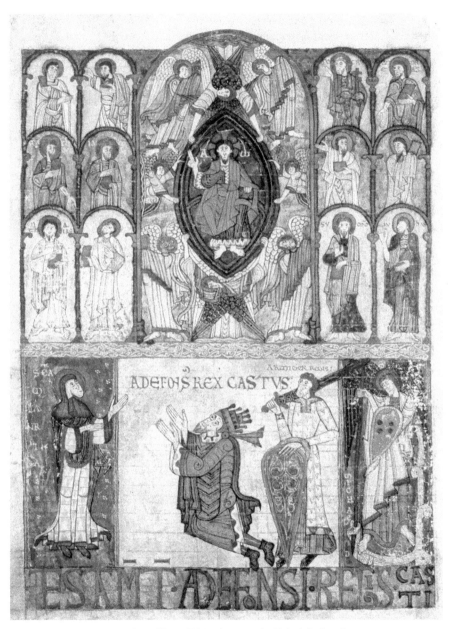

Figure 8.7: Alfonso II Worshipping the Holy Ark. Oviedo,
Archivo de la Catedral, MS 1 *(Liber Testamentorum Ecclesiae Ouetensis)*.
(© Catedral de Oviedo, photo: Lorenzo Arias Páramo).

on this basis. The *Liber Testamentorum* details the first episodes of the journey:[122] a group of disciples of the Apostles would have collected a series of relics in a chest. It is worth noting that the Jerusalemite origins were suggested to Pelagius by the epistle of Osmundo, or another similar story. Fleeing before different threats and wars, the ark was taken first to the north of Africa, and from there, to Toledo. The Muslim invasion forced its later transport to Asturias, to the safety of the impregnable mountains. The story continues in the *Corpus Pelagianum*, as a long interpolation incorporated into the *Adefonsii Tertii Chronica* in its *Ad Sebastianum* version.[123] The Holy Ark reached Asturian territory coinciding with the rebellion of Prince Pelagius against the Muslims, and immediately became the protector of the insurgents. In this way, the relics, the beginning of the Reconquest, and the origins of the Asturian monarchy became closely linked. Alfonso VI, omnipresent in the earlier sources, gives way to characters from remote times more appropriate for the creation of legendary tales. Despite his excellent relations with Bishop Pelagius, the prelate only associates the king with the Holy Ark incidentally, when reporting the finding and relocation of the relics of St. Eulalia.

The following events were registered in a similar way in the *Liber Testamentorum* and the *Corpus Pelagianum*:[124] now in Asturias, the reliquary spent many years *in tabernaculis*, as did the Ark of the Alliance, prior to the building of the church of San Miguel (the modern Cámara Santa) that, like a new Solomon, Alfonso II "the Chaste" took care to erect. It seems this building was initially the *thesaurus* of the church of San Salvador.[125] Pelagius gives it new significance by attributing its construction to the Chaste King with functions as a reliquary.[126] Not by chance, in fol. IVv. of the first booklet (out of foliation) in the *Liber Testamentorum*, Alfonso II worships the depiction of the Holy Ark in the upper section, without caring that the object before him was, in fact, gifted by Alfonso VI centuries later

Following the directives established by the Pelagian version of the installation of the Holy Ark in Oviedo, the information and objects related to Alfonso II take on particular importance. Pelagius made the monarch the protagonist of a new *translatio*. In the twelfth century, the remains of St. Eulalia of Mérida also appeared on the scene. According to the above-mentioned interpolations by Pelagius in the Chronicle of Alfonso III, the relics of the Mérida martyr, extracted from her sepulchre and placed in a little silver box, were taken to Pravia by King Silo (d. 783).[127] Again, Alfonso II took charge of transporting the reliquary to the church of San Salvador, and had it hung from an iron chain "on the ark in which many and various relics of the saints are hidden" (*super archam,*

---

122 Sanz Fuentes, "Transcripción," 456–61 (document 4).

123 According to Madrid, Biblioteca Nacional de España, MS 1513; Prelog, *Die Chronik Alfons' III*, 70–108. The version without interpolating the chronicle in *Crónicas asturianas*, 114–49.

124 Sanz Fuentes, "Transcripción," 456–61 (document 4); Prelog, *Die Chronik Alfons' III*, 92–98.

125 Cristina Godoy, *Arqueología y liturgia. Iglesias hispánicas (siglos IV al VIII)* (Barcelona, 1995), 101; Eduardo Carrero Santamaría, *El conjunto catedralicio de Oviedo durante la Edad Media* (Oviedo, 2003), 43–77.

126 Alonso Álvarez, "El *Corpus Pelagianum* y el *Liber Testamentorum Ecclesiae Ouetensis*," 532.

127 Prelog, *Die Chronik Alfons' III*, 89–90.

in qua diversa et multa sanctorum pignora sunt recondita). On St. Eulalia's feast day, the relics were displayed in the choir for public worship. Over the years, the memory of the contents of the box was lost, until 1102, when Pelagius opened it and found a document inside identifying of the remains of the martyr. After celebrating the finding with a solemn procession, he placed the box "inside a larger silver casket, which had been donated by the lord King Alfonso, son of King Fernando and Queen Sancha, and he placed it in the treasury" (*in alliam capsam maiorem argenteam, que ibi dederat rex dominus Adefonsus, filius Fredenandi regis et Sancie regine, et posuit eam in thesauro iam dicto*): the Holy Ark donated by Alfonso VI, undoubtedly. To celebrate its worship with appropriate pomp, he had the necessary liturgical texts brought from Narbonne province.

I believe that this substantial passage from the *Corpus Pelagianum*, conceived as a shortened version of the great ceremony of 1075, has been given less attention than it deserves. In this case, the monarchs, generally from remote epochs, were given a notable role in the finding or dignification of the relics, but the bishop took over this role in the *inventio* that was denied to Ponce de Tabérnoles in favour of Alfonso VI in 1075. Not by chance, the chest of St. Eulalia was rediscovered precisely a year after the death of Martín, with Pelagius, by then installed at the head of the see, leading the *inventio*, worship, and liturgy of this new devotion without any lay or ecclesiastical rivalry.

The tomb of Alfonso II would also then be subject to renewed attention. The Asturian Chronicles describe how to one side of the church of San Salvador, there was Santa María's tomb, promoted by the Chaste King; the royal pantheon was placed in the west end.[128] Starting with this historical information, Pelagius incorporates into the story of the Holy Ark a succinct but exciting description of the tomb of the founder, probably decorated with a cross.[129] The so-called manuscript of Valenciennes was likely a Pelagian production.[130] In a free sheet in a ninth-century Apocalypse, another version of the story of the Holy Ark was copied, similar to the one in the *Liber Testamentorum*. In the Valenciennes one, another step was taken to incorporate a set of relics *extra arcam* the *corpus Regis Casti, qui ecclesiam Sancti Salvatoris fundavit*.[131]

The *crux gemmata* donated by Alfonso II in 808 also underwent a process of relicization around this time.[132] We do not know its original function, although both its typology and the holes in its arms indicate it was used as a *staurotheca*. The hole in the base, for use in processions, is later than the original work. It is missing the upper rings that allow it to be hung above the altar, as was customary. Noting these characteristics, Schlunk proposed that the cross would have been held aloft in the solemn ceremonies,

---

128 Version *Ad Sebastianum*: "ad recondenda regum adstruxit corpora." From *Crónicas asturianas*, 139.

129 A discussion about this problem in Alonso Álvarez, *"Patria uallata asperitate moncium,"* 26.

130 The reasons for this dependence are explained in Fernández Conde, Alonso Álvarez, "Los catálogos de las reliquias." The passage has been published various times. There is an available edition in Fernández Conde, *La iglesia de Asturias*, 160–62.

131 Alonso Álvarez, "Patria uallata asperitate moncium," 27.

132 Gloria Fernández Somoza, *La Cruz de los Ángeles de la Catedral de Oviedo* (Oviedo, 2004), 47–48. Raquel Alonso Álvarez, "The cruces gemmatae of Oviedo between the eleventh and twelfth centuries," *Journal of Medieval Iberian Studies* 9, no. 1 (2017): 52–71.

as in the depiction in the famous mosaic of San Vitale in Ravenna, in which Bishop Maximian holds a bejewelled cross in the same way.[133]

In the twelfth century, it was said to have been made by angels, hence the origin of its name of "Cruz de los Ángeles," the name it retains today. The legend first appeared in the *Historia Silense*:[134] Alfonso II had precious metals and gems that he decided to use for a cross for the high altar of the church of San Salvador. In very timely fashion, two angels appeared in the court in the guise of pilgrims, requesting to take over the job. When the monarch returned to the room designated for the work, the craftsmen had disappeared, leaving a dazzling cross that he placed above the altar of San Salvador.

Although less extensively, the angelic attribution of the ornament also appears in the Pelagian production, in both the *Liber Testamentorum* and the *Corpus Pelagianum*, with this description: "there is displayed a cross of angelic work, marvellously made," in terms approximate to the "cross made by angelic work" of the *extra arcam* in the Valenciennes work.[135] Although the Silense author remains anonymous, he is believed to have been Leonese, his work showing such detailed knowledge of the Asturian territory that it would have required direct experience, which suggests Oviedo as the origin of the angels story.[136]

In any case, the importance of the legend continued to grow in the city over the following years.[137] It is difficult to accept that the cross, as the Silense indicates, was destined by its promotor to remain hanging over the altar of San Salvador, as it seems that this typology does not date from prior to the late-Carolingian epoch, coinciding with the growth of the worship of the cross in Easter Week.[138] What is interesting about the above description, probably in its initial home, is that the author of the *Historia Silense* was presumably seeing it at a moment in which its new condition of *acheiropoieton* was about to lead to its transfer to the chapel of the relics, the old treasure – as the story contained in MS 804 in Cambrai Library from between the twelfth and thirteenth centuries, seems to indicate.[139] The first part of the manuscript recovers, with variants, the history

---

133 Helmut Schlunk, *Las cruces de Oviedo. El culto de la Vera Cruz en el Reino Asturiano* (Oviedo, 1985), 12–24.

134 *Historia Silense*, 139–40.

135 *Crux ibi monstratur opere angelico fabricata spectabile modo; Crux opere angelico fabricata.* Cited from Sanz Fuentes, "Transcripción," 461 (document 4) (*Liber Testamentorum*). Prelog, *Die Chronik Alfons' III*, 98 (Corpus Pelagianum). Fernández Conde, *La iglesia de Asturias*, 162 (Valenciennes).

136 Alonso Álvarez "La obra histórica del obispo Pelayo de Oviedo." In *e-Spania* 14 (2012), which contains this article, one can find other works that update knowledge about this chronicle (Cavero Domínguez, Escalona, Escobar, Estévez Sola, Henriet, Isla Frez, Jardin, Le Morvan, Luis Corral, Martin, Montaner Frutos, Reglero de la Fuente, Rochwert-Zuili, Sirantoine, and Thielin-Pardo).

137 A detailed analysis of the origin and evolution of the legend of the Cross of the Angels, as well as the evolution of its use, in Alonso Álvarez, "The cruces gemmatae of Oviedo," 56–67.

138 Celia M. Chazelle, "The Cross, the Image, and the Passion in Carolingian Thought and Art" (PhD diss. Yale University, 1985), 342. For the problem in general and in the case of the Cross of the Angels, Alonso Álvarez, "The cruces gemmatae of Oviedo," 62–64.

139 Published as Charles Kohler, "Translation de reliques de Jérusalem à Oviedo," *Revue de l'Orient latin* 5 (1897): 6–21; Fernández Conde, *La Iglesia de Asturias*, 162–78. A recent revision in Adeline

of the Holy Ark and the marvellous story of the Cross of the Angels. The second part narrates the story of the demoniac Oria, taken to Oviedo to be exorcized. One of the objects
used in the ceremony was the Cross of the Angels, taken to the church by the archdeacon
qui thesaurum custodiebat. Once there, it soon became the most important object in the
chapel's treasury, which ended up taking its name: Chapel of the Angels, as indicated in
the founding act of the Brotherhood of the Holy Chamber (1344):

> And in the times that the land was lost to the Moors, archbishops and bishops, those that
> were in Spain, fled to Asturias and brought this Ark with many relics and with holy bod-
> ies, as many as there could be and put them on a mountain much higher that they called
> Montesagro. And when the king, lord Alfonso, who they called the Chaste King, made the
> church of San Salvador in Oviedo, he brought from that mountain very honourably and
> placed it in a chamber that they call chapel of the angels.[140]

In 1385, the cross was stored in a silver box, undoubtedly a reliquary.[141] The concession
of the Jubilee of the Holy Cross, granted by Eugene IV to the cathedral of Oviedo in 1438,
was motivated by its possession of the marvellous Cross of the Angels.[142]

The last case analysed here is not linked to any Asturian monarch but is an example of
the zeal with which Pelagius defended the value and quality of the relics owned by his see.

The oldest inventories contain remains of the blood of Christ, simply mentioned as
de cruore Domini, in the Act of 1075, or *cruore santisimo* in the epigraph of the Holy Ark.[143]
In both cases, it forms part of a Christological collection that also includes a fragment of
the cross, another of the bread from the Last Supper, remains of the sepulchre, and some
similar items. In the Pelagian texts, the original formula disappears in favour of a new
version in which the blood is from the miraculous Christ of Beirut.[144] A simple comparison shows the close relations established between the versions in the *Liber Testamentorum*, the *Corpus Pelagianum,* and Valenciennes:[145]

Rucquoi, "El manuscrito de Cambrai 804: Las reliquias de Oviedo y sus milagros," *Territorio,
Sociedad y Poder* 11(2016): 77–88.

140 *Et en el tiempo que se perdió la tierra con moros, arçobispos e obispos, quantos avía en Espanna,
venieron fugiendo para Asturias e trogieron esta archa con muchas relicas e con cuerpos santos,
quantos podieron aver e alçáronla en hun monte mucho más alto que llaman Montesagro. Et quando
el buen rey don Alfonso, que llaman Rey Casto, fizo la eglesia de San Salvador de Oviedo, trógola de
aquel monte mucho onradamientre e púsola en una cámara que llaman capiella de los ángeles.* Cited
from Soledad Suárez Beltrán, "La Cofradía de la Cámara Santa de Oviedo," *Asturiensia Medievalia* 7
(1993–1994): 171.

141 Fernández Somoza, *La Cruz de los Ángeles*, 140.

142 Enrique López Fernández, *Las Reliquias de San Salvador de Oviedo* (Granada, 2004), 202.

143 Fernández Conde, Alonso Álvarez, "Los catálogos de las reliquias"; Rico Camps, "La inscripción
histórica."

144 A detailed development of this problem in Raquel Alonso Álvarez, "*De cruore Domini*: La
reliquia de la Santa Sangre en la catedral de Oviedo y el Milagro del Cristo de Beirut," in *Medieval
Studies in Honour of Peter Linehan*, ed. Francisco Hernández, Rocío Sánchez Ameijeiras, Emma
Falque (Firenze, 2018), 49–65.

145 The list of the respective relics, in Sanz Fuentes, "Transcripción," 456–61 (document 4);
Prelog, *Die Chronik Alfons' III*, 96–98; Fernández Conde, *La iglesia de Asturias*, 160–62.

Liber Testamentorum

An ampoule of crystal with some blood that poured forth from the Lord, from the side of that image that the treachery of some Jews, carving a waxen image of Christ really crucified, pierced one side from which came out blood and water. So the treachery of the Jews and the faith of the holy church was clear.

Cristallinam ampullam cum de cruore Domini, fuso uidelicet a latare illius imaginis quam quorundam perfidia iudeorum ad pressionem ueritatis Crucifixi Christi cercam affigens ceree cruci, perforauit in latere de quo exiuit sanguis et aqua, ad ipsorum iudeorum perfidiam conuinciendam, et sancte ecclesie fidem roborandam.

Corpus Pelagianum

An ampoule of crystal with some blood that poured forth from the Lord, from the side of that image that a Christian carried with him to the city of Beirut and the perfidy of the Jews, crucifying a true wood effigy in wood, drilled on one side, which came forth blood and water. So it was clear the treachery of the Jews and the faith of the holy church.

Cristallinam ampullam cum de cruore Domini fuso, uidelicet a latere illius imaginis, quam quidam christicola in Beritum urbem secum adduxit, quam quorundam perfidia iudeorum ad depressionem ueritatis Crucifixi Christi ligneam affigens lignee cruci perforauit in latere, de quo exiuit sanguis et aqua ad ipsorum iudeorum perfidiam conuinciendam, et sancte ecclesie fidem roborandam.

Valenciennes

An ampoule of crystal with some blood that poured forth from the side which the faithful made in the likeness of Christ and which treacherous Jews, presevering in their ancient treachery, affixed to wood, the side of which they pierced with a lance as if it had been that of the true living Christ. From this image came forth blood and water to add to the faithful recreation of the Passion of Christ.

Cristallinam ampullam cum cruore fuso de latere illius imaginis quam quidam fideles as similitudinem Christi fecerunt, quam perfidi iudii antiqua perfida obcecati ligno affixerunt et lancea ut veri vivi Christi latus percuserunt, ex qua ad fidem passionis Christi astruendam exivit sanguis et aqua.

The miracle of Christ in Beirut first appears in a Roman florilegium written in Greek in the last quarter of the eighth century, but which spread after its inclusion in the proceedings of the Second Council of Nicaea.[146] On abandoning his home, a Christian in Beirut left an icon of the crucified Christ, to which the new inhabitant, a Jew, paid no attention. When another Jew saw it, he denounced him for having it. The Jews attacked the image, thrusting a spear into its side, from which blood and water flowed. The miracle caused the mass conversion of the Jews in the city, who converted their synagogue into a church dedicated to the Saviour. The conciliar text was translated into Latin in 873, thus favouring its spread through the West.[147]

---

146 Jean-Marie Sansterre, "L'image blessée, l'image souffrante: quelques récits de miracles entre Orient et Occident (VIᵉ-XIIᵉ siècles)," *Bulletin de l'Institut Historique belge de Rome* 69 (1999): 117; Michele Bacci, "The Berardenga antependium and the Passio Imaginis Oifice," *Journal of the Warburg and Courtauld Institute* 61 (1998): 4. For the explanation in the Second Council of Nicaea see: *Sacrorum conciliorum nova amplissima collectio*, ed. Joannes Dominicus Mansi (Firenze-Venezia, 1798), col. 23–31.

147 Sansterre, "L'image blessée," 117.

In the eleventh century, a version was written attributing Christ to Nicodemus, and specifying the way the blood and water from its side had to be collected and distributed around the three continents:

> Finally, he ordered that crystal ampoules be made, and in each of them were introduced the blood and water that came forth from the effigy of our Lord Saviour. The ampoules were sent by his emissaries to Asia, Africa, and Europe.[148]

The detail of the crystalline ampoules, not appearing in the Second Council of Nicaea, guarantees that it was the eleventh-century version known in Oviedo in the twelfth. The mention is really early, contemporary to the first known one in Italy, and very much earlier than those registered in France or England, which did not appear until the thirteenth century.[149]

Ideological motives can be discerned behind this transformation of the blood of Christ into what emanated from the wound on the image of Beirut. From the eleventh century on, there were a series of eucharistic controversies that finally led to the formulation of the doctrine of transubstantiation in the Fourth Lateran Council (1215–1216). One of the issues under discussion was whether, on resuscitating, Christ had recovered all the blood shed in the Passion, a proposal that triumphed and that automatically made any relic of the blood of Christ fake, except those from transubstantiation or wounds inflicted on miraculous images.[150] Converting the *de cruore Domini* into the blood of Beirut stopped any doubts from overshadowing the relic of the Holy Ark in Oviedo, a good example of the energy with which Bishop Pelagius defended the authenticity, validity, and utility of the collection.

Conclusions

The worship of relics in Oviedo originated and was consolidated in two well-defined phases. The first corresponds to the end of the eleventh century and is characterized by Alfonso VI's leading role in their *inventio* and dignification. Directing the opening of the ark and the penitential action that preceded it, he himself donated the luxurious container we know as the Holy Ark. The texts corresponding to this phase aggrandize the figure of the monarch, with the bishops and clergy in the see of Oviedo overshadowed by, or subordinate to him. This exaltation must undoubtedly have enjoyed the consent of Bishop Arias, raised to the episcopal seat by the king and a member of his innermost cir-

---

148 *Denique ampullas praecepit fieri vitreas in quibus portiones misit singulas de sanguine et aqua, quae de imagine Domini Salvatoris nostri decurrerant, quas etiam per Asiam, Africam, Europam, per suos nuntios dirigens.* Cited from Sansterre, "L'image blessée," 117; The text in Athanasii, "De Pass. Imaginis D. N. Jesu Christi," in *Patrologia Graeca*, ed. Jacques-Paul Migne (Paris, 1857), vol. 28, col. 816.

149 Michele Bacci, "Quel bello miacolo onde si fa la festa del santo Salvatore: studio sulle metamorfosi di una leggenda," in *Croce e Santo Volto. Contributi allo studio dell'origine e della fortuna del culto del Salvatore (secoli IX-XIV)*, ed. Gabriella Rossetti (Pisa, 2002), 21; Michele Bacci, "Ad ipsius Christi effigiem. Il Volto Santo come ritratto autentico del Salvatore," in *La Santa Croce di Lucca. Il Volto Santo. Storia, Tradizione, Immagini* (Firenze, 2003), 122.

150 Sansterre, "L'image blessée," 120.

cle. Whilst favouring the link between the king and the relics, and the prestige conferred by these, the prelate also benefited from a ceremony that procured the possession of a valuable reliquary for his see, which, from then on, became the destination of a flow of pilgrims of a certain importance.

Pelagius's rule used this substrate, transforming its meaning, for an ardent defence of the independence and prestige of the see. He was the author of an important set of writings, the *Liber Testamentorum* and the *Corpus Pelagianum*, in which the previously omnipresent figure of Alfonso VI practically disappears. In his place, a new royal personage, Alfonso II, is defined, one more appropriate as a centre for legendary traditions and less threatening to episcopal prestige.

Alfonso II is the real protagonist of the Pelagian production: presented as the builder of the church destined to hold the Holy Ark, as a new Solomon, he took charge of the transfer of the remains of St. Eulalia, initially from Silo to Pravia, then to the church of San Miguel in Oviedo. Lastly, his tomb is described as forming part of a set of relics *extra arcam*.

Thus, Pelagius reactivated worship of relics in Oviedo, definitively united in the figure of the Chaste King. The value he gave to the holy remains is manifested in the operation that converted the blood of Christ into the blood that emanated from the wound in the Christ of Beirut. In an environment of passionate theological disputes, this manoeuvre avoided any doubt being cast on the authenticity of the relic.

As in the rest of Europe, the relics of Oviedo conferred prestige on their owners, donors, *inventores*, and *translatores*. However, while at the end of the eleventh century, Alfonso VI was the main beneficiary of the recognition procured by the collection, from the twelfth century, the bishops, with Pelagius at their head, managed to use them for the greater glory, independence, and benefit of Oviedo Cathedral.

Chapter 9

CHIVALRIC IDEOLOGY IN THE LATE TWELFTH-CENTURY *CHANSON D'ASPREMONT*

DOMINIQUE BARTHÉLEMY

THE *CHANSON DE ROLAND*, although contemporary with the development of chivalry,[1] shows the value system of a highly aristocratic society of revenge, preserved in holy war. It exudes disdain for serfs, used as a foil for the "baron (ber)" and the "vassal," and is not interested in the bulk of the army, largely consisting of "soudoyers." It glorifies the heroic death of great warriors wishing to live up to their lineage and their ancestors, all Franks, and for this reason they are not afraid of dying or killing.

The *Chanson d'Aspremont* was composed shortly before 1190, either in southern Italy or in the French domains of the Plantagenets, or in both. Widely circulated during the Middle Ages,[2] it lacks the poetic force of the *Chanson de Roland.*[3] Perhaps nearer to a romance than an epic poem, it is two and a half times longer. The climate is changing and there is no unity of action. Martí de Riquer was even able to write that, "it had more than a little literary success, but the enormous mass of the chanson makes it tough to read."[4] The tensions and social diversity it reveals are also interesting for the historian: it may be that we can learn more from it than from *Chanson de Roland*, which *Aspremont* wishes to complete by recounting the "enfances" of Roland during one of Charlemagne's great battles in Calabria, on the slopes of Aspromonte. It was fought to defend Roma and the empire against the offensive of King Agoulant, preceded by his son Eaumont.

The *Chanson d'Aspremont* appears to borrow all its great values from the Song of Roland: its elegy of the great but terrible fight to the death in fair combat; its aristo-

---

1 See Dominique Barthélemy, *La chevalerie. De la Germanie antique à la France du XIIe siècle* (Paris, 2012), 195–292.

2 There are several versions: I typically refer to the edition *Aspremont, chanson de geste du XIIè siècle, d'après le manuscrit 25 529 de la BNF*, ed. François Suard (Paris, 2008), not without having also consulted *La Chanson d'Aspremont, chanson de geste du XIIè siècle. Texte du manuscrit de Wollaton Hall*, ed. Louis Brandin (Paris, 1923–1924).

3 It has, however, been of interest to several recent commentators, Dominique Boutet, "Guerre et société au miroir de la *Chanson d'Aspremont,*" in *Guerre et société au moyen âge: Byzance-Occident (VIIIè-XIIIè siècle)*, ed. Dominique Barthélemy, Jean Claude Cheynet (Paris, 2010), 173–83. See the introduction and the literary bibliography in *Aspremont*, ed. Suard

4 *les réussites littéraires ne sont pas rares, bien que l'énorme masse de la chanson rende sa lecture pénible.* Martín de Riquer, *Les chansons de geste françaises* (Paris, 1957), 210. He thinks in particular of the two "wonderful descriptions" (but not pathetic) that are the adventures of Richer and Naimes.

Dominique Barthélemy (dominique.barthelemy@sorbonne-universite.fr) is Professor of Medieval History at the Université Paris–Sorbonne

cratic system; and a number of its formulas and narrative motifs. However, all this is transposed, shifted, and inserted into a more prosaic form,[5] even diluted in a composite ensemble of interesting debates and combats, which are piquant rather than moving. Its composition is more like a game, and it juxtaposes various value systems. Most important, I think, is being able to read into it more truly chivalric elements. In fact, the succession of Frankish victories pushes sacrificial death somewhat into the background; instead, the stress placed on the actual ritual of knighting involves the theme of the promotion of the young, vavasours, and even serfs. One might say, at times, that birth does not count as much as merit, and more than once the knightly accomplishment of the characters overshadows the sacrifice of their associates.

The *Chanson d'Aspremont* follows a general idea mentioned by Dominique Boutet,[6] who refers to the importance of the way victory is achieved based on the sacred union behind royal authority and in the cohesion, almost discipline, of the armies. In the *Chanson de Roland*, the pride of the heroes and Ganelon's hatred for Roland himself lead to a pathetic defeat, for which the Franks make amends by taking revenge. Meanwhile, the death of Roland is so beautiful, so noble, that his reckless refusal to sound his horn might also appear beautiful and perhaps encourage imitators. Here, Charlemagne and the Franks are clear winners. They achieve two victories over the divided Saracens, some of whom are reckless and other deserters. The *Chanson d'Aspremont* borrows the pride and tragic death of Roland for his Saracen double, Eaumont, the previous owner of the sword Durendal, and his refusal to sound the horn, which is solely responsible for his defeat, is that of a son who does not want to call his own father to his rescue.

But this means that in the *Chanson d'Aspremont*, the intrigue and interest are dispersed. A whole series of characters obstruct each other and Roland!

First of all, the Saracens, often visited by the *Chanson de Roland*, play a more important role here. Friendships are woven with them, with a view to converting them, of course, but not without the worldly idea of chivalry common to all peoples. At the same time, they are roundly defeated, even more so than in *Roland*. In this way, Roland has his great tragic scene stolen by his Saracen double, Eaumont and, in the first part, he is relegated to the use of crude burlesque of the kind elsewhere used by Rainouart or Galopin. Charlemagne believes Roland is too young to fight as a knight and shuts him up with his companions in Laon. But Roland's band escape from Laon and he arrives ready to intervene (against the rules of chivalry) in the fight to the death between Charlemagne and Eaumont, knocking the Saracen down with a tree.

Charlemagne is still reluctant to knight Roland, however. And the song has the time to follow the efforts of a vavasour, Richer, on the dangerous slopes of the harsh mountain. He is followed by Duke Naimes, alternating scenes with him. The Duke is shown meeting the Saracens: their messenger Balant becomes Christian and their queen gives him her ring of love. And above all, the *Chanson d'Aspremont* wants to promote the deeds of Girart de Vienne, "a rebellious baron." While he is still resentful of Charlemagne, he

---

5 According to a general evolution of the genre: Dominique Boutet, *La chanson de geste. Forme et signification d'une écriture épique du moyen âge* (Paris, 1993).

6 Dominique Boutet, *Charlemagne et Arthur ou le roi imaginaire* (Paris, 1992), 207ff.

waits until later to express this, and joins the host in the company of his two sons and two nephews. He knights them all and their exploits take up more room than those of Roland. The whole family provides a good example of the successful reproduction of feudal society.

The ritual of knighting is described in its classical form. This involves an essential gesture performed by the nobleman presiding over the accolade ceremony—girding with the sword—together with the preparatory bath[7] and the involvement of two other knights placing spurs on the newly dubbed knight.[8] And knighting is confirmed as part of the reproductive function of feudal society, which is the basis of the songs of lineage vengeance (such as those of Raoul de Cambrai or Garin le Lorrain). Seeing the exploits of his sons and nephews, Girart can exclaim that they are renewing him. When knighting them, he reminds them of the golden rule of the aristocratic system: an accomplished knight is one who does not listen to the advice of a villein, a woman, or a priest.[9] When he knights Roland, and with him, 337 young nobles and twelve peers, he orders them to pay him homage.[10] Like Girart's sons and nephews, Roland is given a particularly beautiful and powerful sword, which also bears memories of the great deeds of its former owner.[11] The remittance of the fief and the wedding follow the knighting when it is done at court (like that of Beuves).[12]

In the songs of vengeance, it is normally a usurped heir who is knighted after he has gained his title and reclaimed the inheritance of a deceased relative (father or uncle). The unusual feature of *Aspremont*, which is not a song of vengeance, sees the opposite problem appear in literature: the coexistence of generations. This problem had been posed for a long time,[13] but the theme of accomplishment brings it out better here than in songs of vengeance, where knighting will produce an heir to avenge the dead baron. In real life, it was not all that unusual in the twelfth century for the son of a nobleman to reach adulthood within his father's lifetime. However, it was costly for a father to recognise his son's state of adulthood by knighting him or having him dubbed knight because this meant giving him part of his inheritance before time.[14] On the other hand, young knighted princes often made their mark with costly enterprises: they asked their fathers for money or rebel against them, as the three eldest sons of Henry Plantagenet did in 1173. With these conditions, a noble father might tend to delay the knighting of his son, as a suzerain lord would delay that of his orphan vassals whose fiefs he held while he

---

7 *Aspremont*, 81, v. 1268.

8 *Aspremont*, 364, vv. 7045–47.

9 *Aspremont*, 82, v. and 83, vv. 1295–97 and 84, vv. 1329–31.

10 *Aspremont*, 364 and 365.

11 *Aspremont*, 83, v. 1300 and 368, vv. 7129–30.

12 *Aspremont*, 83 and 84.

13 See, for example, Dudon de Saint-Quentin, *De moribus et actis primorum Normanniae ducum*, ed. Jules Lair, new ed. (Caen, 1865), 1 and 2, 140–42.

14 This is what the Usages of Touraine-Anjou foresaw in the thirteenth century, *Les Etablissements de saint Louis*, ed. Paul Viollet, 4 vols. (Paris, 1881–86), 2:31.

has them under his protection as minors.[15] Many young men, still "valets" or "children," were therefore waiting to be knighted.[16] They were champing at the bit with impatience, pestering their fathers or lords with demands. This is Roland's position in relation to Charlemagne in the *Chanson d'Aspremont*.[17] This aspect speaks to the audience, and was also a way of enlivening the plot, which risks being weakened by the absence of mortal hate between lineages. As there is no inexpiable quarrel with someone like Ganelon, it remains for "Rolandin" (as he is called until he is knighted) to oppose Charlemagne himself through a misdemeanour, which becomes a form of redemption.

After this, Roland finds room to express himself in a fierce battle showing his bravery. He manages to strike the first blow.[18] He not only has the best sword, received from the lord who knighted him, he is "the best knight in the world" on his own merits.[19] Ultimately it matters little that this title is given to others because in itself it is the sign of an emancipation of personal value.

From now on, in fact, Charlemagne's army is no longer shaped by inter-lineage hatreds. Rivalry exists only in terms of chivalry.[20] There is no longer the risk of dishonour for cowardice because there is the chance to improve: the coward becomes brave.[21] It is very striking to note the point to which, here, perspectives are reversed compared to the *Chanson de Roland*. The landscape itself is semiologically changed: instead of becoming trapped in a defile like that of Roncevaux, where they would be overlooked by menacingly high mountains, the Frankish noble vassals climb the slopes of Aspremont quite cheerfully, assured that any suffering in the harsh mountain conditions will give them the right to recompense.[22] Warriors have the right to gain something: heaven if they die, glory and profit if they survive. The battle against Agoulant may well be a massacre, but the *Chanson d'Aspremont* does not spend much time on that. It tells us in passing that the 337 knights dubbed with Roland are dead, but it does not bother to tell us about it or to

---

15 *La chronique de Gislebert de Mons*, ed. Léon Vanderkindere (Bruxelles, 1904), 85.

16 The phenomenon is hardly perceptible in the twelfth-century archives, but it appears in the thirteenth century, with the multiplication of adult "*écuyers*" or "*damoiseaux*": Philippe Contamine, "Points de vue sur la chevalerie en France à la fin du moyen âge," *Francia* 4 (1976): 255–85 esp. 258; Dominique Barthélemy, *La société dans le comte de Vendôme, de l'an mil au XIVè siècle* (Paris, 1993), 942–52.

17 *Aspremont*, 365. Charlemagne appears very keen to keep Roland under his control, because on this page (and also at the very end, with Florent) the adoubement empowers the government. During the overthrow of his son Louis (the future King Louis VIII) in Compiegne on May 17, 1209, at the age of twenty-two, Philippe Auguste put many restrictions on political emancipation, in the same spirit as this page by *Aspremon*. The problem of the association of the son or the principal heir, on his coming of age, does not arise only for kings, but for all the families of princes and nobles.

18 *Aspremont*, 384, vv. 7385–90. In *Roland*, his command was symbolized by the right to die ahead of others: Roland, 204, v. 2865.

19 *Aspremont*, 449, v. 9086 (title already recognized to the Duke of Ogier: p. 258, v. 4644).

20 *Aspremont*, 416, vv. 8313–14.

21 *Aspremont*, 226, vv. 3747–49.

22 *Aspremont*, 165, vv. 2715–16.

focus on them in an attempt to move us. Instead it repeatedly stresses the gains made by the victorious survivors.[23]

In this, it is well within the spirit of the Norman chronicles of the successes of conquering knights from around 1100: the one written by Geoffroi Malaterra about Roger of Sicily[24] and Raoul de Caen's account of Tancred in the First Crusade.[25] In both cases, the quest for glory and profit (without even being knighted) is given free rein in the war against the Infidel, and plenty of evidence is provided of the tension between young and not-so-young. As I see it, these works are almost synoptic with the *Chanson d'Aspremont.*

A true knightly dynamic would, of course, have been irrelevant in the tale of the defeat of Roncevaux for the *Chanson de Roland*, but in this everything takes second place to the day of the victorious revenge. On the other hand, the *Chanson d'Aspremont* does not celebrate deaths. It shows us those who take up their weapons just as gleefully to replace the dead as they take the first profits from their knightly actions.[26] Moreover, no important character among the Christians dies. This war is not a sacrifice by vassals, as in the *Chanson de Roland* or the cycle of Guillaume; instead it is about knightly accomplishment. The collective honour of the Franks is clearly eclipsed by each man's concern for self-enrichment: at the crucial moment, Charlemagne evokes only this.[27]

Under these conditions, it is quite logical that, by being knighted, one can achieve or begin social promotion. A central episode of the battle against Agoulant is the moment when, in order to obtain new knights (clearly the only combatants who matter), Charlemagne, the Pope, and the Dukes knight everyone who comes forward en masse. Some are sons of serfs, who are offered their freedom[28] so they can deny their origins.[29] All enjoy royal or ducal gifts and will have future knightly fiefs[30]—property taken from the Franks who have refused to fight.[31]

---

23 *Aspremont*, 159.

24 Geoffroi Malaterra, *De rebus gestis Rogerii Calabriae et Siciliae comitis et Roberti Guiscardi ducis fratris sui*, 1, ed. Ernesto Pontieri, new ed. from Muratori, Rerum italicarum scriptores 5, 3 vols. in 2 (Bologna, 1927–1928), 3:3–108. He relates the tension between Jourdain, son of the bastard, Roger, and his father: tome 3, 11 and 36, tome 4.16 (pp. 63, 78 and 94). See Jean-Marie Martin, *Italies normandes, XIè–XIIè siècles* (Paris, 1994).

25 Raoul de Caen, *Gesta Tancredi in expeditione Hierosalymitana*, Recueil des historiens des croisades. Historiens occidentaux 3 (Paris, 1866), 599–716.

26 *Aspremont*, 352

27 *Aspremont*, 351. Moreover, the collective superiority of the Franks is related to that of their equipment: pp. 418, v. 8379–84, and 421, v. 8489.

28 The model for this episode seems to be *L'Histoire de Charlemagne* (also called the chronicle of the pseudo-Turpin): *Turpini historia Karoli Magni*, ed. Ferdinand Castets (Montpellier, 1880), chap. 11. See also *La légende de Compostelle*, ed. Bernard Gicquel (Paris, 2003), 543.

29 The serfs are reputed to have come, among others, from the Franks, who refused to follow the king *pour combatre contre estrange gent*. Philippe de Beaumanoir, *Coutumes de Beauvaisis*, ed. Amédée Salmon, 2 vols. (Paris, 1900), 2:236.

30 *Aspremont*, 360 and 443. Note that the song recognises (420 to 422) the technical superiority that their hauberks conferred on the Franks over the "Africans."

31 *Aspremont*, 46. In the edition of Louis Brandin, the stanza contains an explicit threat to reduce the failing Franks to serfdom (verse 862).

There is no pointless idealism in this prosaic text: the flow of combatants is drawn by possible recompense. Even more than serfs, who are mentioned in passing, the song is happy to promote vavasours.[32] The idea that the most able of them (or the serfs) should be chosen is repeated, putting into practice a suggestion from John of Salisbury in his *Policraticus*,[33] and quite radically calling into question the entire aristocratic system. Fortunately for the hierarchy, at the climax, Girard at least hammers home the idea that a serf cannot be promoted in the clergy.[34] A little like the cycle of Guillaume, which involves the promotion of young "bachelors,"[35] the *Chanson d'Aspremont* is a kind of saga, carrying along conflicting ideas.

Overall, it is not surprising to see the Saracen Balant, who is linked in friendship with Duke Naimes following previous embassies, surrender and become Christian, or the Saracen queen give a ring of love to Naimes, old in his field. Respect for the Saracens and desire to seduce their women were latent in the *Chanson de Roland* and in many texts.[36] In fact, they are aristocratic adversaries of good taste: a functional enemy who always played something of the role of foil for the Frankish nobility. Here their specifically chivalric allure is emphasized,[37] but the trend is not reversed.

What should we think about this casual breach of a fundamental social barrier by knighting serfs on the harsh mountainside? There are few historical equivalents, although Michel Bur has found one in Champagne in 1171.[38] When men of servile origins, or denounced as such, move in the world of knights at court, it is rather surreptitiously, such as in the case of the famous Erembaud de Bruges, and it was through serving the prince or king. The wealth acquired in this way allowed them to equip themselves as knights. In any case, to talk about servile origin is not to refer to the lowest birth: in northern France there are plenty of serfs performing public functions who are, in practice, close to the minor nobles or vavasours and far from the court, which it is dif-

---

32 *Aspremont*, 444: of those who came to the court miserably dressed. The old dream: Ingon.

33 John of Salisbury, *Policraticus*, ed. Clement Webb, 2 vols. (Oxford, 1909), 2:16. See also the theme in Pierre Alfonse, "Disciplina clericalis," in *Patrologiae cursus completus*, ed. Jacques-Paul Migne, 221 vols. (Paris, 1854), 157: col. 677, on the nobility which had to proceed on personal merit rather than from ancestors. Moïse le Sépharade alias Pierre d'Alphonse, *La discipline de clergie*, trans. Jacqueline-Lise Genot-Bismuth (St. Petersburg and Paris, 2001), 222. And the eulogy of the *home bas monté en paraige*, in the middle of the thirteenth century, by Robert de Blois, *L'enseignement des princes*, vv. 380–84 and 1247–54. Robert de Blois, *Sämtliche Werke*, ed. Jacob Ulrich, 3 vols. in 1 (Berlin, 1895; repr. Genève, 1978), 13 and 37.

34 *Aspremont*, 523.

35 Mario Mancini, *Società feudale e ideologia nel "Charroi de Nîmes"* (Firenze, 1972), 97.

36 Huguette Legros, "Entre Chrétiens et Sarrasins, des amitiés paradoxales," in *Aspects de l'épopée romane: mentalités, idéologies, intertextualités*, ed. Hans van Dijk, Willem Noomen (Groningen, 1995), 269–78.

37 *Aspremont*, 510: now speaks about *a lei de chevaler*, it is to spare the enemy queen, not to proclaim a fierce war.

38 Michel Bur, "A propos d'une charte d'Henri le Libéral, ou comment de serf on devient chevalier," in *Droit, administration et justice. Mélanges en l'honneur des professeurs Marie-Thérèse Allemand-Gay et Jean Gay*, ed. Antoine Astaing, François Lormant (Nancy, 2011), 113–27.

ficult for them to access. By confusing the case of serfs a little with that of vavasours, the *Chanson d'Aspremont* is sociologically correct.[39]

The promotion of vavasours is itself uncommon. It is true that the Norman conquests of the late eleventh century (England and Sicily) allowed certain families to rise, but in a limited way; in reality, there were tensions and debates. The chronicle of Geoffroi Mala-terra, for example, while telling the story of the rise of the Hautevilles from their initial poverty through their conquests, also wants to please them by deploring the mediocre origin of Ingelmer, who is the widow of one of them.[40] Undoubtedly, the good vavasour is still the one who dies for his lord, like *Eviscardus* before Taormina.[41] According to a model whose Carolingian origins I have highlighted elsewhere,[42] if a "mediocre" man is allowed to stand out in combat, it is above all for a good death.

In the twelfth century, the vavasours are not a rising class, but a petty knightly aristocracy traditionally below the barons who aspire, always somewhat in vain,[43] to obtain the same considerations and privileges as the barons. After knighting came into existence in the 1060s, it would not be accorded to them as easily as to barons or with the same glitter or the same weapons. This is why those knighted at the same time as Roland remain in the shadows alongside him. Among them there are noble bastards des-tined for social involvement, like Bernier in *Raoul de Cambrai* and Richer in *Aspremont*.

It is a leitmotiv of many chivalric romances in France around 1200 to complain of the lot of the vavasours, urging kings to refill their coffers with largesse and give them the resources to achieve exploits.[44] In real life, kings and princes acted ambivalently.[45] As much in administrative service as in war, or even more so, some men of middling rank—in other words vavasours—did make their fortunes and establish themselves socially.[46]

Neither in real life nor in the *Chanson d'Aspremont* did a few promotions or a few stanzas of social openness really destroy the aristocratic system. On breaching a social barrier, those who have just been promoted do not destroy it.[47] In knightly society, they

---

39 Lamberti Ardensi, "Historia comitum Ghisnensium," ed. Georg Heinrich Pertz, MGH SS 24 (1879), 579–80.

40 Malaterra, *De rebus gestis*, tome 3,31, 76.

41 Malaterra, *De rebus gestis*, tome 3,15 and 16, 66.

42 Dominique Barthélemy, *La mutation de l'an mil a-t-elle eu lieu ? Servage et chevalerie dans la France des Xè et XIè siècles* (Paris, 1997), 204–5 and 222–26.

43 *Usages de Touraine-Anjou.*

44 But not without criticizing, on the other hand, the rise of the "fils de villain" around the 1180s: *Partonopeu de Blois*, ed. Olivier Collet, Pierre-Marie Joris (Paris, 2005). It is more exceptional to join an appeal to King Arthur for generosity to barons and vavasours, and at the same time to praise a sergeant, as did the *Lancelot* in prose in the 1220s (episode of Arquois le Flamand): *Lancelot du Lac*, ed. Elspeth Kennedy (Paris, 1991), 126–37.

45 Like the Count of Champagne, Henry the Liberal, ransoming his own trustworthy Artaud de Nogent, of bourgeois origin, for the benefit of a poor knight around 1170 (which is a counterpoint to the charter of 1173, mentioned above, note 38): Jean de Joinville, *Vie de saint Louis*, ed. Jacques Monfrin (Paris, 1995), 89–91, 200–203.

46 John W. Baldwin, *Philippe Auguste et son gouvernement* (Paris, 1991), 148–58.

47 Edouard Perroy, "Social Mobility among the French Noblesse in the Later Middle Ages," in

could be integrated in small doses and, in fact, a knight of poor origin, Roger, and the Saracen Ferragus, did find their place in Italian chivalric literature. The ideology of earning merit in war despite humble birth does not destroy the prejudice in favour of the higher born. And true subversion, consisting of praising foot soldiers or merits other than those of warriors, had not yet arrived.

In the meantime, the author of *Aspremont* makes a very interesting initial choice for us. In getting away from the outset from the wars of lineages and the vengeful honour of the army of Charlemagne and Girart, he allows expression of the chivalric spirit in its pure form, without the idealization it undergoes in the Arthurian world. I believe he perfectly captures the glorification of individualism of chivalric society, where many are driven to perform in the hope of social advancement. So, despite a still strong tendency to reproduce hierarchies and power, this society is affected by a certain potential mobility. Not everyone stays in his place, as in the *Chanson de Roland*. It is possible to change, notably by royal decision. The individualism of the warrior, which at first sight appears to emancipate him from the weight of lineage and replace the fear of dishonour with the hope of gain, in reality subjects him more to royal (or princely) power than the heroes of the songs of vengeance and "rebel vassals."

Études d'histoire médiévale, ed. Edouard Perroy (Paris, 1979), 225–38.

Chapter 10

ADORATION OF THE MAGI AND AUTHORITY OF THE MEDIEVAL KING: AN AMBIGUOUS CORRELATION

DOINA ELENA CRACIUN

A LITTLE AFTER his coronation as Holy Roman Emperor in 1355, the king of Bohemia and of the Romans, Charles IV, was depicted as the middle-aged Magus on the left wing of the so-called "Morgan Diptych."[1] A similar crypto-portrait is also found on an altarpiece finished in 1464–1465 for the chapel of St. Agatha of the royal palace of Barcelona. In this painting, the youngest Magus bears the physical traits of Peter, Constable of Portugal and pretended king of Aragon (1463–1466). Kings also pursued identification with the Magi by offering gold, frankincense, and myrrh on January 6, as registered in documents for the kings of England, Edward III (1327–1377), and Richard II (1377–1399),[2] for the king of France, Charles V (1364–1380),[3] for the king of Aragon, Pedro IV (1336–1387),[4] and for Felipe II of Spain (1556–1598).[5] Other types of written sources also mention the similitude between medieval kings and the Magi in different contexts. For example, a sermon given in 1273 by Gilles of Orleans at the Saint-Chapel in Paris, in the presence of king Philippe III (1270–1285): "Indeed, I dare say that he is not a real king on Earth the one who did not make this pilgrimage; I mean the one at the place where the King of kings was born, either on the strength of devotion or to bring military help."[6]

---

1 The present chapter develops new aspects and goes further on the same author's 2016 PhD diss. supervised by Pierre Monnet (École des Hautes Études Étudies en Sciences Sociales, Paris) and Prof. Daniel Russo (Université de Bourgogne).

2 Shelagh Mitchell, "Richard II: Kingship and the Cult of Saints," in *The Regal Image of Richard II and the Wilton Diptych*, ed. Dillian Gordon, Lisa Monnas and Caroline Elam (London, 1997), 123 and 314n80; Dillian Gordon, *Making and Meaning: the Wilton Diptych [Exhibition Held at the National Gallery, London, 15 September–12 December 1993]* (London, 1993), 57.

3 Roland Delachenal, ed., *Chronique des règnes de Jean II et de Charles V: les grandes chroniques de France*, 3 vols. (Paris, 1916), 2:233–34.

4 Manuel Mariano Ribera, *Real capilla de Barcelona, la mayor y mas principal de los reynos de la corona de Aragón* (Barcelona, 1698), 55.

5 Jerónimo de Sapúlveda, "Historia de Varios sucesos y de las cosas y de las cosas notables que han acaecido en España y otras naciones desde el año de 1584 hasta el de 1603," *Documentos para la historia del Monasterio de San Lorenzo el Real de El Escorial*, ed. Julián Zarco y Cuevas, 8 vols. (Madrid, 1916–1924), 4:12.

6 *Et uere audeo dicere quod non est uerus rex in terra qui istam peregrinationem non fecit, scilicet*

Doina Elena Craciun (doina.craciun@yahoo.com) was Researcher at the École des Hautes Études en Sciences Sociales, Paris.

Figure 10.1: Master of the "Morgan diptych," *Adoration of the Magi*. Left wing of the diptych, ca. 1355. New York, The Morgan Library & Museum. (© The Morgan Library & Museum, New York).

Figure 10.2:
Jaume Huguet, *Adoration of the Magi*. Part of an altarpiece, 1464–1465. Barcelona, Royal Palace, Chapel of Saint Agata. (© Departament de Cultura de la Generalitat de Catalunya, Barcelona).

These are only some examples in which medieval kings were compared to the biblical Magi, but the phenomenon appears in at least twelve kingdoms between the twelfth and the sixteenth centuries.[7] The identification between the sovereign and these ill-defined biblical figures brings in various important issues related to royal authority and the perception of the king in medieval society. We'll focus here only on the means of accommodating the idea of the king's unique authority with the particular setting of

---

ad locum in quo rex regum fuit natus, et hoc uel causa et ratione deuotionis aut ratione auxilii et cum armis. From Paris, Bibliothèque nationale de France, MS lat. 16481, fol. 71vb. I kindly thank Nicole Bériou for allowing me to use her transcription of this sermon.

7 For a complete list of all the medieval documents, see Doina Elena Craciun, "Les Rois mages, images du pouvoir des rois en Occident (XIIe–XVIe siècles)," 2 vols. (PhD diss., École des Hautes Études Études en Sciences Sociales, Paris, 2016), 1:119–95.

three crowned characters. How can a king be perceived as the ultimate figure of author-ity in a kingdom, while being depicted as a Magus, among at least two other Magi and in the presence of the Virgin and Child? How can his unique authority be maintained among three or even four crowned figures? And is that the only purpose of all medieval authors and commissioners who created this association between kings and Magi, or can other conceptions of royal authority be expressed through this means?

Looking for the use of ideological arguments in medieval power relations, this chapter first focuses on the reticence of kings to use the Magi as a political instrument. Indeed, until the twelfth century, the idea of associating historical kings and the Magi is seldom recorded, and when it is, the association does not aim to highlight royal author-ity. After trying to understand the elements that impede the growth of this correlation, I examine factors that helped overcome this initial hesitation. By examining written and iconographic documents, I will try to reveal the elements that permitted the identifica-tion of kings with the Magi as a means of expressing different—sometimes contradic-tory—conceptions concerning royal authority.

The Three Magi Far from the King's Court

While the Gospel of Matthew (Matt. 2:1–12), the only one mentioning the "Magi from the East," gives very little detail about these figures, the biblical story was enriched in the following centuries with apocryphal writings, Bible commentaries, sermons, or other types of literature. Their number is set at three; they are given names (Melchior, Caspar, and Balthazar) and different geographical origins, each of them receiving an approxi-mate age and specific physical traits. Thus, one of the Magi is seen as old, depicted with a white beard; the second is middle-aged and wears a brown beard; and the third is young and beardless. Their symbolism is very complex: they signify the three ages of life, the three sons of Noah, the three continents; they are messengers of peace and symbols of commerce. Even if they were never consecrated, they are perceived as saints, and their cult is very intense, especially in Köln, where their relics have been kept since 1164. They are seen as ultimate models of conversion and piety, protectors of travellers, and of course, healers, mainly of epilepsy.[8]

Naturally, these popular figures did not fail to reach political rulers. In the famous mosaics of the basilica San Vitale of Ravenna (546–548), the emperor Justinian I (527–565) and his wife, Theodora, (d. 548) carry the eucharistic gifts towards Christ, depicted in the apse of the altar. On the bottom of the Empress Theodora's mantle, one can see the three Magi carrying their own gifts. As Otto Georg von Simson argues, it is the strong eucharistic signification of the Magi's offering that seems to have determined

---

8 For a general view upon the forging of these three figures see Richard Trexler, *The Journey of the Magi: Meanings in History of a Christian Story* (Princeton, 1997) (hereafter Richard Trexler, *The Journey of the Magi*); Hugo Kehrer, *Die Heiligen drei Könige in Literatur und Kunst*, 2 vols. (Leipzig, 1908); Hans Hofmann, *Die Heiligen drei Könige: zur Heiligenverehrung im kirchlichen, gesellschaftlichen und politischen Leben des Mittelalters* (Bonn, 1975); Mathieu Beaud, *Iconographie et art monumental dans l'espace féodal du Xe au XIIe siécle: le thème des Rois mages et sa diffusion* (Dijon, 2012).

the association with the gesture of political rulers.[9] Moreover, Agnès de Lagrange de Baynast sees the Magi as symbols of the recent conversion of the empress from monophysitism.[10] Thus, their depiction on the cloak of the empress is not meant to endorse her position as a political ruler, but only as a recently converted Christian, bringing Christ her eucharistic gift. All in all, the authority of rulers in the East is based upon the image of Christ, never on the Magi, who are not even perceived as kings, as they are in the West.

Indeed, the most important element that permitted the association between Magi and medieval kings in the western world is certainly the royal dignity given to these biblical figures. They were first considered kings by Tertullian, who, at the beginning of the third century, claimed that St. Matthew's Magi are the kings mentioned in Ps. 72:9–11, who bow before the son of God and bring him gifts.[11] The association between the biblical episode of the arrival of the Magi and this psalm is attested throughout the Middle Ages, as these verses are often illustrated with an image of the *Adoration of the Magi.*[12]

As commentaries of Matthew's Gospel and medieval sermons seldom mention the kingship of the Magi, this perception hardly gains ground before the tenth century. As Robert Deshman argues, an important element for the propagation of this idea is their depiction wearing crowns, first seen in the *Benedictional of St. Aethelwold* (963–984).[13] From this moment on, the Magi always appear as crowned figures in western images, plainly establishing their kingship. But it is important to note that the first illustrations of the Magi as kings have a political background.

Even before the tenth century, the image of the *Adoration of the Magi* was inspired by political rituals. As Franz Cumont and J. G. Deckers show, the first sculpted representations of the *Adoration of the Magi* were strongly influenced by imperial ritual and triumphal art in Late Antique Roma. Indeed, the model for the depiction of the Magi bringing gifts was the iconography of the ceremony called *aurum coronarium*, in which conquered people bring the emperor golden crowns as a sign of his triumph.[14] Thus, from the fourth century on, images of the *Adoration of the Magi* became symbols of the

---

9 Otto Georg von Simson, *Sacred Fortress: Byzantine Art and Statecraft in Ravenna* (Chicago, 1948), 29–36. For the correlation between the gesture of the Magi and Eucharist, see Ursula Nilgen, "The Epiphany and the Eucharist: On the Interpretation of Eucharistic Motifs in Mediaeval Epiphany Scenes," *The Art Bulletin* 49, no. 4 (1967): 311–16.

10 Agnès de Lagrange de Baynast, "La conversion au christianisme dans l'antiquité tardive d'après l'exemple des élites italiennes (IVe–Ve s.): sens, formes et manifestations" (Master's diss., Paris, 2008), 493–95.

11 Tertullian, *Contre Marcion. Livre III*, trans. René Braun (Paris, 1994), 126–27.

12 Robert Deshman, "*Christus rex et magi reges*. Kingship and Christology in Ottonian and Anglo-Saxon Art," *Frühmittelalterlichen Studien* (1976): 375–78; Beaud, *Iconographie et art monumental*, 124.

13 Deshman, "Christus rex et magi reges," 377ff.

14 Franz Cumont, "L'Adoration des Mages et l'art triomphal de Rome," *Memorie della pontifical academia romana di archeologia* 3 (1922–1923): 81–105; Johannes G. Deckers, "Die Huldigung der Magier in der Kunst der Spätantike," in *Die Heiligen Drei Könige, Darstellung und Verehrung: Katalog zur Ausstellung des Wallraf-Richartz-Museums in der Josef-Haubrich-Kunsthalle Köln, 1. Dezember 1982 bis 30. Januar 1983*, ed. Rainer Budde (Köln, 1982), 20–32.

imperial politics of expansion and religious renewal. In this early period, when emperors claim to act as Christ on Earth, the Magi are seen as images of people converted to Christianity.[15]

The same idea of the emperor as Christ submitting provinces depicted as Magi was revived during the Ottonian period and seems to account for the Magi bearing crowns in the miniatures Robert Deshman analyses. Indeed, two other images depicting crowned Magi were finished soon after the *Benedictional of St. Aethelwold*, seeming to account for a connection between this iconography and that of the emperor receiving gifts. The *Codex Egberti* (977–993) and the *Poussay Gospels* (ca. 980), both showing crowned Magi, are commissioned by bishop Egbert of Trier (d. 993), also responsible for the famous miniature of the *Registrum Gregorii* (end of the tenth century), in which the emperor Otto (II or III) receives golden gifts from crowned provinces. There is no doubt that for the commissioner and for the painter of these miniatures, the figure of Christ in the *Adoration of the Magi* replicates the one of the Emperor in the *Registrum Gregorii*.[16] Be that as it may, what interests us here is the position of the political ruler which inspired these early Anglo-Saxon and German sources. The conception of the emperor as Christ dominating the Magi seems to prevail in this period, an idea incompatible with that of the ruler as a Magus. Hence, it is not surprising that at this time kings and emperors are never associated with the Magi.

Furthermore, even if their relics are kept in German territory since 1164,[17] these biblical figures remain excluded from the political strategies deployed for promoting the image of rulers, at least until the second half of the thirteenth century.[18] In this phase, the authority of the Emperor relies on the renown of Charlemagne (canonized a year after the translation of the Magi), easier to attach to the person of the sovereign and to the territory of the empire.[19]

Also, besides the specific imperial context that favoured other figures of prestige, the fact that there were three crowned figures probably played its part in the initial reticence observed in all the western kingdoms. Three biblical Magi were difficult to use as a means of enhancing the authority of one king. By comparison, the king as Christ is

---

15 Deckers, "Die Huldigung der Magier," 28.

16 Deshman, "Christus rex et magi reges," 367–405.

17 For the translation of the relics from Milano to Köln, see Heinz Finger, "Die Translation der Dreikönigsreliquien 1164. Ihre politischen und kirchenpolitischen Hintergründe und die mittelalterliche Dreikönigsverehrung in Köln," in *Die Heiligen Drei Könige. Die Translation ihrer Gebeine 1164 und ihre Verehrung in Köln. Eine Ausstellung der Diözesan- und Dombibliothek Köln zum 850jährigen Anniversarium der Translation der Dreikönigsreliquien 2014 (23. Juli 2014 bis 18. März 2015)*, ed. Heinz Finger and Werner Wessel (Köln, 2014), 15–112.

18 Hugo Stehkämper, "Könige und Heilige Drei Könige," in *Die Heiligen Drei Könige. Die Translation ihrer Gebeine 1164 und ihre Verehrung in Köln. Eine Ausstellung der Diözesan- und Dombibliothek Köln zum 850jährigen Anniversarium der Translation der Dreikönigsreliquien 2014 (23. Juli 2014 bis 18. März 2015)*, ed. Heinz Finger and Werner Wessel (Köln, 2014), 38–39.

19 For the context of this canonization and the importance of Charlemagne for the imperial politics, see Robert Folz, *Le souvenir et la légende de Charlemagne dans l'Empire germanique médiéval* (Paris, 1950), 186–213.

definitely an easier and more prestigious association, therefore largely disseminated in the Middle Ages. It is this identification of kings with Christ that brings the possibility of comparing other kings with the Magi.

Christ and Magi: A Hierarchy Showing Supreme Authority

Besides a brief comparison between devoted kings and the Magi in a sermon of St. Augustine (354–430),[20] the first document in which a specific king is associated with these figures dates from around 1190. In his *Chronicle*, Gervase of Canterbury includes a description of the Conference of Montmirail, taking place on January 6, 1169 in the presence of the king of France, Louis VII (1137–1180), and the king of England, Henry II (1154–1189).[21] One of the subjects of this meeting was the homage due from the sons of the king of England to Louis VII for their lands in France.[22] For Gervase of Canterbury, this ritual recalled the biblical episode of the *Adoration of the Magi*. Thus, describing a probably imagined dialogue between Henry II and Louis VII, the monk of Canterbury cites the words the king of England addressed to the king of France: "Lord my king, this day when the three kings have offered gifts to the King of kings, I entrust myself, my sons, and my land to your protection [...]."[23] Accepting the association between himself and "the King of kings," Louis VII endorses this re-enactment of the *Adoration of the Magi* by answering: "Because the King who received the gifts inspired your words, let your sons come before me in order to take possession of their lands on behalf of our kindness."[24]

The text clearly shows that the idea of associating the king with Christ brought up the comparison of other kings with the Magi. Indeed, by the time Gervase of Canterbury finishes this *Chronicle* (begun around 1185–1188),[25] the two sons of Henry II described as Magi have also become kings. Henry the Young (1170–1183) was crowned in the lifetime of his father, while Richard I (1189–1199) was certainly enthroned when Gervase of Canterbury writes this text. Three kings appearing before another one reminds the author of the episode of the three Magi honouring the Christ Child. On January 6, 1169,

---

20 "The current kings are wiser. They do not ask for killing like Herod, but they prefer to worship, like the Magi." (*Quanto consultius nunc reges, non sicut Herodes, interficere quaerunt; sed sicut Magi potius, adorare delectantur.*) Cited from Aurelius Augustinus, "In Epiphania Domini," in *Patrologiae cursus completus*, ed. Jacques-Paul Migne, 221 vols. (Paris, 1845), 38: col. 1029.

21 Gervase of Canterbury, "Chronica de tempore Regum Angliae, Stephani, Hen. II. & Ricardi I," in *Historiae Anglicanae scriptores X*, ed. Roger Twysden, 2 vols. (London, 1652), 2: col. 1404.

22 For the political situation in 1169 and the conference of Montmirail, see Amy Ruth Kelly, *Eleanor of Aquitaine and the Four Kings* (Cambridge, 1978), 134–37.

23 *Hac die domine mi rex qua tres reges Regi regum munera obtulerunt me ipsum, natos meos & terram vestrae commendo custodiae [...].* Cited from Gervase of Canterbury, "Chronica," 2: col. 1404.

24 *Quia vobis hoc inspiravit Rex qui regum munera suscepit, exhibeant nati vestri praesentiam suam ut a mansuetudinis nostrae titulo terras suas possideant.* Cited from Gervase of Canterbury, "Chronica," 2: col. 1404.

25 For the date of this work, see Gervase of Canterbury, *The Chronicle of the Reigns of Stephen, Henry II., and Richard I*, ed. William Stubbs (London, 1879), 15–21.

Figure 10.3:
Façade of the Shrine of
the Three Kings with
Otto IV, ca. 1200. Köln,
St. Peter's Cathedral
Choir (© Hohe Dom-
kirche Köln, Dombau-
hütte Köln, photo: Matz
und Schenk).

Henry and Richard payed homage to the king of France, a ceremony presenting the deference of the two vassal future kings, described here as Magi, to the suzerain, seen as
Christ. Thus, the comparison of kings with the Magi is used here to underline the inferior position of certain kings and the dominating roles of others. The role of Christ is
definitely the prestigious one, while the one of Magus is rather sub-standard. This use
of the *Adoration of the Magi* to show distinction between medieval royal figures is not
specific to this late twelfth century source, but can also be found in later texts.

Describing the birth of Richard II, on January 6, 1367, William Thorne writes in his
Chronicle of Saint Augustine's Canterbury Abbey: "The same year, the day of the Lord's
Epiphany, was born in Bordeaux, Richard, the king of England. Three Magi attended
his birth: the king of Spain, the king of Navarre, and the king of Portugal, all of whom
brought precious gifts to the Child."[26]

---

26 *Eodem anno in epiphania Domini natus est Ricardus rex Angliae apud Burdeywes, in cujus
nativitate fuerunt III. magi, scilicet rex Ispaniae, rex Navernie, et rex Portigalliae, qui quidem reges*

Even if William Thorne invented the episode—because the presence of three kings at the birth of Richard II is not attested by any other documents—[27] his view of this scene is particularly interesting. There is no doubt that the author's purpose is to put his king in a favourable light, and the best way to do this is to give him the role of Christ. Indeed, by the time this chronicle is written, around 1380, Richard is already king of England and William Thorne is very close to the royal court.[28]

The other kings mentioned are probably those with whom the father of Richard II, Edward of Woodstock, was preparing a military intervention in Castile in 1366: Pedro I of Castile (1350–1369), Carlos II of Navarre (1349–1387), and Pedro I of Portugal (1357–1367). Negotiations for this intervention started in Bordeaux in the summer of 1366 and ended with an armed intrusion in Castile and the victory of Nájera on April 3, 1367.[29] There is no doubt that the participation of the father of Richard II temporarily changed the outcome of the conflict in 1367. Hence, one can read the scene of the *Adoration of the Magi* imagined by William Thorne as a transcription of real alliances between four kings in 1366–1367. On the one hand, the kings who search for military help in Bordeaux are seen here as the Magi, and on the other hand, the son of the one who decided to support them takes the role of Christ.

As Gervase of Canterbury does in his *Chronicle*, William Thorne uses the *Adoration of the Magi* and a carefully chosen distribution of the roles in this scene as a means of asserting the superiority of a king upon the others. Yet again, the role of Christ is the one that receives maximum distinction, while the kings seen as Magi share an equal authority, inferior to the one of Christ.

Nevertheless, the role given to medieval kings in a re-enactment of the *Adoration of the Magi* is not always derived from the perception of a ruler as Christ and the desire to show him as superior to other kings. This scene allowed many other means of illustrating a reflection upon royal authority.

An important document introducing the question of authority of the king as a Magus is the façade of the Shrine of the Three Kings, kept in the cathedral of Köln.[30] The left side of the façade is decorated with an unusual *Adoration of the Magi*, in which the three common Kings heading toward the Virgin and Child are followed by another figure, identified by an inscription as "Otto Rex." He is bearing a gift similar to that of the first Magus, but he is inferior in size and has neither a royal mantle nor a crown,[31] while the Magi and

---

dederunt puero munera preciosa. Cited from William Thorne "Chronica Guill. Thorne Monachi S. Augustini Cant," in *Historiae Anglicanae scriptores X*, ed. Roger Twysden, 2 vols. (London, 1652), 2: col. 2142.

27 Gordon, *Making and Meaning*, 57; Trexler, *The Journey of the Magi*, 85.

28 On the chronicle and its author, see the introduction to the English translation *William Thorne's Chronicle of Saint Augustine's Abbey, Canterbury,* trans. A. H. Davis (Oxford, 1934).

29 For the political situation in Castile around 1360, we use here Julio Valdeón Baruque, *Pedro I el Cruel y Enrique de Trastámara: la primera guerra civil española?* (Madrid, 2002), 133–218.

30 For the iconography of the shrine, see Rolf Lauer, *Der Schrein der Heiligen Drei Könige* (Köln, 2006).

31 The lack of a crown is not due to a later loss, but this figure was clearly conceived from the beginning without a crown, Walter Schulten, "Die Restaurierung des Dreikönigenschreines. Ein Vorbericht für die Jahre 1961–71," *Kölner Domblatt* 33/34 (1971): 7–42.

Figure 10.4: Master Theodoric, *Adoration of the Magi*. Fresco, ca. 1365, Karlštejn Castle,
Czech Republic, Chapel of the Holy Cross, north-east window frame.
(© Karlštejn Castle, photo: Doina Elena Craciun.)

the Virgin are sumptuously dressed and crowned. Considering that the decoration of the
shrine started around 1190 and was completed around 1225,[32] there is no doubt that
this fourth Magus is the king of Romans, Otto IV (1198/1209–1215).

Seemingly, a fundamental change took place at this time in people's perception of
the king of the Romans. The sovereign no longer occupies the place belonging to Christ
as in late antique Roman art or in the Ottonian miniatures but is now depicted among
the Magi honouring the Child. What is more, the king of the Romans is shown in a self-
effacing position, inferior even to the Wise men, by his placement behind them and
iconographical details missing, including the crown and mantle. This position is fully
understandable if we see the decoration of the shrine in the context of its completion,
the subject of another article of mine.[33]

Not having the space here to detail this context and the significations of this image
of the king, it is nevertheless important to note once again that identifying a king with a
Magus does not necessarily serve his interests. There is no doubt that, on the façade of
the shrine, the king's authority is largely diminished in favour of the archbishop of Köln,
symbolized by the Virgin and Child.[34] As for the above-mentioned documents, casting a

---

32 Lauer, *Der Schrein*, 7.

33 Doina Elena Craciun, "Représenter la concession du pouvoir: le roi en Roi mage à Cologne
vers l'an 1200," *La représentation politique avant le gouvernement représentatif, Paris–Créteil,
12–14 mars 2015*) (forthcoming).

34 For the Virgin and Child as symbols of the Church and ecclesiastical authorities, especially in
Adorations of the Magi, see Marie-Louise Thérel, *Le Triomphe de la Vierge-Église: à l'origine du décor
du portail occidental de Notre-Dame de Senlis sources historiques, littéraires et iconographiques*
(Paris, 1984), 78–202.

king as Magus is here a strategy used to highlight the distinguished position of the person standing in for Virgin and Child. For Gervase of Canterbury and William Thorne, it was a means of honouring Louis VII or Richard II, whilst on the façade of the shrine the highest dignity is given to the archbishop of Köln, Adolf of Altena (1193–1205).

Even if some documents exploit the dominating position of Christ in the scene of the *Adoration of the Magi*, this is not always the purpose of associating kings with the Magi. On the contrary, most of the documents do not consider the relation between Christ and the Magi, but only concentrate on the depiction of each of the three Kings to emphasize a conception concerning royal authority.

What Authority for One King among Three Kings?

In a commendation addressed around 1235 to the emperor Frederick II, Nicolas, *Barensis ecclesie dyaconus*, writes:

> His ancestor [Frederick I] was a great ruler because he was emperor of the Romans, his father [Henry VI] was greater because he was emperor and king of Sicily, himself [Frederick II] is the greatest of all because he is emperor of the Romans, king of Jerusalem, and of Sicily. Definitely, these three kings are like the three Magi, who came with presents to adore God and the Human, but the last of them is the youngest of the three, on whom the infant Jesus put his blissful hands and his sacred arms.[35]

The author's intention is clearly to praise Frederick II, and the comparison with the Magi perfectly serves this purpose. Nicolas of Bari uses the ages of the Three Wise Men—an old, a mature, and a young one—as a means of chronologically aligning the reigns of the different members of the dynasty: Frederick I (1152/1155–1190), Henry VI (1191–1196), and Frederick II (1212/1220–1250). The contemporary king is thus seen as the youngest of the three Magi. However, what matters above all for Nicolas of Bari is not the dynasty, but the supreme distinction of his king among his ancestors. He then finds a way of showing that Christ himself recognized the particular dignity of Frederick II, the young Magus, by putting upon him "his blissful hands and his sacred arms." Apparently, since it is now possible to show the greater authority of one king among three, the number of the Magi is no longer an obstacle for expressing the emperor's unique power. Undoubtedly, proximity and interaction with the Child are only a few of the instruments used to express the pre-eminence of one king, visual representations of rulers as Magi opening a wide range of other possibilities.

---

35 *Magnus dominus avus suus, quia imperator Romanus [Frederick I], magnus dominus pater, quia imperator et rex Sicilie [Henri VI], ipse maximus, quia imperator Romanus, rex Iherusalem et Sicilie [Frederick II]. Profecto hiis tres imperatores sunt quasi tres magi, qui venerunt cum muneribus Deum et hominem adorare, sed hic est adolescentior illis tribus, super quem puer Ihesus felices manus posuit et brachiola sacrosancta.* Cited from Rudolf M. Kloos, "Nikolaus von Bari, eine neue Quelle zur Entwicklung der Kaiseridee unter Friedrich II," in *Stupor Mundi: zur Geschichte Friedrichs II. von Hohenstaufen*, ed. Gunther Wolf (Darmstadt, 1982), 136. Recently, the text has been edited by Fulvio delle Donne suggests seeing the word *magnus* before *dominus pater* as an error of the copyist and replacing it with the word *maior*, believing it more closely corresponds to the sequence's gradation in the preceding paragraph. Fulvio delle Done, *Il potere e la sua legittimazione: letteratura encomiastica in onore di Federico II di Svevia* (Arce, 2005), 102. We follow here this suggestion.

Figure 10.5:
Master of the Orten-
berg altars, *Adoration of
the Magi*, right wing of
Ortenberger altarpiece,
Workshop at the Mittel-
rhein, probably in Mainz,
around 1420, an altarpiece
originally in Our Lady
Church in Ortenberg,
Darmstadt, Hessisches
Landesmuseum Darm-
stadt, Inv.-Nr. GK 4
(© Hessisches Landes-
museum Darmstadt,
photo: Wolfgang
Fuhrmannek).

By the time crypto-portraits of kings as Magi appeared, not earlier than the fourteenth century, the iconography of the *Adoration of the Magi* was already settled. Most
images show three kings, an old white-bearded one having already removed his crown,
kneeling before the Child and presenting him his gift; a mature brown-bearded king,
standing behind the first one; and finally, a third young beardless Magus waiting in line
to make his own offering. Considering that the elder magus is presented throughout the
Middle Ages—by ecclesiastical sources, legends, and theatrical performances—as the
first of the three to approach the Holy Child, images evidently concur in depicting this
initial moment of the kings' homage. It is in this fixed arrangement of figures that images
of kings depicted as Magi were conceived in the late medieval period.

Manifestly, the order of pre-eminence Nicolas of Bari imagined—with the youngest
Magus blessed by Christ—was not the pattern for visual sources. Thus, unless systematically giving medieval kings the role of the old Magus, the proximity and the interaction with Christ could not be illustrated in images, as in Nicolas of Bari's commendation.
But giving the king the role of the old Magus did not correspond to the need of medieval

Figure 10.6:
Jacquemart de Hesdin,
Adoration of the Magi.
Ca. 1385–1390. Paris,
Bibliothèque nationale
de France, MS. lat. 18014,
fol. 42v. (© Biblio-
thèque nationale de
France, Paris).

authors and artists to create *Adorations of the Magi* in which contemporary kings should be recognized. That is why in medieval images of the *Adoration*, historical kings almost always take the role of the Magus whose age corresponded to the king's own age at the time the image was produced. Deceased kings often appear as the old figure, whilst contemporary rulers mostly play the role of the middle-aged or the young Magus. This role spatially separated them from the Virgin and Child, but other means of showing the greatness of the contemporary king were then employed.

An examination of all the late medieval sources showed that a very common method of emphasizing the contemporary king was that of giving him a particular display to the detriment of the two other Magi. For example, in the so-called "Morgan Diptych," the king of Bohemia Charles IV (1346–1378), depicted as the middle-aged King, is the only one whose figure is entirely visible, standing behind the kneeling elder Magus and in front of the young one, depicted only by half (Fig. 10.1). All the same, as the third Magus in the fresco in Karlštejn, he is also the only one standing, while the other two are bending in front of the child (Fig. 10.4). Also, depicted as the middle-aged Magus in an

Figure 10.7:
Adoration of the Magi.
Fresco, ca. 1390,
Libiš, Czech Republic,
Church of Saint James,
choir, upper register
of the north wall.
(© Saint James Church
Libiš, photo: Doina
Elena Craciun.)

altarpiece from the Church of Our Lady in Ortenberg, his son, Sigismund of Luxemburg (1410/1433–1437), is the only one whose figure and magnificent vestment are entirely displayed (Fig. 10.5). He is also the only Magus standing, while the two others kneel before the Holy Child, a very rare disposition of the three figures. The same method is used to exhibit Charles VI of France (1380–1422) in the manuscript *Les Petites Heures de Jean de Berry* (Fig. 10.6). The king is depicted as the youngest Magus, the only one standing, displayed from the front, unlike the two others, who bend before the Holy Child and are seen in profile.

Besides the standing and front position, the particular distinction of the contemporary king among the Magi could also be signified by the intervention of other figures. For example, in the fresco of Libiš, the king of Bohemia, Wenceslas of Luxemburg (1376–1419), is depicted as the middle-aged Magus in the centre of the image; he is pointed at by King David and is surmounted by an angel (Fig. 10.7). His brother, Sigismund of Luxemburg, is also depicted as the middle-aged Magus in a drawing of Hubertus van Eyck, in which he is emphasized with other means. Not only is seen from the front—unlike the two other Magi—but he is also designated by the arms of the man drawn besides him, maybe a servant who handed him the gift he is holding (Fig. 10.8). This intervention of other figures in order to highlight the king is also present in the Ortenberg Altarpiece mentioned previously (Fig. 10.5). There, one can see a servant on each side of Sigismund of Luxemburg, the one on his right holding his sword and the one on his left handing him the gift. In a last example, four characters draw attention to the middle-aged King in the altarpiece from the Church Santa Maria de Santes Creus: the youngest Magus, St. Joseph, the saint behind the Virgin, and a small figure that hands

Figure 10.8:
Hubertus van Eyck, *Adoration of the Magi*. Ca. 1417, Berlin, Staatliche Museen, Kupferstich-kabinett. (© Staatliche Museen Kupferstichkabinett, Berlin).

him the gift he will present to the Child (Fig. 10.9). Moreover, the magnificent red vestment of the middle-aged Magus is decorated with the letter "A," to signify the figure as a representation of a king of Aragon.

These are only some of the examples showing how visual support offered new and diverse possibilities for highlighting the figure of the contemporary king. Even if the conditions were now different and the possibilities multiplied, it is obvious that the expression of his distinguished authority had the same importance as in the text of Nicolas of Bari. The contemporary king had to be emphasized among the other crowned figures to accredit his supreme authority.

But it is interesting to note that the same strategies were also used to show that the authority of the king is balanced, or even undermined in certain contexts, by the position of local authorities. Thus, in a triptych commissioned by a rich burgher of Köln, Nicasius Hackeney (ca. 1463–1518), the commissioner himself takes the role of the middle-aged Magus on the left wing, whilst the emperor Maximilian I (1486/1508–1519) is depicted as the young King on the right wing. The central panel holds a third crypto-portrait, that of the deceased emperor, Frederick III (1452–1493) (Fig. 10.10). By assuming the role of Magus equal to the two veritable kings, Nicasius Hackeney makes a strong statement concerning his own authority next to that of royalty. Moreover, the distribution of the roles of Magi between Nicasius and Maximilian does not reflect the real ages of the two figures—the former being younger than the latter—but was likely the commissioner's choice. By taking the role of the middle-aged Magus, Nicasius Hackeney comes closer to the Virgin and Child and is shown as the next King who will present his gift after the elder Magus. The mantle of the kneeled figure penetrates the left wing of the triptych,

Figure 10.9:
Lluís Borrassà, *Adoration of the Magi*. Part of an altarpiece originally in the Santes Creus monastery, ca. 1411, Tarragona, Saint Thecla Cathedral, Chapel of the Virgin of Montserrat. (© Catedral de Tarragona).

thus connecting the central scene with the crypto-portrait of the commissioner. Moreover, the Virgin and Child, as well as St. Joseph, are turned towards Nicasius Hackeney, completely ignoring the king on the right wing, crypto-portrait of Maximilian I. Plainly, the *Adoration of the Magi* permitted the commissioner to express his own views on royal authority and show through the crypto-portraits his own position, which surpasses that of King Maximilian I.

To conclude, this chapter has explored the way identification of medieval kings with the biblical Magi became a strategy for expressing different—sometimes contradictory—conceptions of royal authority. Indeed, before the twelfth century, the need to highlight the unique authority of a king seems to hinder the development of the association between kings and the Magi. Nevertheless, this comparison finally found its way, and two important elements in the scene of the *Adoration of the Magi* seem particularly useful for expressing ideas on royal authority.

Figure 10.10: Master of Frankfurt, *Adoration of the Magi*. Ca. 1510–1515,
Stuttgart, Staatsgalerie, Inv. Nr. L 27. (© Staatsgalerie Stuttgart).

The first element is the disposition of three Magi in front of the Virgin and Child.
There is no doubt that when a historical king is described as Christ or when the Virgin
and Child is seen as the symbol of ecclesiastical authority, kings assuming the role of
Magi are put in a position of inferiority. Their authority is then diminished, compared to
that of contemporary figures who receive the distinguished role of Christ.

The image of the Three Kings was of special interest to medieval authors commenting on royal authority through the use of crypto-portraits of kings. Indeed, the superiority of one Magus among the three can easily be underlined in visual documents and
historical kings can thus be shown wielding supreme authority. However, this strategy
is not exclusively used in favour of kings; other figures also take advantage of it, putting
the king in an inferior position compared to their own. Throughout the Middle Ages,
the *Adoration of the Magi* remains an ambiguous reference, able to sustain, but also to
dispute, the king's authority.

Chapter 11

IDEOLOGY AND CIVIC IDEAL IN FRENCH AND GERMAN CITIES IN THE LATE MIDDLE AGES

GISELA NAEGLE

WHEN IT COMES to comparing two countries and two occasionally divergent his-toriographical traditions, the notions of "ideology" and "civic ideal" raise some consid-erations. In Germany, until the reunification of 1990, two separate scientific systems used different terminology. In the former DDR (German Democratic Republic or East Germany), on the basis of Marxist theories, theoretical concepts such as class strug-gle were used, though often rejected or criticized by historians from the former BRD (German Federal Republic or West Germany).[1] The very notion of ideology was linked to this context and its use and definition underwent several changes.[2]

The sociologist Raymond Boudon begins his book on ideology with the observa-tion that "the definitions of the term are very variable from one author to another and the explanations call for heteroclite principles" and that "all in all, it gives the impres-sion that the same word is used to describe a multitude of phenomena."[3] According

---

1 Peter Johanek, "Stadtgeschichtsforschung ein halbes Jahrhundert nach Ennen und Planitz," in *Europäische Städte im Mittelalter*, ed. Ferdinand Opll, Christoph Sonnlechner (Innsbruck, 2010), 45–92; Gerhard Fouquet, "Erich Maschke und die Folgen—Bemerkungen zu sozialgeschichtlichen Aspekten deutscher Stadtgeschichtsforschung seit 1945," in *Die Urbanisierung Europas von der Antike bis in die Moderne*, ed. Gerhard Fouquet, Gabriel Zeilinger (Frankfurt-am-Main, 2009), 15–42; Klaus Schreiner, "Die Stadt des Mittelalters als Faktor bürgerlicher Identitätsbildung," in *Stadt im Wandel. Kunst und Kultur des Bürgertums in Norddeutschland 1150–1650*, ed. Cord Meckseper, 4 vols. (Stuttgart, 1985), 4:517–541; Peter Blickle, "Kommunalismus, Parlamentarismus, Republikanismus," *Historische Zeitschrift* 242 (1986): 529–56; Eva-Maria Engel, "Bürgertum—Bürgerkampf—Bürgerstadt," in *Mittelalterforschung nach der Wende 1989*, ed. Michael Borgolte (München, 1995), 407–25; Eva-Maria Engel, "Stadtgeschichtsforschung zum Mittelalter in der DDR," in *Stadtgeschichtsforschung*, ed. Fritz Mayrhofer (Linz, 1993), 81–99; Pierre Monnet, "L'histoire des villes médiévales en Allemagne: un état de la recherche," *Histoire urbaine* 11, no. 3 (2004): 131–72.

2 Jan Dumolyn, "Urban Ideologies in Later Medieval Flanders. Towards an Analytical Framework," in *The Languages of Political Society, Western Europe, 14th-17th Centuries*, ed. Andrea Gamberini, Jean-Philippe Genet, Andrea Zorzi (Roma, 2011), 69–96; Clifford Geertz, "Ideology as a Cultural System," in *Ideology and Discontent*, ed. David E. Apter (New York, 1967), 47–76.

3 At the beginning of his book, Boudon observes that: "Les définitions du terme sont très variables d'un auteur à l'autre" and that "les explications font appel à des principes hétéroclites." Boudon also writes that "au total, on a l'impression que le même mot sert à décrire une multitude de phénomènes." See Raymond Boudon, *L'idéologie ou l'origine des idées reçues* (Paris, 1986), 29. In the same sense: Terry Eagleton, *Ideology* (London, 2007), 1–2.

Gisela Naegle (Gisela.C.Naegle@geschichte.uni-giessen.de) is Lehrbeauftragte at the Institut für Deutsche Landesgeschichte, Universität Giessen in Germany.

to Boudon, sociologists like Max Weber or Emile Durkheim appear to have carefully avoided this notion.[4] For German historiography, Max Weber's book on the western city[5] exerted an important influence and prompted a whole series of works following its reception.[6] According to the *Dictionnaire de l'Académie française* of 1878, ideology is "the science of ideas" (*la science des idées*): "a system explaining the origin and formation of ideas" (*un système sur l'origine et la formation des idées*).[7] As such, the notion was invented by Antoine-Louis-Claude Destutt de Tracy (1754–1836). For him, "this science can be called 'ideology' if we only pay attention to the subject, 'general grammar' if we only consider the means, and 'logic' if we only consider the goal. Whatever name is given to it, it necessarily contains these three parts."[8] Under the influence of Napoleon I, ideology quickly became a notion of combat with negative connotations. In a speech given in December 1812, during a reception at the *Conseil d'État* he said:

> It is to ideology, to this dark metaphysics which, by subtly seeking the first causes, wishes to base the legislation of the people on these bases, instead of adapting laws to the knowledge of the human heart and the lessons of history, that we must attribute all the misfortunes which our beautiful France has experienced. These mistakes could and indeed did bring about the regime of the men who spilled blood. Indeed, who has proclaimed the principle of insurrection as a duty?[9]

At the time of the Revolution of 1848, in Germany, the word retained the same negative connotation and was used to defame the ideas of revolutionaries. Through Marx and Engels and various adaptations by socialists and social democrats, the concept evolved and became usable in very different contexts.[10] On several occasions, its end had already

---

4 Boudon, *L'Idéologie*, 31.

5 Max Weber, *Gesamtausgabe*, ed. Wilfried Nippel (Tübingen, 1999), 22: *Wirtschaft und Gesellschaft, Teilband 5: Die Stadt;* Max Weber, *La ville*, trans. Philippe Fritsch (Paris, 1982); Max Weber, *La ville*, trans. Aurélien Berlan (Paris, 2014); Max Weber, *The City*, ed. Don Martindale, Gertrud Neuwirth (New York, 1966); Max Weber, *La ciudad*, trans. Julia Varela, Fernando Álvarez-Uría (Madrid, 1987).

6 Hinnerk Bruhns, Wilfried Nippel, eds., *Max Weber und die Stadt im Kulturvergleich* (Göttingen, 2000); Christian Meier, ed., *Die okzidentale Stadt nach Max Weber* (München, 1994); Alain Bourdin, Monique Hirschhorn, eds., *Figures de la ville. Autour de Max Weber* (Paris, 1985).

7 *Dictionnaire de l'Académie française*, 7th ed. (Paris, 1878; repr. Genève, 1994), vol. 2, 3.

8 *Cette science peut s'appeler "idéologie," si l'on ne fait attention qu'au sujet; "grammaire générale," si l'on n'a égard qu'au moyen; et "logique," si l'on ne considère que le but. Quelque nom qu'on lui donne, elle renferme nécessairement ces trois parties.* Cited from Antoine-Louis-Claude Destutt de Tracy, *Éléments d'idéologie*, 2 vols. (Paris, 1800–1815, repr. Pergamon, n.d. [1993]), 1:19n1 (highlighted by Destutt de Tracy).

9 *C'est à l'idéologie, à cette ténébreuse métaphysique qui, en recherchant avec subtilité les causes premières, veut sur ces bases fonder la législation des peuples, au lieu d'approprier les lois à la connaissance du cœur humain et aux leçons de l'histoire, qu'il faut attribuer tous les malheurs qu'a éprouvés notre belle France. Ces erreurs devaient et ont effectivement amené le régime des hommes de sang. En effet, qui a proclamé le principe d'insurrection comme un devoir?* Cited from Napoléon Ier, Discours, le 20 décembre 1812, *Le Moniteur universel*, 356, 21 décembre 1812, 1408.

10 Ulrich Dierse, "Ideologie," in *Geschichtliche Grundbegriffe*, ed. Otto Brunner, Werner Conze, Reinhart Koselleck, 8 vols. (Stuttgart, 1972–1997), 3:131–69.

been observed:[11] to discover a return in force of religious and political ideologies and religious fundamentalism.[12] In the modern German language, the word can still refer to an arbitrary, distorted perception of reality and to forced attempts by totalitarian systems, particularly communist or fascist, at acceptance of their version of the truth.[13] Similar ideas are expressed by Kenneth Minogue, for whom ideology "is the project of creating social perfection by managing society,"[14] which may represent "a direct attack on the modern liberal democratic state."[15] In scientific discourse, a neutral or positive use can also be seen. However, as noted in 1982,[16] surveys in the database of the German historical bibliography reveal a long-time reluctance of German medievalists to resort to this concept. For the period between 1990 and early January 2013, there are 578 titles containing the word "ideology."[17] Most refer to the end of the nineteenth century and especially to the twentieth century, particularly the Nazi era, the communist states of Eastern Europe, or totalitarian systems in general. Studies on scientific theory and terminology, religious and political ideologies, history of ideas, or historiography can be added. For more ancient periods, the word was used very rarely: often applied to antiquity, sometimes to the Carolingian Empire, crusades and holy wars, or in English or French titles. When it came to studying what could be defined as urban ideology, for a long time other qualifiers were chosen, words like "ideas," "thought," "models," "norms and values," or "liberties."[18] In Francophone historiography, Georges Duby also expressed a certain scepticism. For him, ideologies are at the same time "globalizing, distorting, competing" and "stabilizing"[19] and all ideological systems are based on a vision of history or mythical memories of the past. To create a better future, they encourage action. Duby observes that, in general, the historian can only obtain a fuzzy, fragmented,

---

11 Raymond Aron, "Fin de l'âge idéologique?," in *L'opium des intellectuels*, Raymond Aron (Paris, 1956), 315–34; Daniel Bell, *The End of Ideology* (New York, 1965); Otto Brunner, "Das Zeitalter der Ideologien: Anfang und Ende," in *Neue Wege der Verfassungs- und Sozialgeschichte* (Göttingen, 1968), 45–63.

12 Eagleton, *Ideology*, xxi.

13 *Duden, Deutsches Universalwörterbuch*, 7th ed. (Mannheim, 2011), 899–900.

14 Kenneth Minogue, "Ideology after the Collapse of Communism," *Political Studies* 41 (1993): 4–20 at 19.

15 Minogue, "Ideology," 17.

16 Max Kerner, "Einleitung. Zum Ideologieproblem im Mittelalter," in *Ideologie und Herrschaft im Mittelalter*, ed. Max Kerner (Darmstadt, 1982), 1–58 (esp. 50n132).

17 *Historische Bibliographie Online*: accessed January 20, 2013, http://historische-bibliographie. degruyter.com/.

18 Ulrich Meier, *Mensch und Bürger. Die Stadt im Denken spätmittelalterlicher Theologen, Philosophen und Juristen* (Munich, 1994); Ulrich Meier, Klaus Schreiner, eds., *Stadtregiment und Bürgerfreiheit* (Göttingen, 1994); Barbara Frenz, *Gleichheitsdenken in Städten des 12. bis 15. Jahrhunderts* (Köln, 2000); Gudrun Gleba, *Die Gemeinde als alternatives Ordnungsmodell* (Köln, 1989); Heinrich Schmidt, *Die deutschen Städtechroniken als Spiegel des bürgerlichen Selbstverständnisses im Spätmittelalter* (Göttingen, 1958).

19 Georges Duby, "Histoire sociale et idéologies des sociétés," in *Faire de l'histoire*, ed. Jacques Le Goff, Pierre Nora, 3 vols. (Paris, 1974), 1:147–68 at 150.

and distorted impression of the ideologies of the past which, more often than not, were not the subject of coherent and complete comments by their medieval protagonists. He recommends the study of visible signs, figurative objects, emblems, sculpted and painted images, gests, feasts, ceremonies, and suchlike.[20] Criticism about the use of the notion of *Selbstverständnis* (definition or representation of oneself) by Michael Borgolte goes in the same direction. Resulting from a quest for conceptual unity, the outcome would not take account of the contradictions of the medieval urban world; it would be an anachronistic concept and a "modern" interpretation.[21]

Regarding ideology, French and German dictionaries emphasize the importance of the concrete context and the great variability of its definition. According to one of several explanations of the *Trésor de la langue française du XIXe et XXe siècle*, it is about the "more or less coherent set of ideas, beliefs and philosophical, religious, political, economic, and social doctrines specific to an era, a society, a class, that guides the action."[22] Another definition gives the synonyms of "utopia," "dream," and "naive idealism."[23] The common feature of all these explanations is a concept that applies to specific communities at a specific moment in time. Thus, the question raised in the title could also be formulated differently: Have French and German medieval cities had an urban identity marked by a "civic ideal," and to what extent is it expressed in their political activities, their self-image, and their relations with the other actors of their times?

Since the 1990s, the projects of the European Science Foundation and the French National Centre for Scientific Research (CNRS) on the *Origins of the Modern State in Europe: Thirteenth to Eighteenth centuries* have produced the publication of volumes such as *La ville, la bourgeoisie et la genèse de l'État moderne* (1988), *Legislation and Justice* (1997), and *Resistance, Representation and Community* (1997).[24] In the mean-

---

20 Duby, "Histoire sociale," 152–55.

21 Michael Borgolte, "*Selbstverständnis* und *Mentalitäten*. Bewußtsein, Verhalten und Handeln mittelalterlicher Menschen im Verständnis moderner Historiker," *Archiv für Kulturgeschichte* 79 (1997): 189–210; Robert Stein, "Selbstverständnis oder Identität? Städtische Geschichtsschreibung als Quelle für die Identitätsforschung," in *Memoria, Communitas, Civitas*, ed. Hanno Brand, Pierre Monnet, Martial Staub (Ostfildern, 2003), 181–202.

22 According to the definition of the *Trésor de la langue française du XIXe et du XXe siècle (1789–1960)*, ideology is the *ensemble plus ou moins cohérent des idées, des croyances et des doctrines philosophiques, religieuses, politiques, économiques, sociales, propre à une époque, une société, une classe et qui oriente l'action.* Cited from *Trésor de la langue française du XIXe et du XXe siècle (1789–1960)*, ed. Centre National de la Recherche Scientifique, 16 vols. (Paris, 1971–1994), 9:1085.

23 *Trésor de la langue française*, 9:1085; Malcolm B. Hamilton, "The Elements of the Concept of Ideology," *Political Studies* 35 (1987): 18–38, with a list of twenty-seven components to the definition of ideology. The connection between ideology and utopia is the subject of the reflexions by Karl Mannheim, *Ideologie und Utopie*, 5th ed. (Frankfurt-am-Main, 1969).

24 Neithard Bulst, Jean-Philippe Genet, eds., *La ville, la bourgeoisie et la genèse de l'État moderne* (Paris, 1988); Antonio Padoa Schioppa, ed., *Legislation and Justice* (Oxford, 1997); Peter Blickle, ed., *Resistance, Representation and Community* (Oxford, 1997); Jean-Philippe Genet, ed., *L'État moderne. Genèse, bilans et perspectives* (Paris, 1990); Jean-Philippe Genet, "La genèse de l'État moderne. Les enjeux d'un programme de recherche," *Actes de la recherche en sciences sociales* 118 (1997): 3–18;

time, this perspective was modified and the historiographical landscape was marked by the study of rituals, symbols, and ceremonies, communication and interreligious relations, as well as processes of cultural transfer or exchange and the contributions of the anthropological method.[25] In Germany, the discussion was stimulated by Niklas Luhmann's *Systemtheorie*[26] or Jan Assmann's work on cultural memory. However, in France and Germany, the works of Pierre Bourdieu, Michel Foucault, Niklas Luhmann, Jürgen Habermas, and Jan Assmann were discovered only after their translation into the other language.[27]

In France, the concept of "civic religion" referred first to Greco-Latin Antiquity. André Vauchez defines it as "all religious phenomena—cultural, devotional, or institutional—in which the civil power plays a decisive role, mainly through the action of local and municipal authorities."[28] A second condition involves the civil community's right of inspection and certain prerogatives in the religious sphere.[29] Particularly in wartime, processions that pursue the goal of reinforcing the internal cohesion of the city provide a good example, although for the Holy Roman Empire this concept was little used until then. During the Burgundian wars, Strasbourg organized about forty "extraordinary" processions that followed the rhythm of battles: Héricourt, Grandson, Murten, Nancy.[30] For these processions Strasbourg chose the introit *Salus populi*, a votive mass created after the fall of Constantinople, to revive the crusading spirit. Assimilating the duke of Burgundy with the unbeliever and the imminent war with the crusade was a very political choice.[31] In this field, links between religion and politics were close. In Switzerland,

---

Albert Rigaudière, *Penser et construire l'État dans la France du Moyen Âge* (Paris, 2003).

25 Michael Borgolte, ed., *Mittelalter im Labor* (Berlin, 2008); Michael Borgolte, Bernd Schneidmüller, eds., *Hybride Kulturen im mittelalterlichen Europa* (Berlin, 2010); Michael Borgolte, Julia Dücker, Marcel Müllerburg, Bernd Schneidmüller, eds., *Integration und Desintegration der Kulturen im europäischen Mittelalter* (Berlin, 2011).

26 Niklas Luhmann, *Soziale Système: Grundriß einer allgemeinen Theorie*, 15th ed. (Frankfurt-am-Main, 2012); Niklas Luhmann, *Systèmes sociaux: esquisse d'une théorie générale*, trans. Lukas Sosoe (Quebec, 2010); Niklas Luhmann, *Legitimation durch Verfahren*, 3rd ed. (Frankfurt-am-Main, 1993); Niklas Luhmann, *La légitimation par la procédure*, trans. Lukas Sosoe and Stéphane Boucard (Paris, 2001).

27 Jan Assmann, *Das kulturelle Gedächtnis*, 6th ed. (Munich, 2007); Jan Assmann, *La mémoire culturelle*, trans. Danielle Meur (Paris, 2010); Pierre Guibentif, *Foucault, Luhmann, Habermas, Bourdieu. Une génération repense le droit* (Paris, 2010).

28 *L'ensemble des phénomènes religieux—culturels, dévotionnels ou institutionnels—dans lesquels le pouvoir civil joue un rôle déterminant, principalement à travers l'action des autorités locales et municipales.* Cited from André Vauchez, "Introduction," in *La religion civique à l'époque médiévale et moderne*, ed. André Vauchez (Roma, 1995), 1–5 at 1; *Religion civique XVe-XVIe siècle*, ed. Olivier Richard, special issue, *Histoire urbaine* 27 (April 2010); Patrick Boucheron, Jacques Chiffoleau, eds., *Religion et société urbaine au Moyen Âge* (Paris, 2000).

29 Vauchez, "Introduction," 2.

30 Gabriela Signori, "Rituel, événement et propagande: les processions strasbourgeoises durant les guerres bourguignonnes 1474–1477," in *La ville à la Renaissance. Espaces—représentations— pouvoirs*, ed. Gérald Chaix (Paris, 2008), 265–70.

31 Signori, "Rituel," 271; Claudius Sieber-Lehmann, "Teutsche Nation und Eidgenossenschaft.

266   GISELA NAEGLE

there is still commemoration and political instrumentalization of medieval battles and the *Rütlischwur*,[32] and in the collective historical memory of cities like Bern, the victories against the Burgundians occupy an important place. In Fribourg, in 1480, the city ordered a painting of the battle of Murten (1476) for the urban council's hall. In the town halls of Fribourg, Bern, Lucerne, and Solothurn, and the illustrated chronicles of Lucerne and Bern, paintings of battles could be found.[33] The commemoration of battles also existed in German cities and helped to strengthen the collective identity of the inhabitants.[34] In Lübeck, in the fifteenth century, the memory of the Battle of Bornhöved of July 27, 1227 was still cultivated. It was an important victory of a coalition of the city against the Danes. Commemorative ceremonies included a religious service of thanks that was supported by several princes and an annual meal for the poor on July 22, offered by the urban council and the citizens. After the Reformation this religious service was still celebrated, though moved to another date. The meal for the poor existed until 1683. These measures were complemented by a cycle of fifteen images of Lübeck's ancient history in the town hall, five of which were significant in relation to the Empire (they referred to the city's struggle for the legal status of immediacy or *Reichsunmittelbarkeit*) and the Battle of Bornhöved. These images existed from about ca. 1430–1440 until 1795.[35]

The same phenomenon of a close connection between the religious and secular aspects shows itself in the use of urban seals. Of the 434 French cities studied by Christian de Mérindol, eighty-four (or nineteen percent) use religious themes. Most of them are in southern France, the ancient Empire lands, and the north.[36] The most popular motifs are the patron saint of the church, the cathedral, the abbey, or the saint linked to the history of the city, as well as the representation of the saint related to the name of the city.[37]

Der Zusammenhang zwischen Türken- und Burgunderkriegen," *Historische Zeitschrift* 253 (1991): 561–602; for processions in Nürnberg and Erfurt, see: Andrea Löther, *Prozessionen in spätmittelalterlichen Städten* (Köln, 1999).

32 Guy P. Marchal, *Schweizer Gebrauchsgeschichte. Geschichtsbilder, Mythenbildung und nationale Identität* (Basel, 2006); Guy P. Marchal, "Die Schweizer und ihr Mittelalter. Missbrauch der Geschichte?," *Schweizerische Zeitschrift für Geschichte* 55, no. 2 (2005): 131–48.

33 Oliver Landolt, "Eidgenössisches *Heldenzeitalter* zwischen Morgarten 1315 und Marignano 1515?," in *Militärische Erinnerungskulturen vom 14. bis zum 19. Jh.*, ed. Horst Carl, Ute Planert (Göttingen, 2012), 69–97 at 75; Regula Schmid, *Geschichte im Dienst der Stadt. Amtliche Historie und Politik im Spätmittelalter* (Zürich, 2009), 100 and 150–61.

34 Klaus Graf, "Schlachtengedenken in der Stadt," in *Stadt und Krieg*, ed. Berhard Kirchgässner, Günter Scholz (Sigmaringen, 1989), 83–104; Klaus Graf, "Schlachtengedenken im Spätmittelalter: Riten und Medien der Präsentation kollektiver Identität," in *Feste und Feiern im Mittelalter*, ed. Detlef Altenberger, Jörg Jarnut, Hans-Hugo Steinhoff (Sigmaringen, 1991), 63–69.

35 Sascha Möbius, "Die Schlacht bei Bornhöved in der Lübeckischen Erinnerungskultur des 15. Jahrhunderts," in *Militärische Erinnerungskulturen vom 14. bis zum 19. Jh.*, ed. Horst Carl, Ute Planert (Göttingen, 2012), 47–68 at 48–49.

36 Christian de Mérindol, "Iconographie du sceau de ville en France à l'époque médiévale et religion civique," in *La Religion civique à l'époque médiévale et moderne*, ed. André Vauchez (Roma, 1995), 417–18.

37 Christian de Mérindol, "Iconographie du sceau," 419.

Other cities refer to their constitutions with depictions of the mayor or aldermen on horseback, or the landmark buildings of the city.[38]

Legal Foundations and Civic Ideals

At first glance, French and German cities are very different. In part, this is due to the different structure of the medieval Empire and the kingdom of France as elective monarchy and hereditary monarchy. In both countries there were royal cities. The king was their immediate lord, but in the case of the Empire, its status and that of the "free" episcopal cities were more emphasized by contemporaries and later by scientific historiography.[39]

These cities had privileged relations with the king and tried to retain their status. But in spite of many guarantees, kings did not respect their obligations. The emperor, always in need of money, often pawned imperial cities,[40] and in France the cities could become victims of the events of the Hundred Years War, the constitution of appanages, or other political necessities. During the Franco-Burgundian conflict, the question of the cities of the Somme was an important issue. In France, royal enclaves served as a support for royalty and against powerful princes. They could have an important political function, like Montferrand or Tournai. Such cities could use their particular situation to negotiate the granting of extended privileges.[41] Nevertheless, for centuries, cities like Arras or Perpignan had much to suffer from their strategic importance.[42] In the Empire, the royal dynasty changed several times, with implications for the political role of cities. The medieval Empire had several capitals, including Nürnberg and Frankfurt, but there was no uncontested centre that played the same role as Paris.[43] Until its end in 1806, it was marked by a polycentric structure and the development of institutions took place

---

38 Jean-Luc Chassel, Pierre Flandin-Bléty, "La représentation du pouvoir délibératif sur les sceaux des villes au Moyen Âge," in *Le gouvernement des communautés politiques à la fin du Moyen Âge*, ed. Corinne Leveleux-Teixeira, Anne Rousselet-Pimont, Pierre Bonin, Florent Garnier (Paris, 2011), 135–60; *Corpus des sceaux français du Moyen Âge*, ed. Brigitte Bedos-Rezak, 3 vols. (Paris, 1980–2011), Vol. 1 (1980), *Les sceaux des villes*.

39 Gisela Naegle, "'Bonnes villes' et 'güte stete'. Quelques remarques sur le problème des 'villes notables' en France et en Allemagne à la fin du Moyen Âge," *Francia* 35 (2008): 115–48; Eberhard Isenmann, *Die deutsche Stadt im Spätmittelalter 1150–1500* (Wien, 2012); Paul-Joachim Heinig, *Reichsstädte, Freie Städte und Königtum, 1389–1450* (Wiesbaden, 1983); Peter Moraw, "Reichsstadt, Reich und Königtum im späten Mittelalter," *Zeitschrift für Historische Forschung* 6 (1979): 385–424.

40 Götz Landwehr, *Die Verpfändung der deutschen Reichsstädte im Mittelalter* (Köln, 1967).

41 Bernard Chevalier, *Les bonnes villes de France du XIV* au XVI* siècle* (Paris, 1982); Albert Rigaudière, *Gouverner la ville au Moyen Âge* (Paris, 1993); Gisela Naegle, *Stadt, Recht und Krone. Französische Städte, Königtum und Parlement im späten Mittelalter*, 2 vols. (Husum, 2002).

42 Gisela Naegle, "Les châtiments de Toulouse et d'Arras: comparaison des deux villes rebelles au XV* siècle," *Le châtiment des villes dans les espaces méditerranéens*, ed. Patrick Gilli, Jean-Pierre Guilhembet (Turnhout, 2012), 359–72.

43 *Das Hauptstadtproblem in der Geschichte*, Jahrbuch für Geschichte des deutschen Ostens 1 (Tübingen, 1952, repr. Goldbach, 1993); *Les villes capitales au Moyen Âge*, ed. Société des médiévistes de l'enseignement supérieur public (Paris, 2006); Werner Paravicini, Bertrand Schnerb, eds., *Paris, capitale des Ducs de Bourgogne* (Ostfildern, 2007); Gerhard Fouquet, "Hauptorte—Metropolen—

at the level of territorial principalities and cities. The regional diversity of the Empire inspired Alexander de Roes to make an interesting comparison: in his *Memoriale de prerogativa Romani imperii* (1281), he tries to prove that the diversity of political geography does not hinder the fact that it is the same country:

> Therefore in this province called "Gallia" and which is now owned by "Germans" and "French," Franks and "descendants of Franks," there were, in the past, sometimes (only) one, sometimes several kingdoms at the same time or successively, just as it was for a long time the case and as it still is in Spain, where there are several kings, but which, nevertheless, is called the "kingdom of the Spanish."[44]

Later, in 1356, article 31 of the Golden Bull of the Emperor Charles IV contained a similar observation on the Empire's diversity:

> As the magnificence of the Holy Roman Empire has to wield the law and government of diverse nations that differ from each other in their customs, their lifestyle and their vernaculars, it is convenient, and, according to the judgment of all wise men expedient, that the prince electors [...] should be educated in the different varieties of vernaculars and languages, so that they can understand more of them and that they can be understood by numerous people.[45]

Unlike France, where medieval texts and historiography stressed the idea of unity rather than diversity, and where borders remained relatively stable, the medieval Empire included many territories that became independent states. There were several attempts to erect a city as the capital of the Empire, and cities such as Praha or Wien owed much of their prestige and wealth to the presence of the court. Nevertheless, before the sixteenth century and even in the seventeenth century, the weight of cities of residence in the urban network of the Empire was not yet decisive.[46] On the other hand, the role of Paris as an administrative, cultural, and political centre escaped any real challenge at an early stage. Towards 1435, according to the testimony of Jean Juvénal des Ursins,

---

Haupt- und Residenzstädte im Reich," in *Höfe und Residenzen im spätmittelalterlichen Reich*, 1/1, ed. Werner Paravicini (Ostfildern, 2003), 3–15.

44 *In ista igitur provincia, que Gallia dicitur et modo a Germanis et Gallicis, Francis et Francigenis possidetur, quandoque unum, quandoque plura fuerunt regna, aliquando simul, aliquando successive, sicut modo est et diu fuit in Hispania, ubi licet plures sint reges, tamen unum dicitur regnum Hispanorum.* Cited from Alexander von Roes, "Memoriale de Pregrogativa imperii Romani," in *Schriften*, ed. Herbert Grundmann, Hermann Heimpel (Stuttgart, 1958), 91–148 at 115.

45 *Cum sacri Romani celsitudo imperii diversarum nacionum moribus, vita et ydiomate distinctarum leges habeat et gubernacula moderari, dignum est et cunctorum sapientium iudicio censetur expediens, quod electores principes ipsius imperii [...] diversorum ydiomatum et linguarum differenciis instruantur, ut plures intelligant et intelligantur a pluribus.* Cited from "Die Goldene Bulle. Die Metzer Gesetze, 25 december 1356," in *Quellen zur Verfassungsgeschichte des römisch-deutschen Reiches im Spätmittelalter (1250–1500)*, ed. Lorenz Weinrich (Darmstadt, 1983), 392; Gisela Naegle, "Diversité linguistique, identités et mythe de l'Empire à la fin du Moyen Âge," *Revue française d'histoire des idées politiques* 36, no. 2 (2012): 253–79.

46 Étienne François, "Des républiques marchandes aux capitales politiques: remarques sur la hiérarchie urbaine du Saint-Empire à l'époque moderne," *Revue d'Histoire Moderne et contemporaine* 25 (1978): 587–603; Werner Paravicini, Jörg Wettlaufer, eds., *Der Hof und die Stadt* (Ostfildern, 2006).

Paris's importance was based on four factors: the residence of the lords (*demourance de seigneurs*), "the sovereign justice" of the kingdom and that of the Châtelet, the university, and—it is significant that this factor appears last—the merchandise.⁴⁷ Sometimes the central role of Paris was resented by other cities, as in a memorial of the end of the fifteenth century, in which Troyes tried to claim the fairs of Lyon for itself:

> And it would be better to maintain, resolve, and repopulate by instituting the fairs in several towns of the country than to put everything in just one city, as the other parts of the country could not bear the great burdens they should bear, which could lead to the total destruction of Troyes and the region (pays) of Champagne and other surrounding regions (pays) [...].⁴⁸

From the point of view of urban freedoms, too close proximity to the king or the lord and his officers can present a considerable obstacle. For the cities of the Burgundian Netherlands, Marc Boone sees in this circumstance one of the reasons the dream of a city-state was not realized.⁴⁹ One of the capitals of the Empire, Frankfurt, saw this danger and opposed the installation of the *Reichskammergericht* within its walls.⁵⁰ The *Reichskammergericht*, the supreme court of justice of the Empire, was installed in Speyer and later in Wetzlar, not in one of the most important cities. In the late Middle Ages, there was no developed apparatus of imperial officers. Unlike France, where cities were in danger of being controlled by reform commissioners or royal institutions such as the Chamber of Accounts or the supreme court of law, the *Parlement*, German free and imperial cities did not have to fear a too thorough royal administrative control. They had to be wary of the interference of the powerful territorial lords, and in 1388/89 and 1449/50 the *Städtekriege*, wars between cities and princes, ended with the defeat of the cities.⁵¹ In order to carry out armed conflicts and external policy, their margins of manoeuvre were much greater than those of their French counterparts. It is significant that the *Verbundbrief* of Köln (1396), the fundamental text of the medieval urban constitution, contains provisions on the right to make peace and war. According to its provisions, the *Rat* ("council") has no right to conduct warlike enterprises and it cannot

---

47 Jean Juvénal des Ursins, "Audite Celi," (around 1435) in *Écrits politiques de Jean Juvénal des Ursins*, ed. Peter S. Lewis, 3 vols. (Paris, 1978–1992), 1:93–281 at 257; Gisela Naegle, "Vérités contradictoires et réalités constitutionnelles. La ville et le roi en France à la fin du Moyen Âge," *Revue Historique* 632 (2004): 727–62 at 732.

48 *Et vauldroit mieux entretenir, résouldre et repopuler en instituant lesd. foires en plusieurs villes du pays, que de tout mectre en une seulle ville, et ne sauroient les autres pays supporter les grandes charges qui leur convient supporter, mesmement ce seroit la totalle destruction de Troyes et du pays de Champaigne et autres pays à l'environ [...].* Cited from Joseph Pierre, *Quelques notes sur les foires de Champagne et de Brie* (Paris, 1904), 19.

49 Marc Boone, *À la recherche d'une modernité civique* (Bruxelles, 2010), 118–21.

50 Pierre Monnet, "Des juristes en ville: Le *Reichskammergericht* à Francfort, aspects politiques et sociaux d'une brève histoire (1494–1497)," *Publications du Centre européen d'études bourguignonnes*, 40 (2000): 107–27.

51 Alexander Schubert, *Der Stadt Nutz oder Notdurft? Die Reichsstadt Nürnberg und der Städtekrieg 1388/89* (Husum, 2003); Gabriel Zeilinger, *Lebensformen im Krieg. Eine Alltags-und Erfahrungsgeschichte des süddeutschen Städtekrieges 1449/1450* (Stuttgart, 2007).

enter into new alliances or contracts with lords and other cities without informing the *Gemeynde* and obtaining its agreement.[52] In some parts of the Empire and even in those which considered themselves centres, the emperor could be far away. Before becoming emperor, Sigismund had reigned for more than forty years in Hungary,[53] Charles IV was reproached for being too busy with Bohemia, and between 1444 and 1471, for twenty-seven years, Frederick III did not leave his Austrian inheritances.[54] The *Agrippina*, a chronicle of Köln by Heinrich van Beeck (1469–1472), criticizes Charles IV for spending too much time with Bohemia and too little with the Empire, which could cause very serious harm and damage. Charles thought only of his own interests and not of the common good.[55] In this case, it is interesting to look at the chronicler's sources: he uses the Strasbourg chronicle by Jakob Twinger von Königshofen (1346–1420), which also explicitly refers to the Bohemian history by Enea Silvio Piccolomini.[56]

The framework of the elective monarchy allowed cities to make a clear distinction between the Empire and the emperor. In his *Pentalogus* (1443), Enea Silvio Piccolomini, who at that time was also an adviser to the future Emperor Frederick III (d. 1493), emphasizes this strength of urban identity. He makes one of his fictitious interlocutors express fear that the different members of the Empire would not be ready to make financial sacrifices for its interests, and that especially city dwellers would think first about the well-being of their own city.[57] For Johannes Cochlaeus (d. 1552) and other Nürn-

---

52 "[...] not to carry out any military campaign or order it, not to enter into any new alliances, or to accept any letters or contracts with any lords or towns in whatever way." (*[...] geyne hervart zo doin noch zu bestellen, geyne nuwe verbontenisse, brieve noch verdrach mit eyngen herren of steden anzogain off zo machen in eynger wijse.*) Cited from Manfred Huiskes, "Kölns Verfassung für 400 Jahre: Der Verbundbrief vom 14. September 1396," in *Quellen zur Geschichte der Stadt Köln, Förderverein Geschichte in Köln*, ed. Joachim Deeters, 6 vols. (Köln, 1996), 2:6–7 (document 1).

53 Michel Pauly, François Reinert, eds., *Sigismund von Luxemburg* (Mainz, 2006); Sabine Wefers, *Das politische System Kaiser Sigmunds* (Stuttgart, 1989); Josef Macek, ed., *Sigismund von Luxemburg* (Warendorf, 1994); Jörg K. Hoensch, *Kaiser Sigismund, Herrscher an der Schwelle zur Neuzeit, 1387–1437* (München, 1996).

54 Paul-Joachim Heinig, *Kaiser Friedrich III (1440–1493)*, 3 vols. (Köln, 1997), 2:818–19.

55 "Otherwise he [Charles IV] would not have inflicted such severe damage on the Empire; and all empires that are divided in themselves will be destroyed. Selfish interests are the reason why the Holy [Roman] Empire has suffered such hardship and ruin." (*Hey hedde anders sulchen swaren schaden dem Riche nyet zugefu°eget, alle ryche in sich gedeylt wird verderfflichen. Darvmbe viz eygennutze ys dat gemeyne goyt des Hilligen Rychs zu solcher noyt vnd verderfnysse komen*). Cited from Robert Meier, *Heinrich van Beeck und seine Agrippina* (Köln, 1998), 255–56. On the image of Charles IV see: Beat Frey, *Pater Bohemiae—Vitricus Imperii. Böhmens Vater, Stiefvater des Reiches. Kaiser Karl IV in der Geschichtsschreibung* (Bern, 1978).

56 Meier, *Heinrich van Beeck*, 255.

57 "Silvester: Some people say indeed: 'Why should I care for the Empire? I am a citizen of my town. If Frederick wants to get the Empire, he has to assume its charges, because someone who will profit from it has to do so'. Not all the people are in such a state of mind that they care for the honour of the nation." (*Silvester: [...] Aiunt enim nonulli: 'Quid ad me de imperio? Habeat regnum quicumque velit, ego mee civitatis sum civis. Si cupit Fridericus imperium, faciat ipse sumptus, cui commodum redundabit'. Non omnes eius animi sunt, ut honorem nationis attendant*). Cited from Eneas Silvius Piccolomini, *Pentalogus*, ed. Christoph Schingnitz (Hannover, 2009), 262–64.

berg humanists, their city was literally the centre of Europe and the Empire.[58] In spite of his function, even the emperor remained in many respects a territorial prince who protected the interests of his own territories and his family.[59] In the League of Swabia (1488–1534), a league of territorial peace which brought together the most important territories, cities and nobles of the South of the Empire, the emperor was admitted only as an "ordinary" territorial prince.[60] The latter case is particularly interesting because in the context of repressive actions during the Peasants War (1424–1426),[61] member-cities were obliged to act against the rebelling peasants, who often defended ideas much closer to those of the cities than of princes and nobles.[62]

Recently, François Foronda's three volumes on the political contract in Europe showed that it might be interesting to explore the comparative aspect of leagues, urban cooperation, and contract, and their terminology.[63] In situations of royal schism, cities had to define their positions, but also hope to be rewarded for their support. For example, in France, it was necessary to decide between the Anglo-Burgundians and the dauphin, the future Charles VII. In the Empire, the decision was between the Emperor Louis of Bavaria (d. 1347) and the Duke of Austria, Frederick the Fair (d. 1330). Then, elected as anti-King Louis, Charles IV (d. 1378) had in turn to confront Günther von Schwarzburg (d. 1349).[64] Often opposing cities were mired in conflicts that were not theirs. In the Empire, in situations of royal crisis, to ensure their security and defence, cities and sometimes leagues of several princes, lords, and towns acted instead of the king. There were assemblies of cities without the presence of the emperor king, especially from 1471. Nevertheless, these assemblies could also exercise a preparatory or

---

58 "Nürnberg is as well the centre of Europe as that of Germany." (*Norimberga centrum simul Europe simul atque Germanie*). Cited from Johannes Cochlaeus, *Brevis Germanie Descriptio (1512)*, ed. Karl Langosch (Darmstadt, 1976), 74–75.

59 Gisela Naegle, "D'une cité à l'autré: bien commun et réforme de l'État à la fin du Moyen Âge (France/Empire)," *Revue française d'histoire des idées politiques* 32, no. 2 (2010): 325–38 at 337.

60 Horst Carl, *Der Schwäbische Bund 1488–1534* (Leinfelden, 2000), 57.

61 Peter Blickle, *Der Bauernkrieg*, 4th ed. (München, 2012).

62 Carl, *Der Schwäbische Bund*, 486. On the action of the Swabian League during this war, see: Carl, *Der Schwäbische Bund*, 493–97 and Horst Carl, "Landfrieden als Konzept und Realität kollektiver Sicherheit im Heiligen Römischen Reich," in *Frieden schaffen und sich verteidigen im Spätmittelalter/Faire la paix et se défendre à la fin du Moyen Âge*, ed. Gisela Naegle (München, 2012), 121–38 at 132–34.

63 François Foronda, Ana Isabel Carrasco Manchado, eds., *Du contrat d'alliance au contrat politique: cultures et sociétés politiques dans la péninsule Ibérique de la fin du Moyen Âge* (Toulouse, 2007); François Foronda, Ana Isabel Carrasco Manchado, *El contrato político en la Corona de Castilla. Cultura y sociedad politíticas entre los siglos X al XVI* (Madrid, 2008); François Foronda, ed., *Avant le contrat social* (Paris, 2011).

64 Michael Menzel, "Ludwig der Bayer (1314–1347) und Friedrich der Schöne (1314–1330)," in *Die deutschen Herrscher des Mittelalters*, ed. Bernd Schneidmüller, Stefan Weinfurter (Munich, 2003), 393–407 and Martin Kintzinger, "Karl IV (1346–1378) mit Günther von Schwarzburg (1349)," in *Die deutschen Herrscher des Mittelalters*, ed. Bernd Schneidmüller, Stefan Weinfurter (München, 2003), 408–32.

auxiliary role in relation to the diets of the Empire.[65] Urban participants were often experienced "diplomats" who had done a real "apprenticeship."[66] In France, despite the defences of ordinances, cumulation of royal and urban offices was frequent. In 1484, almost two-thirds of the representatives of the third estate at the Estates General of Tours were royal officials.[67] For the imperial diets, we know of a great number of reports that urban ambassadors sent to their native cities. The correspondence of cities provides evidence of coordination regarding decisions about the financial demands of royalty.[68] For example, in 1486, it was feared that the Emperor's request for financial assistance would become so important that most of the Empire and free cities would be saddled with unbearable burdens. In this situation, an assembly of towns in Esslingen decides to convene a second meeting to deliberate on preventive measures and prepare a joint opposition. On this "day" all cities will participate. It will be necessary to make joint decisions and avoid suffering "ruinous and unbearable" burdens" (*so verderblichen schaden und unlidenlichen beswerden*) and the loss of their customary freedoms.[69] As in France, the language of such complaints is deliberately dramatic.

65 Georg Schmidt, *Der Städtetag in der Reichsverfassung* (Stuttgart, 1984), 7, 26, and 33; Gabriele Annas, *Hoftag—Gemeiner Tag—Reichstag* (Göttingen, 2004), 425; Peter Moraw, ed., *Deutscher Königshof, Hoftag und Reichstag im späteren Mittelalter* (Stuttgart, 2002).

66 Christian Jörg, "Gesandte als Spezialisten," in *Spezialisierung und Professionalisierung, Träger und Foren städtischer Außenpolitik während des späten Mittelalters und der frühen Neuzeit*, ed. Christian Jörg, Michael Jucker (Wiesbaden, 2010), 31–64; Bastian Walter, *Informationen, Technik und Macht: Akteure und Techniken städtischer Außenpolitik: Bern, Straßburg und Basel im Kontext der Burgunderkriege (1468–1477)* (Stuttgart, 2012), 80–103 and 148.

67 Neithard Bulst, *Die französischen Generalstände von 1468 und 1484* (Sigmaringen, 1992), 361.

68 See for example, Johannes Jannsen, ed., *Frankfurts Reichskorrespondenz nebst andern verwandten Aktenstücken von 1376–1519* (Freiburg im Breisgau, 1863–1866).

69 "And so, as we should take into consideration and as the royal orders announce, the big (financial) assessment will follow after the little one and this will lead to such charges and burdens for the common free and imperial cities, that it is to fear that, as to their traditional rights, they will be oppressed and that they will suffer an important loss. And it is also to fear that a good number of them will be subject to an almost complete ruin. And, because they are in no ways willing to suffer and to bear this, they think that it is useful and necessary to fix another 'day' [assembly] and to write to all common free and imperial towns, from near and far, in order to deliberate and think about measures to prevent the towns from suffering such damage and unbearable burdens and that by oppression they would lose their traditional rights." (*Und so, als wol zu gedenken ist und die ksl. mandaten anzaigend, der groß anschlag dem klainen wird nachfolgen, und dadurch soliche last und besward auf gemain Fry- und Rstt. erwachsen, das sie dardurch von irem herkomen gedrungen und zu merklichem abgang, und, als zu besorgen ist, etlich zu gruntlichem verderben gebracht werden, sie auch solhs in kainen wegen erliden noch erzugen mogen, habend sie nutz und notturftig sein bedacht, das ain ander tag furgenomen und gemainlich all Fry- und Rstt., fern und nach, darauf beschrieben werden, zu erwegen und zu ratschlagen, was sy furzunemen, damit die stett nit zu so verderblichen schaden und unlidenlichen beswerden gebracht und von irem alten herkomen gedrungen werden.*) Cited from "Abschied des Städtetages zu Esslingen am 4. August 1486," in *Deutsche Reichstagsakten unter Maximilian I. 1. Band: Reichstag zu Frankfurt 1486*, ed. Heinz Angermeier, Reinhard Seyboth, Deutsche Reichstagsakten. Mittlere Reihe 1, 2 vols. (Göttingen, 1989), documents 440, 459.

The subject of the forms of urban cooperation and solidarity in France has received little attention from researchers until now. Despite the active cooperation of the cities of the Midi in times of crisis, which were the subject of studies on Rouergue and Quercy,[70] there were no highly institutionalized urban leagues as in Italy, Germany, or the *hermandades* in Spain.[71] It seems interesting to compare the latter and,[72] theoretically, the concept of *pactisme*,[73] with the studies of corporatism and *Genossenschaft,* as well as with the theory of "communalism." In these leagues of a horizontal nature, the terminology of fraternity and mutual aid played an important part, and in 1383, at the time of the Rhine League, the Strasbourg Urban Council wrote to its "dear special friends and confederates" (*unsern sundern guten frunden unt eitgenoszen*), mayors and councils of the cities of Mainz, Frankfurt, Hagenau, Wissembourg, Wetzlar, Friedberg, Gelnhausen, and Pfeddersheim, by inciting them to military measures against Worms and Speyer.[74] Military and punitive actions by German cities are the subject of some comments made by Philippe de Commynes:

> [...] because a man with only one servant will defy a big city or a duke, that he may have a pretence to rob, especially if he has a little castle, perched upon a rock, to retreat to [...]. Here, these people are seldom punished by the German princes [...]; but the towns punish them severely whenever they catch any of them, and have often besieged and blown up such castles, and they employ generally a certain number of armed men.[75]

---

70 Pierre Flandin-Bléty, "Essai sur le rôle politique du Tiers-État dans les Pays de Quercy et de Rouergue (XIIIe-XVe siècle)," 2 vols. (PhD diss., Université Paris-2, 1979); Elizabeth Brown, *Customary Aids and Royal Finance in Capetian France* (Cambridge, MA, 1992); Elizabeth Brown, *Politics and Institutions in Capetian France* (Aldershot, 1991).

71 Gisela Naegle, "*Omne regnum in se divisum desolabitur?* Coopération urbaine en France et dans l'Empire médiéval," in *Ligues urbaines et espaces à la fin du Moyen Âge,* ed. Laurence Buchholzer, Olivier Richard (Strasbourg, 2012), 53–69.

72 Gisela Naegle, "Einleitung," in *Frieden schaffen und sich verteidigen im Spätmittelalter/Faire la paix et se défendre à la fin du Moyen Âge,* ed. Gisela Naegle (Munich, 2012), 31–40, Máximo Diago Hernando, "Die politische Rolle der Städtebünde im spätmittelalterlichen Kastilien (13.–16. Jh.)," in *Frieden schaffen und sich verteidigen im Spätmittelalter/Faire la paix et se défendre à la fin du Moyen Âge,* ed. Gisela Naegle (München, 2012), 139–59; Máximo Diago Hernando, "Transformaciones sociopolíticas en las ciudades de la Corona de Castilla y en las del Imperio alemán durante el siglo XIII," *Anuario de estudios medievales* 27, no. 1 (1997): 103–46.

73 María Asenjo González, "Ciudades y Hermandades en la Corona de Castilla. Aproximación sociopolítica," *Anuario de Estudios Medievales* 27, no. 1 (1997): 103–46; Jaume Sobrequés y Callicó, *El pactisme a Catalunya* (Barcelona, 1982); Gregorio Colás Latorre, "El pactismo en Aragón. Propuestas para un estudio," in *La Corona de Aragón y el Mediterráneo siglos XV–XVI,* ed. Esteban Sarasa, Eliseo Serrano (Zaragoza, 1997), 269–93; Luiz Legaz y Lacambra, ed., *El pactismo en la Historia de España* (Madrid, 1980).

74 *Frankfurts Reichskorrespondenz,* 1, no. 30, 10.

75 *[...] car ung homme qui n'aura que luy et son varlet deffiera une grosse cité ou ung duc, pour myeulx pouvoir robber, avecques le port de quelque petit chasteau rochier ou il se sera retraict, [...]. Ces gens icy ne sont gueres de foiz puniz des princes d'Almaigne, [...]; mais les villes, quant ilz les peuvent tenir, les punissent cruellement, et aulcunes foiz ont bien assiégé de telz chasteaulx et abatuz: et aussi tiennent lesdictes villes ordinairement des gens d'armes paiéz.* Cited from Philippe de Commynes, *Mémoires,* ed. Joël Blanchard, 2 vols. (Genève, 2007), 1:402–3.

This medieval observation again highlights the differences between German and French cities and their respective margins for manoeuvre. Nevertheless, the comparative study of urban revolts and their punishments shows a good number of elements which were important for the definition of the cities themselves: In France and Germany, the actual course of such insurrections presented many parallels. In both cases, the symbolic sites of urban power were the main focus. The intention is to penetrate the places of power, the city hall, the council headquarters, or the seats of the urban assemblies. Then, possession of the city's keys, archives, and control of the bell, treasure, and seals are among the main objectives. In the case of punitive measures after revolts, these objects also become privileged targets of repression. In addition, the lord of the city in question attacks the walls, the privileges of commune or consulate, the composition of the urban government, etc. In some cases, he imposes the installation of a garrison, builds a citadel, or confiscates the town hall.[76]

When it comes to ideology and civic ideals, one thinks first about cities of the Empire (*Reichsstädte*), free cities and communal towns in the north and centre, or of consulates in the south of France. Increasingly interested in territorial cities, cities of residence, and small towns, modern researchers are reassessing the traditional picture.[77] They point out that important territorial cities such as Braunschweig had succeeded in gaining a much more influential place than some of the small imperial cities.[78] The criterion of the concession of urban law played a large part in the definition of the city in German historiography. It is much less valid for France, where consulates could also be tiny and where Paris was not a commune in the legal sense.[79] On the theoretical level, law was largely prefigured by the constructions of learned law, such as the idea of the *civitas sibi princeps* of Bartole, the maxim *quod omnes tangit*, and the works of the great Italian jurists and theologians.[80] However, in the field of judicial practice, it is difficult to measure the exact influence of the reception of the Roman–canonical law[81] and, unlike in the Empire, in France, there were no real city-states. In the different regions of the Empire and France the chronological moment and the actual degree of reception of the learned law is very different, with important differences between the north and the south.[82] For the Empire, the fact that for a long time the academically trained jurists had to study in Italy or, more rarely, in France, exercised an important influence.[83] For a long

---

76 See Patrick Gilli, Jean-Pierre Guilhembet, eds., *Le châtiment des villes*.

77 On this typology, see Isenmann, *Die deutsche Stadt*, 281–315.

78 Bernd Schneidmüller, "Reichsnähe - Königsferne: Goslar, Braunschweig und das Reich im späten Mittelalter," *Niedersächsisches Jahrbuch für Landesgeschichte* 64 (1992): 1–52 at 29–41.

79 Naegle, "Bonnes villes," 115–48.

80 On these legal maxims, see Christian Meier, *Stadt und Bürger*.

81 Helmut G. Walther, "Die Macht der Gelehrsamkeit. Über die Meßbarkeit des Einflusses politischer Theorien gelehrter Juristen des Spätmittelalters," in *Political Thought and the Realities of Power in the Middle Ages*, ed. Otto Gerhard Oexle, Joseph Canning (Göttingen,1998), 241–67.

82 Gerhard Dilcher, "Die Rechtsgeschichte der Stadt," in *Deutsche Rechtsgeschichte*, ed. Karl S. Bader, Gerhard Dilcher (Berlin, 1999), 249–827.

83 Peter Moraw, "Universitätsbesucher und Gelehrte im deutschen Reich," in *Gesammelte Beiträge*

time, and especially for the liberal historians of the nineteenth century, the medieval commune represented a democratic and egalitarian ideal opposed to the hierarchies of the feudal world. In this respect, the *conjuratio*, the oath, and the link between the beginnings of the institutional and legal organization of cities and that of other forms of horizontal corporate organization such as guilds or trades have been highlighted.[84] In Germany and Switzerland, there were cities commemorating this oath in the form of a public repetition or renewal of the act on the occasion of urban government change or elections, which was designated as *Schwörtag* and contributed to reinforcing the cohesion of the urban community.[85] Nowadays, in several cities like Ulm, this date still gives rise to folkloric festivals. Since 1990 the city of Esslingen has tried to reconnect with this tradition which, as in other cities, had disappeared with the loss of the quality of imperial city (*Reichsstadt*) in 1802.[86] Since 2004, the same resumption of this day took place in Reutlingen where, besides a speech of the mayor and a Protestant religious ceremony, there was also a fair with "medieval" shows.[87]

Regarding the participation of the population in its leaders' decisions, it was long believed that it was possible to establish a direct continuity between the small urban republics and the modern democratic states. This factor also explained researchers' great attraction to Hanseatic studies.[88] In the twentieth century, this prospect of "democratic" continuity was increasingly challenged by a growing interest in marginalized and excluded groups. It was found that most cities were governed by urban oligarchies, elites,

---

zur deutschen und europäischen Universitätsgeschichte, Peter Moraw (Leiden, 2008), 435–574; Jürg Schmutz, *Juristen für das Reich* (Basel, 2000).

84 Karl Kroeschell, Albrecht Cordes, "Bürger," in *Handwörterbuch zur deutschen Rechtsgeschichte*, 2nd ed. (Berlin, 2008), 1:col. 738–47; Gerhard Fouquet, "Gilde," in *Handwörterbuch zur deutschen Rechtsgeschichte*, 2nd ed. (Berlin, 2012), 2: col. 383–86; Otto Gerhard Oexle, "Soziale Gruppen in der Ständegesellschaft: Lebensformen des Mittelalters und ihre historischen Wirkungen," in *Die Repräsentationen der Gruppen*, ed. Otto Gerhard Oexle, Andrea von Hülsen-Esch (Göttingen, 1998), 9–44; Wilhelm Ebel, *Der Bürgereid als Geltungsgrund und Gestaltungsprinzip des mittelalterlichen deutschen Stadtrechts* (Weimar, 1958); Paolo Prodi, *Il sacramento del potere* (Bologna, 1992), 192–225; Albrecht Cordes, Joachim Rückert, Reiner Schulze, eds., *Stadt - Gemeinde - Genossenschaft* (Berlin, 2003).

85 Isenmann, *Die deutsche Stadt*, 213; Rainer Jooß, "Schwören und Schwörtage in süddeutschen Reichsstädten," in *Die Visualierung städtischer Ordnung, Anzeiger des Germanischen Nationalmuseums* (Nürnberg, 1993), 153–68.

86 On its website, the city of Esslingen gives explanations on the resumption of this tradition (accessed April 25, 2017, www.esslingen.de/site/Esslingen-Internet-2016/node/629568/Lde?QUERYSTRING=schw%C3%B6rtag) and presents the speeches made on this occasion since 2005 (accessed April 25, 2017, www.esslingen.de/,Lde/start/es_themen/archiv-schwoertag.html).

87 Presentation of this event on the city's website, accessed April 25, 2017, www.reutlingen.de/de/Leben-in-Reutlingen/Unsere-Stadt/Reutlinger-Besonderheiten/Reutlinger-Schw%C3%B6rtag.

88 Summary and bibliographic overview in Rolf Hammel-Kiesow, *Die Hanse*, 4th ed. (München, 2008); Albrecht Cordes, ed., *Hansisches und hansestädtisches Recht* (Trier, 2008); Eckhard Müller-Mertens, Heidelore Böcker, eds., *Konzeptionelle Ansätze der Hanse-Historiographie* (Trier, 2003); Isabelle Richefort, ed., *Les relations entre la France et les villes hanséatiques de Hambourg, Brême et Lübeck* (Bruxelles, 2006). Synthesis in French: Philippe Dollinger, *La Hanse, (XIIᵉ-XVIIᵉ siècles)* (Paris, 1988).

patricians or, in any case, small groups. The convening of large assemblies was rather rare and reserved for difficult cases which required special legitimacy to avoid disturbances. The debate on the scientific terminology to be used is revealing and shows fluctuations. There were discussions about the notion of "patriciate," elite, "strata," or ruling classes, *Stadtadel* (urban nobility), and suchlike.[89] For Germany, forms of urban sociability, such as brotherhoods, patrician societies, and their social life such as banquets, dance events, etc., have attracted much attention from researchers.[90] Particularly for the ruling elites, these types of meetings were often restricted to a small circle of families. They also served as preparation ground for alliances and marriages and were an important means of reinforcing their coherence. With regard to the social structure of cities in both countries, there are important regional differences. In the north and centre of France[91] and in Germany, the nobility does not live in cities as in Italy. A "true" noble must live nobly and must not participate in trade or exercise a trade. The social stratification can be very noticeable. Members of the elite sometimes marry surrounding nobles, but cities remain dominated by commoners. In Austria, there are even cities explicitly prohibiting marriage with nobles, as was the case in the *Wiener Stadtrecht* (Urban Law of Vienna) of 1221.[92] Unlike some parts of Spain, in relation to the total population the percentage of the nobles was low.[93]

The transformation of urban governments into "authorities" (*Obrigkeit*)[94] can be observed in both French and German cities. In the French case, this phenomenon is

89 Jean-Philippe Genet, Günther Lottes, eds., *L'État moderne et les élites* (Paris, 1996); Reinhard Elze, Gina Fasoli, eds., *Stadtadel und Bürgertum in den italienischen und deutschen Städten des Spätmittelalters* (Berlin, 1991); Gerhard Fouquet, "Stadt—Adel. Chancen und Risiken sozialer Mobilität im späten Mittelalter," in *Sozialer Aufstieg. Funktionseliten im Spätmittelalter und in der frühen Neuzeit*, ed. Günther Schulz (München, 2002), 171–92; Philippe Braunstein, "Pour une histoire des élites urbaines: vocabulaire, réalités et représentations," in *Les élites urbaines au Moyen Âge* (Paris, 1997), 29–38; Claude Petitfrère, ed., *Construction, reproduction et représentation des patriciats urbains de l'Antiquité au XXᵉ siècle* (Tours, 1999); Thierry Dutour, ed., *Les nobles et la ville dans l'espace francophone (XIIᵉ-XVIᵉ siècles)* (Paris, 2010); Guido Castelnuovo, *Être noble dans la cité. Les noblesses italiennes en quête d'identité (XIIIᵉ-XVᵉ siècle)* (Paris, 2014).

90 Gerhard Fouquet, ed., *Geschlechtergesellschaften, Zunft-Trinkstuben und Bruderschaften in spätmittelalterlichen und frühneuzeitlichen Städten* (Ostfildern, 2003).

91 For the comparison, see Dutour, *Les nobles*; Werner Paravicini, Otto Gerhard Oexle, eds., *Nobilitas. Funktion und Repräsentation des Adels in Alteuropa* (Göttingen, 1997).

92 Herwig Ebner, "Zur Ideologie des mittelalterlichen Städtebürgertums aufgrund österreichischer Stadtrechte des späten Mittelalters," *Jahrbuch für Geschichte des Feudalismus* 7 (1983): 156–84 at 176.

93 Máximo Diago Hernando, "La participación de la nobleza en el gobierno de las ciudades europeas bajomedievales," *Anuario de estudios medievales*, 37, no. 2 (2007): 781–822; Máximo Diago Hernando, "El perfil socioeconómico de los grupos gobernantes en la ciudades medievales: análisis comparativo de los ejemplos castellano y alemán," *En la España medieval* 18 (1995): 85–134; Adeline Rucquoi, "*Caballeros* et *hidalgos*: la noblesse et la ville en Castille," in *Les nobles et la ville dans l'espace francophone (XIIᵉ-XVIᵉ siècles)*, ed Thierry Dutour (Paris, 2010), 312; Ludolf Pelizaeus, *Dynamik der Macht. Städtischer Widerstand und Konfliktbewältigung im Reich Karls V.* (Münster, 2007), 89–146.

94 Eberhard Isenmann, "Obrigkeit und Stadtgemeinde in der frühen Neuzeit," in *Einwohner und Bürger auf dem Weg zur Demokratie*, ed. Hans Eugen Specker (Ulm, 1997), 74–126.

reflected in the terminology of the "mayor's subjects."[95] After the confessional split in the Empire, this strength of urban governments became even more visible. According to the provisions of the Peace of Augsburg (1555) and the famous adage *cuius regio eius religio*, the governments of the cities of the Empire asserted the decisions of their own city's religion. More often than not, attempts by members of the urban elite to enlarge their personal power and to emerge definitively from the ranks of the ruling class of their city were doomed to failure. The patricians of German cities were careful that none of them got too powerful.[96] Unlike French cities, some of the Imperial cities possessed territories.[97] The latter remained more modest than the *contados* of the Italian city-states, but in the end several of the large state cities succeeded in safeguarding their state quality until the twentieth century (Lübeck, until 1937), and even the twenty-first (Bremen and Hamburg).[98]

Medieval Historiography and Urban Identities

Questions of origin and self-image are essential to the definition of urban identity. In Germany, almost every city of some importance has one or more urban chronicles,[99] while in France, with a few exceptions, this type of source hardly exists. Urban lawsuits kept in the records of the *Parlement* provide interesting information on the definition of medieval urban identity. They contain "presentations" of cities that have the same function as those of individual people.[100] It was necessary to establish the "good fame

---

95 "[...] in the city [i.e., Limoges], there are [urban] councillors who are [its] lords, and Gauthier was their subject." (*[...] en la ville a consulz qui sont seigneurs, et estoit Gaultier leur subgiet*). Cited from Naegle, *Stadt, Recht und Krone*, 2:404 and 632 (the example of La Rochelle).

96 See the cases of Niklas Muffel in Nürnberg (Gerhard Fouquet, "Die Affäre Niklas Muffel. Die Hinrichtung eines Nürnberger Patriziers im Jahre 1469," *Vierteljahrschrift für Sozial- und Wirtschaftsgeschichte* 83 (1996): 459–500) and the mayor of Zurich, Hans Waldmann (Michael Jucker, "Der gestürzte Tyrann. Befriedung von Aufständen durch Gestik, Symbolik und Recht," in *Integration und Konkurrenz. Symbolische Kommunikation in der spätmittelalterlichen Stadt*, ed. Stefanie Rüther (Münster, 2009), 177–204; Hartmut Boockmann, "Mittelalterliche deutsche Stadt-Tyrannen," *Blätter für deutsche Landesgeschichte* 119 (1994): 73–91.

97 On the comparison of Germany and Castile, see Máximo Diago Hernando, "Los señoríos territoriales de las ciudades europeas bajomedievales. Análisis comparativo de los ejemplos castellano y alemán," *Hispania* 188 (1994): 791–844 (examples of Nürnberg, Bern, etc.); Gisela Naegle, Jesús Ángel Solórzano Telechea, "Geschlechter und Zünfte, *Prinçipales* und *Común*. Städtische Konflikte in Kastilien und dem spätmittelalterlichen Reich," *Zeitschrift für Historische Forschung* 41, no. 4 (2014): 561–618.

98 Naegle, "Bonnes villes," 144.

99 See, for example, Historische Kommission bei der bayerischen Akademie der Wissenschaften, ed., *Die Chroniken der deutschen Städte vom 14. bis zum 16. Jahrhundert* (Leipzig, 1862–1931; repr. Göttingen, 1961–1968); Peter Johanek, ed., *Städtische Geschichtsschreibung im Spätmittelalter und in der frühen Neuzeit* (Köln, 2000); Volker Henn, "Städtische Geschichtsschreibung in Köln und im Hanseraum," in *Spätmittelalterliche Städtische Geschichtsschreibung in Köln und im Reich*, ed. Georg Mölich, Uwe Neddermeyer, Wolfgang Schmitz (Köln, 2001), 29–55.

100 Claude Gauvard, "La fama une parole fondatrice," *Médiévales* 24 (1993): 5–13; Annick Porteau-Bitker, Annie Talazac-Laurent, "La renommée dans le droit pénal laïque du XIIIe au XVe siècle," *Médiévales* 24 (1993): 67–80.

and renown" of a city. These presentations emphasize aspects such as the age and privileges of a city, its unwavering fidelity to the king, its strategic, economic, religious or legal importance as the seat of institutions and courts of law, the existence of a university, etc.[101] In the medieval Empire, cities used similar arguments. During a quarrel of precedence between Köln and Aachen at the Diet of Regensburg on May 7 or 8, 1454, according to the account of Enea Silvio Piccolomini, Köln used the following arguments: its foundation by Agrippa, Augustus's son-in-law; its ancient possession of *ius italicum* at a time when Aachen was not even founded; its status as the seat of the archbishop who crowns the king; many noble families descending from the Roman patricians; the university (at which Albert the Great taught); its image as holy city (possession of the relics of the Three Wise Men and the eleven thousand virgins); its size; its large buildings; and its position on the Rhine.[102]

Other interesting sources are the deliberative records. However, in France, for a long time they were restricted to the decisions of urban government and to provide a kind of short "protocol." In the event of insurrections or conflicts, the records are often silent, as urban governments tried to cultivate an image of inner concord and harmony.[103] Another central value of medieval cities, the common good, has been the subject of several recent collective volumes.[104] It was a double-edged sword that was widely used in arguments between cities. It could be used for revolutionary purposes, for negotiations with the prince or king, but also to justify sacrifices, taxes, and measures of expropriation, or simply to guarantee high quality and availability of goods and products of craftsmen.[105] Accounting sources can add significantly to urban identity research because they identify communication and messenger networks. Unfortunately, quite often, they do not give very detailed information on the content, conduct, and results of the missions of urban

---

101 Naegle, "Bonnes villes," 139–43.

102 Johannes Helmrath, "Kölner Geschichstbewußtsein," in *Quellen zur Geschichte der Stadt Köln, Förderverein Geschichte in Köln, 2. Spätes Mittelalter und frühe Neuzeit*, ed. Joachim Deeters (Köln, 1996), 85–89.

103 Noël Coulet, "Les délibérations communales en Provence au Moyen Âge," in *Le Médiéviste devant ses sources*, ed. Claude Carozzi, Huguette Taviani-Carozzi (Aix-en-Provence, 2004), 227–48; Caroline Fargeix, *Les élites lyonnaises du XVe siècle au miroir de leur langage* (Paris, 2007); Michel Hébert, Kouky Fianu, eds., *L'écrit et la ville*, Memini. Travaux et documents 12 (Ottawa, 2008); Graeme Small, "Municipal Registers of Deliberations in the Fourteenth and Fifteenth Centuries: Cross-Channel Observations," in *Les idées passent-elles la Manche?*, ed. Jean-Philippe Genet, François-Joseph Ruggiu (Paris, 2007), 37–66; Naegle, *Stadt, Recht und Krone*, 1:40–48. List of texts edited in Gisela Naegle, *La ville, le droit et la couronne. Bibliographie thématique*, Ménestrel, accessed January 21, 2013, www.menestrel.fr/spip.php?rubrique443.

104 Élodie Lecuppre-Desjardin, Anne-Laure van Bruaene, eds., *De bono communi* (Turnhout, 2010); Franck Collard, "Pouvoir d'un seul et bien commun (VIe-XVIe siècles)," *Revue française d'histoire des idées politiques* 32, no. 2 (2010): 227–30; Herfried Münkler, Harald Bluhm, eds., *Gemeinwohl und Gemeinsinn. Historische Semantiken politischer Leitbegriffe* (Berlin, 2001).

105 Gisela Naegle, "Bien commun et chose publique: Traités et procès à la fin du Moyen Âge," *Histoire de l'intérêt général, Histoire et archives* 19 (2006): 87–111, and Gisela Naegle, "Armes à double tranchant? Bien commun et chose publique dans les villes françaises au Moyen Âge," in *De bono communi*, ed. Élodie Lecuppre-Desjardin, Anne-Laure van Bruaene (Turnhout, 2010), 55–70.

ambassadors. But it is often possible to reconstruct the composition of the embassies and the stages of the journey.[106] For German cities there are reports of urban messengers sent to the imperial diets, which give interesting insights into the urban interpretation of the kingdom's *grand* policy.[107] In many respects, the perspectives of French and German narrative sources are very different and, unlike the French *Grandes Chroniques*, in the Empire there was no "official" royal or imperial medieval historiography. Jean-Marie Moeglin points out that in the medieval Empire, universal/imperial history and the regional historiography of territories and cities coexisted. Writers such as Johannes Rothe (ca. 1360–1434)[108] or Jakob Twinger von Königshofen[109] wrote about the history of the world, of the Empire, and of their territories, princes, and cities. Wigand Gerstenberg (1457–1522), to choose a less famous example, wrote a chronicle of the territories of Hesse and Thuringia and a chronicle of the small town of Frankenberg.[110] Often, these authors integrate universal history, that of the popes and especially that of the emperors, in the history of their own cities, a combination that better justifies the defence of their freedoms and privileges. There was also a specific literature for urban rulers: sources such as Johannes Rothe's *Ratsgedichte*[111] or Johann von Soest's *Wie man eyn Stadt regieren soll* ("How to govern a city").[112] Authors like Rothe were deeply involved

---

106 Albert Rigaudière, "Voyager pour administrer. Les émissaires sanflorains en Auvergne et dans le royaume (1393–1394)," in *La ville médiévale en deçà et au-delà de ses murs. Mélanges Jean-Pierre Leguay*, ed. Philippe Lardin, Jean-Louis Roch (Rouen, 2000), 291–314; Florent Garnier, "Deux représentants millavois en mission à Paris (2 octobre 1439–28 février 1440, n.s.)," *Annales de Midi* 116, no. 246 (2004): 205–24; Florent Garnier, "Représenter la ville en Rouergue au bas Moyen Âge: réglementation et pratique des voyages consulaires," in *Rouergue, carrefour d'histoire de nature*, Fédération Historique de Midi-Pyrénées et la Societé des Lettres, Sciences et Arts de l'Aveyron (Rodez, 2003), 41–54; Flandin-Bléty, *Essai*.

107 Pierre Monnet, "Courriers et messages: un réseau de communication à l'échelle urbaine dans les pays d'Empire à la fin du Moyen Âge," in *Information et société en Occident à la fin du Moyen Âge*, ed. Claire Boudreau, Kouky Fianu, Claude Gauvard, Michel Hébert (Paris, 2004), 281–306; Pierre Monnet, "Jalons pour une histoire de la diplomatie urbaine dans l'Allemagne de la fin du Moyen Âge," in *Auswärtige Politik und internationale Beziehungen im Mittelalter*, ed. Dieter Berg, Martin Kintzinger, Pierre Monnet (Bochum, 2002), 151–74; Rainer C. Schwinges, Klaus Wriedt, eds., *Gesandtschafts- und Botenwesen im spätmittelalterlichen Europa* (Stuttgart, 2003).

108 Stefan Tebruck, "Rothe, Johannes," *Neue Deutsche Biographie* 22 (2005): 118–19. Online version accessed January 21, 2013, www.deutsche-biographie.de/pnd118603191.html; Ursula Peters, ed., *Literatur in der Stadt* (Tübingen, 1983), 242–48.

109 Jean-Marie Moeglin, "Die historiographische Konstruktion der Nation—'französische Nation' und 'deutsche Nation' im Vergleich," in *Deutschland und der Westen Europas im Mittelalter*, ed. Joachim Ehlers (Stuttgart, 2002), 353–77; Jean-Marie Moeglin, "Sentiment d'identité régionale et historiographie en Thuringe à la fin du Moyen Âge," in *Identité régionale et conscience nationale en France et en Allemagne du Moyen Âge à l'époque moderne*, ed. Jean-Marie Moeglin, Rainer Babel (Sigmaringen, 1997), 325–63; Jean-Marie Moeglin, *L'Empire et le Royaume. Entre indifférence et fascination, 1214–1500* (Villeneuve d'Ascq, 2011).

110 Ursula Braasch-Schwersmann, Axel Halle, eds., *Wigand Gerstenberg von Frankenberg 1457–1522* (Marburg, 2007).

111 Herbert Wolf, ed., *Johannes Rothes Ratsgedichte* (Berlin, 1971).

112 Heike Bierschwale, Jacqueline van Leeuwen, eds., *Wie man eine Stadt regieren soll. Deutsche*

with the daily life of medieval cities. His *Ratsgedichte*, poems addressed to the Council of the city of Eisenach, compare the different urban offices with the human body and refer to the organization of the Empire and the Church. The *Ratsmeister* is presented as its head, board members are its heart, finance officers its hands, and clerks its eyes. The aldermen who must ensure the publication of the laws and ordinances of the council are its throat and mouth.[113] Rothe praises the concord which makes small cities grow, while discord would even lead large cities to ruin and impoverishment.[114] The *Ratsgedichte* already propagates a sort of deontology of the good urban officer. The common good of the city, its well-being, and honour are central values. Certain crimes and vices will be punished by exclusion from the council (capital crimes, incest, protection of notorious criminals, felony, calumny, theft, crimes against clergy and nuns, alienation of properties of the city, etc.). It is necessary to keep deliberations secret, to render fair justice, to protect the innocent, widows, and the poor. Corruption is severely criticized. The Council must ensure that the law and good customs are safeguarded. Its sittings and the exercise of justice must take place as though God himself was present. The list of moral qualities for urban officers is long and contains an enumeration of the traditional virtues required for every ruler (wisdom, temperance, sobriety, prudence, etc.). Adultery, playing dice, and ostentatious clothing are forbidden. One must know how to speak wisely, listen attentively to supplicants, not to yield to uncontrolled anger. To this Rothe adds some typically bourgeois virtues and a positive appreciation of economic activities. Finance officers must possess the qualities of a good and honest housekeeper.[115] However, Rothe also wrote a book of advice addressed to knights and historiographical texts dedicated to the regent of the territory and her officials.[116] Thus, the boundaries between manifestations of urban ideals and values and the service of the prince or the Church were sometimes blurred.

For several European regions, the foundation myths provide a basis for comparison and show common ground. According to the *Annales manuscrites de Limoges*, Trojans founded Limoges, Clermont, Poitiers, and Toulouse.[117] According to Philippe de Vigneulles, Paris, Reims, and Troyes also had Trojan founders.[118] In the Empire, it was believed that Bonn, Xanthen, Bern, and Augsburg were Trojan foundations, even if,

---

und niederländische Stadtregimentslehren des Mittelalters (Frankfurt-am-Main, 2005); Eberhard Isenmann, "Ratsliteratur und städtische Ratsordnungen des Mittelalters und der frühen Neuzeit," in *Stadt und Recht im Mittelalter*, ed. Pierre Monnet, Otto Gerhard Oexle (Göttingen, 2003), 215–479.

113 Gisela Naegle, "Rothe, Johannes," in *Écrivains juristes et juristes écrivains du Moyen Âge au siècle des Lumières*, ed. Bruno Méniel (Paris, 2015), 1097–1103.

114 Friedrich Ortloff, ed., *Das Rechtsbuch Johannes Purgoldts nebst statuarischen Rechten von Gotha und Eisenach* (Jena, 1860; repr. Aalen, 1967), 314n41.

115 Naegle, "Johannes Rothe."

116 Volker Honemann, "Rothe, Johannes," in *Die Deutsche Literatur des Mittelalters—Verfasserlexikon*, ed. Kurt Ruh, Burghart Wachinger, Gundolf Keil, Werner Schröder, Franz Josef Worstbrock (Berlin, 1978–2008), Vol. 8 (1992), 277–85.

117 Naegle, *Stadt, Recht und Krone*, 2:403.

118 *La Chronique de Philippe de Vigneulles*, ed. Charles Bruneau, 4 vols. (Metz, 1927–1933), 1:23.

later on, they tried to find indigenous founders.[119] In France and Germany, these myths are sometimes derived from the same sources as the *Chroniques de Frédégaire* (660) and the *Gesta regum Francorum* (ca. 726/737).[120] A third widespread model rested on the attempt to build a biblical filiation by referring to Japheth, Noah's son. According to Maria Asenjo González, in Spain another of Noah's descendants, the Egyptian Osiris, was said to be responsible for the foundation of Cádiz, Sevilla, Toledo, Ávila, Segovia, and Barcelona.[121] Philippe de Vigneulles describes several re-foundations of Metz that would become the mother of Trier, Verdun, and Toul in pre-Roman and Roman times.[122] He celebrates the urban freedoms of the "noble citizens" of Metz, who "would not suffer a prince or king over them, but wished to live and die in their frankness and liberty, as long as it was possible for them."[123] In the *Agrippina*, Heinrich van Beeck traces the origins of Köln as far away as possible and rejects more realistic versions. Trebeta, the son-in-law of the Babylonian Queen Semiramis, fled and founded Trier. This foundation is followed by that of Köln, Mainz, Worms, Strasbourg, and Basel. Thus, in relation to its age, Köln becomes at least the second city in Europe. Its foundation at a time when there was not yet an archbishop makes it possible to better justify its freedom.[124] Köln is presented as a member of the group of *Reichsstädte*. Van Beeck lists eighty-nine names that are linked to the image of the imperial eagle. He also lists episcopal cities and some without this legal status. He does not know all the *Reichsstädte* that were to appear, so some are omitted.[125]

For the German-speaking cities, the medieval historiographical situation varies from one city to another. Swiss cities such as Bern and Zürich had official chronicles and some orders are placed by the Council (*Rat*).[126] In other cities, there was a historiography car-

---

119 Michael Borgolte, "Europas Geschichten und Troia. Der Mythos im Mittelalter," in *Troia. Traum und Wirklichkeit*, ed. Michael Siebler (Stuttgart, 2001), 192.

120 "'Quod non sit honor Augustensibus si dicantur a Teucris ducere originem'. Humanistische Aspekte in der *Chronographia Augustensium* des Sigismund Meisterlin," in *Humanismus und Renaissance in Augsburg*, ed. Gernot Michael Müller (Berlin, 2010), 247–48; Karl Schnith, "Mittelalterliche Augsburger Gründungslegenden," in *Fälschungen im Mittelalter. Internationaler Kongreß der Monumenta Germaniae Historica*, 6 vols. (Hannover, 1988–1990), 1:497–517.

121 María Asenjo González, "La représentation de l'origine mythique de la ville de Valladolid," in *Ab urbe condita...: Fonder et refonder la ville: récits et représentations*, ed. Véronique Lamazou-Duplan (Pau, 2011), 94.

122 *La Chronique de Philippe de Vigneulles*, 1, 8, 12–13, 25. On this author and Metz, see Gisela Naegle, "Divergences et convergences: Identités urbaines en France et en Allemagne à la fin du Moyen Âge," in *Mundos medievales. Espacios, sociedades y poder. Homenaje al profesor José Ángel García de Cortázar y Ruiz de Aguirre*, ed. Beatriz Arízaga Bolumburu, Dolores Mariño Veiras, Carmen Díez Herrera, Esther Peña Bocos, Jesús Ángel Solórzano Telechea, Susana Guijarro González, Javier Añíbarro Rodríguez, 2 vols. (Santander, 2014), 2:1663–76.

123 *[N]obles citains [...] ne voulurent souffrir prince ne roy sur eulx, ains volrent vivre et morir en leur franchise et liberalité, tant et cy longuement qu'il leur fust possible.* Cited from *La Chronique de Philippe de Vigneulles*, 1, 25.

124 Meier, *Agrippina*, 95–96.

125 Meier, *Agrippina*, 109.

126 Schmid, *Geschichte*.

ried by circles close to urban power or the patrician class.[127] In Nürnberg, Frankfurt am Main, or Augsburg, autobiographical documents provided an interesting complement to this set.[128] The book by Matthäus Schwarz, a citizen of Augsburg, born in 1497, is one of the most interesting texts because it contains many images that make one think of a photo album. The author presents himself in the form of colourful images during the different ages of his life, from the period of his mother's pregnancy to his own old age.[129] At the dawn of modern times, large patrician families such as the Augsburg Fuggers or the Nürnberg Tuchers employed writers and artists to create a representative image of the history of their families.[130] Sometimes, especially during periods of internal unrest that create a need for justification and legitimacy, there are even texts emanating from different political camps. Wars between Nürnberg and the *Markgrafen* of the House of Hohenzollern (1449–1453) and the *Städtekriege* brought about songs and poems by the two parties of the conflict.[131] Recent research has shown that Nürnberg took care of its own image and sometimes bought the works of authors on the history of the city, but also that it was not a true "identity policy" in the narrow sense, and that the "private" initiative of the authors and especially the cultivated patricians of the city remained decisive. In the case of Nürnberg, the historiographical and literary discovery of its own identity owes much to personalities like Hartmann Schedel or Christoph Scheurl and other humanist authors.[132] In the fifteenth and early sixteenth centuries, there was a whole group of jurists strongly involved in the life of their cities or cities in a certain region: Sebastian Brant (1457–1521), for example, author of the *Narrenschiff / Nef des Fous*, who was also very active at the beginning of the University of Basel and in the service of the city of Strasbourg.[133] It is significant that Christoph Scheurl, a humanist, jurist, and patrician from Nürnberg also played an important role in the history of the University of Wittenberg. Scheurl taught there between 1507 and 1512, and is considered the author of the statutes of this university, which are drafted according to the models of those of Tübingen (1477)

---

127 For Nürnberg, see Carla Meyer, *Die Stadt als Thema. Nürnbergs Entdeckung in Texten um 1500* (Ostfildern, 2009); Jean-Marie Moeglin, "Les élites urbaines et l'histoire de leur ville en Allemagne (XIVᵉ-XVᵉ siècles)," in *Les élites urbaines au Moyen Âge*, ed. Société des médiévistes de l'enseignement supérieur public (Paris, 1997), 351–81.

128 Pierre Monnet, "Reale und ideale Stadt. Die oberdeutschen Städte im Spiegel autobiographischer Zeugnisse des Spätmittelalters," in *Von der dargestellten Person zum erinnerten Ich*, ed. Kaspar von Greyerz, Hans Medick, Patrice Veit (Köln, 2001), 395–430; Pierre Monnet, "Das Selbst und die Stadt in Selbstzeugnissen aus deutschen Städten des Spätmittelalters," in *Kommunikation mit dem Ich*, ed. Heinz-Dieter Heimann, Pierre Monnet (Bochum, 2004), 19–37.

129 Philippe Braunstein, *Un banquier mis à nu. Autobiographie de Matthäus Schwarz bourgeois d'Augsbourg* (Paris, 1992).

130 See, for example, Haus der Bayerischen Geschichte, Staatsarchiv Nürnberg, eds., *Das Große Tucherbuch, Stadtarchiv Nürnberg, E 29/3 Nr. 258* (Nürnberg, 2004).

131 Karina Kellermann, *"Abschied vom, historischen Volkslied." Studien zu Funktion, Ästhetik und Publizität der Gattung historisch-politischer Ereignisdichtung* (Tübingen, 2000).

132 Meyer, *Die Stadt als Thema.*

133 Klaus Bergdolt, Joachim Knape, Anton Schindling, Gerrit Walther, eds., *Sebastian Brant und die Kommunikationskultur um 1500* (Wiesbaden, 2010).

and Bologna.[134] The evolution of Wittenberg, which was originally a very small seigneur-ial city of about two thousand inhabitants, illustrates very well the difference between French and German university cities. During the first decade of the university there were about nine hundred students. In 1528, the city had about four thousand inhabitants,[135] but it attracted personalities like Luther, Melanchthon, and the painter Lucas Cranach. The image of the city also appeared in iconography. The chronicle of Hartmann Schedel (1440–1514), a humanist physician from Nürnberg, contains many engravings, including a very famous image of Nürnberg.[136] In the Swiss cities of Bern, Zürich, and Spiez, several members of the Schilling family wrote illustrated chronicles (*Bilderchroniken*).[137] At the same time, inspired by Italian models, the literary genre of the eulogy was an important success.[138] This development not only affected the great cities of the Empire or the free cities, as shown by the example of the small seigniorial city of Frankenberg in Hesse. Like those of Bern and Zürich, Wigand Gerstenberg's chronicle contains images and some instructions for their execution. These images show important events in the life of this small city, including a very serious fire in 1476 and the city's reconstruction.[139] There are also representations of Frankenberg's battles, of *faides* or quarrels with noble leagues, such as a representation of the defeat of 1381 against the noble societies *Im Horne* and *Im Falken*.[140] In 1505–1506, the humanist Helius Eobanus Hessus wrote some lines in a Latin poem in honour of the city where he had been educated.[141]

As for France, we find much earlier examples of this kind of city eulogy. According to Eustache Deschamps (1346–1407), "Riens ne peut se comparer à Paris" and the Paris-paradise comparison became a literary *topos*.[142] This literary genre could claim ancient

---

134 Heiner Lück, "Das ernestinische Wittenberg: Universität und Stadt (1486–1547)," in *Das ernestinische Wittenberg: Universität und Stadt (1486–1547)* (Petersberg, 2011), 12.

135 Lück, "Das ernestinische Wittenberg," 16.

136 "Nuremberg," in Hartmann Schedel, *La chronique universelle de Nuremberg, l'édition de 1493*, ed. Stephan Füssel (Köln, 2001), fol. 100.

137 Diebold Schilling (der Ältere), *Berner-Chronik. Faksimile*, ed. Hans Bloesch, Paul Hilber (Bern, 1942–1945); Bendicht Tschachtlan, *Tschachtlans Bilderchronik. Faksimile-Ausgabe der Handschrift Ms. A 120 der Zentralbibliothek Zürich*, ed. Alfred A. Schmid (Lucerne, 1988); Diebold Schilling (der Ältere), *Spiezer Bilderchronik. Faksimile-Ausgabe der Handschrift Mss. Hist. helv. I 16 der Burgerbibliothek Bern*, ed. Hans Haeberli, Christoph von Steiger (Lucerne, 1990).

138 See, for example, Meyer, *Die Stadt als Thema*, 245–341; Klaus Arnold, "Städtelob und Stadt-beschreibung im späteren Mittelalter und in der frühen Neuzeit," in *Städtische Geschichtsschreibung im Spätmittelalter und in der frühen Neuzeit* (Köln, 2000), 247–68; Naegle, "Bonnes villes," 120.

139 Braasch-Schwersmann, *Wigand Gerstenberg*, "Stadtchronik," (unnumbered), image 14, (Frankenberg), SAbb.14 and image 15, SAbb.15.

140 Braasch-Schwersmann, *Wigand Gerstenberg*, "Stadtchronik," image 11, SAbb.11.

141 Ulrich Ritzerfeld, "Zwischen Stagnation und Wandel. Frankenberg an der Eder zur Zeit Wigand Gerstenbergs," in *Wigand Gerstenberg von Frankenberg 1457–1522*, ed. Ursula Braasch-Schwersmann, Axel Halle (Marburg, 2007), 25–41 at 25.

142 Eustache Deschamps, "Riens ne peut se comparer à Paris" (balade 169), in *Œuvres complètes d'Eustache Deschamps*, ed. Marquis de Queux de Saint-Hilaire, Gaston Raynaud, 11 vols. (Paris, 1878–1903), 1:301–2 and balade 170, *Œuvres complètes*, 1:302–3.

ancestors and by 1065–1070, Sigebert de Gembloux composed a eulogy of the city of Metz.[143] In 1323, Jean de Jandun wrote a eulogy of Senlis. He claims that an anonymous author responded to him, saying an honest man could not live and exist anywhere else but Paris, and that such a man would have written, "I concede to you that I am of the opinion that to be in Paris is simply 'to be' and that staying elsewhere means 'not to be'."[144]

Jandun appreciates the beauty of the nearby forests of "his" city of Senlis, the fertility of the land, the abundance of its wines, the excellence of its bread, the cleanliness of its cobblestoned streets, the salubrity of its temperature, the amiable and solid qualities of its inhabitants, and so on.[145] He does not intend to deny the merits of Paris. However, to reach the conclusion that Paris is the best city in the world, it is necessary to make comparisons: "I conclude that according to the experts of grammar [...] there are three degrees of comparison [...]. So I prove now: whoever says that nothing can be compared to Paris, admits that it is not good, and, if this is the case, logically, it cannot be 'better' or 'the best'."[146] Jandun also wrote a eulogy of Paris, but refuted the bad jokes and denigrations against Senlis (his opponent had spoken of the abundance of frogs and flies).[147]

Travel stories are also interesting sources: through the lens of a foreign country or city, they contain information that reflects the perceptions of the time. From this point of view, it might be interesting to compare cities with trade relations, such as Nürnberg, Lyon, and Barcelona. For many medieval German travellers, their home city was the point of comparison. Hieronymus Münzer observes that Barcelona was twice as large as Nürnberg and, to describe Madrid, he says the city has very extensive suburbs which are the same size as Biberach.[148] His compatriot Gabriel Tetzel crossed the country during the period of the Catalan civil war and highlighted the insecurity caused by this conflict. He enjoyed Barcelona, which he described as a great and powerful city and the capital of Catalonia, where an honourable reception was given for his master, Ambassador Leo de Rozmital, and his entourage. His observations mainly concern commercial activity, maritime trade, and the belief that Barcelona had as many ships as Venezia.[149] Before

143 Mireille Chazan, *L'Empire et l'histoire universelle* (Paris, 1999), 56–58.

144 *Opinor te conftiteri quod esse Parisius est esse simpliciter; Esse alibi, esse non nisi secundum quid.* Cited from *Éloge de Paris composé en 1323 par un habitant de Senlis, Jean de Jandun*, ed. Nicolas-Rodolphe Taranne, Antoine Leroux de Lincy (Paris, 1856), 30.

145 Summary of the eulogy of Senlis by the publishers, in *Éloge de Paris*, 1.

146 *Suppono secundum grammaticos, [...] tres esse gradus comparationis [...]. Nunc arguo: Quicumque dicit Parisius in nullo gradu comparationis esse ponendam, concedit eam non esse bonam, et ex consequenti nec meliorem nec optimam.* Cited from *Éloge de Paris*, text, 27–28.

147 *Éloge de Paris*, 26.

148 Klaus Herbers, "Vom Bodensee nach Spanien. Eigenes und Fremdes im Blick eines Reisenden um 1500," in *Oberschwaben und Spanien an der Schwelle zur Neuzeit*, ed. Dieter R. Bauer, Klaus Herbers, Elmar L. Kuhn (Ostfildern, 2006); see also Pedro Martínez García, "El Sacro Imperio y la diplomacia atlántica: el itinerario de Hieronymus Münzer," in *Diplomacia y comercio en la Europa Atlántica medieval*, ed. Jesús Ángel Solórzano Telechea, Beatriz Arízaga Bolumburu, Louis Sicking (Logroño, 2015), 103–22.

149 Johann Andreas Schmeller, ed., *Des böhmischen Herrn Leo's von Rozmital Ritter- Hof- und Pilger-Reise durch die Abendlande 1465–1467* (Stuttgart, 1844), 133–34.

the civil war, Sebastian Ilsung admired Catalan cities and Barcelona, which he compared with Venezia.[150] For Pero Tafur, there were parallels between Nürnberg and Toledo; Nürnberg is "a very old city and it is populated in the same way as Toledo."[151] From his point of view, Köln was more impressive than Nürnberg: "This one is the most important [mayor] city and the richest and the most famous of all German towns and […] the city is very well fortified by walls, with a good moat and barricades and it has very nice streets and many craftsmen from all kinds of mechanical arts […]."[152] His criteria in the case of Köln were the same we find in other travellers who very often mention the presence of fortifications or walls. Some visited the defensive works and admired the artillery or the *Zeughaus*. For Gabriel Tetzel, in this case, the absence of walls on one side of the city of Ghent even justified doubts that, despite the city's impressive size, this agglomeration could be designated a "city."[153]

In summary, as these medieval observations show, despite many differences, the comparative study of cities, their argumentative techniques, and constructions of identity can still offer many promising and interesting lines of research.

---

150 Volker Honemann, "Sebastian Ilsung," in *Deutsche Jakobspilger und ihre Berichte*, ed. Klaus Herbers (Tübingen, 1988), 85: "Then I came across many beautiful towns in Catalonia, and I came to the big city of Barcelona; this is the most magnificient one that I ever visited and with great lords and there are also big ships and it is equal to Venice with all this preciousness, and it is the capital of Catalonia and there would be a lot to say about it" (*Dar nach kam ich durch vil schener stet in Katelonia und kam in die grose stat Parselone, daz ist die herlichest stat, da ich ey ein kam, von mechtigen herren, und grosse scheffung komt da zuo, und gelicht gar zuo Fenedig mit aller kostlichhaid, und ist die habstadt in Katelonia, da wer vil dar von zuo sagen*).

151 For Pero Tafur, Nürnberg is *a muy antigua çibdat es a la manera de Toledo poblada*. Cited from *Andanças é viajes de Pero Tafur por diversas partes del mundo avidos (1435–1439)*, ed. Marcos Jiménez de la Espada (Madrid, 1874), 269.

152 *Ésta es la mayor çibdat é la más rica é la más fermosa que ay en toda Alemaña, é […] la çibdat muy bien murada, con buen fossado é barrera, é muy gentiles calles, é muchos artesanos de todas artes mecánicas […]*. Cited from *Andanças é viajes de Pero Tafur*, 240–41.

153 Johann Andreas Schmeller, ed., *Des böhmischen Herrn Leo's von Rozmital*, 152.

Chapter 12

ECONOMY AND RELIGION IN LATE MEDIEVAL ITALY: MARKETS IN THE CHRISTIAN CITY

GIACOMO TODESCHINI

OFFICIAL EXCHANGE OF goods and money in fourteenth- and fifteenth-century Italian cities took place against the backdrop of a rhetorical discourse of salvation and thus a Christian religious framework. However, despite what we might be tempted to believe, this does not mean that the form taken by the market or a Western trading economy emerged in a Christian context from a social framework established by objectively Christian urban communities, nor by Christians being present in a given area as inhabitants or residents. As has now been amply demonstrated by studies devoted to clarifying what citizenship effectively meant in late medieval Italy, being a citizen of a city could mean very different things, as degrees of citizenship were varied and ambiguous. Rather, institutional dynamics and governmental powers set up to control Christian cities in Italy defined and imposed the forms of belonging to the Christian community, and the languages which defined what were authentic, or rather legitimate, methods of commercial aggregation.

In other words, Christian commercial dynamics would seem—in actual daily life in the sources—to have been the result of pressure exerted by politics on economics or, more precisely, the consequence of political choices characterized by the preliminary adoption of Christian charismata drawn from a long documentary tradition as the badge of all conceivable authenticity and legitimacy. While it is normal historiographical practice to limit analyses of the markets of a given period to an examination of the relationship between the specifically local context of the market and its political and cultural structures as a whole, in analyses of late medieval Italian markets, it seems much more useful and meaningful to break out of the straitjacket of an exclusively locally-based approach to understand the long-term perspective against the backdrop where markets were located. All this in an Italy like that of the fourteenth- and fifteenth centuries, at least as far as north-central Italy is concerned, which was specifically marked out by the interweaving of local and international policies and the overweening presence of the Church and canon law imposed by Roma or Avignon. And, last but not least, it was also marked by the dissemination of legal analysis of economic practices by contemporary lawyers and theologians.[1] On the other hand, any analysis of fourteenth- and fifteenth-

---

[1] Andrea Gamberini, Jean-Philippe Genet, Andrea Zorzi, eds., *The Languages of Political Society. Western Europe, 14th–17th Centuries* (Roma, 2011).

Giacomo Todeschini (todeschinigiacomo@gmail.com) is Emeritus Professor at the Università di Trieste in Italy

century Italian cities has to take account of the profound changes that took place from both the economic and the conceptual and political perspectives as a result of the systematic spread of Jewish communities and the legal and political baggage they brought with them.[2]

Language, Images, and Metaphors of Christianity and the Spread of the Market

In Italian city markets, the tangible outcomes of political and intellectual systems were partly conscious developments and partly the outcome of a highly stratified theological and legal textual accretion. For an understanding of this, we need to know that natural practices of economic exchange had been substantially re-codified and overlain in the Christian context to the point of transformation in the Late Middle Ages into a gargantuan metaphor for the divine order, mirrored by earthly order. The roots of the political and institutional character of markets in Italy from the ninth century onwards went deepest here, with ancient and traditional theological overwriting of the markets as a dialectic of exchange. The invitation to trade and invest one's riches for a profit, present in the Holy Scriptures as a metaphor for investment in salvation, was effectively transformed by means of a system of commentaries which modified Christian discourse on the path to salvation from the fifth to the tenth centuries into the prescriptive rhetoric of the policies of lordships. In this context the founding ideology of the markets themselves were seen as emanating from sacred powers, which controlled them in jurisdictional terms.[3]

Metaphors of celestial salvation imposed from the outset the inexorable logic of trading and credit exchange at a time when the work of canon lawyers and glossarists from the eleventh century onwards was giving them exemplary status in the economic context and making them a model of optimal economic dimensions. This process produced the linguistic basis of a potential political reading in a social context of everything to do with the dynamics and objects which could determine accumulation of wealth, investment, profit, and, in short, economic organization, and what could be depicted as morally and institutionally valid.[4]

The markets assumed an early importance from a governing perspective which on one hand touched on economic utilitarianism and on the other coincided in the finest detail with the will of these sacred powers to affirm their territorial control. Commercial practices, lending, interest, and merchant associations came to the fore in the language of the European Christian powers as a type of rhetoric to describe the social functioning which these powers saw as sacred, following their Christian definition. Urban markets,

---

2 Julius Kirshner, Osavaldo Cavallar, "Jews as citizens in late medieval and Renaissance Italy: the case of Isacco da Pisa," *Jewish History* 25 (2011): 269–318.

3 Valentina Toneatto, *Les Banquiers du Seigneur. Évêques et moines face à la richesse (IVe–début IXe siècle)* (Rennes, 2012).

4 François Bougard, "Le crédit dans l'Occident du haut Moyen Âge: documentation et pratique," in *Les élites et la richesse au Haut Moyen Age*, ed. Jean-Pierre Devroey, Laurent Feller, Régine Le Jan (Turnhout, 2010), 439–78.

or rather the markets within Christian jurisdictions and thus those legitimated as such by the authorities, presented themselves to the world as invested with Christocentric holiness and, from the eleventh century onwards in particular, as always in harmony with the Roman papacy. Italian royal, seigneurial, and ecclesiastical sources present a recapitulation of the daily exchange practices encompassed by the codes and rituals of official Christianity in the language of the holy or consecrated institutions.

Economic and social historians have to take careful account of the institutional limits of this representation. This is the only way to avoid confusing markets that were in fact active but only partially present in the sources from those which, while understood as legitimate by those who governed and issued laws, did appea in legal, theological, notarial, sovereign, or statutory documentation. These markets in any event took account of and defined them as the materialization of a collective wealth of which the city's or the local government's holiness was the charismatic synthesis.[5]

The Meaning of *commercium, nundinae,* and *mercatum*

The significant doubling up of the word used in the European but especially Italian administration from the twelfth century to indicate the place where public contracting took place, *nundinae* but also *mercatum*, immediately reveals the structural ambiguity of the notion of market. This is clear when used outside the legislative sphere in the legal and theological or moral contexts, in the language from which the late Middle Ages was to build its narratives and codes relating to the life of the markets. The period-specific nature of market days (*nundinae*), a term which originated from a Roman desire to designate the chronologically concrete and provisional nature of the market is contradicted by the word *mercatum*. Certainly, it was packed with implicit references to the language of religious holiness and thus to the *commercium* and *mercatum* spoken of in the fields of liturgy and theology.

In fact, the *mercatum* was spoken of first by royal diplomats from the area of Italy and then by jurists who commented on the Code of Justinian and lastly in Italian city statutes. Nevertheless, the infinite series of notarial records do not simply record a periodic event or some established local situation. It was actually an economic state of affairs made up as much of contractual behaviours and models as it was of their incorporation into the legal and thus religious framework that legalized them as elements of the life and growth of an institutionalized and sacred collectivity. While *nundinae* speaks of a market as a moment in time incorporated within a longer timeframe, *mercatum* is suffused with the authorized political substance of an existing system of exchange even when it was neither perceptible nor visible, even when not physically materialized by the interplay of contracts and prices. The ambiguity which was such a feature of Italian—and not only Italian—urban markets even in their names, above all after the

---

5 Giacomo Todeschini, *Il prezzo della salvezza. Lessici medievali del pensiero economico* (Roma, 1994); Giacomo Todeschini, "Ecclesia e mercato nei linguaggi dottrinali di Tommaso d'Aquino," in *Etiche economiche,* ed. Maria Luisa Pesante, special issue, *Quaderni Storici* 105, no. 3 (2000): 573–621; Paolo Prodi, ed. *La fiducia secondo i linguaggi del potere* (Bologna, 2007).

mid-twelfth century, grew, if account is taken of the role markets assumed in the documentation made up as much by chronicle narratives as by series of local laws. If, in fact, instead of abstracting from these sources the information relating to the life of markets—leaving aside their context—we pay attention to the events which determined the appearance of markets as narrative subjects or legal frameworks, we soon find that this documentary manifestation of the institutional economic state of affairs serves to throw light on a political, ecclesiastical, and rhetorical discourse or one concerning the confines of deliberating or judging power. From time to time *mercatum* is an opportunity to speak of jurisdictional subjugation, as in the case of the conflict between Lodi and Milano or, as in the case of many papal letters in the same period, the term to use when indicating the space in which a non-simoniacal exchange was legitimated, that is, one which did not contravene the economic norms which safeguarded ecclesiastical assets. The contractual space granted jurisdictionally by a higher to a subordinate power was called *mercatum*, but this word also indicated, in the textual sphere fenced in by the city statutes, both urban areas set aside for exchange and the rights of cities to control that space. And in the theological textual milieu, the whole dense web of conceptual associations which gave a name to the economic circumstances understood as functional or otherwise to the growth of the *res ecclesiarum*, or rather *patrimonia pauperum*, revolved around *mercatum* to *mercari*.

In this last case, which effectively comes across in the sources as being intimately linked to the public legislative framework, the market was explicitly one and the same as a form of daily sociality of which theologians, jurists, and legislators wanted to ensure compatibility or rather continuity with a social order that was at all times represented as a ritual and sacred order. The institutional nature of the Italian markets from the thirteenth century onwards would thus appear very clear. Enlarging on Mathieu Arnoux's conclusions, their identification with jurisdictional space meant, at the same time, their incorporation into Christian religious space.[6] It was, in fact, precisely the contractual dimension which made a pre-eminently element of trust within the market that made possible the codification of the markets as defined and reliable systems from the starting point of the faith of their participants. The word "*fides*" was understood both as the reliability of those trading, selling, and contracting and the fact that they belonged to an environment of credibility that was indistinguishable from the spheres of official religion and political friendship.

Market and *bonum commune*

The overlapping of the dimensions of contract and trust translated in concrete terms both into those recognisably within the validated institutional network of trust that was seen as more trustworthy, and in the development of a systematic political and eco-

---

6 Mathieu Arnoux, "Vérité et questions des marchés médiévaux," in *L'activité marchande sans le marché?*, Armand Hatchuel, Olivier Favereau, Franck Aggeri, ed. (Paris, 2010), 27–43; Mathieu Arnoux, *Le temps des laboureurs. Travail, ordre social et croissance en Europe (XIe–XIVe siècle)* (Paris, 2012).

nomic pedagogy available both in intellectually sophisticated treatises and at the same time on the marketplaces. The objective of the latter was to promote publicly significant trade for profit and equate this with religion, which saw salvation in the afterlife as the ultimate, incalculable form of profit achievable by means of investment in good works, customarily described, above all by Franciscan preachers, as "a mountain of golden ducats reaching up to the skies."[7]

Such a complex interweaving of doctrine and practice, between the mechanisms of Christian identification and the road from economic assets to its investment with a view to growth in capital, generated a representation of "the common good"—*bonum commune*—in Italian cities viewed as both economic and cultural organisms capable of connecting private possessions with public prosperity. In such a context, the wealth of individuals seen to all intents and purposes as citizens of the city of God was the starting point for collective wealth. This type of political and religious overemphasis on the private patrimonies of those recognized as champions of public and especially religious institutions—like the members of the great thirteenth and fourteenth century commercial dynasties—inevitably led to the exclusion from the market scene as a stage for the *bonum commune*. It became difficult or impossible for churches or the Roman Church to see as Christian and thus legal some of the economic activities in such a Christian city. The story of the ejection of the merchants from the temple, as told by the Gospels, was—and not coincidentally—much analysed and commented on in the Italy of the thirteenth and fourteenth centuries, as it had become of crucial importance to establish which merchants had no right to trade in the temple built by the Christian city market.[8]

Christian Society, Circulation of Currency, and Jewish Moneylending

The spread of Jewish moneylending in the cities and markets of north-central Italy from the thirteenth century onwards was replete with complex and ambiguous meanings.[9] However, when seen close up, it is an element capable of throwing light on the distinctly political and ideological character of the fourteenth- and fifteenth-century Italian markets. At first sight the proliferation of Jewish lending houses meant delegating a prohibited activity—"manifest and public usury"—to those not subject to Christian law and thus not recognized as citizens in the full sense of the word and people suspected of moral infamy. At the same time, in the specific urban context, this provided a provisional solution, more political than economic, to the problem involving an increasingly visible differentiation between the sphere of higher credit loans and that of consumption loans, which led inexorably to an increase in the cost of money and a consequent loss in the buying power of the non-privileged majority. The so-called Jewish monopoly on

---

7 Giacomo Todeschini, "Il Medioevo tra etica e profitto," in *Enciclopedia Italiana: Il Contributo italiano alla Storia del Pensiero. Ottava Appendice. Economia*, ed. Vera Negri Zamagni, Pier Luigi Porta (Roma, 2012), 3–15.

8 Giacomo Todeschini, *Les marchands et le temple* (Paris, 2017).

9 Giacomo Todeschini, "Eccezioni e usura nel duecento osservazioni sulla cultura economica medievale come realtà non dottrinaria," *Quaderni Storici* 131, no. 2 (2009): 443–60.

consumption loans, in this context, was actually a temporary and unsatisfactory solution to an economic and social crisis, or rather an imbalance in the market system, which the local oligarchs managed to neither control nor understand, but which they attempted to regulate using the conceptual strategies at their disposal. This solution was characterized by an ambiguous dual approach, both economic and ideological, to the insolvency of the less wealthy. On one hand, in fact, local rulers developed, expressed, and disseminated a belief that the need for money by so many was the effect of a shortfall in circulation, when it was actually the consequence of a growing economic and political imbalance. On the other hand, these new, more restricted civic oligarchies generated and disseminated the idea by which the solution to the monetary shortage and thus of exchange malfunction was a question of entrusting consumption loan management to a non-Christian minority traditionally perceived and publicly represented as greedy and money-hoarding: thus rich in what the weaker social classes—and sometimes also the local ruling elites—felt they lacked: liquid cash.[10]

Historiographical difficulties in connecting the theological and administrative lexicon generated by late medieval culture and politics have often obscured evidence of their connections. In fourteenth- and fifteenth-century Italian cities, a nexus linked traditional theological stereotypes, which indicated the Jewish resistance to conversion as a form of perfidious avarice, with the widespread administrative notion so characteristic of Italian civic cultures from the onset of economic change, according to which cash liquidity must be triggered by groups of lenders outside the city and for this reason imagined as fabulously wealthy.

This twofold misunderstanding—of the cause of the crisis and real Jewish wealth—not only failed to alleviate the problem of the growing impoverishment of the population, but actually worsened it at this point. This placed blame for wrong-headed economic policies squarely on the shoulders of Jewish communities, or rather their bankers, when the policies were actually implemented by local governments and determined by the economic culture and the image of the market that they generated and disseminated. Effectively, systematic recourse to consumption loans managed by a minority without full citizenship rights generated a series of substantially negative consequences for urban economies and the markets they generated. On one side, loans for interest understood as pure sale of money by a group which was not incorporated into the urban social system, and thus alien to the logic of civic relationships and networks of trust relationship, did not lead to decreases in the cost of money because it made of consumption loans a sale of money linked to pawn values whose current prices were entirely uncertain. On the other hand, such trade continued to highlight the existing economic and political difference between the socially significant credit managed by the trading elites on the one hand and the semi-legal or illegal credit networks on the other, the latter consisting of a vast system of loans and repayments which, generically, anyone—citizen or foreigner, *civis* or *alienus*—could give or receive.

---

10 *Gli ebrei nell'Italia centro settentrionale fra tardo Medioevo ed età moderna (secoli XV–XVIII)*, ed. Marina Romani, Elisabetta Traniello, special issue, *Cheiron* 57–58 (2012).

The fact that the permission to lend involved local rulers granting fixed-term citizenship, which could be revoked at any time, to Jewish communities meant that trading in money had to take the form of high and rapid profits to lenders who could only marginally see themselves (and be seen as) effective, long term participants in the economy and urban markets.

Whilst the at least partial integration of Jewish minorities into Italian Christian cities in the fourteenth and fifteenth centuries has rightly been noted, the highly significant fact from the point of view of an analysis of economic and credit relations remains that these lending activities were largely alien in civic terms and thus unable to reinforce the city's economic fabric or reduce poverty in any way. Discrimination against Jewish communities as social and economic groups, namely the civic de-legitimation of these groups, thus had negative consequences for the economic impact of the transactions delegated to these groups.

At the same time, loans managed by Jews and entrusted by fourteenth- and fifteenth-century city oligarchies to these *infideles* involved reiterating the profound and entirely political and religious differences which intersected formalized credit relationships in Tuscan, Emilian, Lombard, Piedmontese, Ligurian, and Veneto cities. Here, full-blown citizens took centre stage between what was referred to as *simpliciter cives* or *cives originarii*—a narrow circle of important artisans and merchants, courtiers and functionaries—and the vast, indistinct maze of non-formalized and frequently unregistered credit and trading relationships which were the norm for the majority of the population to whom the exclusive world of full citizenship was closed. Both the Italian urban laws of this period and doctrinal conceptions relating to markets generated above all in Dominican and Franciscan milieux highlighted the impropriety of these networks of economic relationship. They pointed the finger at small traders, servants charging interest, and women doing small-scale local business and retail and its effect on social disorder, a danger to the health of a body politic publicly founded on the success of large-scale merchants and sacred institutions.[11]

Civic Identity, Observant Franciscans, and the Economy

The conceptual framework we have just sketched was essentially defined by dividing markets between the political and religious legitimacy of business networks controlled by what was publicly affirmed and economic practices that were illegitimate, albeit provisionally useful, and conducted by infidels and commoners of doubtful origin. In this difficult situation, a complex and contradictory Franciscan representation of a credit system, or rather market, took shape and came to the fore. It was understood as organized by the trust of citizens and charitable assistance and thus totally internal to the city

---

11 Giacomo Todeschini, "Usury in Christian Middle Ages. A Reconsideration of the Historiographical Tradition (1949–2010)," in *Religione e istituzioni religiose nell'economia europea. 1000–1800 / Religion and religious institutions in the European economy. 1000–1800, Atti della Quarantatreesima Settimana di Studi dell'Istituto F. Datini,* ed. Francesco Ammannati (Firenze, 2012), 119–30.

and for this reason capable of activating systems of loans which were in turn exclusive and selective.[12]

This political and economic distinction requires highlighting, as there was a significant difference of scale in late medieval Italian cities between forms of credit put forward by Observant Franciscans and the reality of pawn loans by bankers from the Jewish community. Jewish loans effectively existed as the result of economic difficulties in the institutional city sphere. We might say that this took place "in the heat of the moment," responding to a real demand for such loans by citizens looking for guarantees which could be generated solely by the sale of money. On the other hand, the Franciscan credit and market notion response to the fifteenth century crisis was the outcome of two centuries of economic development typical of the school of the Friars Minor.[13] From the perspective of primarily doctrinal discussions, pawn loans contracted out to the Jewish community seemed a loophole in the system of trust required to hold together the Christian market and make it functional, a system intended to be total and pervasive. The market and thus the network of credit relations it required was examined by thirteenth- and fourteenth-century Franciscan economists as a quantifiable aspect of a political and religious framework.[14] Based on *fides*, or rather reciprocal faith, between those in business together, substantially deriving from a shared cultural and religious history, then it was a serious problem to have the active presence in the market and in the credit system of culturally diverse and religiously alternative elements to the Christian model. As we have seen, loans managed by Jewish lenders seemed to the city rulers, on the basis of a mistaken analysis, to be the solution to an imbalance between poverty and wealth. At the same time, the Franciscan school saw these Jewish loans as a crisis in the nexus of economics and politics, that is, the relationship between ethics and economics which this school held to be the only possible route to public happiness. If the local ruling class saw contributions of Jewish money as a revitalization of the city economy, an emergency measure, Franciscan thinkers with Bernardino di Siena in the forefront saw Jewish loans as an economic malaise the outcome of which could only be a halt in the circulation of wealth and paralysis of the body politic. Characteristically, this deconstruction of the Jewish presence in Italian cities by the Franciscans coincided with a description, once again by the Friars Minor, of the civic disorder created by their presence. Franciscan economists saw Jewish loans as an open door to the proliferation of uncontrolled economic relationships and the undisciplined participation in the market of immoral and unclassifiable elements whose sole objective was the acquisition of personal wealth.[15]

Between these two diverse but, as we shall see, not entirely conflicting perceptions and representations of pawn loans managed by Jewish bankers, was the vision of eco-

---

12 Giacomo Todeschini, *Franciscan Wealth* (New York, 2009).

13 Odd Langholm, *Economics in the Medieval Schools. Wealth, Exchange, Value, Money and Usury according to the Paris Theological Tradition, 1200–1350* (Leiden, 1992).

14 Amleto Spicciani, *Capitale e interesse tra mercatura e povertà nei teologi e canonisti dei secoli XIII–XIV* (Roma, 1990).

15 Diego Quaglioni, Giacomo Todeschini, Gian Maria Varanini, eds., *Credito e usura fra teologia, diritto e amministrazione. Linguaggi a confronto (sec. XII–XVI)* (Roma, 2005).

nomic relations specific to the Jewish cultural tradition in its Jewish variant. In this case, the potential for trading in money like any other goods offered to Jewish bankers by the Christian ruling elites responded to the specific legal Jewish notion that money was an object of trading value (not an indication of value in itself) as well as a need by Jewish communities of Italian or German origin to settle in cities and acquire citizenship or something close to it. This specific point of view, whilst presumably not perceived clearly by city rulers and the Franciscan economic school, was reconstructed as the origin of the logic of markets by the Franciscans. In this way, loans managed by non- or semi-citizens were directly connected to a trading activism which was apparently a danger to the established economic and social balance of the Christian city. On the other hand, it seemed to dissolve the network of personal relationships based on trust and strongly institutionalized in a Christian sense on which the market should rest.

City rulers and Franciscan intellectual elites, then, whilst reaching different conclusions on the meaning of Jewish loans in the short and medium term for strongly rooted local contexts and thus of narrow and institutional social groups in the widest sense of the term, in any case shared a number of assumptions on the presence of both Jews and commoners in markets in Christian lands. It was from the starting point of these premises that a sometimes difficult dialogue developed between the city ruling elite and the Franciscan order, one capable in the fifteenth and sixteenth centuries of reaching agreement on the role of some form of urban institution providing credit. As both the local ruling class and the Franciscan school saw the Jewish community and the bankers working within it as culturally and economically alien in the same way they saw small-scale artisans, salespeople, the non-free, and in general the unknown and the *minores* as alien to the market, the problem essentially consisted of the short- or long-term benefits this world could be acknowledged to have.

It was thus not difficult for the cultured Franciscan milieu—on the strength of a well-established tradition of Roman and canon law—to demonstrate to a local ruling elite, which derived its compact nature and credibility from the Christian lexicon of identity and a political rationale built on the language of religion and theology, that the presence of Jewish moneylenders on Christian land equalled the breakdown of credit and economic trust between businessmen and institutional bodies, and thus blocked all potential development. According to this logic, gradually taken on board by civic communities, loans were the opposite of credit and civic recognition of those who needed not simply money but also, and above all, access to credit became the only acceptable basis for banking transactions.[16]

The struggle against lending managed by Jewish bankers carried out by the Observant Franciscans thus established a juxtaposition between trade in money and granting credit and a clear difference between the apparent solvency of a debtor and credibility, or rather the civic identity of those needing money. In the event that a member of the civic community was in need of liquid cash it became of fundamental importance from a Franciscan point of view to judge the nature of this individual's citizenship, namely his

---

16 Giacomo Todeschini, Come Giuda, *La gente comune e i giochi dell'economia all'inizio dell'epoca moderna* (Bologna, 2011).

or her membership of the community and thus reliability. The guarantee constituted by the pawn itself was substituted with a less visible guarantee consisting of the much higher value of certifiable civic identity, that is, membership by the individual requiring access to credit to the urban body politic and the market. It was on this basis that the Monte di Pietà, as a Franciscan institution which substituted pawnbroking with public savings, selected its clientele, establishing that not everyone had a right to credit or deserved it, because not all the people in the city had the right to be there or were recognized as wholly reliable individuals.[17]

Jewish loans intended by the local ruling class as an emergency measure in situations of crisis were a resort for those who could offer the guarantee of a pawned asset or tradeable item whatever their social or citizenship status. By contrast, the credit offered by the Franciscans and the Italian trading cities from the second half of the fifteenth century onwards activated an economic judgment. The overall object of this was to link the right to a loan, that is, the access to credit, with recognized status as a full citizen. The legality of a banking transaction and thus the right to be active in the credit market was rooted at this point in the verifiable civic condition of those requiring economic assistance for economic survival and to take public part in the market. It thus became fundamentally important to recognisably belong to the community which generated the market, whatever the specific circumstances of an individual's private business.[18]

Conclusions

The active and lively marketplace which was such a feature of late medieval Italian cities was thus neither a natural economic organization nor the effect of an interplay of relationships which corresponded to the objective form taken by city trading and financial transactions. Quite the contrary, it was the outcome of a complex, slow to develop interweaving between the lexicons of profit and religious election, the socio-economic practices imposed by privileged family-based networks, and the dynamics of public prosperity legitimated by fundamental charismatic powers such as, first and foremost, the papacy. The result of this institutional and linguistic journey at the beginning of the Early Modern period was an Italian financial market capable of measuring the effective political and civic citizenship of those active in the market. The market thus functioned as a clearly institutional and selective context well-suited to reflect social order and hierarchies, and became the material and immaterial environment in which the right to profit and political supremacy of certain exclusive minorities was affirmed and guaranteed.[19]

---

17 Maria Giuseppina Muzzarelli, *Il denaro e la salvezza. L'invenzione del Monte di Pietà* (Bologna, 2001); Lawrin Armstrong, *Usury and Public Debt in Early Renaissance Florence: Lorenzo Ridolfi on the Monte Comune* (Toronto, 2003).

18 Joel Kaye, *Economy and Nature in the Fourteenth Century. Money Market Exchange, and the Emergence of Scientific Thought* (Cambridge, MA, 1998).

19 Paolo Prodi, *Settimo non rubare. Furto e mercato nella storia dell'Occidente* (Bologna, 2009).

Part Three

IDEOLOGY IN THE MIND

Chapter 13

THE RELATIONSHIP BETWEEN MENTALITY AND IDEOLOGY: ACCULTURATION AND CHRISTIANIZATION IN GALICIA, 500–1100

JUAN COIRA POCIÑA

THE MIDDLE AGES was a time of contrasts and opposites (God and the devil, Christianity and paganism, and so on), a time that can be viewed as one of many contradictions. However, when analysing other societies, specifically societies from the past, it must be remembered that our way of viewing them is very much conditioned by our own way of understanding the world. It is precisely at this intersection between past and present that contradictions arise. Indeed, "historical knowledge is always, in one way or another, self-consciousness: when studying the history of other times men cannot but compare it with their own time."[1] Therefore, it is our contemporary mentality that sits at the origin of historical curiosity and perception of difference.[2]

Our mentality leads us to perceive medieval culture as a combination of oppositions that may appear irresolvable, similar to understanding life and death as irreversible. However, there was no space for such impossibilities in the medieval world. Integrity and belief in the uniqueness of creation were the characteristic features of this period, though this did not necessarily mean complete harmony. The contrasts that existed were very much rooted in social life, in those irreconcilable oppositions between wealth and poverty, privilege and humiliation, and suchlike. Here is where Christianity played an essential role precisely because the Christian world "eliminated" these very real contradictions by moving them to the higher plane of celestial universal categories. On this plane, solutions could be found.[3]

It might seem, therefore, that Christianity and its doctrine of a just and perfect heavenly life after one's earthly life were the solution to these contradictions. Ultimately, temporal inequalities pale into insignificance when compared with eternal privileges. However, this was not the case. Many reasons contributed to this, including the fact that Christianity itself was one of the reasons behind such contradictions, as it superimposed

---

1 *El conocimiento histórico representa siempre, de una u otra manera, conciencia de sí: al estudiar la historia de otra época los hombres no pueden dejar de compararla con su tiempo.* Cited from Aron Gurevich, *Las categorías de la cultura medieval* (Madrid, 1990), 25.

2 Philippe Ariès, "La historia de las mentalidades," in *La Nueva Historia*, ed. Jacques Le Goff (Bilbao, 1988), 460–81 at 478.

3 Gurevich, *Las categorías*, 31–34.

Juan Coira Pociña (juancoirapocinha@gmail.com) is Researcher at the Universidade de Santiago de Compostela, Spain.

itself onto other visions of the world in places where it became the official religion.[4] Christianity had its own ideology and the population its own mentality.

This chapter examines some of the most important parts of the relationship between mentality and ideology during the Early Middle Ages (sixth to eleventh centuries), how they were formulated and how they influenced pre-Christian mentality and Christian thought during this period and up until the consolidation of the acculturation process. It draws from several written sources, including the works of St. Martin of Braga, Visigothic councils, penitentials, and hagiographies. During these centuries, popular mentality reached its greatest influence over Christian doctrine and practice with the consolidation of the existence of purgatory, folkloric motifs, the marvellous in hagiography, and practices of pre-Christian origin during festivities. However, the Church also began to implement a firmer and more structured programme for the reform of its traditions. The spatial and referential framework taken here is the northwest of the Iberian Peninsula, though this framework could be applied elsewhere.

Ideology and Mentality

This section clarifies what "ideology" and "mentality" mean to me. Both are complex terms, related to each other and overlapping in some instances, according to positions inspired by Marxist theories or the *Annales* school of thought. Existing definitions can sometimes be confusing.[5]

Despite difficulties that might arise when trying to reach a definition of ideology and mentality, some authors coincide and these instances serve to differentiate the two concepts. However, this is not true of Marxists, who include both concepts within ideology at the same time, recognizing that they function on different levels.

Ideology for Marxists is a constituted and organized speech that is both systematic and elaborate. It can match the worldview of a social group or several groups (collective

---

4 One example of these contradictions is the existence of revenge. In the Middle Ages it was a right, almost an obligation, belonging to the aggrieved social group. Christianity advocates forgiveness and rejects the notion of revenge, yet God or the saints could seek revenge when they were aggrieved. See for example Ordoño de Celanova, *Vida y milagros de San Rosendo*, ed. Manuel Díaz y Díaz, María Virtudes Pardo Gómez, Daría Vilariño Pintos (A Coruña, 1990), 173ff.

5 There is abundant bibliography focused on both concepts. For reasons of size, this bibliography is not the subject here, but I leave here a list of the books I used for reference: Ariès, "La historia de las mentalidades," 460–81; Roger Chartier, *El mundo como representación. Historia cultural: entre práctica y representación* (Barcelona, 1995); Georges Duby, *Historia social e ideologías de las sociedades* (Barcelona, 1976); Ana Rosa Fernández Pérez, Araceli Otero Fernández, César Quelle Vidal, "A historia das mentalidades na recente historiografía española," in *Historia a Debate. Galicia*, ed. Carlos Barros (Santiago de Compostela, 1995), 143–63; Domingo González Lopo, "Historia de las mentalidades. Evolución historiográfica de un concepto complejo y polémico," *Obradoiro de Historia Moderna* 11 (2002): 135–90; Jacques Le Goff, "Las mentalidades. Una historia ambigua," in *Hacer la Historia* 3, ed. Jacques Le Goff, Pierre Nora (Barcelona, 1980), 81–98; Hervé Martin, *Mentalités médiévales. XIe–XVe siècle* (Paris, 1996); Julio Antonio Vaquero Iglesias, "Mentalidades e ideologías," in *Historia a debate: actas del Congreso internacional "A historia a debate" celebrado el 7–11 de julio de 1993 en Santiago de Compostela*, ed. Carlos Barros, 3 vols. (A Coruña, 1995), 2:25–35; Michel Vovelle, *Ideologías y mentalidades* (Barcelona, 1985).

speech, not merely individual) and it usually has the support of specialized institutions with the necessary instruments in place to be able to impose that ideology on other visions of reality (mainly Church and State). By contrast, mentality is a less elaborate, organized, or systematic discourse that is acquired from non-conscious (better than unconscious)[6] ways carried through from the early years of life. Eminently collective and linked to gestures, behaviour, habits and customs (that is to say, to tradition and daily life), mentality "evolves slowly, changes progressively, and passes from one generation to another until the moment in which it loses, sometimes sharply, all consistency."[7] It is a worldview that often does not have the support of specialized institutions and whose central axis is the home and family/lineage.

Ideology and mentality never exist separately but interact and evolve within a given society. It is complex to differentiate one from the other since there are conscious elements that combine harmoniously with unconscious elements to form the mental structures of an individual or group.[8]

Human beings are influenced by both ideology and mentality. Mentality plays a role from our early years, during our upbringing and throughout our life, as we acquire habits, verbs and manners that fit together more or less harmoniously. Ideology is added on top of this as each individual joins new networks, from work (professional organizations) to residential communities (the parish). These networks try to reshape those now traditional initial habits we adopted and adapt them to new models. It is important to note that the elementary ideological networks lie under the jurisdiction of the Church and the State.[9]

The Early Centuries of Christianity

From the year 313, with the "Edict of Milan," Christianity went from being a prohibited sect to a consolidated body in the state, ultimately replacing paganism as the official religion. From then on, the Church was able to expand its doctrine with support from the authorities.

> [...] We grant Christians and everyone else the right to freely practise religion that everyone desired, in order that all that is divine in the celestial world show itself favourable and conducive to us and to all those under our authority." Although this edict recognized that all religions were legal, the real purpose was to legalise the Christian religion, the only one mentioned.[10]

---

6 "The collective unconscious? It would be better to say the collective non-conscious." (*¿Qué es el inconsciente colectivo? Sin duda sería preferible decir el no-consciemte colectivo.*) Cited from Ariès, "La historia de las mentalidades," 481.

7 *évoluent lentement, s'infléchissant progressivement en passant d'une génération à une autre, jusqu'au moment où elles perdent, parfois brusquement, toute consistance.* Cited from Jacques Paul, *L'Eglise et la culture en Occident*, 2 vols. (Paris, 1986), 2:522.

8 Martin, *Mentalités médiévales*, 7. I reiterate my disagreement with the concept of "unconscious." I judge the concept "non-conscious," used by Ariès, to be more appropriate.

9 Martin, *Mentalités médiévales*, 14–15.

10 *[...] conceder a los cristianos y a todos los demás la facultad de practicar libremente la religión*

Christianity created a whole structure with its own rites, liturgy, doctrine, morals, and dogmas in which everyone had to believe. All of this existed under the umbrella of ecclesiastical authority. Supporting the Church became one of the main tasks of imperial power, with the often-repeated notion that God himself ordered for Caesar to be given what belonged to him. But this, stating that all temporal power comes from God, gave him a power with divine roots. Relationships forged between religion and power were no longer sporadic, but systematic: "God and Caesar stopped acting by themselves; God began to have influence on Caesar, so Caesar had to give God what he owed him."[11]

From that time on, the Christian Church had freedom to impose its message on a vast territory: Christianization began. The Fathers of the Church set the dogma and attacked the ancient religion, branding it false and demonized.[12] Space was Christianized, as was time (parish networks, parish churches, calendars, etc.); and a new language with new concepts (sin, hell, salvation, etc.) was introduced into the mind of the population. In short, a new conception of the world and reality surfaced, supported and shared by both those who held power and by a highly specialized group, the clergy. With this came an elaborate and systematic doctrine. That is to say, an ideology came into being.

Over the course of these centuries and in spite of instability, the Church not only maintained its alliance with political power but began to acquire it too.[13] Allied with the State, part of the power structure, and established as the only true and official faith, Christianity continued the evangelization process.

Obtaining a quick conversion, as was the case with the monarchs (whose motivations were not strictly religious), would not have been possible in a traditional society. These are societies that constantly look towards the past as a time that offers confidence

---

que cada uno desease, con la finalidad de que todo lo que hay de divino en la sede celestial se mostrase favorable y propicio tanto a nosotros como a todos los que están bajo nuestra autoridad. Cited from Raúl González Salinero, *Las persecuciones contra los cristianos en el Imperio romano* (Madrid, 2005), 73–74. About the process of consolidation of Christianity until Teodosio and the edict of Thessalonica, and the beginning of the repression against paganism, see 73ff.

11 *Dios y César dejaron de actuar cada cual por su lado, Dios empezó a pesar sobre César, era preciso que César diera a Dios lo que a Dios se debía.* Cited from Paul Veyne, *El sueño de Constantino. El fin del imperio pagano y el nacimiento del mundo cristiano* (Barcelona, 2008), 165–70.

12 Eusebius of Cesarea wrote: "Thus after all tyranny had been purged away, the empire which belonged to them was preserved firm and without a rival for Constantine and his sons alone. And having obliterated the godlessness of their predecessors, recognizing the benefits conferred upon them by God, they exhibited their love of virtue and their love of God, and their piety and gratitude to the Deity, by the deeds which they performed in the sight of all men." (*Expurgada así, realmente, toda tiranía, el imperio que les correspondía se reservaba seguro e indiscutible solamente para Constantino y sus hijos, quienes, después de eliminar del mundo antes que nada el odio a Dios, conscientes de los bienes que Dios les había otorgado, pusieron de manifiesto su amor a la virtud, su amor a Dios, su piedad para con Dios y su gratitud, mediante obras que realizaban públicamente a la vista de todos los hombres.*) Cited from the closing paragraph of Eusebius of Caesarea, *Historia Eclesiástica* (Madrid, 1997), 646 (bk. 10, chap. 9, §9).

13 Hidacio, bishop in Chaves in the fifth century, was an example of this in the northwest of the Iberian Peninsula, since he acted as a political representative of his community. See César Candelas Colodrón, *O mundo de Hidacio de Chaves* (Santiago de Compostela, 2006).

and stability in the face of an uncertain future. Conversion meant denying oneself and one's ancestors,[14] so it was difficult to achieve and the Church had to apply an innovative methodology to a process that was also new. Firstly, on a theoretical level, the Fathers of the Church, who were cultured and had excellent theological knowledge, were responsible for setting a dogma. Secondly, the lowest sector of the parish network, the parish clergy, was fundamental on a practical level and sought to introduce Christianity in the day-to-day lives of many people. On both levels, the methodology was faced with some customs, rituals, and beliefs that did not fit harmoniously with Christian doctrine.

Mentality and Ideology in the Sixth to Eighth Centuries

As in the rest of Europe, acceptance of Christian ideology was hampered by a different kind of mentality. Incompatibilities between that ideology and the mentality held by the population were reflected in the sources we have, especially in Visigothic councils and the work of St. Martin de Braga.[15] These sources were written from the point of view of Christian ideology, since the religious group was the only one with the power of the written word. They were written with the aim of reforming and debasing the beliefs and customs held dear by the population.

St. Martin of Braga

St. Martin of Braga made one of the greatest evangelistic efforts in the northwest of the Iberian Peninsula. His work *De correctione rusticorum* reveals the most noted superstitions of Galician people in the sixth century.[16] Indeed, traces of this mentality can still be seen today.

His work begins with basic information about theology and then the author explains the origin of idolatrous cults. The ancient pagan gods were among the false idols, demons serving the Devil. However, the bishop of Braga shows himself to be "benevolent" and even paternalistic in the sense that he understands the idolatrous and demonic cults as a result of the Devil's deception of ignorant people, rather than as a manifestation of faith in a religion that is obviously considered false:[17]

---

14 Oronzo Giordano, *Religiosidad popular en la alta Edad Media* (Madrid, 1983).

15 *Concilios visigóticos e hispano-romanos*, ed. José Vives (Barcelona, 1963); Xosé Eduardo López Pereira, ed., *Cultura, relixión e supersticións na Galicia sueva. Martiño de Braga. De Correctione Rusticorum* (A Coruña, 1996); Martín de Braga, *Obras completas/Martín de Braga*, trans. Ursicino Domínguez del Val (Madrid, 1990).

16 Superstitions that were shared with the population of other regions. See Cesáire d'Arles, *Sermons au people / Cesáreo de Arlés*, ed. Marie-José Delage (París, 1971–1986); Fabrizio Nicoli, *Cristianesimo, superstizione e magia nell'alto Medioevo: Cesario di Arles, Martino di Braga, Isidoro di Siviglia* (Bagni di Lucca, 1992).

17 St. Martin of Braga was one of the leading figures fighting against the Priscillian heresy, deeply rooted in Galicia. He tried to correct the errors not for doctrinal reasons (the heresy had already been banned), but to challenge ignorance, as he says in the beginning of *De correctione*. About Priscillianism, see Francisco Javier Fernández Conde, *Prisciliano y el priscilianismo: historiografía y realidad* (Gijón, 2007).

Then the Devil or his ministers, the demons, which had been thrown out of Heaven, on seeing men who out of ignorance disregarded their creator, started to serve him through creatures. And they started to appear in different figures, speaking with them and asking them to offer sacrifices on the high hills and in the leafy woods.[18] And also asking them to honour them as though they were God, giving them the names of evildoers, who had spent their whole lives committing crimes and evil acts.[19]

In this fragment, the idea of a sacred space, namely mountains and forests (nature), can also be noted. This is a space not accepted by the Church. The new ideology had its own places of worship (churches) where divinity was manifested in a privileged way. However, ecclesiastical authorities soon realized the difficulty involved in eradicating certain conceptions of sacred mountains, forests, springs, rivers, stones, etc. from the mentality held by the population. For this reason, the tactic was to try to Christianize these areas by building churches, shrines, altars, crosses, etc. However, these acts also served to create confusion.[20]

Idols have to be destroyed, but *fana*, the sacred places where idols are kept, do not have to be destroyed. *Fana* must be purified with holy water after altars have been erected and relics installed. Christian worship at ancient sacred places will immediately familiarize novices with the new faith. Even traditional festivities must be maintained, transforming, for example, animal sacrifices into a banquet [...].[21]

Other violations are related to the calendar. The Church tried to instil its own conception of time and rationalization. It attempted both to change the names of days (to avoid them being dedicated to pagan gods) and to modify the date of the first day of the year. St. Martin wanted to change January 1 to March 25, the day of the Incarnation). These attempts were largely unsuccessful, though fruitful in some territories.[22]

---

18 *Entonces el diablo, o los demonios sus ministros, que fueron arrojados del cielo, viendo a los hombres que por ignorancia despreciaron a su Creador, empezaron a servirlo por medio de las criaturas. Y empezaron a manifestarse en diversas figures, a hablar con ellos y pedirles que les ofreciesen sacrificios en los montes altos y en los bosques frondosos.*Strabo already spoke about sacrifices to gods, by referring to Galician, Asturian, and Cantabrian people of the first century: "They feed above all on the goat's meat and they sacrifice a he-goat, prisoners, and horses to Ares" (*Se alimentan sobre todo de carne de cabra y sacrifican a Ares un macho cabrío, prisioneros y caballos*). Strabo, *Geografía de Iberia* 3.3.7, trans. Javier Gómez Espelosín (Madrid, 2007), 204ff.

19 *[Y] a honrarlos como a Dios, poniéndoles los nombres de hombres malhechores, que habían llevado una vida de toda clase de crímenes y de maldades.* Cited from Martín de Braga, *Obras completas*, 146.

20 Giordano, *Religiosidad popular*, 232–34.

21 *Los ídolos han de destruirse; pero no los fana, los lugares sagrados donde aquéllos se custodian. Éstos, por el contrario, han de purificarse con agua bendita después de que se alcen altares y se instalen reliquias. El culto cristiano celebrado en los antiguos lugares sacros familiarizará inmediatamente a los neófitos con la nueva fe. Incluso las fiestas tradicionales deberán mantenerse, por ejemplo transformando el sacrificio de animals en un banquete [...].* Words of Gregory the Great cited by Franco Cardini, *Magia, brujería y superstición en el Occidente medieval* (Barcelona, 1982), 23.

22 As in Portugal, for example, where Monday is called "segunda-feira" (second day), Tuesday "terça-feira" (third day), etc.

In the same way, the mistake of thinking that the year begins at the Calends of January was introduced to those ignorant and uncouth people. This is entirely fake. For, as the Holy Scripture says, the first day of the year was the equinox on March 25.[23]

Then it moves on to speaking about omens. Divination practices were the most readily persecuted because they meant denying God one of his essential attributes, foreknowledge and therefore, omniscience:

> God did not allow men to know the future, but did allow that in living in fear of God man would see in him the government and aid that would carry him through life. Knowledge of things before they happen is exclusive to God. However, demons use several arguments to delude vain men into offending God and they even take the souls of these vain men with them to Hell.[24]

St. Martin speaks of various ways of divining the future. One that clearly stands out is the importance attached to omens garnered from the voices of animals or their flights. However, these were not the only kind of divination practices used in the northwest of the Iberian Peninsula.[25]

The bishop of Braga includes many other practices and beliefs. For him, many of these practices and beliefs were nothing more than superstitions, making them entirely dispensable. However, these very beliefs were rooted in the mentality of the people and so would not be easy to eradicate. They included celebrating the day of the moths and rats;[26] lighting candles next to stones,[27] trees,[28] fountains,[29] and cross-

---

23 *Igualmente se introdujo entre los ignorantes y rústicos aquel otro error por el que piensan que el principio del año son las calendas de enero, lo cual es falsísimo. En efecto, como dice la Santa Escritura, en el mismo punto de equinoccio fue el principio del primer año [...]. En toda división recta hay igualdad, como sucede en los veinticinco de marzo, en el que tanto espacio de horas tiene el día como la noche.* Cited from Martín de Braga, *Obras completas*, 148.

24 *Dios no mandó conocer las cosas futuras, sino que viviendo siempre en el temor de Dios, esperasen en Él el gobierno y el auxilio de su vida. Es propio de solo Dios el conocer los acontecimientos antes de que sucedan; sin embargo, los demonios engañan a los hombres vanos con diversos argumentos hasta conducirlos a la ofensa de Dios, y hasta arrastrar consigo a las almas al infierno.* Cited from Martín de Braga, *Obras completas*, 148.

25 "Lusitanian people are fond of sacrifices, and they examine the entrails without removing them; also they examined besides the veins and discover signs by touching. Also they predict by inspecting the entrails of their prisoners, which they cover with assays: [...] from the entrails, they get a first omen for how they will fall" (*Los lusitanos son aficionados a los sacrificios, y examinan las entrañas sin necesidad de extraerlas; también examinan además las venas del costado, y descubren los indicios mediante el tacto. Predicen también mediante la inspección de las entrañas de sus prisioneros, a los que cubren con sayos: [...] de las entrañas obtienen un primer presagio por la forma en que caen*). Strabo, *Geografía*, 217–18.

26 About the cult to mice, rats, or moles in Antiquity, see José Carlos Bermejo Barrera, *Sociedade e relixión na Galicia antiga* (Santiago de Compostela, 2008), 145ff.

27 About the cult to stones in Galicia, see Xesús Taboada Chivite, *O culto ás pedras no noroeste peninsular* (Verín, 2008), 9–44.

28 Dendrology survived for many centuries; its roots lie in Antiquity. Caesarius of Arles was already against these practices. López, *Cultura, relixión*, 91.

29 The cult of water is highly visible in Latin epigraphy; water, precisely because of its healthy

roads;[30] celebrating the *calendas* (first day of the month)[31]; spilling grain and wine over a log burning in the heat;[32] pouring bread on a spring;[33] paying attention to the day when someone started a journey;[34] enchanting herbs for charms;[35] and others like decorating the tables for certain festivities or paying attention to feet (when entering a building, for example).

St. Martin also laments that people underestimate the sign of the cross before which no omen or devil has any power, and laments that people turn away from the faith, that is to say, the symbol received in baptism:

> And so he who disdains the sign of the cross of Christ and looks for other signs lost the sign of the cross he received at Baptism. Equally, he who practices enchantments invented by magicians and other evil practitioners lost the enchantment of the holy symbol and the dominical prayer which he had received in the faith of Christ and also trampled Christian faith at his feet because one cannot serve God and the Devil at the same time.[36]

As we can see, the amount of pre-Christian practices rooted in the traditions and mentality of the Galician people was plentiful.[37] The initial position of Christian ideology

---

virtues, is a capital element in lots of rites. Many divinities and mythical beings live around springs and rivers. St. Martin of Braga cites Neptune, nymphs, or "Lamias." In addition, some rivers could have magic properties, like the Limia river ("river of forgetting"), which is mentioned by Strabo, *Geografía*, 211.

30 For more information on the cult to crossroads, so specific to the northwest of the Iberian Peninsula, see Bermejo, *Sociedade e relixión*, 158ff.; and Xesús Taboada Chivite, "La encrucijada en el folclore de Galicia," *Boletín Auriense* 5 (1975): 101–12.

31 Not only the *calends* of January, but the *calends* of every month.

32 For more information on the tradition called "Tizón de Navidad," see Manuel A. Castiñeiras González, *Os traballos e os días na Galicia medieval* (Santiago de Compostela, 1995), 9ff.

33 This rite is still alive at the shrine of San Andrés de Teixido (Cedeira, A Coruña, in the north of Galicia). It is made to divine the future (*hidromántico*): if the bread floats, the desire of the pilgrim will be accomplished.

34 Superstitions related to the day on which some activities are carried out remained prevalent throughout the Middle Ages. Indeed, a current Spanish saying reminds us that "on Tuesday, neither marry nor board a boat" (*en martes, ni te cases ni te embarques*).

35 St. Martin criticizes their bad use in spells, not in medicinal usage. During the ensuing medieval centuries the tradition of collecting herbs for some festivities remained strong, believing that these herbs had special virtues on these specific days. Nowadays, we still collect herbs and flowers on the eve of St. John's feast-day (June 23 to 24).

36 *Por eso todo aquello que despreciando la señal de la cruz de Cristo, y mira a otras señales, perdió la señal de la cruz que recibió en el bautismo. Igualmente, el que guarda otros encantamientos inventados por magos y maléficos, perdió el encantamiento del símbolo santo y de la oración dominical que recibió en la fe de Cristo, pisoteó la fe de Cristo, porque no puede dar culto juntamente a Dios y al diablo.* Cited from Martín de Braga, *Obras completas*, 151. "The Church did not condemn the principle of symbolic efficacy, since it was also the foundation of its practices. The Church condemned it because they were not its practices, but in the background they were the same ones." Translated from Jean-Claude Schmitt, *História das superstições* (Mem Martins, 1997), 48–49.

37 The work of St. Martin of Braga must be analysed carefully. Its similarity with the works of other missionaries, of which the bishop of Braga was undoubtedly aware (Caesarius of Arles, for example), is evident. However, the majority of the practices that he cites are testified at one time or

was condemnation, but some of these practices did indeed become part of Christian ideology.

St. Martin offers more information on these kinds of beliefs and practices in another of his works, *Capitula Martini*.[38] However, this work no longer refers explicitly to the Galician territory and is instead a compilation of previous councils.[39] In this work, we can appreciate other practices. As is the case with the bishop of Bragas' work, some of the practices and beliefs are attested in later sources; they are particularly interesting in terms of their representation of the relationship between Christian ideology and the mentality held by the Galicians, not only by farmers, but also by the clergy. There is some coincidence between both works. Of all these coincidences, I highlight one that survives throughout the Middle Ages without the Church managing to stop it: the practice of bringing food to graves (canon 69). This is a practice related to the belief in life after death that Julio Caro Baroja explained as faith in a kind of life taken by the body of the dead (without separating the body and the soul), by which the living must provide housing, food, and even light or face possible harm from the dead.[40]

Hispanic-Visigothic Councils

The other sources used are the Hispanic-Visigothic councils.[41] These provide a series of interesting customs, allowing us to expand the geographical and chronological contexts. These customs include not fasting on All Souls' Day (council of Braga II, canon 10); work on Sunday but rest on the fifth day, dedicated to Jupiter; divination and sorcery (Narbonne); idolatry, dances, and festivities on the birthdays of saints, and funeral songs and beating the breast at funerals (Toledo III, 16, 22 and 23); not fasting during Lent or other Ember days, such as the *calendas* of January, and clerics who go to magicians and soothsayers (Toledo IV, 11, 29, 41 and 53); gluttony, even during Lent (Toledo VIII, 9); the faithful who give offerings for their own souls before having died (Toledo XI, 12); clerics who sacrifice with milk instead of wine (Braga III, 1); venerated stones and worship for springs and trees (Toledo XII, 11); despoliation of altars (Toledo XIII, 7); and onwards.

As we have seen, Christian ideology faced a series of practices and rituals that were rooted in the mentality not just of the general population but also of the clergy, whose

---

another, so it is possible to believe that these practices really did exist. As an example of a practice which was probably not contemporary, St. Martin mentions human sacrifices: they were prohibited by the Romans in the year 97 BCE, which would suggest that in the sixth century they did not take place, but in reality they did. Strabo mentions it, although his imperialist position in favour of the Roman traditions is evident also: "Also they predict by inspecting the entrails of their prisoners." Strabo, *Geografía*, 218.

38 Martín de Braga, *Obras completas*, 115–32.

39 Councils of Nicaea, Laodicea, Antioch, Ancira, Neocesarea, Braga, Cartago, Toledo, etc. See José Carbajal Sobral, *Los concilios de Braga en los siglos VI y VII, reflejo de la vida en la Gallaecia de la época* (Porriño, 1999), 387–94.

40 Julio Caro Baroja, *Análisis de la cultura. Etnología, historia, folklore* (Murcia, 2011), 214. This book also offers an explanation about the customs of lighting candles and building tombs.

41 *Concilios visigóticos*.

social background and mentality often coincided. They had to contend not only with practices but beliefs. Some of the council canons and works of St. Martin were written against the heresy of Priscillian.[42] Indeed, they lead us towards learning about beliefs involving death and the afterlife.

At the beginning, the Church showed, unlike in Antiquity, little concern about the ways in which dead people were treated. It allowed rituals to take place, but did not give space to certain beliefs regarding the superstitious care of bodies.[43] Not only do we have the aforementioned example of bringing food to tombs and offering sacrifices in honour of the deceased, but the Church also condemned acts of sorrow at funerals (those in attendance should not be saddened by hopelessness, or beat their breasts),[44] as well as the lighting of candles in cemeteries and the holding of Masses for the deceased in fields, etc.[45]

> It is not allowed to light candles during the daytime, because we must not disturb the spirits of the righteous. It is not convenient that ignorant and daring clergymen both move the offices and distribute the sacraments on the fields over the tombs, but the masses for the deceased must be offered into the churches, or where the relics of the martyrs are deposited.[46]

---

42 For example, in the first Council of Toledo, in the second (400 and 527 respectively), or in the first and second Council of Braga (561 and 572 respectively). In the case of the works of St. Martin, the 58th canon in *Capitula Martini* is revealing: "If a person, not because of abstinence but just out of a loathing towards food, abstains from meat, this holy Council thinks it good that he first try the meat and then if he wants, abstain from it. But if he hates it, to such an extent that he will not try vegetables cooked with meat, he, in not obeying, if he does not remove himself from heretical suspicion, will be deposed from the order of the priesthood" (*Si alguno, no a causa de las leyes de la abstinencia, se abstiene de tomar carne, tuvo por bien este santo concilio que primeramente las pruebe, y después si quiere se abstenga de ellas. Pero si rehusa, de tal modo que no prueba las legumbres cocidas con carne, este desobediente, si no aleja de sí la sospecha de herejía, sera depuesto del orden del clericato*). According to the bishop, God made human beings in order to feed themselves with vegetables and seeds; when killing for food, the spirit loses its sensitivity and God's inspiration does not reach people who eat meat. Carbajal, *Los Concilios de Braga*, 170.

43 Schmitt, *História das superstições*, 64.

44 Council of Toledo III, canon 13.

45 Nor was St. Augustine himself in favour of funerary luxuries because it meant people acting as though in pagan rituals; minimal cares were enough for deceased. Neither moaning nor sobbing was necessary. "[...] For we thought it not fitting to solemnize that funeral with tearful lament and groanings: for thereby do they for the most part express grief for the departed, as though unhappy, or altogether dead; whereas she was neither unhappy in her death nor altogether dead." Or "[...] For she, the day of her dissolution now at hand, took no thought to have her body sumptuously wound up, or embalmed with spices; nor desired she a choice monument, or to be buried in her own land. These things she enjoined us not; but desired only to have her name commemorated at Thy Altar, which she had served without intermission of one day" (*The Confessions*, 9, 12–13). Augustine of Hippo, *The Confessions. The City of God. On Christian Doctrine* (Chicago, 1984), 69 and 71.

46 *No deben durante el día encenderse en el cementerio cirios, porque no se ha de molestar a los espíritus de los justos. No está bien que clérigos ignorantes y osados, trasladen los oficios y distribuyan los sacramentos en el campo sobre las tumbas, sino que se debe ofrecer las misas por los difuntos en las basílicas o allí donde están depositadas las reliquias de los mártires.* Cited from the Council of Elvira, 34, in the case of candles; *Capitula Martini*, 68, or the Council of Braga II, 68 in the case of the masses. These practices still exist.

These references confirm the belief of the Galician people, and of men and women of the Early Middle Ages in general, in the afterlife. The Christian Church had no problem with accepting this part of its doctrine (inherited from Judaism and Greco-Roman religion), but it had to adapt to the specific circumstances of the time. However, this part of the chapter focuses in more depth on just one of the practices mentioned above, the Masses for the deceased and the ceremonies carried out in their honour. This leads us inevitably to consider the possibility of intervening in the fate of the souls of the dead; that is, the belief, perhaps vague, in an intermediate state between Heaven and Hell:

> Christians took, very soon, the habit of preaching for their deceased. In Antiquity, such an attitude was something completely new. According to a beautiful sentence of Salomon Reinach, "pagans preached to the dead, while Christians preached for them." Actually, as the manifestations of beliefs and mentality do not appear suddenly, the intervention of the living in favour of the dead who suffer in the afterlife is found in some pagan circles, above all in the common people.[47]

During the first of the medieval centuries, having the backing of power allowed Christian doctrine to start finding its place in mentality. However, the success of this process was obviously not so simple. Christianity took advantage of belief in the afterlife from the very start. However, other elements of its theology were not yet understood, and at the level of practice and rituals, much evangelization work still lay ahead for the Church hierarchy. In these centuries, very few Galician people could have reached Paradise.

Mentality and Ideology in the Ninth to Eleventh Centuries

Let us now turn to three literary sources: penitentials, hagiographies, and visions of the afterlife.

Penitentials

Firstly, let us analyse a series of penitentials, in particular the *Cordubense*, whose probable origins can be placed in Galicia in the first half of the eleventh century.[48] This text gives us a vision of religious life at this time. These types of documents were born in the Early Middle Ages: the most ancient penitentials that we preserve were created in the seventh century and written in vulgar Latin. They were intended to help the priest dur-

---

47 *Les chrétiens prirent, très tôt semble-t-il, l'habitude de prier pour leurs morts. Par rapport à l'Antiquité cette attitude était une nouveauté. Selon une heureuse formule de Salomon Reinach "les païens priaient les morts, tandis que les chrétiens prient pour les morts." Certes, comme les phénomènes de croyance et de mentalité n'apparaissent pas soudainement, l'intervention des vivants en faveur de leurs morts souffrants dans l'au-delà se rencontre dans certains milieux païens, surtout à niveau populaire.* Cited from Jacques Le Goff, *La naissance du Purgatoire* (Paris, 1981), 61.

48 Francis Bezler, *Les pénitentiels espagnols* (Münster, 1994), 32ff. Penitentials are a source created by clergymen and intended for clergymen. Their point of view is tendentious and they offer a distorted image of popular mentality: Aron Gurevich, *Medieval Popular Culture: Problems of Belief and Perception* (Cambridge, 1988), 34. However, clergymen knew very well the conditions in which their parishioners lived. In addition, like St. Martin of Braga, the information they offer us agrees with other contemporary, earlier, and later sources.

ing confession, in this case a private confession. The penitentials were also adapted to a common language.[49]

The idea of penance is inextricably linked to the notion of sin; penance cannot exist without sin and the belief in the effectiveness of expiation as a way to cleanse the sins of the soul. The very fact of questioning the faithful to discover their flaws is a new strategy in the attempt to understand and better control society. It is also an attempt to render the concept of sin more intelligible and to introduce its language in people's minds.[50]

A type of sin usually highlighted in penitentials are sexual ones. Sexual misconduct from the point of view of the Church was already plentiful in the first sources analysed.[51] In the eleventh century, we face a similar reality: adultery, fornication, copulation at prohibited times, masturbation, sodomy, and so on, all practices for which clerics still reproached the faithful, but also that clergymen themselves committed. The population showed a carefree mentality toward sexuality and marriage, a mentality that had not yet been consolidated by the Church.

Especially interesting are the practices related to death and the transcendental moment of entombment. Thus, in the *Cordubense* penitential the following acts appear: kissing the corpse, entombment near the saints (in the temple), and unorthodox songs to accompany the corpse.[52]

There are also numerous faults committed against the Eucharist, especially by clergymen responsible for handling the body of Christ: hosts that fall to the ground, hosts that are eaten by animals or spat at, bad liturgies.[53] These kinds of acts occupy an important part of the penitential.

Other condemned practices are related to the lack of temperance and moderation in eating and drinking. These are particularly prevalent concerning drinking since drunkenness was considered to cause more serious sins, such as lust. Both clergymen and laymen committed this sin, but penance was greater for clergymen, especially in the case of the hierarchy of the Church.[54]

---

49 Gurevich, *Medieval Popular Culture*, 25ff. and especially 78ff.

50 Penitentials can be understood as simple theoretical works and collections of previous canons without connection to reality. It is true that their authors tried to include all types of sins to serve as an effective guide for confessors. However, every penitential shows its particularities and every author compiles previous canons, but he chooses among them the most suitable to the context in which he lives. See Mercedes López-Mayán Navarrete, "El *Corrector et Medicus* de Burcardo de Worms," *Rudesindus* 5 (2009): 103–34.

51 *Capitula Martini*: 27: "on fornicating clergymen" (*De fornicatione clerigis*); 44: "if the deacon were to marry twice" (*Si subdiaconus secundam duxerit uxorem*); 76: "on the adulterous" (*De adulteris*); 81: "on those who have sex with animals" (*De his qui se animalibus conmiscuerant*). Council of Toledo III, 10: "nobody can impose the chastity of widows" (*Ut viduis pro castitate violentiam ullus inferat*); Council of Toledo XVI, 3: "on sodomites" (*De sodomitis*)

52 The Council of Braga I had prohibited these entombments, and the Council of Toledo III the unorthodox songs.

53 The *Cordubense* penitential mentions the maleficent eucharist, characteristic of a mentality which believes in magic rather than in Christ: Bezler, *Les pénitentiels*, 248. We should remember that also the Council of Braga III referred to the eucharist with grapes or even milk instead of wine.

54 If the offender were a bishop, the penance was seven weeks only eating bread and drinking

Another violation the Church tried to eradicate was the lack of respect shown towards Sunday rest. In an attempt to sanctify time in its main manifestation (the calendar), the Church wanted to impose rest on the seventh day, as God had ordered. However, work on Sunday took place, as did other practices.[55] This was also the day on which to attend and participate in Mass, as was well established by the commandments of God: "sanctify the holidays." Attendance at Mass was obligatory (although communion only acquired attendance three times a year). However, the *Cordubense* penitential establishes forty days of penance for those who missed three Sundays in a row, indicating that this obligation was not always fulfilled.[56]

As has been shown, men and women of the first half of the eleventh century performed many actions that conflicted with Christian ideology. The vicars of Christ did not manage to conquer time or space, nor did they control mentality. Therefore, it was not only practices, but also beliefs that were still linked to a worldview based in pre-Christian thought. However, this worldview did include some additions from the official religion. These additions, little by little, were settling into everyday life (penance, worship of saints albeit from a "popular" view, some festivities of the calendar, etc.).

This fusion of beliefs manifested in the celebration of Masses for the dead.[57] These celebrations also crystallized in the official Christian doctrine through the commemoration of the Day of the Dead, driven from the tenth century by the order of Cluny.[58] We have already seen that belief in the afterlife was not something new, just like the belief in the effectiveness of certain offerings to calm the dead or favour their souls. These acts demonstrate a belief in a Christian afterlife, but no longer one with the traditional division of Heaven and Hell, because celebrating mass for the soul condemned to Hell does not make sense. In fact, the *Cordubense* specifies, in the case of masses for lay people, that they are celebrated for a "good lay person."[59] But was this good lay person good enough to be saved? Probably not, since Paradise was initially reserved for martyrs and saints and this is what led to the different versions of it presented by the "Fathers of purgatory" about the categories of sinners, as for example in St. Augustine:

> During the time between man's death and the final resurrection, souls are held in secret places [purgatory as a physical location does not yet exist], and every soul is worthy of rest or punishment, according to the choice it has made while living in the flesh. It cannot be denied that the souls of the deceased are relieved by the piety of their living relatives [...]. But these things are beneficial to those who, when living, deserved that these same

---

water; if the offender were a priest the penance was five weeks with the same punishment; four weeks if the offender was a deacon, etc. Bezler, *Les pénitentiels*, 251.

55 Nevertheless, people respected other days in order to carry out other activities; for example, they observed the "Venus day" to get married, St. Martin informs us. Martín de Braga, *Obras completas*, 151. The *Cordubense* penitential also considers the confiscation of the properties if anyone committed the offence of not respecting Sunday rest three times. Bezler, *Les pénitentiels*, 273.

56 Bezler, *Les pénitentiels*, 246.

57 Bezler, *Les pénitentiels*, 249.

58 About this commemoration, see Marcel Pacaut, *L'ordre de Cluny (909–1789)* (Paris, 1991), 134–35.

59 Bezler, *Les pénitentiels*, 249.

things could be then beneficial after [hence the *Cordubense* penitential says "pro layco bono"] [...]. Therefore, in life man acquires all the merit with which he can be alleviated or oppressed after death.[60]

Although Heaven and Hell were the only places fully accepted in Christian theology, the community of believers conceived at least one other state, halfway between salvation and damnation, in which souls awaited the Last Judgment and benefited from the prayers and offerings of their living loved ones.[61] Those who offered these prayers could be relieved by remembering and believing in the benefit of their actions towards the deceased.[62] In this state, those who were not good enough, but had corrected them-

---

60 *Durante el tiempo que media entre la muerte del hombre y la final resurrección, las almas se hallan retenidas en ocultos lugares, según que cada una es digna de reposo o castigo, conforme a la elección que hubiese hecho mientras vivía en la carne. No se puede negar que las almas de los difuntos son aliviadas por la piedad de sus parientes vivos [...]. Pero estas cosas aprovechan a aquellos que, cuando vivían, merecieron que les pudiesen aprovechar después [...]. Por lo tanto, aquí se adquiere el hombre todo el mérito con que pueda ser aliviado u oprimido después de la muerte.* Cited from Augustine of Hippo, *Manual de fe, esperanza y caridad*, trans. P. Andrés Centeno (Madrid, 1979–1990), accessed December 15, 2015, www.augustinus.it/spagnolo/enchiridion/index2.htm. Clarifications between brackets are the present author's.

61 Le Goff himself accepts the importance of the popular tradition surrounding the creation of purgatory. "The purgative fire involves rites and beliefs that popular tales, legends, and spectacles help us to understand. Voyages to the afterlife belong to a genre that blends erudite and folkloric elements, *exempla* about purgatory stem from the frequency of popular tales or ones that are related to them" (*Le feu purgatoire [...] participe de rites et de croyances que les conyes, legéndes et spectacles populaires permettent de comprendre; les voyages dans l'au-delá ressortissent à un genre où éléments savants et éléments folkloriques sont étroitement mêlés; les* exempla *sur le Purgatoire sont souvent issus de contes populaires ou apparentés avec eux*). Le Goff accepts as well that there are "too many uncertainties to be able to specify, explore in depth, or interpret the undeniable part that corresponds to popular culture" (*trop d'incertitudes pour qu'on puisse aisément préciser, approfondir, interpréter la part indéniable de la culture populaire*). Le Goff, *La naissance*, 26. Gurevich, however, says that the idea of purgatory "first arose not in the theology of the late twelfth century, but much earlier [...]. The notion of an otherworldly place or places where souls are subjected not merely to torments but also to expiatory procedures arose already at the beginning of the Middle Ages, as a product of the irresistible need of believers to retain hope of salvation. Hence, it would be incorrect to attribute the initiative for the idea of purgatory to the scholastics." Erudite clergymen opposed this idea because it was not in the bible, but since it was so deeply rooted in the people, the Church accepted it little by little. See Gurevich, *Medieval Popular Culture*, 148–49.

62 "Those who have not been completely good can (perhaps) save themselves through the purgative fire. What's more, they can achieve mitigation of their punishments through the offerings of living people prepared to intercede before God and thanks to finally deserving, despite one's own sins, salvation. These merits are acquired through a good life and a constant effort to improve it through the observance of mercy actions and through the practice of *penitence*. The relationship established this way between penitence and "purgatory," so important during the twelfth and thirteenth centuries, clearly appears for the first time in the works of St. Augustine" (*[...] ceux qui n'ont pas été tout a fais bons peuvent (peut-être) se sauver à travers un feu purgatoire. [...] On peut d'autre part obtenir une mitigation des peines grâce aux suffrages de vivants habilités à intervenir auprès de Dieu et à la condition d'avoir, malgré ces péchés, mérité finalement le salut. Ces mérites s'acquièrent par une vie généralement bonne et un effort constant pour l'améliorer, par l'accomplissement d'oeuvres de miséricorde, et par la pratique de la pénitence. Cette mise en relation*

selves during their lives could be saved through the action of the "fire of purgatory." It served to expiate their venial sins:

> But if it be said that in the interval of time between the death of this body and that last day of judgment and retribution which shall follow the resurrection, the bodies of the dead shall be exposed to a fire of such a nature that it shall not affect those who have not in this life indulged in such pleasures and pursuits as shall be consumed like wood, hay, stubble, but shall affect those others who have carried with them structures of that kind; if it be said that such worldliness, being venial, shall be consumed in the fire of tribulation either here only, or here and hereafter both, or here that it may not be hereafter—this I do not contradict, because possibly it is true.[63]

To conclude this section on penitentials, we should highlight certain practices related to magic, superstitions, and celebrations of pre-Christian origin. Without a doubt, they transmit to us the traditional mentality characteristic of a society closely linked to nature. People felt as though they were an indissoluble part of nature, believing they had the ability to influence it without turning to God and his mediators. The *Cordubense* penitential does not give us any information about these beliefs and practices. However, this does not mean that in Galicia those practices and beliefs did not exist. For that reason, they are only mentioned here: magic and medicine related to each other, magic bathrooms (with spiritual and physical regeneration, as baptism symbolized as well); collecting herbs with magic phrases; certain funeral rites; soothsayers and divination; magic related to meteorology and sex; masquerades or May festivities; and agrarian fertility rites.[64]

These are practices that were difficult to eradicate because, as Gurevich says, "it was possible to destroy or discredit the old gods, but not to eliminate traditional habits of thinking, embedded as they were in the eternally repetitive cycle of agrarian life."[65] The key lies in understanding nature as neither different nor opposite to the human being. The human being included himself in nature and both constantly interacted, hence the need for festivals and rituals to maintain a certain kind of order. Ritual, magic, and festivity were intended to properly manipulate the forces of nature and manifest unity with it; the natural and the supernatural were connected in one indissoluble whole. With Christianity, nature and the human being were no longer the same thing. The union between them was no longer organic but symbolic.[66]

---

de la pénitence et du « purgatoire, » qui sera si importante aux XIIe-XIIIe siècles, apparaît pour la première fois avec netteté chez Augustin). Cited from Le Goff, *La naissance*, 101.

63 *The City of God*, 21.26. Augustine of Hippo, *The Confessions*, 582.

64 Bezler, *Les pénitentiels*, 287ff. St. Martin mentioned some of these practices, such as collecting herbs or divination. The Galician synods of the fifteenth and sixteenth centuries also include information about these beliefs and practices.

65 Gurevich, *Medieval Popular Culture*, 90.

66 Gurevich, *Medieval Popular Culture*, 96.

Hagiography and Visions of the Other World

Penitentials, created by clergymen, show an apparent confrontation between Christian ideology and popular mentality. It is necessary, therefore, to be cautious with the information they provide. This is not to say that it is false information, but there are other sources which provide a fusion between ideology and mentality. In these sources, the narrator shares ideas and worldviews with his audience. That is the case with hagiography, particularly so in collections of miracles and in some visions of the afterlife in Galicia compiled in the eleventh century. However, in some cases they are visions relating to experiences of previous centuries.[67]

Hagiography is a type of literature born with the first Christian martyrs, the primary purpose of which is to perpetuate the memory of saints' lives to instruct readers in the emulation of their virtues. Later, it was used to reinforce the cult of the saints. Hagiographic work is centred around a presumably historical figure and in its core contains some facts about his life that were considered to be credible.[68]

The most interesting aspect of these works is precisely the audience to whom they are directed and their aim. They had to be comprehensible, or they would not achieve their function. There is then a kind of dialogue (not opposition, as in the case of the penitential) between the clergymen and the audience of believers. On this level, there is a strong connection between worldview and social and religious precepts. The Church was gaining a better understanding of popular mentality, and Christianity found a way to penetrate the consciousness of the people and also to instil its ideology. This was done through a precise channel, through the vision of the world held by the population, especially through folklore and the marvellous. This process also meant adapting to traditionally popular orality.[69] The word of God tried, for the first time, to really approach the faithful. Through this interaction, elements of pre-Christian mentality entered into Christian literature,[70] and also into ideology.

Saints' lives were written with the aim of promoting a cult around a particular saint, as has been previously noted. However, this was not always necessary: throughout the Middle Ages we can see the success of the cult surrounding these figures, intermediaries between human beings and divinity, covering the ungraspable distance between divine and human worlds. They were more accessible figures, as humans who had been on

---

67 Aymerich Picaud, *Liber Sancti Iacobi. "Codex Calixtinus"*, ed. Abelardo Moralejo, Casimiro Torres, Julio Feo (A Coruña, 2004); Manuel Díaz y Díaz, *Visiones del Más Allá en Galicia durante la alta Edad Media* (Santiago de Compostela, 1985).

68 Isabel Velázquez, *Hagiografía y culto a los santos en la Hispania visigoda: aproximación a sus manifestaciones literarias* (Mérida, 2005), 26. On the cult of saints, see Peter Brown, *The Cult of the Saints: Its Rise and Function in Latin Christianity* (Chicago, 1982); or Stephen Wilson, *Saints and their Cults: Studies in Religious Sociology, Folklore and History* (Cambridge, 1983).

69 "Actually, the motifs of saints' lives, legends, visions of the Other World, and miracle stories were frequently borrowed from folklore." Gurevich, *Medieval Popular Culture*, 4.

70 Hagiography was also based in popular tradition, with topics and concepts removed from its folklore and mythology. This literature is an individual creation, but in this case it takes motifs from folklore and orality, both collective creations. Their limits are not clear, because an interaction between ideology and mentality is produced.

earth, and whose relics could be seen and even touched by the faithful; the saint "was the most popular hero of medieval society; his feat was the highest feat that could be accomplished on earth."[71] The Church tried to exemplify models of life through saints, using their rejection of the world, asceticism, moral perfection, and contact with the higher powers as representation of their sanctity. However, to the faithful, the most attractive aspect of these lives were the miracles.[72]

The world of the marvellous was deeply rooted in popular mentality. The Church had tried to suppress it or, in some ways, transform it, by giving it a new meaning. Ecclesiastical authorities adapted their ideological system to include the possibility of the marvellous in Christian doctrine but, of course, only when produced by God. They could then distinguish between *mirabilis* (the marvellous itself, with pre-Christian roots), *magicus* (the supernatural maleficent), and *miraculosus* (the supernatural Christian). The marvellous was constituted as a form of resistance to Christian ideology by favouring the animal and vegetable world ahead of Christian humanism.[73] The Church rejected it in principle, but did not do the same with its miraculous version, which was made through the saints: "All the marvellous, whatever its nature, could be assimilated, used and eventually distorted by the dominant discourse."[74]

Both forms co-existed in the Early Middle Ages and the marvellous retained its own channels for expression: dreams, journey stories, appearances and, above all, profane and court literature.

Let us now turn to the *Liber Sancti Iacobi*. This compilation, written in the first half of the twelfth century, but based on miracles well known in the eleventh century,[75] is a

---

71 Gurevich, *Medieval Popular Culture*, 43.

72 "Medieval men did not believe in everything indiscriminately, and there is no basis for suspecting that they were completely lacking in critical attitudes towards certain information. But the border between the likely and the unlikely did not lie where it does today. Confidence in the possibility of the miraculous was exceptionally strong, [...] It was primarily from collective beliefs and notions that he drew his convictions, including criteria for truth and falsehood. Truth was what the collective believed." Cited from Gurevich, *Medieval Popular Culture*, 55. "The most visible part of saintly cults lies clearly in the need for miracles since many compilations have nothing to say about this practice, much like hagiography, a literary genre illustrated prolifically by clergymen and monks" (*La partie la plus visible du culte des saints est à l'évidence la demande de miracles, car les nombreux recueils ne laissent rien ignorer de cette pratique tout comme l'hagiographie, genre littéraire que les clercs et les moines ont illustré de manière prolifique*). Cited from Paul, *L'Eglise et la culture en Occident*, 2:669.

73 Jacques Le Goff, *Lo maravilloso y lo cotidiano en el Occidente medieval* (Barcelona, 1996), 12ff.

74 Martin, *Mentalités médiévales*, 208.

75 "From the dawn of the cult of St. James and from the first formation of the Hispanic traditions, there is already information about the tomb of James and veneration to him in some of the martyrologies of the ninth and tenth centuries. This information included the miraculous power of the Apostle" (*Ya desde los albores del culto jacobeo y desde la primera formación de las tradiciones hispánicas, se encuentran en algunos de los martirologios del siglo IX y X noticias sobre la tumba de Santiago y su veneración. Estas noticias ya incluían el poder milagroso del Apóstol*). Cited from Klaus Herbers, "Mentalidad y milagro. Protagonistas, autores y lectores," *Compostellanum* 40, no. 3–4 (1995): 323. See also Manuel Díaz y Díaz, "La literatura jacobea anterior al Códice Calixtino," *Compostellanum* 10, no. 4 (1965): 283–305.

good example of the relationship between popular culture and mentality within Christian culture. It is a text that stands in service of the "official" ideology of the Church.

Firstly, we must remember that saints can perform miracles, but only when ordered to do so by God: "before and after dying, any saint by order of God can resurrect dead people."[76]

The ability to predict the future was also a property of the saints. It is also something that is supernatural, something which according to popular mentality could be found in divination, but that Christianity admitted only as divine power:[77] "when you have seen the funeral rites of your deceased deservedly accomplished, and after spending a night praying, as usual, and you go back to the city called León, you will find your companions."[78] This prediction was fulfilled.

Another characteristic of hagiography is the longing of the presence of divine justice where justice of a secular variety failed. A child came to life after being unjustly hanged for a crime he had not committed, and "when people were coming and saw the child still alive after having been hung so long, they realized he had been accused of avarice, but saved by the mercy of God."[79]

More evidence can be found in prayers for the deceased. We have an example in the fourth book of the *Liber* (called the *Pseudo-Turpin*), where an executor failed to fulfil his commission and the dead person appeared to him in a dream, saying:

> Since I have commended to you all my goods so that you might give them in alms for the redemption of my soul, you must know that all of my sins have been forgiven before God; but as unjustly as you saved my alms, understand that I have suffered infernal punishment for 30 days; and you must know therefore that tomorrow you will be placed in the same place from where I have left, and I will sit in Paradise.[80]

The features of the system of offerings for the deceased were being defined shortly before the definitive configuration of purgatory as a physical place.

---

76 *[A]ntes y después de la muerte cualquier santo por don de Dios puede resucitar a un muerto.* Cited from Picaud, *Liber Sancti Iacobi*, 336.

77 The supernatural acts of the saints were not easy to distinguish from pagan magic; both were inseparable in popular mentality. The clergymen themselves had doubts, so they fixed the border according to the performer of the action: the true miracle was worked by the saint, while false miracles—*maleficia*—were performed by the devil or his agents. Gurevich, *Medieval Popular Culture*, 74.

78 *cuando hayas visto cumplidas dignamente las exequias de tu difunto y tras haber pasado una noche en oración completa, según costumbre, y vayas de regreso, en la ciudad llamada León te encontrarás con tus compañeros.* Cited from Picaud, *Liber Sancti Iacobi*, 338.

79 *viniendo la gente y viendo vivo todavía a quien llevaba colgado tanto tiempo, comprendieron que había sido acusado por la insaciable avaricia del huésped, pero salvado por la misericordia de Dios.* Cited from Picaud, *Liber Sancti Iacobi*, 342.

80 *Puesto que te encomendé todas mis cosas para que las dieses en limosnas por la redención de mi alma, sábete que todos mis pecados me han sido perdonados ante Dios; pero como retuviste injustamente mi limosna, entiende que he padecido durante treinta días las penas infernales; y sabe, pues, que mañana serás colocado tú en el mismo lugar del infierno de donde yo he salido, y yo me sentaré en el paraíso.* Cited from Picaud, *Liber Sancti Iacobi*, 433.

In the *Liber* the salvation of men who either went to Jerusalem or fought against the Saracens is frequent. We must not forget that popular mentality saw St. James as a leader against Muslims.[81]

The idea that saints, to fulfil their promises, demand veneration and something in return is also present. If not given veneration and something in return, they can be vindictive and cruel. The apostle gives too much power to a knight in his struggle against the Turks, "But as every man is said to be false, the knight forgot what he had offered to the apostle; so deservedly he fell sick unto death."[82]

Another aspect of holiness is thaumaturgy. The belief in the healing ability of the saints (even resurrections), either by direct intervention or through their relics, is rooted in popular mentality even today. In the case of Santiago, a man who had an illness connected to his throat was healed when touched by a shell: pilgrims to Santiago usually carry shells.[83]

Another circumstance is the (almost) eternal struggle of saints against demons, against whose attacks they defended men: a defence that occurs during men's lives, but also after their deaths, as the saints could release a soul from Hell after the corporeal death.[84] However, saints not only defend men from demons, but also against other wild creatures (which can symbolize the forces of Evil): lions, bears, leopards, and dragons.[85]

Especially interesting is the popular legend surrounding Santiago *Caballero*, leader of the Christian host in the Spanish Reconquista. He appears with his attributes (pure white clothes, encircling arms, and with two keys in his hand) to a Greek bishop who had reprimanded some peasants for having worshipped Santiago as a warrior. The miracle took place in the year 1064, when the Christian army conquered Coimbra, and thanks to the supposed miraculous intervention of Santiago.[86]

Popular legends have importance once again in the book of *Traslatio* (as, for example, the legend of "Queen Lupa") or *Pseudo-Turpin*, which connects the figure of James the Apostle to Charlemagne. Legends and beliefs that are rooted in popular mentality[87] and were accepted and considered true also by the Church of the city of Santiago. The

---

81 Picaud, *Liber Sancti Iacobi*, 347 and 349–59. I discuss this legend below.

82 *Mas como todo hombre se dice que es falso, el caballero da al olvido lo que había ofrecido al Apóstol; por lo cual cayó merecidamente enfermo de muerte.* Cited from Picaud, *Liber Sancti Iacobi*, 349.

83 Picaud, *Liber Sancti Iacobi*, 355.

84 Picaud, *Liber Sancti Iacobi*, 367–71.

85 Picaud, *Liber Sancti Iacobi*, 383–84, respectively. Dragons are animals which are present in the Christian tradition (symbol of the devil in the Apocalypse, such as snakes in other contexts). They appear again in the *Liber* in the story of the *Translatio*: the disciples of Santiago, looking for an adequate place to bury the Apostle, confronted some legendary threats. Between them, they confronted a dragon. But dragons also belong to both the marvellous world and popular mentality (Celtic folklore, for example).

86 Picaud, *Liber Sancti Iacobi*, 376 and 377n473.

87 This is similar to a legend that is very important in Galician popular imagination, that of the mythical being called *mouros* who lived under the dolmens and forts (Iron Age settlements) hiding huge wealth. See Mar Llinares García, *Os mouros no imaxinario popular galego* (Santiago de Compostela, 1990).

compiler did not hesitate to include these legends in the *Liber* to increase the prestige of the see.[88]

The second of the literary sources considered are the Visions of Other World and apparitions of the deceased in medieval Galicia. In those sources, we can see how the population conceived the geography of the afterlife: Hell and Paradise mainly, but also a third place was suggested.

Medieval visions were shaped on both a literary and popular level. The popular level was based on the beliefs and needs of the population even though its popular origins were hard to clarify. Although already before Christianity and ancient mythologies the existence of visions (and prophecies) was relatively common, these took a completely original character in the Christian ambient by introducing eschatological nuance, the necessity of both imagining the Afterlife and communicating with it, especially through offerings.[89]

First, let us analyse visions experienced by Valerius of Bierzo (685 CE) with the configuration of Paradise as one of the main motifs. Certain aspects of this Paradise are underlined, including its lush vegetation, never-withered flowers, red roses, and stunning white lilies, surrounded by the splendours of spring and rivers of prodigious beauty. The concept of Paradise as a splendid well-stocked garden is already present in the Bible. However, motifs of flowers and wonderful greenery were deeply rooted in popular mentality and it was in this way that the people imagined the heavenly Paradise.[90]

The same concept appears in the Vision of Trezenzonio, whose beginning of the "adventure" is located in the eighth century. On a trip through Galicia after the Arab invasion, he arrived at A Coruña and saw an island from the lighthouse. After sighting it, he travelled to it. Heavenly features characterize this island: abundant vegetation and food, warm weather, etc. Its inhabitants are angels and blessed figures who sing constantly. During his stay, he ate herbs and meat from animals he hunted, honey, etc., and the scent of herbs and fruits is indescribable. Once again, this is a "paradisiacal" vision of Paradise. He returned to his world after seven years in a magically prepared boat, but Galicia was already more populous. Indeed, in this vision we face one of the features of the medieval concept of time that is different to our contemporary conception of time. In the Middle Ages, several centuries could pass almost in some hours without this being illogical or inconceivable.[91]

---

88 Another example of popular legend but related to ecclesiastical culture is the arriving of St. James in a stone small boat. About this legend, see José María Andrade Cernadas, "Cultura clerical y cultura popular en el legendario jacobeo: la barca de piedra," *El extramundi y los papeles de Iria Flavia* 63 (2010): 115–24.

89 Díaz, *Visiones del Más Allá*, 9–11.

90 Díaz, *Visiones del Más Allá*, 33ff.

91 Díaz, *Visiones del Más Allá*, 107–8. About the conception of the time in hagiography and similar works, see Gurevich, *Medieval Popular Culture*, 17–18. In these works, concrete time is hardly important. On "literary time," see Gurevich, *Las categorías*, 158ff. "The epic consciousness found no contradiction in the divergences between the usual course of the time and the course in the

Finally, we'll look at some visions which confirm the existence of a third place where the souls go, between Heaven and Hell. However, as has been said, this is a place that is still not consolidated in the geography of the Afterlife. The first of them is a vision of the queen Godo, wife of the King of Galicia, Sancho Ordóñez (written in the first half of the eleventh century). The basic thesis raises the question of the value of prayers and offerings made in suffrage for the dead. The king's soul itself took advantage of them, since he appeared to the queen to tell her she had to continue with the suffrages. The apparitions took place on Saturday.[92]

In another of these experiences, the vision of Gundesindo, Bishop of Iria, the visions are also associated with premonitory dreams, which during the Middle Ages constituted practically the same phenomenon.[93] In the Early Middle Ages, dreams of premonitions belonged to the phantasmagoric. However, in the Bible it was not this way because they were an instrument of divine revelation (mainly in the Old Testament). Christianity had interest in dreams in a first phase but distrusted them later[94] when they were associated with heresy, with both the demonic and the sexual, and accused of attempting to appropriate one of the divine abilities: to know the future.[95]

In this vision, the idea that Gundesindo had had a bad life is emphasized. On his deathbed, his mother stayed awake beside him and a voice spoke to her when she was half asleep, halfway between vision and dream. The deep sense of maternal charity, a mother concerned about the eternal destiny of her son, led her to test the effectiveness of her prayers. The voice spoke to her in the middle of a fire (fire of purgation?),[96] saying: "Know that your son has been admitted tonight in the company of the chosen by God."[97] The idea of purgatory was already present.

---

legends" (*La conciencia épica no encontraba contradicción alguna en las divergencias entre el curso habitual del tiempo y la marcha del mismo en la leyenda*): Gurevich, *Las categorías*, 158.

92 The belief that on one day per week infernal punishments could not take place existed. This was a tradition that was rooted in popular mentality. Díaz, *Visiones del Más Allá*, 70n88.

93 Paul, *L'Eglise et la culture en Occident*, 2:660–61.

94 Jacques Le Goff, *O imaginário medieval* (Lisboa, 1994), 299ff.

95 We can distinguish three types of dreams: true dreams, which come from God (saints' dreams or from the monastic spaces); false dreams (they come from the devil); and human dreams, involved in suspicion by the Christian morals. Schmitt, *História das superstições*, 92–93. In the daily life, dreams were a common experience, but caused plenty of anguish because of the occult sense of the future. Dreams always worried human beings; in order to get their meaning, people went to men and women who were considered saints or even witches, and the Church had a new reason to demonize them.

96 Concept of St. Augustine. Le Goff, *La naissance*, 114ff. and 181ff.

97 *Sábete que tu hijo ha sido admitido esta noche en la compañía de los elegidos.* Díaz, *Visiones del Más Allá*, 92.

320 JUAN COIRA POCIÑA

Conclusion

During the Early Middle Ages, popular mentality exerted a significant influence on Christian ideology. Above all, this influence was due to the attitude of the Church. The Church began a dialogue with its audience of believers through the kinds of literature just analysed, directed precisely at this audience. By the end of this period, the Word of God tried to approach the faithful, this time both by penetrating their consciousness and by instilling ideology through its own conception of reality, by means of, for example, folklore and the marvellous world.

While considering the aforementioned consequences of popular mentality on Christian ideology, it is important that we do not forget other "achievements" of this mentality, such as the "birth of purgatory" or the survival of fertility rites, magic, divination, funeral practices, and similar.

However, the Church did not just make concessions. It also brought its doctrine closer to the faithful, so that people were born, lived, and died being Christian. They believed in the Afterlife and, above all, in the Last Judgment; they were devoted to the saints (it would be correct to speak of a popular religiosity); they attended Christian festivities (although less frequently than they should do); they received the sacraments; they largely assumed the Christian calendar (which was based on the pagan calendar), and so on. Also, the Church continued more exhaustively than before to promote renewal so as to eradicate all practices and beliefs considered to be dangerous for doctrine (and consequently, for ideology). This process began with the Gregorian reform in the second half of the eleventh century and continued throughout some of the great church councils (especially the Fourth Lateran in 1215).

Therefore, the relationship between popular mentality with Christian ideology ("popular" culture and "official" culture), cannot be understood simply in terms of opposition. As we have shown, the permeability between them took place along a process of acculturation in which mentality and ideology contributed to each other, forming an original medieval culture with which people and Church could identify. This permeability and relationship would garner strength to a larger extent from the twelfth century onwards.

Chapter 14

THE FOUNDATION OF THE FRANCISCAN FRIARY OF THE SANT ESPERIT, VALENCIA: RULE, ECONOMY, AND ROYAL POWER IN THE FIFTEENTH-CENTURY CROWN OF ARAGON

CHIARA MANCINELLI

THE FOUNDING OF a new monastery in the early fifteenth century in the north of the Kingdom of Valencia enables us to review poverty as an ideology aimed to renew the Christianity that dominated late-medieval society. The monastery of the *Sant Esperit* ("Holy Spirit") was one of the first of the observant type in the Crown of Aragon. The Observant movement arose from an ideal of poverty propounded by the same Franciscan friars who, at the same time, were combining economics with urban activities in a Christian market society and working to influence the ruling elites, beginning with the monarchy. It was a new approach to Christianity, but examining it enables us to appreciate how the notion of poverty changed rapidly at the start of the fifteenth century, fully affecting the ideological basis with which Christianity influenced society.

Introduction: Monastic Income according to the New Poverty

Ten kilometres from Sagunto and thirty-five from València, on the border of Gilet, lies the friary of *Sant Esperit del Mont*. While the Franciscan friary, still open today, retains very little of its medieval grandeur, one fundamental characteristic remains: its remote location. Surrounded by mountains and woods, it is not difficult to understand why, even centuries later, at the beginning of the fifteenth century it was built in this location for a group of Franciscans who advocated strict observance of the Franciscan Rule, constituting one of the first observant communities in the Crown of Aragon. If the isolated character of the friary encouraged adherence to the ideal of poverty, at the same time it was incapable of sustaining itself by practising alms. In fact, in addition to being far from Christian populations, the friars were surrounded by Muslims and the largest Jewish community in the Kingdom of Valencia, in Sagunto. To provide for the needs of the friars, Queen Maria de Luna, patroness of the friary, gave them a total of seven thousand shillings in the form of a perpetual income (i.e., *censals*) over lands from her family inheritance and populated mostly by Muslims.

At that time, censals were not considered contrary to the Franciscan Rule, but rather they were at the base of what the thinker and friar Francesc Eiximenis, involved in the

Chiara Mancinelli (chiara.mancinelli.svigelj@gmail.com) is Researcher at the Universitat Autònoma de Barcelona. She records her thanks to Isabelle Lherondel for her help in the translation of this chapter.

new foundation from its inception, described theoretically in his works. Eiximenis, whilst warning merchants about the excessive use of *censals* considered them a lawful economic instrument if administered by the Church.[1] For him, the financial foundation of the friary rested on Maria de Luna's great work of charity, demonstrating her administrative capacity while avoiding the sin of greed, as Eiximenis repeatedly states in his *Scala dei*, the book dedicated to the queen. If we recall that Eiximenis participated in the early phases of the community and chose the first guardian, we can appreciate his role in the institution of the Sant Esperit in Valencia and thus in the Observance Movement in the Province of Aragon, both from the theoretical and practical points of view.

Approximately fifty years after its foundation, however, doctrinal considerations on this kind of income, the *censals*, changed. Sant Esperit del Monte's source of income was now held to be inconsistent with the vow of poverty. For this reason, a chapter of Franciscans in Barcelona in December 1456 withdrew these *censals* from the friary and later transferred them to the convent of Poor Clares in València. The protagonist of this new phase was another queen, Maria of Castile, whom by royal inheritance governed Sant Esperit and was also the patroness of the convent of the Sant Esperit. Maria of Castile was not only a great supporter of the Franciscan Observance, then more powerful than it had been at the beginning of the century, but also of the Franciscan figures who spearheaded this movement, amongst whom was Matteo d'Agrigento, who, unlike Eiximenis, did not approve of *censals*. We have to go deeper into the analysis of how the Franciscan and royal interests intervened in the founding of the Sant Esperit in light of the religious, political, and economic aspects in order to understand this evolution of thought about poverty.[2]

Political Ways of Imposing Strong New Standards of Christian Poverty

The foundation of the Sant Esperit followed the institution of two communities which were exemplary for the return of the Franciscan Rule to the Crown of Aragon: Xelva and Manzanera. After having settled in the hermitages nearby, on October 30, 1388, the friars obtained permission to build the friaries of San Francisco in Xelva and Nuestra Señora de los Ángeles in Manzanera.[3] In 1402, Maria de Luna subsidized the friary of Xelva by granting it fifty gold florins.[4] That same year, the queen asked Pope Benedict XIII in Avignon for licence to build a notable monastery in the Tuliu Valley, where the friars would live in

---

1 Francesc Eiximenis, *El* Tractat d'usura *de Francesc Eiximenis*, ed. Josep Hernando i Delgado (Barcelona, 1985), 77–85.

2 For a thorough examination of this subject, see Chiara Mancinelli, "Francesc Eiximenis y el convento del Santo Espíritu del Monte: la cuestión de un modelo económico, político y religioso" (PhD diss., Universitat Autònoma de Barcelona, 2014), accessed January 21, 2016, www.tdx.cat/handle/10803/285460?show=full and Chiara Mancinelli, *Teoria e pratica economica francescana. Il convento del Santo Spirito del Monte (Gilet, Valencia)* (Roma, 2017).

3 José Antonio Hebrera y Esmir, *Crónica de la provincia franciscana de Aragón*, ed. Luis Falcón Aller, Antolín, Abad García, Cisneros (Madrid, 1991), 46–49; Vicente Martínez Colomer, *Historia de la provincia de Valencia de la Regular Observancia de san Francisco por el p. fr. Martinez Colomer, tomo I*, ed. Salvador Fauli (València, 1803), 59–76.

4 Pedro Sanahuja, *Historia de la seráfica provincia de Cataluña* (Barcelona, 1959), 282.

strict observance of the Rule of St. Francis. Maria de Luna's request shows the purpose of the Sant Esperit, and through her plea, laid the basis to ensure the legal autonomy necessary to carry it out.[5] Before receiving an official answer from the pontiff, the queen made a series of donations to the friary. Many of them were through intermediaries, like Eiximenis and Bartomeu Borràs.[6] Maria de Luna sent Borràs himself as ambassador, probably in 1403, to the pope in Avignon. In one of the chapters of the embassy, the queen requested that, once the Sant Esperit was built, said friary and those of Xelva and Manzanera, which belonged to the same Rule, and all future friaries, should constitute an independent and separate vicariate. The friars who live in those friaries should choose their vicar without any confirmation by the Minister or the General Minister.[7]

The queen's petition to establish a separate vicariate represents a clear and remarkable declaration of intentions that allows this embassy and the foundation of Sant Esperit to be considered the beginning of an organized project of diffusion of the Franciscan reform movement, later known as the Observance, based on royal support. In August 1403, Pope Benedict XIII responded to Maria de Luna's request by issuing the papal bulls, *Eximiae devotionis* and *Dum sincere*. With these two bulls, the pope granted the queen the right to found a friary of any order recognized by the Holy See in the territories of the king[8] and asked the bishop of València to verify that she had carried out her wish.[9] It was established that through Francesc Eiximenis, Maria de Luna was to appoint the first guardian, who thereafter would be selected every three years by the friars of the community, according to the usual jurisdiction and other particulars or privileges granted with the bulls. The first guardian of the Sant Esperit was Borràs. Later, on October 21, 1404, Maria de Luna donated the friary to the Franciscans. In consideration of its isolated position, and so the friars could not seek alms, in exchange the queen assigned five thousand shillings from València. The rents were collected from the Vall de Almo-

---

5 For example, she asked that neither minister nor other superiors could change or obstruct decisions made by friars the queen selected.

6 Jill R. Webster, Andrés Ivars Cardona, "Franciscanismo de la reina de Aragón, doña María de Luna (1396- 1406)," *Archivo Ibero Americano* 42 (1982): 81–123 (documents 5–7); *Francesc Eiximenis i la casa reial. Diplomatari 1373–1409*, ed. Jaume Riera i Sans, Jaume Torró Torrent, 5–7 (documents 5, 6, 7); 12–13, 14, 21, 23–24, 26–27, 38–39, 41–43 (documents 16–17, 19, 29, 34–35, 39–40, 54, 58–60); Benjamín Agulló Pascual, "Fundación y dotación del convento de Santo Espíritu del Monte (Valencia)," *Archivo Ibero Americano* 42 (1982): 126–55 (documents 5–7); *Francesc Eiximenis i la casa reial*, ed. Riera and Torró, 55 (document 83); Mancinelli, *Francesc Eiximenis*, 425–27 (documents 48, 50–51).

7 Áurea L. Javierre Mur, *María de Luna, reina de Aragón (1396–1406)* (Madrid, 1942), 291. Later, in April 1407, King Martín reiterated Maria de Luna's request to the Pope: Mancinelli, *Francesc Eiximenis*, 415 (document 41).

8 Ovidio Cuella Esteban, *Bulario aragonés de Benedicto XIII, 1. La curia de Aviñón (1394–1403)* (Zaragoza, 2003), 438.

9 Ovidio Cuella Esteban, *Bulario aragonés de Benedicto XIII, 4. El papa Luna (1392–1423), promotor de la religiosidad hispana* (Zaragoza, 2003), 96; *Bullarium Franciscanum Romanorum Pontificum constitutiones, epistolas, ac diplomata continens: tribus ordinibus Minorum, Clarissarum, et Poenitentium a seraphico patriarcha Sancto Francisco institutit concessa ab illorum exordio ad nostra usque tempora*, ed. J. H. Sbaralea, 7 vols. (Roma, 1759), no. 947; Martínez, *Historia del Real*, 15–17.

nacid, which belonged to the queen's heritage.[10] In 1404, the queen suffered many ills, and two years later died of a stroke. In her will, Maria bequeathed another two thousand *sous* to the Sant Espirit: fifteen hundred shillings collected from the Vall de Almonacid to cover the necessities of the friars who could not provide for themselves and five hundred shillings collected from the town of Paterna for the restoration of the friary.[11] Among the executors of her will, Maria de Luna appointed three Franciscans: Francesc Eiximenis, Bartomeu Borràs, and Joan Eximeno.

Although the word "Observance" is found in documents following the foundation of Sant Espirit, we believe that its purpose, its remote location, and the privileges of the granted autonomies make Sant Espirit exemplary for the beginnings of the Franciscan Observance in the Crown of Aragon. This development, with the decisive support of the Crown, gave renewed vigour to the attempts to reform Xelva and Manzanera. Among the acts of royal support, it is necessary to emphasize the proposal of Borràs as minister supported by Maria de Luna.[12] The occupation of a high position in the hierarchy of the order by a friar supporter guaranteed the support of the hierarchy to the incipient Observance.

The close relationship of the Franciscans with the Crown can be defined as "mutual dependence," as David Viera states in one of his works on Eiximenis.[13] On one hand, the Crown and local governments favoured some friars for their experience and political knowledge; on the other hand, the Franciscans received substantial support from the Crown for the construction of friaries or funding for their studies. Based on the analysis of royal patrimony during the first half of the fourteenth century, Jill Webster refers to the many forms of donations made to the Franciscans, including their appointment as advisors or ambassadors.[14] According to Paolo Evangelisti, this documented evidence allows us to evaluate the extent of the presence of the Franciscans in the Court or in the communities of the Crown of Aragon. This presence was genuinely political because of the existence of elite *viri evangelici*, culturally and technically prepared to define the practices and transfer them to a political class through teaching, written works, and their presence in institutional policies.[15] During the reign of Martin and Maria de Luna, one of the most emblematic acts that testifies to the relationship between the royal family and the Franciscan order was the resolution taken by the king according to which all confessors of the royal house had to be chosen from among the friars. The clergymen who fulfilled the post of confessor were considered counsellors and also held the office of ambassador.[16]

---

10 Agulló, "Fundación y dotación," 145–49 (document 3).

11 Despite the fact that Maria de Luna's will has not been found, this information is reported by chronicler Pedro Martínez and corroborated by King Martin's management of the friary. Martínez, *Historia del Real*, 31–33.

12 Webster and Ivars Cardona, "Franciscanismo de la reina," 112–16 (documents 66–70).

13 David J. Viera, "Francesc Eiximenis and the royal house of Aragon: a mutual dependence," separated from *Catalan Review. International Journal of Catalan Culture* 3, no. 2 (1989): 183–89.

14 Jill R. Webster, "La contribución de los registros del Patrimonio Real a la historia de los frailes menores durante la primera mitad del siglo XIV," *Archivo Ibero Americano* 53, nos. 209–12 (1993): 525–48.

15 Paolo Evangelisti, *I francescani e la costruzione di uno stato* (Padova, 2006), 9–12.

16 Lluís Fullana, "Rescripto de Martín el Humano ordenando perpetuamente que los confesores

In the case of Maria de Luna, although Francesc Eiximenis was not her confessor,[17] the relationship between the queen and the Franciscan was very strong. The missions conducted by Eiximenis and the queen's request for spiritual support in times of illness confirm Maria's reliance on the friar from a political and religious point of view.[18]

To Eiximenis, Maria de Luna's character seemed perfectly adapted to the ideal of a devout, charitable, God-fearing woman and faithful counsellor to the king. The friar dedicated his book *Tractat de contemplació* or *Scala Dei*[19] to her and described her virtues in a letter to Martin while in Sicily.[20] It should be noted that in this same letter, Eiximenis asked Martin to build a Franciscan friary in Segorbe,[21] which would be established by the same community of the Sant Esperit in 1413 and for which the term "Observance" was first used in its papal confirmation.[22] It is necessary to keep in mind that Maria de Luna's devotion had a clear political dimension: apart from consolidating her fame through her patronage of donations and charity work, the mendicant orders became an extension of the Court. On the other hand, the commitment and political participation of the Franciscans with the royals should not be interpreted as the fruit of manipulation or a lack of faith, but as the product of mutual trust.[23] In the case of Eiximenis, for example, the relationship with the Crown was not submissive, since he distanced himself from behaviour and political decisions he did not approve of.[24] In the case of the Sant Esperit,

---

de la Casa Real de Aragón sean franciscanos. Zaragoza, 1° Agosto 1398," *Archivo Ibero Americano* 16 (1921): 250–55.

17 *Francesc Eiximenis i la casa reial*, ed. Riera and Torró, 8 (document 10).

18 Nuria Silleras Fernández, *María de Luna: poder, piedad y patronazgo de una reina bajomedieval*, trans. Virginia Tabuenca Cortés (Zaragoza, 2012), 114, 135–48; *Francesc Eiximenis i la casa reial*, ed. Riera and Torró, 51 (document 76); Daniel Girona Llagostera, *La derrera malaltia de la reyna María de Luna: 1406* (Barcelona, 1922), 18–19 (documents 10, 12); Webster and Ivars Cardona, "Franciscanismo de la reina," 112 (document 64).

19 Francesc Eiximenis, *Scala dei*, ed. Curt J. Wittlin, Elisabet Ràfols (Barcelona, 1985), 8.

20 Sadurni Martí, "Les cartes autògrafes de Francesc Eiximenis," *Estudi General* 22 (2002): 235–49, accessed January 21, 2016, www.narpan.net/documents/autografseiximenis.pdf.

21 "You must convert if you wish to follow St. Francis. Or you will neglect him. For little money you can, my lord, construct a building in Segorbe which I hope you will want to do." (*Mester que us convertiatz un poch a sent Francesch que no·l laxetz de tots puns. Ab pocha mesió porietz fer una casa a Sogorb; per què, seyor, plàcie-us que ley fasatz*). Cited from Martí, "Les cartes autògrafes," 247.

22 *Bullarium Franciscanum (1759)*, vol. 7, no. 1109. Eiximenis's aspirations came true when, in 1413, the Sant Esperit community obtained a papal bull to found a new friary in Segorbe. Bartomeu Borràs, ex guardian, and Bernat Escoriola, the new guardian, are authorized to establish a Franciscan and observant house called Santa María de los Ángeles. The privileges of the Sant Esperit were transferred to the new friary. In 1414, in Avignon, Pope Benedict XIII granted the Sant Esperit friars permission to found another friary in Llíria. Nevertheless, Franciscan chronicles date this friary from the sixteenth century. Mancinelli, *Francesc Eiximenis*, 433–38 (document 59); València. Arxiu General i Fotogràfic de la Diputació Provincial de València, *Historia del Real Colegio de Santo Espíritu del Monte por el Padre Fr. Pedro Martínez, morador y cronista del dicho*, typed copy, 1980, 203–13.

23 Silleras, *María de Luna*, 129–48.

24 For example, we can mention Eiximenis's refusal of the request from King Juan (John) I to be his confessor.

the location of the community was not only due to spiritual needs, but to a precise political and economic need. Sagunto, in fact, was part of the feudal territorial basis for Maria
in the kingdom, so that the presence of a friary patronized by her in those territories
reinforced her power there. In addition, the fact that the Sant Esperit depended on the
diocese of Zaragoza and not on that of València kept it out of the conflicts between *ban-
dositats*, in which the ecclesiastics of València were involved.[25]

The Ideal of Poverty, Economic Knowledge, and Conversion of Infidels

From Eiximenis's point of view, the foundation of a friary close to Gilet which sought
to follow the Franciscan Rule to the letter coincided with many of the considerations
put forward in his works: criticism of opulence and avarice among the clergy;[26] lifestyle
change for the clergy for the new millennialism;[27] the need to support churchmen living outside the city who dedicated themselves to prayer;[28] and the diffusion of religious
centres in the still little converted Kingdom of Valencia.[29]

In addition, to understand the institution of the first observant friaries north of the
city of València, it is necessary to take into account other factors, such as the scant Franciscan presence in that area, proximity to the territories of the Luna family's heritage
("Patrimonio de Luna"), the existence of trade routes, and the presence of Muslims and
Jews in the territory where the friaries were founded. Because of their position, the first

---

25 With regard to this matter, we have to consider Eiximenis's participation on the Queen's Council
to solve conflicts between factions in València. Silleras, *María de Luna*, 114–48.

26 Francesc Eiximenis, *La societat catalana al segle XIV*, ed. Jill R. Webster (Barcelona, 1967),
75–77; *Llibre dels àngels*, book 3, chapter 17, accessed January 21, 2016, www.antiblavers.org/
galeria/thumbnails.php?album=14&page=2; Francesc Eiximenis, *Lo libre de les dones*, ed. Frank
Naccarato (Barcelona, 1981), 359–60; Montserrat Martínez Checa, "Francesc Eiximenis. Pastorale:
edició i traducció" (PhD diss., Universitat Autònoma de Barcelona, 1995), 317–36; Francesc
Eiximenis, *Vida de Jesucrist*, treaties 9 and 10, treaty 10, chapter 46, accessed January 21, 2016,
www.antiblavers.org/galeria/thumbnails.php?album=14&page=9.

27 Robert E. Lerner, "Eiximenis i la tradició profètica," *Llengua i literatura: Revista anual de la
Societat Catalana de Llengua i literatura* 17 (2006): 18.

28 "And here they were favoured and honoured and maintained all spiritual people and fearful
of God, and especially those that were fed and maintained outside the city, in the mountains or in
other places, devout hermits or persons alone servant of God, who through prayers and alms were
forced to continually pray for the city" (*E aquí fossen favorejades, e honrades e sostengudes totes
persones spirituals e tements Déu, e en special fossen nodrits e conservats, fora la ciutat, en muntanyes
o en lochs altres, devots hermitans o persones en solitud sirvents a Déu, les quals tinguen per prechs
e per almoynes obligades a contínuament orar per la ciutat*). Cited from Francesc Eiximenis *Dotzè
llibre del Crestià*, ed. Xavier Renedo (Girona, 2005), chap. 9, 18.

29 "In thirteenth place, given that the so-called city became again Christian, as it is explained,
it is appropriate that you often help in church buildings, as well as in building churches and
monasteries, and their decoration, and to satisfy clergy more than any other city the kingdom"
(*Tretzenament, car com la dita ciutat sia novellament cristiana, així com dit és, per tal cové que sovín
ajudets a edificis eclesiàstiques, així com són fer esglésies e monestirs, e llur ornaments, e a satisfer
a religiosos més que altra ciutat del regne*). Cited from Francesc Eiximenis, *Regiment de la cosa
pública*, ed. Daniel de Molins de Rei (Barcelona, 1927), 20:1–6.

observant foundations constituted a true extension of the Franciscan presence into the northern part of the Crown of Aragon, helping to reduce the distance separating the other friaries from the one in Játiva, the most southerly in the Crown. The first reformed friaries were also along the trade routes connecting Teruel and València, the interior of the kingdom, and the Mediterranean coast, and economically relevant places, such as Segorbe. The economic dynamism of the territories where these friaries were found is often repeated in Franciscan foundations, economically interesting regions being the ideal field of action and preaching of the friars. Unlike Xelva and Manzanera, where it was impossible to determine the influence of Eiximenis and the role of the Crown in their foundation, with the Franciscan letter of 1392 to Martin, we can consider the hypothesis of a project to situate the community of Segorbe, and then of the Sant Esperit, inside or near Luna territories. This way, the friary could enjoy the protection granted by Maria de Luna's jurisdiction, while also being close to the first two foundations, namely Xelva and Manzanera.

The presence of Jews and Muslims in the areas around the Franciscan friaries and, in general, where the first phase of the observance in the Kingdom of Valencia took place, is an important element, considering the pastoral task of the Franciscans. Although there are no documents to tell us about the relationship between Jews and Muslims and the friars of Xelva, Manzanera, the Sant Esperit, and Segorbe, the position of those friaries can be considered an indicator of the observants' pastoral purpose. In the case of the Jews, what set them apart from Christians was not only their lack of understanding of the Christological message, but their otherness in terms of their practices. They became a focus for the Franciscans. In the fifteenth century, the Franciscans turned out to be experts in the use and ownership of lexical techniques, perfect economists, and ideal directors of local Christian economies. All these reasons make conflict with the Jewish presence in the economic field understandable, as can be seen in Italian, Provençal, and Aragonese cities of the time. This controversial approach, adopted by the mendicant orders but considerably strengthened by the observants, is linked to a fundamental economic notion: of the flow of wealth as the key to perfect Franciscan spirituality for Christian infidels and the notion of immobile wealth as a typical attribute of the infidels' carnality and greed.[30] In the case of the Sant Esperit, near the most important Jewish community and self-governing community (or *aljama*) in the kingdom, this mission was not limited to conversion to Christianity in the strict sense, but also included a broader attempt to control and normalize the social and economic behaviour of the infidels.

The need to Christianize the Kingdom of Valencia, still with an excessively Moorish aspect, was emphasized by Eiximenis in his *Regiment de la cosa pública*, the 1383 work addressed to the councillors (jurats) of València in which he explained how to govern the city. According to the friar, it was necessary for the councillors to support the construction of religious buildings, churches, and Christian monasteries.[31] The opin-

---

30 Giacomo Todeschini, "Franciscan Economics and Jews in the Middle Ages: From a Theological to an Economic Lexicon," in *Friars and Jews in the Middle Ages and Renaissance* (Boston, 2004), 99–117.

31 See note 29.

ion of Eiximenis is based on data indicating that, by the middle of the fifteenth century, the total population of the Kingdom of Valencia was about a quarter of a million, about thirty percent of whom were Muslims. Indeed, in the territories of the Crown of Aragon, the Kingdom of Valencia was the area with the highest proportion of Islamic population, due to its frontier position. The northern part of Valencia had the greatest concentration of Muslims (*mudéjares*), mainly in the inland valleys of the Millars and Palancia rivers and in the Serra d'Espadán, location of the Vall de Almonacid. As we have seen, this was the area where most of the revenues for the Sant Esperit were collected.[32]

Christian Poverty, Credit, and Rent from *censals*

The allocation of *censal* incomes from Vall de Almonacid and Paterna to the Sant Esperit has some similarities with the process of imposition of the *censal* on the income of royal rents collected by seigneurial tax collectors or bailiffs. As early as the twelfth century the Crown assigned payment of credits on feudal rents received each year. A *censal* was a fixed income that one contractually received (the *carregament*) after lending some capital. In the fourteenth century, we find the *censal* arrangement growing via those charged with collecting income for the Crown:[33] the allocation of a sum of money, the value of the services rendered, or a pious action were converted into a perpetual income to deduct from the respective bailiffs. Only in the first case was there a physical loan of money, while in the others, the capital was "in kind," for services the beneficiary lent to the Crown. In the examples offered by García Marsilla regarding the General Bailiff who collected the king's incomes in the Kingdom of Valencia, these *perpetuals* granted these *censals* incomes to religious institutions.[34] In the case of the legacy of the Sant Esperit, we are faced with a particular case. In fact, the "Patrimony of Luna" was part of the Crown, but was still administered by Maria de Luna, the feudal lord of lands inherited

---

32 María Teresa Ferrer i Mallol, "Las comunidades mudéjares de la Corona de Aragón en el siglo XV: la Población," in *VIII Simposio internacional de mudejarismo. De mudéjares a moriscos: una conversión forzada: actas, Teruel, 15–17 de setiembre de 1999*, 2 vols. (Teruel, 2003), 1:27–154.

33 A *censal* takes the form of a trade contract or *carregament* made before a notary. The seller (or lender) sells to a buyer (or creditor) the right to receive periodically a pension (the income or *censal*) for a determined price (the capital lent). The type of interest, the *for*, which expresses the relation between the pension and the price, is rarely indicated in the *carregament* and tends to be included in a separate document, where you find an *apoca* or receipt and where the seller recognizes receipt of the capital. The settlement of annual incomes in the terms established is contained in another type of document, the *apoca* of pension, which is issued by the creditor in acknowledgement of the payment. In the case of a *censal mort*, there is no *lluïsme* or *fadiga*, the element which allows the holders to intervene in the management of assets. Antoni Furió, "Crédito y endeudamiento: el censal en la sociedad rural valenciana (siglos XIV–XV)," in *Señorío y feudalismo en la Península Ibérica (ss. XII–XIX)*, ed. Eliseo Serrano Martín, Esteban Sarasa Sánchez, 4 vols. (Zaragoza, 1993), 1:501–534; Juan Vicente García Marsilla, "La formació d'un mercat del crèdit. Orígens i difusió del censal en la societat valenciana (segles XIII–XV)," *Butlletí de la Societat Catalana d'Estudis Històrics* 12 (2001): 135–44.

34 Juan Vicente García Marsilla, *Vivir a crédito en la Valencia medieval. De los orígenes del sistema censal al endeudamiento del municipio* (València, 2002), 301–8.

from her father. We have found no indications on the *carregament de censal* of Maria de Luna's legacy to the friary. However, we believe that, while it was not a case of real financial capital but of economic–spiritual capital, that is to say, the financial endowment of a friary, it is probable that this type of document was not produced.

We have no document explicitly stating that the *censal* rents to the Sant Esperit were perpetual incomes (*censal mort*), but in her donation, the queen describes the rent as perpetual and for this reason we have considered the *censal* assigned to the friary as *censal mort*. In addition, we should bear in mind that in the Kingdom of Valencia *censals morts* were usually called simply *censals*.[35] Likewise, the subsidy of the incipient observant movement has some parallels with the Crown's financing of the campaigns in the Mediterranean, also sustained through the imposition of *censals* in the territories of the Kingdom.[36] The growth of the *censal* credit system in the Crown of Aragon stimulated a long theological, ethical, and legal debate.[37]

Incomes without dominion arose in the Kingdom of Valencia in the thirteenth century, although much fewer than other *censals*, which were based on incomes from land, in line with the emphyteusis land-tenure model. However, from 1330 to 1340 the volume of *censal* rents increased due to economic development and the demographic saturation that preceded the Plague, a set of factors that made access to land more difficult, generating the need to create rents and new incomes for the monasteries. The *censal* was also used as a credit instrument in the political sphere and especially by municipal institutions. The fiscal pressure exerted by the monarchy, which needed to finance its military campaigns, accelerated the process of consolidating the *censal* to finance royal necessities. From 1370, the *censal* entered the sphere of private credit, permitting the circulation of large sums which otherwise would have remained immobilized in the hands of widows, nobles, or the clergy. In addition, those sold *censals* were later invested in the purchase of other *censal* rents. The rapid development of the credit mar-

---

35 García Marsilla, *Vivir a crédito*, 185.

36 Francisco Javier Cervantes Peris, *La herencia de María de Luna. Una empresa feudal en el tardo medioevo valenciano* (Segorbe, 1998); Francisco Javier Cervantes Peris, "La receptoría general del Antiguo Patrimonio de María de Luna. La gestión de la deuda censal en unos estados feudales del XV valenciano," *Pedralbes* 13, no. 2 (1993): 249–54.

37 For example, we can mention the manuscript containing Eiximenis's *Tractat d'usura* and other authors who discussed the legality of these rents, like Bernat Puigcercós, Ramon Saera, Richard of Middleton and Henry of Ghent. Josep Hernando i Delgado, "El contracte de venda de rendes perpètues i vitalícies (censals morts i violaris), personals i redimibles (amb carta de gràcia). El tractat d'autor anònim "Pulchriores allegationes super contractibus censualium (segle XIV). Edició i estudi del text," *Arxiu de Textos Catalans Antics* 11 (1992): 137–79; Josep Hernando i Delgado, "Quaestio disputata de licitudine contractus emptionis et venditionis censualis cum conditione revenditionis. Un tratado sobre la licitud del contrato de compraventa de rentas personales y redimibles. Bernat de Puigcercós, O.P. (siglo XIV)," *Acta histórica et archaelogica mediaevalia* 10 (1989): 9–87; Josep Hernando i Delgado, "Les controvèrsies teològiques sobre la licitud del crèdit a llarg termini," in *El món del crèdit a la Barcelona medieval*, ed. Manuel Sánchez Martínez (Barcelona, 2007), 213–38; Josep Hernando i Delgado, Josep Ignasi Padilla, "Un tractat d'autor anònim sobre la licitud del contracte de venda de censals amb carta de gràcia (segle XIV)," in *Miscel·lània. Homenatge a Josep Lladonosa* (Lleida, 1992), 275–91.

ket also led to a gradual decrease in interest rates: from ten percent in the middle of the fourteenth century to five percent at the end of fifteenth. At the beginning of the latter century, the sale of *censals* was the main income for the city of València, but it must be considered that the payment of interest was the main expense, leading to a significant increase in public debt.[38]

The allocation of *censal* rents to a religious community was not an isolated event. Financial concessions to the Valldecrist, a Charterhouse just south of Segorbe, for example, were remarkably similar to those of the Sant Esperit. When Peter Despujol was prior, eighteen hundred shillings came from Segorbe, eighteen hundred *solidos* sent by the Muslim community (*aljama*) of Segorbe, and three thousand shillings that the same *aljama* sent for the feast of St. John and for Christmas. All these amounts are arranged in Maria de Luna's will.[39] The "Patrimony Book" of the General Bailiff of Valencia in 1412 indicates that the Charterhouse of Valldecrist received two thousand shillings and thirty-five hundred censal shillings from Segorbe.[40] In addition, it received three thousand censal shillings from the Vall de Almonacid.[41] Nunneries also received *censal* rents, such as the Cistercian convent of Saida,[42] the Poor Clares of Perpignan,[43] Pedralbes in Barcelona,[44] and St. Clare in Mallorca.[45] In 1442, Maria of Castile defended the Poor Clares of Catalayud before the judges and juries of the city, because they did not want to pay the *censals* assigned to the abbess.[46] As we know, in 1457, the Poor Clares of the Holy Trinity received the *censals* previously assigned to the Sant Esperit. Other Franciscan friaries also received this type of rents. We know, for example, that, in 1422, the friary of Barcelona received *censals* through a testamentary legacy.[47] In 1432, Maria of Castile defended the right of the Franciscans of Vic because they were not receiving the per-

---

38 García Marsilla, "La formació d'un mercat del crèdit."

39 Jill R. Webster, "La cartuja de Vall de Crist. Los primeros años, los monjes y la casa real," *Estudis Castellonencs* 10 (2003– 2005): 341–60.

40 València, Arxiu del Regne de València, Bailía, appendix, no. 61, fol. 318r.

41 María Milagros Cárcel Ortí, Vicente Pons Alós, "Las rentas del monasterio de la Vall de Crist en 1444 a través de la décima apostólica de Segorbe – Albarracín," *Boletín de la Sociedad Castellonense de Cultura* 81, no. 1 (2005): 305–15; ARV, Bailía, appendix, n. 61, fol. 319r.

42 Pau Viciano Navarro, "La gestió econòmica d'un monestir cistercenc femení. La Saïda de València a la fi del segle XV," *Revista d'historia medieval* 2 (1991): 111–32.

43 Barcelona, Arxiu de Corona d'Aragó, Cancillería, r. 3001, fols. 68v, 69r.

44 Juan Carlos Sastre Barceló, "Aproximació a l'economia del monestir de Santa Clara (segles XIII-XV)," in *Abadies, cartoixes, convents i monestirs: aspectes demogràfics, socioeconòmics i culturals de les comunitats religioses (segles XIII al XIX), XXII Jornades d'Estudis Històrics Locals, Palma, del 19 al 21 de novembre de 2003*, ed. Maria Barceló Crespí, Isabel Moll Blanes (Palma, 2004), 269–85.

45 Esther Cruz Perez, "Notes per a l'estudi de bases economiques del convent de Santa Clara als segles XV i XVI," in *Abadies, cartoixes, convents i monestirs: aspectes demogràfics, socioeconòmics i culturals de les comunitats religioses (segles XIII al XIX), XXII Jornades d'Estudis Històrics Locals, Palma, del 19 al 21 de novembre de 2003*, ed. Maria Barceló Crespí, Isabel Moll Blanes (Palma, 2004), 359–73.

46 Barcelona, Arxiu de Corona d'Aragó, Cancillería, r. 3184, fol. 67v.

47 Barcelona, Arxiu de Corona d'Aragó, Cancillería, r. 2960, fols. 169r–v, 170r.

petual rent called *censals morts* received from Galcerando and Salvador de Villardello.[48] The law of the Order nevertheless prohibited this type of income, if it was perpetual and founded on earthly goods. However, in 1279, Pope Nicholas III had established that legacies on behalf of friars were lawful in some situations, as when they were formulated like alms arranged in wills for the friars' needs without constituting an income in their favour.[49] This is exactly how the allocation of the rents from Maria de Luna to the Sant Esperit was made. The donation act specifies that, because of the friary's seclusion and the friars' inability to beg, they were granted a rent instead of alms.

Approximately fifty years after the grant by Maria de Luna, however, the allocation of rents to the Sant Esperit was considered contrary to the observance of the vow of poverty. The *censals* granted by the queen so the new friary could begin its life were now condemned by that same movement, now more developed and structured, now under, Maria of Castile.[50] From the appearance of Matteo d'Agrigento in the Crown in 1426, a "mature" phase of the observance had begun, characterized by the progressive increase of the observant friaries, the appearance of institutions of their own, such as the vicariate and the observant vicar, and the normalization of independent behaviour within the organizational frameworks in action.[51] The Sant Esperit seemed to remain beyond thanks to the autonomy granted to the foundation by the donation and the papal bulls. In November 1443, Maria showed an interest in the privileges of the friaries, asking the guardian to secretly deal with them. Later, in December 1444, she asked the pope for the friars of Sant Esperit to be included in the observant vicariate. It would not be until 1457 that the rents granted to the Sant Esperit were removed. They represented a real impediment to the Franciscans' acceptance in the Observance because they constituted a violation of the vow of poverty. In January 1457, Maria notified noble Bernat Prats that she had received the letters from the vicar general and other friars in the recent chapter meeting in which she was informed of the transfer of the revenues. This removal, decided during the Franciscan Chapter held in the friary of Santa María de Jesús in Barcelona on December 4, 1456, was ratified by King Alfonso, who, in March 1457 authorized the exchange of the legacy of Sant Esperit in favour of the Poor Clares of the Holy Trinity in València.[52] In June of the same year, Pope Callixtus III, formerly bishop of València, who had blessed the first stone of the Poor Clare community, confirmed the decision with the bull *In domo domini*.

By this time attitudes to *censals* had also changed. Unlike Eiximenis, the friar Matteo d'Agrigento, also linked to a queen close to the Franciscan Order and a supporter of the

---

48 Barcelona, Arxiu de Corona d'Aragó, Cancillería, r. 2971, fols. 94r–v.

49 Clément Lenoble, *L'exercice de la pauvreté. Économie et religion chez les franciscains d'Avignon (XIIIe–XVe siècle)* (Rennes, 2013), 150–51, 171–73.

50 She intervened in Sant Esperit by participating in the election of friary procurators and in the administration of rents and was committed to adapting Sant Esperit to the Observance.

51 For additional information, see Chiara Mancinelli, "Un lugar donde ser pobres: la Observancia franciscana en la Corona de Aragón (1380 ca.–1460 ca.)," *Memoria Europae* 1 (2015): 95–123.

52 Joaquín Sanchis Alventosa, *Santo Espíritu del Monte. Historia del real monasterio* (València, 1948), 219–23 (document 100).

Observance, disapproved of the use of *censals*. The proximity to and influence of Matteo on Maria of Castile, involved personally in the transfer of the rents of the Sant Esperit, was probably a determining factor in her action. Matteo d'Agrigento preached against *censals* in Barcelona and València and the queen suggested to her court jester, Antonio Tallander, that he listen to Matteo's sermons. The friar's sermons would have helped him to understand the illegality of these contracts, so that "you will be enlightened to reduce and define the censals mentioned in correction and amendment from any gained evil."[53]

Conclusions

The example of the founding of the Sant Esperit, a friary which emerged under royal patronage and the influence of Francesc Eiximenis at the beginning of the fifteenth century for the purpose of observing the Franciscan Rule to the letter, shows us that Franciscan and royal interests coincided in the institution of a community which would develop a reform movement, expand royal power and, at the same time, advance the Franciscans in an area with little Franciscan presence and a large community of infidels. However, the Sant Esperit also shows the royal founding depending on *censal* rents, a financial instrument widespread in the Crown of Aragon, widely present in the "Patrimony of Luna," and already used by the king to finance his military campaigns. The *censal* rents were approved by Eiximenis if managed by the Church and, as a form of patronage, allowed Maria de Luna to perform a great act of charity, showing her good administrative capacity. The revenues of the Sant Esperit were collected in an area mainly populated by Muslims who financed a friary which could not have subsisted because of its isolation from Christians and the presence of Muslims and Jews in its vicinity. The request by Maria de Luna, reiterated again by King Martin, to establish a separate vicariate formed by the first observant friaries and future communities, allows all these elements to be placed in the picture of a project with a clear long-term perspective—the diffusion of the Observance—in which Franciscan and royal interests converged in the wider context of religious, political, and financial issues in the Crown of Aragon in the first half of the fifteenth century. It highlights the presence of Muslims and Jews, the spread of *censals* and concerns over this instrument of credit, and the relations between the Crown and the Franciscan Order. The later transformation of the income of the Sant Esperit constituted a turning point because it shows the evolution of a political, religious, and economic practice from half a century before and, therefore, illustrates the evolution in the notion of poverty within the context of credit and the late medieval Christian market economy.

---

53 *Fossets illuminat per relexar e diffinir los dits censals en esmena e satisfació alguna del mal guanyat.* Agostino Amore, "La predicazione del B. Matteo d'Agrigento a Barcellona e Valenza," *Archivum franciscanum historicum* 49, nos. 3–4 (1956): 255–333 (document 3).

Chapter 15

METAMORPHOSIS OF THE GREEN MAN AND THE WILD MAN IN PORTUGUESE MEDIEVAL ART

JOANA FILIPA FONSECA ANTUNES

IN A WORLD closely dependent on nature, the Wild Man and the Green Man played important yet seemingly opposite roles in the art, literature, and imagination of the Middle Ages. The irrationality and violence of animal force, destructive when untamed, collides with and complements the supposedly benevolent and joyous presence of vegetable life, passive and quiet. What are, then, the real differences and similarities between these two figures, both the offspring of nature and of the medieval mind, and what is their importance?

Working in the context of the present historiographical concerns with marginalization and margins, this chapter opens with a discussion about the conceptual and visual relation between the Wild Man and the Green Man, from a broader, European context, and then moves to the specific circumstances of some Portuguese examples.

I often talk here of the Middle Ages as if it were a single block of cultural history, mainly for practical purposes. This doesn't mean, however, that one should forget the huge discrepancies caused by distances of place and time in a period that lasted a thousand years, assuming different shapes in different territories of the Old Continent. Also, the subliminal differences between what one may call the Romanesque and the Gothic Middle Ages must always be considered, especially while referring to mental attitudes towards nature in each of the cultural contexts. But, since the differences and changes operated in the human imaginary and the material realms are as interesting as its similarities and continuities, I choose to open the chronological spectrum to the all-encompassing nature of medieval art and culture.[1]

Setting the Stage: Nature, Wilderness, and Wildness

The long period historiographically identified with the Middle Ages is, interestingly enough, marked by two dramatically opposed climatic phases. The first one, commonly known as the "little optimum" or medieval warm period, occurred between the eleventh and the fourteenth centuries. During this time, nature was often kind, allowing bountiful harvests and providing the ideal background for huge population growth, both in rural

---

1 This chapter, first submitted in 2012, is in its original form, with only minor changes and updates to the content and bibliography.

Joana Filipa Fonseca Antunes (joana.filipa.antunes@gmail.com) is Professora Auxiliar at the Universidade de Coimbra in Portugal.

and urban areas. By this time, the wilderness was being tamed through massive assart-ing, and the woods progressively submitted to order imposed by humans.[2]

But from the fourteenth century on, a progressive change took place, replacing the warm and mild weather with colder, harder conditions. The beginning of this "Little Ice Age" coincides with periods of famine and epidemics, such as the Black Death, reshap-ing the relationship between humanity and nature, and leading to a rethinking of man's own place in the world.[3] The order previously imposed over the woodland—reflective of an encyclopaedic vision of the world best exemplified by medieval bestiaries—is then transformed into a shape-shifting attitude of rationalization and re-mystification. Lying between the progressive privatization of the forest space, with its chivalric whimsies, and the search for a rational understanding of natural forces and creatures,[4] the late medieval wilderness was still an ambivalent place.

Despite the dramatic changes in natural conditions, the relationship between medi-eval man and the wilderness of European woods was constantly tense. While humans struggled for control of these woodlands, progressively domesticating it and conse-quently reducing its area, the need for a rational management of natural resources became self-evident.[5] And, while successfully taming the woods, they managed to turn irrational fear into wonder, admiration, and fantasy, transforming the lurking creatures of the forest into images capable of conveying complex stories, messages, and images.

Such an example is provided by imaginary figures such as the Green Man, whose demonic Romanesque features give place to a multitude of natural expressions from the fourteenth century on. Also, the Wild Man, the traditional inhabitant of woods, moun-tains, and caves, begins its literary development precisely at the end of the favourable warm period. This *coincidence* could be expressive enough to show how reality has a fluid counterpart in the mind of a culture particularly prone to symbolic thought.

The appeal of the *silva* and its vital force was, in fact, common across the whole medieval period and society. Jacques Le Goff is particularly assertive in summarizing how forests could be a desirable space for everyone: it provided nobles a place to hunt and a stage for their chivalric endeavours; it answered the religious cravings for an ere-mitic life, only conceivable in a desert; and, to common people, it offered a whole range of raw materials which complemented an essentially domestic economy.[6] But, sublimi-

---

2 Brian M. Fagan, *The Little Ice Age: How Climate Made History, 1300–1850* (New York, 2000), 16–17. Jacques Le Goff explores the idea of the desert–forest through medieval literature, also pointing out literary clues to a phase of deforestation in two particular chapters of his book on the medieval imagination, namely "Le désert-forêt dans l'Occident médiéval" and "Lévi-Strauss en Brocéliande." See Jacques Le Goff, *L'Imaginaire médiéval: Essais* (Paris, 1985), 60–75 and 152–87.

3 See John Aberth, *An Environmental History of the Middle Ages: The Crucible of Nature* (London, 2012), 1–4 and 49–50.

4 This renewed approach to nature is well exemplified by the attitude towards animals. As Aberth pointedly described, the fantasist and allegorical character of medieval bestiaries seems to give place to "a rationality and near human equivalence to animals that is reminiscent of the Orphic school of Pythagoras during classical times." See Aberth, *An Environmental History*, 10.

5 See Aberth, *An Environmental History*, 2.

6 Le Goff, *L'Imaginaire médiéval*, 66.

nally, there's another possibility offered by the forest to everyone who "went there to marginalize themselves, to comport themselves as men of nature who had fled from the world of culture."[7]

In spite of being part of the Divine Creation, as much as man himself, nature was still a strange force, unpredictable and hard to deal with. Though the traditional approach to medieval culture and economy through the binomial nature *versus* culture, or wildness *versus* anything built, ploughed, or inhabited,[8] can no longer be sustained without many nuances, the flight from an ordered and culturally developed world towards wilderness is still a meaningful and stimulating phenomenon. And, needless to say, the experience and perception of nature and its unpredictable outputs—whether in agricultural fields or untamed woods—must have been different for a townsman or a villager. Although one should not be led to believe that people who lived in the cities were as detached from nature's cycles and innermost forces as we are now,[9] it becomes quite evident that their lives were not as "centered on the endless processions of seasons, on the routines of planting and harvest, cycles of good years and bad"[10] as the peasants from the countryside. One may suppose, then, that in a rural context an image like that of the Green Man could evoke the sharpness of a life-and-death cycle which was closely tied to each person's life, while in the city it might be only a distant reminder of that vital cycle, whose poetic references could be emphasized over its tragic ones. Thus, the potential of the wilderness as a "way" of marginalization may be better understood through one of its agents: an urban elite interested in projecting its whimsies and desires (as much as its fears) onto the woods.

But even before the imaginary of troubadours, the *chansons de geste*, or Renaissance utopian returns to an idyllic nature, people did search the wilderness to marginalize themselves. And this could happen literally or symbolically, by means of a physical flight, an inspirational one, or even a symbolical projection into mythical beings. Whatever the reason or the process implied, people felt compelled to transpose the limits of untamed nature and *experience* it. St. Bernard himself—the founder of a community that would be one of the most industrious in the exploitation of woodlands—is quite clear about the epistemological, and also symbolic, importance of this very experience: "you shall find something further in the forests than in books. The trees and rocks will teach you that which you will never be able to hear from the masters of science."[11] Nature as an effective catalyst to human perfecting is, in fact, inseparable from the psychological potential

---

7 *Il est allé là pour se marginaliser, afin d'avoir le comportement des hommes de la nature qui ont fui du monde de la culture.* Cited from Le Goff, *L'Imaginaire médiéval*, 66.

8 See Le Goff, *L'Imaginaire médiéval*, 74.

9 John Aberth also points to this "modern alienation from nature" as one of the many factors that demonstrate a deep sense of distance between the medieval world and ours. See Alberth, *An Environmental History*, 15.

10 Fagan, *The Little Ice Age*, 16.

11 *Aliquid amplius invenies in silvis quam in libris. Ligna et lapides docebunt te, quod a magistri audire non possis.* Cited from Bernard of Clairvaux, Epistle 106, in Corrine J. Saunders *The Forest of Medieval Romance: Avernus, Broceliande, Arden*, (Cambridge, 1993), 17.

of a solitary experience in the woods. To quote once again Jacques Le Goff: "Thus, the Judaic and eastern tradition of the desert was joined by a 'barbarian or Celtic' tradition as well as a Germanic–Scandinavian one." [12]

This mythological and pagan character of the forest was, doubtlessly, one of the main reasons for its symbolic potential of marginalization.[13] Besides this natural inclination to the presence of *deviant* cults and spiritual attitudes, the forest could be an actual destination of physical flight, receiving and protecting within its realms people in search of purification through penitence, or triumph through adventure. And it could also be the refuge of pure "marginals": convicts, bandits, and adventurers[14] who found in the wilderness a temporary suspension of law and human imposed order. The forest becomes then, during the long time between the twelfth and the fifteenth centuries, a place of solitude, mystical experience, and life on the edge—a place of liminality. There, characters such as Merlin or Sir Yvain, *le chevalier au lion*, experience a temporary madness that turns them into Wild Men.[15] There, the exiled Tristan and Iseult are subjected to the harshness of the wild life, also meeting a suggestively named fellow, Ogrin.[16] And there, hermit saints such as St. John Chrysostom, St. Onuphrius, St. Mary of Egypt, or even St. Mary Magdalene, find solace for the torments of a sinful life—and they too become physically close to the Wild Folk prototype.[17]

Closer to medieval man's daily life is the idea of the forest as a mischievous trickster.[18] These aspects may not be totally distant from the fact that woods, although sometimes controlled by the elites, are indeed the place where the social hierarchical chains are broken.[19] And it is not uncommon to find literary narratives and artworks which offer

---

12 *À la tradition judaïque et orientale du désert s'est ainsi ajoutée une tradition "barbare celtique" [...], mais aussi germanique et scandinave de la forêt-désert.* Cited from Le Goff, *L'Imaginaire médiéval*, 69.

13 See, for example, Alberth, *An Environmental History*, 18–25 and 70–83.

14 See Le Goff, *L'Imaginaire médiéval*, 66. /

15 For references about Chrétien de Troyes' characters and their metamorphosis into Wild Men, see, for example: Le Goff, *L'Imaginaire médiéval*, 70–74 and 152–87; Timothy Husband, *The Wild Man: Medieval Myth and Symbolism* (New York, 1980), 3 and 59–61.

16 Molly Kelly presents diverse attitudes towards the Morois forest as they appear in different versions of Tristan's romance, proving how some authors see the exile from society as positive (this is the case of Gottfried), and liberating, while others (Béroul is an example) emphasize the distress imposed by the natural *milieu* over the exiled lovers. See Molly Robinson Kelly, *The Hero's Place: Medieval Literary Traditions of Space and Belonging* (Washington DC, 2009), 237–47.

17 For a brief reference to these saints and their relation to Wild Folk imagery see, for example, Husband, *The Wild Man*, 95–109; Nicolas Adell-Gombert, "Marthe et Marie-Madeleine ou le partage de la destiné feminine," in *Marthe et Marie-Madeleine. Deux Modèles de Dévotion et d'Accueil Chrétien*, ed. Bruno Phalip, Céline Perol, Pascale Quincy-Lefebvre (Clermont-Ferrand, 2009), 84; Dany Sandron, "Un modèle de rédemption: La représentation de Sainte Madeleine," in *Mariage et Sexualité au Moyen âge: Accord ou Crise?*, ed. Michel Rouche (Paris, 2000), 267–68.

18 See Robert Fossier, *Ces Gens du Moyen Âge* (Paris, 2007), 190–208; Le Goff, *L'Imaginaire médiéval*, 73.

19 Originally "the place where, in a way, the central axis of the feudal hierarchy breaks" (*le lieu où se brisent, en quelque sorte, les mailles de la hiérarchie féodale*). Cited from Le Goff, *L'Imaginaire médiéval*, 156.

us a glimpse of this inversion of the common social order, by presenting the Wild Man as the lord of the forest, ruling over animals and exerting his power over every forester who dares to dwell in his domain.[20]

In fact, an antinomic vision of nature in its wild state is as frequent in literature as it is in art, and some of its best examples involve both the characters who are subjects of this chapter. The Green Man is, in fact, one of the most durable expressions of nature's ever changing qualities: sometimes he smiles benevolently, perhaps to signify the fertile and amenable seasons of its eternally renewed cycle; other times, he frowns and grimaces violently, simultaneously denouncing and exorcizing the coldest, hardest periods of the year.[21] The Green Man is the implacable nature that threatens, imprisons, and ravishes humans and animals alike in so many Romanesque capitals, corbels, and inhabited initials. But he is also the nurturing nature that feeds the Holy Family during the flight to Egypt or provides shelter to hermits and holy persons in so many gothic works.

The beneficial, purifying, and spiritually enhancing properties of the European forest as the immediate counterpart of the oriental desert is, in fact, one of the most striking features of the medieval imaginary and its relationship with nature.[22] If creatures like the Wild Man are not yet playing the positive role of the Good Savage, still embodying the impetuousness and irrationality of beastly behaviour, the transformation of sinful humans into wild men, by their exile in the wilderness of woods, is synonymous with the achievement of holiness.

By the end of the Middle Ages, as it is conventionalized, the mental attitude towards the woods changes and the positive vision of the wilderness seems to ultimately win over the negative one. Part of the explanation for this (which is the climax of a long-term process, more than an acute change) lies in the historical context itself, as control over the forest's territories increases and urban life becomes more and more asphyxiating for humankind at the dawn of a humanist consciousness of its own society's drawbacks. The forest becomes tendentiously an idyllic place, not always exempted from danger, but mostly a place of freedom, where humanity can hope to have a simple life.[23] This life is progressively identified with the Wild Man's, who ceases to be a truculent, hideous, and

---

20 Once again, Chrétien de Troyes provides one of the best examples, by presenting the wild man (*homme sauvage*) met by Yvain in the forest as the lord of the beasts. See Le Goff, *L'Imaginaire médiéval*, 71. Some of the most interesting visual counterparts are a set of tapestries made between 1400 and 1450 in Germany and Switzerland, where the Wild Man appears surrounded by animals and a familiar entourage, acting like a leader or a ruler. These and other examples may be found in Husband, *The Wild Man*, 6, 77–82 and 122–24.

21 For a compilation of numerous examples of different Green Men imagery, see Kathleen Basford, *The Green Man* (Cambridge, 1978, repr. 2000).

22 Le Goff, *L'Imaginaire médiéval*, 59–75.

23 Apropos of this idyllic longing for a simple life in direct contact with nature see, for example, the illuminations of Jean Bourdichon, depicting the *Four Conditions of Society*, 1457–1521, Paris, École nationale supérieure des Beaux-Arts; and also *La Ballade des Quatre États de la Société*, where the wild man is presented speaking about his natural condition. The transcription and translation of this text may be found in may be found in Husband, *The Wild Man*, 201–2.

Figure 15.1: Dedication stone from the Church of Nossa Senhora da Oliveira, (detail, 1401, Guimarães, Portugal. Museu de Alberto Sampaio, L5 (© Museu de Alberto Sampaio, Guimarães)).

violently lustful creature, to become a rustic character, a good husband, and a caring father, capable of ploughing the land or improvising a home.[24]

Similarly, the elusive character that is the Green Man becomes a less frightful reminder of nature's crudeness, death, and decay, returning to his first association with Silvanus, fauns, and satyrs, the merry escort of the Bacchic parades which amused the men of the Renaissance.

But, at the verge of this change, a whole discovery of a new world is taking place, providing the forest with a new counterpart of wilderness. In art, literature, and thought, nature wasn't always a real place and, the more inaccessible it was the more permeable it became to invention and fantasy. The burst of imagination which one expects to find in poetry, romance, folk tales, or even hagiographical texts appears then in another type of work, supposedly credible by its scientific nature. This is the case with travel reports which, in territories such as the Iberian kingdoms, enjoyed great literary success since at least the fourteenth century. One of these earlier examples is the Castilian *Libro del conocimiento*, whose author emphatically states, while talking about the cynocephali: "and I saw one of them."[25] Likewise, over the next two centuries, Portuguese travellers and authors preach that "experience is the mother of all things,"[26] while

---

24 The previously solitary figure of the Wild Man begins to be accompanied by his own folks, and even his family, in works such as the fifteenth century sets of Swiss tapestries, and later in woodcuts like the one used to illustrate Hans Sachs' poem on the Wild Man. Both works may be found in Husband, *The Wild Man*, 122–27 and 132–33.

25 *Et yo vi vno dellos.* Paulo Lopes, "A representação do corpo dos habitantes dos confins do mundo no Libro Del Conosçimiento," in *O Corpo e o Gesto na Civilização Medieval*, Ana Isabel Buescu, João Silva de Sousa, Maria Adelaide Miranda (Lisboa, 2006), 90–91.

26 Originally "a experiência é a madre de todas as cousas." Cited from Duarte Pacheco Pereira, *Esmeraldo de Situ Orbis* (Lisboa, 1892)

still writing about their encounters with monstrous beings from the edges of the world. Quoting Paulo Lopes, one must agree that in a time when "the distinction between real and imaginary wasn't even looked for, this kind of account was not taken as fictional."[27] And if this is true for travel literature, it must also be applied to other kinds of narratives and its respective visual counterparts. The Wild Man wasn't simply a fictional and literary character, or a strange figure used to ornament church capitals. Until the fifteenth century, he was an actual embodiment of an ancestral fear of dense forests and rough mountains, a fear already personalized by the rational Greeks and Romans in beings such as satyrs and fauns.[28] As an imaginary character, he was useful to inspire respect of the forest, on which everybody depended, but also to warn young women away from a place where they could easily fall prey to (true) men's wilder appetites. Occasionally, short narratives and homilies would evoke the story of one of these young women who would try to use this figure to her advantage, claiming her pregnancy was the result of rape by a lustful Wild Man.[29]

Most frequently, the spirit of these inhabitants of the woods would be incarnated by men, usually young ones, who periodically would mask themselves with animal skins, leaves, and/or moss, marking a popular calendar closely dependant on the performance of fertility or exorcism rites.[30] These secular parades and performances were once also practised by the elites, who used them as exotic moments of courtly amusement, as shown by the sadly celebrated example of the *Bal des Ardents*. And, in a popular context, the use of a disguise close to the features of Green and Wild Men still happens today in many European countries, evoking fertility and prophylactic rites, and also the cyclical life of the natural world to which man is hopelessly connected, from birth and growth to death and rebirth.

The *reinvention* of the natural world suggested by the embodiment of these figures answers a dynamic relation between centre and periphery in which the centre (the known, civilized, and mainly urbanized world) is synonymous with order and perfection, and the periphery is chaotic, imperfect, strange, and monstrous in its distance from the centre. This is important because the humanity that is virtually absent in the inhabitants of the far east of the medieval world, for example, is strongly present in both Green and Wild Men, as one of their most striking physical features. For the medieval man, the figure we now call Green Man could have been a simple nature spirit or even an archetype, coherently meaning life but also death, and the Wild Man could be the antithesis of human decency. But whether spitting leaves or brandishing a club, with the body fully naked or covered in fur, Wild Men remained essentially men.

---

27 For his work see http://iem.fcsh.unl.pt/section.aspx?kind=investigador&id=345.

28 See Lynn Frier Kaufmann, *The Noble Savage: Satyrs and Satyr Families in Renaissance Art* (Michigan, 1984).

29 Helen Young, "Wodewoses: The (In)Humanity of Medieval Wild Men," *AUMLA: Journal of the Australian Universities Modern Language Association*, special issue (2009): 40.

30 Claude Gaignebet, Jean Dominique Lajoux, *Art profane et religion populaire au Moyen Âge* (Vendôme, 1985), 90–95.

Green Men and Wild Men: Inhabitants of the Margin

Whether in manuscript folios, architectural structures, or decorative arts, these figures often appear in the physical margins as secondary characters or as complements to a main discourse. Portuguese art provides us with a great number of examples of this formal peripheral condition: in church dedication stones, misericords on choir stalls, and decorated capitals, just to count a few.[31] Usually neatly separated from sacred figures and themes, they are charged with the negativity of the borders, spaces for sinners, demons, and forbidden behaviours, but also with the vitality and freedom of otherness offered by that space, a space of hope, exorcism, and salvation.[32]

When trying to evaluate how images such as the Green Man and the Wild Man can provide us a glimpse of man's own instincts, fears, thoughts, and feelings, one must pose an inevitable question: can we assume these images as *other natures* of mankind? How can one see "other natures" of man in characters "commonly read as an Other, the antithesis of humanity?"[33] As Helen Young puts it, we are dealing with a *porous* territory "on the borders of humanity."[34] And it is porous, as medieval man was able to express his fear of himself through a mirroring process. By reflecting his own ugliness, wickedness, and guilt in a being that is his own antithesis, he could better exorcize his demons and enclose them in a distant place. This place could be an exotic, unexplored land at the edges of the world, as well as a secluded corner of his imagination, where figures like the Green Man or the Wild Man would be imprisoned in plays and stories, or immobilized in the stone of a capital, or constrained by the parchment folio of a lavishly illuminated manuscript. As far as he could deny the complete humanity of these vicious creatures, he would be safe from comparison, identification, and condemnation. As William Caxton puts it in his version of Aesop's fable *The Man and the Satyr*: "a wodewose is a monster lyke to the man/as hit appiereth by hys figure."[35]

The denial of the human nature of the *wodewose*, Middle English for Wild Man, is quite clear from his qualification as a monster whose only resemblance with humanity is his body and posture. But this denial has probably more of an automatic self-defensive process than a conscious segregation. Regardless, it shouldn't prevent us from reading medieval man's nature and integral humanity through the semi-human creations of his mind. On the contrary, one must agree that "This liminality calls into question any fixity of medieval and early modern conceptualizations of humanity",[36] thus expanding the borders of our own conceptualization about the medieval and early modern mind.

---

31 Examples of these works include: the consecration stone from the church of Nossa Senhora ra Oliveira, offered by King John I in 1401, Museu de Alberto Sampaio (Guimarães); a misericord from the choir stall of the monastery of Santa Cruz (Coimbra), ca. 1513; a corbel from the façade of the church of Conceição Velha (Lisboa), ca. 1534.

32 Maria de Lurdes Craveiro, "O Anjo Moderno. The Modern Angel," in *Angelorum: Anjos em Portugal*, ed. Manuel de Sampayo Graça (Guimarães, 2012), 59–60.

33 Young, "Wodewoses," 37.

34 Young, "Wodewoses," 37.

35 Young, "Wodewoses," 42.

36 Young, "Wodewoses," 37.

Although the basic criterion for humanity formulated by thinkers like St. Augustine was rationality,[37] man always knew that sometimes he could be as irrational as any other animal from Creation. Momentary glimpses of this purely animal nature, though immediately associated with mental or physical illness (and, quite immediately, with sin), were at least as constant then as they are now. And, although corporeal expression was less constrained than today's, as the various medieval and early modern manuals of good manners exemplify, strange behaviour, exasperation, incongruence, and insanity certainly brought shame and disapproval.[38] But, symbolically, how could people deal with this non-human irrationality? If one looks for the answer in literature and art, there seems to be at least two alternatives: exorcism or marginalization, both of them options that fit the Green and the Wild Man. Through them, and other imaginary beings, medieval man could conceptualize, rationalize, analyse, and, most important of all, objectify his own irrationality. Thus, is it possible to presume that, by being the antithesis of humanity, these beings cannot express a repressed humanity? They certainly can, as far as they are both embodiments of another nature of man: a physiological, corporeal, animal, and mostly irrational one, but still a human nature. But, more than seeking humanity in these figures, maybe one should try to find in them the animal features that men felt compelled to express.

Green Men: Not that Green and Often Wild

The "Green Man" is one of the most constant iconographical motifs of medieval art, and a figure well known to almost every medievalist.[39] Lady Ragland gave the name (1939) to strange humanoid faces carved or painted between leaves and branches, either smiling or frowning, or instead spitting or swallowing plants. The basic, visual scheme of the Green Man is simple and ancient: a foliate head, mix of human and plant, animal and vegetal. This foliate head appears in Roman art during the first century with similar features and, probably similar symbolic and mythological implications, since it may be related with embodiments of wild nature like Silvanus (god of the forests).[40] And this indeed is one of the most successful formulas to express men's harmony with nature, a relationship with good and bad outcomes, as mortality comes along with it.

But the "green" character of these figures should be regarded with some caution. First of all, they were certainly not always painted in green. The first known Green Man to appear in a Christian context was actually painted in yellow-gold over a red background. What may seem information of secondary importance is, in fact, a relevant

---

37 Young, "Wodewoses," 37–38.

38 The texts containing advice on good manners and moral restraint, especially aimed at a courtly environment, are vastly represented from the fifteenth century on. Some examples are Christine de Pisan's *Enseignements à Son Filz Jean de Castel*, France, ca. 1430; D. Duarte, *Leal Conselheiro*, Portugal, ca. 1438; *The Boke of Curtasye*, England, 1440; Erasmus of Rotterdam, *De Civilitate Morum Puerilium*, 1530; and Giovanni della Casa, *Il Galateo*, Venezia, 1558.

39 For further information on the Green Man's features, prototypes, literary developments, or iconographic ancestries, see Basford, *The Green Man*.

40 See Basford, *The Green Man*, 9–10.

pointer to the symbolic sense of this enigmatic figure, since it forcibly points to the possibility, already advanced by Kathleen Basford,[41] that the leaves sprouting from these creatures' mouths may be green and fresh leaves (signs of life force and renewal), as well as yellow and decaying autumnal branches (reminders of a life that withers and runs to an end). Alternatively, if one insists in the association between the foliate heads and the green colour, it must be taken into account that the symbolism of this colour was ambivalent: it could be a liturgical colour as well as that of a slithery demon's skin.

Similarly, the easy and kind character of the Green Man must be put in context: frequently bestialized and demonized by Romanesque art, it becomes more human, varied, and natural in Gothic chronologies. But even then, and to quote Kathleen Basford, "There are very few benevolent or serenely smiling faces: more typically they frown. [...] Sometimes the eyes are squinting, the expressions suggesting various levels of inebriation; bellicose, morose, even comatose, but seldom jocose."[42]

Thus, the impartial view of these nature forces, as benevolent and violent as Nature may be, doesn't seem to remain untouched by medieval art. While some authors believe that the change in the perception and depiction of the natural world—which doubtlessly occurred from Antiquity to the early Middle Ages—was due to its negativization through new theological points of view,[43] I believe the explanation must be found elsewhere. In fact, medieval theology was a highly structured reflex of the medieval mind, comprising a global, ambivalent, and all-encompassing view of the world. A tree, a root, a branch, would have been used as a literary image, a symbol, or an allegory of things good and bad alike.[44] Similarly, almost every animal presented in a bestiary would have a double symbolic meaning.

Nevertheless, some of the Green Men carved in much medieval churches are indeed menacing in their expression, and are most likely to be seen as "demons and specters of the demon wood."[45] Indeed, the Church's early recognition of persisting animist rites, and the consequent demonization of natural forces and pagan gods, all attest to the crystallization of symbolic and archetypal figures which would have a long lasting presence in medieval literature and iconography.[46] Thus, even if in a context of battle

---

41 See Basford, *The Green Man*, 11.

42 Basford, *The Green Man*, 7.

43 This is the opinion of Kathleen Basford, who presents Hrabannus Maurus's eighth-century interpretation of biblical allegories as a decisive turning point on the vision of nature and, consequently, the image of the Green Man. See Basford, *The Green Man*, 12.

44 This is precisely what we find in Hrabannus Maurus's interpretation of biblical allegories, identified by Kathleen Basford as a decisive source of the negative vision of nature through the first centuries of the medieval period. A thorough analysis of this work will quickly reveal that the positive interpretations of natural elements such as branches and roots outnumber the negative ones. See "Beati Rabani Mauri," in *Patrologiae cursus completus*, ed. Jacques-Paul Migne, 221 vols. (Paris, 1852), 6:1036–37.

45 Basford, *The Green Man*, 14.

46 For the long-lasting presence of pagan practices through the early Middle Ages and the establishment of conversion strategies by the Church, see, for example Ludo J. R. Milis, ed., *The Pagan Middle Ages* (Woodbridge, 1998), 54–56 and 134–36; Carl S. Watkins, *History and the Supernatural in Medieval England* (Cambridge, 2007), 68–106.

against paganism and superstition, one may expect to find depictions of ancient tree spirits in the decoration of Romanesque works of art, as green men and green beasts pop up between twigs and tree branches. Whether this means a condemnation of the belief in deified nature forces—similar to the one which led to the systematic cutting down of the Celtic people's sacred trees until the tenth century—or even a triumphant remark on the Church's victory over paganism, one cannot surely tell. But from the iconographical point of view, these green men peeking beneath the leaves of a Romanesque capital, seem to have the same ancestry as, for example, the tree spirits of St. Amand's (584–675) legend. This saint, in his effort to Christianise pagan peoples in Gaul, is said to have found a blind woman who worshipped trees. He convinced her to renounce that sinful behaviour by cutting down one of her sacred trees, being rewarded with the recovery of her sight.[47] In one illuminated manuscript, a miniature depicts the tree spirits as little human heads appearing between the tree branches while the woman cuts the tree,[48] as they would appear in architectural decorations and marginal paintings. This particular depiction will have, as we will see, a huge importance in the comprehension of the Green Man as a symbolic connection between trees and vegetation as cyclical life forces, and human head as the source of consciousness.

The grimacing devilish Green Beasts found in works such as the Codex Egberti (ca. 980) or the Folkunge Psalter (twelfth century), the capitals of St. Kyneburgha Church (twelfth and thirteenth centuries) or the tympanum of Saint-Julien Church in Mars-sur-Allier (late eleventh or early twelfth century),[49] may be, thus, embodiments of demonized pagan gods and spirits subdued by the institutionalized Church. But they may just as well be simple depictions of the purely animal, unpredictable, and uncontrollable side of forests, glens, marshes, and mountains. In this sense, both Green Man and Green Beast become the forest itself, making nature present through a simple symbolic image, instead of complex scenery or landscape. This is what happens, for example, at one of the carved stone capitals of Saint-Lazare Cathedral at Autun (twelfth century),[50] where a leonine Green Beast works as the stage for a bear-hunting scene. Since the bear itself is a symbol of the winter that needs to die to give rise to a new period of light,[51] the role of the Green Beast (and thus the Green Man) as a symbol of the vital and cyclical force of nature becomes easy to understand. And this is also the case, I believe, of many other

---

47 The Life of St. Amand was translated in Jocelyn N. Hillgarth, *Christianity and Paganism, 350–750: The Conversion of Western Europe* (Philadelphia, 1986), 147–48. St. Amand's struggle for the eradication of the tree cult is also mentioned in Alberth, *An Environmental History*, 81.

48 Gaignebet, *Art profane et religion populaire*, 76. These miniatures are part of a manuscript now kept at the Bibliothèque de Valenciennes, as *Troisième Vie de Saint Amand*, ca. 1175, fol. 66v, accessed April 23, 2019, https://patrimoine-numerique.ville-valenciennes.fr/ark:/29755/B_596066101_MS_0500.

49 Codex Egberti, Reichenau (Southern Germany), late tenth century, now Trier, Stadtbibliothek, MS 24. All these works may be found in Basford, *The Green Man*, plates 14, 18a, b, c, 19a, and 19b.

50 This capital is also menioned in Gaignebet, *Art profane et religion populaire*, 79.

51 The bear is also frequently presented in close interaction, and familiar proximity, with the Wild Man. For the symbolic role of the bear during medieval times see, for example, Gaignebet, *Art profane et religion populaire*, 79–91; Michel Pastoureau, *L'ours: Histoire d'un roi déchu* (Paris, 2007).

Figure 15.2: Two Green Men, fifteenth century, Batalha, Portugal,
Church of Santa Maria da Vitória (© Mosteiro de Batalha).

Green Men figures, like the one that supports the Bamberg Rider[52]—the knight who
rides through the realm of the unknown by embroiling himself in the thick woodland.

From the thirteenth century on, the expression of these foliate figures becomes more
human and less frightful. Nevertheless, one can hardly see the Green Man as an intrinsi-
cally good or peaceful figure, as it brings up the idea of an uneasy symbiosis between
man and plant, and an opposition between Heaven, longed for by the human soul, and
Earth, the dramatic prison of the human body. In some way, the idea of the Green Man
implies "the darkness of unredeemed nature as opposed to the shimmering light of
Christian revelation."[53] As shown at the end of this chapter, this idea has old roots and
we will find some of them firmly grounded in Portuguese late medieval literature.

Likewise, the use of foliate heads on funerary monuments suggests the idea of death
and rebirth, through the example of the fast decay and transformation occurring in the
vegetable world. St. Peter himself enunciates this ephemeral nature in terms of its comparison with human vainglory: "For all flesh is as grass and all the glory of man as the
flower of grass. The grass withered and the flower thereof falleth away."[54] Whether acting as a *memento mori*, a metaphor of nature's ambivalent qualities, an embodiment of
pagan cults, a synthetic depiction of the wilderness, or even a symbol of natural life force

---

52 Also published in Basford, *The Green Man*, plates 37 and 38.

53 Basford, *The Green Man*, 21.

54 Quoted in Basford, *The Green Man*, 21.

and fertility,[55] the fact is that the simple presence of the Green Man summons the attitude of fascination and fear inspired by wild nature in the medieval mind. Medieval art in general, and Portuguese medieval art in particular, are valuable sources for a better knowledge of such relationship. Let us look at some of the more representative buildings of the Portuguese Middle Ages; we'll find—with the exceptions that always define the prolixity that goes beyond the establishment of artificial chronologies in art—that precise metamorphic process seen in Green Man imagery. At Sé Velha, the Romanesque Old Cathedral of Coimbra (twelfth century), there are numerous capitals, and even corbels, decorated with sculpted Green Beasts sprouting wavy branches or geometrized crochets, but not even one Green Man. At Batalha Monastery (fourteenth century), one of the finest examples of Gothic architecture in Portugal, human faces appear between or above the foliage on many capitals, without fusing with it, just like the tree spirits of St. Amand's legend. At the same time, here is the first known appearance of a full-bodied Green Man (a rather rare typology) in Portuguese art. And, finally, at the sixteenth-century church of São João Baptista (St. John the Baptist) in Tomar, the Manueline capitals display a great variety of Green Men with fleshy leaves cropping up from their mouths. In this precise timeframe, Portuguese art achieves its greatest variety of Green Men types in sculpture. Therefore, one may find a grotesque, grinning man's face appearing between two bare twigs, in a choir stall's misericord, as well as a spectral and ghostly face surrounded by leaves, in the corbels of a church.

But it is precisely at the São João Baptista Church that we find some of the most intriguing—and simultaneously enlightening—aspects of the Green Man's iconology. First of all, their stunning variety provides a kind of summary of the symbolic potential of the Green type. There, we find ogre-like figures sprouting leaves, together with stylized Green Beasts, and anthropologically inspired Green Men, with Brazilian Indian and African facial features. This multiplicity of Green Men versions in the same space, unparalleled in Portuguese medieval art, suggests the enactment of a cosmological cycle, in which devouring Time expresses itself through foliate masks and faces with an open mouth. These were images particularly significant in a church such as the one of São João Baptista in Tomar, for its own invocation, closely related to solstitial celebrations.[56] This connection may be further explored through the presence of a trycephalous Green Man,[57] whose immediate relation to the succession of past, present, and future is highly significant in the context of this symbology of natural cycles.

---

55 The Green Man is sometimes seen as a counterpart of female fertility figures such as the Sheela-na-gig. Images such as the one carved in the tympanum of St. Leonard Church in Shropshire, which shows a full-length depiction of a green man's body exhibiting his genitalia, seem to confirm the plausibility of this hypothesis. See Basford, *The Green Man*, plate 20b; Antony Weir, James Jerman, *Images of Lust. Sexual Carvings on Medieval Churches* (London, 1993).

56 Paulo Pereira, "A Obra Silvestre e a Esfera do Rei. Iconologia da Arquitectura do Período Manuelino na Grande Estremadura" (master's thesis, Universidade Nova de Lisboa, 1987).

57 One immediate counterpart of this carving may be found in a misericord of the Church of St. Mary and All Saints' choir stall (ca. 1418–1434), at Whalley in Lancashire (north-west England). Other examples are provided in Gaignebet, *Art profane et religion populaire*, 66–71.

Figure 15.3:
One of the African Green
Men carved on the capitals
of the Church of S. João
Baptista (St. John the
Baptist), sixteenth century,
Tomar, Portugal. Igreja
de São João Baptista
(© Diocese de Santarém).

The Summer Solstice becomes then one of the strongest links between this green imagery and the dedication of the church itself, since it coincides with the religious celebrations of St. John the Baptist. And yet another subliminal connection may be found through another common feature of the foliate heads and the cult of this saint, himself a man on the margin, and a man of the wilderness. In the *Legenda Aurea*, Jacobus de Voragine tells how the head of the saint, beheaded as a result of Salome's wiles, was afterwards brought to Jerusalem and buried in a secret place by Herod himself. After being found and then hidden again in a cave, later rediscovered and transported to Constantinople, it finally arrived at the Poitou (France) during the reign of Pepin, and "by his powers many dead men were resurrected."[58] Already depicted in eleventh-century Byzantine manuscripts,[59] the head of St. John the Baptist becomes a subject commonly found in medieval art and iconography, whether in an extremely schematic form, as in numerous pilgrim's badges, or in a naturalist rendering of the saint's injured and lifeless face. This last version was particularly cherished in German lands between the fourteenth and the sixteenth centuries, where it was known as *Johannesschüssel*.[60] The head of the saint, carved in wood, metal, and alabaster, was displayed over a platter, with a livid expression, eyes half or totally closed, and semi-open mouth. Many of these sculp-

---

58 *Et inde Gallias apuc Pictaviam regnante Pipino postmodum est translatum, ubi ejus meritis multi mortui sunt resuscitati.* Cited from Jacobus de Voragine, *Legenda Aurea vulgo Historia Lombardica dicta* (Osnabrück, 1969), 573.

59 From the Victoria and Albert Museum, London; accessed February 4, 2013, http://collections.vam.ac.uk/item/O120641/head-of-st-john-the-head-unknown/.

60 See, for instance, the work of Barbara Baert on this iconographical type: Barbara Baert, *Caput Johannis in Disco. Essay on a Man's Head* (Leiden, 2012); Barbara Baert, "The Johannesschüssel as Andachtsbild. The Gaze, the Medium and the Senses," *Disembodied Heads in Medieval and Early Modern Culture*, ed. Catrien Santing, B. Baert, A. Traninger (Leiden, 2013), 117–60.

tures were provided a hollow back, with an opening that leads precisely to the mouth, and there is some evidence to support the hypothesis that this was a device to hide a candle, providing dramatic illumination for the saint's face.[61]

In another source, the so-called Taymouth Hours (second quarter of the fourteenth century), a queen is depicted as discovering the head of St. John, buried under a tree.[62] Such a depiction of the saint's head between the green grass of the *erber* ("garden") is immediately suggestive of both the *Johannesschüssel* type and the Green Man, leading us to question if the open mouth of the sculptures could not have been alternately filled with candle light, and with still living branches and leaves, depending on the liturgical calendar.[63] In any case, the coincidence displayed in medieval folklore, literature, and art, between the cult of the Baptist's head, Green Men, and also Wild Men, is obvious and quite easy to explain: the head is the active principle, the ultimate focus of life, the lodging of the spirit, and the source of creative power.[64] Such a connection is still found in the fourteenth-century Middle English poem *Sir Gawain and the Green Knight.* Here the head is once again an extreme symbol of life and supernatural power, as the otherworldly figure of the Green Man is linked with a cephalophore by his ability to recover his own severed head and put it back in place as though nothing had happened.[65]

Popular symbols of life, death, and rebirth, the foliate heads that pullulate in many Christian buildings, such as the Portuguese church of São João Baptista in Tomar, are part of an ancient lineage whose potential symbolism seems deeply rooted in human imagination. A solution to the problem of making nature present and visible, the Green Man appears with striking similitude in different places at different times.[66] Other times, it suffers a metamorphosis in a continuum of space and time, as seems to happen in places such as the actual basilica of *San Silvestro in Capite* (Roma), where the pre-existence of a temple with strong animistic influences seems to have never been erased. Thus, the ancient Aurelian Temple of the Sun, the walls of which were decorated with foliage friezes and highly detailed green men sculptures,[67] would become a church dedi-

---

61 This is the case for at least two of the Victoria and Albert Museum's *Johannesschüssel* alabaster sculptures (one made in Germany, between 1430 and 1450, and the other made in England between 1470 and 1490), which still bear wax remains on the hollow backs. Information available online, accessed February 4, 2013, http://collections.vam.ac.uk/item/O120641/head-of-st-john-the-head-unknown/.

62 London, British Library, Taymouth Hours, MS Yates Thompson 13, fol. 108r.

63 This is also suggested by sculptures like the Baptist's head of the Cathedral of Naumburg (thirteenth century), whose expression is strikingly similar to that of so many Green Men; his mouth open, the tongue slightly pulled out, and the plate decorated with flowers.

64 See Jean Chevalier, Alain Gheerbrant, *Dicionário dos Símbolos* (Lisboa, 1994), 136–37; Baert, *Caput Johannis in Disco.*

65 See *Sir Gawain and the Green Knight,* trans. Joseph Glaser (Indianapolis, 2011), 16–17.

66 See Basford, *The Green Man,* 9–14 (see also plates 1–10); Phyllis Araneo, "Green Man Resurrected: An Examination of the Underlying Meanings and Messages of the Re-Emergence of the Ancient Image of the Green Man in Contemporary, Western, Visual Culture" (master's thesis, University of the Sunshine Coast, 2006), 7–12.

67 Accessed February 4, 2013, www.gerty.ncl.ac.uk/photo_details.php?photo_id=1469.

cated to St. Sylvester, and some centuries later, would have received a relic said to be the head of St. John the Baptist himself.

As another nature of man, and a personification of nature, the Green Man will accompany the urges of his own time, absorbing new realities and conflating with his animal counterpart, the Wild Man.

Wild Men: Not Always Wild and Sometimes Green

When compared with the Green Man, the Wild Man seems to be a much more complex character, since his features are outlined with greater clarity. He was certainly the object of a long literary and iconographic construction that endowed him with a specific psychological and physical profile, with narratives of his own, and an important role in tales and popular festivities.

Symbol of rude masculinity, overwhelming strength, and uncontrolled lust, he descends from characters as disparate as (or as similar as) the Mesopotamian Enkidu, the Greek Herakles, Silenus, and satyrs, the Roman fauns, the Biblical Samson, or even Elijah.[68] Alien to civilization, for his inability to speak, his wild behaviour, and his beastly appearance, with a body covered in dense fur, he is protagonist of the monstrous races, the medieval inhabitants of the borders of the (un)known world.[69]

In the medieval imagination, Wild Men were a frightening race of people that haunted forests, mountains, and wild places, commanding animals (and occasionally fighting them), killing the men who dared to enter their realms, and abducting the women who passed nearby. In art, they fulfil that same need for projecting men's inner fears: the fear of the forest, with animals that could kill him, plants that could hurt him, and evil spirits that could deprive him of salvation; but also the fear of himself, of his own irrationality, his violent and impulsive behaviour, and his sexual urges, so hard to repress. No one has summarized it better than Richard Bernheimer:

> It happens that the notion of the wild man must respond and be due to a persistent psychological urge. We may define this urge as the need to give external expression and symbolically valid form to the impulses of reckless physical self-assertion which are hidden in all of us, but are normally kept under control.[70]

By opposing himself to a wild counterpart, man could feel his own behaviour as a proper one—for as irrational as he could be, he would never be as bad as a *wodewose*. By projecting his own anxieties onto another being, with a specific name and shape, he would be rationalizing and self-exorcizing them.

This exercise of self-control through otherness is quite clear in art, as we find so many depictions of fights between men (usually knights) and Wild Men. Some of them

---

68 For the long lineage of the medieval Wild Man see, for example, Richard Bernheimer, *Wild Men in the Middle Ages: A Study in Art, Sentiment, and Demonology* (Cambridge, MA, 1952), 22–49; Husband, *The Wild Man*, 7–12; Gabriel Cusac Sánchez, José Muñoz Domínguez, *Los Hombres de Musgo y su parentela salvaje: el mito silenciado* (Salamanca, 2011), 23–33; Kaufmann, *The Noble Savage*, 29–43.

69 See Husband, *The Wild Man*, 1–18; Bernheimer, *Wild Men*, 12 and 33.

70 Bernheimer, *Wild Men*, 3.

are depictions of fights caused by the shameless lust of the Wild Man, who kidnaps a lady to keep her as a sexual object and is later punished by a knight who shows up to save her. Here too, one is able to see men projecting their own behaviour in their wild counterpart, for although we know sexual aggression toward women was frequent in the Middle Ages, the only surviving visual depictions of this phenomena seem to be the ones that feature the Wild Man as the perpetrator of rape. This is perfectly exemplified by the narrative developed in some of the folios of the above-mentioned Taymouth Hours. In the first two scenes, we see a crawling *wodewose*, peering furtively at two maidens chatting behind the security of a castle's walls. Once they decide to leave the castle for a walk in the woods, the lustful Wild Man rushes in and eagerly grabs one of them. As she screams and struggles to get free from the brute's arms, an old man appears and kills the Wild Man.[71]

On other occasions, the cause of the fight is unknown, but iconography is explicit regarding the superiority of the knight[72] that, following the literary example of Alexander the Great himself,[73] kills the beast without mercy—in yet another psychological purgative process. Hunting the Wild Man and ultimately killing him is, thus, a moral duty of the good knight, whether he goes in defence of a lady or simply in search of adventure. To rationalise one's fears, vices, and sins, and ultimately eliminate them is, thus, a process of perfection that only the civilized man can reach.

Obviously, this is only one of the possible readings of this characters' wildness, for the deep immersion of the Wild Man in the purifying experience of solitude and communion with nature was frequently seen as a means of remitting human sin. In the so-called Smithfield Decretals (ca. 1340) marginal narratives, wilderness and wildness are equated with spiritual improvement. One of the many moralizing stories on display is that of a lustful hermit and an adulterous woman: her husband discovers their affair and the monk kills him. Then, consumed by guilt, he confesses himself, strips off his clothes, and hides in a cave, where he becomes a wild man. Depicted with the body covered in fur, surrounded by animals, he is compared to the figure of the Wild Man as lord of the animals and noble savage: this is, indeed, the moment of his beatitude and forgiveness, since the next scene shows him already dressed (sign of recovered civilization), leaving his cave while another monk leads him back to the monastery.[74] Another lavish example of the redeeming character of wildness is the depiction of the life of St. Mary of Egypt in the desert: through twelve different folios of the same Decretals, the Egyptian sinner is presented as a Wild Woman, queen of the beasts; she feeds them with her own three loaves of bread. The harshness of her desert is suggested by the multiplication of trees

---

71 BL, Taymouth Hours, Yates Thompson 13, fols. 60v–63v.

72 This is clearly visible, for instance, at the scene of the Wild Man hunt in the *Queen Mary Psalter*, 1310–1320, London, British Library, MS Royal 2 B VII, fols. 172v–173.

73 *Le Roman d'Alexandre* was widely read throughout the Middle Ages, since at least the twelfth century. It appeared in numerous editions and versions and was the source of various depictions of Alexander's life and deed. See, for example, Gaignebet, *Art profane et religion populaire*, 122 and 124; Husband, *The Wild Man*, 51–8.

74 *Smithfield Decretals* (Decretals of Gregory IX), ca. 1340, France; MS Royal 10 E IV, fols. 114v–118v.

Figure 15.4:
Olivier de Gand and Jean
d'Ypres, Wild Man at
the altarpiece of the Old
Cathedral of Coimbra,
1498–1502, Coimbra,
Sé Velha (© Diocese
de Coimbra).

and the layers of green grass, although the whole experience of penance is presented as an Edenic one.[75]

Despite these exceptions, which would only become the rule from the end of the fifteenth century onwards, Wild Folk represented a negative counterpart of civilized man and his world. One particularly interesting example may be found in a sixteenth century Portuguese silver dish depicting a *psychomachia* in the form of a confrontation between Wild Men, wild beasts, and knights.[76] Through the relief frieze, one can see Wild Men in their traditional activity of fighting animals such as lions, dragons, and even unicorns. They are closely followed by three knights, or soldiers, that seem to be there not to fight the wild animals (because the Wild Man, being their lord, could do this better than anyone), but to catch, tame, and civilise Wild Men themselves. The progression of that control and domestication seems to be illustrated by different stages of beastliness, pointed out by the different kinds of hair covering the *wodewoses*.[77] One of them—the one that seems to have been made captive—is very close to a huge snail, which reinforces the superiority of the knight, stating implicitly that the Wild Man, though brave when in confrontation with wild animals, may become a coward once put before a sword.[78]

In fact, when he is not brandishing his wooden club, the Wild Man uses a more sophisticated, but possibly not a more prestigious weapon: the bow and arrow. As one may see in various works of art, such as a capital from the collegiate church of Santa

---

75 *Smithfield Decretals*, BL, Royal 10 E IV, fols. 274v–280v.

76 Standing dish (*salva*), sixteenth century, silver-gilt, Lisboa, Museu Nacional de Arte Antiga.

77 Alternatively, these different types of fur could suggest the presence of different, highly imaginative sub-species of Wild Men.

78 The connection of snails and cowardice is easy to grasp in many medieval illuminated manuscripts and sculpted reliefs, where the size of the animal is enhanced in comparison with his counterpart, usually a frightened knight. For further information on this theme see, for example, Lilian Randall, "The Snail in Gothic Marginal Warfare," *Speculum* 37, no. 3 (1962): 358–67.

Maria da Oliveira (in Guimarães), and the altarpiece of the aforementioned Old Cathedral of Coimbra,[79] Wild Men were considered to be proficient users of bow and arrow, a weapon that was condemned by the Church and disdained by the noble knight, for being mostly used by cowards and marginals, sometimes curiously called "wild boys."[80]

A similar statement of civilization and superiority through the taming of Wild Folk is suggested by the heraldic role of the Wild Man. During the fifteenth and sixteenth centuries, Wild Men and Women were abundantly used as heraldic tenants on the shields of great families of the time. Appearing in illuminated books, engravings, stained glass, caskets, goldsmith works, and wood and stone sculptures, they imply an obedience to their "owners" that, in previous centuries, could hardly be imagined. Although Spanish art is by far more lavish in examples of this kind, some eloquent examples may be found in Portuguese art. One of them is the fifteenth-century limestone tomb of João de Albuquerque,[81] which dis-

Figure 15.5: Wild couple from the renovation of the rotunda. Convent of Christ, sixteenth century, Tomar, Portugal. (© Convento de Cristo, Tomar).

plays a wild couple holding the heraldic shield of the deceased's family on one of its faces. Entangled with sinuous branches of wild rose bushes, their childish bodies and facial features make them nature's children more than embodiments of woodland terrors. They are already tamed and thus they share with the *putti* and angels that inhabit

---

79 Capital from the main portal of the Church of Santa Maria da Oliveira (Guimarães), fourteenth century; Altarpiece of the Old Cathedral (Coimbra), made by Olivier de Gand and Jean d'Ypres between 1498 and 1502. This work is also mentioned in Maria José Goulão, "Do mito do Homem Selvagem à descoberta do 'Homem Novo': a representação do Negro e do Índio na Escultura Manuelina," in *IV Simpósio Luso-Espanhol de História da Arte. Portugal e Espanha entre a Europa e Além Mar* (Coimbra, 1988), 326.

80 Le Goff, *L'Imaginaire médiéval*, 157–61.

81 Tomb of D. João de Albuquerque, fifteenth century, Museu de Aveiro (Aveiro). This work is also mentioned in Goulão, "Do mito do Homem Selvagem," 326–28.

the other faces of the tomb the positive role of intermediaries between life and death, sin and salvation.[82]

Wild Men, now frequently accompanied by their female counterparts, as in the famous wild couples of the *rotunda* of the templar Convent of Christ at Tomar (ca. 1515),[83] become thus more familiar, less hirsute and violent, bringing an exotic quality to the lives of the elite—the same elite that used to *chase* them and soon would be envying them for their ingenuity, and their simple and natural way of life.[84]

The next step in the iconography of both Green and Wild Men in Portugal, from the end of the fifteenth century on, is the progressive (though not univocal) merging of these imaginary beings with the real men that Portuguese navigators met in newly discovered contexts of wilderness.[85] This fusion is clearly visible in the re-invention of Green and Wild Men with their typical elements, but with Brazilian, Indian, or African features, as in the capitals of São João Baptista church. Later on, these real men will definitely take the iconographical, as well as the mental, place of the medieval Wild Men, and will return to a margin that is either allegorical and paradisiacal or simply ornamental. This is, in fact, a very interesting example of the progressive replacement of a proto-anthropology—the so-called "monstrous anthropology" (*antropología monstruosa*),[86] perfectly illustrated by Hartmann Schedel's map—[87] to a modern, ethnographical, and positive approach to the Other. The space occupied by a folkloric, sometimes quite mythological character that embodied men's fears and anxieties about the vastness of his own world and self, will be progressively filled with references—some more truthful and impartial than others—to strange, uncivilized, impulse-driven beings that seemed (at least) real humans. Even though this transformation is quite clear, this conceptual distinction, which is mainly operative, could never imply an absolute separation between two ways of perception that coexisted for a long time.

Two of the best iconographic examples of this process in Portuguese art come from Coimbra and Tomar. The first one is the church of the monastery of São Marcos, frequently called the "pantheon of the Silva family," for housing various tombs of its founders. In one of them, the fifteenth-century tomb of Fernão Teles de Meneses,[88] two Wild

---

82 Craveiro, "O Anjo Moderno," 59–60.

83 Capitals, sixteenth century, Templar Convent of Christ (Tomar).

84 Goulão, "Do mito do Homem Selvagem," 322–23.

85 For a synthesis of these transformations, particularly their influence on Wild Man imagery, Goulão, "Do mito do Homem Selvagem," 321–45. Though directly related to the Spanish discoveries, the following essay is worthy of further attention: Stanley L. Robe, "Wild Men and Spain's Brave New World," in *The Wild Man Within. An Image in Western Thought from the Renaissance to Romanticism*, ed. Edward Dudley, Maximilian Novak (Pittsburgh, 1972), 39–54.

86 Maria José Goulão, "Do Homem Selvagem ao Índio Brasileiro. A construção de uma nova imagem da humanidade na arte europeia de Quinhentos," in *A Carta de Pero Vaz de Caminha. Documentos e ensaios sobre o achamento do Brasil*, ed. Luís Donisete Benzi Grupioni (Rio de Janeiro, 2000), 173.

87 Hartmann Schedel, *Liber Chronicarum* (Nürnberg Chronicle), woodcut illustrations by Michael Wolgemut and Wilhelm Pleydenwurff (Nürnberg, 1993), fol. 12v.

88 Tomb of Fernão Teles de Meneses, Diogo Pires-o-Velho, 1490, Church of São Marcos (Coimbra). This work is also mentioned in Goulão, "Do mito do Homem Selvagem," 326–28.

Men are dramatically presented, in a marginal though clearly visible location, opening the curtains of the funerary niche to unveil the effigy of the deceased. On the lower frieze of the tomb, a Green Man disgorges vigorous foliage inhabited by inconspicuous animals. While the location and the physical features of the Wild Men are typical, this Green Man is far more singular, since he was given the face of an African negro, a ubiquitous character of Portuguese late medieval (or early modern) society, that by then is also becoming a usual presence in visual art, literature, theatre, and music. Likewise, another two tombs of the same family depict two Wild Men as heraldic tenants, and two Brazilian Indians.

Though this connection between real and imaginary *savages* deserves a thorough and exclusive enquiry, it nevertheless points to common schemes of categorization and apprehension of the novelty of things never seen before (and thus described through analogy and comparison to known realities), as much as it deals with the projection of the self through the many faces of alterity.

Green and Wild: The *Silvestre* and the *Salvagem*

Thus, even the most superficial analysis of the metamorphosis that both Green and Wild Men went through in medieval art, discloses the symbolic, and sometimes even visual, ambiguity of these two supposedly different characters. In fact, not only do they seem to share a common symbolic ground—that of a vital, untamed, and amoral Nature—and even some physical features—the *wodewose* is sometimes a green and leafy creature, for instance—as they occasionally merge into one single character. This happens, for instance, in a depiction of the month of September in the Bedford Hours. Enclosed in a round orchard, an old man, with white hair and beard and a body fully covered in bright green leaves, contemplates the fruits of his own time and labour. Over his head, a caption reads *vertõpnus*, a name that becomes more explicit in the text inscribed at the bas-de-page: "How in the month of September Vertumnus yields his fruits."[89] As a survival of the roman god Vertumnus, this personification of the seasonal fertility of nature, both tamed and wild, is neither a wild nor a green man, but a fusion of both—a *silvestre*.

In Portugal, this iconographic fusion between the Green and the Wild Man doesn't seem to have clear expression. Nevertheless, some images show us that the distance between these figures may be very tenuous and artificial. For instance, in the same standing dish mentioned above, one of the Wild Men is completely deprived of bodily fur (despite the long beard and hair), and is wearing a kind of foliage jacket. A very similar figure appears in one of the carved corbels of Conceição Velha's façade, at Lisboa (sixteenth century), but this time it seems like a Green Child, dressed in leaves, and accompanied by a hound and a hare. Likewise, the identification of real "wild men," such as sub-Saharan Africans and Brazilian Indians, with both the role of the Green and the Wild Man seems to point in that same direction, suggesting the possibility of a conceptual conflation of both figures.

---

89 *Comment ou moys de semptembre vertompnus rent son fruit*, Bedford Hours, Book of Hours, Use of Paris, ca. 1410–1430, British Library, MS Add. 18850, fol. 9v.

Although this phenomenon deserves further research and attention, it is worth noting the contribution of another way of imagining and depicting these same figures, materialized in late medieval literature and, especially, theatre and novels.[90] In various works of Gil Vicente, official playwright of kings Manuel (1495–1521) and his son, John III (1521–1557), we notice a great fluidity in the portrait of the Wild Man, commonly present in medieval and early modern plays, parties, and parades. Through the plays, one finds references to names or titles such as *São João o verde* ("St. John the Green") and *Juan de la Greña* ("John of the Bush"), that put us either in the presence of a Wild Man disguised in leaves (the *folhudo*) or a hirsute one. This single creature, both green and wild, is thus metamorphosed through the natural cycles of the year and imbued with a "double symbolic role"[91] that Spanish folklore itself knows very well, for example, in the figures of the Moss Men of Béjar.[92]

In the tragi-comedy *Triunfo do Inverno* ("Triumph of the Winter"), presented to King John III in Lisboa (1529),[93] the author introduces Winter's character by saying: "the winter enters wild, speaking Castilian."[94] This Winter is thus a Wild Man who reinforces this introduction by presenting himself as *Juan de la Greña*.[95] Eager to intensify his rude, hairy, and wild appearance, he indirectly confirms his identification with the common type of the medieval Wild Man. In fact, not only the word *grenha* immediately evokes (either in Portuguese or in Castilian) the hirsute aspect of the *wodewose*, but also the linguistic derivations of that word remind us of that same impetuous and violent character: *grenha* may refer to a dense forest or wood; *desgrenhado* is an adjective applied to a shaggy look; and in Spain, the expression *andar a la greña* meant to fight or to discuss violently.[96]

Proud of himself, this winter archetype assumes his own being as a portent, a gigantic presence that, despite his look of "brute wild man",[97] is able to dominate the elements and throw chaos and discomfort in men's lives, especially in the lives of those who are more dependent on nature's benevolence, such as the shepherds. In fact, if the ancestors of the medieval Wild Man can be traced back to the ancient spirits of nature, protectors of flocks and shepherds—such as fauns and satyrs—this offspring seems to consciously ignore that benign side, assuming only the most harsh and violent aspects that Nature may assume.

------

90 For an excellent contextual analysis of Portuguese medieval literature, folklore, and iconography, see Ana Cristina Leite, Paulo Pereira, "São João o Verde, o Selvagem e o Gigante em Gil Vicente – apontamento iconológico," in *Estudos Portugueses. Homenagem a Luciana Stegagno Picchio*, ed. Francisco Bethencourt, Diogo Ramada Curto (Lisboa, 1991), 371–88.

91 Leite, "São João o Verde," 371–88.

92 Cusac, Los Hombres de Musgo, 65–133.

93 Gil Vicente, *Copilaçam de todalas obras de Gil Vicente a qual se reparte em cinco liuros* (Lisboa, 1586), fols. 204–15.

94 *O Inverno vem salvagem castellano en su dezir.* Roughly translated from Vicente, *Copilaçam de todalas obras*, fol. 203.

95 Vicente, *Copilaçam de todalas obras*, fol. 203.

96 Vicente, *Copilaçam de todalas obras*, fol. 203.

97 *Salvage bruto.* From Vicente, *Copilaçam de todalas obras*, fol. 203.

We know, though, that this personification of Winter is actually presented as a pure force of Nature, deprived of any sense of justice, of good or evil, when he says that his icy, windy presence is real for good and bad people alike: "I make the good and the bad close windows and doors, and I make the orchards weep for the death of the gardens."[98] The further dialogues show us that Winter is a period of natural violence which is not welcomed by men, much less for those who are forced to work without shelter.

Later, and in the middle of the torments that form the Triumph of Winter, the *wodewose* doesn't want to be limited to earthly realms and, extending his power over the seas and those who navigate its waters, evokes his allies, the sirens/mermaids, that usually appear in iconography as close neighbours of both Green and Wild Men: "I want to demonstrate my power on the sea because the earth likes the cold storms I want to command. I will make the sirens sing and endanger the ships."[99] Curiously enough, this same entourage has its iconographical counterpart in works such as the Flemish altarpiece in the Old Cathedral of Coimbra, whose foliate frame shows vain, mirror- gazing mermaids next to rushing Wild Men and fabulous creatures of symbolic nature.[100] Certainly aware of the old, mythological, and almost archetypal fights between Winter and Summer, Gil Vicente brings this one onstage, not bragging, but singing instead. This character is not immediately described or presented, but appears as a symbol of regeneration and renewal, a positive force that returns to replace the order stolen by Winter: "Return the beauty to every thing in its degree to the flowers their whiteness to the earth its greenness that the wild weather has stolen."[101]

In spite of this positive attitude towards Summer, in contrast with the unpleasant Winter, the text goes on to a kind of Christian acknowledgement that Nature, even in its most favourable and kind temper, is still very weak when compared with Divine perfection. When the Mountain (another character of the play) decides to offer the king a garden, an "earthly heaven," a group of young men and women appear, singing: "Who says that he is not St. John the green",[102] as if saying, "Is this not St. John the Green?" These two verses, not very explicit, may play an ambiguous part in this whole metamorphic cycle of seasons: are these young people addressing Summer, personified in St. John the Green (predictable counterpart of *Juan de la Greña*), or are they addressing the king himself? The ambivalence seems to be intentional.

---

98 *Hago a buenos y a roynes cerrar ventanas y puertas y hago llorar las huertas la muerte de los jardines.* Cited from Vicente, *Copilaçam de todalas obras*, fol. 203.

99 *Yo quiero sobre la mar demonstrar mi poderio pues la tierra gusta el frío tormentas quiero ordenar. Haré cantar las serenas y peligrar a las naves.* V Cited from icente, *Copilaçam de todalas obras*, fol. 210.

100 Altarpiece of the Old Cathedral (Coimbra), made between 1498 and 1502 by Olivier de Gand and Jean d'Ypres.

101 *Buelvase la hermosura a cada cosa en su grado a las flores su blancura ala tierra su verdura quel bravo tiempo a robado.* Cited from Vicente, *Copilaçam de todalas obras*, fol. 212v.

102 *Quem diz que nam he este sam Joam o verde.* Cited from Vicente, *Copilaçam de todalas obras*, fol. 214v.

But, even more important than this is a clear expression of an awareness of the transience of life, of the frailty of all beauty, even those born with the Triumph of Summer, for "all the things created have their end determined some for a long time, others shorter and others for a medium time."[103] These verses are close to the thirteenth-century English verses that Kathleen Basford related to the image of the Green Man as a symbol of death and cyclical renewal: "So here's a thought your teeth should clench 'All greenness comes to withering'."[104] And indeed they provoke the indignation of Summer, who cannot help remarking that the beauty of flowers and gardens is possible only through him. In a kind of moralizing climax, the character of the Infant states the superiority of a symbolic garden of God, almost as if recalling that all personifications and allegories, so dear to theatre and literature as well as visual arts, are nothing more than reminders of old naturalist cults, acceptable from the point of view of man himself, a natural being, but offensive when considered as something superior to God's Law. Summer may create beautiful flowers, of course, but he doesn't have the power to endow them with an eternal beauty, nor preserve them from decay and death. Nature itself lives with that commitment to transience and the only way to Salvation comes from the stability of God's power:

> If by this you say pieces / because these flowers you make / you make and unmake them / you make them bloom and dry.

> And the holy garden of God / blossoms without fading / that are then no longer] / is the work of weak skies / which have no fixed power.[105]

Paulo Pereira saw in this idea of a garden, heaven or a Golden Age, a connection with the socio-cultural role of the *Sylvan* Man (*homo silvestris*, no longer simply *homo selvaticus*). This same connection is, in fact, one we can apply to the symbolic reading of the presence of wild couples in the circular apse of the Church of the Convent of Christ in Tomar, also a symbolic "Orient," inhabited by these decayed creatures that were formerly linked to Heaven (like the first couple) and for whom the word of God may provide Salvation.[106] But, besides this moral role of the new Wild Man—whether or not merged with his green counterpart—there's a sociological role that helps to understand his growing popularity, as it will appear in festivities, parades, churches, and domestic settings alike, at the hands of the urban elites of late medieval Europe.[107] Simultaneously a favourite

---

103 *Todalas cousas criadas tem seu fim determinado dellas per tempo alongado dellas mais abreviadas delas per curso meado.* Cited from Vicente, *Copilaçam de todalas obras*, fol. 214v.

104 Basford, *The Green Man*, 18.

105 *Se por este dizes pecas / porque essas flores que fazes / tu as fazes e desfazes / tu as floreces e secas. E o santo jardim de Deos / florece sem fenecer / que o ser e logo nam ser / é obra de fracos céus / que nam tem fixo poder.* Cited from Vicente, *Copilaçam de todalas obras*, fol. 215.

106 See Craveiro, "O Anjo Moderno," 59–60; Pereira, *A Obra Silvestre e a Esfera do Rei*, 255–260.

107 Previously pointed out by Richard Bernheimer, the sociological and ideological implications of the late medieval domestication of the Wild Man have been further and thoroughly developed by Florent Pouvreau in a comprehensive study on the Wild Man: Florent Pouvreau, *Du poil et de la bête. Iconographie du corps sauvage en Occident à la fin du Moyen Age (XIIIe–XVIe siècle)* (Paris, 2015), 172–74.

heraldic device, a highly entertaining character, and a moralizing tool, he serves the purposes of an empowered king, a languishing aristocracy, and a rising bourgeoisie:

> By the mise-en-scène of the wild body, the nobles affirm their symbolic domination over the forest while displaying, to a larger audience, the values on which their ethics and identity are built (courage, strength, devoutness, fidelity), along with their erotic courtliness. By assimilating and appropriating courtly values and aesthetics, the great urban bourgeoisie also participates in the success of this figure. Festivities and city entries, tomb slabs or tapestries are some of the many mediums that testify the fondness of the urban patriciate for the wild man in the last century of the Middle Ages.[108]

In any case, the gradual identification of the Wild Man as the Good Savage brings forth this eminently urban setting of his rehabilitation and domestication. By corresponding to the bucolic idyll of a modest and frugal life, in direct contact with raw Nature and uncompromised with the artificial codes of urban society, the wild man (even if still a *brute savage*, to quote Gil Vicente once again) provides a counter-example to the futility and vice of life in the world.[109]

Conclusions

As long-lasting products of the medieval imagination, Green and Wild Men are figures deeply compromised by the ideological framework of a period that was neither uniform nor paradoxical. No more, at least, than any other period beyond its chronological range.

Thus, despite their secular connection to chivalric literature and courtly amusements, their intrinsic connection to a self-directed projection of humanity in its biological and physical, but also cultural and moral nature, makes them the feral offspring of an all-encompassing religious view of the world. Though apparently disruptive, these embodiments of the wildest aspects of nature and mankind are precious pieces in the complex gear of ecclesiastical rhetoric, working within the framework of the dominant Christian ideology; reinstating its triumph over paganism and superstition; confirming its role in the atavic cycle of life, death, and rebirth; confronting men and women with their irrational and amoral counterparts, just to progressively domesticate them and put them at service. Both exotic and fearsome, the hirsute *wodewoses* and the enigmatic leafy faces that lurk in the corners, sides, frames, and borders of churches, books, liturgical vessels and luxury items, tapestries, and frescoes, are alluring props of a scenery carefully planned to impress and overwhelm the viewer. And, in medieval Portugal as in any other place in what would become Europe, this viewer was invariably a believer. So, it is not surprising to find in the metamorphoses outlined above a close connection to the paths and strategies of a Church in a constant quest for ideological uniformity and stability.

---

108 *Par la mise en scène du corps sauvage, les nobles affirment leur domination symbolique sur l'espace forestier et diffusent auprès d'un public plus large les valeurs qui constituent son éthique et son identité (courage, force, dévouement, fidélité), ainsi que son érotique courtoise. La grande bourgeoisie urbaine, en même temps qu'elle assimile et s'approprie des valeurs et l'esthétique courtoise, participe également au succès de la figure. Fêtes et entrées de villes, lames funéraires ou tapisseries sont autant de médiums qui témoignent du goût du patriciat urbain pour l'homme sauvage au dernier siècle du Moyen Âge.* Cited from Pouvreau, *Du poil et de la bête*, 270.

109 See Pouvreau, *Du Poil et de la Bête*, 143–145, 172.

This ideological manipulation becomes quite clear in Portuguese occurrences of the Wild and the Green Men in the period corresponding to the government of King Manuel. Placed at the porous border between late medieval and early modern art and history, this period is marked by a clear centralization of royal power, anchored in visual propaganda in which the King, the Kingdom, and the Church are presented as inseparable entities, working as a triumphant triad ready to civilize and evangelize a newly discovered mankind, along with the old antagonists of Christian faith, such as Muslims and Jews. And in Portugal, there is no other period more fertile in depictions of the Green and the Wild Man in the visual and the performing arts, than the last decades of the fifteenth century and the first quarter of the sixteenth. Though this frequency cannot be explained by the more or less subtle changes occurring in the anthropological mindset of contemporary men, or the ideological positioning of the Church regarding the need for conversion and reception of the soon-to-be new Christians, it is nevertheless clear that these are major forces at play. Between this role as the embodiment of men's fear of his own irrationality, imaginary counterparts of real *wild people*, allegories of the vitality and harshness of untamed Nature, both Green and Wild Men seem to depart from the illustration of vice and sin to become instruments of a moral commitment to humility, resilience, and contempt by a defiled world. And this was a timely metamorphosis in a moment when, all over Europe to some extent, devotion was becoming an increasingly intimate affair, at the verge of the first protestant advances. Neither uniform nor paradoxical, though, this is also a time when the reinforcement of powerful monarchies—as in Portugal and Spain—grows along with the protagonism of the Church, playing a key role in the establishment of values such as uniformity, orthodoxy, civility, and civilization. And between the blooming of a Christian humanism and the rooting of a Catholic Reformation, there was still time to explore other natures of man.

Chapter 16

MILITARY MODELS FOR NOBLES IN ZURARA'S NORTHERN AFRICAN CHRONICLES

ANDRÉ LUIZ BERTOLI

GOMES EANES DE Zurara (1410?–1474) wrote four works about the Portuguese in Africa:[1] *Crónica da Tomada de Ceuta* (1449–1450); *Crónica de Guiné* (1452–1454); *Crónica do Conde D. Pedro de Meneses*, composed between 1458 and 1464, which tells us about the Captain of Ceuta during the years 1415–1437; and *Crónica do Conde D. Duarte de Meneses*, a chronicle written between the years 1464 and 1468 that highlight the Captain of Ksar es-Seghir[2] in the period 1458 to 1464.[3] We will examine here the ideal models held up for Christian military personnel, particularly what it meant to be a "Good Captain" and to be "Daring Warriors."

---

1 This chapter is a broader and more detailed study of a text presented to the Seminar II–Doctoral Classes in Medieval History at the Faculdade de Ciências Sociais e Humanas da Universidade Nova de Lisboa (FCSH–UNL). The author is grateful to Dr. Maria de Lurdes Rosa, who helped shape the original text; Dr. Marcella Lopes Guimarães for her suggestions; and Begoña Farré, who helped with the English.

2 A small, fortified town (known as *Alcácer Ceguer* to the Portuguese) on the northernmost tip of Morocco opposite Portugal.

3 For this chapter I have made use of Gomes Eanes de Zurara, *Crónica da Tomada de Ceuta*, ed. Reis Brasil (Sintra, 1992). This chronicle is composed of one hundred and five chapters divided into five parts: prologue and introduction; the decision and preparations to attack Ceuta; the struggle between Christians and Muslims; the knighting of the Portuguese Princes, and also King João I's decision to keep the conquered city; at the end, their return to Portugal; and a conclusion. I made use too of Gomes Eanes de Zurara, *Crónica do Conde D. Pedro de Meneses*, ed. Maria Teresa Brocardo (Braga, 1997). This version is the book that began as Maria Teresa Brocardo's doctoral thesis. It was based primarily on MS 439 produced in the beginning of the sixteenth century, which can be found in the Biblioteca Geral of the Universidade de Coimbra. This chronicle is divided into two books, for a total of one hundred and twenty-two chapters (eighty-two in the first book and forty in the second), and they are divided into four parts, two in each book (Maria Teresa Brocardo, "Introdução," 9–10): prologue; Pedro de Meneses' men's actions to defend Ceuta; a narrative of events from Ceuta and in the kingdom; and Duarte de Meneses' deeds leading the warriors' actions during the last years of his father's captaincy. Finally, I made use of Gomes Eanes de Zurara, *Crónica do Conde D. Duarte de Meneses*, ed. Larry King (Lisboa, 1978). Originally this chronicle contained one hundred and fifty-six chapters, but in manuscripts preserved today, thirty-eight entire chapters are missing and twenty-one are incomplete. In other words, there are ninety-seven complete chapters that can be divided into three parts: prologue; Duarte's actions alongside his father; and the narrative of battles against the Moors in North Africa from 1437 until 1464, when Duarte died. Among the sources used as the basis for Zurara's narratives, oral testimonial accounts and official documents should be mentioned. Their use allowed the chronicler to present a history favourable to royal interests (Brocardo, "Introdução," 11).

André Luiz Bertoli (andrelbertoli@gmail.com) is Researcher at the Universidade Nova in Lisboa.

Zurara's works were part of a writing project to legitimize the power of the Portuguese royalty and nobility, as well as to justify their actions in a specific place, Africa. This project is explicit in his Northern African chronicles, which, sometimes, have stretches in common. His Moroccan trilogy tells of the Lusitanians' achievements in North Africa from the conquest of Ceuta in 1415 until the death of Count Duarte de Meneses in 1464. All Zurara's chronicles together—including the West African *Crónica de Guiné*—describe the Portuguese conquests in North Africa and their voyages and raids along the African coasts.

The context described (1415–1464) is wider than the time in which Zurara wrote his works (1449–1468). The former witnessed several political upheavals: agreements and alliances—or their breaking—in the Iberian Peninsula and Christendom; conflicts between Christians; the war against Muslims; and successful or ill-fated adventures, including conquests and sacrifices.[4] The chronicler sought to legitimize Portugal's expansionist policy in North Africa. However, what really matters for this research is that, within the context of warfare marked by the clash between Christians and Muslims, acts of bravery, cowardice, violence, and clemency were used by Zurara to impose ideal models on the Portuguese Christian nobility. Based on this thesis, I shall present preliminary research on these "Northern African" chronicles, with a particular focus on the depiction of warriors aimed at those who fought for the Portuguese king in Africa.

I will then go on to explore more closely several chapters in these chronicles, all of them expounding the martial values that defined the Lusitanian nobility's chivalric profiles. These chapters focus on actions or orders of five individuals: King Afonso V; Prince Henrique; Pedro de Meneses, Captain of Ceuta; Duarte de Meneses, Captain of Ksar es-Seghir; and Rodrigo Afonso, Afonso V's squire, who fought alongside Captain Duarte.

---

4 The resumption of the war against Muslims since the conquest of Ceuta (1415); the beginning of an expansionary policy beyond the Iberian Peninsula, confronting Castilian interests in the Atlantic and Africa; getting politically closer to Aragon; crossing the *Bojador* (1434) and travels along the African coast; the disaster of Tangier (1437) and Prince Fernando's captivity; a succession crisis following the death of King Duarte (1438) and Afonso V's minority; a Portuguese Regency that turns its back on Aragon and moves closer to Castile; the death of Fernando in captivity (1443); the Regency ends, followed by an intestine crisis that resulted in the battle of *Alfarrobeira* (1449); seeking papal support—with the pope sometimes supporting Portugal, other times Castile—for Portuguese conquests and occupations in Africa and the islands in the Atlantic; the intention to start a crusade in the east after the Turks take Constantinople (1453); the conquest of Ksar es-Seghir (1458); and so on. We see a fifteenth century marked by the pressure that various groups exercised on the Crown, which did not decrease, but changed in in relation to different interests (see further Luís F. F. R. Thomaz, *De Ceuta a Timor* (Lisboa, 1994), 60; Fátima R. Fernandes, "A participação da nobreza na expansão ultramarina portuguesa," *Revista de Estudos Ibero Americanos* 26 (2000): 119; Humberto B. Moreno, "Balanço de um século no Portugal anterior ao encontro do Brasil," *Arquipélago – História* 5 (2001): 554; Renata C. de S. Nascimento, "Os privilégios e os abusos da nobreza em um período de transição: o reinado de D. Afonso V em Portugal (1448–1481)" (PhD diss., Universidade Federal do Paraná, 2005), 9). In this troubled milieu, the initial expansion into North Africa depended much more on a number of individual initiatives than from any planning made by the Crown (see Thomaz, *De Ceuta a Timor*, 205; João P. O. e Costa, "D. Afonso V e o Atlântico, a base do projecto expansionista de D. João II," *Mare Liberum* 17 (1999): 40–41 and 57–58). Even before the 1430s, divergent interests relating to war in Morocco had already been reported in Portuguese documents, such as *Livro dos Conselhos de El-Rei D. Duarte*.

Essentially, these chapters were selected because Zurara highlights exemplary warlike attitudes that were part of the whole relationship of medieval man to war: obedience to the captain versus performance of chivalric prowess. The chronicler did not retell the events in a simple way since there were other variables in setting out "reality" in his historical-literary description.

Consequently, this paper draws attention to archetypes defined for the Portuguese warriors who must fight in North Africa. In the episodes I show, what Zurara presents are models of action in war: sometimes the faithful and diligent warrior who does not abandon his lord regardless of the risks; elsewhere, the captain who faced all adversities while maintaining his prudence, thus becoming the most exemplary leader for a threatened outpost in North Africa; sometimes, also, the archetype of the valiant and stubborn knight, the "New Crusader" represented first by Prince Henrique and later by King Afonso V.

The first and second models represent primarily the captain and his men, who must constantly defend the Portuguese outposts in the Maghreb: prudence and fortitude being the virtues highlighted. The third model was normally exalted in attacks and conquest situations, being the embattled Christian knight who displays courage and strong commitment to the Christian faith while facing the "unfaithful" Muslim. Generally, but not always, those who represented the last model did not live in or guard the settlements in North Africa, but rather went there accompanying a noble, prince, or king to accomplish military deeds for their own honour and glory.

The Representation of Portuguese Noble Warriors

Before describing particular models let us first examine Zurara's objectives (and by implication those of Afonso V) and the importance of memory and writing in constructing these ideals. Marcella Lopes Guimarães considers the texts produced under the king's orders and commissioned by the Avis dynasty as "medieval codices which aim perhaps to answer the aspirations of the old nobility and to educate the new one."[5] So, employing the quill, the *literati* preserved the memory of royal power and legitimized its exercise, as well as justifying the use of violence by the nobility. Zurara's situation matches the definition by Guimarães—based itself on Jacques Verger's conceptual framework[6]—whereby the chroniclers Fernão Lopes and Gomes Eanes de Zurara were men of learning in the court, being part of a group committed to producing tailored knowledge.[7] While continuing Lopes's work as the kingdom's chronicler, Zurara's goals diverged from Lopes's objectives.[8]

---

5 Marcella Lopes Guimarães, "A ensinança de evitar o Pecado na prosa de D. João I e D. Duarte," *Revista de História da UPIS* 1 (2005): 25.

6 Jacques Verger, *Homens e saber na Idade Média* (Bauru, 1999).

7 Marcella Lopes Guimarães, "Estudo das representações de monarca nas Crônicas de Fernão Lopes (séculos XIV e XV): o espelho do rei – 'Decifra-me e te devoro'" (PhD diss., Universidade Federal do Paraná, 2004), 45.

8 They had different objectives simply because the interests varied in each period. In the 1430s, Fernão Lopes legitimized the dynasty itself, building a victorious history and an image of union

But both focused on narratives of internal conflicts, wars, and models of conduct.[9]

Zurara's depictions of Portuguese society, nobility, and royalty reflected the interests of the Avis dynasty. Thus, according to Daniel Orta, this chronicler wrote about royalty and nobility, under the auspices of and at the request of the king because "the inclusion of some men in these texts meant not only their heroic representation, but also the possibility that others of their lineage could receive benefits and have an example to follow",[10] as seen in the following excerpt from the *Crónica da Tomada de Ceuta*:

> Do not assume that I did not employ great diligence seeking and knowing all the deeds of other Lords. Not only the main Lords, but either, I would write their deeds if I found worthiness, or should I know anyhow, knowing that the will of the King, my Lord, is to know perfectly all the merits of his naturals to honour the memory of the dead and to remunerate the living by their work or their parents' work.[11]

Similarly, in *Crónica do Conde D. Duarte de Meneses*, the letter sent by Afonso V to Gomes Eanes de Zurara while he was in Ksar es-Seghir is significant. This letter highlights the importance of writing in terms of preserving the memory of men and their deeds. This made it easier for the king to know who was worthy of receiving favours and benefits as a result of the actions they performed in his service.[12] So, the actions reported in or omitted from the chronicles were important with regard to benefits and losses that could affect some nobles.

Consequently, warfare and the gift of benefits or favours (*mercês*) were necessary strategies used by the newly-established Avis dynasty to gain the nobility's support because those nobles who fought for the king expected to receive privileges.[13] Thus, the conquests in Africa offered the location and the opportunity for part of the Portuguese nobility to rise socially, as well as offering a way to relieve tensions within the kingdom.[14] This warrior movement resulted in a renewal of relations between royalty

---

between different subjects: monarchy, nobility, clergy, and the third state, the last, in Lopes's words, being the *arraia miúda*; but from 1449, in his narratives, Gomes Eanes de Zurara legitimized a royal policy choice—the expansion to North Africa—almost totally excluding the action of certain subjects like the *arraia miúda* and primarily Prince Pedro, his kin, and followers.

9 King, "Introdução," 25.

10 Daniel A. Arpelau Orta, "Escrita, poder e glória: cronistas tardo-medievais portugueses e a nobreza no primeiro movimento expansionista no noroeste africano (c. 1385–1464)" (master's thesis, Universidade Federal do Paraná, 2007), 67.

11 *Nem presuma algum que eu não pus tamanha diligência em requerer e buscar todos os aquecimentos dos outros senhores. E não ainda daqueles principais, mas de qualquer outro do povo, escrevera seu feito, se o achava em merecimento, ou o pudera saber por qualquer guisa conhecendo bem que a vontade de el-Rei meu senhor é perfeitamente saber todos os merecimentos de seus naturais para honrar a memória dos mortos, e remunerar aos vivos por os trabalhos de seus padres ou deles mesmos.* Cited from Eanes de Zurara, *Crónica da Tomada*, 248.

12 Eanes de Zurara, *Crónica do Conde D. Duarte*, 41–43.

13 José Mattoso, *Fragmentos de uma composição Medieval* (Lisboa, 1993), 137, and Fernanda Olival, "The Military Orders and the Nobility in Portugal, 1500–1800," *Mediterranean Studies* 11 (2002) 75.

14 Arpelau Orta, "Escrita, poder e glória," 71.

and nobility because, with certain limits, the Crown was able to increase the nobility's dependence as a result of the royal favours granted to those who served the king.[15]

Apart from the benefits granted to those considered worthy, Zurara also intended to exalt and promote profiles of the noble warrior. Silvio Queirós has drawn attention to the pedagogic character of Zurara's texts as he used chivalric images in his description of some members of the royal household as an additional resource to strengthen their power.[16] From King Afonso's letter mentioned above and the chronicles, one can more clearly perceive the value that Afonso V gave to such writings, especially those that dealt with the "history" of great heroes, kings, and lords.[17]

Besides the *Crónica da Tomada de Ceuta*, Zurara's last two chronicles also narrate in a certain sense "a family saga" in North Africa—they are royal chronicles that highlight the actions of two members of the Meneses noble family. Along with Zurara's prior works, these texts about the Meneses contributed to the kingdom's "official chronicles," which represented the Portuguese project of conquering North Africa, the exercise of Christian chivalry, and the triumph over the Muslims.[18] Brocardo considered these texts as "private chronicles,"[19] aimed at chivalric and noble glorification.[20] Authorized and commissioned by Afonso V, one intention of Zurara's chronicles was to extol the main characters' virtues in the exercise of chivalry and war.[21] As a result—conforming to the monarch's will—Zurara praised the warrior nobility, creating and disseminating examples to be followed.[22]

To build warrior models contemporary to his time, the chronicler found their basis in archetypes shown in earlier works: the *Crónica Geral de Espanha*, *Livro de Linhagens do Conde Pedro Afonso*, Lopes's chronicles, and similar. So, in Zurara's texts we find references to military actions of certain exemplary individuals who exercised leadership and were militarily prominent against Muslims: notably Rodrigo Díaz de Vivar, *el Cid*;[23] Alfonso VI, King of Leon and Castile, *Imperator totius Hispaniae*;[24] Afonso Henriques

---

15 António Dias Farinha, *Os portugueses em Marrocos* (Lisboa, 1999), 27–28; Nascimento, "Os privilégios e os abusos," 88; and Arpelau Orta, "Escrita, poder e glória," 71.

16 Silvio de Galvão Queirós, "'Pera Espelho de Todollos Uiuos' – A imagem do Infante D. Henrique na Crônica da Tomada de Ceuta" (master's thesis, Universidade Federal Fluminense, 1997), 196.

17 Eanes de Zurara, *Crónica do Conde D. Duarte*, 42–43.

18 Luís Krus, "Crónica," *Dicionário da Literatura Medieval Galega e Portuguesa*, ed. Giulia Lanciani, Giuseppe Tavani (Lisboa, 1993), 174.

19 Brocardo, "Introdução," 10.

20 Krus, "Crónica," 174.

21 Costa Gomes, "Zurara, Gomes Eanes de," *Dicionário da Literatura Medieval*, 687–88.

22 Krus, "Crónica," 174; André Luiz Bertoli, "O Cronista e o Cruzado: a revivescência do ideal da cavalaria no outono da Idade Média Portuguesa (séc. XV)" (master's thesis, Universidade Federal do Paraná, 2009), 147–48.

23 Eanes de Zurara, *Crónica da Tomada*, chap. 11, 65. I provide here and elsewhere the part and/or chapter of the original work, with the pagination from the edition afterwards.

24 Eanes de Zurara, *Crónica da Tomada*, chap. 11, 65.

(Afonso I), the first Portuguese King;[25] Alfonso VIII, King of Castile who led the Iberian Christian coalition in the battle of Navas de Tolosa;[26] Paio Peres Correia, the master of the the Order of Santiago Order, who had a key role in the conquest of the Algarve.[27] But we might ask: to whom were those models aimed? On this topic,[28] Zurara's ideological references and constructions of models were directed at reaffirming the renewing the nobility,[29] but mostly, to the rising nobility in carrying out services in the Maghreb and along the coasts of Africa.

The Good Captains: Pedro and Duarte de Meneses as Models of Prudence

Let us now focus on the actions of the two Meneses, through Zurara's eyes. He high-lighted the following aspects: prudence, faithfulness, and obedience.

In the fifth chapter of *Crónica do Conde D. Pedro de Meneses* when the chronicler named who was chosen by João I to become the captain of Ceuta, Zurara listed the ideal qualities: to be a good knight; to be noble; to have many followers; and to be brave, tough, and prudent in war.[30] Some men turned down this position of great responsibil-ity and honour—or debacle, but Zurara wrote that Pedro de Meneses offered himself to take on the captaincy of Ceuta if it were to please the king.[31] Being supported by the Master of the Order of Christ—his uncle—and by the prior of the hospital and Prince Duarte—to whom he was ensign—Pedro received this captaincy from João I.[32] He took on a difficult post, captain and defender of Ceuta, a city nestled in Muslim territory. Zur-ara's narratives present Pedro as being successful in his tasks.

Zurara made clear that prudence was one of the main virtues for the captain of Ceuta in order to defend this African city.[33] This is reinforced in the eighth chapter, when Zur-

---

25 Eanes de Zurara, *Crónica da Tomada*, chap. 11, 66; Eanes de Zurara, *Crónica do Conde D. Pedro*, pt. 1, chap. 12, 217.

26 Eanes de Zurara, *Crónica da Tomada*, chap. 11, 65.

27 Eanes de Zurara, *Crónica do Conde D. Pedro*, pt. 1, chap. 12, 218.

28 Also seen Marcella Lopes Guimarães, "A ensinança."

29 Taken from María Concepción Quintanilla Raso, "La renovación nobiliaria en la Castilla Bajomedieval: entre el debate y la propuesta," in *La nobleza peninsular en la Edad Media. Actas del VI Congreso de Estudios Medievales*, ed. Juan Ignacio Ruiz de la Peña Solar (León, 1999), 259 and 277.

30 "Needed here are not only strong and resilient men, but also prudent and versed in war" (*[...] caa nõ soomemte hera neçessario homem ardido e forte, mas aymda prudemte e avisado no auto da guerra*). Cited from Eanes de Zurara, *Crónica do Conde D. Pedro*, pt. 1, chap. 5, 197.

31 Also narrated in Eanes de Zurara, *Crónica da Tomada*, chap. 100, 283.

32 Eanes de Zurara, *Crónica do Conde D. Pedro*, pt. 1, chap. 5, 198.

33 "[Y]ou should consider that the job you have requires, first, that you be a good Captain, then a good Knight, and [...] must work to let all thy deeds be made with great care. Vegetius says in the *Livro da Arte da Cavalaria* that prudence belongs more to Princes and host rulers than to any other Knight, not only because their doctrine and example all others would copy, but, also, your damage could hinder many others" (*[...] caa deveis de cõsyrar que o carrego que temdes rrequere que primeiro sejaes boom capitão e depois bõo cavaleiro, e [...] vos deveis de trabalhar que todos vossos feitos façam co gramde rresguardo e avisamemto, ca diz Vegecio no "Llyvro da Arte da Cavalaria" que aos // primçipes e rregedores da oste pertemçe mais a prudemçia que a cada h~u dos outros*

ara "gave literary voice" to King João I, who supposedly said those who stay in Ceuta had to be tough, prudent, and must obey the Captain in this city defence, their main task.[34] But it can be seen through the *Crónica do Conde D. Pedro de Meneses* that they did not just defend their outpost; they also attacked Muslims villages and cities, sometimes under Pedro de Meneses' leadership, at others without the captain's orders, but always exercising their prowess in chivalry.

The first struggle between Christians and Muslims appears in Chapter 14.[35] Some Portuguese noblemen boldly attacked the enemies, even without Pedro's order,[36] an act of disordered chivalry. After that, in the same chapter, we see the prudence in Pedro and in the decision of the noble council. They determined not to let the nobles and soldiers go out to attack the Muslims—described as a daring and devious enemy—[37] without the captain's orders. Otherwise, they could lose Ceuta faster than the Portuguese army had conquered it.[38]

So, intending to warn the Portuguese in Ceuta, Zurara recounted Captain Pedro's reprimands and, in some cases, punishments directed to particular disobedient and reckless defenders of Ceuta. The chronicler also explores the consequences of indisci-

---

cavalleiros, porque não soomemte o seu emxemplo e doutrina à-d'aproveitar a todollos outros, mas aymda o seu dano pode empecer a muitos). Cited from Eanes de Zurara, *Crónica do Conde D. Pedro*, pt. 1, chap. 29, 292.

34 Eanes de Zurara, *Crónica do Conde D. Pedro*, pt. 1, chap. 8, 205–6.

35 Eanes de Zurara, *Crónica do Conde D. Pedro*, pt. 1, chap. 14, 226–29.

36 "But who were on the wall, seeing such audacity, did not wait the Captain's order, but as they could, they grabbed their weapons and got out very boldly against them, where there occurred a strong and large skirmish. [...] And because Earl Pedro was far away, in another part of town against *Almina*, he belatedly knew about that clash, and mainly because those who wanted to be in the fight did not dare to tell him, fearing he would contradict them. But the rumour ran through the town and reached him, who rapidly hastened there and did not want to give way for Christians to depart from the wall, because it was all surrounded by trees, as we have already said, and he feared that perhaps there were other Moors hidden with the intention to make a trap, and so he did remove all Christians" ([...] *Mas os nossos que estavão sobre o muro, vemdo tall atrevimemto, nom quiseram esperar liçemça n~e mamdado do capitão, mas assy como poderam tomarão suas armas e muy ousadamente sairõ a elles, omde se volveo h~ua forte e gramde escaramuça. [...] E porque o comde dom Pedro hera lomge dally, na outra parte da çidade comtra // a Allmina, ouve rrazão de saber tarde as novas daquelle rrebate, e primçipallmemte porque aquelles que desejavam ser na pelleja nõ ousavam de lhas hir dizer, tememdo-se que os contrariasse da sayda. Peroo ho rrumor correo pella çidade e chegou omde elle estava, o qual trigosamente acudio pera aquella parte e nõ quis dar lugar que se os cristãos allomgassem do muro, porque hera todo cercado d'arvoredos, como jaa dissemos, e temeo que porvemtura estevessem outros mouros emcubertos com temção de lhes fazer allg~u e~gano, e por e~ fez rrecolher todos cristãos*). Cited from Eanes de Zurara, *Crónica do Conde D. Pedro*, pt. 1, chap. 14, 227–29.

37 On the one hand, Zurara exalts the enemy in order to aggrandize the Portuguese achievements; on the other hand, his depiction of them as evil justifies their attacks on Muslims. So, while the chronicler represents the Muslims as a great enemy—either in number or in honour of those who led them, such as Aabu (see Eanes de Zurara, *Crónica do Conde D. Pedro*, pt. 1, chap. 17), they are also represented as treacherous, volatile infidels.

38 Eanes de Zurara, *Crónica do Conde D. Pedro*, pt. 1, chap. 15, 229–31.

pline, well characterized in the narrative of Álvaro Afonso's death.[39] In *Crónica do Conde D. Pedro de Meneses*, the latter died because he went out to ransack Muslim villages, disobeying Pedro de Meneses' orders. Zurara considered his death as an example of "bad fate" for those who are too bold and undisciplined. A bad outome, yes; but in certain moments, a fate exalted by the chronicler when he writes, "the good and virtuous always chose the fields in front of the enemies' weapons as their graves."[40]

In his chronicles, Zurara shows that the guardians (note, not conquerors) of North African settlements should not take too many risks nor be undisciplined and disobey the captain; otherwise they would diminish their defensive capacity, an inglorious action. Thus, the captain should find the balance between military aggression and prudence, sometimes stimulating boldness and at other times caution in order to defend and hold Ceuta.

Concerning the *Crónica do Conde D. Duarte de Meneses*, the key chapters for this study are chapter 44, in which Captain Duarte de Meneses challenges his half-brother to one-to-one combat so that he might gain honour and fame;[41] and chapter 154, in which the Captain—albeit reluctant and fearful, he is loyal—accepts the king's command that he join a dangerous attack even though it could cost his life.

Earlier, in the third chapter of the *Crónica do Conde D. Duarte de Meneses*, Zurara describes the character, virtues, and physical appearance of Count Duarte, portraying him as a man destined to bear arms; having great authority and lordly qualities; devoted to God; fair, honourable, and loyal. This illegitimate son grew up in an environment (Ceuta) marked by constant hostility with the Moors. Zurara attests this in the fourth chapter,[42] when the chronicler connects father and son in his storyline.[43] Brought up close to Pedro, Duarte supposedly followed his father's example in terms of character and conduct. Therefore, in Zurara's narratives, Pedro had a martial and audacious, yet still cautious personality, which is the image Zurara reflected in Duarte too.

I shall focus now on chapter 44[44] for its clear dichotomy between Christian and Muslim. Zurara describes a one-to-one combat, unique in this text, with each warrior representing one side: Portugal and Fez. The Christian warrior was Rodrigo

---

39 Eanes de Zurara, *Crónica do Conde D. Pedro*, pt. 1, chap. 53, 397–404.

40 *Os bõos e virtuosos escolheram sempre por sepulltura os campos que estam amte as armas dos ymigos.* Cited from Eanes de Zurara, *Crónica do Conde D. Pedro*, pt. 1, chap. 34, 310.

41 According to José Mattoso, honour was what differentiated the nobility from the rest of population. Honour meant honesty, but it was more than that because it had been converted, in the most typical ideological expression of aristocratic superiority, into senses of dignity, prestige, strength, authority, or valour. Mattoso, *Fragmentos de uma composição*, 158.

42 Eanes de Zurara, *Crónica do Conde D. Duarte*, chap. 4, 51–55.

43 Zurara had already stated this proximity: "[A]nd he also had a son by the name of Duarte, who later was Earl of *Viana de Caminha* and Captain of Ksar es-Seghir, that in the knightly deeds showed that he had the good blood of his father" (*[...] E ove tamb~e h~u filho a que chamarão dom Duarte, que depois foy comde de Viana de Caminha e capitão da villa d'Allcaçer, o quall nos feitos da cavalaria mostrou// bem a bomdade do samgue que trazia do padre*). Cited from Eanes de Zurara, *Crónica do Conde D. Pedro*, Part 1, Chapter 3, 184.

44 Eanes de Zurara, *Crónica do Conde D. Duarte*, chap. 44, 136–37.

Afonso,[45] King Afonso V's squire and Duarte de Meneses' brother on the maternal side;[46] the Muslim warrior was anonymous. Furthermore, the chronicler presents an ancestral ideal of warrior behaviour that still resonated in the nobility and chivalry of the late medieval period, as we shall now see.

Zurara begins his account of the siege of Ksar es-Seghir by emphasizing the magnitude of the military force behind the King of Fez, as this makes the Portuguese triumph the more glorious.[47] Allegedly, it was a huge force defeated by less than two thousand men who were defending Ksar es-Seghir. Besides the scale of the opposing force,[48] the chronicler also underlines the noble status of forty-two captains, *Alcaides*, and *Marins*, who led various groups under the king of Fez.

From here on, the one-to-one combat takes centre-stage. At the beginning of the Muslim siege of Ksar es-Seghir,[49] as described by Zurara, a Moor approached the town to challenge Portuguese defenders, seeking to discourage them and to glorify himself in front of his peers.[50] This enemy's courage did not deter the chronicler from comparing

---

45 Rodrigo Afonso appears sixteen times in *Crónica do Conde D. Duarte de Meneses*, all of them in combat as a man who carried out daring actions, fighting against Muslims and any other threat to the Portuguese domains in North Africa. He was under the orders of Duarte de Meneses and his son, Henrique. Therefore, one can point to Rodrigo Afonso as a "special subordinate" in the military actions of his brother and nephew, as he appears in Zurara's narrative as always willing to follow their orders in combat.

46 Eanes de Zurara, *Crónica do Conde D. Duarte*, chap. 42, 131.

47 Eanes de Zurara, *Crónica do Conde D. Duarte*, chap. 44, 136.

48 Supposedly more than twenty thousand men, but readers should question these numbers. In a different study, it would be interesting to reflect on who those people were, because they probably were not all combatants. References give the impression that actions of non-combatants in military activities were of no importance, but this does not tally with reality, because even those who did not take a direct part in the conflict became involved in war (Christopher Allmand, "War and the non-combatant in the middle ages," in *Medieval Warfare: A History*, ed. Maurice Keen (Oxford, 1999), 254; Miguel Gomes Martins, "*Para bellum*. Organização e Prática da Guerra em Portugal durante a Idade Média (1245–1367)" (PhD diss., Universidade de Coimbra, 2007), 755). As Christopher Allmand and Miguel Martins have observed, many of the men present in a conflict situation would have been peasants who brought food supplies, while others were workers needed to build materials to keep an offensive or defensive position. In addition, one cannot forget the "marginals," those who accompanied a military campaign in search of some profit—all kinds of marginalized people and criminals convicted in their own lands. But, as we know, medieval chroniclers generally extrapolated the value of individual or small cavalry/nobility groups. Obviously, in the Portuguese Ksar es-Seghir ranks, there would also be camp-followers and non-combatants, but since they were surrounded, everyone had to fight. If the enemy took Ksar es-Seghir, it would not differentiate between combatants and non-combatants. For possible outcomes of medieval sieges, see: João Gouveia Monteiro, *A guerra em Portugal nos finais da Idade Média* (Lisboa, 1998), 368; Joseph F. O'Callaghan, *Reconquest and Crusade in Medieval Spain* (Philadelphia, 2004), 135–40; Gomes, "*Para Bellum*," 643–44.

49 This fortified place had been conquered by the Portuguese on October 24, 1458. Later that year, on November 13, 1458, Ksar es-Seghir was besieged by the Marinid Sultan Abd al-Haqq II, the king of Fez, who tried to recover it (Eanes de Zurara, *Crónica do Conde D. Duarte*, Chapter 44, 136). The one-to-one combat is set during this siege.

50 Eanes de Zurara, *Crónica do Conde D. Duarte*, chap. 44, 137.

the Moor's image to servants of the devil.[51] In this way, Zurara represented the Moors as being more susceptible to passions and temptations, which led them to act rashly and underestimate their enemies. Zurara's representation of the ideal warrior is completely the opposite, because he should be Christian and prudent—though not always, as seen in some actions of Prince Henrique and King Afonso V.

The Christian response was rapid, as the captain realized that if this enemy was not punished, such Portuguese inaction would encourage others to come forward and risk an attack on the walls of Ksar es-Seghir. The chronicler said that the captain's order to Rodrigo Afonso was to capture or kill this audacious Moor, as an example to deter others. The squire—who was of less important lineage—accepted the order.[52] Clearly victory in battle would increase the value of his lineage and the honour of this warrior; even so, if he were defeated, at least his family could collect the "value" of his death and honour from the king through "recognition of the legal effects of 'martyrdom,' including fixed remuneration and various kinds of compensation, particularly for physical injuries."[53]

Furthermore, from our knowledge of martial practices in such a context, if Rodrigo Afonso had not followed the captain's order, he would be in a dishonourable situation that could disqualify him in front of the warrior nobility, because he would be going against warrior values of honour, courage, loyalty, and obedience. This reinforced the image of the Portuguese warrior that the chronicler had built up in his earlier works, because showing ability on the battlefield was most important, defining the honour of a knight or a squire.[54]

This struggle might simply be an allegory used by Zurara as a narrative strategy to represent the Portuguese victory over the Muslims who besieged Ksar es-Seghir. Who knows if it really happened?[55] Regardless, this episode served Zurara's panegyric

---

51 Eanes de Zurara, *Crónica do Conde D. Duarte*, chap. 44, 137.

52 Eanes de Zurara, *Crónica do Conde D. Duarte*, chap. 44, 137.

53 Maria de Lurdes Rosa, "Por detrás de Santiago e além das feridas bélicas. Mitologias perdidas da função guerreira," in *Actas das VI Jornadas Luso-Espanholas de Estudos Medievais. A guerra e a sociedade na Idade Média. 6 a 8 de Novembro de 2008*, ed. Maria Helena da Cruz Coelho, Saul António Gomes, António Manuel Rebelo, 2 vols. (Coimbra, 2009), 2:383–84.

54 Richard W. Kaeuper, *Chivalry and Violence in Medieval Europe* (New York, 1999), 130.

55 It is worth noting that Zurara does not indicate his source for this episode, nor indicate if it was reported to him by a witness or if he found it in some written source, but he (re)constructed the episode as follows: "And so, Rodrigo Afonso left and headed firmly against the Moor, with whom he fought. The Moor, with bold action, wished to show that he had heart. And then, with strong courage, he fought against his opponent. Rodrigo Afonso, from his side, remembered the reason he had been sent out, worked hard to make the Moor acknowledge his inferiority, and with many wounds he sent his soul to the other world as a messenger of many that soon would make that trip. And the body was lying there without a head, because Rodrigo Afonso, at his brother's request, or to settle himself, took it by the hair in his hand" (*E // assy Rodrigo Affonso foy fora assy aderençou riJamente ao mouro com o qual ouue sua pelleia. ca o mouro assy como tomara antre os outros aquelle atreuymento assy quis mostrar que o nom fezera sem myngua de coraçom. E assy com animo forte se combateo com seu contrayro. Rodrigo Affonso doutra parte nembrado da fim pera que ally fora enuyado trabalhou tanto que fez ao mouro conhecer a melhorya que auya sobre elle E com muytas feridas mandou a ssua alma ao outro mundo assy como por messegeyra das muytas que*

discourse. As read in the narrative, both combatants were committed to defeating the adversary and, consequently, providing a tough lesson for the enemies' morale. Each character represented—with his sword and his life—a belief, a culture, a realm, and a king. In this fight, there would be no mercy for the defeated, contrary to the religious values of both sides, but they would honour their warrior values.[56]

This can be seen when Rodrigo Afonso, the Christian, not satisfied with killing the enemy, decapitated him and left his body while he took the head as a reward after the Moor's defeat. This outrageous act enraged those Moors who witnessed it. In war situations, and especially in medieval sieges, any act of violent intimidation could affect the enemies' morale.[57] Quoting Sean McGlynn, "everywhere, terror and atrocity are present as a manifestation of the military imperative."[58] Even if reality matched the narrative, the account of the combat can be read in terms of narrative strategies aiming to exalt the Christian warrior and his greatness as a combatant—perhaps exaggerating it.

Now let us turn to chapters 153 and 154 of the in *Crónica do Conde D. Duarte de Meneses*. What is important here is the portrayal of acts of disordered chivalry in contrast to the caution advocated by the captain of Ksar es-Seghir. Ironically, the king himself leads the risky action. Before describing the tragic death of Duarte,[59] Gomes Eanes de Zurara wrote about Afonso V's willingness to carry out raids. He decided to launch an attack on Benacofu Sierra. As a Portuguese captain serving Afonso V in North Africa, Duarte is summoned to join his king. Even though he was against this idea because he knew the dangers of the Benacofu region, he did not refuse the king's request, as an obedient vassal described.[60]

It is perhaps worth noting in this chronicle the fact that, apparently, Duarte considered himself to be under the influence of a prophecy that foretold his death if he fought under another's command.[61] This is how Zurara announced the tragedy that would befall

---

em breue auyam de fazer aquella uyagem. e o corpo ficou ally tendido sem cabeça por que Rodrigo Affonso. Ou auisado per seu yrmãao ou por contentar a ssy meesmo a leuou cortada pellos cabellos na mãao). Cited from Eanes de Zurara, *Crónica do Conde D. Duarte,* chap. 44, 137.

56 The perception of this paradoxical relationship between warrior values and Christian piety must have guided some knights and chroniclers—who praised the warriors' actions—to seek to bridge this gap, incorporating only some religious ideas into their own. Jean Flori, *A cavalaria: a origem dos nobres guerreiros da Idade Média* (São Paulo, 2005), 92 and 138; Kaeuper, *Chivalry,* 4 and 9; Richard W. Kaeuper, *Holy Warriors: the Religious Ideology of Chilvary* (Philadelphia, 2009), 32, 35 and 36, 66–93, 94–115. Consequently, this tension between different ideals—secular and spiritual—was constant (Rosa, "Por detrás de Santiago," 384), as Christian *caritas* was confronted with the warrior conception of honour, skill with weapons, and triumph over enemies, which usually resulted in extreme violence (Kaeuper, *Holy Warriors,* 6–7).

57 Gomes, *"Para Bellum,"* 764–75.

58 Sean McGlynn, *By Sword and Fire: Cruelty and Atrocity in Medieval Warfare* (London, 2008), 252.

59 Eanes de Zurara, *Crónica do Conde D. Duarte,* chap. 153, 349–50.

60 Eanes de Zurara, *Crónica do Conde D. Duarte,* chap. 153, 350.

61 The following prophecy was made by a monk who had spiritual and "prophetic" authority: ("[F] urther, he knew that he would not die except under other's captaincy, because where he was the main Captain he would always have blessed deeds, he also knew the place where he would be hurt

the royal quest. The prudent Duarte perished while he was under the king's command.[62] Paradoxically, according to the "mirrors of princes" genre, kings should set the example of nobility, chivalry, prudence, and justice. But in the action described by Zurara, it is Afonso V who represents disordered chivalry.

At the beginning of the endeavour, the Portuguese had the advantage: separated into smaller groups, they won a few skirmishes against the unsuspecting local population.[63] If at first the king had been prudent in not sending infantry, crossbowmen, and harquebusiers to expel the Moors hiding in the forest, later he was reckless when he sent that military support to Tétouan while in a hostile environment.[64]

From this point on, the chronicler stops foreshadowing the tragedy and begins narrating it. With the falling numbers of Portuguese ready to fight, the Moors hidden in the woods started to come out and attack. When Afonso V realized this, he returned to defend his ranks. But without military support and with enemy numbers increasing, the situation became more difficult for the Portuguese forces.[65]

Besides defending King Afonso, Duarte knew how important the Royal Standard was to maintain cohesion and morale of those who were fighting.[66] As one of the most experienced men in raids against Berbers, Duarte was chosen to cover the king's retreat. He accepted, even knowing that almost everyone would leave as soon as Afonso V had gone.[67]

---

and that he would not have any of his men there, that was told to him by a monk from Sarzeda who was called Fray Luis, a man from another land who said many things, that to the experts have good or bad prophetic spirit" (*[...] quanto mais que elle tijnha sabido muitos annos auya que nom auya de morrer senom sob capitanya alhea. ca onde elle fosse capitam principal sempre auerya bem auenturados aqueecimentos. e per aquelle meesmo lugar per que auya de seer ferido. assy lhe // era dicto e como nom auya de teer ally nehuum dos seus a qual cousa lhe fora dicta per huum monge da çarzeda que se chamaua Frey luis homem doutra terra que muytas cousas taaes que segundo as particolaridades que dezia parecya aos entendidos que auya spirito profetico ou de boa parte ou de maa*). Cited from Eanes de Zurara, *Crónica do Conde D. Duarte*, chap.154, 350.

62 Eanes de Zurara, *Crónica do Conde D. Duarte*, chap. 154, 350–55.

63 Eanes de Zurara, *Crónica do Conde D. Duarte*, chap. 154, 351–52.

64 Eanes de Zurara, *Crónica do Conde D. Duarte*, chap. 154, 352.

65 Eanes de Zurara, *Crónica do Conde D. Duarte*, chap. 154, 353.

66 He was King Duarte's Ensign since the death of his father, Pedro de Meneses, who had occupied that post before him. During the Afonso V's reign, Duarte de Meneses was also made the King's Ensign. Besides, he was an experienced warrior who knows the Standard's importance in any battle.

67 "And because the danger was growing, the people kept going, and then the Earl Duarte shouted very tightly that they should be ashamed and must not abandon their King and his banner. But it was no use. The King, fighting the Moors, was advised to summon the Earl of Viana [Duarte] who, some said, spoke to Diego da Salveira 'if my predictions are true, it is my final hour.' Earl, said the King, stay with these Moors because you know their tricks and warn these people. I did not want you to say what you said at that time and gave me this work, mainly because I do not have any of my men here, because those who are here do not do your command, so they will not do mine. But, just because you ask for your service, I accept whatever happens to me. And then the King left, and the Earl was not wrong in what he had said, because almost everyone was gone" (*E por que o perigoo cada uez era mayor hyasse a gente quanto mais podya. tanto que o conde dom Duarte braadaua muy riJa / mente que ouuessem uergonha e nom desemparassem seu Rey e seu stendarte. mas aquello nom*

Trying to protect Afonso's withdrawal, Duarte was wounded and his horse was killed;[68] his destiny had already been decided. Narrating his end in a grandiloquent way, Zurara emphasized Duarte's military virtue in his last stand, surrendering his own life to save the king.[69]

In this chronicle, the captain of Ksar es-Seghir is the "mirror" of Portuguese nobility, representing the loyal, prudent, courageous, and honourable vassal. What is exposed in these episodes is a true warrior hero model, transformed into an exemplary Portuguese captain in North African territory—a position no doubt hard to occupy—permanently dealing with warrior violence and recklessness while exercising a captain's military duties. Thus, Duarte encourages temerity, but to a moderate degree, as it could benefit some less fortunate warriors; he tries to instil military prudence into soldiers and also restrain offensive war excesses, but does not refuse to follow the king's orders. He is not a coward in battle, defending Afonso right up to his death. Zurara exalts Duarte without hiding the fact that it was royal recklessness that led him to disaster. Perhaps, this was a message for the Portuguese nobility about their relationship with an over-interventionist royal power in the overseas possessions.[70]

From the actions of these captains, father and son, above all, Zurara could emphasize the profile of the warrior nobility valued by the Portuguese king. In Zurara's chronicles, he profiled the main military virtues—prudence, loyalty, obedience, and faithfulness—the ideal model for those who wished to be captains and soldiers in African settlements during the fifteenth century.

Daring Warriors: Prince Henrique and Afonso V— Models of Chivalry, Boldness, and Loyalty

A great part of the *Crónica da Tomada de Ceuta* was written based on Prince Henrique's testimonies, especially events of war. This chronicle highlights the main characters that were fighting during the Ceuta conquest, primarily Prince Henrique and the heir Duarte. In Zurara's words, Henrique was the protagonist of great deeds during the Ceuta conquest, focusing on courage, determination, and his willingness to fight Muslims.[71] While part of the nobility were glorified in war, Zurara presents the masses—Fernão Lopes's *arraia miúda*—ruthless and only interested in riches, stealing to satisfy their greed.[72]

---

prestaua nada. E veendosse elRey em trabalho com os mouros foy conselhado que mandasse chamar o conde de uyana [Duarte]. o qual dizem que disse a diego da salueyra com que hya fallando se as minhas profecyas som uerdadeyras agora he a minha derradeyra hora. Conde disse elRey ficaae com estes mouros por que lhe conhecees as manhas e acaudellaae esta gente. Eu nom quisera dizem que disse elle que em tal tempo me derees tal cuydado. principalmente por que nom tenho aquy nehuum dos meus. Ca pois estes que som presentes nom fazem uosso mandado menos faram o meu. pero pois que o uos assy auees por uosso seruiço ey por muyto bem empregado mym meesmo em qual quer // cousa que me acontecer. E entom aballou elRey e o conde nom foy enganado em seu dito. por que caasy todos partyram). Cited from Eanes de Zurara, *Crónica do Conde D. Duarte*, chap. 154, 354.

68   Eanes de Zurara, *Crónica do Conde D. Duarte*, chap. 154, 354.

69   Eanes de Zurara, *Crónica do Conde D. Duarte*, chap. 154, 355.

70   As noted by Oliveira, "D. Afonso V e o Atlântico," 63–64.

71   Eanes de Zurara, *Crónica da Tomada*, chap. 76, 232–33.

72   Eanes de Zurara, *Crónica da Tomada*, chap. 77, 234.

In *Crónica da Tomada de Ceuta*, the chronicler explored Henrique's warrior personality and martial ideas to show his commitment to fighting the Muslims. Consequently, Prince Henrique is always represented as a fearless and embattled warrior who takes action in his hands, facing dangerous situations while leading part of the Portuguese forces in Ceuta.[73] Their fight is represented as just and holy, because they were Christian warriors facing the *infidels* to recover territory for Christendom.[74]

After they had split into two groups, one led by Prince Duarte and the other by Prince Henrique, many of those who accompanied the latter were looking for fortunes and ransacking Muslim houses. Because of this, Zurara considered some of them as dishonourable people—generally the common people; but others were simply weak, morally and physically, and not real warriors;[75] and, accordingly, many perished in battle. Thus, says the chronicle, from the men who accompanied Prince Henrique, only four survived. On the contrary, Henrique and those four who kept fighting side by side are depicted as honourable, tough Christian warriors.[76] Moreover,

---

73 "What's the point of being the first Captain that the King, my lord and father, sent to occupy the land, because with so little work I had my victory, or what glory that I could have in the day of my knighting if my sword was not soaked in the infidels' blood / [...] And when the Moors came, or because they were helped by others, or because they felt that the Christians would make no great effort like the first time, they turned on them again. And made them turn their backs harder than the first time. And at their front, the Prince stumbled again, who at that time was twenty years old and had thick and strong arms and a heart to support the work. / And when he saw Christians again fleeing, this doubled his fury and he jumped again between them, attacking with such force that made them spread from one part to another. But the Christians had great fear, that most part of them passed by the prince without knowing him, not returning anymore. / [...] the Christians and the Moors could not fight, but only a few, from which the first was always the prince, whose blows were well known among all the others" (*Que me prestou a mym seer o primeiro capitam, que elRey meu senhor e padre mamdou que filhasse terra, pois com tam pouco trabalho ayia dauer a minha uitoria, ou que gloria poderey teer no dia da minha cauallaria, sse a minha espada nom for molhada no samgue dos jmfiees. / [...] E, quando ali chegaram os mouros, ou por haverem outros de novo em sua ajuda, ou por sentirem que os cristãos não traziam tamanho esforço como da primeira, voltaram outra vez os rostos sobre eles. E fizeram-lhes virar as costas com muito maior força que da primeira E, trazendo-o ante si, toparam outra vez com o Infante, o qual àquele tempo, era de idade de vinte e um anos. E havia os nembros grossos e fortes, e coração não lhe falecia nem ponto para lhe fazer suportar os trabalhos. / E, quando assim viu, outra vez, os cristãos desbaratados, dobrou-se-lhe a sanha, e saltou outra vez entre eles, e tão fortemente os cometeu que os fez desborralhar para uma parte e para a outra. Mas os cristãos traziam consigo tamanho temor, que a maior parte deles passaram pelo Infante sem haver dele nenhum conhecimento, e não tornarão mais atrás. / [...] os cristãos primeiros e os mouros derradeiros não podiam pelejar senão mui poucos, dos quais o dianteiro foi sempre o Infante, cujos golpes eram bem conhecidos entre todos os outros*). Cited from Eanes de Zurara, *Crónica da Tomada*, chap. 78, 236–37.

74 In short, the war against the infidel combined, simultaneously, religious and political aspects. Maria do Rosário Pimentel, "A expansão ultramarina e a lógica da guerra justa," in *O reino, as ilhas e o mar-oceano*, ed. Avelino de Freitas de Meneses, João Paulo Oliveira e Costa (Ponta Delgado, 2007), 301. The recovery of land for Christendom, being considered just and holy, legitimized legal, political, and military actions in war against Muslims. Dias, *Os portugueses em Marrocos*, 27–28.

75 Eanes de Zurara, *Crónica da Tomada*, chap. 79, 238.

76 "But from those seventeen who accompanied him, no more than four followed [...] But

in Zurara's words, Henrique should be the warrior example to everyone, including future kings.[77]

In chapter 79 of the *Crónica da Tomada de Ceuta*, Henrique and these four honourable warriors faced a huge number of Muslims. While they were fighting and resisting, none of them wanted to abandon the prince, even when he asked someone to look for help.[78] In this dangerous situation, fidelity and solidarity between lord and subordinates are shown, because these warrior peers were fighting for their group and captain.

---

who would have thought that the prince or any of those four who were with him could escape alive, because over that door is the wall, that is thick and strong. [...] there were many Moors that they left between them and the walls, which were full [of Moors] whose concern was none other than to disturb those Christians where they could reach with their weapons. [...] But God wants a result that they [the Moors] did not want. And, despite all their strength, the prince passed by those Moors who faced him. [...] Surely this is not a small signal, when the power of only five men had power to push a crowd with so much damage to the enemies' blood" (*Mas daqueles dez e sete que primeiramente o acompanhavam, não seguiram mais de quatro [...] Mas quem havia de cuidar que o Infante nem nenhum daqueles quatro que com ele foram, pudesse escapar, daquele feito vivo, porque sobre aquela porta está o muro, que é grosso e forte. [...] Ora seria que, cá os mouros que eles leixavam ante si eram muitos, e os muros, isso mesmo estavam cheios, cujo cuidado não era outro senão empecer àqueles cristãos, onde eles podiam chegar com suas armas. [...] Mas quis Deus que o seu desejo não houve aquela enxecução que eles com tão boa vontade quiseram. E, a despeito de toda sua força, passou o Infante além com aqueles mouros que levava ante si. [...] Por certo não é este pequeno sinal, quando o poderio de cinco homens somente teve esforço e ardileza de empuxar tamanha multidão com tamanho dano e estrago do seu sangue [...]*). Cited from Eanes de Zurara, *Crónica da Tomada*, chap. 79, 238–39.

77 "But I do not want to assign all this deed to your [Prince Henrique] strength, because I believe that our Lord God wanted to bring [him] to the world to defend his holy temple, which is His Holy Church, and to revenge the mistakes of those enemies of the faith and what they did so often against the Christians. This prince, who as His knight armoured with the Holy Cross, fought in His name. And to prove my intention, I put before my eyes the process of his [Henrique's] life, in which I found such wonderful virtues that, considering them, I think that he is a man brought into this world to be the mirror to everyone alive. Which virtues, God willing, I will tell distinctly in his own place, so you can truly know the truth of my words. 'Great Prince,' says the author, 'flower of chivalry of our realm, heart and fortitude worthy of great memory! And who else can I praise in superlative degree, that had real fortitude, but to say that this is Prince Henrique?'" (*[...] Empero não quero este feito de todo atribuir à sua força, porque considero que quis Nosso Senhor Deus trazer ao mundo por defensão do seu santo templo, que é a Sua santa Igreja, e por vingança dos erros e cometimentos que aqueles inimigos da Fé fizeram por muitas vezes aos seus fiéis cristãos, a este príncipe, que assim como Seu cavaleiro, armado das armas da Santa Cruz, pelejasse no Seu nome. E, para provar minha intenção, ponho, ante meus olhos, o processo da sua vida, no qual acho tais e tão maravilhosas virtudes, que, considerando em elas, não me parecem senão se algum homem trazido a este mundo para espelho de todos os vivos. As quais virtudes, a Deus prazendo eu contarei distintamente, em seu próprio lugar, porque possais verdadeiramente conhecer a provação de minhas palavras "O excelente príncipe," diz o autor, "frol da cavalaria do nosso reino, coração e fortaleza digna de grande memória! E qual outro posso eu louvar em superlativo grau, que houvesse a verdadeira fortaleza, salvo se disser este é outro Infante Dom Henrique?"*). Cited from Eanes de Zurara, *Crónica da Tomada*, chap. 80, 240–41.

78 "[S]ir, they answered, none of us have the insolence to leave you here, even if you were in a room, safe from all danger, we would be ashamed if we leave you being so few. And none of them ever wanted to leave, saying that fate would determine that someone would find them, dead or alive, close to him" (*[...] senhor, responderam eles, que nenhum de nós haja de filhar atrevimento para*

In 1433 Prince Pedro sent a letter to his brother and king, Duarte. In this letter, the prince wrote that it was really important to be protected by loyal servants.[79] Loyalty was a key virtue for all subordinates, particularly for the kings' vassals. It was through benevolence and loyalty in the relationship between lord and vassal that the pact of solidarity was established.[80] In a letter presented in the *Livro da Cartuxa*, King Duarte also wrote to the captains—especially those who were to go to Tangier in 1436—"remembering that I ordered my flag to you, which you must save and defend as my own person."[81] So, theoretically, everybody should be obedient and loyal to those who carried the king's authority.[82]

In the *Crónica da Tomada de Ceuta*, Zurara constructed a noble warrior model through chivalric and crusader ideals. This model is represented mainly by Prince Henrique, a fearless and resilient warrior fighting the enemy of Christendom. Consequently, Henrique's depiction is as the noble knight who has the most important Christian virtues and martial values, respecting all social rules inherent to his position. The same archetype is clear in the previous text, *Livro da Cartuxa*, especially in chapter 21, when King Duarte advises his brother Henrique about his leadership while facing the Muslim enemy at Tangier. So, in Zurara's narratives, Henrique embodied a noble warrior ideal in the African conquests, but, in some way, different from the ideal represented by the two Meneses.

Returning to the narrative in chapter 155 of the *Crónica do Conde D. Duarte de Meneses*,[83] after Duarte's death, Zurara presents more characteristics of fearlessness and—in the context of that battle—the reckless warrior, but now represented by Afonso V. After the losses just described, King Afonso only left at the insistence of those who forced him away. According to the chronicler, Afonso V did not want to retreat; on the contrary, he wanted to fight till the death against the Muslims, which he considered an honourable death and fate.[84] During the retreat, other Portuguese knights were killed, being named by Zurara because of their "honourable death" in defending the king.[85] Afonso V's warfaring and "crusading" character appears prominently in the following extract:

> Thus the King arrived at the foot of that hill followed by many Moors, where he wanted to return and fight them, but Rui Melo, who was an admiral, and João Freire, asked him to withdraw. And he, not valuing their request, turned against the Moors, who were increas-

---

vos leixar aqui, cá ainda que estivésseis em uma sala, seguro de todo perigo, vergonha haveríamos de vos leixar sendo tão poucos E, brevemente nenhum deles nunca se dali quis partir, dizendo que, pois que os a ventura assim acertara, que mortos ou vivos a par dele os haviam de achar). Cited from Eanes de Zurara, *Crónica da Tomada*, chap. 81, 243.

79 King Duarte, *Livro dos Conselhos de El-Rei D. Duarte (Livro da Cartuxa)* (Lisboa, 1982), chap. 6, 44.

80 Mattoso, *Fragmentos de uma composição*, 152.

81 *Lembrando vos que vos encomendey minha bandeira a qual deves gardar e defender como minha propria pesoa.* From Duarte, *Livro dos Conselho*, chap.21, 124.

82 Duarte, *Livro dos Conselho*, chap. 21, 122 and 124–25.

83 Eanes de Zurara, *Crónica do Conde D. Duarte*, chap.155, 355–57.

84 The same is considered in Eanes de Zurara, *Crónica do Conde D. Pedro*, pt. 1, chap. 34, 310, quoted here.

85 Eanes de Zurara, *Crónica do Conde D. Duarte*, chap. 155, 355.

ing. Oh Lord, they said, please, get out of here, due to the danger. Do not take the chance of losing the inheritance that your grandparents gained with so much work. And he, not listening to their requests, stuck the stump of the spear in the ground and leaning against it, he said: Shut up, if you knew me you would not talk like that. This is not something that I would fear, to suffer and wait for death for the faith of our Lord Jesus Christ. Whoever wants can go, because I want to die here in the service of God and the exaltation of his Holy Faith. When they heard those words, the others said among themselves, this man has the purpose of dying here. Regardless, we will take him from here. And then, each one climbed onto his horse and, almost by force, tore him away, saying, Lord, you can kill us, but you will not die here, please, hear reason, because God gave you a good understanding. And so, they took him until the horses put their feet in the river and went beyond.[86]

According to the "Crusader" image represented by Zurara, King Afonso's intention was to confront the enemies of Christianity with force and courage.[87] To do so, he sometimes put the value of prudence—so exalted by his father, King Duarte—beneath the "service to God" in his fearlessness to do battle with the Muslims. For Duarte, and also in Zurara's chronicles about the Meneses, prudence was essential for everyone, particularly for kings. They should govern their kingdoms; listen to their council; protect their lands and people; and also exercise justice, but they should not fall into temptation, nor be vicious and unfair. Neither should they risk their kingdoms for vain glories in uncertain adventures.[88]

In Zurara's *Crónica do Conde D. Duarte de Meneses*, the prudent, courageous, and honourable Duarte de Meneses took the role of a faithful servant to the king and his

---

86 *Assy chegou elRey ao pee daquelle monte muy seguydo dos mouros. onde quisera fazer a uolta a pelleiar com elles senom foram Ruy de meelloo que era almyrante e Joham Freyre que lhe pedyram por mercee que se tyrasse dally E elle menos preçando seus requerimentos uoltou contra os mouros que eram // [219r] cada uez mais. Oo Senhor disseram elles por mercee tyraaeuos daquy de tam magnifesto perigoo nom queyraaes seer aazo de se perder a erdade que uossos auoos com tanto trabalho guaanharom E elle aficado de seus requerimentos. Ficou o conto da lança no chaão e encostandosse a Ella disse callaaeuos ca se me conhecessees nom fallaryees assy. Jsto nom he cousa de que me eu aJa despantar. mas sofrer e sperar aquy morte polla ffe de nosso Senhor Jesu christo quem quiser podesse yr que eu aquy quero morrer em seruiço de deos e exalçamento de sua santa ffe. E os outros quando ouuyram aquellas palauras disseram antre ssy. este homem de preposito sta de morrer aquy. Seia de nos o que deos e o que elle quiser. mas nos todauya tyremollo daquy. E entom se enuyrom aas cambas do cauallo cada huum per sua parte. e caasy per força o arrancarom dizendo Senhor assy nos podees / matar mas per nehuum modo uos nom morreres aquy. por mercee soJugaaeuos aa rrezom pois uos deos deu tal e tam boo entender. E assy o lleuarom ataa que lhe meterom os pees do cauallo na ribeyra e passou aallem. Cited from Eanes de Zurara, Crónica do Conde D. Duarte, chap. 155, 355–56.*

87 Some years earlier, in 1456, the fall of Constantinople (1453) prompted Pope Calixtus III to proclaim a crusade against the Turks. This was welcomed by Afonso V, as evident in papal bulls and letters exchanged between him and the papacy (see documents in the *Monumenta Henricina* (Coimbra, 1960–1974). When this "mission" was frustrated, Afonso V returned to his campaigns in Africa. Portuguese forces conquered Ksar es-Seghir (1458), *Anafé* (1464), and *Arzila* (1471). The same year, the Moors abandoned *Larache* and Tangier, which were soon occupied by the Portuguese. However, if on the one hand these military endeavours benefited some of the warrior nobility who were rewarded by the king, on the other hand they led to financial and human problems. Moreno, "Balanço de um século," 554.

88 Duarte, *Livro dos Conselho*, chap. 6, 43 and 45; Eanes de Zurara, *Crónica da Tomada*, chap. 11, 66.

aims; while Afonso V took the role in use by his uncle Henrique in *Crónica da Tomada de Ceuta*,[89] the leader and main knight of the Portuguese "New Crusade." The captain of Ksar es-Seghir is praised by the chronicler but, beyond that, Zurara delineated a noble profile desired by King Afonso V for those who wished to fight for him in Africa.

A recurrent factor in this and other medieval chronicles is the role of "disordered chivalry" and "ordered chivalry" and ancestral cultural reminiscences,[90] all of which derived from the attempt to control physical strength and violence through Christianizing war and moralizing warriors.[91] It also can be seen in Zurara's chronicles, showing the paradox that defined chivalry. Even the kings, including Afonso V, can be examples of this paradox. Monarchs, captains, and knights are idealized in Christian chronicles, but in any medieval martial action the reality was rougher than the ideal.

The chronicles selected for this analysis were written between 1449 and 1468 by a contemporary chronicler. Gomes Eanes de Zurara wrote at the request of a king who sought to strengthen his power through writing and sword, and by legitimizing his expansionist strategy. In this context, the idea of Christian chivalry was ever-present and its projected virtues and values were enormously important for the nobility, besides also influencing royal policies themselves. According to Duby:

> The culture of feudal aristocracy was ordered around two basic concepts: nobility, which had spread from the upper level to the small elite of nobilities in the year one thousand; and, on the other hand, chivalry which, in turn, undoubtedly emanates from the lesser aristocracy.[92]

These cultural features are mixed, because the lower level of the nobility also influenced the whole of noble society. At the same time, as a chronicler who favoured the nobility surrounding the king, Zurara intensified the role of nobility and chivalry in his narratives. Consequently, he highlighted the Christian noble ideal opposed to the "devious" Moors.[93] This Christian/Muslim antithesis is one of the main themes of these chroni-

---

89 Bertoli, "O Cronista e o Cruzado," 149.

90 The problem of ordered versus disordered chivalry also appears in Eanes de Zurara, *Crónica do Conde D. Pedro*, Chapter 4, when Zurara writes about the supposed reasons King João I kept Ceuta. One of them was to fight "infidels" to keep the Portuguese soldiers disciplined and exercised in war, and prevent disorderly warlike action and idleness. Eanes de Zurara, *Crónica do Conde D. Pedro*, chap. 4, 193–94.

91 Rosa, "Por detrás de Santiago," 384–85 and 394. For ancestral cultural reminiscences, see also: Georges Dumezil, *Heur et malheur du guerrier. Aspects mythiques de la fonction guerrière chez les Indo-Européens* (Paris, 1999); Joël H. Grisward, *Archéologie de l'épopée médiévale. Structures trifonctionelles et mythes indo-européens dans le Cycle des Narbonnais* (Paris, 1981).

92 *A cultura da aristocracia feudal se ordena em torno de duas noções básicas: a noção de nobreza, que se difundiu a partir do nível superior, a partir da pequena elite dos nobiles do ano mil, e, por outro lado, a noção de cavalaria que, por sua vez, emana incontestavelmente das camadas menos elevadas da aristocracia.* Cited from Georges Duby, *A sociedade cavaleiresca* (São Paulo, 1989), 150.

93 Renata C. de S. Nascimento, Sylnier M. Cardoso, "História e Literatura: A Crônica do Conde D. Duarte de Meneses (Século XV)," in *Anais XXIII Congresso de Educação do Sudoeste Goiano. Educação e Meio Ambiente, Cerrado – Patrimônio em Extinção* (Goiânia, 2007), 4.

cles—as Larry King said, referring to *Crónica do Conde D. Duarte de Meneses*[94]—and the backdrop to Zurara (re)constructs the way nobility should act. In this way, Zurara tried to define an ideal of chivalry adapted to the needs of Portuguese expansion in North Africa during the fifteenth century, which, in turn, would serve as a model for military nobility elsewhere in Africa.

This study is far from complete. It can be enlarged in various aspects: for example, studying other models depicted by Zurara. Further research could analyse archetypes represented by other fifteenth-century chroniclers. Comparing different models and their contexts, it becomes easier to perceive and understand these models' continuities, ruptures, and evolutions. Furthermore, one may want to focus further on the ideals, values, and virtues linked to these models. All of these show the further potential of investigation into these chronicles and the ideologies that they present.

---

94 King, "Introdução," 34–35.

Chapter 17

LORENZO THE MAGNIFICENT: FROM PSEUDO-DYNASTIC POLITY TO THE OTTOMAN MODEL

SOPHIE SALVIATI

DURING THE PERIOD following Cosimo the Elder's return from exile to Firenze, in October 1434, until the coming to power of his grand-son Lorenzo the Magnificent, the members of the Medici family did their utmost to ensure the establishment of a dynastic policy. Indeed, Cosimo remained in the background of political life but he developed his influence among his fellow countrymen and implicitly celebrated his descendants. As for Lorenzo, he followed a political line centred more on his own person, influenced by the Ottoman model, with whom he had closer and closer diplomatic links during the years 1470 to 1480. This chapter looks at these two competing models during Lorenzo's period as de facto ruler of the Florentine republic.

Ensuring the Continuity of Medici Policy

In the years 1420–1430, the groups opposed to the Medici, led by Rinaldo degli Albizzi,[1] jealous of their own political power, were a constant menace for Cosimo de Medici.

---

1 The opposition between the two families, Medici and Albizzi, dates back to the pretentions of Rinaldo's father, Maso, who was at the centre of the Florentine oligarchy as early as 1382. After the *Balìa* in 1426, the rivalry between the two groups became violent; see "Il regime di Cosimo de' Medici e il suo avvento al potere," in *Italia quattrocentesca: politica e diplomazia nell'eta di Lorenzo il Magnifico*, ed. Riccardo Fubini (Milano, 1994), chap. 3, 62–86. As for Rinaldo degli Albizzi (1370–1442), he was sent by the Signoria to Volterra to curb a rebellion in 1428, then to Lucca; he was accused of trying to increase his riches through plundering and was called back to Firenze. In the early 1430s, he paid the debts of Bernardo Guadagni, who because of them could not get the function he coveted within the Florentine government. Guadagni, whose family home had been burnt down during the revolt of the Ciompi led by Salvestro de' Medici among others in 1378, ferociously hated Cosimo. Once Guadagni had been elected *Gonfaloniere di Giustizia*, Rinaldo degli Albizzi did not fail, through him, to oust his main rival Cosimo de' Medici, whose influence worried him, and had him exiled as it is well known. See: Antonio Rado, *Dalla repubblica fiorentina alla signoria medicea: Maso degli Albizzi e il partito oligarchico, in Firenze dal 1382 al 1393* (Firenze, 1926). Benedetto Dei also gave his vision of the events, quite a pro-Medici one: "In the year of Christ 1433, when in Florence there was a change of state between citizens and citizens, for fear and suspicion of each other and to be the greatest of the city, at the time Bernardo Ghuadagni was 'Gonfaloniere' of Justice. There was two parts and civilian bodies in Firenze, and one of them was Messer Ball of the Strozzi and Messer Rinaldo of the Albizzi and Ridolfo Peruzzi chose many other major and worthy citizens, and on the other was Cosimo de' Medi[ci] and Neri di Gino Chapponi and Messrs Agnolo Acciaiuoli and Ridolfi and Pitti and Ghuicciardini and Soderini and Martegli and

---

Sophie Salviati (sonushka.salviati@orange.fr) is Researcher at the Université Toulouse Jean Jaurès in France.

Indeed, when the time came for the members of the Signoria to change,[2] the pro-Medici party no longer had a majority; on the contrary, the new government was very much opposed to it. On September 5, 1433, Cosimo was imprisoned then exiled to Venezia. He was nevertheless called back to Firenze the following year (October 5, 1434) thanks to the evolution of the political life in Firenze and the intervention of Pope Eugene IV, and he participated discreetly but efficiently in the work of the Signoria. Without getting foreground functions, he unquestionably acquired a strong political weight. Buying the support of a few followers, he was already planning to establish a governing dynasty in Firenze, which would be destined to his descendants, a dynasty of "Firenze lovers" and not "spouses," as Pope Pius II liked to ironically emphasize.[3] Even if Cosimo had important functions in the republic of Firenze, that was not evident. He never was one of the nine priors of the Signoria, but between 1434 and 1455 he held significant offices: in 1435, 1439, and 1445, he was a *Gonfaloniere di Giustizia* three times and a member of the *Dieci di balìa* (the "War Committee") seven times; from October 1440 to February 1441 he became *accoppiatore*, replacing his brother Lorenzo who had died while filling those functions, and that was to be the only time. In 1445 and 1449 he was a member of the *Otto di Guardia* ("Police Committee"), but in accordance with the Medici speciality and tradition in financial affairs, he became an officer of the public treasury several times, from 1445 to 1448 then from 1453 to 1455.[4] Such omnipresence, albeit in the shadows, later brought him the nickname of "great puppeteer."[5]

Thanks to its *protector*, Firenze soon appeared as the *baluardo della cristianità* and showed the urgent necessity to re-establish Greco-Latin unity in order to block the

---

other great citizens, who sent the Florentine Signoria to Cosimo de' Medici and, put in tension, the practice was to make him die. Onde la parte sua provide he was condemned to be banished for all life, him and all his family. But he was confined on the road outside Firenze" (*Correvano gli anni di Cristo1433, quando in Firenze fe' mutamento di stato fra cittadini e cittadini, per paura e sospetto l'uno dell'altro e per essere i maggiori della città, al tempo ch'era Ghofaloniere di Giustizia Bernardo Ghuadagni. Erono in Firenze due parti e ssete civili, e chapo d'esse erano dall'una parte messer Palla degli Strozzi e messer Rinaldo degli Albizzi e Ridolfo Peruzzi cho' molt'altri principali e degni cittadini, e d'altra parte era Cosimo de' Medi[ci] e Neri di Gino Chapponi e messer Agnolo Acciaiuoli e Ridolfi e Pitti e Ghuicciardini e Soderini e Martegli e altri grandissimi cittadini, che lla Signoria fiorentina mando un di per Chosimo de' Medici, e, messolo in distresso, si tenne praticha farllo morire. Onde la parte sua provide si e in tal modo chondanariche lla vita sua glifuchampata e a lui e a tutta sua famiglia. Ma e' fuchonfinato via fuori di Firenze*). Cited from Benedetto Dei, *La Cronicadall'anno 1400 all'anno 1500*, ed. Roberto Barducci (Firenze, 1985), 50–51.

2 The Florentine political system was composed of the *accoppiatori*, who were in charge of making the lists of citizens that could be elected as magistrates, the *balia* made up of the ten citizens controlling the access to public functions of those chosen or elected, and the *Gonfaloniere di Giustizia*. Selected among the inhabitants of the various districts in Firenze, the politicians were often neighbours and clients of the great families of the town. See: Ivan Cloulas, *Laurent le Magnifique* (Paris, 1982), 27–30 and 54–55.

3 Franco Cardini, *La cavalcatad'oriente, I magi di Benozzo a PalazzoMedici* (Roma, 1991), 11.

4 Cloulas, *Laurent le Magnifique*, 62.

5 *Gran burattinaio*. Interview of Franco Cardini by Manuela Zadro, "L'anno che Cosimo creo l'Umanesimo," *La Repubblica*, September 28, 1989, in the Cronaca di Firenze, 3–4.

Ottomans who represented a serious menace for Occidental peace and culture. Particularly at the time of the diplomatic negotiations about its hosting of the church council in 1439 (with the Holy See, Pope Eugene IV, and the Byzantine Emperor John VIII Palaiologos), Cosimo intended to be seen as the one organizing a magnificent reception and lending the necessary money to penniless princes, whether to pay for the crusade or the expenses due to the stay of the Eastern Orthodox delegates in the city: when, with the bull *Sicut pia mater*, dated September 9, 1434, the Supreme Pontiff hesitated about the financing the Council, the cost was two hundred thousand ducats, or one hundred and twenty-five thousand florins.[6] And without hesitating, Cosimo the Elder's city agreed to lend the money. A loan was subsequently launched and on April 17, 1438, Cosimo and his brother Lorenzo lent Eugene IV ten thousand gold florins. Gradually, secure in his status of administrator of the papal court and friend of the pope, and with a strategy to give Firenze an exceptional prestige in crucial historical circumstances, Cosimo de' Medici planned considerable expenses aimed at showing Firenze as the last bulwark of Christendom. In June 1439, Firenze lent the Pope the equivalent of ten thousand ducats, and in July 1439, the Medici brothers granted him six thousand florins from their personal casket. After unity was reached with the Eastern Church (July 6, 1439), by October 9, twelve thousand ducats were owed to the Medici in Constantinople, after papal troops had defended the city thanks to financial help from the Florentine family.

While the economic aspect played a particularly important role in the ascent of the Medici family, there was also a more strictly political value in their actions: when Cosimo was a *Gonfaloniere di Giustizia*, he welcomed the pope when he entered Firenze at the beginning of the year 1439; that was one of his few public functions, but it put him in the limelight. When John VIII Palaiologos left in August of the same year, it was Cosimo again who had the honour of being allowed to add the imperial insignia to the family coat-of-arms, as a sign of gratitude.[7] Thus the hosting of the Council and the functions bestowed upon Cosimo gave the bankers' family *un' iniezione di prestigio*,[8] as Roberto Bizzocchi so well worded it. The Medici started to use the Orient and the presence of its representatives in Firenze to establish their dynasty.

It is remarkable that when the Curia was solicited into choosing Firenze as the seat of the Council after it had left Ferrara, Cosimo did not personally visit Ferrara, the city of the Estes; he preferred sending his brother there and waiting for the delegates in his own town in order to give them a better welcome, thus showing to all his own tacit and undisputed power:

> Cosimo [...] had renounced in favour of his brother precisely to be found in Firenze under
> the appearance, somewhat formal, of head of state: having come to power four years

---

6 Nicolae Jorga, *Notes et extraits pour servir à l'histoire des Croisades au XVème siècle* (Paris, 1899).
7 Raffaella Maria Zaccaria, "Documenti e testimonianze inedite sul concilio: linee per una ricerca," in *Firenze e il concilio del 1439*, ed. Paolo Viti, 2 vols. (Firenze, 1994), 1:98.
8 Roberto Bizzocchi, "Concilio, papato e Firenze," in *Firenze e il concilio del 1439*, ed. Paolo Viti (Firenze, 1994), 119.

earlier, probably with the pope's complicity, the Medici seized the opportunity of Eugene IV's return to Firenze to solemnly establish a recently implanted regime.[9]

The pope indeed left to no one else than the Medici the care of dealing with the move of the Council from Ferrara to Firenze, and even neglected consulting the Signoria as was expected, since it was the only official political and diplomatic organ.

> A significant point is that, when they came to the decisive question, those most concerned—the Pontiff and his partisans—did not address the Signoria, who on many occasions had guaranteed the promise of hosting the pope and the whole Curia in Firenze, but the Medici themselves, just as concerned as the legitimate government of the Florentine state, and maybe more, in the possibility of Firenze becoming the seat of the Council.[10]

Henceforth Cosimo intended his son Piero and above all his grandson Lorenzo to be the heirs of this key position at the heart of Florentine political life: the palace he had had built by Michelozzo on the Via Larga concentrated a whole network of clients around him, thus forming a district entirely devoted to the cause of the Medici family.

In the Line of Emperors

In the heart of the Medici palace, and functioning as a reception-room, lies the chapel, the decoration of which was commissioned to Benozzo Gozzoli and bears the unmistakable mark of Cosimo's dynastic project: in the painter's depiction of the Wise Men's pageant, everything is symbolical of the ascent of the family; even though Cosimo is only very discreetly shown, Benozzo puts three contemporaries of the Medici in a manner that fully reflects the will of Cosimo to see his grandson succeed the greatest of emperors. Thus, on the eastern wall of the chapel, on the side of the rising sun, the upcoming generation is represented by Lorenzo as a very young man dressed as the king Caspar as in the festivities of the year when the fresco was painted.[11] Behind him is a crowd of friends and connections: Galeazzo Maria Sforza, duke of Pavia, recently allied after half a century of staunch fighting against Firenze; Sigismondo Pandolfo Malatesta, lord of Rimini; the preceptors of Lorenzo and Giulano; the members of the Platonic Academy, Ficino, Salviati, and the three Pulci brothers. On that eastern wall, it is the representa-

---

9 *Cosimo [...] aveva rinunciato a favore del fratello per farsi appunto ritrovare a Firenze nelle vesti anche formali di capo dello stato: venuti al potere quattro anni innanzi non senza sospetto di complicità papale [...], i Medici approfittavano del ritorno di Eugenio IV in città per una consacrazione solenne del regime recentemente impiantato.* Cited from Riccardo Fubini, "Problemi di politica fiorentina all'epoca del concilio," in *Firenze e il concilio del 1439*, ed. Paolo Viti (Firenze, 1994), 27.

10 *È [...] estremamente significativo il fatto che, giunti al momento decisivo della questione, i più diretti interessati (cioè il pontefice e i suoi sostenitori) si rivolgessero non alla Signoria, ma ai Medici, interessati quanto il legittimo governo dello stato fiorentino, e forse anche in misura maggiore, all'eventualità che Firenze divenisse sede dell'assise conciliare.* Cited from Gianfranco Rolfi, Ludovica Sabregondi, Paolo Viti, eds., *La Chiesa e la città a Firenze nel XV° secolo* (Firenze, 1992), 70.

11 Cardini, *La cavalcata d'Oriente*. Whereas this study is by some aspects debatable and challenged by other critics, we should not forget that interpreting pictures always presents a risk of extrapolation. Therefore, we shall be careful to underline that our opinion, through Cardini's work, is a mere possibility, admittedly subjective although plausible.

tion of dawn, of renewal, of those that have chosen the right side, the faithful followers of Lorenzo, the new hope of the Medici family, crowned with the laurels reflecting his glory: the painter played on the words *Laurentius a lauro* and bestowed on Lorenzo the laurels of emperors.

On the south wall, Caspar comes just behind the emperor John VIII Palaiologos, the heir to the dying Byzantine empire, who can be recognized under his costume of middle-aged king (Balthazar), with his double-pointed beard typical of Greek sovereigns; the oldest king, Melchior, probably the emperor Sigismund of Luxemburg, the heir of the Roman-German Empire, one that was already on the wane, appears on the western wall, therefore looking at the setting sun. Lorenzo, dressed in white (*candidus*), becomes *candidatus* and rides behind John VIII Palaiologos (the middle-aged king), the fallen emperor of Constantinople, and Sigismund of Luxemburg (the oldest king), the emperor of the Holy Roman empire who died in 1437. As Richard Trexler points out, it seems quite likely that the grandson of Cosimo should become in this landscape the only heir of the *partes orientis et occidentis* of the Roman empire. The laurels form an aura around his face and chest. He is not actually wearing a crown but a laurel wreath, as if he were wrapped in the symbolical foliage. Those laurels suggest nothing less than the triumph of Roman emperors, an idea corroborated by the choice of the antique theme of the triumphal pageant of the emperor coming back victoriously from a military campaign.[12] As for the inheritance of the two parts of the empire, it might be implicit in a verse from Matthew's gospel ("they went back another way into their country") when he mentions their country [that of the Magi], using the possessive in the singular, thus suggesting the unity of their land, and through them, the East and the West reunited under the leadership of Lorenzo.

The eastern wall is all the more striking as with its bright morning light it stands in opposition to the western wall, more narrow, showing the oldest king, followed by the portraits of Medici enemies such as Maso degli Albizzi, Niccolo da Uzzano, Gino Capponi or, as usual, the most feared and most prestigious Palla Strozzi, finally eliminated by Cosimo in 1434 when back to Firenze from exile. Those are indeed powerful rivals, possible competitors, but they belong to a past generation, a declining one in the original meaning of the word, from now on eliminated and without importance. With marked allegorical allusions, the cycle of the *Cavalcata dei Magi* thus intends to show the Medici's guests (who, as mentioned before, were received in this chapel, in front of this fresco) that the Florentine landscape was changing to their advantage. No doubt, the use of historical elements to celebrate a dynasty turns this fresco into an imposing metaphor, a landscape transfigured by the ambitions of the family in power in Firenze. It is to be kept in mind that one of the main dimensions of the fresco lies in the presence of the whole *gens medicea*: indeed it is a presentation by Cosimo of his family to the Child, in the perspective of a civil engagement over several generations. Lorenzo comes first before Cosimo. Moreover, as Christian Bec points out in his booklet *Le Siècle des Médicis*, the fifteenth century was marked by a renewal of the notion of youth: a particular care

---

12 Richard C. Trexler, "Les mages à la fin du Moyen-Âge: un duo dynamique," *Les Cahiers du Centre de Recherches Historiques* 5 (1990), accessed March 7, 2013, http://ccrh.revues.org/2887.

was from then on given to children and their education, for in them lay the glory of the family and the survival of the name. Cosimo stands in the background behind Lorenzo, because the grandson is the future of the *casato*. Besides there is a legend that Nicola da Bari mentions when he compares the emperor Frederick II to the youngest king, "on whom the Child Jesus has laid his holy hands and sacred arms"[13] thus turning the young man into the Lord's anointed.

So this is a long-term investment: the fresco was ordered not for himself, but for his family and his city. That was to be the difference between the conception of art in the middle of the century and at the end of the century, when Lorenzo became a prince for whom courtiers were working.

Beyond the implicit claim for pre-eminence within the city, the Medici established their intellectual domination by assuming the position of heirs of the different empires of the history of the world. The presence of eagles (or falcons) refers both to the Roman empire and to power: they are the only birds able to ascend quite vertically towards the sun, like the Medici who were at that time undertaking a brilliantly successful social rise. In the fresco by Benozzo Gozzolli, everything tends to underline the power, both discreet and efficient, of the Florentine family.

In 1459, when Cosimo received Galeazzo Maria Sforza, the son and ambassador of his father the duke of Milano, in this very private chapel that he used as a reception-room, he addressed him a short poem showing his wish to establish a dynasty:

> Lord, those who are before you,
> as much as I can I recommend to you,
> so that you recommend them to your father,
> to whose orders they always will be.[14]

Lorenzo, in the wake of the great emperors in the northern and southern Christian world, already stood as their heir, and as a grown man relentlessly confirmed that function and privilege by appropriating the power thanks to a well-thought political, diplomatic and cultural system.

Addictissimi et observandissimi figliuoli di Sua Maestà il gran Turco

After the fall of the Byzantine capital of Constantinople in May 1453, however, symbolic affiliation of the Medici with the Emperor Palaiologos was no longer on the agenda for Lorenzo: he then turned toward the Ottoman oriental model, since Sultan Mehmet II was the new ruler of the Mediterranean world. Lorenzo stressed his pro-Turkish policy even more when he answered the pope, who solicited him about a crusade, that Florence would only take part in it when European princes could find common agreement to

---

13 *Super quem Ihesus felices manus posuit et brachio la sacrosancta.* Cited from Rudolf M. Kloos, "Nikolaus von Bari, eine neue Quelle zur Entwicklung der Kaiseridee unter Friedricht II," *Deutches Archiv für des Mittelalters* 11 (1954–1955): 166–90.

14 *Singniore, chostoro che avete avantj, / Quantun que io posso io ve gli racchomando, / Che gli racchomandiate al vostro padre,/ Del quel sempre saranno al suo chomando.* From Cosimo de' Medici, *Stanze*, 1459.

carry out a joint action, which was clearly unlikely or impossible. For instance, when in 1476 the Italian powers (Milan excepted) signed an agreement to finance the campaign of Matthias, King of Hungary, Florence promised to contribute to that new crusade; but on June 14, 1477, the Florentine government became reluctant, considering the conditions were not met to lead an action against the Turks:

> As for us, we think the conditions in Italy have changed a lot since that tax was decided, and this is why we are not able to pay for anything, except if the whole of Italy brought its contribution.[15]

Under the pretext of other preoccupations, the plague, the famine, or economic difficulties, citing division in the Italian peninsula, Firenze always evaded its promises: on July 8, 1477, Lorenzo who was answering the Venetian orator Piero Molin, declared that the Signoria, to its great regret, would not be able to engage against the Turks:

> Magnificent ambassador, etc. We highly regret what we hear from your mouth about the daily growing perils due to the attacks and successes of the Turks [...]. However, considering the present conditions in Italy and at home, we think we should attend to the most urgent things first [...] Nevertheless, as we said before, if the rest of Italy came to an agreement, we know where we stand and what our duty is, and, uniting with the others, we would participate to the best of our ability and we would fulfil our duty as friends and Christians, etc.[16]

Meanwhile, Lorenzo the Magnificent was sealing with the Sultan a closer and closer unofficial alliance through more and more intimate and obsequious diplomatic letters: whereas in 1470 they started curtly with *Turcho* to address Mehmet II, ten years later they ended with sheer flattery. The language used in the official reports with the Sultan was more and more fawning. For instance, after the Pazzi plot against the Medicis in 1478, Lorenzo wanted to carry out his own justice and sentence to death Bernardo Bandini who had taken refuge in Constantinople; he therefore told the Sultan that the Florentines were "the very thankful and very faithful sons of His Majesty."[17] In the same letter, the sovereign was mentioned as an emperor showing unrivalled kindness to the inhabitants of Firenze, incomparable leniency, and eternal glory. Some extracts of letters sent between 1472 and 1476 from Firenze to the *Magno Turcho* deserve to be quoted for their flattering and bombastic style. On September 3, 1472, the Signoria in recom-

---

15 *A noi pare che siano molto mutate le conditioni in Italia da quello tempo che tale contributione fu ordinata, et per questo non siamo in animo di pagaré alcuna cosa per tale cagione, se non ne quando il resto d'Italia concorressi.* Letter to the Signoria Tommaso Soderini, June 14, 1477, 50, 19, c. 104v; Lorenzo de' Medici, *Lettere, 6 (1481–1482)*, ed. Michael Mallett (Firenze, 1990), 373 (document 4).

16 *Magnifico imbasciadore, etc. Molto ci dispiace quello che intendiamo da voi, de' periculi ogni dì maggiori che per gli apparati et successi del Turcho [...] Ma considerandole presenti conditioni di Italia et nostre, ci pare da pensaré alle cose più presso [...] Et nondimeno, come come latra volta dicemo, quando el resto d'Italia concorresse, sappiamo il luogo nostro et faremo il nostro debito, et insieme cogli altri concorreremo secundo le forze nostre, et satisfaremo al debito della amicitia et della relligione christiana, etc.* Letter from Lorenzo de' Medici to Piero Molin, July 8, 1477, Lorenzo de' Medici, *Lettere, 6 (1481–1482)*, 374–75.

17 *Addictissimi et observandissimi figliuoli di Sua Maesta.* Firenze, Archivio di Firenze, Riformagioni, Carteggio della Signoria, missive, 47, Minutari, 11; Legazioni e Commissarie, 20, June 18, 1479.

mending Carlo Baroncelli, the new Florentine consul in the East, to Mehmet II, took the opportunity to praise the sovereign in the following words: "Every day, we admire your humaneness more, most glorious prince [...]. The usual duties and your benevolence towards our nation and our city continually lead us into more submission to you."[18]

Another example of that obsequious attitude of the Florentines is the letter dated April 10, 1476, addressed to the *Turchorum imperatori*:

> Immense is your power, immense too is your glory, which spreads widely through the universe, illuminated by the greatness of your feats and your admirable courage. Yet to our opinion there is nothing more glorious and more divine in you than your humaneness, your kindness and your leniency—immortal qualities of your spirit that we have experienced, most of the time with the utmost admiration. So we eagerly wish you to remain in the same dispositions towards us and our nation.[19]

Besides, the whole circle of the Medici shared this craze for the Orient: Luigi Pulci surprisingly addressed his friend, the chronicler Benedetto Dei, like this: "to my beloved Benedict of Salamalec"[20] or, iconoclastically wrote "I've been shaken by the bells from time to time, and I wish we had an agreement for ten years for 'subaci' and 'nascia'; and Benedetto Dei will not tell you the opposite."[21]

He thus openly proclaimed his fascination for the Ottoman orient which he had come to know during his journeys as well as his complicity with Benedetto Dei who, like him, seemed to prefer the Sultans' kingdom to his own country. Pulci even declared "I will come to un-baptize myself at the fonts where I was at that cursed time and place shamefully baptized; for my destiny was certainly the turban rather than the frock",[22] thus risking being seen as a renegade. His *Morgante*, first published in 1483, contained

---

18 *Quotidie magis admiramur humanitatem tuam, gloriosissime princeps [...] consuetis officiis et benignitate tua in nationem et urbem nostram, continuo magis ob noxii reddamur.* Firenze, Archivio di Stato di Firenze, Riformagioni, Carteggio della Signoria, missive, 45, Minutari, 10, September 3, 1472.

19 *Maximum imperium est tuum, maxima et per universum orbem propagata gloria et magnitudine rerum gestarum admirabilique virtute tua illustrata. Nos tamen nihil habere te putamus gloriosius, nihil divinius humanitate, affabilitate, clementia, quas nos animi tui immortalissimas dotes saepe maxima cum admiratione animorum sumus experti, et affecti saepe multis magnis que beneficiis. Vehementer autem cupimus, eundem te sempre experiri erga nos et nostram nationem.* Firenze, Archivio di Stato di Firenze, Riformagioni, Carteggio della Signoria, missive, 47, Minutari, 10, April 10, 1476.

20 *Al mio caro Benedetto Dei salamalec.* Letter 48. Luigi Pulci, *Morgante e lettere*, ed. Domenico De Robertis (Firenze, 1962).

21 *Mi sono rincresciute le campane da un tempo in qua, e vorrei che noi ci reggessimo un tratto X anni a subaci e nascia; e Benedetto Dei non ti dirà il contrario.* "Probably, I was bothered by the controversies between the various states concerning the "holy and righteous enterprise." 'Subacce' and 'birth' [zoubaschi et pacha]: perhaps the Italian names of Turks, as read in the *Chronicle* of Benedetto Dei, so subasci "e 'Podestà and captains of the Grand Turk," and birth is perhaps for "Basque," "and is greater beside him"; so Pulci would like the Christians to have ten years of Ottoman government. Letter 17 (19), to Firenze, from Napoli, March 18, 1471.

22 *Io verro' costi' in su le fonte a sbattezzarmi dove fui in maladetta ora e punto indegnamente batezzato; che certoio era piuttosto distinato al turbante che al cappuccino.* Cited from Letter 3. Pulci, *Morgante e lettere*, 1216.

numerous Arabic references. Under the cover of a chivalric epic, he obviously delights in quoting the Orient. To mention only a few lines, in *cantari* 26 and 27, there are numerous examples of the author's pleasure in quoting the Muslim culture. Under the pretext of praising Orlando, the angel who appears to him and voices his merits finally only talks to him about the lands of the infidels:

> [...] and Sansonetto
> and so many others in Mecca that you have baptized,
> and you have brought back to the son of Mary
> Jerusalem, Persia and Syria.[23]

The association, within the same line, of the antinomic words *nella Mecche* and *battezzasti*, almost forming an oxymoron, finally shows the syncretic reunion of two religions rather than their opposition, and the question could almost be raised: were they "baptized in Mecca?" He also loves repeating Muslim-sounding words, judging from the various examples of the Arabic greeting he seems to be fond of:

> Such is the faith of Melchizedek,
> A man with tongues more numerous than Babel
> To be addressed with alecsalam salamalec.[24]

More dogmatically, Pico della Mirandola was introduced to the Quran through his master of Arabic and Aramaic, Guglielmo Raimondo Monchates,[25] then tried to read it in the original: "I hope I shall soon read the Koran itself in its original language."[26]

More than anything, however, political interests and internal quarrels in Italy induced Lorenzo himself to express his rapprochement with the Turks and his estrangement from his fellow-citizens. Lorenzo Tanzini points out that Firenze as well as Venezia were accused by a sixteenth-century southern chronicler, Michele Laggetto, of participating in the Otranto massacre (1480) by not reacting, and worse than that, sending the Sultan an embassy possibly led by Giuliano de' Medici:[27]

> We come to the wicked, profane conclusion that, as they could find no remedy more efficient to their needs [the needs of Venezia and Firenze], they turned to the Great Turk as

---

23 *[...] e Sansonetto/ e tanti nella Mecche battezzasti/ e reducesti al figliuol di Maria/ Gerusalem e Persia, e la Soria.* Cited from Pulci, *Morgante e lettere,* cantare 27, § 136.

24 *Ecco la fede di Melchisedecche,/ Un uomch'è di più lingue che Babelle/ Da dir gli alecsalam salamalecche.* Cited from Pulci, *Morgante e lettere,* cantare 26, §26.

25 The Sicilian scholar Monchates, sometimes called Flavius Mithridates, or even Mithridates—a nickname intended to give the character an esoteric touch—was first to introduce the Kabbalah into Christian theology. See Shlomo Simonsohn, "Alcuni noti convertiti del Rinascimento," in *Ebrei e Cristiani nell'Italia Medievale e moderna: Conversioni, scambi contrasti,* ed. Michele Luzzati, Michele Olivari, Alessandra Veronese (Roma, 1988).

26 *Quo me prope diem Mahumethem ipsum patria lingua loquentem auditurum spero.* Cited from *Supplementum Ficinianum,* ed. Paul Oscar Kristeller, 2 vols. (Firenze, 1937), 2:272–73.

27 Lorenzo Tanzini, "Il Magnifico e il Turco. Elementi politici, economici e culturali nelle relazioni tra Firenze e Impero Ottomano al tempo di Lorenzo de' Medici," *Rivista dell'Istituto di Storia dell'Europa Mediterranea* 4 (2010): 277.

powerful lord, wishing to acquire kingdoms, to persuade him to realise that kingdom. [...] After receiving that embassy, and at the request of the Florentines and persuaded by the Venetians, Mehmet sent an army over to that kingdom and finally conquered it, as the above-mentioned Venetian lords had cleared the way for him.[28]

Although there is no proof of a possible embassy or a would-be agreement of the Florentines, it is however sure that the very unstable political situation Lorenzo de' Medici had to face might explain such a sign of alliance. The impasse in which the Magnificent found himself spurred him into writing a few lines that are quite essential in the perspective of our research-work: in the late 1470s and in the 1480s, the tensions between Firenze and the rest of Christendom, especially the kingdom of Napoli and Pope Sixtus IV, reached such a climax that Lorenzo, in a desperate letter, exclaimed:

> Is it not unthinkable—shall we turn Turks ourselves?—that the leader of the Christians should see the Turk in Italy and should not be more affected? Quite the contrary, his main worry is to increase the power and territory of the conte Hieronymo [Riario, the Pope's nephew].[29]

Finally, following the Ottoman model, Lorenzo concentrated power around his own person: although the style of power in Firenze had nothing to do with true established absolutism, the real permanent tightening of electoral control enabled the Medici, through a stronger concentration of power within the narrower circle of the regime, to claim legitimacy. The continuity of the transmission of the political power within the same family also deserves to create a parallel between Firenze and the Ottoman world, since the influence of the Medici on their city lasted for three generations, thus faintly, though in reality, echoing the Osmânli dynasty.

On July 5, 1470, in order to prepare the reform of the *Consiglio dei Cento* Lorenzo established a list of the families that had filled the function since 1434, naturally favouring the *accoppiatori* (those chosen among members of the *Consiglio*) whom he knew as staunch supporters of his family. Bartolomeo Scala, the chancellor of the republic, found the project too oligarchical. The reform, an ambitious one, was twice rejected by the *Consiglio dei Cento* but was finally adopted by the *balìa* that met in July 1471 and was composed of two hundred of Lorenzo's followers. From then on, the *Consiglio* became the only organ that could decide tax changes in Firenze, as well as political and military actions. Its permanent part, composed of forty members, all of them fervent supporters

---

28 *Si venne in questa scellerata e profana conclusione, che non trovando rimedio più efficace a lor bisogno [of Venice and Florence] che invocare il gran Turco come signore potente e desideroso d'acquistar regni e metterli in animo di far l'impresa del regno [...]. Hauta questa imbasciata Maumeth, e richiesto dai Fiorentini e confortato e persuaso dai veneziani di mandare un'armata in regno, e finalmente di avria potuto insignorire, offerendo li detti signori veneziani il passo libero e sicuro.* Quoted by Aulo Greco, "Il lamento d'Italia per la presa d'Otranto di Vespasiano da Bisticci," in *Otranto 1480. Atti del convegno internazionale di studio promosso in occasione del V centenario della caduta di Otranto ad opera dei Turchi,* ed. Cosimo Damiano Fonseca, 2 vols. (Galatina, 1986), 2:345.

29 *È pure gran cosa et da di ventare turchi noi altri, che il capo de' cristiani vegga i Turchi in Italia et non se ne risenta, anzi, la principal cura sua è in accrescere signoria et stato al conte Hieronymo.* Cited from Lorenzo de' Medici, *Lettere, 5 (1480–1481),* ed. Michael Mallett (Firenze, 1989), 58.

of the Medici, meant for Lorenzo a power on which he could rely.[30] On August 8, 1472, the *Signoria* gave full powers to the ten *accoppiatori*, one of whom was Lorenzo.[31]

The wish for personal power appears in the *Sacra Rappresentazione de Pietro e Paolo*,[32] in which the author, Lorenzo, likes to compare himself to Constantine, Emperor of the East. Indeed the best-known lines in that work develop the theme of the solitude of the prince and the difficulty of governing, as well as the traditional protestations of detachment:

> Let him that shall inherit your kingdom
> know that reigning is sheer trouble,
> complete exhaustion of body and mind;
> there is no sweetness in governing, as one might first believe.[33]

That wish to concentrate power into his own hands appears also on a medal engraved by Bertoldo di Giovanni after the Pazzi conspiracy in 1478, in honour of Lorenzo and in memory of his brother Giuliano, in order to remind everyone of the merit of the Medici, just as Pisanello or Constanzo da Ferrara had respectively engraved on bronze the effigy of John VIII and that of Mehmet II.[34] Indeed the sultan, on the medal by Constanzo da Ferrara, is compared to an emperor, a re-use of Roman greatness, thus indicating the centralization of power on his person. Besides, as Julian Raby points out, the choice of the engraver seems quite meaningful: in his oriental passion for medals, Mehmet II several times hired followers of Pisanello who, as we said before, had made the portrait of the Byzantine emperor John VIII Palaiologos. It is then likely that for the Great Turk it would have been a new way of appearing as the successor of the greatest emperors,[35] just like Lorenzo on the medal commemorating his victory over the conspiracy.

---

30 About the complex question of the control of institutions and the modification of the *Consiglio dei Cento*, see Cloulas, *Laurent le Magnifique*, 128–9.

31 Nicolai Rubinstein, *The Government of Florence under the Medici (1434 to 1494)* (Oxford, 1997), 215.

32 The work was performed for the first time on February 17, 1491 by the Compagnia del Vangelista, in the presence of Lorenzo, on the occasion of the election of his son Giuliano as *messere* of the Company; the *messere* was "the dignitary in charge of the financial organization and setting of the pageant," See Ilaria Taddei, "L'Encadrement des jeunes à Florence au XVème siècle," *Histoire Urbaine* 3 (2001): 119–32. The online version, accessed April 19, 2015, is at www.cairn.info/revue-histoire-urbaine-2001-1-page-119.htm. The setting to music of the performance was done by Enrico Isaac, for which see Federico Ghisi, "Le musiche di Isaac per il *S. Giovanni e Paolo* di Lorenzo di Medici," *La Rassegna musicale* 16 (1943): 264–73.

33 *E chi sarà di voi del regno erede,/ sappi che'l regno altro non è che affanno,/ fatica assai di corpo e di pensiero;/ né, come par di fuor, dolce è l'impero.* Cited from Lorenzo de'Medici, "Rappresentazione di S. Giovanni e Paolo," in *Scritti scelti*, ed. Emilio Bigi (Torino, 1965), § 98 and 101, 585–86.

34 About the fashion of medals in Firenze, see: Alois Hess, *Les Médailleurs de la Renaissance, Florence et les Florentins* (Paris, 1891).

35 Julian Raby, "A Sultan of Paradox: Mehmed II the Conqueror as a Patron of the Arts," *Oxford Art Journal* 5, no. 1 (1982): 4.

Conclusion

Cosimo's patient building of a power entirely centred on his lineage in the early fifteenth century was fully achieved with the accession of his grandson. Taking as model the Sultan's power and establishing a diplomatic and cultural complicity with him, Lorenzo fully realized his grandfather's plans. Even the name of "Magnificent" was bestowed on Lorenzo as well as Suleiman a few years later, thus confirming the full political success of the Medici and their aspiration to rise to the highest spheres.

Their success, in spite of the difficulties at the end of the fifteenth century and at the beginning of the sixteenth, proved unfailing. When the dynasty returned to power, the creation of the Medici Oriental Press (*Typographia Medicea*) is emblematic of the ongoing, strong, unofficial relations between Firenze and the Muslim lands. In 1590, the press printed about ten Arabic books: naturally among them were the four Gospels, republished the following year, illustrated with engravings by the Florentine Antonio Tempesta. There were also a dictionary and two grammars (1592), *The Canon of Medicine* by Avicenna (1593), *The Elements* by Euclid (1594), and so on. The interest in all forms of oriental culture remained obvious. So much so that the Sultan Murad III, who was supposed to be the target of the enterprise, allowed the books to be imported into Ottoman territory. So, the texts started to circulate widely, reopening, in spite of all, the doors of mutual knowledge.[36]

---

[36] For this whole paragraph, see Angelo Michele Piemontese, "I fondi dei manoscritti arabi, persiani e turchi in Italia," in *Gli Arabi in Italia: cultura, contatti e tradizioni*, ed. Francesco Gabrieli, Umberto Scerrato (Milano, 1985), 664–77.

Chapter 18

POLITICAL IDEOLOGY AND LEGAL IDENTITY: THE REFORM OF JURIDICAL DELIBERATION IN ARAGON IN THE FIFTEENTH AND SIXTEENTH CENTURIES

MARTINE CHARAGEAT

THE MEDIEVAL KING[1] has been called "the source of justice."[2] But in the kingdom of Aragon, kings could not readily perform this role due to the peculiar legal character of this kingdom, with collections of historic laws, or *fueros*, taking a preeminent role over a town, locality, or civil estate, and which as a system is known as the *foralidad*.[3] So this chapter will explore concepts such as power and authority but without engaging explicitly with the framework of Christian ideology that underpins much of the rest of this book. It focuses on the extension of judicial sovereignty of the Aragon kings; parallel to this Christian ideology is relevant in the context of the project of religious unification of Iberia at the time of the Catholic Kings, Fernando and Isabella. The inquisition courts at the service of building a Catholic Spain also served the royal assumption of plenipotential power (*merum imperium*) in Aragon, despite strong resistance.[4] In this sense, judicial submission of the Aragon kingdom to royal power can be seen as the counterpart of forced insertion elsewhere in Spain of the political plan to achieve religious unity. As we shall show, one way to break the power of territorial rights in Aragon was to control the exercise of criminal justice through an obligation to consult the jurists of the king.

Legal practice in Aragon can be partly inferred from the kingdom's legislation, which, occasionally, regulates its institutional workings, often at the king's instigation, but documents relating to judicial practice can also be revealing. Some trial documents, relating to a juncture in the proceedings, and, more so, the texts of sentences, show that judges, when taking a decision, could consult experts in law whose designation varied

---

1 This chapter is a recast version of a text from Martine Charageat, "Rois, juges et consultation juridique en Aragon (XIIIe–XVIe siècle)," in *Conseiller les juges au Moyen Âge*, ed. Martine Charageat (Toulouse, 2014), 217–43.

2 See Silvère Menagaldo, Bernard Ribémont, eds., *Le roi fontaine de justice. Pouvoir justicier et pouvoir royal au Moyen Âge et à la Renaissance* (Paris, 2012).

3 Jesús Morales Arrizabalaga, "La foralidad aragonesa como modelo político: su formacíon y consolidación hasta las crísis forales del siglo XVI," *Cuadernos de Estudios Borjanos* 27–28 (1992): 99–175. The author explains how the *foralidad* (body of *fueros*) became a judicial system with or against the *ius commune* according to the supporters of one or the other.

4 José Angel Sesma Muñoz, "Violencia institucionalizada. El establecimiento de la Inquisición por los Reyes Católicos en la Corona de Aragón," *Aragón en la Edad Media* 8 (1989): 659–74.

Martine Charageat (mcharageat@free.fr) is Maître de conférences at the Université Bordeaux Montaigne in France.

from one court to another. Study of trials and Aragonese legislative texts demonstrates when and why legal consultation took place. Sources indicate that consultation could be demanded by the different parties or by the judge. It could also be imposed by the will of the king when he believed such activity useful in establishing sovereignty where it was not yet acquired in the late fifteenth century. Consequently, between an ideal of justice and day-to-day realities, we can see that juridical, institutional, and ideological concerns, as well as those pertaining to identity, were intimately mingled, initially and certainly, in the choice of counsellors, and then in the decision of whether or not to compel the judge and/or the conflicting parties to consult. Coercion can be employed by obliging the judge to make his final decision dependent upon a vote by the counsellors.

Advisory activities in the system of justice may be closely entwined with conflicts over jurisdiction and (re)present a forceful means of power between the king and those liable to his justice within the kingdom. The nature and political interest of the juridical consultation is more important than simply its functional aspects. The political nature of a consultation is evident when it is accepted or refused, whether it is consensual or enforced, making it a government instrument for confrontation and the construction of conflictual relations between distinct jurisdictions (local officials, urban tribunals, the Aragon court of *justicia*), or between the king and his judges. It poses the question of the judges' independence and what resistance was required to preserve what we shall call, for convenience, their autonomy or jurisdictional sovereignty. As Arrizabalaga has written, the whole process, which no only sets the king against kingdom, but frequently *reino* and *reino*, plays a large part in the "creation" of Aragonese subjects, their subjugation being felt more and more strongly in a region where their subjugation had been, without doubt, felt less than in Castile.

Studying the way legal consultation became an instrument in the hands of the Aragon kings, serving their reconquest of the *merum imperium* in a kingdom where the inhabitants swore by their *fueros*, is an approach which mixes political, as well as legal, ideology and identity.[5] Use of the terms "ideology" and "identity" is bound to the fundamental concept of *foralidad* (the body of historical rights, privileges, and freedoms). This term refers to the standard body of laws in the kingdom (*fueros, leyes, costumbres, libertades, actos de cortes, observancias*) as well as the means of producing current norms (king versus *cortes*), and how they work alongside each other (royal law, rights, *fueros*).[6] It demonstrates a way, notably after 1301 in Aragon, of conceiving government as a form of contract.[7]

---

5 Jesús Lalinde Abadia, "¿Es el derecho la esencia del ser aragonés?," *Anales de la Fundación Joaquín Costa* 11 (1994), 85–100.

6 Morales "La foralidad aragonesa," 99–175.

7 For a renewed approach to government as a form of contract, see the following studies: François Foronda, Ana Isabel Carrasco, eds., *Du contrat d'alliance au contrat politique. Cultures et sociétés politiques dans la péninsule ibérique à la fin du Moyen Âge* (Toulouse, 2007); François Foronda, Ana Isabel Carrasco, eds., *El contrato político en la Corona de Castilla. Cultura y sociedad politicas entre los siglos X al XVI* (Madrid, 2008); François Foronda, ed., *Avant le contrat social. Le contrat politique en Occident médiéval XIIIe-XVe siècle* (Paris, 2011).

However, the history of the Aragonese *foralidad* unfolds as part of a dialogue, often antagonistic, between successive kings and the kingdom, which calls on, sometimes fictional, memories of the past, such as the Trastamara's arrival as head of state.[8] If the relationship between the kings and their kingdoms can be considered a confrontation it is because, from the fourteenth century, the defenders of the Aragonese *foralidad* clash with the monarchy's ambitions of repairing defects, in terms of administration, in the sovereignty of justice (*iudicare*) in Aragon. At the crossroads of the conflicts between the king and kingdom, or opposing different parties, lies the *justicia*, a figure whose court exercises considerable authority within the Aragonese kingdom. The backdrop of the confrontation is the basic notion of *contrafuero*, about which some remarks should be made before tackling the utilization of juridical consultation to assert the monarchy's judicial authority in terms of *merum imperium*.

Foralidad, contrafuero, and Monarchical Sovereignty

The figure who embodied the force of Aragonese *foralidad* wass that of the *justicia mayor*.[9] This individual and his court had the wherewithal to restrain the monarchy's judicial sovereignty due to the competence of this institution (*justiciazgo*) over the creation of law and because the *justicia* tribunal was in charge of secular justice throughout the kingdom. The monarchy, deprived to some extent by custom and usage of its supreme jurisdiction over a great part of the kingdom after the *Reconquista* against the Muslims, had to begin another war of conquest, for its *merum imperium*.[10] The monarchy's recovery of control of its *iurisdictio* consequently implies a reformation of the power bases of the Aragonese *justicia*. Beginning with Peter the Ceremonious, serious limits started to be placed on this officer's jurisdictional remit (*arbitrium*), restraining his capacity to "produce" legal norms, which inevitably compete with the king's law, by means of the *observancias*.[11] In future, the *justicia* was no longer permitted to create, but simply formulate, the *fuero*, in the sense of Aragonese law. In order to do this, the

---

8 Jesús Morales Arrizabalaga, "Los fueros de Sobrarbe como discurso politico. Consideraciones de método y documentos para su interpretación," *Huarte de San Juan: Revista de la facultad de Ciencias Humanas y Sociales de la Universidad Publica de Navarra*, Serie Derecho 1 (1994): 161–88.

9 Luis González Antón, "El Justicia de Aragón en el siglo XVI (según los Fueros del Reino)," *Anuario de Historia del Derecho Español* 62 (1992): 565–86; Guillermo Redondo Veintemillas, "El Justicia de Aragón: entre el mito y el antihéroe (datos para 1591 y 1710)," in *Tercer encuentro de estudios sobre el Justicia de Aragón* (Zaragoza, 2003), 33–45; Esteban Sarasa Sánchez, "La historiografía sobre la institución del Justicia de Aragón en la Edad Media: un panorama retrospectivo," in *Sexto encuentro de estudios sobre el Justicia de Aragón. Instrumentos para el conocimiento de los orígenes y desarollo de una institución clave en la Edad Media* (Zaragoza, 2005), 53–63; Àngel Bonet Navarro, "La actividad procesal del Justicia de Aragón," in *Sexto encuentro de estudios sobre el Justicia de Aragón*, 65–77.

10 Jesús Morales Arrizabalaga, "Formulación y hermenéutica de la foralidad aragonesa (1247–1437)," in *Estudios de derecho Aragonés* (Zaragoza, 1994), 47–99.

11 Jesús Morales Arrizabalaga, "La intervención de la Corte del Justicia y las Cortes del reino en la formulación del Fuero de Aragón," in *Cuarto encuentro de estudios sobre el Justicia de Aragón* (Zaragoza, 2003), 133–53.

need to undermine the Aragonese *justicia*'s authority was undertaken by neutralizing the *contrafuero* and its multiple effects, a process that is familiar to historians of law.

The term *contrafuero* denotes the violation of *foral* (provincial) law par excellence. It represented a transgression of the very essence of Aragonese *foralidad*. The *contrafuero* only existed because it is recognized as such, as an attack on a person's rights or as protection of their property. The process authorized, when a *contrafuero* was committed, the application of specific procedures.[12] The ultimate effect of the *contrafuero* lay in feeding resistance to the monarch's jurisdictional sovereignty without it enjoying a particular authoritative formulation.

In consequence, it is not so much the authority of the Aragonese *justicia* which represents an obstacle to the monarch's jurisdictional sovereignty; it was the entire legal system to which he could refer that made his role problematic, in addition to the fact that his magistracy was a long-term, personal one. The solution for the monarchy was to free itself from the traps of the *contrafuero* by rendering, from 1348, the *justicia* himself susceptible to commit them and making him responsible for the correct application of the *fueros*.[13]

This undermining process continued, notably during Fernando the Catholic's reign in the late fifteenth century, provoking legal crises caused by the establishment of Inquisition tribunals in the kingdom of Aragon. The inquisitorial process inevitably upset Aragonese "judiciary habits" because it authorized *ex officio* procedure, solitary confinement, and torture, and practised the incarceration of people or confiscation of possessions, arbitrarily in both cases, in short, everything which had been prohibited since 1283.[14] The Aragonese deputies reproached the king for letting the inquisitors contravene, with impunity, the principles of the *foralidad*, and so to act extra-judicially or *contrafueros*. The criticism was occasionally severe, almost suggesting that the monarch was perjuring himself and breaking the contract made in his coronation oath to govern the kingdom with respect for the *fueros*.[15] Thus, Fernando the Catholic found it difficult to impose the Inquisition in the late fifteenth century in the rebellious zones near Teruel and then in the rest of the kingdom, with some members of the Inquisition even being murdered.[16]

---

12 Ángel Bonet Navarro, *Procesos ante el Justicia de Aragón* (Zaragoza, 1982).

13 Morales, "Formulación y hermenéutica," 87–89.

14 Gonzalo Martínez Díez, "La estructura del procedimiento inquisitorial," in *Historia de la Inquisición en España y América*, ed. Joaquín Pérez Vullanueva, Bartolomé Escandell Bonet, 3 vols. (Madrid, 1993), 2:275–300; José Manuel Perez-Prendes Muñoz de Arraco, "El procedimiento inquisitorial (esquema y significado)," in *Inquisición y conversos: conferencias pronunciadas en el III Curso de cultura hispano-judía y sefardí de la Universidad de Castilla - La Mancha, celebrado en Toledo del 6 al 9 de septiembre de 1993* (Toledo, 1994), 147–89.

15 José Ángel Sesma Muñoz, *El establecimiento de la Inquisición en Aragón (1484–1486). Documentos para su estudio* (Zaragoza, 1987), 97–100, esp. 98 (document 61, dated November 29, 1484). There the kingdom's deputies remind the sovereign that he has always encouraged the Aragonese to call on him to protect their *fueros* and their freedoms: *los sobredichos Fueros e otros que son por Vuestra Magestat iurados* ("the aforementioned *fueros* and others that are sworn to by Your Majesty").

16 Antonio C. Floriano Cumbreño, "El tribunal del Santo Officio en Aragón: establecimiento de

These "*foral* crises" reveal the refusal of the Aragonese to lose control of the administration of justice with regard to their traditional privileges and personal freedoms, even if the monarchs do eventually become their masters, albeit later in Aragon than elsewhere in the Christian West.[17] To assert their justice plenipotentially on Aragonese soil, the monarchs had to find a way to neutralize the legal impact of the frequently invoked *contrafuero*. One of the most formidable strategies employed was to reinforce control over the judges, not only through their nomination but above all by controlling their juridical judgments, and thereby the sentences. This would allow the monarch to reclaim, for example, his monopoly over capital punishment.[18]

Rendering juridical consultation obligatory in certain cases led to control over the exercise of justice, at least in part. Not to put too fine a point on it: if the interpreters of the *fueros* no longer recognize the *contrafuero*, it will disappear, and if the interpreters are the king's men, this should happen even more easily. Fernando the Catholic quickened the process of reaffirmation of his jurisdictional sovereignty by imposing new consultative constraints on the kingdom's judges and on the *justicia*, as well as reorganizing the circuits of legal consultation to benefit the higher authorities of the kingdom and its officers of justice, Aragonese of course.

The *Justicia* of Aragon: Judge, Interpreter, and Counsellor

After the *Cortes* of Ejea (1265), the *Justicia* of Aragon acted as interpreter of the *fueros*, empowered to render the law's intention or non-literal meaning, liable to escape a particular judge.[19] He was also defined as the judge of *contrafueros*, notably when the general privilege was granted in 1283. He was solely competent to resolve disputes generated by infringements of the Aragonese laws. Finally, he acted as arbiter in conflicts between the king, the royal administration, and the Aragonese in general.[20] From an established institutional figure close to the monarch, notably during the reign of James II, after 1265 he became the defender of the Aragonese nobility's interests in the face of royal jurisdiction.[21] This quick summary could be subtler, but, lacking time, should set the scene for understanding why the Aragonese *justicia* is, a priori, the best placed, in

---

la Inquisición en Teruel," *Boletín de la Real Academia de la Historia* 86 (1925): 544–605; Jacqueline Guiral-Hadziiossif, *Meurtre dans la cathédrale. Les débuts de l'Inquisition espagnole* (Saint-Denis, 2012).

17 Jesús Morales Arrizabalaga, *Fueros y libertades del reino de Aragon. De su formación medieval a la crisis preconstitucional (1076–1800)* (Zaragoza, 2007), 61–63.

18 Martine Charageat, "Notes introductives sur la peine de mort en Occident médiéval. État de la question," in *La mort pénale. Les enjeux historiques et contemporains*, ed. Mathieu Soula, Jean-Pierre Alline (Rennes, 2015), 83–94.

19 Esteban Sarasa Sánchez, "El Justicia de Aragón y las Cortes en la Edad Media," in *Cuarto encuentro de estudios sobre el Justicia de Aragón* (Zaragoza, 2003), 187–94.

20 Ángel Bonet, Esteban Sarasa Sánchez, Guillermo Redondo Veintemillas, *El Justicia de Aragón: Historia y derecho (breve estudio introductorio)* (Zaragoza, 1985).

21 González, "El Justicia de Aragón," 565–85.

institutional terms, to counsel and enlighten anybody within the realm with questions on the *fueros* and/or Aragonese law.

We should also recall that, from 1348, where there are legal queries or *dudas no crasas* (à propos *fueros*, freedoms, privileges, usages, and customs of the realm), any officer could interrupt a proceeding and consult the *justicia* within the following three days. The *justicia* had eight days to reply and, according to this legal opinion, must determine whether the officer was justified in his doubt.[22] If it appears that it was one of the parties who, by his actions, had aroused the officer's doubt, that party must pay the expenses of the consultation. Such expenses were, on the other hand, to be charged to the officer or judicial consultant, if the *justicia*'s legal opinion proved there was no good reason for doubt.[23] It would seem that the primary concern of the public authority was to prevent abuses in the consultation, possibly proceeding from a manipulation of legal texts with a view to influencing the course of a case in progress. Finally, if the judge did not respect the time allowed for consultation, if he continued the proceedings before the *justicia* had responded, or if the consulting magistrate did not take into account or gainsaid the *justicia*'s legal opinion, he must be punished.[24] He would incur punishments aimed at officials who do not respect their oath, namely the death penalty, mutilation of limbs, or other corporal punishment, but also exile or prison.[25] The *justicia*'s competence con-

---

22 "Within eight days of receiving the consultation, the Justice must respond to the governor, the judges, and other officers, or even before he can" (*Qui Iustitia infra octo dies, postquam dubium illud receperit, debeat & teneatur praedictos Regentem officium Gubernationis, Iudices, & alios officiales, de dicto dubio certificare, & eisdem per suas literas super eo respondere vel ante, si facere potuerit*). Cited from *Fueros, Observancias y Actos de Corte del Reyno de Aragón*, 1, 45b.

23 "And in the same way, the governor, the judges, or the officers will have to pay the costs of procedure entailed by the consultation if it appears in the answer of the *Justicia* that there was no reason to doubt" (*Et eodem modo solvant dicti gerens vice Gubernatoris, Iudices vel officiales expensas praedictas parti, quae ipsas fecerit in casu, in quo per certificationem & responsionem dicti Iustitiae, apparuerit dictos officiales, non habuisse iustitiam causam dubitandi*). Cited from *Fueros, Observancias*, 1, 45b.

24 "We decree and ordain, that if the Regent of the office of the government, judges, and other officials, in case that it has been said the doubts have happened to them in the premises, they had to consult the Justice of Aragon: and they do not pursue the lawsuit or the case; moreover, if the judge continues the procedure for which he has consulted the Justice during the three-day period available to the Justice to give his advice: if the judges do not apply the advice or proceed contrary to the counsel of the Justice, all and each of them will have to be punished." (*Statuimus & ordinamus, quod si dicti Regens officium Gubernationis, Iudices, & alii officiales praedicti, in casu quo dicta dubia eis evenerit super praedictis, habuerint consulere Iustitiam Aragonum: & non supersedebunt procedere in dictis causis, seu negociis: imo processerint in eisdem, vel infra triduum non consultaverint Iustitiam Aragonum prout dictum est, vel non expectata consultatione, seu certificatione dicti Iustiae, in casu quo ipsum consultaverint: processerint in causis, seu negociis praedictis, vel habita certificatione ab ipso Iustitia, ipsam non servaverint, vel processerint contra certificationem dicti Iusticiae in toto , vel in parte in dictis casibus, & quolibet ipsorum praedicti officiales, & quilibet ipsorum puniantur.*) Cited from *Fueros, Observancias*, 1, 45b.

25 *Fueros, Observancias*, 1, 71a, the information is found under the heading *De iuramento praestando per Officiales, de servando Foros, Privilegia, libertates, usus & consuetudines Regni Aragonum*.

ferred a legally-binding authority so that the response to any consultation he provided must take effect.

The formulated legal opinion is termed a *pronunciato* or *declaratio*, as a sort of preliminary to the sentence, but it was never referred to by the term *consilium*. The penalties evoked previously are executed as soon as the *justicia* decreed, at the close of the plenary procedure, if the officers had not respected all or part of his *declaratio*. It was impossible to appeal against these punishments, if the *justicia* pronounced them, just as the contending parties could lodge no appeal to the legal opinion of the *justicia*, drafted within the scope of a juridical consultation.[26] The king also anticipated the case of the *justicia* eluding his duty of counsel or non-respect existing regulations, such as those imposing time limits. He also provided for situations in which the *justicia* may commit a *contrafuero* as judge or may be unable to prevent an inferior judge from committing one. Peter the Ceremonious let it be known and ordered that if the contravention occurred in the context of criminal acts, the *justicia* would himself undergo the corresponding penalties: death, exile, mutilation, corporal punishment, prison.[27] When a penalty was not enforced due to the *justicia* or if his failure concerned a civil suit and, in either case, was detrimental to one of the contending parties, the *justicia* must compensate the said party for double the damages. Moreover, he would lose his position, could obtain no other, would no longer belong to the king's court and could not do so in future, and could not benefit from royal favour.

However, the position of counsellor must have become excessively burdensome because, after 1352, it was established that the *justicia*'s obligation to advise on absolutely every type of doubt was only to be exercised in favour of the *sobrejunteros*. These were officers appointed by the king and placed at the head of a new territorial division (*junta*) established around 1260. Initially they were responsible for carrying out the sentences of the *justicia* or of any other judge within their circumscription. Their role was simply to implement sentences; they had no jurisdictional authority so, by the end of the Middle Ages, their essential activity was to track down criminals and maintain public order.[28] Beyond the *sobrejunteros* the *justicia*'s counselling obligation to other officers and judges of the realm was limited to criminal or difficult civil suits.[29] In the

---

26 "Taking into account only the truth, a pronunciation or declaration, whose Justice in the above cases, the parties or some of them cannot appeal and where there is an appeal to judgment, it's frivolous appeal, though would not be honoured: he can pursue who appeal." (*sola facti veritate attenta, a pronunciatione, vel declaratione, cuius Iustitiae in casibus supradictis, per partes, vel aliquam ipsarum non possit appellari, & ubi appellaretur, dictae appellationi tanquam frivolae, nullatenus deferatur: nec eam prosequi possit appellans.*) Cited from *Fueros, Observancias*, 1, 46a.

27 "In the event of a criminal offence punishable by death, exile, amputation of limbs, corporal punishment, or incarceration, the Justice incurs the equivalent sentence [...]." (*si factum erit criminale, & mors, exilium, extema membrorum, poena corporalis, vel captio fuerit subsecuta: dictus Iustitia Aragonum substineat, & poenam similem habeat sustinere.*) Cited from *Fueros, Observancias*, 1, 46a–b.

28 Ricardo del Arco y Garay, *Reseña histórica de la villa de Ejea de los Caballeros* (Zaragoza, 1972); Antonio Álvarez Morales, "Hermandades concejiles y orden público. Las Hermandades en Aragón," *Clio & Crimen* 3 (2006): 195–208.

29 "The Justice is obliged to provide advice to the *sobrejunteros* of our kingdom in every case

1352 *fuero*, it was written that requests for counselling were delaying the *justicia* from completing his other tasks. Consultations were probably too numerous, they certainly lengthened proceedings and, moreover, delay may have been the reason for them being requested, explaining the need to reduce their number.

However, why were the *sobrejunteros* to be assisted in this way? They seem to be people simply carrying out sentences emanating from the *justicia* or ordinary judges. But the realm's legislation shows how frequently they were led to consult the *justicia* because of the resistance they met in the field, where they represented the face of the judicial executive. In 1398, it was stipulated that the position of *sobrejuntero* be entrusted to noteworthy, honourable, and capable persons, but no mention is made of their legal competence. Counsel from the *justicia* would provide a very important aid to the king's men, probably legally powerless when faced with professionals in justice, well-appointed with assessors expert on *fueros*. Indeed, the *sobrejunteros* had to be sure that resistors could not claim they were acting against the *fueros* (i.e., *contra-fuero*), especially in places outside their *junta*. The practice of *consultatio* depended on requiring inhabitants to submit to decisions of justice that were enforced by officers who were perhaps perceived as primarily the king's men. It is important, therefore, because they were not judges, that they could apply the decisions of the magistrates, in whose name they acted, without risk of being prevented by any privilege, such as immunity inherent to the status of *infanzón* for example, or by any procedure anticipated in legal texts related to the *fueros* (e.g., *iurisfima, privilege de manifestación*). Undoubtedly, this explains why the *justicia* must reply to all their requests regardless of the nature of the procedure undertaken. Resistance from those liable to the king's justice was the core issue in this category of *consultatio*. Where opposition occurred, the process of consultation allowed the *justicia* to intervene judicially against lords or municipal magistrates who tried to block the enforcement of measures to be carried out by the *sobrejunteros*.

Also in 1398, at the Zaragoza meeting under Martin I, steps were taken to regulate methods of consultation with the *justicia*. The aim was to render the legal opinion beyond further discussion or appeal, above all by the opposing party, when it had taken place during a trial. The opposing party, unable to appeal against the *justicia*'s legal opinion, must be informed of its application. On the other hand, the party was entitled to oppose the process of consultation, but only before the legal opinion was handed down, and he must justify his opposition by bringing the litigious acts to the *justicia*'s knowledge. If these conditions were fulfilled but one of the parties in the case still felt wronged, he could appeal to the king. Lastly, in the case where a party could not appeal against the legal opinion but discovered that the consultation did not follow established

---

where they consult him, and to the other judges and officers of justice of our kingdom, in cases and doubts of a criminal nature and in arduous civil cases." (*quod dictus Iustitia teneatur dare solummodo consilium Supraiunctaris nostris dicti regni, in casibus in quibus eundem Iustitiam duxerint consultandum. Et aliis Iustitiis & Iudicibus dicti regni, in casibus & dubitationibus criminalibus, & criminaliter intentatis: & in aliis civilibus causis, quae eidem Iustitiae arduae videbuntur.*) Cited from *Fueros, Observancias*, 1, 46b–47a.

rules, he could call on an exception, which could be presented before a competent judge of his choice.[30]

The *justicia*'s authority was hereby preserved insofar as possible; opposition to the consultation process was preferred to objection or appeal against his *pronunciatio*. From these first pieces of information gleaned from texts concerning the *fueros*, it is possible to understand and comprehend how much power and influence the Aragonese *justicia* had over the administration of justice within the kingdom. He exercised a real monopoly of control over the application of texts in the domain of legal counsel. He was truly the cornerstone of the Aragonese system of justice.

As far back as 1979, Victor Fairén Guillén had posed the question whether or not the Aragonese *justicia* counselled the king.[31] In fact, we simply have to read the official designation of the *justicia* in texts on judiciary practice for this role of counsellor to appear expressly, at least in the fifteenth century: he was *milites, serenissimi domini regis consiliarii ac justicia Aragonum*. In more concrete terms, royal consultations exist. In the fourteenth century, in his collection of *Observancias*, the *justicia* Jimeno Pérez de Salanova (1294–1330), left a written trace of the activity of counsel in the form of *dictámenes* and *consultas* dispensed to everybody including the king. Jésus Delgado Echeverría produced a survey establishing the list of consultants from King Jaime (Jaume) II to municipal judges.[32] He noted that Pérez de Salanova, in his legal opinions, occasionally took care to indicate that he had called for the advice of *sabios*, experts in law of the *fueros*, or even of *jurisperitos*. Arguments or counter-arguments were rarely given for the solutions proposed. Jésus Delgado Echeverría also remarks that the *Observancias*, when used to resolve occasional doubts, never resulted from an interpretation of the *fueros* and that Pérez de Salanova never cited authors of references.[33]

However, the *justicia* was not alone in this task; he was assisted by his own counsellor, who helped in taking decisions, and by lieutenants to whom he delegated a part of his activity. Ten or so books, conserved between 1446 and 1539, record the activity of consultation and deliberation of the counsellors to the Aragonese *justicia*'s court.[34] The counsellors took an oath in the same way as any other public officer. Only one reference is made to this oath in 1446, the day a new *jurisperitus* arrived at the session. However, it is worthwhile citing as it is particularly explicit about the function of the oath-taker; for example, a certain Martín de Polo swore on the four gospels and the cross to: "directly

30 *Fueros, Observancias*, 1, 272–73.

31 Víctor Fairén Guillén, *Antecedentes aragoneses de los juicios de amparo* (Ciudad de México, 1971), 39–59.

32 Antonio Pérez Martín, *Las observancias de Jimeno Pérez de Salanova, Justicia de Aragón* (Zaragoza, 2000); Jesús Delgado Echeverría, "El Justicia Jimeno Pérez de Salanova, experto en fuero y derecho," in *Segundo Encuentro de Estudios sobre el Justicia de Aragón* (Zaragoza, 2002), 61–92.

33 The *Observancias* form a body of literature resulting from judiciary practice, closely related to the *fueros*, but in no way a glossary. Some are sentences delivered by the *justicia* and become a source of law; others are forms of advice, intended to clarify doubt on specific points of Aragonese law, thus enabling judges to act according to the situation after a consultation.

34 The books conserved are those for 1446, 1456, 1459, 1467, 1484, and 1497, followed by 1521, 1529, and 1539 during the period of interest.

advise the justicia and its lieutenants and keep secret the votes of the council."[35] The members of this council were almost always solicited in civil suits. Criminal procedures were very rarely mentioned, although at this time, no detailed and methodical study of such has been undertaken.[36] As for the *justicia*'s lieutenants, one of their roles was to oversee the contradictory debates held within the council of the tribunal court. Initially having just one lieutenant, the *justicia* was awarded a second in 1348, distinguishing him from other judges of the realm who had only one assessor.[37] Luis González Antón considers that this corresponds to a depersonalization and mechanization of the *justicia*'s functions. Until 1467, the two lieutenants are appointed and dismissed by the *justicia* himself, before becoming the prerogative of the *disputación* until 1528, when the monarch regained control of their election.[38] When Queen Joanna, lieutenant of the kingdom, decided to reform, by depriving the *justicia* of the nomination of the lieutenants, she justified her decision by a desire to hereby assure a better and freer administration of justice.[39] Such a formula is not insignificant in the face of a major institution which had been hereditary since 1442.[40] The lieutenants were drawn from two *bolsas*, the first containing the names of *juristas y letrados*, the second the names of laymen said to be discreet and experienced.

The two lieutenants help to relieve the *justicia* of a part of his workload by advising lower judges on points of law and procedure. For example, the lieutenant Joan de Luna deliberated on a doubt submitted by the Huesca judge, Joan Cepero. The written trace of the demand for consultation is interesting because it unveils the manner in which the doubt was expressed, here regarding the execution of an order concerning the fate of a field. The land was sold by one of the parties implicated in the suit, but was claimed to be owned by another person. All the rhetoric of the petition, displayed for the benefit of the person from whom advice was expected, can be discovered.[41] In this case, Joan Cepero did not know whether he must complete the initial procedure or interrupt it because a *iurisfirma* had been deposed at the *justicia*'s court by the person who claimed to have

---

35 *recte consulare dominum iusticiam et eius locumtenentes et tenere secreti vota consilii.* From Zaragoza, Archivo Histórico Diocesano de Zaragoza, Liber consilii, 1446, fol. 5v.

36 Martine Charageat, "Délibération et justice à la cour du Justicia d'Aragon (1456)," in *L'espace public au Moyen Âge. Débats autour de Jürgen Habermas*, ed. Patrick Boucheron, Nicolas Offenstadt (Paris, 2011), 205–19.

37 *Fueros, Observancias*, 2, 117a–b.

38 Encarna Jarque Martínez, José Antonio Salas Ausens, "Los lugartenientes del Justicia de Aragón," in *Cuarto encuentro de estudios sobre el Justicia de Aragón* (Zaragoza, 2003), 155–72.

39 *Fueros, Observancias*, 2, 143b (*Forus inquisitionis officii Iustitiae Aragonum*).

40 Luis González Antón, "La vinculación familiar del cargo de Justicia y sus consecuencias institucionales," in *Tercer encuentro de estudios sobre el Justicia de Aragón* (Zaragoza, 2003), 9–31.

41 Huesca, Archivo Histórico Provincial de Huesca, Sección papeles de Justicia, caja 1301–5, 1510, no fol.: "thus advising that it be done in the best form and way that it can and should be done, I beseech and require by your lieutenant of Justice of Aragon that you advise and order what should be done about the mentioned theme" (*Por tanto consulendo en en aquellas mejores via modo et forma que fazerla deve y puede, suplico y requiero por vos senor lugarteniente de Justicia de Aragon le consejeis y mandeis que es lo que es tenido y deve esser cerqua lo susodicho*).

bought the field, Joan Ximénez. It is not surprising that the lieutenant instructed Joan Cepero not to continue the initial procedure in the meantime.[42] Nevertheless, this type of indication remains rare in judicial documents and, at this time, it is difficult to claim to analyse legal consultations from the Aragonese *justicia*'s court.

The Aragonese *justicia*'s particular competence over juridical consultation, at the summit of the legal system, certainly constituted a real monopoly. The monarchs, especially from Fernando the Catholic onwards, would try to break it in order to impose their own jurisdictional authority throughout the kingdom of Aragon, notably by forcing the *justicia* himself to consult when exercising his duties as judge and by partly transferring this exclusivity towards people other than the *justicia*. But before tackling this point, which is an essential milestone in the history of the takeover of plenipotential legal powers by the Aragonese monarchs, it is advisable to look into the realities, perceptible in the sources, concerning the political stakes of consultation in terms of rivalries and jurisdictional competition.

Fernando I's Decision to Reform Aragonese Juridical Consultation Circuits

Fernando the Catholic dealt seriously with the task of reforming the Aragonese consultation system between 1493 and 1510, seeking to bypass and restrict the omnipotence of the *justicia* as interpreter of *fueros* and sole judge of *contrafueros*, by rendering counsel compulsory in certain circumstances. The objective was to subject the conclusion of lawsuits, in particular criminal, to the counsel of new experts. He had the aim of reinforcing the application of law, the efficiency of justice, and his own judicial authority within the realm, so the monarch established a council of five experts, or *letrados*, annexed to the Aragonese *justicia*'s court. Their specific function was to counsel higher and lower judges across the entire kingdom in criminal suits.[43] This measure commenced in 1493 and was expected to last five years. It was later renewed, in 1510, with some changes. Today the 1493 text is classified *fori non in usu*, which undoubtedly explains why histo-

---

42 Huesca, Archivo Histórico Provincial de Huesca, Sección papeles de Justicia, caja 1301–5, 1510.

43 *Fueros, Observancias*, 2, 173–74: "which sentence has to be given by the council of five Jurists experts in Law, and in the Fueros, and practices of the Reign, natives, and resident in said Reign: who have to reside all the time infrascripto in the City of Zaragoza, or wherever the Court of the Justice of Aragon goes: Who have been and are obliged to advise, deliberate, and vote on all the definitive sentences by the major and minor officials of said Kingdom, and for each of them they have to give in the trials, and criminal cases, that by virtue of this Fuero they will do and maintain in all the articles, that according to these Fueros these officials have to consult with said Jurists" (*la qual sentencia se haya de dar de Consejo de cinco Iuristas expertos en Derecho, y en los Fueros, y praticas del Regno, naturales, é domiciliados en el dicho Regno: los quales hayan de residir todo el tiempo infrascripto en la Ciudad de Çaragoça, ó allà do se mudará la Cort del Justicia de Aragon: los quales sean tenidos, é obligado de consejar, deliberar, é votar sobre todas las sentencias diffinitivas que por los officiales del dicho Regno, mayores et menores, y por cada uno dellos se havran de dar en los processos, é causas criminales, que por virtud del dicho Fuero se farán, é proseguirán en todos los articulos, que segund los presentes Fueros los dichos officiales son tenidos consultar.con los dichos Iuristas*).

rians in law and institutions are more interested in the second version, the 1510 one.[44] The records of judicial practice give information about judges practising the aforesaid consultation imposed by the monarch's will, as expressed at the Zaragoza *Cortes* as early as 1493. In future, the rubric entitled *super causis criminalibus* stipulated that, at the end of every criminal proceeding, the judge had twenty days to pronounce sentence, which must be elaborated after consulting the five expert jurists, *fueros*, and Aragonese judicial practice. The five men must be born in the kingdom of Aragon and live there, either in Zaragoza or in the place where the Aragonese *justicia's* court was situated, the court to which they were primarily attached. They were obliged to counsel, deliberate, and vote on the sentences to be pronounced in criminal affairs by the kingdom's judges. To do so, they would act as soon as the demand was made and the procedure, or its copy, transmitted. They had ten days to deliberate and decide the sentence, which must, a priori, be pronounced by the consulting judge. The *fuero* envisaged the possibility that the five jurists be divided. In case of parity, here in case of disagreement between two possible sentences, the judge would make his decision in accordance with the votes he considered the most just. In cases of greater divergence, the majority view would prevail. Collegiality now took precedence over the individual nature of the advice given by assessors.

Nevertheless, all the kingdom's judges were not equal in the face of this consultation imposed by royal authority. The realm's superior magistrates (the vice-chancellor, the regent of the king's chancellery, the lieutenant general, the *primogenitor*, and the regent of the office of *gobernación*) had an advantage. They could also participate in the vote of the five jurists and, undoubtedly, had more influence in the choice of the final sentence. Other, lower judges underwent the procedure. Finally, the text stipulated that in criminal cases where the defendant was not liable to incur the death penalty or bodily mutilation, the judges were exempted from consulting the five *letrados*. The obligation of counsel is thus reduced to the most serious affairs, those crimes listed in the *fuero* titled *De homicidis*, but this liberty was accompanied by a warning: judges who do not consult do so at their own risk and peril.[45]

The king named the five jurists, who followed him on his journeys throughout the realm and who helped expedite legal matters. This tradition was ancient, confirmed by the 1348 *fuero*.[46] It stressed that these five assessors or counsellors must perfectly master the kingdom's law and customs. In the case of absence, illness, or death of a jurist, the others must notify the kingdom's deputies, who then had fifteen days to nominate three

---

44 *Fueros, Observancias*, 2, 173–76 (*Super causis criminalibus*).

45 *Fueros, Observancias*, 2, 174b.

46 "In addition to the Justice of Aragon, we conduct and must have in our course as advisers two militia and two lawyers, who know the fueros, the privileges, the liberties, and customs of the kingdom, with the advice of which present at the court are dispatched and we send all the cases of the Kingdom concerning Justicia, those which have reached our course and which we shall have to send" (*quod ultra dictum iudicem Aragonum ducemus, & teneamur ducere in Curia nostra in Consiliarios, duos milites, necnon & duos iurisperitos, qui sciant Foros, Privilegia, libertates, usus & consuetudines dicti Regni, cum Consilio quorum qui in Curia praesentes erunt expediemus, & et faciemus expediri omnia et singula negocia dicti Regni concernentia Justiciam, quae ad Curiam nostram venerint, & expediri habebunt*). Cited from *Fueros, Observancias*, 1, 26b.

(if one jurist is lacking) or six persons (if two), amongst whom the king must choose the replacements within ten days.[47] Finally, undoubtedly the most important effect sought by the monarch in his conquest of the *merum imperium* within the realm of Aragon, the sentences handed out by the five jurists must be executed with no possibility of opposition originating from a traditional obstacle, namely *foral* law. The aim was to render these sentences completely *desaforadas*, that is, out of reach of Aragonese privileges which ordinarily protected those liable to trial, by letting them be placed under the *justicia*'s protection (*manifestación*) or by blocking a court proceeding by a prohibitory appeal. The true reason for this measure is thus explained. Disguised as apparent exclusivity, a verticality in the institutional mechanism is created, so that one category of sentence, the most serious, is delivered by the king's men and thus appears to emanate from the king himself.

At least one Aragonese judge escaped the obligation to consult the five *letrados*, the *justicia* peculiar to the Zaragoza brotherhood of stockbreeders.[48] Having his own jurisdiction and his own sinister pitchforks at his disposal, the judge of this powerful organization, greatly privileged by the monarchy since the late thirteenth century, was permitted to judge alone or by consulting his own, four or six, assessors, the *prohombres*.[49] The authority of the magistrate of the Zaragoza brotherhood of stockbreeders was extremely important and the sentences he pronounced could not be appealed against, unlike those of the Aragonese *justicia*.

In fact, the new political restrictions on juridical consultation seemed to work well, and quite quickly, from traces we find in sources of actual judicial practice. On October 27, 1494, Pedro de Moro, the Huesca *justicia*, appeared before Joan Dalgas and Pedro de la Cavallería to demand their advice on a current affair. On October 31 of the same year, the legal experts (*jurisperiti*) Joan López, Joan Dalgas, Pedro de la Cavallería, and Gaspar Manent, counsellors (*letrados*) on criminal cases, named by the king and sitting at the royal chamber of the kingdom's *Diputación,* communicated their reply. There are actually five counsellors, but Miguel Molón was for some reason prevented from participating. The counsellors deliberated and voted, which decision became the object of an official instrument.[50]

---

47 *Fueros, Observancias*, 2, 174b–175a.

48 José Antonio Fernandez Otal, "El Justicia de de ganaderos en la Edad Media," in *Cuarto encuentro de estudios sobre el Justicia de Aragón* (Zaragoza, 2003), 23–59.

49 Daniel Gracia Armissen, David Ramos Amigo, "Una manifestación de poder en el Aragón del quinientos: la horca de los ganaderos," *Revista Zurita* 75 (2000): 133–58.

50 "October 31, 1494, in Zaragoza. On this day, Joan López, Joan Dalgas, Pedro de la Cavallería, and Gaspar Manent, legal advisers in the criminal cases given and assigned by the king and the general assembly of Aragon recently gathered in the city of Zaragoza, in the Royal Palace of the deputies of the Kingdom of Aragon, answering and advising the judge of the city of Huesca on the final sentence of the present trial and other consultations made by him, all agreed without Miguel Molón who, because of an impediment, could not be present, were and are of opinion and advice considering the contents of the trial and other things in *fueros* and in law that the Justice must absolve Pedro del Punyal accused on the things contained in the denunciation against him asked by Francisco Oliva [...] On the same day, the counsellors, who answered and advised the judge of the

In 1497, Martín de Almorabet consulted counsellors, incidentally refuting the assertion by legal historians who consider Fernando's reform to be effective only after 1510 using the argument that the 1493 measure is classified today as being among the non-used *fueros*. The text of the sentence is explicit.[51] The death sentence pronounced against Juan Ortiz was a result of the type of consultation now imposed by the king. On the other hand, this example contradicts the observation regarding the tribunal of the officialty and also that the gospels disappeared from the judge's table at the same time as the appearance of the counsel of experts in the elaboration of judiciary decisions.[52] Without doubt, the 1493 political measure was sudden, leaving no time for the

---

city of Huesca on the final sentence in the present proceedings, Miguel Molón excepted, deliberated on the written act of my hand Joan Prat, notary, and signed by the advisers. And they ordered by me notary that it be handed over and delivered to Garsia de la Fuente notary [...] of which he made a public instrument, etc: witnesses: Jaime Molón, notary of the city [...], and Joan Romeu, merchant, inhabitant of the city of Zaragoza." (*Die XXXI mensis octobris anno 1494 Cesarauguste. Eadem die domini Joanes Lopez, Joanes Dalgas, Petrus de la Cavallería et Gaspar de Manent jurisperiti consiliarii ad consulendum in causis criminalibus datis et asignatis per excellentissimum dominum nostrum regem et curiam generalem aragonum ultimo celebratam in civitate Cesarauguste congregari in camera regia domorum diputacionis regni aragonum respondendo et / v / consulendo domino justicie dictis civitatis Osce super sentencia diffinitiva ferendam in presenti processu et aliis consultatis per eum omnes concordes dempto Michaelle Molo qui propter impedimentum sue persone interesse non potuit in negocio presenti fuerunt et sunt opinionis et voci atentis contentis in presenti procesu et aliis in foro et racionis consistenti dictus Justicia debet absolvere dictum Petrum del Punyal acusatum a contentis in peticione contra eum oblata pro parte dicti Francisci Oliva [...]. Eadem die dicti domini consiliarii respondendo et consulendo dicto justicie dictis civitatis Osce super sentencia diffinitiva in presenti processu ferenda omnes concordes dempto dicto Michaelle Molo fecerunt deliberacionem supra scriptam scripta manu mei Joannis Prat notarius et firmata manibus dictorum consiliarorum Et mandarunt per me dictus notarius tradidi et liberari huiusmodi processum Garcie de la Fuente notarius [...] ex quibus fecit instrumentum publicum etc. Testes: Jacobus Malo notarius civis [...] et Joan Romeu mercator habitator civitatis Cesarauguste.*) From Huesca, Archivo Histórico Provincial de Huesca, 1494, Sección papeles de Justicia, caja 261–3.

51 "In the name of Christ [...] Martín de Almorabet, citizen and judge of the city of Huesca has seen the information and the criminal petition [...] against Antonio Ripol, prisoner and accused and seen the questions and answers of the accused, seen the depositions, witnesses, and evidence and the publication of testimonies [...] and with the advice of the magnificent Miguel Molón, Pablo López, Joan Dalgas, and Gaspar Manent, legal advisers for the King and the Royal Court and the deputies of the Kingdom of Aragon, [...] we pronounce and condemn Antonio Ripol to natural death, to be hanged on the gallows of the Alquibla or St. George so that he finishes his days and by way of example for the others [...]." (*Cristi nomine invocato [...] Martinus de Almorabet civis et iusticia civitatis osce visis appellitu et petitione criminalibus [...]contra et adversus Anthonium Ripol captum et acusatum oblat visis in super interrogationibus et responsionibus dicti acusati visis testium deposicionibus et probationibus et publicatione dictorum testimonium [...] et cum consilio magnificorum Micellis Molón Paulus Lopez Johannis de Algas et Gasparis Manent iuris consultorum per dictum regem et curiam generalem regni aragonum diputatorum [...] pronunciamus et dictum Anthonium Ripol acusatum ad mortem naturalem condempnamus videlicet ad infurcandum eum cum capistro in collo in patibula bocata de la alquibla vel sancti jeorgi taliter que dies suios extremos et naturales ybidem fineat ut ey cedat in penam aliis in exempla.*) From Huesca, Archivo Histórico Provincial de Huesca, Sección papeles de Justicia, caja 263–4, 1497.

52 Martine Charageat, "Les sentences de l'official à Saragosse et à Barcelone à la fin du Moyen Âge," *Cahiers de Fanjeaux* 42 (2007): 317–42.

lay judges to effect this transition on their own initiative. The difference of form between the two texts cited, 1494 and 1497, demonstrates that the new consultation process was still in its teething stages. Or at least the style is not set or fixed when, in the sentence, an account is given of the consultation and its strict observation by judge on post. The manner of exposing the legitimacy of the process by invoking the king's authority is variable. The experience is novel and not necessarily comfortable, which may explain why the consultation is always presented as an act of unavoidable obedience to an institution owing its existence to the king.

Another proceeding, conducted in 1498, demonstrates the full remit of the five *letrados* and gives an idea of the duration of a consultation. A certain Martín Soler, accused at the court of the Aragonese *justicia* of various crimes by the magnificent Juan Pérez d'Urries, lord of Ayerbe, had been condemned to perpetual exile by the lieutenant of the *justicia*, after consulting the five *letrados*. Soler broke his exile and found himself in the gaol of the municipal judge of Huesca in 1498. He incurred, as stipulated in the final sentence pronounced by the Aragonese *justicia*'s court, the penalty of death by hanging, which is what the procurator for the initial plaintiff tried to obtain from Joan Serra, the Huescan judge, threatening to resort to accusing the official of delinquency if he did not execute the initial sentence.[53] The judge, however, did not comply immediately. He presented the procedure for consultation to the counsellors Miguel Molón and Pedro Dola on September 19. On the 28th, Joan Dalgas, Miguel Molón, and Pedro de la Cavallería gathered in the royal chamber of the House of the *Diputación*, in response to the request from the Huesca judge, and informed him, after a unanimous vote, that he must give a copy of the *petitio* deposed by the opposing party to the prisoner and enjoin him to pres-

---

53 Huesca, Archivo Histórico Provincial de Huesca, Sección papeles de Justicia, caja 263–4, 1498, no fol.: "said Martín Soler prisoner and criminal by the said lieutenant of Justice of Aragon on the advice of the five jurists to the King and the general court in the criminal cases delegated, was definitively / and by definitive sentence passed in the thing judged condemned to perpetual banishment from all the kingdom of Aragon with [the] condition that if he were found within said reign that in that case I condemn him to natural death in such a way that he die in his final days [...] and as said Martín Soler is on record notoriously for having breached the exile for reason of the banishment imposed on him [...] and thus has fallen as in a punishment of corporal death [...] and that he is detained in your power and according to the fuero of Aragon and if he is held by others and they are obliged to continue and comply with the sentence given by said lieutenant of Justice of Aragon against said Martín Soler [...] you are obliged to do so in another way and the procurator shall protest as well against the official who fails to comply in his position" (*el dicho Martin Soler reo y criminoso por el dicho lugarteniente de Justicia de Aragon a conseio de los cinco letrados por el Rey y corte general en las causas criminales diputados, fue difinitibamente / e por sentencia difinitiva pasada en cosa juzgada condempnado a exilio perpetuo de todo el regno de Aragon con cominacion que si fuese trobado dentro del dicho regno que en tal caso lo condempno a muerte natural en tal manera que sus dias feneciese extremos / e naturales [...] e como el dicho Martin Soler conste notoriamente aver quebrado el exilio siquiere destierro a el imposado [...] y asi aya caydo en pena de muerte corporal [...] e aquel st preso en vuestro poder et vos segun fuero de Aragon et aliis seays tenido et obligado exseguir e complir la sentencia dada por el dicho lugarteniente de Justicia de Aragon contra el dicho Martin Soler [...] seays tenido fazelo en otra manera el dicho procurador protiesta asi como contra official délinquente en su officio*).

ent his defence within the allowed time.[54] A second consultation took place in October the same year, this time on the final sentence to be rendered by Joan Serra. On the 30th, Miguel Molón, Pedro de la Cavallería, and Gaspar Manent consulted and decreed that the Huesca judge must pronounce or conclude the case and the prisoner must be freed.[55] Martín Soler left prison on November 3, but nothing is said about the executory nature of the clause, concerning the death penalty in case of rupture or exile, contained in the initial sentence, that of the lieutenant of the Aragonese *justicia*. In any case, thanks to the king's counsellors, Martín Soler would not be executed by the municipal judge of Huesca. It would be tempting to find herein a form of opposition between the king's men and the figure of the *justicia*, if it were not that the lieutenant's initial sentence was delivered with the counsel of the same jurists, or, at least, this may be supposed with little risk.[56] Undoubtedly, the threat of the death penalty must remain a simple threat: the road was long for the king of Aragon in his conquest of the *merum imperium* within the realm. He did not succeed straightaway, even with the help of these new experts, by whom he certainly intended indirectly to extend his omnipotence over criminal justice.

In 1510, the document *De modo et forma procendi in criminali* repeated the one of 1493 with a slight alteration, illustrating a climb-down by Fernando the Catholic in the domain of justice. The *fuero* gives the impression of having been thoughtfully rewritten to improve, refine, and lighten the use of consultation of the five *letrados* in criminal cases. The judges now got the right to determine the sentence themselves, *a peligro suyo*, but could consult the jurists without referring to the defendant. On the other hand, in cases where the sentence may be the death penalty, the mutilation of a limb,

---

54 "Joan Dalgas, Miguel Molón, etc. Chancery advisers for the King appointed to criminal cases under the law, gathered in the royal chamber of the houses of the deputies of the Kingdom of Aragon, answering and advising the judge of the city of Huesca on the sentence to be proposed by him in this trial / all unanimous were and are of opinion and advice. And given the merits of the trial [...] the judge must pronounce and grant to the accused a copy of the request to justice and the requests of the opposite party and assign it to respond in writing and present his defence within the legal period." (*Johannes de Algas, Miguel el Molón et steteris de la cancilleria consiliarii per dictum dominum regem nominati in causis criminalibus iuxta dictum forum congregati in camera regia domorum diputationis regni aragonum, respondendo et consulendo dicti justicie civitatis Osce consultanti super sentenciam per eum ferendam in presenti processu / omnes concordes fuerunt et sunt opinonis et voti Et attentis meritis dicti processus[...] dictus justicie tenetur et debet pronunciare et concedere dicto capto copiam de petitis et requisitis per partem adversam et asignari sibi ad rescribendum et suis defensiones offerendum tempus competens.*) From Huesca, Archivo Histórico Provincial de Huesca, Sección papeles de Justicia, caja 263–4, 1498, no fol., September 28, 1498.

55 Huesca, Archivo Histórico Provincial de Huesca, Sección papeles de Justicia, caja 263–4, 1498, no fol., October 30, 1498.

56 Here it must be pointed out that the three counsellors cited are also members of the council of the Aragonese Justicia's court, Pedro de la Cavallería in 1484, and Miguel Molón, Joan Dalgas, and Gaspar Manent in 1497. The series of registers being intermittent, these are the dates closest to the case where the lists of members could be verified. No rupture can be seen between the provenance of the men of the Justicia's court and those who might appear as the king's men, which corresponds to the method of their recruitment. It, therefore, remains difficult to define their political discrimination.

or exile exceeding two years, the procedure was modified.[57] The judge must inquire whether the prisoner wished the sentence to be pronounced with or without the counsel of the five jurists. This time, the type of sentence to be submitted for consultation is more clearly defined, but, seventeen years after the initial measure, a major change is found: the judge must ask the prisoner whether or not he will accept a sentence voted by the five *letrados*. His reply must figure clearly in the procedure by an official act. The prisoner can refuse the consultation and claim a sentence delivered directly by the judge charged with the affair, but if the defendant requests the assistance of the jurists, the consultation is at his expense. If he is too poor, the *universitas* is liable for the costs.[58] Possibly this arrangement benefited wealthier defendants able to negotiate a more favourable outcome to the process than that expected by the nature of the aforementioned penalties. Above all, by choosing not to be judged by the intervention of the five *letrados'* consultation, the *desaforado* nature of this particular regime of voted sentence can be avoided and the defendant can try to assert traditional rights and privileges belonging to the Aragonese *foralidad*. Once again, it would seem that the attempts of Fernando the Catholic to impose an authoritarian state justice collided with resistance of those who had the means of eluding the officers charged with applying royal justice within the kingdom of Aragon. By contrast, the king did make progress on the matter of coercion by ordering that sentences pronounced with the counsel of the jurists must be executed and could not be opposed.

> [...] and said sentence and the execution of it, nor the trial, nor those intervening in it, can be impeded by manifestation, guarantees of rights of any nature, evocation, attachment, appeal, and inhibitions of those obtained, and that will be obtained, nor any other impediment.[59]

The king thus assumed, indirectly at first, the right of life and death over his Aragonese subjects, by means of a form of authoritarianism whose legitimacy relied on a process developed by the Aragonese themselves, the *desaforamiento*. He had perfectly understood the benefit in bypassing that to which he was bound by his oath at the time of his coronation, namely to respect the *fueros*, and had managed to do so in indisputable legality. This new manner of organizing juridical counselling undermined the foun-

---

57 *Fueros, Observancias*, 1, 299a: "And that the judges at their own risk can pronounce and decide in all the criminal cases of the crimes that are brought before them and dealt with under the present Fueros, remaining in their power, consult the opinion of the five Jurists [...] or at their own risk sentence in said cases, that are not so in the cases where they had to impose [the] the death penalty, or mutilation of [a] limb, or exile exceeding a time of two years" (*E que los juezes à peligro suyo puedan pronunciar y dezidir en todas las causas criminales de los delictos que por los presentes Fueros delante dellos seran levadas y tractadas, restando en facultad suya, arbitrio consultar a los cinco Iuristas [...] o a peligro suyo pronunciar en las dichas causas, pues no sea en la s causas donde se hoviesse de imponer pena de muerte, ó mutilacion de miembro, ó exilio excedient tiempo de dos años*).

58 *Fueros, Observancias*, 1, 299b.

59 *e la dicha sentencia y execucion de aquella, ni el processo, ni los intermedios de aquella, no se puedan empachar por manifestacion, Firmas de derecho qualquiere natura sean, evocación, adjunción, apelación, e inhibiciones de aquellas obtenidas, e obtenederas, ni otro empacho alguno.* Cited from *Fueros, Observancias*, 1, 300a.

dations of the Aragonese system of, in a broad sense, compact and contract.[60] It had contributed to the progressive affirmation of the king's authority without immediately provoking direct opposition.[61]

Conclusions

The decision to attach these counsellors to the *justicia* is part of a process set in motion to deprive the institution, little by little, of its power, so that the *justicia* lost some of its political and juridical authority.[62] However, during Fernando the Catholic's reign, the networks and alliances were such that the king's men, on the spot, who would be directly facing supporters of the realm's judicial and procedural autonomy, could not be distinguished. We do see, however, some fleeting indications of solidarity. In 1511, one of the five *letrados* belonged to the *viente*, the twenty citizens of Zaragoza charged with occasionally applying a swift form of municipal justice called *de fecho y mano armada*, justified by the duty of vengeance in name of the honour of the municipal body.[63] The state of relations between the capital of the realm and the monarch may be judged from this type of evidence. Here the city of Zaragoza showed its desire to administer municipal justice as independently as possible, freed (*desaforado*) when necessary from the

---

60 Enric Guinot y Rodríguez, "Sobre la génesis del modelo político de la Corona de Aragón en el siglo XIII: pactismo, corona y municipios," *Res publica. Revista de filosofía política* 17 (2007): 151–76; Gregorio Colás Latorre, "El pactismo en Aragón. Propuestas para un estudio," in *La corona de Aragón y el Mediterraneo*, ed. Esteban Sarasa Sánchez, Eliseo Serrano Martín (Zaragoza, 1997), 269–94.

61 Direct opposition resulting in aggressive activity is found at the time of the dispute about the foreign viceroy (see Luis González Antón, "La monarquía y el reino de Aragon en el siglo XVI: consideraciones entorno al pleyto del virrey extranjero," *Principe de Viana*, anejo 2–3 (1986): 251–68); the *alteraciones* in the late sixteenth century (Jesús Gascón Pérez, "De las alteraciones a la rebelión: una alternativa a la interpretación 'aristocrática' del conflicto entre Felipe II y Aragón en 1591," *Pedralbes. Revista d'història moderna* 21 (2001): 165–91; Gregorio Colás Latorre, José Antonio Salas Ausens, *Aragón en el siglo XVI. Alteraciones sociales y conflictos políticos* (Zaragoza, 1982)); or the affair of king Felipe II's secretary (Antonio Pérez (Gregorio Colás Latorre, "Antonio Pérez: el último episodio del enfrentamiento entre Aragón y Felipe II," *Antonio Pérez: semana Marañón '98*, ed. Antonio Fernández de Molina (Zaragoza, 1999), 105–126; Joseph Pérez, "El secretario Antonio Pérez y las alteraciones de Aragón," *La monarquía hispánica Felipe II, un monarca y su época: Real Monasterio de San Lorenzo del Escorial, 1 de junio, 10 de octubre*, (Madrid, 1998), 377–86).

62 González, "El Justicia de Aragón," 566–85.

63 This case concerns the abduction of the son of the king's first secretary, Juan de Coloma. The town activates the privilege of the veinte, who are authorized to destroy the goods and bodies of the kidnappers if they do not return the child (AHPZ, 1511, procedure n. 201). One of the veinte who votes for the activation of the privilege is also one of the five letrados consulted in this matter: "And first the said Bernaldino Spital, one of the mentioned twenty, voted the same as in the present trial have voted, who is present above on the 13th day of the month of October of the year 1511" (*Et primo el dicho Bernaldino Spital uno de los dichos veinte dixo e voto lo mesmo que en el dicho y presente processo havia votado el qual esta de presente de arriba a xiiii dias del mes de octubre anyo de mil quinientos y onze*).

restrictions of the kingdom's law.[64] By leaning on this ambition of the Aragonese capital and by imposing the installation of the Inquisition's tribunals, for motives which are far from simply religious, Fernando the Catholic struck a blow which eventually shook the foundations of the kingdom's juridical system. This was an orchestrated attack against the Aragonese *foralidad*, because the procedure linked to the privilege of the *veinte* and to inquisitorial justice authorized all that *foral* law prohibited since the thirteenth century: ex officio procedures, solitary confinement, torture, and *arbitrium judicis* concerning imprisonment of individuals and confiscation, even destruction, of their goods. The extraordinary inquisitory procedure made headway intrusively and eventually contaminated other jurisdictions. However, it was not until the reign of Emperor Charles V that still more radical measures, which stripped the *justicia* of all exclusive competence after 1528, were taken in the domain of juridical consultation. The emperor chose to attack the problem at its roots by introducing five *letrados* into the *justicia*'s council. He appointed them himself and they were designated "lieutenant" in the documents. They must be reputable, expert, and knowledgeable in law and in *fueros*, over thirty, and have four years professional experience. But, above all, the *justicia* of Aragon could no longer deliver sentence without their counsel, under pain of seeing it annulled.[65]

Legal consultation had become an activity that the monarchs appropriated progressively as a government instrument, to serve a vertical hierarchy of authority far from the older contractual inclinations, still dreamed of in the sixteenth century by some Aragonese supporters of a compact system. It is not easy to trace a line between the logic of delegation or representation in the activity of the counsellors placed at the summit of the Aragonese institutions. But, at the turn of the fifteenth century, the consultation process must be considered in tandem with Aragonese *foralidad* in order to understand how the choice, imposed on the judge or contending parties, of consultation, carried a double impact, judicial and political: the will to judge well, to integrate the respect of royal justice for some, to defend Aragonese liberties for others. Consultation did not take place in isolation, as a simple source of legal advice, refined by the problems of interpretation of standard law. The relationship between consultation and *foralidad* may

---

64 Martine Charageat, "Légaliser la transgression: la fabrique d'un droit de vengeance à Saragosse (XVᵉ-XVIᵉ siècle)," in *La fabrique de la norme*, ed. Véronique Beaulande, Julie Claustre, Elsa Marmursztejn (Rennes, 2012), 145–61; Martine Charageat, "Fonder et refonder la ville par la justice. Saragosse et son Privilège des Vingt," in *Ab urbe condita. Fonder et refonder la ville: récits et représentations (second Moyen Âge- premier XVIᵉ siècle)*, ed. Véronique Lamazou-Duplan (Toulouse, 2011), 463–75.

65 *Fueros, Observancias*, 1, 139a: "We order that if the justice of Aragon wishes to deliver a trial or trials that in its Court have been activated or intend to activate: that this cannot be done without the advice of the five Lieutenants, or the majority of them. And if they did the contrary, that said sentence, would be declared null ipso. And that it be respected that the mentioned justice can only revoke it, in said trial, on request by the party against whom the sentence has been given" (*Item ordenamos que si el iusticia de Aragon querra pronunciar algun processo o processos que en su Corte se huvieren actitado, o actitaran: que aquello no lo pueda hazer sin consejo de los cinco Lugartenientes, o de la mayor parte dellos. E si el contrario hazia, que la dicha sentencia, que havra dado sea nula ipso Foro. E sea tenido el dicho Iusticia en el mismo processo aquella revocar, à solo pedimiento de la parte contra quien fuere dada*).

be purely jurisprudential, but it may also be the fruit of more elaborate strategies, concerned with gaining the reins of power. This infernal duo represented both the strength and weakness in the dynamics of defence of the famous Aragonese liberties opposed to a monarchic state heading towards political and judicial centralization and religious unity. On the one hand, judicial sovereignty and religious unity were forged in the crucible of the Christian ideology of royal power; on the other side, changing the rules of juridical consultation in the late fifteenth century was also simply a way of annihilating the political pact system (*pactismo*) in the kingdom of Aragon. The Christian king must be a source of justice for all, under divine control. Accordingly the right to order executions must appear as a royal prerogative simply delegated to the lower judges.

Part Four

THE MIDDLE AGES AS IDEOLOGY IN LATER ERAS

Chapter 19

THE MIDDLE AGES: SUPPORT FOR A COUNTER-REVOLUTIONARY AND REACTIONARY IDEOLOGY, 1830–1944

CHRISTIAN AMALVI

IN HIS WORK *La Chevalerie*, published in 1884 and aimed at a mass audience beyond the scholarly community, Léon Gautier, a graduate of the École nationale des Chartes, declared that

> It really is no exaggeration to compare the Church during the Middle Ages to a sun penetrating everything with its rays and from which no living thing could permanently remove itself. [...] A true idea of the Middle Ages can only ever be obtained if the beautiful, shining church is represented behind each man of this harsh age.[1]

This judgment, by no means an isolated one in the religious literature of the nineteenth century and even in the first half of the twentieth until the Second Vatican Council, is a good summary of the deep feelings of legitimist Catholics, convinced that the medieval period was not just a rainbow of bright colours, but also a religious ideal to be followed. It provided an exemplary social model: that of an organic society unified under the benevolent supervision of a protective monarch, who, like St. Louis (King Louis IX), respected the rights of all his subjects, and a paternalist clergy, who, through charity, made sure no one was left by the wayside. This was a harmonious world on a European scale—Christendom—in which everyone had the place assigned them by providence, knowing nothing of the dire contemporary class struggles.

In our contribution, we look at how and why Catholic elites used the idealized Middle Ages in this way, brandishing it as a weapon against revolutionary modern times accused, by smashing the social unity of the Ancien Régime, of having left the individual alone and isolated against an all-powerful State. We will analyse this veritable Catholic crusade against the France stemming from the Revolution in four successive sequences:

1. The period of nostalgia for the Middle Ages reconstructed in the colours of Romanticism, from about 1830 to 1860.

2. The *time of Frédéric Le Play*, from 1860 to 1890, when the Middle Ages was reclaimed by the social science developed by this former mining engineer.

---

1 *Il n'y a vraiment aucune exagération à comparer l'Eglise durant le Moyen Age à un soleil qui pénètre tout de son rayonnement et auquel rien de vivant ne peut définitivement se soustraire. [...] On ne se fera jamais une idée vraie du Moyen Age si l'on ne se représente l'Eglise lumineuse et belle, derrière chacun des hommes de cette dure époque.* Cited from Léon Gautier, *La Chevalerie* (Paris, 1884), 350–51.

Christian Amalvi (christian.amalvi@univ-montp3.fr) is Professor at the Université Paul-Valéry Montpellier 3 in France.

3. The medieval crusade under the banner of Joan of Arc undertaken against the parliamentary, lay, masonic Republic of the years 1890 to 1940.

4. A dream of the restoration of Christianity under Vichy, which eventually became a nightmare.

Nostalgia in Romanticism for the Middle Ages, ca. 1830 to 1860

Nostalgia for a period of organization based on the king and the nobility under the sign of the cross was expressed particularly after the revolution of July 1830. So as not to have to serve the king of the barricades, Louis-Philippe, considered a vile usurper of the French throne, or to respect the tricolour flag of 1789, the legitimists retreated to their castles, particularly in the west of France, in a kind of internal emigration. Withdrawn within their lands of Anjou, these aristocrats were concerned to show that, taking a long view from the Middle Ages to the nineteenth century, their lineage had always maintained a mutual understanding with the farmers who lived on their land and that, as in the "good old days" of feudalism, they were always their most effective and benevolent protectors. In this spirit, they undertook to restore or reconstruct their homes, always in the medieval style. They were inspired by the work of one of their number, Count Théodore de Quatrebarbes, an admirer of the model enlightened monarch "Good King" René of Anjou, whose *Œuvres complètes* he published from 1844 to 1846 and to whom he devoted a biography in 1853: the *Histoire de René d'Anjou*. Théodore de Quatrebarbes declared such admiration for the century of his heroes that he had his castle at Chanzeaux restored in the flamboyant Gothic style favoured by the aristocracy. Inside, exuberant neo-Gothic decoration provided a setting for paintings boasting of his family's continuity since the Crusades. The neo-Gothic library was presided over by a statue of King René. Another illustrious family, the Dreux-Brézé, had their castle at Brézé restored in medieval style and asked Cicéri, the decorator of the Paris Opéra, for a neo-Gothic setting to set off their collection of old weapons. Finally, the La Rochefoucauld family had an extravagant medieval castle built at Challain-la-Potherie, decorated with many corner towers, bartizans, and finials. The tops of the towers, pointing skywards with steeply sloping slate roofs, symbolized the continuity of these aristocratic families in the same place since medieval times and their capacity to overcome the revolutionary rupture. An architect from Anjou, René Hodé, the creator of Challain-le-Potherie, spent his career bringing to life the dreams of the local nobility to reconstruct an idealized Middle Ages. His work included three types of constructions offered as standard: classical manor houses provided with medieval towers; genuine medieval or Renaissance castles with attractive neo-Gothic decoration, and, finally, entirely new buildings harking back to a utopian, dreamlike Middle Ages.[2]

To refute Voltaire's calumnies against a Middle Ages sunk in clerical obscurantism under the Second Empire (1852–1870) another aristocrat, the Count of Montalembert (1810–1870), leader of the liberal Catholics, undertook to write an enormous

---

2 Christian Derouet, *L'œuvre de René Hodé: 1840–1870* (Paris, 1977), s.p.

Histoire générale des moines d'Occident de saint Benoît à saint Bernard. He understood and showed that the Benedictines were the true founders of civilization for three main reasons. Firstly, they had transmitted the cultural heritage of Antiquity to Europe by sheltering it in their monasteries at the time of the great barbarian invasions. Secondly, their land clearances and technical innovations (water mills, for example), contributed to an economic take-off in the West and transformed a poor region into an enlightened, prosperous society: Christendom. Finally, they ensured the protection of farming populations from the harsh feudal world and arbitrary lay power and, for the weak, they were the incarnation of justice. This hagiographic picture allowed Montalembert to implicitly legitimate the reincorporation of the regular clergy into contemporary society to combat their disenchantment. In fact, just as the monks saved Christian society from despair following the fall of the Roman Empire, if we allow them to come back, they will pull French society from the abyss of decadence into which it has sunk since the Satanic revolutionary rupture, or so he implied.[3]

However, Montalembert's work is another example of nostalgia for a world which is (perhaps) ultimately a lost one. At the same time, Frédéric Le Play was offering another approach drawn from these medieval adventures with some relevance for the future.

The Middle Ages Reclaimed by Social Science, from about 1860 to 1890

The works of Frédéric Le Play (1806–1882) in fact originate from the all-conquering scientific rationalism of the second half of the nineteenth century, based on the prestige of the Saint-Simoniens and the followers of Auguste Comte. Le Play, a graduate in mining engineering from the École Polytechnique, carried out many solidly documented monographic studies throughout Europe in order to understand the living conditions of *Ouvriers européens* ("European workers"), the title of his first famous work, and to find solutions to their poverty. Rejecting revolutionary syndicalism, which was recruiting workers, and the absolute liberalism arising from the Le Chapelier law of 1791, which left workers utterly isolated against the power of the State and the employers, he intended to regenerate contemporary society by restoring the old natural certainties: those of the extended family headed by the paterfamilias and of groups of workers, notably the old medieval guilds. In his view, modern workers should line up behind their bosses just as craftsmen in medieval cities were grouped in their workshops behind the master, who, along with their professional training, ensured they would have their daily bread and provided them with very effective social protection against unemployment and sickness. Although Le Play always denied the accusation of wanting to revive the old corporations of the Ancien Régime, he did always explicitly state his admiration for medieval society. Here is some advice he gave the *Unions de la paix sociale* (Unions for Social Peace) set up after the Paris Commune:

---

3 Christian Amalvi, "Notice Charles Forbes de Montalembert," in *Dictionnaire biographique des historiens français et francophones*, ed. Christian Amalvi (Paris, 2004), 229.

FEUDALISM.

The system that best ensures the well-being of the lower class. It is characterized by reciprocal dependence between bosses and workers; the boss's duty to help, and workers' families enjoying perpetual usufruct of their homes and workshops. [...]

THE MIDDLE AGES.

Considered as the age which, through social links, best guaranteed the existence of improvident populations and, in general, the lower classes.[4]

Frédéric Le Play wanted to convince men of goodwill from the political left and right of the accuracy of his observations. However, it must be acknowledged that his thought attracted the approval, above all, of legitimist Catholics, hostile to the republicans, who saw in Frédéric Le Play's work a reactionary utopia aimed at reclaiming a clerical, feudal, and monarchical Middle Ages.[5]

The Medieval Crusade Against the Parliamentary Republic, from 1890 to 1940

To effectively undertake their crusade against "La Gueuse" (the Whore)—in other words the Republic, which they saw as the deserving heir of the Terror and the Committee of Public Safety—the Catholics found, in the banner of Joan of Arc, a standard capable of bringing together all "good" Frenchmen against the Freemasons, guilty of wanting to laicize French society by chasing God out of the state schools, the courts, hospitals, and so on. It is true that, following Michelet and Jules Quicherat, Joan of Arc had many followers in the republican camp, and not only in eastern France. However, the successive stages of her religious promotion towards sainthood—in 1894 she was declared venerable by Rome, in 1909 she was beatified, and canonized in 1920—gradually turned the radical and socialist left away from a heroine who from then on was a prisoner of the clerics and the nationalists. In fact, with the Dreyfus affair, Joan appeared as a hostage of the nationalists, notably the recently founded Action Française, which proclaimed the need to "kick out" of France those whom Charles Maurras tirelessly denounced as the "four federated States": the Jews, the Freemasons, the reformed Christians, and the "foreign scum." In 1895, in the anonymous preface to a *Vie populaire de Jeanne d'Arc*, written by the Viscountess Olga de Pitray, daughter of the famous Countess of Ségur, we find congratulations directed at the author because she

---

4 FEODALITE./ *Le régime qui assure le mieux le bien-être de la classe inférieure. Il a pour caractères: la dépendance réciproque du patron et de l'ouvrier; les devoirs d'assistance du patron; l'usufruit perpétuel du foyer et de l'atelier, assuré à la famille de l'ouvrier.[...]/ MOYEN AGE./ Considéré comme l'époque qui a le mieux garanti, par les rapports sociaux, l'existence des populations imprévoyantes, et, en général, de la classe inférieure.* Cited from Frédéric Le Play, *La bibliothèque de la paix sociale: notices comprenant le précis historique des travaux accomplis, depuis 1830, par les fondateurs et le comité de cette bibliothèque*, 2nd ed. (Tours, 1876), 39 and 42 (*correspondance n° 2: l'accord des partis politiques. Lettre de M. Lucien Brun, député de l'Ain et réponse de Le Play*).

5 The best work about Frédéric Le Play is that of Maguelone Nouvel-Kirschléger, *Frédéric Le Play: une réforme sociale sous le Second Empire* (Paris, 2009), 265.

Deals pitilessly with the Jews, the Freemasons, the English, enemies of her religion and her country, and (because) above all she stigmatizes the executioners, the judges of the heroine and, in particular, Bishop Cauchon, whom she declares was a converted Jew who sold out to the English.[6]

After the beatification of the shepherdess from Lorraine in 1909, the troops of Action Française began the habit of parading in front of her statue by Frémiet in the Place des Pyramides in Paris, a tradition taken up again between the wars and then updated again since the 1970s by the Front National.

Action Française was not content to use the figure of Joan, the incarnation of the doctrine of full nationalism maintained by Charles Maurras and Léon Daudet. After the Great War, it took up for its own purposes the conclusions of Frédéric Le Play on the need to draw inspiration from the organization of work in the Middle Ages to restore social peace against the threat of revolutionary syndicalism and Bolshevism. It also based itself on scholarly research carried out by the graduate of the École nationale des Chartes Léopold Delisle (1826–1910) entitled *La Condition de la classe agricole et l'état de l'agriculture en Normandie au Moyen Age*. It quotes his thesis, dating from 1851, one of the first great studies of medieval social history:

> Scholars zealous for historical truth have been happy to pore over everything: old documents, old leases, and old archives and they have not been afraid to conclude that peasants were never happier than they were then. In particular, Mr. Léopold Delisle has made the same reflection in his important report […]. In particular, he states that a peasant in the Middle Ages would be absolutely astonished to visit our farms.[7]

Although, after 1919, the Catholic Church was resigned to recognizing the legitimacy of the victorious Republic, some intransigent priests did not give up their dream of rebuilding a Christianity shining with spiritual and social unity on the ruins of a modern society rotted by the false values of laicism. The highly consistent initiatives between 1930 and 1940 of a Jesuit, Father Doncoeur (1880–1961), a brave chaplain during the Great War, should be highlighted. He was an advocate of "cleaning up" the Panthéon by getting rid of its impious characters like Voltaire and Rousseau and giving it over to "the saints of France," mostly great medieval figures of St. Genevieve, St. Clotilde, Blanche of Castile, St. Louis, and Joan of Arc, whose faces and actions are represented on the walls. In 1930, he founded the *Cahiers du cercle de sainte Jeanne d'Arc* to train the mothers of Christian families and he put on performances of many medieval mystery plays, like the *Passion* by Arnoul Gréban, outside humble churches and cathedrals, notably in Chartres

---

6 *Traite sans pitié les juifs, les francs-maçons, les Anglais, ennemis de sa religion et de son pays; et (parce qu') elle stigmatise surtout les bourreaux, les juges de l'Héroïne, et en particulier l'évêque Cauchon qu'elle affirme avoir été un juif converti et vendu aux Anglais […].* Cited from lga de Pitray, *Vie populaire de Jeanne d'Arc* (Lille, 1895).

7 *Des savants pleins de zèle pour la vérité historique se sont plu à dépouiller partout les vieux actes, les vieux baux, les vieilles archives, et ils n'ont pas craint de conclure que jamais le paysan ne fut plus heureux qu'autrefois. M. Léopold Delisle notamment fait la même réflexion dans son important mémoire […]. Il affirme notamment qu'un paysan du Moyen Age visiterait sans grand étonnement beaucoup de nos fermes.* Cited from Xavier Lévrier, *Les Préjugés sur l'Ancien Régime: la prétendue ignorance et la prétendue misère de nos pères* (Paris, 1922), 38–40.

and Paris. In August 1933, as chaplain to the senior scouts, he led his *cadets* to the Holy Land, where they presented themselves as descendants of the crusaders defeated by Saladin in 1187: "on behalf of our brother Scouts of France, we prayed overlooking this battlefield where the Christian realm was lost. With St. Louis, in 1253, a brief victory passed over this desolation."[8]

Seen in this way, we can better understand how, traumatized by the disaster of 1940 and at the risk of losing his soul, along with a good number of the French bishops, Father Doncoeur, should welcome as a "divine surprise" the accession to power of Marshal Pétain, a charismatic leader, and the beginning of the Révolution Nationale.

A Dream of the Restoration of Christianity Turned Nightmare, 1940–1944

At least until the end of 1942, the French clergy found good reasons to rejoice in the direction of the Révolution Nationale, an authoritarian regime, hostile to the lay, parliamentary republic and grouped around a charismatic leader sent by providence who, at least initially, seemed in the eyes of Catholics to be the incarnation of the virtues of Joan of Arc.[9] Two decisions in particular seduced a number of Catholics who, like Father Doncoeur, was nostalgic for an organic period such as the Middle Ages: the willingness to draw inspiration from the medieval theories of Frédéric Le Play to resolve the issue of the class struggle on one hand, and, on the other, the many official festivals in honour of Joan of Arc organized by the new regime between 1941 and 1944, both in the southern ("Vichy") zone and in the German-occupied north.

Promulgated in October 1941, the Labour Charter brought together blue- and white-collar workers and bosses in the same structure. Vichy also expressed its interest in the re-establishment of corporations. However, beyond the farmers' corporation, its action in this sphere remained limited. In fact, Vichy's desire to restore medievalism was shown above all by the lustre given to the festival of Joan of Arc, voted for on July 10, 1920 by the markedly right-wing "Blue Horizon" Chamber and reactivated by Vichy. This celebration, held on a Sunday between May 8 and 12, served as a kind of political shop window for the new regime, stressing five fundamental themes for the Révolution Nationale.

The destruction of the French fleet at anchor in Mers-El-Kebir on July 3, 1940 fed the regime's natural Anglophobia. The example of a humble country girl made it possible to extol the role of the peasant so dear to the heart of Marshal Pétain, together with the "land of France" supposedly uncorrupted by the masonic, parliamentary republic. Associating religious and lay organizations including teenagers, notably scouts, with

---

8 *Au nom de nos frères Scouts de France, nous avons prié face à ce champ de bataille où sombra le royaume chrétien. Avec Saint Louis, en 1253, passe sur cette désolation une brève victoire.* Cited from Dominique Avon, *Paul Doncoeur s.j. Un croisé dans le siècle* (Paris, 2001), 220.

9 Jean-Louis Clément, "Entre symbole, mythe et exemple: Jeanne d'Arc en zone libre: 1940–1942," in *Jeanne d'Arc entre la terre et le ciel du Midi. Regards méridionaux sur la bonne lorraine (XVe-XXIe siècle)*, ed. Christian Amalvi, Julie Deramond (Paris, 2012), 137–52.

the manifestations of the cult of Joan demonstrated Vichy's real interest in the young people, who bore all France's hopes for the future. It expresses better than a long speech the sincere support that the clergy, who were strongly present on the ground, gave to the French State, which had officially reintegrated them into national life after they had been excluded by the republicans following the end of the moral order promoted by another marshal. Finally, the recovery of the figure of the shepherdess from Lorraine contributed to highlighting the continuity of the history of France, transcending the disaster of May 1940, demonstrating to everyone that the legitimacy of power did not rest with the Gaullist dissidents in London but in Vichy, at the heart of a regenerated France. Despite the hardships of wartime, a propaganda effort was therefore agreed. In 1941, six hundred medium-sized posters per *département* were distributed, and popular success undoubtedly came at the get-togethers from 1941 to 1944 in both the southern zone and the northern zone occupied by the Germans, who tolerated the festival out of Anglophobia.[10] Here is an appeal from May 1942 to the population of Provence to celebrate the memory of *Jeanne, libératrice de la Patrie*:

> Join in the mass ceremonies of hope to mark the day. In the fifteenth century a young peasant from our country chased out the invader and saved France. Unfortunately, today, the country, torn by divisions, has gone to war and from war to disaster. Throughout history, what has made France has been the unity of French people around their leader. Still today, only the unity of everyone can maintain and save France. Unity behind the Marshal, and with the Marshal and his Government. In these tragic days, the Virgin of Lorraine is providing the Great Marshal with invisible aid. LEGIONNAIRES AND VOLUNTEERS, do not allow discord, worry, and depression to penetrate into your hearts. COURAGE, TRUST, HOPE. Fear nothing; if you can remain united and can unite others, health will come as surely as the sun comes back up over the horizon. Protect our homeland, revive it, and make the proud, burning soul of France resound here. France IS IMMORTAL. LONG LIVE THE MARSHAL; LONG LIVE FRANCE.[11]

The highpoint of the manifestations of loyalty of the French clergy towards Vichy probably came with the pilgrimage organized by Father Doncoeur, as chaplain to the senior scouts, on August 15, 1942 and with the firm support of the regime, to the sanctuary of the black Virgin of Puy, venerated since the Middle Ages and an important staging post on the road to Santiago de Compostela. With ten thousand participants from reli-

---

10 Rémi Dalisson, *Les Fêtes du Maréchal. Propagande festive et imaginaire dans la France de Vichy; préface de Pascal Ory* (Paris, 2007), 300.

11 *Unissez-vous aux cérémonies de recueillement et d'espoir qui marquent cette journée. Au XVe sicle, une jeune paysanne de chez nous a chassé l'envahisseur et sauvé la France. Aujourd'hui, hélas, le pays déchiré par les divisions est allé à la guerre et de la guerre au désastre. Dans l'histoire, l'union des Français autour de leur chef a fait la France. Aujourd'hui encore, seule l'union de tous peut maintenir la France et la sauver. L'union derrière le Maréchal, avec le Maréchal et son Gouvernement. En ces jours tragiques, la Vierge de Lorraine assiste invisiblement le Grand Maréchal. LEGIONNAIRES ET VOLONTAIRES, ne laissez pas pénétrer en vous la discorde, l'inquiétude, la dépression. COURAGE, CONFIANCE, ESPOIR. Ne craignez rien, le salut viendra aussi immanquablement que le soleil remonte à l'horizon si vous savez rester unis et unir. Gardez la Patrie, faites la revivre, faites y vibrer l'âme ardente et fière de la France. LA France EST IMMORTELLE. VIVE LE MARECHAL, VIVE LA FRANCE.* Cited from Dalisson, *Les Fêtes du Maréchal*, 149–50.

gious youth movements, it demonstrated faith in a government clerics believed would ensure the re-establishment of a Christian order largely inspired by the principles of the century of St. Louis.[12] However, before the end of 1942, important and tragic events demonstrated to growing numbers of Catholics the duplicity of Vichy and its criminal involvement with the occupying Germans, particularly the hunting down of the Jews. The Vélodrome d'Hiver round-up, organized in Paris on July 21 and 22, provoked an indignant reaction from many Catholics, notably Mgr. Saliège, Archbishop of Toulouse, who, on August 23, had a pastoral letter read in the churches of his diocese in Haute-Garonne. Mgr. Théas did the same in the neighbouring diocese of Tarn-et-Garonne. Moreover, lay people reacted by challenging the chimera of the improbable contemporary restoration of Christianity maintained by Father Doncoeur, upholding human rights inspired by an absolutely different conception of the Middle Ages. A Catholic tract also invoking Joan of Arc denounced the Vélodrome d'Hiver round-up:

> During the early centuries of barbarian invasions, the bishops of the Gauls, such as Gregory of Tours and Prætextatus, opposed the ferocious instincts of the Germanic tribes, sometimes at the cost of their own lives. [...] Catholics of France: these nearby or far-off examples dictate your duty.[13]

In May 1943, without even referring to Father Doncoeur, some drivers from Savoy refused to take part in the festival of Joan of Arc in Annecy because it was being run by uniformed members of the Legion's Military Police, an openly collaborationist institution which served as a recruiting ground for Joseph Darnand's militia, a French auxiliary arm of the Gestapo.[14] From then on, without even asking the opinion of their spiritual leader, many scout leaders went over to the Resistance. After that same year, 1943, Father Doncoeur, whose decisions were challenged by his Jesuit brothers, began to understand, a little late in the day, that his dreams of the Révolution Nationale restoring medieval Christendom had come to a tragic impasse. Finally realizing it was a game of deception benefiting the occupier, he fell silent until the Liberation of France. He only emerged to organize the 800th anniversary of the Second Crusade preached by St. Bernard on the hill at Vézelay, on July 21 and 22, 1946. This time, however, he stressed the federative theme of peace and, at this late stage, refrained from any impulse towards the reconquest of French society by the Catholic religion.[15]

After 1945, the French clergy certainly rallied to the Republic, discreetly abandoning their grandiose dream of restoring medieval values in French society, but this nostalgia, which had beguiled generations of Christians since 1830, continued to operate, probably until Vatican II (1962–1965). We find a revealing example in the granddaughter of the

---

12 Avon, *Paul Doncoeur*, 288.

13 *Pendant les premiers siècles des invasions barbares, les évêques des Gaules comme Grégoire de Tours et Prétextat s'opposèrent, parfois au prix de leur vie, aux instincts féroces des tribus germaniques. [...] Catholiques de France: ces exemples proches ou lointains vous dictent votre devoir.* Cited from Gérard Silvain, *La Question juive en Europe: 1939–1945*, with preface by Marie-Madeleine Fourcade (Paris, 1985), 93.

14 Avon, *Paul Doncoeur*, 300.

15 Avon, *Paul Doncoeur*, 307.

great philosopher Gabriel Marcel (1889–1973), the father of Christian existentialism. Born in 1946, in *Une éducation française* she ironically describes her family's medieval nostalgia, recounting that they dreamed of "living like the Middle Ages, the time of faith, miracles, and society kneeling before the Redeemer as on the spandrels of cathedrals!" and where their litany was, "the France of Joan of Arc, St. Louis, and the cathedrals." [16]

Finally, we should make it clear that, although most Catholic scholars who studied the Middle Ages from the Romantic period to the 1940s dreamed of building on their scholarly work to restore the spirit of the medieval period in the society of their time, not all of them shared this reactionary attitude. Frédéric Ozanam (1813–1853), for example, who, through his work on Dante and the Franciscan poets contributed to reclaiming the Middle Ages by stressing that it was a period characterized by the beauty of Gothic art and literature, in particular, never sought to revive its institutions. However, their historical approach still persists today. Because of its desire to bridge the artificial chronological gap between the end of the ancient world and the birth of the Middle Ages, it seems to prefigure Henri-Irénée Marrou's fruitful line of questioning expressed in *Décadence romaine ou Antiquité tardive?*[17] And through its capacity to see medieval history from the comparative perspective of the long view, on a European scale, it appears to anticipate the far-reaching ambitions of the colloquium at the University of Lleida in June 2012 that is the basis of the present volume.

---

16 *Vivre comme au Moyen Age, l'époque de la foi, des miracles et de la société agenouillée devant le Rédempteur comme au tympan des cathédrales!; la France de Jeanne d'Arc, de Saint Louis et des cathédrales [...]*. Cited from Odile Marcel, *Une Education française* (Paris, 1984), 51–52.

17 Christian Amalvi, "Notice Frédéric Ozanam," in *Dictionnaire biographique des historiens*, 243–44.

Chapter 20

THE MIDDLE AGES AMONG SPANISH INTELLECTUALS OF THE FIRST HALF OF THE TWENTIETH CENTURY

ANTONIO DE MURCIA CONESA

INTERPRETING THE DIFFERENT ways Spanish intellectuals of the first half of the twentieth century used the Middle Ages issue is a risky and selective task, not without some arbitrariness. The first of these regards the extent and intention of who we classify as "Spanish intellectuals" and which temporal boundaries are relevant for the history of thought. Indeed, if it is difficult to define what a European intellectual is (despite the important contributions of authors like François Dosse or Wolf Lepenies[1]), it is much more difficult in the case of Hispanic thought, where the uses of the concept have had no founding myths like the Dreyfus case in France (whose influence dwarfs the scandal of the Process of Montjuïc) nor apostles as energetic as the Frenchman Julien Benda. The second aspect of arbitrariness consists in reducing the role of these intellectuals to a more or less homogeneous discourse, even though almost all of them contributed to the narrative of the "novel of Spain" (*novela de España*).[2] And finally, equally arbitrary would be to turn the Middle Ages into the core argument of that discourse.

Nonetheless, let us attempt to approach these concepts with these caveats in mind. Thus, notwithstanding its vagueness, the omnipresence of the term "intellectual" during the period covered confirms its role as a weapon in the battles of culture and war. A weapon which, like all rhetorical devices, has a double edge; thus, Unamuno himself, who was acclaimed by the public attending his lecture at the Zarzuela theatre against the "Law of Jurisdictions" (*ley de jurisdicciones*) in Catalonia, shouted "Long live the intellectuals!" (*¡Vivan los intelectuales!*) but was attacked at the end of his life by an audience of legionnaires in the University of Salamanca, shouting "Death to intellectuals!" (*¡Mueran los intelectuales!*).[3] That double-edged concept was shared by some advocates who liked

---

1 François Dosse, *La marche des idées. Histoire intelellectuelle et histoire des intellectuels* (Paris, 2003); Wolf Lepenies, *¿Qué es un intelectual europeo? Los intelectuales y la política del espíritu en la historia europea* (Madrid, 2008).

2 Javier Varela, *La novela de España: los intelectuales y el problema español* (Madrid, 1999).

3 The 1906 "law of jurisdictions" gave military courts the power to prosecute any civilian spokesman or publication judged to have insulted the military. This law caused the grouping of most of the Catalan parties around the *Solidaritat Catalana* coalition. Miguel de Unamuno gave a lecture against the law at the Teatro de la Zarzuela. The President of the Second Republic, Manuel Azaña, abolished this law in 1931. During the Spanish civil war, Unamuno, who had supported at

Antonio de Murcia (Antonio.deMurcia@ua.es) is Profesor Ayudante Doctor at the Universidad de Alicante in Spain.

to oscillate between political disinvolvement and political intervention, sometimes as dramatically as Ramiro de Maeztu did. Ramiro was a particular Hispanic embodiment of a *bendiano* cleric (after Julien Benda), who dreamed of making journalists "a religious order" (*una orden religiosa*) that was closed to those who "distort the truth or judgment to serve a cause" (*falseen la verdad o el juicio por servir a una causa*) but who, at the same time, considered the term "intellectual" "repulsive" (*repulsiva*), if only because he thought the Russians had coined it.[4] Moreover, the discursive heterogeneity of the Hispanic version of the modern *clerc* has its stylistic boundaries in the shared preference for writing essays in articles and books, newspaper articles and scholarly texts, and critical and historiographical writings. Suitable for literary self-presentation of elites who are eager for popularity but fearful of the masses, this hegemony—also double-edged— of the essay, or the mere attempt at writing an essay, reached the boastful dispersion of Unamuno or the agonizing collapse of the desire of being systematic in the work of Ortega, who in a letter of 1925, confessed to Ernst Robert Curtius that "this double-edged paradox, according to which, the fact that the little that is done in philosophy in Spain takes the guise of popular newspaper articles, is one of the most curious and interesting points of the spiritual structure of Spain."[5] What we want to emphasize here is the fact that this frenzy for essay-writing has determined for decades the forms of writing and thinking about the Middle Ages much more than typical historiography, not only among intellectuals in the broad sense, but also among medievalists in the narrow one.

Much has been written on the national uniqueness of some "ways to dream of the Middle Ages," in the late Umberto Eco's words. This exceptionalism cannot be separated from the question of Spain, be it considered a novel, a moral problem, or even a real philosophical problem. Nevertheless, my intention here is to qualify this singularity (given as incontrovertible proof of the theorem of Spain against Europe) and instead emphasize the international character, or more precisely, the European connections of the medieval argument among Hispanic intellectuals. In my view, those connections are inseparable from modern thinking on "the crisis": a mindset that, despite its heteroge-

---

first the reasons for the military uprising against the Republic, started a nasty incident with the fascist general Millán-Astray at the University of Salamanca. The professor firmly told the fascists: "You will win, but you will not convince!" (*vencereis, pero no convencereis*). The soldiers of Millán-Astray shouted: "Death to intellectuals!" (*¡Mueran los intelectuales!*). The incident ended with the writer's removal as rector of the University of Salamanca. He spent his final months, from October to December 1936, under house arrest.

4 Ramiro de Maeztu, *España y Europa* (Madrid, 1959), 62–64. Maeztu (1875–1936) wrote several important works about Spain and Europe. He wrote a book that was published in English under the title *Authority, Liberty, and Function in Light of the War* (in Spanish *La crisis del humanismo*), in which he called for a reliance on authority, tradition, and the institutions of the Roman Catholic Church. Vehement opponent of the Spanish Republic—he wrote in 1934 a strongly conservative book *En defensa de la Hispanidad*—, he was shouted down by Republicans from the first days of the Civil War.

5 *Esta paradoja—de doble filo—en virtud de la cual lo poco que se haga de filosofía en España tome el disfraz de artículo para diario popular, es uno de los puntos más curiosos e interesantes de la estructura espiritual de España.* Cited from José Ortega y Gasset, Ernest Robert Curtius, "Epistolario entre Ortega y Curtius," *Revista de Occidente* 6 (1963): 332.

neity, either in its neo-humanist or anti-humanist formulations, attributed the reasons for the physical self-destruction of the West to forgetting its genuine cultural tradition. Both diagnoses, self-destruction and oblivion, were associated with the gloomy expectations of a future that seemed to go beyond all the historic ups and downs suffered by the European experience in history since the beginning of modernity. For the intellectuals who upheld those diagnoses and forecasts, the Middle Ages offered exciting arguments for building a trans-historical morphology and a rhetorical space from which the most fearsome effects of the dominant celebration of that movement as an aesthetic and political imperative should be offset or redirected. However, an important part of the "elites" finally succumbed to this approach. In this context, the image of the Middle Ages ranged from a persuasive, but peripheral, function to a central and substantive presence that was, in any case, an essential structure for different discursive practices. It can probably be found in the work of Américo Castro, even more than in Menéndez Pidal and Sánchez-Albornoz, where the humanist link between political and cultural reflection and what we might call the "medieval argument" reached its high point.[6] Apart from its various developments, this argument aspired to become a key for interpreting the historical uniqueness of Spain as a remedy for the bouts of national culture and politics. In this sense, notwithstanding its dialogue or confrontation with Europe, the special feature of the medieval presence in Spanish essays on the "problem of Spain" was determined by the prospects of civil war, even many years after the end of the armed conflict. From such perspectives, the medievalism of intellectuals such as Castro was a valuable and ductile scholarly instrument to explore the lines of convergence between the drama of his own self-awareness and the conscience of the nation.

The following pages are not a survey, more or less complete, of the uses of medievalism in promotional writings of Hispanic intellectuals and in historical-literary essay writing, although some reference to these is required. Its purpose is to test a conceptual approach to the medieval argument through three concepts that, although selective, are

---

6 Claudio Sánchez-Albornoz (1893–1984) was a crucial figure for the development of Spanish medieval historiography, and even more so for the Latin-American; see the excellent book: Ariel Guiance, ed., *La influencia de la historiografía española en la producción americana* (Madrid, 2011). However, his great work of medieval essayism (Claudio Sánchez-Albornoz, *España, un enigma histórico* (Buenos Aires, 1957)), cannot be considered—nor Americo Castro, *España en su historia* (Buenos Aires, 1948)—a culmination of the "medieval argument" among the intellectuals of the first half of the twentieth century, as we consider it here. The interpretation of the Hispanic reality from the Middle Ages in Castro, as in Pidal, concerns the language and literature and anthropological, philosophical, and critical-literary concepts whose structure demanded essayistic forms, that the rigorous Pidal also cultivated, for example, to justify his essentialist theses on the Hispanic character or his evolutionary category of the "latent state." The "Anti-Castro," as Sánchez-Albornoz called him in his *opus magnum*, is not the result of thoughts obsessed with the perspectives of civil war like those of Castro or—very differently—Maeztu or Xirau, nor the result of literary humanism disposed to articulate heterogeneous categories for a totalizing interpretation of his subject. It is rather the work—undoubtedly also essayistic and ideological, reluctantly—of an academic determined to cancel any possibility of interpreting the history of Spain outside the historiographical channels he considered unquestioned and thus to determine the scientific orientation of academic medievalism in the Hispanic setting.

not arbitrary. First, the concept of Subject, particularly the Hispanic Subject, associated with, but not reducible to, the concept of national identity, whose invention or reconstruction was a central task in the diagnosis and therapy of the Spanish and European crisis. Secondly, the issue of Mediation, an old ideal for the critics, concerning the proper task of those who, from the authority of their erudition or position as privileged observers of reality, make attempts to rebuild the links between the individual and community, experience, and expectations, or tradition and the present. In this regard, we are interested in the intellectual who, whether a historian or not, resorts to the Middle Ages in their role of a "medium" in the struggle for memory. Thirdly, the concept of Memory which, turned into a regulative idea of historiography, looks at the Middle Ages to overcome the oversights of history, fuelling what we might call a medievalization of the historical world. But first, let me contextualize some aspects that favoured the multiplication of these more or less oblique presences from the Middle Ages.

Presences of the Middle Ages

Ortega's damning statement in his *España invertebrada*, "The secret of the great Spanish problems lies in the Middle Ages",[7] synthesizes the persuasive power that the Spanish intelligentsia entrusted to the medieval argument: an argument, historical and ahistorical at the same time, that was established as key to a true reading of the present. We find examples of this rhetoric in the aforementioned book by Ortega as well as in his *La Rebelión de las masas*, with its penchant for Gothicism *a contrario sensu*, or in the defence by Maeztu, in his *Crisis del Humanismo*, of the Middle Ages as anti-Pelagian and anti-Averroist, whose theology in the thirteenth century would be the antidote to the ills of modernity. Or in describing the benefits of the Hispanic medieval crucible, creator of "habits of liberality and democracy" as Joaquim Xirau did in his monograph about Ramon Llull.[8] Along with this presence, mainly rhetorical, the Middle Ages maintained a substantial presence in historical-philological essays that, via an interdisciplinary methodology, eventually turned it into an exemplary trans-historical constellation. This sort of "science of the Middle Ages," close to the name Curtius[9] gave to it, forms the core of

---

7 *El secreto de los grandes problemas españoles está en la Edad Media.* Cited from José Ortega y Gasset, *España invertebrada*, ed. Paulino Garagorri (Madrid, 1981), 105.

8 *Hábitos de liberalidad y democrácia.* From Joaquim Xirau, *Obras completas II: Vida y obra de Ramón Llull* (Madrid, 1999), 215–349. Joaquim Xirau Palau (1895–1946) was a Spanish philosopher and teacher. Dean of the Faculty of Philosophy and Letters of the University of Barcelona, he went into exile in Mexico after the Spanish civil war, where he taught at the National Autonomous University of Mexico. In Madrid he was a disciple of Ortega y Gasset, García Morente, and especially of Manuel Bartolomé Cossío, with whom he formed his philosophical-pedagogical vocation following the principles of the Institución Libre de Enseñanza, founded by Francisco Giner de los Ríos.

9 For this Alsatian Romanist, it was, at root, a "regulative idea," that had to orient the medieval interpretation of Europe, and one of whose parts would be "literary science." Ernst Robert Curtius, *Gesammelte Aufsätze zur Romanischen Philologie* (Bern, 1960), 109; and Ernst Robert Curtius, *Literatura europea y Edad Media latina* (Ciudad de México, 1955), 747ff.

the works conceived in the *Centro de Estudios Históricos* created in 1910 by the *Junta para Ampliación de Estudios*.[10] The fact that, notwithstanding their belief in positivism, most of the concepts and arguments of this erudite production were generated, and could only be generated, through the essay is due, on the one hand, to the disciplinary overflow of objectives and methods, and on the other, to constant discussion with intellectual positions which fall within a wider ideological debate. However, what essay-writing required in a more decisive way was a convincing identification between history and memory, for which the humanist-literary origin of its practitioners, trained in philology and literary criticism rather than in historiography, was crucial.

This literary memory culminated in the works of Menéndez Pidal and Américo Castro and is difficult to separate from the rhetorical-persuasive efforts to make the Middle Ages, sometimes rather opportunistically, into the founding moment of the modern crisis. Such efforts appear sporadically, but also paradigmatically, in Ortega, garnering the admiration of Castro and contempt by Pidal, although not as much as the contempt that the latter received from the philosopher.[11]

In parallel with these national debates, some of the best European literary thought promoted significant interpretations of Spanish medieval studies and the "problem of Spain" at an international level. In 1931, in an impassioned speech in honour of the newly proclaimed Spanish Republic before the Society of Friends and Sponsors of the University of Bonn, Curtius, then better known for his critical and promotional writings than for his medieval research, reeled off the names of some of the greatest minds that constituted, in his words, "*la vida española del espíritu*". Among them, besides his friend Ortega, he listed Unamuno, Ganivet, Marañón, Pérez de Ayala, and Américo Castro, then

---

10 La *Junta para Ampliación de Estudios e Investigaciones Científicas* ("Board for Further Studies and Scientific Research") established in 1907 and presided over by the Nobel prize winner Ramón y Cajal, thought science an essential ingredient of knowledge, culture, and social progress. For its founders, like for those of the Institución Libre de Enseñanza, education and science would play a central and ever-increasing role in the development and well-being of society.

11 Ortega's sharp criticism of Pidal, so bleak for the latter, who understood them generally as the forays of a layman into his materials, not only concerned the determination of the philologist, Pidal, to trace Hispanic essence to the beginning of time, or his Castilianist interpretation of the country's history (an interpretation, however, that Ortega also proclaimed in his own way, certainly with less constancy but sometimes more virulently), but rather for what the philosopher considered a sterile and irritating tendency of the scholar to entertain the north of the national-medieval issues in labyrinths of literary research. It was an old reproach. In one of the first and probably endless interventions by the author of *La España del Cid* in the Ateneo in Madrid, the bright and flowery pen of Navarro Ledesma commented that he was the "excellent lad whose only defect is his assiduity with which he dedicated himself to the chronicles of the Middle Ages, believing with the most utter simplicity, that this was also of use for something [...] A shame that the sharp and perspicacious intelligences like his are wasted on such mousy necessities, having as there is here such a necessity for a general *sursum corda* to move out of ordinariness and irritating morass that dominates everywhere nowadays." See Joaquín Pérez Villanueva, *Ramón Menéndez Pidal: su vida y su tiempo* (Madrid, 1991), 112ff. A few decades later, Pidal himself, for example, in his lectures in Havana, zealously wanted to fulfil the functions of the *sursum corda*, adopting the *hybris* of *excitator hispaniae* that had earlier been cultivated by other representatives of the Spanish intelligentsia like Unamuno or Ortega himself.

ambassador to Berlin. In the year of the proclamation of the Republic, according to the Alsatian Romanist "that intelligence embodied the will for national renewal" (*esta inteligencia encarnaba la voluntad de una renovación nacional*). However, as he would state a year later at the Seminar of Pedagogy at the University of Barcelona, invited by Joaquim Xirau, Curtius did not view the Spanish intellectual republic through the lenses of the tradition of the *regenerationism* movement, but through the lens of a Weimar Republic on the verge of succumbing. Spain was thus an extraordinary laboratory to reformulate the great questions of interwar Europe, since its rise "is part of the great process of balance between cultures, which can provide a stable basis for spiritual renewal—at the same time Restoration and Renaissance—of Europe."[12] Once expurgated the anti-European excesses of Ganivet and the later Unamuno, what the Romanist called "national questions of life" (*nationalen Lebensfragen*), rather than vital questions about the nation, would become the only particular manifestation of the question about the survival of Europe. As in early Romanticism, in the interwar period, medieval Hispanic culture (which lasted until the Baroque of Calderón) was a recurring theme among those who, on the eve of European destruction, imagined Spain as a model for a special or alternative path, a *Sonderweg* that would allow Europe to leave its unending crises and to rewrite the guidelines for its modern tradition. This is undoubtedly a literary model, which subordinates political and social history to the history and critics of literature, and which found its most passionate formulation in a speech entitled "Literature as a spiritual space of the nation" (*La literatura como espacio espiritual de la nación*)[13] that the Austrian poet Hofmannsthal read in 1927 at the University of Munich before his rector, the Hispanist Karl Vossler.

In Europe, and especially in Germany, a humanism existed that substituted the Greek mirror for the medieval one and which wanted to find in the Spanish national question the modern imprint of an essential European Latinity. As is well known, Curtius traced this Latinity to the poetry of Jorge Manrique, who he considered a champion of

---

12 *Es parte del gran proceso de equilibrio entre culturas, que puede facilitar bases estables para la renovación espiritual—a un tiempo restauración y renacimiento—de Europa.* Cited from Ernst Robert Curtius, "Problemas de la cultura española actual," in *Escritos de humanismo e hispanismo*, ed. Antonio de Murcia Conesa (Madrid, 2011), 18.

13 Hugo von Hofmannsthal, "Das Schrifftum als geistiger Raum der Nation," in *Erfundene Gespräche und Briefe* (Frankfurt-am-Main, 1999), 122. This Catholic view close to the "conservative revolution" struggled with people like Víctor Klemperer and Ludwig Pfland who considered that Spanish literature was condemned to isolation, or, with the very different fascist or philo-nazi interpretations of Spanish culture, saw in its exceptionalism the model for German exceptionalism. A paradigmatic and sinister example of the latter was the playwright Joseph Gregor who, in *El teatro español del mundo* of 1937 and especially in the epilogue from 1943, talked about the Spanish as the only culture that was aware of all the European contradictions, of the abyss between the north and the south, and of all the tensions in the world of thought. This life of contradictions, forged in the Middle Ages, would have led it to a suicidal and anti-modern struggle for the *idea*, culminated in a civil war that the author celebrated as an act of reaffirmation against the civilized Europe: a revenge for the destruction of its empire, that had prefigured the Hitlerian idea of Europe: "Spain experienced the tragedy of Europe before anyone and in a model way." From Joseph Gregor, *Das spanische Welttheater* (München, 1943), 474ff.

the idea of empire. In 1948, the same year the Romanist published *Literatura europea y Edad Media latina*, Castro published in Mexico the first edition of *España en su historia*. In the same magazine where Curtius published the first research for his *opus magnum, Zeitschrift für romanische Philologie*, Ramón Menéndez Pidal had vigorously defended an interpretation of the Hispanic epic and, in particular, the topics about el Cid, directly confronting the interpretation of the German Romanist, and, therefore, that of a European representation of the Hispanic spirit.[14]

Indeed, the Middle Ages had taken centre stage in the discourse of some intellectuals who had abandoned the contemporary debates to search for the real keys to the present in the cultural and literary traditions. What distinguishes the Spanish scholars and polygraphs, who also followed this old romantic detour through the Middle Ages, is the resolution with which they assumed its national specificity and their commitment to distance it from any cosmopolitan idea of history.

(Re)Constructing the Spanish Middle Ages as Subject

When Pidal wrote the preface to his *Historia de España* with the title of "Spaniards in history" (*Españoles en la historia*), or the essay on "Spaniards in literature" (*Españoles en la literatura*), he was undoubtedly identifying a common subject for the phenomena that had occupied most of his already countless studies. We can say the same thing, perhaps even more explicitly, of Castro's invocation, since the prologue of *España en su historia*, of the individual and social man, an emaciated subject who was the agent of the history-biography of Spain.

Nevertheless, it is not entirely accurate to consider that the aim of these studies by medievalists on the Hispanic reality was to prove the existence of a collective identity. This is so, at least, if, according to the authoritative definition by Jan Assmann, we understand "collective identity" as the "image that a group forms of itself and with which its members identify"; that is, if we understand that, far from existing by itself or by the projection of the internal needs of the researcher, "the collective identity is a matter of 'identification' by the individuals concerned" so that it only exists "to the extent that certain individuals profess it."[15] Despite the explicit commitment of Castro to identifying the subject who is the agent of the history of Spain, such a subject could hardly identify itself without the generous hermeneutics of the historian. Something similar can be said of the author of *La España del Cid*, for whom the historical subject is necessarily anonymous and, therefore, unable to express its own self-consciousness, something

---

14 Ramón Menéndez Pidal, "La épica española y la '*Literaturästhetik des Mittelalters*' de E. R. Curtius," *Zeitschrift für romanische Philologie* 69 (1939): 1–9; Spanish edition in: Ramón Menéndez Pidal, *Castilla. La tradición, el idioma* (Madrid, 1955), 75–93.

15 *La imagen que un grupo se forma de sí mismo y con la que se identifican sus integrantes; la identidad colectiva es una cuestión de "identificación" por parte de los individuos afectados; en la medida en que la profesan determinados individuos.* Cited from Jan Asmann, *Historia y mito en el mundo antiguo. Los orígenes de la cultura en Egipto, Israel y Grecia* (Madrid, 2011), 121ff. The title of the Spanish edition is surprising, when that of the original work was *Das kulturelle Gedächtniss. Schrift, Erinnerung und politische Identität in frühen Hochkulturen* (München: Beck, 1999).

only noticeable to those who know how to pursue its deployment in the high-level structures that surround it.

Contrary to what is often claimed, these hermeneutical syntheses on the Hispanic Medieval Ages did not have as their sole objective the foundation of a centralist nation-state. Admittedly, the reference to Spain is unequivocal. References to the word "nation" are, however, fewer than we might think. In a recent essay on the ideological backgrounds of Hispanism, Joan Ramon Resina noted a fundamental epistemological and ideological split between the medievalism of Menéndez Pelayo and Milà i Fontanals, and that of the subsequent generation of Pidal.[16] The former would be primarily guided by aesthetic ideals, while the obsession of Pidal for Castilianism would be guided by a political principle, which is confirmed by his fight against Basque and Catalan nationalisms during the Republic. That would explain the lack of interest of the Cantabrian scholar in medieval culture. In fact, despite his appreciative reception of the first great work of Pidal on the princes of Lara, Menéndez Pelayo[17] could state with contempt, "Let others extol the Middle Ages!" (*¡Que ensalcen otros la Edad Media!*), and devote his "Toast of the Retiro" (*Brindis del Retiro*) speech to the Spain of Calderón; in so doing, he was honouring the catholicity of the Empire and the Church rather than a national community.[18] Perhaps this interest was behind the close relationship between Menéndez Pelayo and Catalan intellectuals, encouraged by their common traditionalist view of European modernity. Disdainful of the liberal Gothicism of the *doceañistas* (politically moderate supporters of the Spanish Constitution of 1812), this neo-Catholic traditionalism was not so obsessed with the national question as the liberal scholars of the *Centro de Estudios Históricos*. Pidal belongs to the class of intellectuals convinced of what his most enthusiastic biographer, the scholar Pérez Villanueva, summarized: "Spain must go back

---

16 Joan Ramon Resina, *Del hispanismo a los estudios ibéricos. Una propuesta federativa para el ámbito cultural* (Madrid, 2009), especially the chapter: "¿Qué hispanismo? Trauma cultural, memoria disciplinada e imaginación simbólica," 101–26.

17 The scholar, historian, and literary critic Marcelino Menéndez Pelayo (1856–1912) is indispensable for understanding the contradictions of Spanish conservative thinking. On the one hand, his work provided intellectual and historical arguments for Spanish (and Catalan) Catholic traditionalism; on the other, it preserved and transmitted the knowledge of marginal but fundamental figures of Spanish thought despised if not persecuted by the official Spanish culture. It is important to read his important *Historia de los heterodoxos españoles* (1880–1882).

18 At least since the period of the Restoration and in parallel to the writing of national histories of Spain and its literature, the essayism of a constellation of polygraphs (teachers, lawyers, politicians, journalists, literary critics), either in the service of traditionalism, progressivism and, above all, moderantism, had contributed to symbolizing the articulation between the political idea of nation and the interests of an increasingly hegemonic bourgeoisie, through a terminology of undoubted aesthetic power. We must not forget that these terms translated some of those that had already been brandished by those who (like the neo-Catholics, including those from the Catalan intelligentsia) had identified Spain with the most universal structures of the Empire or the Church. Retranslated to the conceptual construction of a national structure, such concepts are in the orbit of what we would nowadays call collective identity. Together with the cited works by Javier Varela and Joan Ramon Resina, valuable information about the concepts of nation and memory can be found in: Ricardo García Cárcel, *La herencia del pasado. Las memorias históricas de España* (Barcelona, 2011).

to itself. Because of this, they all share a Medievalism, where they seek the roots."[19] That conviction, rather than being linked to nineteenth-century national-liberal projects was a product of the great fractures that the twentieth century brought. These required not only an account of institutional unity, but also one of cultural unity.

That may be why Menéndez Pidal much more frequently used the term "Spanish people" (*pueblo español*)—rather than "Spanish nation" (*nación española*)—since the former was an obvious legacy of the old romantic *Volk* which, more sensitive to the latent traits of culture, allowed the artificial political dimension of the national structure to be replaced with the natural purity of its popular form. From Pidal's logic, the oral character of medieval culture was the most direct way to reach the ethno-forming elements of the community.

Beyond the expression *nación española* and along with the term *pueblo español*, the substantial medievalism of our essay-writers also used, with particular emphasis, the concept of *civilización española*. It is no coincidence that in his first lecture at Princeton University, entitled "The Meaning of Spanish Civilization" (*El significado de la civilización española*), Castro significantly did not use the term "culture." We will soon return to this important text. Prior to that, it is worth recalling that in the previous decade, Ortega had condemned *culturalism*, the ideology of the culture, and its "false immanence" (*falsa inmanencia*), thus taking a stand in the European dispute between *Kultur* and *Zivilisation* that runs through the intellectual debate in the interwar period. In this debate, the use of the term "civilization" was an unequivocal sign of an allergy to nationalisms.[20] Therefore, it is striking that Castro uses it in a text that ends by looking at the medieval sources for Spanish national uniqueness. Spengler, with whom Castro had an acknowledged debt, was, of course, a precursor. However, it seems fair to look first for a precursor in the Spanish context, namely the figure of Rafael Altamira.[21]

Indeed, this scholar and politician from Alicante understood perfectly (in a very different way from Spengler) that the idea of civilization was inseparable from cosmopolitanism and, therefore, that the question of Spain was also a European issue. For Altamira, the nation was a variation on the common construction of a civilization or, in his words, "the global division of labour for civilization" (*la division del trabajo mundial por la civilización*). Such a position is thus at the antipodes of the nationalist discourse of Fichte, whose works Altamira himself translated. That is why he called his general history of Spain, published in 1945, *Historia de la Civilización española*, but which he had sketched out many years earlier: "for me, to say civilization is the same as saying

---

19 *España debe volver a sí misma. Por ello, todos comparten un medievalismo, donde buscan las raíces.* Pérez Villanueva, *Ramón Menéndez Pidal*, 157.

20 José Ortega y Gasset, *El tema de nuestro tiempo*, ed. Paulino Garagorri (Madrid, 1981), 98–105.

21 Rafael Altamira (1866–1951), is one of the most significant Spanish historians of the twentieth century. Professor at the University of Oviedo he gave courses and conferences in many universities both in Spain and abroad. He was also a judge at The International Court of Justice, at The Hague in the Netherlands, where he concentrated his efforts on working for peace and international dialogue. For his work and career he was nominated as candidate for the Nobel Peace Prize in 1933. The same year, he was elected a Foreign Honorary Member of the American Academy of Arts and Sciences.

history", he says in his preface.[22] The term "civilization" contained for him, as it did for Castro, that particular integrating force which was basically intended to put an end to the hegemony of political and chronological history. Altamira also explored the medieval Hispanic sources of that civilization, but not its uniqueness, as Castro or Pidal, and, in his own way, Ortega did too. That is why he wanted to emphasize that all the Hispanic epic literature was a product of Latin literature, and that Italianism and Classicism, rather than Muslim influence, determined Hispanic literary writing. When Castro presented the medieval sources of the problem of Spain to his American listeners, now translated into the catastrophe of civil war, he also insisted on the idea of a particular Spanish civilization, saying "civilization" was for him the same as saying "subject" and, with this in mind, it was also the same as saying "history." Its intended compensatory effect was specifically medieval in this idea of civilization. Indeed, the need to know and understand the Hispanic subject was a central strategy for understanding how, in the mid-twentieth century, the certainties of a medieval subject could compensate for the depths of the modern subject. This idea was defended before an audience composed, among others, of US military personnel who wanted to study before a possible invasion of Spain.

The "Ticklish" Medieval Subject

A few years ago, the Slovenian philosopher Slavoj Žižek, with no connection to Hispanic studies nor medievalism, began one of his most lucid books saying: "A spectre is haunting western academia: the Cartesian subject."[23] After this parody of the famous Marxist saying, he recited the list of contemporary enemies of that spectre, from deconstructionism to post-Marxist critics and feminism. Aptly, he traced the history of that exorcism to Heidegger, who, from his chair in Freiburg, not only held forth against the Cartesian subject but, in general, against all European intellectuals, whose impenitent humanism would have helped to conceal the true presence of being. For certain, if Žižek had known the lecture that Américo Castro gave at Princeton[24] soon after occupying the chair of Spanish Literature, and in which he presented his idea on the history of Spain, he could have included that lecture in the anti-Cartesian list. With the significant title of *The Meaning of Spanish Civilization*, this text, which we have already referred to, is a model for understanding the scope of the medieval argument in Spanish thought and rewriting the history of European anti-Cartesianism, and anti-modernism. Indeed, in it, the philologist exclaimed: "The Spanish self is not the *cogito ergo sum* [...] The Spanish self is *La vida es sueño* of Calderón, the self of Segismundo." The author continued:

---

22 *Para mí decir "civilización" es lo mismo que decir "historia."* From Rafael Altamira, *Historia de la civilización española* (Barcelona, 2008), 8.

23 *Un espectro ronda la academia occidental: el sujeto cartesiano.* Cited from Slavov Žižek, *The Ticklish Subject* (London, 1999).

24 Américo Castro (1885–1972) became ambassador to Germany during the Spanish Republic. When the Spanish civil war broke out in 1936 he moved to the United States, teaching literature at the University of Wisconsin–Madison from 1937 to 1939, at the University of Texas from 1939 to 1940, and at Princeton University from 1940 to 1953. There, Castro continued and developed his transformative and suggestive theses on the Jewish and Islamic identity of Spanish culture. His influence on American Hispanism was and remains remarkable.

The Spanish self is that of Cervantes: an ego that prolongs the will of existence in the most opposite directions, because it thinks that the exclusionary or partial attitudes will lead it to endless mazes. It is the self of Francisco Giner, who wanted Spain's present time to consist in its traditional past and its bright future, at the same time. Or that of Goya, wherein beauty and horror, hell and paradise coexist [...] And that of Lope, with his love and duty [...] The list [he concludes] could be extended from the Middle Ages to the present.[25]

In his lecture, Castro reiterates the crucial distance between the Spanish subject, a polymorphic one, coined in the Middle Ages, which is the agent of its own historical reality, and the modern European subject, which he considers, in a compact form, a rational subject, overwhelmed by science and technology that it has itself generated, and in doing so, triggered the great crisis of modernity. The terms in which he outlines that crisis are not very different from those used by philosophers and humanists from Central Europe shortly before World War II, such as Husserl, Huizinga, or the aforementioned Curtius:

Today, Western civilization is going through a crisis from which we do not know how we will survive. The illusory faith in reason has collapsed. Its place has been replaced by the brutal action which, via dark forms of collective will, disintegrates and annihilates the individual.[26]

On top of all modern dangers, against which the subject which is the agent of Spanish history would be an alternative, Castro points to an idea of science, identified with technology, as primarily responsible for western violence and war: "From the spontaneity of natural man to dehumanized technology, through the 'humanized technology': a world that dominates us, a force that can influence our actions and destinations. Paradoxically, this leads to a new primitivism."[27] The naive faith in technology and science was thus, for the philologist, cause and effect of an enlightened faith in progress from which the war had brutally healed us:

Modern man has been living in an order that makes him similar to perfection, towards the utopia of 'infinite progress' [...] Over the past three centuries, Europe has lived thinking

---

25 *El yo español no es el del cogito ergo sum [...]. el yo español es el de "La vida es sueño" de Calderón, el yo de Segismundo; El yo español es el de Cervantes: un ego que prolonga la voluntad de la existencia en las direcciones más opuestas, pues piensa que las actitudes exclusivistas o parciales le llevarán a laberintos inacabables. Es el yo de Francisco Giner, que quería para España un presente que fuese al mismo tiempo su pasado tradicional y su espléndido futuro. O el de Goya, en el que convivían belleza y horror, infierno y paraíso... Y el de Lope, con su amor y su deber [...] La lista [concluye] podría alargarse hasta el presente desde la Edad Media.* Cited from Américo Castro, "The Meaning of the Spanish Civilization," in *Américo Castro and the Meaning of Spanish Civilization*, ed. José Rubia Barcia (Berkeley, 1976), 30. In another work, he explicitly denies any possible Cartesian interpretation of Cervantes: Américo Castro, *El pensamiento de Cervantes* (Barcelona, 1972), 90.

26 *Hoy la civilización occidental atraviesa una crisis a la que no sabemos cómo vamos a sobrevivir. La fe ilusoria en la razón se ha colapsado. Su lugar se ha sustituido por la acción brutal, mediante oscuras formas de voluntad colectiva que desintegran y aniquilan al individuo.* From Castro, "The Meaning," 28.

27 *De la espontaneidad del hombre natural a la técnica deshumanizada, pasando por la "técnica humanizada": un mundo que nos domina, una fuerza que puede condicionar nuestros actos y destinos. Paradójicamente esto nos lleva a un nuevo primitivismo.* Cited from Castro, "The Meaning," 27.

that what escaped reason did not exist or was not worth being known. Today, however, we cannot help but smile at the attempt of the nineteenth century to make science into a religion, and believe that progress, the result of a social mechanism, was unstoppable.[28]

Such arguments converge with much of European neo-humanism of their time, but they are inseparable from a debate that is specifically Spanish. Indeed, from Menéndez Pelayo to Unamuno, the controversy over science in Spain had fluctuated between two central arguments: the special feature of Spanish science, consisting of theology, poetic and mystic, against the monotonous Cartesian definition of modern science; or the absence of Spanish science, understood mostly as techno-science, under the singularity of the Hispanic *ethos*. On several occasions, Castro chided those who claimed a science that was characteristic of Spain, reminding them of the titanic task the *Centro de Estudios Históricos* had assumed in the development of a historiography and a philology comparable to those cultivated in Europe. In fact, the arguments in this debate, isolated outbreaks of which can still be found in Spain's national intelligentsia, were dependent on opposition to what or whom they were put forward. For Castro, it was above all about claiming a special form of knowledge, a *Sonderweg* of Spanish science suitable to justify his particular historiographic hermeneutics, i.e., the idea of a history of the Hispanic subject by a Hispanic subject:

> In this atmosphere of applied science, technology, and welfare, Spanish values suffered a huge depreciation. The main Spanish issue has always been the man as an absolute and naked reality, and the products with which he tries to mark the consciousness of his existence are secondary. For a Spaniard, human beings are more important for what they are than for their social function and their production. If a Spaniard does not find a vital connection between what a person does and what he is, that person will not interest him in the least.[29]

The key to the "substantive" medievalization of the Hispanic subject is to be found in this anthropological framework, a moral and anthropological medievalization, very different from the rhetorical and theological one that Ramiro de Maeztu emphasized from his *Crisis del humanismo* to his posthumous *Defensa del espíritu*.[30] Associated with his defence of Hispanity, Maeztu's theological medievalization should be understood as the confrontation not only with the modern Cartesian subject, but also, and espe-

---

28 *El hombre moderno ha estado viviendo en un orden que lo hace semejante a la perfección, hacia la utopía del "progreso infinito" [...] Durante los tres últimos siglos Europa ha vivido pensando que lo que escapaba a la razón no existía o no era digno de conocer. Hoy, sin embargo, no podemos sino sonreír ante el intento del siglo XIX por hacer de la ciencia una religión y al creer que el progreso, resultado de un mecanismo social, era imparable.* Cited from Castro, "The Meaning," 27.

29 *En esa atmósfera de ciencia aplicada, tecnología y bienestar, los valores españoles sufrieron una gran depreciación. El principal tema español ha sido siempre el hombre como realidad absoluta y desnuda, y sólo secundariamente, los productos con los que intenta situar la conciencia de su existencia. Para un español, los seres humanos son más importantes por lo que son que por su función social y su producción. Si un español no encuentra una relación vital entre lo que una persona hace y lo que es, esa persona no le interesará lo más mínimo.* Cited from Castro, "The Meaning," 27.

30 Ramiro de Maeztu, *La crisis del humanismo* (Barcelona, 1919); Ramiro de Maeztu, *Defensa del espíritu* (Madrid, 1958).

cially, with the Lutheran subject. In this field, Maeztu insists on a transfer of contents from the thirteenth to the twentieth centuries, allowing him to imagine the naive updating in the modernity of the anti-Pelagian and anti-Averroist Middle Ages, an antidote against Renaissance humanism, Protestant voluntarism and, finally, the individualistic narcissism of the masses. Not in vain, Maeztu was a regular reader of Max Weber and Ernst Troeltsch, but, above all, he was an attentive reader of Kant. So attentive that he could not help but fear the subjective foundation of law. "The German liberals ("like the Spanish liberals," we might add) forgot that there is no other means to realize the law in this world than maintaining it by means of arms." Otherwise, and that is what he really feared, scattered individuals would seek its foundation in an all-encompassing and divine subjectivity, identified with the Hegelian State and embodied in the Bolshevik State.[31] The medievalism of the thirteenth century claimed by Maeztu, foreshadowing post-Tridentine Catholicism, was, in short, a salutary lesson against individualistic narcissism, a transcript of Ortega's Revolt of the Masses. And it is also so against the parliamentary democracy of the "argumentative class." It is no accident that Maeztu read Donoso Cortés in depth, mainly through Carl Schmitt. Actually, the Middle Ages of Maeztu were a trans-historical incarnation of the Catholic form as a legal form, something Schmitt admired. But their natural place was the modern empire or what Schmitt himself considered the Hispanic *nomos* of the earth.

Nevertheless, the medievalist essayism of philologists was not looking for patterns of theological orthodoxy in the medieval mirror of the Hispanic subject. In this respect, the teachings of Menéndez Pelayo, who, as a good humanist, was involved in violent debates with representatives of the Spanish Scholastics (unbearable for him and unrelated to his ideal of aesthetic and literary tradition), are always present. Their primary goal was to find symbolic vestiges of a permanent *ethos*. Pidal, rather a late advocate of imperial Spain, provides an interesting example of his medieval concept of the Hispanic subject in an early and comprehensive comparative work on the origins of *El condenado por desconfiado*.[32]

In this paper, Pidal, like the Spanish theologians, rejected the repugnance of some European critics towards the fanatic triumph of faith in personal salvation above one's

---

31 *Los liberales alemanes [habría que añadir: "como los liberales españoles"] se olvidaron de que no hay otro medio para realizar el derecho en este mundo que mantenerlo con las armas.* From De Maeztu, *Defensa del espíritu*, chap. 6. The immediate connection between Kant and the totalitarian state is a habitual exercise even nowadays among defenders of the Spanish philosophical exceptionalism. It was easy to do it then, especially because the Krausist mysticism soon took charge of erasing the imprint of the nineteenth-century Spanish neo-Kantians, like del Perojo. For the history of Spanish Kantism it is essential to see the study by José Luis Villacañas "Historia de una historia olvidada," in *Kant en España. El neokantismo en el siglo XIX*, ed. José Luis Villacañas (Madrid, 2006), 13–139. It is not by chance that in the same lecture at Princeton, on praising Ortega—presented as a Hispanic Kantian without precursors, as he never or almost never quoted José del Perojo or Manuel de la Revilla—Castro celebrates his distance from neo-Kantism which he argued had so often and so erroneously been following in Spain through positivism, on which, by the way, Castro only omits the most mystical Comte.

32 Ramón Menéndez Pidal, "El condenado por desconfiado," in *Estudios literarios* (Madrid, 1973), 9–46.

works. However, he also questions the theological reading of the Romantic scholar Agustín Durán, who, in the drama of Tirso, appreciated a reaction "against the fatal and heart-breaking rigidity of Protestantism."[33] Pidal does appreciate a distinctly theological issue: reformulating Molina's theme of sufficient grace and effective grace, but always through an original assimilation of the old legend on the comparison of merits, of Oriental origin, to which Tirso added modifications. The philologist gives us valuable information about the different variants of the issue. Above the theological and poetic synthesis, for Pidal "it is necessary to draw attention to the traditional facet" (*es preciso llamar la atención sobre el aspecto tradicional*), which "constitutes the storyline of the work" (*dio trama entera en la obra*). That's where the *ethos* of the drama lies, its moral value over its theological value. In contrast with Molina, the orthodox Catholic scholar, Pidal the philologist considered it an error that this theological work was "impossible to taste in the modern age, characterized by scepticism" (*imposible de saborear en una época de escepticismo como la moderna*) in an age "seething with ideas of humanity and altruism" (*bullen ideas de humanidad y altruismo*). The figure of Paul, anxious about predestination, was for Pidal:

> A real, living figure in all ages, not invented by a single abstraction, but the slow result of the contact with races and civilizations, of migration, of the struggle for life; in short, the figure of Paul is the child of a secular legendary generation whose antiquity is ennobling.[34]

The important thing is that the legendary theme of comparing merits can serve different religions, the Christian as well as the Muslim and the Hebrew, as it already did with the Brahmin. "That hermit devoured by anxieties of the soul, searcher of the divine secrets, who interrogates a mute and impenetrable sky [...] will forever retain his grandeur and interest, even after the death of our religious theatre."[35]

What is important here, in order to understand the scope of Pidal's "medieval argument," is that he places *El condenado* by Tirso much closer to a medieval subject, to a conciliatory *ethos* of permanent human characters, than to a Tridentine Catholic subject which, according to Pidal, and contrasting with Ramiro de Maeztu and even Menéndez Pelayo, was something that was historically unrecoverable, or, in other words, belonging to history, but not to memory. The Spanish-ness of Paul / Tirso de Molina lies precisely in the human, anthropological level, which drives his desperate actions.

Over time, Pidal refined the uniquely Hispanic features of these human characters, reducing the Catholic structure of the empire of Charles V to these. In turn, Castro would do the same thing with the subject of Spanish civilization, that anti-Cartesian self, which

---

33 *Contra la fatal y desconsoladora rigidez del protestantismo.* From Menéndez Pidal, "El condenado por desconfiado," 42.

34 *Una figura real y viviente en todas las edades, no inventada por una abstracción individual, sino producto lento del contacto con razas y civilizaciones, de la emigración, de la lucha por la vida; hija, en fin, de una secular generación legendaria con cuya antigüedad se ennoblece.* Cited from Menéndez Pidal, "El condenado por desconfiado," 9–46.

35 *Ese ermitaño devorado por ansiedades del alma, escudriñador de los secretos divinos, que interroga a un cielo mudo e impenetrable [...] conservará eternamente su grandeza e interés, aun después de muerto nuestro teatro religioso.* Cited from Menéndez Pidal, "El condenado por desconfiado," 44.

is that of Calderón, but only to the extent that Calderón did not represent the divine creature of Tridentine orthodoxy, but the "essential man" who "has been and is the main subject of Spanish civilization."[36]

That whole man, *con su seguridad y oscilaciones*, an alternative model to the man of the crisis, is not eternal for Castro, as he seems to be for Pidal, since he cannot ignore the vital basis on which he is founded: his entirety is prefigured in the Hispano-Arabs who created, in southern Spain, a culture superior to that of the lands from which they came and determined a marked Spanish interest in all questions of existence, even before the essence. That is why this subject is so paradigmatic, as proclaimed in the conference on *meaning*, on the epic of the Cid, which puts the depiction of everyday life ahead of the mythic tale.

Mediation

In his *Ensayo sobre historiología*,[37] written shortly after *España en su historia*, following the methodological discussions on this work, Castro compared the role of the historian, and therefore himself, with a *medium*. The term is not accidental. The task of the media-tor was indeed what many European intellectuals, particularly the so-called "human-ists," had entrusted themselves with in response to the "crisis of mediation," which can be defined as the dissolution of shared forms (legal-political, religious, aesthetic) from which relations between subjects themselves, and between them and their objects of knowledge, could be organized. Against the excessively political reaction of dictator-ship, the humanist intellectual elites trusted in literary knowledge (criticism, philology, hermeneutics, but also journalism) for the continuing generation of meaning. As Castro repeated in his lecture at Princeton, this generation of meaning should also be the true mission of science, as opposed to the technique, and, therefore, the goal of historical knowledge against the sociological and political.

Spanish philosophers cited by Castro, thinkers about the "polymorphism" of life, represented the Spanish response to the crisis of mediation: an unrepentant and some-times agonizing effort, from Unamuno to Ortega, to integrate the individual and the col-lective, science and life, culture and civilization. Castro relayed it to the Americans as "an ego that prolongs the will of existence in the most opposite directions, because it thinks that the exclusionary or partial attitudes will lead to endless labyrinths." It is, in short, the subject of a story of mediation summarized in the desire of Francisco Giner, "who wanted for Spain a present time consisting in its traditional past and its bright future, both at the same time."[38] The Spanish way, the special path that the history of Spain had

---

36 *Hombre esencial; ha sido y es el asunto principal de la civilización española.* Cited from Castro, *España en su historia.*

37 Américo Castro, *Ensayo sobre historiología. Analogías y diferencias entre hispanos y musulmanes* (New York, 1950).

38 *Un ego que prolonga la voluntad de la existencia en las direcciones más opuestas, pues piensa que las actitudes exclusivistas o parciales le llevarán a laberintos inacabables; que quería para España un presente que fuese al mismo tiempo su pasado tradicional y su espléndido futuro.*

undertaken since the Middle Ages was not only an exception but, as some German intellectuals had perceived, a guide to avoiding the dissolution Spanish philosophers talked about. Therefore, he concluded his lecture on Spanish civilization advising the American public to get in contact with it, for "contact with Spanish civilization will pave the way for a fruitful new humanism."[39]

The purpose of this humanism and its historical interpretation of the culture and life of nations was certainly a compensatory response to disenchantment in the world, due to the separation of disciplines and values, in which Max Weber saw the essence of modernity. Castro had read Max Scheler admiringly, a declared enemy of Weber's diagnosis, from whom he took his theory of values to merge it with what he had learned from his reading of Dilthey. The result was a double epistemological operation: raising the concept of "convivial value" to a central category of literary hermeneutics and converting it into its main historiographical technique. Although the coexistence of the value is not natural in itself, but depends on certain historical conditions, it is always mediated, it always needs a "medium," a mediator. To tell the story of Spain is to explain the origins of its mediations, but also to contribute to its survival, in short, to contribute to the medievalization of its entire history, its present and its future; in other words, to the restitution of a historical time opposed to the modern acceleration of time. And this can only be done by turning historiography into a sort of autobiographical projection, which means transforming history into memory.

The Memory or Memories of the Middle Ages

In 1942, Joaquín Xirau published an article in Mexico entitled *Humanismo español (Ensayo de interpretación histórica)*, which categorically stated: "Spain is a nation without history."[40] He blamed this lack of history on the serious spiritual problems of the Hispanic world which he described in similar terms, except those derived from the fervent Christianity of the Catalan philosopher, to those expressed by Castro, two years earlier, in his conference at Princeton. What did Xirau mean with that "lack of history" (*falta de historia*) with such pathetic consequences? He meant: "the absence of clear ideas about our past and our future," in other words, the lack of "continuity of a serene and

---

Castro's reference to Giner when showing the Americans the origin of his thought is essential, as his conception of the historical reality is inseparable from the organic thesis of the founder of the Institución Libre for whom "in the intellectual order, begets the common historical sense, by the irreflexive interpenetration of all the social activities that, crossing in multiple directions according to laws unknown or forgotten by the collaborators in the same general culture form the plot of this," and was extremely concerned by the fact that "the spirit of the peoples" took "ever more eccentric directions" until it dissolved "in a wild atomism, that does away with any common action, with all social links and still with all objective elements." From Francisco Giner de los Ríos, "La política antigua y la política nueva," in *Obras selectas*, ed. Isabel Pérez Villanueva (Madrid, 2004), 118–27.

39 *El contacto con la civilización española allanará el camino para un nuevo y fructífero humanism.* Cited from Giner de los Ríos, "La política antigua," 127.

40 *España es un pueblo sin historia.* From Joaquim Xirau, "Humanismo español (ensayo de interpretación)," in *Obras completas*, ed. Ramón Xirau, 4 vols. (Madrid, 1999), 2:534–51.

critical judgment on the meaning contained in its presence and temporal development in the Western world." Not that the Christian thinker denied the absence of historiographies, but that he denied them the minimum historical value, because they held onto the "blind amorphous erudition," "the simple handling of big issues" and "the patient stacking of facts."[41] However, the proposed remedy against this scholarship was not a new methodology, more subtle and attentive to the complexity of the historiographical narrative, but rather the understanding of the "spirit" that "creates the Hispanic world" (*informa el mundo hispánico*) acting on its agents without them knowing. Just accepting that *a priori*, we will be in a position to understand, for example, that the Bolívar's revolution was caused by the same "liberal spirit" "we already find in the political and social institutions of all nations of medieval Spain [...]."[42] The methodological question is how and where to find this shaping spirit, how to give scientific substance to that *a priori*. All responses ultimately converge in memory.

Indeed, the belief that memory must be the ultimate goal of history underlies the diagnosis of the absence of history. This was a conviction shared by almost all intellectuals who passed through the Middle Ages in search of their Hispanic subject, including philosophers like Xirau and Ortega, and which represent, in a paradigmatic way, the works of historiographical synthesis undertaken by the philologists. The historical memory developed by these men of letters is, as we have said, a literary memory.

Its root, proto-Romantic, goes back to a discovery of modern literary criticism and history which consists of matching the words to the land or, more specifically, to the

---

41 *La ausencia de ideas claras sobre nuestro pasado y sobre nuestro futuro [...]; la continuidad de un juicio sereno y crítico sobre el sentido que encierra su presencia y su desarrollo temporal en el mundo de Occidente [...]; ciega erudición amorfa; el fácil manejo de grandes tópicos; el paciente amontonamiento de hechos.* Cited from Joaquim Xirau, "Humanismo español (ensayo de interpretación)," in *Obras completas*, ed. Ramón Xirau, 4 vols. (Madrid, 1999), 2:534–51. In a very similar way to the cited speech by Castro, Xirau here defines "Spanish humanism" as the "heroic attempt to save, in spirit and in action, the ecumenical unity of a world that is splitting apart."

42 *Encontramos ya en las instituciones políticas y sociales de todos los pueblos de la España medieval [...].* From Xirau, *Obras completas*, 2:551. Thus, in his opinion, Bolívar denied that what was behind his war against a supposed Hispanity were not enlightened French ideals, but rather those that Hispanity itself had generated; the same that moved his enemy Riego: Xirau's perception is bedecked with Christianity that seeks lines of mediation, of unification of the critical subject born from Humanism. However, in any case, what this is about is to "seek in the deepest depths of history the integrating breath capable of incorporating into the organism of a tradition, progressive and creative, the innovations brusquely introduced" (*buscar en lo más profundo de la historia el aliento integrador capaz de incorporar al organismo de una tradición, progresiva y creadora, las innovaciones bruscamente introducidas*). Another sentence by Xirau is extremely significant for the question of the subject and its relation with the medieval argument: "Hispanic humanism is not a resonance of foreignizing voices as perhaps spirits exempt from profundity believe. We have fathers, we have old and illustrious fathers, and we have to honour them. Only in this way will we fulfil our destiny and contribute to the salvation of the world. And we can say in truth: 'I know who I am'" (*El humanismo hispánico no es una resonancia de voces extranjerizantes como lo creen acaso espíritus exentos de profundidad. Tenemos padres, tenemos viejos e ilustres padres y es preciso que les hagamos honor. Sólo así cumpliremos nuestro destino y coadyuvaremos a la salvación del mundo. Y podremos decir con verdad: "Yo sé quién soy"*). Cited from Xirau, *Obras completas*, 2:551.

stones. The key is to look for the eloquence of the written words, like that of the stones which make up a Church, not so much in what they say and do not say, but in what they retain in their own mute shape as a testimony, or, rather, a metonymic expression of an attitude, of a subject or of a bygone world, always available and ever present. To ensure this presence, the philologist "medium" highlights the direct link between the uniqueness of the work and the community that the work represents. Moreover, he turns the formula "a people creates a poem, a poem creates a people"[43] into an infinitely reversible one. Be it called "spirit," "character," "nation," "people," or "civilization," the subject of this literary memory merely names the interchangeable roles of the power of expression that is evident in the text and the collective power that the text expresses. Herder vindicated this formula to set the basis for a national literature, not in the name of particularism, but rather the liberalization of universalism, one that ceased to be the monopoly of cultural empires (especially the French). Therefore, the formation of the concept of universal literature (*Weltliteratur*) is parallel to that of national literatures. Both required a rewriting of tradition, new mirrors or mirages of history, which placed the ideal setting to reinvent the relationship with classicism and the dispute between the ancients and moderns in the Middle Ages, or, more precisely, between the recent moderns, who sought their sources in classicism, and ancient moderns who, rebelling against the present, looked for theirs in the Middle Ages.[44]

For a while, at least in France, the construction of an idea of civilization from a literary memory was a liberal endeavour, a third way which, affirming the analogy between mind, language, and community, mediated between the social, moral, and cultural organicism of the counter-revolutionaries and the anti-traditionalism and faith in progress of the revolutionaries. Later, it was the preferred route of supporters of an idea for civilization that linked the European nations around the *uchronia* of an evergreen "Romania."

In Spanish literary thought, the Middle Ages paradoxically became the place where the keys to all the oversights of history stood, but also the keys to all recovery of memory. In the appendix to his controversial text *Los españoles en la historia*, significantly entitled "duties of history" (*Los deberes de la historia*),[45] Pidal lamented the injustice of what he called "enhancement of memories" (*realce de memorias*) at the expense of forgetting other memories. An injustice perpetrated by historians, from the same Middle

---

43 *Un pueblo crea un poema, un poema crea un pueblo.* We find this expression in Jacques Rancière, *La palabra muda* (Buenos Aires, 2009), 71.

44 In his *Fragmentos*, Friedrich Schlegel distinguishes between the oldest moderns and the recent moderns; in other words, between those who, from their particular chemistry, long for the oriental organic model and those who pursue the abstract Greek model. The interest of Romanticism in the Germanic Middle Ages—an interest that can only be deployed from the chemistry and the irony of the criticism—appears not only as a rejection of classicism, but also, at the same time, as a return to the orient, both worlds linked by the religious. From this perspective, there is no incoherence in the Catholic drift of a modern consciousness sustained by aesthetic and literary criticism. Peter Szondi, *Poética y filosofía de la historia*, 2 vols. (Madrid, 1992), 1:71ff.; and Hans-Robert Jauss, "La réplica de la 'querelle des anciennes et des modernes' in Schlegel y Schiller," in *La historia de la literatura como provocación* (Barcelona, 2000), 75ff.

45 Ramón Menéndez Pidal, *Los españoles en la historia* (Madrid, 1947), 255–58.

Ages which, with their institutional disintegration, would have prevented the Spaniards from remembering the history of their unitary "ethos." The medieval chronicles from the Alfonso Castilian king chronicles would have suffered the consequences of ignoring earlier historians. And, as Pidal argues, the writing of history is always partial, selective, and more so if it is guided by political interests.[46] Hence the "oversight of archiving memories" (*descuido en archivar memorias*) more prevalent in the Crown of Castile than in Aragon and Navarre, and the inveterate tendency of writers to forgetfulness, beyond the selection of information required by the historical account.

Notwithstanding his essential contributions to the history of language and philological criticism, Pidal's hermeneutics of medieval history stands on three epistemological and ideological assumptions: first, memories experienced are more numerous, more diverse, and more real than memories recounted. In other words, what is forgotten always exceeds what is remembered in the same way as what is latent is always greater than the conscious; second, historical truth is always on the side of what is forgotten or latent; and, third, these heterogeneous memories that underlie history hold an "indissoluble unity," which is the ultimate measure of historical knowledge. Finally, truth lies in this unity, understood as a kind of *complexio oppositorum* of the different memories of each period, forgotten or enhanced "according to the pressure of circumstances" (*según el apremio de las circunstancias ambientes*). Such unity within the heterogeneity is analogous to the unity of the subject of history. It is also analogous to a concept of the Middle Ages understood as the authentic *complexio oppositorum* of the most heterogeneous interests of history. Only that conception of medieval memory can be erected as an unquestionable truth; for example,

> The provincial Hispanic feeling, facing the [cosmopolitan] city, arises within the Roman Empire, representing the beginning of a national consciousness; or the institution of the Hispanic-Leonese Empire, which had been ignored since the late Middle Ages; or the grouping of the five kingdoms conceived under their dynastic unity.[47]

That desire to rebuild *the* historical memory of *a* Hispanic subject in the Middle Ages also underlies the project of Américo Castro, and the assumptions of those beyond philology and historiography, such as Ortega, Xirau, and before them, Giner or Fernando de los Ríos, who interpreted the history of Spain as the history of an all-encompassing unity.

Faced with the problem of how to make the genealogy of a memory that goes beyond any of its writings into a science, the solution is to decouple history from historiography or, rather, to subordinate the interpretation of the historiographical text to the context

---

46 "All historiographic works imply a necessary enhancement of some bygone memories, and necessary silence regarding others [...] What then was highlighted is transmitted unchanged to the following centuries, and with this, some are determined to forget what was then discarded" (*Toda obra historiográfica implica necesario realce de algunas memorias pretéritas, y necesario silencio respecto de otras [...] Lo que entonces fue destacado se transmite inalterable a los siglos siguientes, y con esto, se determinan cierto olvido para lo que entonces fue desechado*).

47 *El sentimiento provincial hispánico que, frente a la urbe, surge en el seno del Imperio romano, representando el comienzo de una conciencia nacional; o la institución del Imperio hispano-leonés, ignorada ya desde la Baja Edad Media; o la agrupación de los cinco reinos concebidos bajo su unidad dinástica.* Cited from Menéndez Pidal, *Los españoles*, 257.

of its literary production, placing it within the limits of an original and pervasive oral expression. This is the basic assumption of philological traditionalism: the unity of a historical memory based on a poetic oral use, which is not based on the biological or racial essentialism of the subject, but rather on the morphology, equally biological, of its language. However, according to Pidal's terminology, that emphasis on *a specific* historical memory as a lived memory which has been experienced involves a "partial selection" (*escogimiento parcial*) of memories: a calculated enhancement of those which allows the fusion of the communicative, psychological memory typical of the brief history, and the founding cultural memory typical of long history.[48] Reduced to poetry, this historical memory unifies the various memories, psychological, profane, religious, moral or legal, ignoring the different modes in which they are written and transmitted, as well as their internal tensions.

A paradigm of this strategy of "Memory" against "Memories" is found in the interpretation of medieval historiography and, particularly, in the Alfonsine chronicles. If, as Pidal says in his studies on the *Romancero*, "literature is born and grows ignoring itself",[49] the same is true of memory, which is never born as a historiographical enterprise but as poetry: a vulgar historiography, I must say, spontaneous, such as that of "journalist" minstrels. The reading that Pidal, and to an extent, Castro, make of the *Primera Crónica General* or *Estoria de España* weighs the historiographical value of the text for its ability to express the collective memory. Thus what is most relevant, even more than the contents of the texts, is its expressive value, the form of its writing, its "texture" in the words of Castro, which becomes a metonymy of the collective "ethos" that unconsciously encouraged its development. In contrast to earlier chronicles like the *De rebus Hispaniae* by Jiménez de Rada or the *Chronicon mundi* by Lucas de Tuy, the chronicle of Alfonso was written in the vernacular language, and a great part of it by various authors, especially the part written under the reign of Sancho IV, where the influence of the epic is much greater. Castro perceived a "varied and sylvan frond" (*fronda varia y selvática*) in the *Primera Crónica general* or *Estoria de España*, the same that Pidal perceived as a "confusing jungle of tangled fronds" (*selva confusa de enmarañada fronda*) full of arguments for that "vital overflow"[50] of what is Spanish regarding the linguistic, legal, and spiritual tradition that constituted the framework of Christian-Roman Europe. We cannot go deeper to show the methodological weakness of these interpretations; we refer to an earlier work in which we accept the observations of Georges Martin and Isabel Fernández Ordóñez on the relationships between the historian and the king, and between them and the kingdom ("the historiographical power") to focus attention on the pedagogical and political functions of the chronicles serving a crown keen to reconcile the supremacy of the royal order with the legitimacy of the judges representative of the Castilian nobility against the tyranny of Leon.[51]

---

48 Asmann, *Historia y mito*; and García Cárcel, *La herencia del pasado*.

49 *La literatura nace y crece ignorándose a sí misma*. From Menéndez Pidal, *Los españoles*, 255.

50 *Desborde vital*. From Menéndez Pidal, *Los españoles*, 255–58.

51 Antonio de Murcia, "Memoria histórica de la Edad Media e idea de tradición en Menéndez Pidal y Américo Castro," *Res publica* 17 (2007): 309–28.

Together with Francisco Rico, José Luis Villacañas has emphasized the nature of the *Estoria de España* as "family history" (*historia de familia*), which allows the expression of the transmission of power, and has insisted on its imperial nature which, as Fernández Ordóñez argues, determines that the protagonist is not the people, but the lords who exercised the empire; hence the pedagogical sense. However, Villacañas underscores an essential aspect, which Pidal and Castro had significantly overlooked: the constitution of the *Estoria* as a book, in imitation of the Bible, the ultimate cornerstone of the continuity, stability, transcendence, and therefore, the vicariousness of kings in relation to God.[52] But all these issues require a critical eye and enter directly into political issues, which, for these philologists, are incompatible with memory, as they require stepping away from the past to analyse it rather than to keep it in mind. And, of course, they are not compatible with what Castro called the "apolitical vitality of the Spaniards."[53]

From the perspective of a genuine conceptual history, the main problem with that memory is that of its hermeneutical limits. In other words, how can a historian establish himself as guardian and interpreter of a memory regardless of the awareness that the agents themselves have of it? How can we continually refer to an agent subject of history, as Castro does, ignoring the fragmentary subjects of "the histories"? The solution is simply to roll back memory to its pre-literary time, either to its dormant state or its existential foundation. Pidal rendered great importance to the biological metaphor of latency, which is brilliant and operational even today when it comes to describing the communication processes between oral use and literacy.[54] What is problematic is not to turn the latent memory into a regulative principle of the production processes and poetic transmission in oral cultures; the problem is to make it into a real principle for the historical continuity and ethno-formation of a subject of history that is anything more than a rhetorical subject.

---

52 José Luis Villacañas Berlanga, "Apéndice VI: Legitimidad, poder y religión en el Islam. Debate con Américo Castro," in *La formación de los reinos hispánicos* (Madrid, 2006), 85–123.

53 *Vitalidad apolítica de los españoles*. From Castro, *España en su historia*.

54 Thus, Paul Zumthor has adopted this concept of the latent state as that of a "deep oral use" (*oralidad profunda*), which he defines as "a complex set of common conducts and discursive modalities, that determine a system of depictions and a faculty of all the members of the social body to produce certain signs, to identify and interpret them in the same way" (*un conjunto complejo de conductas y modalidades discursivas comunes, que determinan un sistema de representaciones y una facultad de todos los miembros del cuerpo social de producir ciertos signos, de identificar y de interpretarlos de la misma manera*), thus an oral use that "refers to the first source of the authority that governs the practice (in the absence of ideology) of a society" (*hace referencia a la fuente primera de la autoridad que rige la práctica (a falta de ideología) de una sociedad*). For Zumthor, this is a question of perceiving the cultural productions in a space-time framework that includes them in a perpetual movement made up of collisions, interferences, exchanges, and ruptures in which history is not perceived, in which it remains unaware, as "in the word heard nothing separates what is conditioned by time and what depends on the place" (*nada separa todavía en la palabra oída lo que el tiempo condiciona y lo que depende del lugar*). From Paul Zumthor, *La letra y la voz. De la literatura medieval* (Madrid, 1989), 167–91.

This problem brings us back to the endless dialectic between forgetfulness and memory. If, as Pidal maintains, also in his studies on the *Romancero*, "what is lost is more than what can be found," and if historical knowledge is based on the excess of what is forgotten, then, rather than a custodian of memory, the medievalist becomes a manager of oversights. Similarly, the philologist officiates as an oracle of what is latent, that which does not have "tangible" truth, like Vulgar Latin, "it has [thanks to hermeneutic media-tion] a logical reality as 'tangible' as if it were before the eyes."[55] Thus, the true subject of history is, paradoxically, that which has been forgotten by it. The latency of what is Hispanic among the Goths does not admit as a rejoinder the fragility and instability, the inability of a patrimonial system in the Visigothic kingdom of Hispania, nor the subse-quent documented processes of ethno-formation closer to the constitution of a State. Similarly, the unquestionable existence of a vanished folk poetry on which the *Poema del Cid* is built is precisely because of its disappearance, much more accessible to the memory than the tangible, historical existence of the *Historia Roderici* or the *Carmen Campidoctoris*.

In his methodological justification, Pidal denounced the recalcitrant individual-ism of those who deny the powers of latency, rescuing the aforementioned reversible formula of the poem that makes the people, and the people that make the poem from proto-Romanticism. However, curiously, this operation has a limit, just where collec-tive authorship is attributed to the written tradition, that is, to an institutionalized conception of literature, such as that applied by Curtius to the reading of the Spanish epic, which closely links its genesis not to a process of national ethno-formation but to an international tradition mediated by the *translatio* of Latin culture. Curiously, that is where Pidal and most Spanish critics, from Lida de Malkiel to Dámaso Alonso, redis-covered the concept of individual creativity, of poetic originality, not in the name of individualism, but of the ethnographic and poetic analogy between subject, language, and culture, a counterpoint to the homology between *imperium*, *ecclesia*, and *studium*. In this controversy, Pidal suddenly becomes an avowed anti-traditionalist.[56] Thus, he shows that not only are historical memories selective, but also their supposed collective subjects. Given a choice, Pidal here sides with life even if he has to give up tradition; or rather, he redefines the true tradition, one that is not written and, therefore, absent from histories, just as in life, against whose truth any other argument pales.

---

55 *Lo perdido es más de lo que se puede encontrar; posee [gracias a la mediación hermenéutica] una realidad lógica tan "tangible" como si lo tuviera delante de los ojos.* Cited from Menéndez Pidal, *Los españoles*, 255–58.

56 For the controversy between Curtius and Pidal, see: Antonio de Murcia Conesa, "Estudio preliminar," in *Escritos de humanismo e hispanismo*, ed. Antonio de Murcia Conesa (Madrid, 2011), 13–74. Also the work of: Ernst Robert Curtius "El *Carmen Campidoctoris (Cid-Rhytmus)*," in *Escritos de humanismo e hispanismo*, ed. Antonio de Murcia Conesa (Madrid, 2011), 143–55. The controversy is very instructive for evaluating the concepts of memory and tradition applied to history from philology.

Medievalization of Time: Experience and Expectation of the Civil War

In a virulent essay of 1932, *Años decisivos* (translated into Spanish during the civil war, of course, in the fascist-controlled area), Oswald Spengler held that the modern historian

> Confuses his mother tongue with the written language of the great cities in which every-one learns to read and write, that is, with the language of newspapers and magazines, which indoctrinate citizens about the "law" of the nation,[57]

while the oral language, that of the common people, expresses the "inner form of an important life which, unconsciously and inadvertently, is performed in each deed and every word."[58] Contempt for this orality would be the result of modern liberalism and individualism, which replace individuals with the masses. This reference seems sig-nificant because it comes from someone who has been widely read in Spain and who inspired several of the categories in Américo Castro, and by linking the essential word, the one reflecting collective oral memory rather than the written one, with villages rather than with the city. This conception of memory is undoubtedly decidedly anti-urban. None of the defenders of that memory, which rests on oral use and the literature generated by it, could recognise that, in fact, apart from the remembrance of the dead (present in the "memorials" of the churches, in which the living and dead appear almost equally by virtue of their importance or contributions to the church community, and in the remembrance of the souls in purgatory through an organized system of prayers and alms), the first obvious manifestation of a will to build a community memory was the "urban memory," contemporary with the development of the cities. Here, one could talk about the need to preserve an identity against other forms of domination not through immediate oral communication, but by the written mediation of municipal archives.

Since his lecture at Princeton, Castro stated on numerous occasions that the Spanish soul always has something of primary humanity in its struggle with the basic problems of human geology. That soul was clearly hardly urban and ill-fits a type of modernity in which "every gesture of true manhood, of free life, is something outrageous, ridiculous, and reprehensible" (*todo gesto de auténtica virilidad, de vida libre, es algo extravagante, ridículo y rechazable*). For Castro, the gesture of life is also the subject of a history of Spain, which manifests itself in the "heart of the language" (*meollo de la lengua*). Against Pidal, the author of *España en su historia* emphasized the existential and experiential nature of historical memory. That was the reason why the subject should not be sought in pre-medieval figurations. But it was also the reason why it endured forever prefig-ured in the Middle Ages. History has an obligation not only to know the past but to bear in mind that the Middle Ages are not only an imprecise historical epoch but, above all, the point of intersection between the vertical and horizontal planes of history, that is, between the planes of succession and continuity. The collective subject is formed pre-

---

57 *Confunde su lengua madre con el lenguaje escrito de las grandes ciudades en el que cada uno aprende a leer y escribir, esto es, con el lenguaje de los periódicos y revistas, que iluminan al ciudadano sobre el "derecho" de la nación.* Cited from Oswald Spengler, *Años decisivos* (Granada, 1938), 42–43.

58 *Forma interior de una vida importante que, inconsciente e inadvertidamente se realiza en cada hecho y cada palabra.* From Spengler, *Años decisivos*, 43.

cisely where succession crosses continuity, which has its individual reflection in the intersection, or rather the merging of interiority and externality:

> The functional structure of Hispania, its reality, is given in the expression "I woke up feeling sick" and in a thousand other manifestations, which those who had dealings with Spaniards of the eleventh century in the sanctuary of Compostela or of the twentieth century in the Puerta del Sol of Madrid, can see.[59]

In this horizontal plane "past moments experienced by those who were and continue to be numerators of the broad common denominator of their own history survive and take on their own existence."[60] The horizontality between author and reader is presented as proof not only of the possibility of receiving the texts, but also of the common vital abode between past and future and, therefore, of the futility of a history whose purpose is not to reveal our entanglement in the "palimpsest of past life" (*palimpsesto de la vida pasada*). The common abode is associated with the structure of personal existence, which, for example, with Muslims, is what allowed them to adopt the ancient technologies and sciences, but not the revival of Homer or Sophocles. Only literature can testify to this structure, in the literary use of language, which, not because it is literary (*littera*), but by being interwoven into life, style, and consciousness, becomes a privileged reflection of expressions of life's experience in the common abode. To that end, once again, Pidal's disciple must remind us of the cultural, collective origin of national literature. An origin in which legal custom and poetic oral life are mixed up, as in Pidal, although with many nuances, as Eduardo de Hinojosa has taught in his work on law in the *Poema del Cid*.

Castro, like Pidal, and in general all those who questioned the Middle Ages (and also ultimately Ortega himself), solely from a consideration of historical memory as a "living arrangement," tended towards a geographical rather than a chronological conception of history. According to this conception, the philologist could move between different moments in history. Therefore, in his response to Leo Spitzer's objections to the poor attention to the genesis of the concepts used in *España en su historia*, Castro said, "The question of how it was possible for a structure to be set up over the centuries is independent, secondary, to the reality of the structure itself once set up."[61] That is why he did not take into account, for example, the historical times involved in the wars of medieval Spain, nor that Christian warfare, the inheritance of Constantine, was declared before the *jihad*, even before the early Christians could understand the Muslim world. Therefore, he insisted on attributing to the cult of Santiago a crucial role as a generator of

---

59 *La funcional estructura de Hispania—su realidad—se da en "amanecí enfermo," y en mil otras manifestaciones que puede observar quien trate a hispanos del siglo XI en el santuario de Compostela, o a los del siglo XX en la Puerta del Sol de Madrid.* Cited from Américo Castro, "Respuesta a Leo Spitzer," *Nueva revista de filología hispánica*, 3 (1949): 152.

60 *Sobreviven como propios los momentos del pasado vividos por quienes fueron y continúan siendo numeradores del amplio común denominador de su historia propia.* From Américo Castro, *Sobre el nombre y el quién de los españoles* (Madrid, 1965), 81.

61 *La cuestión de cómo haya sido posible que una estructura se constituya a lo largo de los siglos es independiente, secundaria, respecto de la realidad de la estructura misma una vez fijada.* From Américo Castro, *De la España que aún no conocía*, 3 vols. (Ciudad de México, 1972), 2:249–66.

military endeavours, symmetrical to the Muslim *jihad*, and of an idea of empire whose European source he disregarded. Thus, he paid scant attention to the way the idea of apocalypse determined the historical times of the Christian kingdoms.

This geographical conception of historical times tried to bridge the gap between historical experience and the horizon of expectations, typical of modernity. Hispanic uniqueness consisted of demonstrating that the terrible and modern experience of the civil war was fully integrated into a historical experience, whose terrible expectations could only be neutralized by a knowledge of the Middle Ages, whose permanent memory becomes the key to overcoming it.

As Castro told his audience in Princeton, only a cataclysm, with the intervention of another superior historical agent, can modify the common abode and reconstitute it in another form. However, he told his audience little or nothing about the conditions and material consequences (technical, political, economic, or social) of this "cataclysm." How is the abode maintained after the expulsion of the Jews and the Moriscos? How can we keep it, especially after the civil war? Castro's response, in line with other intellectuals of his time, stands on the finding that the Hispanic subject had survived, even after the war, oblivious to the acceleration of time that was threatening to destroy civilization. And precisely by also being oblivious to the crisis of modern Europe and its rationalist science, that subject would have to continue contributing to that civilization something that neither German culture with its *Wissenschaft*, nor the French one with its *clarité*, could provide: its tenacious approach to life as a problem and its even more tenacious willingness to face death.

The itineraries of Hispanic thought in the twentieth century are inseparable from this phenomenon, perhaps specific to Spain, but always measured against or confronted with a European idea of modernity. It was against this idea that, for much of the century, before and after the civil war, an essential part of the Spanish intelligentsia strove to understand the Hispanic "historical being" as a singular essence for death, whose trans-historical permanence was revealed in a constant disposition for civil war. The fact that the dramatic self-consciousness of this destiny was inseparable from what we have called the "medieval argument" indicates the important role played by historical memory in the work of some "elites" who placed their own survival and that of their nation in it.